Public Finance and Economic Welfare

Kenyon E. Poole

PROFESSOR OF ECONOMICS, NORTHWESTERN UNIVERSITY

RINEHART & COMPANY, INC., NEW YORK

Preface

In recent years the need for a closer integration of public finance with the main body of economics has been stressed by a growing number of economists. The newer books in the field of public finance and fiscal policy often call attention in their titles to this change in orientation. The emphasis varies, however. Thus some texts center the interest on the impact of taxes, public spending, and debt management on the level and distribution of national product. Others stress the relation of public finance to economic, political, and social welfare. In any event, the reader is sensible of the fact that government finance is no longer dealt with solely as an end in itself but is treated as part of the economic and social organism. Attention is being paid, moreover, to modern advances in theoretical economics. For example, in discussing the tax burden recent authors have presented broader and more dynamic treatments of the incidence and economic effects of taxes than were formally available. Again, in line with present-day emphasis on the factors which determine the levels of income and spending, use has been made of refinements in the analytical tools of price and income theory. By devoting increasing attention to the reciprocal relationships between public finance and economic growth, writers in the field of public finance have shown awareness of the long-term economic effects of the fiscal policies of federal, state, and local governments.

The present author is in wholehearted agreement with the attempt to place the great mass of detail characterizing the study of public finance into a general framework of economic, political, and social thought. The focus of the present book is on the welfare aspects of public finance. Welfare is construed here in a broad sense and therefore not only includes the direct and immediate effects of fiscal measures on the relative satisfactions of individuals and groups in the national economy but also embraces the cyclical and long-term growth implications as well. Within the scope of the welfare approach, however, room exists for considerable difference in emphasis. The salient features of the present volume are a

v

strong emphasis on monetary and fiscal theory, special attention to the relation of public finance to the distribution of income, and a striving to place the issues in their historical setting. In addition, particular emphasis has been given to the following special problems: the technique of budgeting, the meaning of economic equilibrium as a basis for an understanding of monetary and fiscal policy for economic control, the practical and institutional problems facing the use of fiscal measures for full employment without inflation, and the economics of social security.

Despite the changes in emphasis to be found in recent public finance texts, these works retain a strong family resemblance to those of earlier authors. The reason for this is not far to seek. It is neither possible nor desirable to circumvent the task of discussing a respectable proportion of the huge mass of disparate financial problems of the several governmental levels. These problems are the inevitable accompaniment of government finance in a highly industrialized economy operating under a federal system of government. Public finance is a many-faceted study, and readers who want to understand the American fiscal system quite naturally insist on full coverage.

At the same time, each instructor will have his own conception of the relative emphasis that he wishes to place on different aspects of the complex field of public finance. For this reason special subjects can be dealt with independently. Thus, for example, separate chapters are devoted to Budgeting, Intergovernmental Fiscal Relations, Economic Equilibrium, the Art of Fiscal Policy, Fiscal Policy and the Distribution of Income, and the Economics of Social Security. In a shorter course in public finance one or more of these subjects may be omitted without breaking the chain of thought, or they may be treated as outside reading.

The author feels a deep sense of gratitude for the very helpful advice and criticism which he has received from a large number of readers at various stages of the work. The manuscript was read in its entirety by Howard R. Bowen, President of Grinnell College, and E. Gordon Keith, Professor of Finance at the Wharton School of Finance and Commerce. In addition, various individual chapters were given special readings, including the latter half of Chapter 3 (Robert Eisner, Associate Professor of Economics, Northwestern University, Robert Strotz, Associate Professor of Economics, Northwestern University, and Lawrence Werboff, Assistant Professor of Economics, Cornell College), Chapter 4 (Jesse Burkhead, Professor of Economics, Syracuse University), Chapter 7 (James M. Buchanan, Professor of Economics, Florida State University, and Fred Westfield, Lecturer in Economics, Northwestern University), Chapters 8, 9, and 10 (Richard E. Slitor, United States Treasury Department), Chapters 14 and 15 (Ronald Welch, California State Board of Equalization), Chapter 16 (Joseph A. Pechman, Council of Economic Advisors), Chapter 17 (Leon Rothenberg, Research Director, Federation of Tax Administrators), Chapter 18 (Robert Eisner), Chapter 19 (Robert Eisner and Alvin Marty, Assistant Professor of Economics, Northwestern University), Chapters 20, 21, and 23 (Robert Eisner), Chapter 24 (Wilbur J. Cohen, Director, Division of Research and Statistics, Social Security Administration, and Ray Nordstrand, Department of Economics, Northwestern University), and Chapter 25 (Roland I. Robinson, Professor of Finance, Northwestern University). Moreover, thanks are due to the many individuals, unfortunately too numerous to mention here, who have been so kind as to comment on doubtful passages, as well as to those who have provided items of information difficult to acquire. Dudley Johnson gave valuable assistance in the collection of statistical and bibliographical data, especially for the income and property tax chapters. After all this help and encouragement, it goes without saying that the author bears sole responsibility for any shortcomings that may remain.

K.E.P.

Evanston, Illinois
January 1, 1956

Contents

▶ GOVERNMENTAL REVENUE

► SOCIAL SECURITY, PUBLIC DEBT, AND
ECONOMIC GROWTH

Figures

Tables

Public Finance and Economic Welfare

1 The Scope and Growth of Public Finance

► GOVERNMENT AND THE ECONOMY

The federal, state, and local governments of the United States are engaged in an enormous collection of activities. A highly complex and growing society demands a constantly increasing complement of those goods and services which can only be provided by government. Of such government services, by far the most costly is national defense. In the neighborhood of 85 per cent of the federal budget is at the present time devoted to national defense, including the cost of maintaining the military establishment, foreign aid, atomic energy, veterans' aid, and interest on the war debt. Other federal programs, though dwarfed by national defense, have nevertheless become very large in absolute terms. Aid to agriculture, development of natural resources, free services to business and labor groups, aid to education, continental highways, and a host of other activities that have been added as public need for them developed—all these make tremendous demands on the tax resources of the national government.

The states and the municipalities likewise have felt a constant pressure to expand their services. A hundred years ago over 80 per cent of the American population was rural; today only approximately 40 per cent remains in this category. This extraordinary migration to the larger centers, which is still continuing, has naturally led to an ever-increasing specialization of economic functions; and government activity has been one of the forms that this specialization has taken. Moreover, with the development of transportation and communications, rural areas have likewise participated in the expansion of public services. The consolidated school and the county hospital are examples. But the cost of government is not limited to the need of the three levels of government for revenues in order to finance the purchases of goods and services from the private sector of the economy. Government agencies also make transfer payments and subsidies, such as veterans' benefits and farm price supports, for which no

3

equivalent value is demanded of the recipient. Public finance is concerned with how these manifold functions are financed, and with the economic effects of the methods of financing that are employed.

Public finance deals with four major governmental functions. These are the determination of the level and direction of public spending, the search for tax revenues, public borrowing, and the management of the public debt. At the federal level a fifth function of public finance has come to receive much attention during the years since the economic collapse of the thirties and the appearance of the *General Theory* of John Maynard Keynes. This is the impact of public spending, taxation, borrowing, and debt management on the level and distribution of income. The great growth in the importance of government, particularly the national government, in the economy during the last generation has necessitated much preoccupation with the effects of government finance on income and employment, and, more positively, with deliberate changes in tax rates and rates of government spending in order to compensate for fluctuations in private investment and consumption spending. On the taxation side, more and more attention has been paid to the economic effects of taxes, as contrasted with the former restriction of emphasis to taxes as a means of obtaining revenues.

Public expenditures are covered largely with revenues derived from taxes; but governments also receive income from the sale of services, for example, from toll roads and from the sale of electricity, gas, and water, and the like. Moreover, they frequently find it necessary to borrow. Large public works programs and wars usually require long-term borrowing; and even in the short period, the flow of tax receipts is not perfectly synchronized with the dates on which cash payments by government must be made. Therefore governments must market public issues in competition with private securities. A rate of interest must be fixed for each type of public security, the needs of the government and of potential investors taken into account in the terms of issue, and maturities spaced so that the securities falling due for repayment in each year can be financed out of budgetary surpluses or converted into new issues. Because of the enormous growth in the importance of government in the last twenty-five years, its economic and financial functions have likewise vastly increased in importance and complexity.

▶ THE GROWTH IN GOVERNMENT ECONOMIC ACTIVITY

The great growth in the magnitude and scope of the economic activities of all levels of government (particularly the federal) in recent years has changed radically our concept of the meaning of public finance. No longer can we think of it as merely the technical problem of matching expenditures and revenues. Public finance has come to include the economic significance of the activities of government. This is a much broader concept, for it implies that the measures taken to finance government cannot be regarded as more or less detached from the economy as a whole. The economic welfare of society demands that governments consider the impact of their financial activities on the economy. Government finance affects the level of national product, and therefore employment. It also modifies the distribution of income and wealth. Some conception of the trends in the magnitudes involved will assist in an appreciation of the extent of the impact of government on the economic life of the nation.

The last half century has seen a tremendous rise in the dollar expenditures of all levels of government in the United States. From 1902 to 1953 total expenditures rose almost seventyfold; expenditures of the federal government were about 150 times the 1902 figure, state expenditures rose by 85 times, and local expenditures increased by 21 times.

Table 1. Federal, State, and Local Expenditures, Selected Fiscal Years, 1902–1953

(Dollar amounts in millions)

Fiscal Year	Total	Federal	State	Local
1902	1,500	485	136	879
1913	2,789	725	297	1,767
1927	10,255	2,974	1,451	5,830
1934	14,009	6,694	2,143	5,172
1940	19,116	9,062	3,555	6,499
1944	104,675	95,059	3,319	6,197
1948	52,464	33,069	7,897	11,498
1952	93,642	65,408	10,790	17,444
1953	104,356	74,274	11,466	18,616

SOURCES: *Annual Reports* of the Secretary of the Treasury; Bureau of the Census, *Historical Statistics on State and Local Government Finances, 1902–1953.*

The rapidly increasing size and complexity of the American economy have necessitated an enormous expansion in the services provided by all levels of government. But the greatest rise has come in federal spending. This is partly due to the modest financial and economic role of the federal government before World War I, and even into the twenties, and partly due to the fact that a large proportion of the additional public services required in a modern complex industrial economy can be provided most efficiently, and in important instances (e.g., national defense, industrial regulation) only, by the central government. Likewise the importance of state spending has increased in relation to that of the local governments. The steady movement toward centralization of public functions is strongly illuminated by the trends depicted in Table 1.

Uncorrected dollar figures for government expenditures can easily lead to misconceptions concerning the extent of the secular rise in public spending. An obvious correction that must be made is for changes in the price level. The wholesale price index of the Bureau of Labor Statistics stood at 58.9 in 1902; it had reached a postwar peak of 180.4 by 1951. Thus the wholesale price level had about tripled during the fifty-year period, accounting for two thirds of the rise in public spending. Another correction is for population growth. With a growing population a given level of public spending is a declining level of per capita public spending. Still another correction is that for the growth in national income. The relative importance of a given level of public spending becomes smaller the larger is national income.

The phenomenon of economic growth makes it difficult to place an interpretation upon the significance of a secular rise in public expenditures. A rise in public spending is to be anticipated as population rises. Police and fire departments, educational facilities, hospitals, roads, national defense, and so on, all bear a relation to the size of the population to be served. But economic growth also means a higher degree of specialization and a greater complexity of life. Consequently the amount of public services needed *per person* rises, because a greater variety and intensity of government services must be provided as people become more and more crowded together, as more business and personal relationships have to be policed and controlled by government agencies, and as urbanization and increasing economic, political, and social sophistication on the part of the public create demands for ever higher standards of public services. As we shall see in a later chapter, there is no easy way to determine if in some sense government expenditures have risen *too* rapidly over the years.

Table 2 corrects the dollar changes in public expenditures since 1913 for changes in the price level, population, and national income. This table reveals a number of interesting facts with respect to the trend of public expenditures in the United States. It will be noted, for example, that despite the attempts of the economy-minded Coolidge and Hoover administrations in the twenties to hold down federal spending, total public spending as a proportion of national income was substantially greater than it had been before World War I. Again, it is interesting to note the great rise in the ratio in the early thirties. This reflects several aspects of depression phenomena. Expenditures in current dollars rose moderately, from $10.26 billion to $12.83 billion between 1927 and 1934. But because of the sharp decline in prices, *real* government expenditures rose substantially. National income declined greatly, though less so in constant dollars (not indicated in the table). The net result of the depression rise in federal public works spending and the decline in national income was the doubling of total government expenditures taken as a proportion of national income.

The effects of the tremendous expenditures incurred during World War II are reflected in the rise of each of the indices of government activity as revealed by Table 2, in current and real dollars, in per capita expenditures, in national income in terms of current dollars, and in gov-

Table 2. Total Federal, State, and Local Government Expenditures, Selected Years, 1913–1953

(Adjusted for changes in the price level, population, and national income)

Cal-endar Year (1)	Total Expendi-tures ($ billion) (2)	Whole-sale Price Index (1926 = 100) (3)	Total Expendi-tures in 1926 Dollars (4)	Popu-lation July 1 (5)	Per Capita Expendi-tures 1926 Dollars (6)	National Income ($ billion) (7)	Total Current Expendi-tures as a Percent-age of National Income (8)
1913	2.79	69.8	4.09	97.2	42.1	34.8	8.0
1927	10.26	95.4	10.75	119.0	90.3	75.9	13.5
1934	12.83	74.9	17.12	126.4	135.7	49.0	26.2
1940	18.47	78.6	23.46	132.1	178.0	81.6	22.6
1944	103.07	104.0	99.18	138.4	716.5	182.6	56.5
1948	51.40	165.1	31.13	146.6	212.6	221.6	23.2
1952	93.92	176.5	53.31	157.0	337.5	291.0	32.3
1953	102.53	174.1	58.86	159.6	369.3	305.0	33.6

SOURCES: Expenditures for 1913 and 1927 are fiscal year. Calendar year expenditures for the later years are from *Survey of Current Business*, 1954 Supplement, p. 172. National income data: for 1913 and 1927, Department of Commerce figures for national income produced, 1909–1941 (cf. National Industrial Conference Board, *Economic Almanac*, published annually, which are fairly comparable with national income figures for later years, *Survey of Current Business*, cited above, pp. 162–163.

ernment expenditures as a percentage of national income. The sharp decline in the ratio in 1948 reflected the post–World War II version of "back to normalcy," and the subsequent rise to what may prove to be a fairly stable ratio, of about one third of national income accounted for by public expenditures, in large part reflects American disillusion with hopes for a relatively unarmed peace. But it also in part reflects the urgency of an expansion of state and local expenditures in response to a growing public demand for services.

Before having done with Table 2, it is important also to note some of the matters which it conceals. Per capita expenditures, popular as they are and probably always will be with publicists and propagandists, do not give much information on the extent of the burden of rising public expenditures on the average citizen. They throw no light on the distribution of the population by age brackets, military and civilian status, sex, and so on. Consequently per capita expenditures do not provide any very accurate basis for judging the burden of public spending. A rise in the proportion of those above the age of sixty-five and below working age (which has actually occurred in recent years) would represent a greater burden on the working population even if no rise in public spending and taxing took place.

Attention should also be called to the question of the appropriateness of using the wholesale price index for deflating current public expenditures. Since different types of price index do not move in parallel fashion, either cyclically or secularly, it makes a difference which one is used. Governments by no means spend all their money on goods sold at wholesale. At the present time approximately ten million persons are employed by the government or are in military service. To correct government purchases of these services for changes in the price level, then, an index of wage rates would be more appropriate than an index of wholesale prices. Nevertheless, since *some* price index must be used, the wholesale index is the most nearly appropriate. Another point should be noted. Column 2 in Table 2 presents over-all data on government spending. No distinction is made between direct purchases of goods and services, on the one hand, and subsidies and other transfer payments (for example, interest on the debt), on the other. Thus a great deal of information is concealed that is important to have if we are to make any inferences on the burden of public expenditures. This problem will be discussed at greater length in Chapter 3.

Finally, attention should perhaps be called to the fact that in a growing economy it may be considered normal for both private and public expenditures to rise. When an organism grows, all its members also develop. It is another question, however, whether all economic institutions, including the government, should grow at an equal rate. In terms of our table, the question arises whether public spending as a proportion of national income should remain constant over the years. A detailed answer to this question must be deferred until the functions of government in the economy have been examined further. A *definite* answer, however, agreed to by all parties, is hardly an attainable objective.

▶ PUBLIC OPINION AND THE LEVEL OF EXPENDITURES

All of us are taxpayers, and taxpayers are frequently concerned whether or not we are approaching the limits of taxable capacity in the United States. This issue is reserved for later discussion, but the fact that it is so frequently raised by newspaper editorials, in Congressional hearings, and during election campaigns, leads one to ask the question whether public demands for economy in government are ever heard, and if heard, whether cries for economy are effective in reducing public spending. As a preface to this discussion it is helpful to bear in mind that demands for additional public services, as well as demands for economy in government, must be addressed separately to each of the three levels of government. The federal government is responsible for military protection, public works expenditures for combating depression, major economic programs, and other services which transcend state lines or state fiscal capacities. States, in turn, make expenditures on public safety and welfare, education, highways, health and hospitals, penal institutions, and the development of natural resources. The counties and localities are concerned with public safety, schools, highways, sanitation and health, libraries, and the like.

An argument that is made again and again by those who deplore the great rise in public spending, particularly that of the federal government, is that expenditures can be cut if Congress and the President will simply take the bull by the horns. This is certainly true. Much waste can always be eliminated, and many public expenditures could be curtailed without visible loss of services to the public. Note, for example, the earnest efforts of the administration in the spring of 1953 to curb federal expenditures, which provide evidence that public expenditures are by no means impervious to reduction.

On the other hand, a very considerable proportion of public expenditures is not easily subject to reduction. Society comes to expect the retention of various public services to which it has grown accustomed. As changing economic and social conditions require the addition of new types that were never thought of before, the list tends to grow. The impact of this circumstance on the growth of public spending can be appreciated by a brief survey of the course of federal, state, and local expenditures, and the public attitude toward this development, since the founding of the Republic.

► THE GROWTH OF PUBLIC EXPENDITURES IN THE
UNITED STATES

CONFLICTING VIEWS ON FEDERAL SPENDING AFTER 1789

The cleavage of opinion between those who desire an important role for government in the economy and those who believe that "that government is best that governs least" has roots deep in the past. Alexander Hamilton favored an important role for the central government. One reason for his view was that only if the central government were to have responsibility for a substantial volume of expenditures could the states be persuaded to yield to it the wide power to levy taxes that advocates of a strong central government regarded as indispensable. The Constitution reflected the views of the Hamiltonians, since it not only gave the federal government exclusive jurisdiction over the customs, but also concurrent powers with the states in most areas of taxation. Although it was then believed that the federal government would have no reason to make full use of this power, it was significant that fiscal obstacles to such extension were removed.

Two important factors convinced the opponents of Hamilton's position that concentration of the spending power in the central government was undesirable. First was the view that had received much currency in England after the appearance of Adam Smith's *Wealth of Nations* (1776), namely, that expenditures by the central government are unproductive. The wastefulness and conspicuous consumption of most of the courts of Europe during the eighteenth century, when no distinction was made between the king's personal household and the budget of the nation, led to a feeling that government spending was of necessity wasteful. The second was the fact that even those who did not share the view that public expenditures are necessarily unproductive could not agree on whether the central government or the states should have major responsibility for public works expenditures.

The first of these views could not withstand the onslaught of public demand for the economic expansion of a rapidly growing country. Many projects had to be undertaken that were impossible to private enterprise. Thus the Louisiana Purchase was made under the administration of Jefferson, a sturdy opponent of a strong federal government. The Cumberland Road was begun in 1806 to hasten the opening of the West. Moreover, Jefferson and Gallatin, his Secretary of the Treasury, hesitated to adhere dogmatically to the view that government expenditures are unproductive. Both advocated federal aid to the states for financing such improvements as building roads in newly developed territories, dredging rivers, and building canals. Again, federal budgetary surpluses in the latter part of the decade turned the attention of the administration in the direction of plans for systematic internal improvements. Thus political predilections had to give way to the swiftly moving events of the times.

THE ERA OF WESTWARD EXPANSION

The rapid westward expansion after 1815 introduced a new element into the struggle over federal expenditures. The new states were impatient of any obstacle to their rapid growth. Therefore, in their opinion, expenditures should be undertaken by the states, which felt they could act more quickly, and more clearly in their own interest. This strong emphasis on state rights, though not the exclusive property of either party, became most pronounced under Jackson. He feared that increased federal spending (and taxing) would not only confer an undesirable uniformity on the states, but would encroach on their sovereignty. This view, strengthened by the widening cleavage between North and South during the thirty years that preceded the Civil War, helped to retard the growth of federal expenditures during the first half of the century.[1]

Despite Jackson's opposition to federal spending, expenditures under his administration on public works were higher than ever, for the same factors which caused the new states to resent federal interference made them dependent upon it. Although he vetoed a number of bills for the construction of interstate highways, the ever-widening settled area of the United States made rising federal expenditures on public works inevitable. It was finally necessary, in 1836, for Jackson to swallow his dislike for a distribution of the federal surplus, which was made in the form of a loan to the states. Thus indirectly the federal government financed a considerable part of the expenditures undertaken by the states. It was tacitly agreed that the "loan" should never be repaid.

The constantly recurring budgetary surpluses of the decades before the Civil War provided a continuing impetus to Congress to seek out new spending projects. These surpluses resulted from a tax system based almost exclusively on the protective tariff, which did not protect, and consequently furnished unneeded revenues. An unspent cash budgetary surplus was found to be a constant threat to financial stability, since it drained cash out of the hands of the public into the vaults of the Treasury. In the years immediately before the Civil War, however, sentiment again turned against the increasing volume of federal expenditures. Economic difficulties reduced the frequency of the surpluses, and preoccupation with the problem of agrarianism arrested the development of sentiment in favor of an extended use of federal spending powers.

EVENTS AFTER THE CIVIL WAR

The Civil War greatly affected the struggle between the federal government and the states for political and fiscal supremacy. The necessity for a full battery of taxes, including the personal income tax, gave the former experience with the types of taxes that are basic to a high level of public spending. The physical and economic dislocations caused by the war lessened the objections to federal assistance, and the growth of big business necessitated increased federal controls.

---

[1] Protectionists of the period, however, favored a high level of federal expenditures, financed by the customs. Henry Clay was the leader of this group, whose platform he called the "American System." (Cf. P. Studenski and H. Krooss, *Financial History of the United States* [New York: McGraw, 1952],, pp. 90–91.) The protectionists favored veterans' pensions, distribution of the proceeds of the sales of federal lands among the states, and internal improvements. To assure the retention of a high tariff they also advocated the reduction of revenues other than the customs. For the reaction of the South to this program, and for an appreciation of its tremendous significance for the growing economic cleavage that paved the way for the Civil War, refer to Calhoun's famous speech delivered in Congress in 1850.

On the other hand, sentiment did not yet exist for the entrance of the federal government into new forms of public investment, and throughout much of the last quarter of the century the Treasury was hampered by the reappearance of the surpluses that had characterized many of the prewar years. President Cleveland, however, proved a staunch opponent of increased federal spending. In the face of repeated surpluses that threatened a financial crisis and deflation, he refused to accept the view that the federal government should increase expenditures on internal improvements. The recurring surpluses were "a condition which confronts us, not a theory," and something should be done about them. Nevertheless, it was the people that should support the government; the government should not support the people. Congress must reduce the tariff, not increase appropriations. As always in the nineteenth century, federal expenditures were bound up with the cause of protection.

The situation began to change, however, after the conclusion of the great monetary struggle that had occupied the attention of the public and Congress since the Civil War, and had been settled by the passage of the Gold Standard Act of 1900. Under Theodore Roosevelt's administration a wider group of publicists began to join in the chorus of complaint raised in earlier years by the Grangers, the Populists, and others, against the numerous social abuses that had sprung up unchecked as the nation industrialized after the Civil War.

These abuses were largely outside the power of the states to correct. Federal legislation for the control of business and the protection of labor was necessary, and implied in this legislation was a great increase in federal spending. Of equal importance was the growth of a new concept of the role of the federal government at home and in the world at large. Expenditures increased for the conservation of natural resources and for agriculture; the Great Powers were to be impressed with the size of the United States Navy; and millions were spent on the Panama Canal. The Spanish-American War was itself a manifestation of the changing mood. These prewar developments have to be borne in mind in assessing the public spending aspects of the "back to normalcy" movement of the Harding administration.

THE ATTEMPT TO CURTAIL FEDERAL SPENDING AFTER WORLD WAR I

As in the case of every great war, the rise in expenditures during World War I gave birth to many governmental functions that would never be surrendered. Wars and great depressions both produce a number of irreversible trends in public spending. They also tend to accelerate earlier trends. On the one hand, gaps are discovered in the nation's ability to provide certain materials necessary for carrying on a war: witness the interest in the public development of hydroelectric power and synthetic nitrates in the twenties. On the other hand, the war itself creates dislocations and problems that have to be solved with the help of public spending during the ensuing years of peace. Examples are veterans' pensions and medical care, support to farmers who have been attracted to submarginal land by high wartime food prices, and the protection of markets for industrial products created during the war. Some expenditures are temporary, like those made in order to help industry to reconvert to peacetime production. Others, however, continue indefinitely, and may open up new federal spending opportunities. These developments were more marked after World War I than had been the case after the Civil War, and they have been still more noticeable after World War II.

The course of federal spending during the twenties was determined jointly by underlying forces not greatly subject to control, and by the attitude of the Harding, Coolidge, and Hoover administrations and of the public toward the relation between the central government and the individual. As we have seen, "back to normalcy" could at most mean a return to the trend of federal spending that had been established in the quarter century before the war, with superimposed upon it the irreducible expenditures made necessary to liquidate the aftereffects of the war itself. On the other hand, President Coolidge applied the test of economy to all requests for federal appropriations; the Bureau of the Budget was established in 1921 in order to reduce waste and inefficiency in government expenditures; and the Directors of the Bureau took it to be their main function to hold down expenditures rather than to compare the relative advantages of given amounts of public and private spending. An element of major importance was the speedy return to isolationism after the war, which brought with it an immediate cessation of foreign loans and a rejection of any official participation in the reconstruction of Europe. Federal expenditures hardly rose from 1924 to 1929.

THE GREAT DEPRESSION AND AFTER

After the 1929 crash the level of federal spending increased despite the attempt of both the Hoover and Roosevelt administrations to reduce public spending in order to minimize the deficit. By 1934 federal spending was more than twice the 1929 level, even though the price level had fallen sharply; and there was a further large increase by 1939. Relief expenditures necessarily rose regardless of spending philosophies, and shortly after assuming office Roosevelt inaugurated a large program of public works spending. Since 1939 the immense increase in federal spending has been dominated by war and preparation for war, foreign aid, and a vast complex of programs (veterans' aid, farm relief, and so on) which transfer purchasing power from one group to another. Another prominent development has been the growth in the importance of government enterprise. The federal government is in business in a big way with such enterprises as the Commodity Credit Corporation, the Tennessee Valley Authority, the Atomic Energy Commission, and the like. States are heavily involved in the tourist industry. Cities and states set up authorities, like the Port of New York Authority, which engage in a wide range of economic activities. Even small localities are in the public-utility business.

► SPENDING BY THE STATES AND MUNICIPALITIES

Expenditures of the states and cities have likewise increased substantially in recent decades. Although the trend has risen as both levels of government have taken on many new functions, periods of rapidly rising expenditures have been interspersed with periods of curtailment. The latter have occurred for the most part during time of war, when the federal government has not only pre-empted most of the tax sources but has also diverted factors of production from the states and the cities as well as from the private sector of the economy.

As we have seen, the states displayed great interest in spending for internal improvements during the second quarter of the nineteenth century. As a result of overextension, however, some states incurred an excessive volume of debt. In a number of cases the states refused to honor their debt, and the revulsion against irresponsible financial methods led some of them to write prohibitions into their constitutions against borrowing for internal improvements. The cities also vastly increased their expenditures, mainly for protective services against disease, crime, and fire. Like the states, many of the municipalities exceeded their borrowing capacity, and sentiment grew for limitations on their spending programs. A serious obstacle to curtailment, however, was the widespread corruption of the city political machine.

After 1880 expenditures of the states for social services, education, conservation of resources, and for state institutions began to rise. The state general property tax, which had been introduced to finance the expansion of state spending earlier in the century, was found inadequate to meet the claims of expanded activities. Taxes on transportation, insurance companies, public utilities, and corporations, together with liquor and inheritance taxes, provided the required revenues, and state tax commissions were formed to make assessment and collection of taxes more efficient.

From 1900 to 1930 by far the greatest relative increase in public expenditures was at the state level. It was a period of incipient breakdown in the capacity of the localities to provide the rapidly increasing number of services needed in a society that was rapidly increasing in complexity. The phenomenon was most marked in the twenties, particularly because of the expansion in automobile traffic, the democratization of higher education, the realization that health control is not a local matter, and the recognition of the role of the states in public relief. Moreover, the time had not yet come when public sentiment favored a further centralization of functions into the hands of the federal government.

Once again an entirely new set of state taxes was required. In the absence of a federal income tax before 1913 some states were able to exploit this tax, while the rapid development of automobile transport permitted increasing reliance on gasoline and vehicle taxes. Finally, experiments began to be made with various types of sales taxes. Owing to the inadequacy of the local property tax for financing the rising demands for local services, despite rapidly increasing rates and yield, some states surrendered their own real-estate taxes and in addition made grants-in-aid to the localities.

The depression created difficulties for the states and towns with respect to both revenues and expenditures. Expenditures increased for relief, while revenues fell off sharply. The municipalities were harder hit than the states, for they depended primarily on the property tax. The latter were fortunate in having the gasoline and motor vehicle taxes, as well as the relatively inelastic business taxes. Since 1930, however, federal spending has vastly risen in comparison with both state and local spending. Moreover, the federal government has inaugurated a system of grants-in-aid to the states, and the localities have become increasingly dependent on the latter. In brief, not only has government spending greatly increased in recent years, but governmental finances have become more and more centralized.

► TRENDS IN THE DISTRIBUTION OF FEDERAL EXPENDITURES

As of 1953 federal expenditures for national defense vastly outstripped other federal spending activities. The change in public awareness of defense needs is sharply illustrated by the rise in the proportion of total federal spending taken by this item from 13.8 per cent in 1939 to 59.8 per cent in 1953. It should be noted, however, that percentage comparisons may be misleading. In 1914, for example, defense expenditures had accounted for as much as 36 per cent of total federal expenditures. The reason, however, was that spending for other purposes was at a low level. In view of the huge rise in dollar spending on certain other items of federal expenditure, it is noteworthy that their relative magnitude has declined since 1932. Thus veterans' benefits, which accounted for about 22 per cent of federal spending in 1932, had dropped to below 7 per cent by 1939, and were at about the same level in 1953. A somewhat similar trend characterizes payments on the national debt.

A glance at Table 3 will show that major changes have occurred in the types and relative importance of the expenditures that the federal government has been called upon to make in the past twenty years. Subsidies to agriculture, which had declined as a result of high war and postwar demand for farm products, rose sharply in 1953 ($3.1 billion as compared with $1.2 billion in 1939.) International financial aid and atomic energy, two items that did not exist before World War II, accounted for about 10 per cent of the federal budget in 1953. Another item of federal expenditure that has risen steadily since 1936 is social security. This will continue to rise in terms of dollars, though of course not neces-

Table 3. The Functional Distribution of Federal Spending

(Fiscal years; dollar amounts in billions)

	1932		1939		1953	
	$	%	$	%	$	%
TOTAL	4.5	100.0	8.7	100.0	74.6	100.0
National defense and related activities	0.8	17.8	1.2	13.8	44.6	59.8
International financial aid	—	—	—	—	5.8	7.8
Interest	0.6	13.3	0.9	10.3	6.5	8.7
Veterans	1.0	22.2	0.6	6.9	4.3	5.7
Agriculture	0.4	8.9	1.2	13.8	3.1	4.2
Public works	0.5	11.1	1.0	11.5	1.7	2.3
Social security	—	—	0.5	5.8	2.3	3.1
Atomic energy	—	—	—	—	1.8	2.4
Work relief	—	—	2.5	28.7	—	—
Direct relief	0.3	6.7	—	—	—	—
Other	0.9	20.0	0.8	9.2	4.5	6.0

SOURCES: *Annual Reports* of the Secretary of the Treasury, "Budget Expenditures by Major Classifications."

sarily relatively to other expenditures, as the social security system includes more and more workers, and as annual retirements increase. It is of passing interest to note that even in 1939, when the impact of war spending, especially by European nations, was beginning to make itself felt, relief expenditures totaled $2.5 billion, or nearly 30 per cent of the federal budget.

International financial aid may be expected to decline as Western Europe becomes more nearly self-supporting. This item has taken different forms as circumstances have altered. During the war the lend-lease program totaled nearly $50 billion, though partly offset by about $7 billion of reverse lend-lease by Allied countries in the form of support of American troops. After the war, loans were granted to Britain and France, and relief payments were made through the United Nations Relief and Rehabilitation Administration. The United States participated in the International Monetary Fund and in the International Bank for Reconstruction and Development. Direct loans were made by certain United States government agencies, as well as by the Export-Import Bank. Between 1946 and 1950 federal expenditures on international finance totaled $23 billion. Too many intangible factors in the world political and military situation exist for it to be safe to venture any predictions on the likelihood that American financial aid can be held to a low level.

▶ TRENDS IN THE DISTRIBUTION OF STATE EXPENDITURES

ALL EXPENDITURES

Table 4 indicates the changes in the level and relative importance of the major types of current expenditures of the states during the period 1915–1953.

Table 4. Expenditures of the States by Function
(Dollar amounts in millions)

	1915		1932		1940		1953	
	$	%	$	%	$	%	$	%
TOTAL	470	100.0	2597	100.0	4097	100.0	14,677	100.0
Public safety	62	13.2	178	6.9	220	5.4	414	2.8
Public welfare	34	7.2	128	4.9	947	23.1	2514	17.1
Education	157	33.4	621	23.9	939	22.9	4382	29.9
Highways	77	16.4	1071	41.3	1134	27.7	3584	24.4
Health and hospitals	61	13.1	216	8.3	318	7.8	1313	8.9
Housing	—	—	—	—	—	—	13	0.1
Natural resources	18	3.8	79	3.0	107	2.6	543	3.7
Employment security	—	—	—	—	—	—	187	1.3
General control	50	10.6	138	5.3	172	4.2	406	2.8
Miscellaneous	11	2.3	166	6.4	260	6.3	1322	9.0

SOURCES: Bureau of the Census, *Historical Statistics of the United States*, p. 316; *State Government Finances in 1953*, pp. 22, 26.

The first thing to note about Table 4 is that it presents only totals for all states.[2] Wide variations occur in both total and per capita expenditures on different functions in the several states. For the states as a whole a number of changes have taken place since 1915, and again since 1932. A great increase in the proportion of state expenditures devoted to highways took place between 1915 and 1932. The rise was from 16.4 per cent

---

[2] The Bureau of the Census also presents these data by individual states.

to 41.3 per cent of total expenditures. Although the relative importance of this type of expenditure declined as progress was made on the completion of the highway network of the states and as the federal government interested itself in national highways, the proportion was still as high as 24.4 per cent in 1953. The tremendous growth in the number of automobiles on the highway in the postwar years has again made the highway system inadequate, and the immense financial problems involved in the construction of modern through roads have popularized the use of revenue bonds serviced from the proceeds of tolls.

Declines have occurred in the relative importance of expenditures for public safety and for general control, and these declines have been fairly continuous throughout the entire period. The reason is, of course, that as the states have taken on added functions, the traditional services have necessarily declined in relative terms. Substantial increases have taken place in public welfare. The states have participated heavily in the programs for relief and assistance that were initiated or expanded during the depression. These include aid to the disabled, public assistance, welfare institutions, as well as grants to the localities for public relief. In 1953 three fifths of total state expenditures on public assistance were devoted to old-age assistance, while one fifth went to dependent children.

EDUCATION

State expenditures on education are of particular interest because of their role as a bulwark against undue centralization of educational policy at the national level. A large proportion of state expenditure for education consists of grants to the localities. In 1953, for example, somewhat less than one third of the $4.4 billion spent by the states on education went to their own institutions of higher learning, while approximately $2.7 billion, or 62 per cent, consisted of intergovernmental expenditure.

Two species of grant have been made to the locality or school district. One is the flat grant, which is not geared to the differences in taxpaying capacity of the lower level of government. The other, now in use in the majority of states, is the equalization grant. The grant may be contingent on increased efficiency. For example, consolidation of a number of one-room school buildings into a central unit may be required. In this case the effect is not only to raise the standard of education but to reduce costs as well. An important aspect of state aid to the localities in the field of education is the desire to retain responsibility for public education in the hands of the states and the municipalities. In the highly mobile society that characterizes the modern state, the necessity for a high minimum educational standard throughout the country is obvious. State aid to the communities for education not only relieves the burden on local property taxes but reduces the pressure for federal aid (and consequently the imposition of federal standards) in the field of education.

► THE DISTRIBUTION OF LOCAL EXPENDITURES

Table 5 shows the distribution of general expenditures of 481 cities with a population of 25,000 or more in the fiscal year 1952.[3] For a number of reasons it is difficult to compare the distribution of local expenditures with earlier years.[4] A few general remarks may be made, however. The cities have placed greater emphasis in recent years on expenditures for

Table 5. General Expenditures by Function, 1952

(For 481 cities of 25,000 or more; dollar amounts in millions)

	$	%
TOTAL GENERAL EXPENDITURES	5,184	100.0
Police and fire	945	18.4
Highways	587	11.3
Sanitation	534	10.3
Public welfare	424	8.1
Education and libraries	982	18.9
Health and hospitals	454	8.8
Recreation	234	4.5
General control	260	5.0
Interest on debt	173	3.3
Other	591	11.4

SOURCE: Bureau of the Census, *City Government Finances in 1952*, p. 13.

health and hospitals and on recreation. Public welfare expenditures have likewise increased in importance. On the other hand, the proportion of total local expenditures on general control, education, and public safety has fallen. The relative importance of various types of local expenditures varies sharply in accordance with nation-wide economic changes. During major wars, for example, the capital expenditures of the localities naturally decline sharply. The deficiency is later made up in postwar years of abnormally high capital investment. Highway and other types of maintenance are similarly affected. Again, certain types of expenditures are more vulnerable to depression than others.

[3] Thus much local expenditure is not included. Moreover, variations in the structure of city governments create problems of comparability.

[4] Statistics are not gathered for all the localities. Therefore the Bureau of the Census restricts its coverage to cities over 25,000. But the number of cities in this group changes with the growth and redistribution of population. Also, the classification of expenditures has changed over the years.

▶ SUMMARY

The rapid dynamic changes associated with the modern industrial state have resulted in a substantial increase in the relative economic importance of government. This phenomenon has been particularly marked in the United States at the federal level, although the states and localities have substantially expanded their services in the last fifty years. Because of the great rise in the proportion of national income taxed and spent by government, the study of public finance must be concerned with broader considerations than merely technical aspects of government finance. Public finance must also deal with the economic significance of government activities. However, in a general survey much that might be included must be left to more specialized studies. The major subjects not treated are the finances of nationalized industries and the economics of the government corporation.

A survey of the trends in federal, state, and local expenditures indicates that while some types of spending appear likely to remain with each level of government, there is a constant tendency for higher governmental jurisdictions to undermine the fiscal powers of lower levels. This tendency stems in part from the widespread belief that some centralization of spending powers is necessary in order to reduce the impact of differences in the wealth and taxpaying capacity of different states and, within the states, of different municipalities. An equally important consideration is the fact that many of the modern expensive forms of public service cannot be provided by the lower levels of government. Similarly, the encroachment of the public sphere on the *private* sector of the economy is largely explainable on the ground that the latter cannot provide certain services that the public insists on having. A brief survey of the history of public spending in the United States indicated that the ratio of public spending to national income tends to rise even in the face of administration and Congressional philosophies opposing the trend. Finally, recent trends in the distribution of expenditures at the federal, state, and local levels were examined. At all levels growing population, urbanization, and the demand by the public for a variety of new services have resulted in substantial changes in the relative importance of different types of expenditures in the last few decades. Dominating the whole picture has been the rise in military expenditures.

▶ REFERENCES

DUE, JOHN F. "Government Expenditures and Their Significance for the Economy," in K. E. Poole, ed., *Fiscal Policies and the American Economy*. New York: Prentice-Hall, Inc., 1951.

FABRICANT, S. *The Trend of Government Activity in the United States since 1900*. New York: National Bureau of Economic Research, 1952.

MUSGRAVE, R. A., and J. M. CULBERTSON. "The Growth of Public Expenditures in the United States, 1890–1948," *National Tax Journal*, June, 1953, pp. 97–115.

RATNER, S. *American Taxation: Its History as a Social Force in Democracy*. New York: W. W. Norton & Company, 1942.

STUDENSKI, P., and H. KROOSS. *Financial History of the United States*. New York: McGraw-Hill Book Company, Inc., 1952.

2 The Financing of the Federal, State, and Local Governments: Historical Perspective

► TRENDS IN FEDERAL, STATE, AND LOCAL TAXATION

The extraordinary increase in the level and variety of the functions of government in the past fifty years, described in Chapter 1, has necessitated a comparable rise in the proportion of national income taken in taxes. The greatly increased revenue needs have required the introduction of new types of highly productive taxes. Since the federal government has enjoyed considerable freedom in tax experimentation, it is at the national level that the changes have been most marked.

To be sure, the states have the constitutional and legal authority to levy such taxes as they desire (except customs). Their freedom of action is limited, however, by the extremely high rates of similar federal taxes. The corporate and personal income taxes are the major examples of a large degree of federal pre-emption. The localities, in addition, are limited in their search for tax sources by the fact that they are creatures of the states. State constitutions sometimes impose limits on the types of taxes that the cities and towns may use, as well as on maximum rates. This means that it is often insufficient for the cities to appeal to state legislatures for permission to introduce new taxes or to raise rates of old ones. The much more difficult task of amending the state constitution may have to be faced.[1]

The tremendous growth in the tax-revenues of all levels of government in the United States has already been implied in the discussion of the

---

[1] New York City, for example, has felt these restrictions acutely in recent years. See the Report by R. M. Haig and Carl S. Shoup to the Mayor's Committee on Management Survey, *The Financial Problem of the City of New York* (New York; June, 1952). Eight states imposed over-all rate limits in the thirties, six constitutionally and two through legislation. No new rate limitations have been imposed since then.

Table 6. The Relative Growth of Federal, State, and Local Tax Revenues, Selected Fiscal Years, 1913–1953

(Dollar amounts in millions)

	1913		1927		1934		1940		1944		1953	
	$	%	$	%	$	%	$	%	$	%	$	%
Federal	663	29.2	3,471	36.3	2,986	33.6	5,689	42.2	40,553	82.3	70,300	71.1
State	301	13.3	1,608	16.8	1,979	22.2	3,313	24.5	4,071	8.2	10,552	11.6
Local	1,308	57.5	4,479	46.9	3,933	44.2	4,497	33.3	4,703	9.5	10,356	11.3
TOTAL	2,272	100.0	9,558	100.0	8,898	100.0	13,499	100.0	49,327	100.0	91,208	100.0

SOURCES: *Annual Reports* of the Secretary of the Treasury; Bureau of the Census, *Historical Statistics on State and Local Government Finances, 1902–1953; Statistical Abstract of the United States.*

expenditure growth in the previous chapter. The same corrections must be made, of course, for price-level changes, population growth, and the rise in national output, that were made for expenditures. Changes in the percentage of total tax revenues accounted for by each level of government are also striking. In 1913 the tax revenues of the municipalities were over half of total taxes. Despite the steady growth in the importance of both federal and state taxes, local revenues still maintained their pre-eminence into the depression. The relative importance of state taxes had increased slightly at the expense of local taxes, while the relative position of federal tax revenues remained substantially unchanged.

The events of the depression, however, altered the picture substantially. By 1940, federal tax revenues had sharply increased their percentage importance at the expense of the localities. Relationships were once more altered, this time drastically, as a result of World War II and its aftermath. Percentagewise, the tax receipts of the federal government rose tremendously at the expense of both the states and the localities; but the relative decline in local tax revenues after 1940 was substantially greater than that in state revenues. Clearly, such massive changes in the relative fiscal positions of the three levels of government, occurring within a comparatively brief space of time, could not fail to have important effects on the distribution of economic and political power among the governmental units.

▶ FEDERAL TAXATION

The passage of the Corporation Excise Tax of 1909 inaugurated a new era in federal taxation. This was the first step toward de-emphasizing the customs, which had dominated the federal revenue system up to that time, and toward the inclusion in the tax system of a permanent system of income taxes. In foreshadowing the adoption of the first permanent personal income tax in 1913, it introduced what has since then been the settled policy of relying on the corporate and personal income taxes for the bulk of federal revenues.[2] The transition from the customs to income taxes as the major source of revenue made possible the use of tax progression, in the sense that the tax is a larger percentage of a higher income than it is of a smaller one. Under the corporation income tax, this would be true to the extent that the tax reduces dividends and that dividends accrue primarily to individuals in the higher income brackets. Under the personal income tax, progression could be achieved directly through a schedule of rates graduated according to income.

Table 7 indicates the nature of the changes. Virtually the entire

---

[2] The Sixteenth Amendment specifically exempted the federal income tax from the requirement that direct taxes be apportioned among the states according to population. Without such an exemption an income tax would be an impossibility. A poor but populous state would be liable for a larger tax than would a wealthy but more thinly populated state.

federal tax revenue in 1913 was derived from customs and excises. Since these taxes are largely ultimately paid by the consumer, very little of the burden of the federal tax system rested on savers prior to World War I. Furthermore, because savers comprise the middle and high income receivers, the burden of federal taxes was on the lower income groups.

Table 7. Trends in Federal Taxes by Tax Sources, 1913–1954

(Dollar amounts in millions)

	1913		1929		1939		1954	
	$	%	$	%	$	%	$	%
TOTAL TAX COLLECTIONS	663	100.0	3,455	100.0	5,191	100.0	70,482	100.0
Customs	319	48.1	602	17.4	319	6.2	562	0.8
Excises	309	46.7	459	13.3	1,619	31.0	9,214	13.1
Liquor	—	—	13	—	588	—	2,783	—
Tobacco	—	—	434	—	580	—	1,580	—
Manufacturers'	—	—	6	—	397	—	2,688	—
Retailers'	—	—	—	—	35	—	438	—
Transportation and communications	—	—	—	—	—	—	1,415	—
Admissions	—	—	6	—	19	—	310	—
Corporation income and excess profits	35	5.2	1,236	35.7	1,123	21.7	21,546	30.7
Personal income	—	—	1,096	31.8	1,029	19.8	32,813	46.8
Estate and gift	—	—	62	1.8	361	7.0	935	1.3
Employment	—	—	—	—	740	14.3	5,108	7.3

SOURCE: *Annual Reports* of the Secretary of the Treasury.

TRENDS IN RECEIPTS FROM CUSTOMS AND EXCISES

Customs and excises still accounted for about 30 per cent of federal revenues in 1929. This was about the same percentage of total federal taxes as that contributed by the personal income tax. The decade of the twenties was a period of domination by the groups that opposed what they thought was excessive reliance on personal and corporate income taxes, and the high personal income tax rates of World War I were gradually reduced. Yet determined attempts to bring about the introduction of a general federal sales tax were unsuccessful both during the twenties and again during the depression. It is extremely difficult to get rid of a general sales tax once it has come into operation. Consequently, opposition forces can be fairly easily marshaled when such a fundamental fiscal decision is up for consideration. On the other hand, the Revenue Act of 1932 did make heavy use of selective excises. The opposition to excises is ordinarily less than that to a general sales tax. The reason is that selective sales taxes can be made to distinguish between spending on subsistence goods (housing, food, and the like) and the commodities bought by the middle- and higher-income classes.

To those who valued budgetary balance above all other considerations, circumstances seemed to weigh heavily in favor of consumption taxes of some sort during the depression, along with increased corporate and personal income tax rates. When national income falls, consumption spending falls less than income. In other words, the public strives to maintain previous consumption standards by reducing its liquid savings. Thus excise tax yields tend to fall less than national income. In a strenuous attempt to restore budgetary balance the Hoover administration set in motion a trend toward greater permanent use of excise taxation. The percentage of total federal tax revenues accounted for by excises more than doubled from 1929 to 1939. Moreover, the reversal of this process between 1939 and 1954 (when by coincidence the percentage had dropped again to about that of 1929, or 13.1 per cent) was brought about by the great increases in income tax rates rather than by more modest use of excises.

Finally, attention is called to two interesting developments within the area of federal consumption taxation. The first is the extraordinary decline in the importance of the tariff. The decline has been both absolute (in constant or price-deflated dollars) and relative, and this source of revenue is now insignificant. The second is the tremendous rise in liquor taxation. The rise is partly explainable, of course, by the existence of prohibition in 1929, when alcohol revenues were unimportant. Heavy increases in liquor tax rates during and after World War II, however, coupled with a relatively inelastic demand during a period of very high income, have caused this tax to pull well ahead of the tobacco tax.

THE RAPID DEVELOPMENT OF PERSONAL AND CORPORATE INCOME TAXATION

Nearly one half of federal revenues was derived from the personal income tax in 1954. The heavy requirements of the federal government for tax revenue make it unlikely that the relative importance of this tax will decline in the foreseeable future. Indeed, if the argument were accepted that corporate income tax rates should be substantially lowered, much of the decline in revenues from this source would have to be made up from the personal income tax. This tax, denounced by its opponents at the time of its adoption as a "class" tax,[3] has been converted into an obligation payable by the bulk of the working population. Exemptions have been lowered, and the rate on the first taxable bracket is high (20 per cent in 1956). The consequence has been that despite a highly progressive rate schedule, a large proportion of the receipts now comes from individuals in the lower middle-income brackets. Moreover, deduction of the tax from

---

[3] That is, a tax that was believed to discriminate unfairly against those with higher incomes by making them pay higher *rates*. This was thought by the wealthy to be "unreasonable classification" of individuals for tax purposes.

wages and salaries at the source has enhanced the difficulty of evasion by the lower-income receivers. Increasingly, therefore, the personal income tax has come to be a tax on lower incomes, and therefore on consumption, as well as on saving.

Almost as spectacular as the growth of the personal income tax has been that of the corporate income tax. Introduced at the rate of 1 per cent in 1909, it had reached a rate of 52 per cent by 1951.[4] In 1954 it accounted for over 30 per cent of federal revenues. The corporate income tax is not as clearly a tax on ability to pay as the personal income tax. Although it is probable that the burden of the tax in the short run falls on profits, and therefore on the stockholder, the situation is by no means as clear over longer periods of time.[5] To the extent that investors are discouraged from buying equities in the taxed corporations, interest cost to the latter rises, output declines, and price tends to rise. To some extent, then, the corporate income tax is probably passed on to the consumer, at least in the long run.

Another characteristic of the corporate income tax is that ownership of stock is distributed over a wide range of income groups. Although it is true that the bulk of the stocks are held by those in the higher-income brackets, a flat 52 per cent corporate income tax means that high- and low-income stockholders are treated alike. This reduces the progressivity of the corporate income tax, as well as that of the entire tax system, which makes heavy use of this form of tax.

Detailed discussion of these complex issues is reserved until later. Suffice it to say here that many tax experts believe that the corporate income tax should be abolished as an independent tax, and that the resulting increased income left in the hands of stockholders should be taxed under the personal income tax at rates applying to the income of each particular stockholder. This argument presupposes, of course, that all profits are actually distributed, or, if they are reinvested, that the stockholder is required to pay a tax on his share of the profits as if they had been distributed to him.

RELATIVE NEGLECT OF DEATH AND GIFT TAXATION

A glance at the proportion of total federal revenues contributed by the estate and gift taxes will indicate that the federal government is not very interested in this revenue source. Despite a highly graduated set of rates, the proportion was only 1.3 per cent in 1954. The exemption is high (as of 1955, $60,000), so that the great bulk of estates escape taxation. Moreover, death and gift taxes have been regarded as primarily

---

[4] The rate was 25 per cent on the first $25,000 of earnings, and 52 per cent on the rest. These rates were extended for another year in the Internal Revenue Code revision of 1954.

[5] This question is discussed in Chapter 11.

the domain of the states.[6] The first permanent federal estate tax was enacted in 1916, and after repeal in 1926 of the gift tax of 1924, a permanent gift tax was enacted in 1932. The retention of the estate tax after the fiscal crisis of World War I is attributable to popular sentiment against excessive concentration of wealth.

Part of the failure of the death tax as a revenue producer must be attributed to the variety of legal means whereby the tax can be avoided. A still more important point, however, is the fact that if death taxes are to be productive, they must be subject to very low exemptions and high rates in relatively low tax brackets. Naturally this would be unpopular. Even in Great Britain, where far more emphasis is laid on death taxes than is the case in the United States, not quite 5 per cent of total revenues came from this source in 1950, as compared with less than 2 per cent in the United States (including both the state and federal taxes). The purpose of the gift tax is to discourage avoidance of the estate tax, and its importance is not to be measured by its revenues.

PAYROLL TAXES

A final distinguishing characteristic of the federal tax system since 1936 has been the rapid growth in payroll taxes. In fiscal 1954 they had reached $5.1 billion. The incidence of payroll taxes depends partly on the level and direction of business activity. To the extent that payroll taxes are borne by the wage earner, or by the consumer in the form of higher prices, they constitute a highly regressive element in the federal tax system. On the other hand, in so far as they provide the occasion for increases in wage rates at the expense of profits (probably an unlikely effect of the tax in the long run) they are likely to be somewhat progressive.

One thing is certain. If social security should be expanded to cover all the human risks that are incurred from cradle to grave, the cost will be very great. This will mean that benefits will have to be largely financed by a combination of (1) taxes on those who will ultimately benefit and (2) higher prices paid by consumers. In other words, the costs of a social security system that really offers security will probably have to be met largely by the masses of the population, without any substantial downward redistribution of income.[7]

CONCLUSION

Two conflicting trends have appeared in recent years in the federal tax system. The first is the tremendous development of income taxation.

---

[6] The states, however, have also made relatively little use of this revenue source. As we shall see in Chapter 16, the major interest of the federal government in death taxes is their economic, social, and political effects, which far outdistance their revenue significance. Because of the importance of death taxes for control, Congress has been unwilling to retire from the taxation of estates.

[7] The problem is discussed further in Chapter 24.

This has made possible the introduction of progressivity into the tax system. The second is the enormous, and evidently permanent, rise in federal spending and taxing, which makes it impossible to finance the federal government solely, or even largely, through progressive taxes. A corollary of the increased economic role of the federal government has been its great use of the most lucrative taxes, to the embarrassment of the states and municipalities. Thus fiscal developments in the last two decades have made urgent a complete re-examination of the tax and spending relationships of the federal, state, and local governments.

▶ THE TAX SYSTEMS OF THE STATES

The outstanding characteristics of state taxation from 1915 to the present time have been (1) the virtual elimination of the property tax as a source of state revenue, (2) the development, since the depression, of a complex system of taxation on sales and gross receipts, and (3) the rapid increase, particularly since 1939, in the importance of the corporate and personal income taxes.

Wide differences exist among the states, of course, in the relative importance of different taxes. Noteworthy also is the fact that despite the disposition of the federal government to avoid pre-empting death taxes as a revenue source, the rise in state revenues from this source between 1929 and 1954 was not very great, and its relative importance steadily fell. A new type of tax, the severance tax imposed on the removal of ore and oil from the ground, has achieved increasing importance in the past twenty years. Although still of minor importance for *all* the states, this tax is an important source of revenues in those states which possess mineral resources.

NONTAX REVENUES

The fiscal picture of the states cannot be appreciated by looking at taxes alone. Total state revenue and borrowing in 1954 amounted to $21.1 billion, of which borrowing totaled $2.2 billion.[8] Of the remainder, tax revenue was $11.1 billion. Thus an important part of state revenues comes from nontax sources. In 1954 subsidies from the federal government totaled $2.7 billion. They were made for public welfare, education, highways, health and hospitals, and unemployment benefits. By far the most important item was public welfare grants, which were $1.4 billion in 1954. Grants for highways were $542 million, and for education, $277 million.

In one form or another subsidies to the states by the federal government have been made throughout much of our history. For example, a distribution was made to the states, under the guise of a loan out of the

---

[8] Bureau of the Census, *Summary of State Government Finances in 1954*, p. 6.

federal surplus, as early as 1837. Successive Presidents, however, vetoed Congressional attempts to develop a system of federal grants to the states. Buchanan vetoed a bill that proposed to give federal land to the states as a subsidy to education. The issue grew hot again, however, as a result of the persistent federal surpluses under the Cleveland administration.

Table 8. Trends in State Taxes, 1915–1954

(Dollar amounts in millions)

	1915		1929		1939		1954	
	$	%	$	%	$	%	$	%
TOTAL TAX COLLECTIONS	368	100.0	1,951	100.0	3,085	100.0	11,089	100.0
General sales, use or gross receipts[a]	—	—	—	—	440	14.3	2,540	22.9
Motor-vehicle fuels	—	—	431	22.1	801	26.0	2,218	20.0
Tobacco	—	—	—	—	60	1.9	464	4.2
Liquor	21	5.7	—	—	228	7.4	463	4.2
Motor-vehicle licenses	15	4.1	348	17.9	364	11.8	1,031	9.3
Income	2	—	204	10.5	331	10.7	1,776	16.0
Corporate	—	—	—	—	134	—	772	—
Individual	—	—	—	—	197	—	1,004	—
Property	186	50.6	350	17.9	259	8.4	391	3.5
Death and gift	29	7.9	149	7.7	133	4.3	247	2.2
Severance	—	—	—	—	47	1.5	312	2.8
Other[a]	115	31.3	469	24.1	422	13.7	1,647	14.9

[a] Includes a wide variety of minor taxes, miscellaneous licenses, sales taxes, and the like.

SOURCES: Bureau of the Census, *Historical Review of State and Local Government Finances; Summary of State Government Finances in 1954.* Exclusive of insurance trust revenue.

It was not until the depression of the nineteen thirties that the financial difficulties of the states led them to exert pressure for a regular system of grants-in-aid. In 1913 federal grants were negligible. The central issue raised by the multiplication of federal grants to the states is that of the preservation of the federal system of government. He who accepts money from another also accepts control.

SERVICE CHARGES

The states derive considerable revenues from charges for services. Receipts of educational institutions and hospitals, together with highway tolls and earnings on property and investments, totaled $1.3 billion in 1954. Gross revenues from the operation of state liquor stores were $974 million, and social insurance trust revenue over $2.5 billion. The excess of revenues over expenditures in these latter two areas was, respectively, $171 million and $464 million. The former represented revenues in the form of profits; the latter arose out of the good employment record in the postwar period, together with the excess of social security in-payments over benefits normally to be expected in the earlier years of an old-age social security system.

CONCLUSION

In conclusion, two important features of state taxation should be mentioned. First, the multiplication of state taxes has not been accompanied by a significant increase in progressivity. By all odds the greatest source of state tax revenues is the complex of sales taxes and use and gross receipts taxes, including the taxes on gasoline, tobacco, and liquor. Even the gasoline and liquor taxes do not contribute substantially to the progressivity of a tax system. Again, the state personal income tax cannot be subject to much progression. The rapidly rising scale of rates under the federal income tax schedule reduces the possibilities in this direction.[9] Second, the wide discrepancy in the taxable capacity of different states that existed before the war has now been markedly lessened. This has resulted from the tremendous movement of capital into Southern and Western states, partly in response to shifting populations and the discovery of new natural resources, and partly as a result of huge wartime and post-war federal spending.

► LOCAL REVENUES

LOCAL TAX REVENUES

The basic tax revenue source of the localities has always been the property tax. In recent years, however, as municipal expenditures have multiplied, many cities have resorted increasingly to other forms of taxation. A few cities have introduced a crude form of income tax, and some have instituted sales taxes. Nevertheless, the property tax remains by all odds the most important municipal tax. The property tax yielded 87.1 per cent of total municipal tax revenues in 1953. (See Table 9.) In 1932 the property tax had provided the localities with 97 per cent of their total tax revenues of $4.3 billion. In 1913 the ratio was 91 per cent. Therefore, despite the addition of new tax sources, the property tax continues to bear most of the burden at the local level.

NONTAX REVENUES

The major development in the local revenue system has come, not in the area of taxes, but in that of nontax revenues. Total tax receipts of the localities were $10.4 billion in 1953, but total revenue was $21.0 billion,

---

[9] This would not be so, of course, if highly graduated state taxes were deductible from the federal income tax base. This device would, however, greatly reduce the federal income tax base and would also necessitate relatively low rates applicable to an individual's top taxable bracket. It is of interest to note that the separatist-minded province of Quebec regards deduction of provincial from central government income taxes as a important device for retaining political power.

or just about double.[10] Miscellaneous charges for services brought in $2.3 billion, and $2.4 billion was derived from revenues from public utilities and liquor stores. The major nontax revenue source, however, was $5.7 billion of intergovernmental revenues, of which $5.4 billion was from the states. The magnitude of these grants from the states is an indicator of the potential threat to home rule by the municipalities. Because a healthy political system requires an active political life at the local level, some states have taken steps to provide the cities and towns with additional

Table 9. Local Tax Collections, 1953
(Dollar amounts in millions)

Source	$	%
TOTAL TAX COLLECTIONS	10,356	100.0
By type of source		
Individual income	96	0.9
Corporate income	7	0.1
Sales and gross receipts	718	6.9
Property	9,010	87.1
Licenses and permits, and other	519	5.0
By form of local government		
County	2,051	19.8
City	4,552	44.0
Township	592	5.7
School district[a]	2,954	28.5
Special district	205	2.0

a Excluding school systems operated as segments of state, county, city, or township governments.

SOURCE: Bureau of the Census, *State and Local Government Revenue in 1953.*

taxing powers. Maryland, Pennsylvania, and New York have been leaders in this field. The consequence in Pennsylvania, for example, has been the widespread adoption of local general sales taxes, admissions and amusement taxes, and taxes on income, tobacco, and public utilities. These taxes have not, however, been able to make a real dent in the dominance of the property tax.

► FEDERAL, STATE, AND LOCAL DEBT

FEDERAL BORROWING

By the end of 1953 total federal, state, and local debt had reached nearly $300 billion. By comparison, gross national product in 1953 was

---

[10] Bureau of the Census, *Historical Statistics on State and Local Government Finances, 1902–1953.*

about $365 billion. There is, of course, no particular significance in this comparison, except that, huge as the debt appears, countries have survived national debts that were still larger in relation to gross national product. The British national debt was twice national income at the end of both

Table 10. Federal, State, and Local Debt, End of Fiscal Year
(Dollar amounts in billions)

	1914		1929		1939		1952	
	$	%	$	%	$	%	$	%
Federal	1.2	21.0	16.9	49.6	40.4	66.9	266.1	88.7
State	0.4	7.0	2.3	6.7	3.3	5.5	7.8	2.7
Local	4.1	72.0	14.9	43.7	16.7	27.6	25.7	8.6
TOTAL	5.7	100.0	34.1	100.0	60.4	100.0	299.6	100.0

SOURCES: Bureau of the Census, *Historical Statistics of the United States, 1789–1945*, p. 305; *Historical Review of State and Local Government Finances*, p. 18; Department of Commerce, *Indebtedness in the United States, 1929–1941*, pp. 24–25; Bureau of the Census, *Historical Statistics on State and Local Government Finances, 1902–1953*.

Napoleonic Wars and World War I.[11] By far the greatest absolute, as well as relative, increase in debt has been at the federal level. Most of this increase has been incurred during time of war. The decline in national income and the increased relief spending during the depression, however, led to a rise in the debt of $24 billion from 1931 to 1939.

A large federal debt has both advantages and disadvantages, one of the former being the fact that an elastic money supply may depend on the availability of large amounts of either public or private debt for purchase by the banks. Too large holdings, however, can result in an excessive money supply.[12] The most frequently discussed disadvantage of the debt is the tax burden involved in transferring purchasing power from taxpayers to those who own government securities. Another disadvantage is the onerous task of managing a large debt. The size of the debt is determined largely by political considerations connected only indirectly with good or bad *effects* of the debt. Federal borrowing is the resultant of decisions already made by Congress on the level of public spending and the level of tax rates. To the general public the really disturbing aspect of the growth in the federal debt is the fact that in recent years rises tend to occur alike during periods of depression, war, and cold war. But as we shall see in a later chapter, this may or may not be a matter for concern.

[11] See A. W. Acworth, *Financial Reconstruction in England, 1815–1822* (London: King, 1925), p. 136.

[12] In the long run, however, financial institutions and business credit practices are likely to be adaptable to changes in monetary requirements. Thus the point made above applies primarily to short-term elasticity of the money supply.

TRENDS IN STATE AND LOCAL BORROWING

Measured in terms of national income, debt of the municipalities has declined from 17 per cent to about 8 per cent since 1929. The percentage for the states has remained stable at about 3 per cent. The great era of state and local borrowing was the second and third quarters of the nineteenth century. The localities were forced to borrow heavily, however, to build new roads and improve their school systems during the years through 1929. With the financial pressure relieved by increasing state aid (and federal aid directly to relief recipients), the cities and towns weathered the depression fairly well. The small size of the increase in local debt from 1929 to 1939 was partly fictitious, however, since 1939 dollars were worth more than 1929 dollars.[13]

Local debt has nevertheless remained remarkably stable since 1939. The municipalities were able to repay much of their debt during World War II, when high revenue yields were accompanied by a low priority on municipal capital development projects. With the lifting of controls after the war, local spending rose again. The continued high level of national income, together with gradually rising property tax assessments and rates, has helped to keep the increase in local debt to relatively modest proportions. On the other hand, physical plant and city streets have often been allowed to deteriorate, and a significant decline in business activity might cut into tax revenues at a time when capital projects could hardly be deferred any longer.

► CONCLUSION

Since the turn of the century the importance of government in the national economy has vastly increased. Again, since 1930 the role of the federal government has risen sharply in importance as compared with that of the states and municipalities. The impact of these developments has been felt in all phases of economic life. The growth in public expenditures and taxes means that changes in taxes and public expenditures now have important effects on the level and distribution of national income. The rise in the public debt has made the federal government an important competitor of private industry for the nation's savings. Moreover, the banking system now holds substantial amounts of federal securities. In other words, the money supply has come to be based largely on public debt.

Because of the rise in the relative importance of federal finance in recent years it has been necessary to re-examine the nature of its effects on the economy. Formerly it sufficed, when additional public expenditures were to be undertaken, to raise tax rates and impose new taxes without much regard for their economic effects. Today account must be taken of

---

[13] However, population growth means a decline in *per capita* debt.

the effects on consumption, saving, and investment. More than this, the possibility must be investigated that variations in federal taxes and expenditures can be made to compensate for variations in the rate of private consumption and investment spending, and therefore in the level of employment.

▶ REFERENCES

See also references at end of Chapter 1.

BUREAU OF THE CENSUS. Annual publications on state and local finances.
———. *Historical Review of State and Local Government Finances,* June, 1948; *Historical Statistics on State and Local Government Finances,* 1902–1953.
HANSEN, A. H., and H. S. PERLOFF. *State and Local Finance in the National Economy.* New York: W. W. Norton & Company, 1944.
SECRETARY OF THE TREASURY. *Annual Reports.*
UNITED STATES TREASURY DEPARTMENT. *Treasury Bulletin,* monthly.

3 Government Expenditures and Public Welfare

► THE NATURE OF THE PROBLEM

We saw in Chapter 1 that the great growth in public expenditures in recent years, particularly at the federal level, has taken place in the face of much official and public opposition. Because of the ineffectiveness of this opposition, certain fundamental questions arise with respect to the underlying social and economic significance of the trend. Is the continuance of a more or less unplanned rise in public expenditures desirable? Whether or not it is desirable, is it inevitable? Could this trend lead to state social-ism? Or can criteria be set up that will assist us in a democratic society to determine the optimum levels and directions of federal, state, and local expenditures?

In considering the above questions, we shall aim in this chapter to examine the relative functions of the public and private sectors of the economy in the production of the national output, and therefore in the use of resources.

► A "LAW OF INCREASING PUBLIC EXPENDITURES"?

Some economists have in fact tried to test the existence of a law of increasing public expenditures. The German economist Adolph Wagner, writing in the second half of the nineteenth century, became impressed by the seemingly persistent tendency for government expenditures to increase in all countries. He derived from this observation a "law of increasing state activity."

Wagner wished to explain the fact that, in the countries which he studied, public expenditures tended to rise more than in proportion to the increase in population. He ascribed this phenomenon to the apparent rule that increasing density of population requires the state to accept functions previously performed by individuals for themselves, or not needed at all

36

in sparsely populated areas. Examples come readily to mind: police and fire protection, sewage disposal, state institutions, museums, and the like.

Under proper assumptions there is a measure of truth in the reason Wagner assigned to the growth in public expenditures. Nevertheless, the causes of increases in public expenditures are too complex to conform to any simple law. In any event, it is more important to know whether a long-term tendency actually exists for public expenditures to increase *in relation to private spending.* For if such a tendency exists, whether or not it attains the dignity of a law, this question at once arises: Does a persistent increase in the ratio of public to private expenditures imply a movement in the direction of state socialism? Or does it merely mean that there is a tendency toward increasing public expenditures without a corresponding increase in control over the economic and political life of private individuals?

RISING PUBLIC EXPENDITURES AND STATE DOMINANCE

The contention has frequently been made that rising federal spending in the United States could lead to state socialism.[1] It cannot be denied that if virtually 100 per cent of national income were paid to the factors of production by the Treasury, and then returned to it in taxes and purchases of the products of nationalized industries, we should be living under a planned economy. Moreover, it is obvious that at some percentage substantially short of this figure the federal government would be the dominant influence in our economic lives, and consequently of most other aspects of our private lives as well. Beyond this, however, it is not possible to say much about the role of the government on the basis of the ratio alone. An extensive inquiry would have to be conducted into the use actually made by the federal government of its spending and taxing powers in order to coerce the individual.

It is clear that no single index can give an unambiguous measure of the relative importance of government in the economy.[2] Even if such an index were found, it could hardly perform the additional function of indicating the extent of any trend toward state domination of the individual. The ratio of total government spending to national income, for example, is an aggregative measure that relates to the over-all economic effects of

---

[1] Senator Byrd of Virginia has carried on a campaign to reduce Federal expenditures, in part in order to "turn the tide away from state socialism." As chairman of the Joint Committee on Reduction of Nonessential Federal Expenditures, he has constantly urged the adoption of budgets far short of those recommended by the executive branch.

[2] It will be noted that state and local spending is largely irrelevant to the problem of measuring the impact of government finance on the economic and political independence of the individual. For state and local spending and taxing are, at least to a large extent, independent of central control. On the other hand, spending at all levels of government has the same effect in restricting the range of goods purchasable in private markets.

government activities. It makes no distinction between government spending for factors of production in the pursuit of its own functions, and subsidies to other levels of government and to pressure groups and individuals in the quest of their objectives. As a measure of the importance of government, therefore, it is highly ambiguous.

If transfer expenditures are eliminated from total government spending, the ratio becomes one of the cost of government services to national income. This ratio recognizes that the recipient of a government subsidy, unless it is tied to some action on his part, makes the decision on how to spend it. But federal subsidies may involve more of an encroachment on the freedom of the individual than does, for example, military spending. A subsidy is very apt to be made contingent upon some act by the recipient. Even if it is not, the government is in the position of encouraging a given pattern of resource use in its subsidy policy.

Another measure of the economic importance of government is the ratio of value added by government production to national product. This measure takes account of the fact that the final value of government services includes a large amount of value created actually by the private sector, for example, building materials used in government installations. Still other possible measures are the ratio of government-owned property to total property, the percentage of total workers employed by all levels of government, and the share of government in the total sales of final product by industry.[3] Even if all these measures moved in the same direction, they would do so at different rates. Each has its own conceptual characteristics that make it more useful for one purpose than for another. Thus there is no single measure of the economic importance of government or of the extent of its encroachment on the private sector.

► FACTOR-PURCHASE AND TRANSFER EXPENDITURES

As implied above, government expenditures consist broadly of two types, factor purchases and transfer expenditures. The first comprise the expenditures incurred in the purchase of the intermediate goods and services required by the government in the production of public goods and services. The second are those which merely transfer purchasing power from one segment of the private sector to another. The latter may be either a gratuitous transfer (i.e., no *quid pro quo* is required from the recipient) or a payment for existing property rights.[4] Examples of the former are

---

[3] Cf. S. Fabricant, *The Trend of Government Activity in the United States since 1900* (New York: National Bureau of Economic Research, 1952), Chap. II.

[4] Cf. A. C. Pigou, *Public Finance* (3rd ed.; London: Macmillan, 1947), p. 19. Pigou points out that he has called the first type, in successive editions, exhaustive, real, and non-transfer expenditures. He now favors the last, probably because it is the only term that is fully coordinate with the term "transfer." The term "factor-purchase" is used by John Due (K. E. Poole, ed., *Fiscal Policies and the American*

the costs incurred in maintaining government agencies, the cost of public works, and military expenditures. Examples of the latter are interest payments on the public debt, veterans' benefits, farm subsidies, and unemployment relief. Clearly, factor-purchase and transfer expenditures may differ substantially in the nature and degree of their interference with the private sector.

The distinction between factor-purchase and transfer expenditures is of major significance in a discussion of the allocation of resources between the public and private sectors of the economy. The former represent a direct use of resources by the government. The latter involve simply a redirection of resources from one segment of the private sector of the economy to another. The government makes the basic decision, but it does not itself determine the use of the resources.

FACTOR-PURCHASE EXPENDITURES

When resources are fully employed, a decision on the part of the government to increase its expenditure on factors of production means that either consumption or factor-purchase expenditures (i.e., investment) by firms must fall. Let us consider the latter alternative. In the absence of excess inventories, the result will be a decline in the output of commodities purchasable by consumers in the private markets. If there is unemployment, however, an increase in government factor payments can occur without a matching decline in the resources available to the private sector. Indeed, if the factors purchased by the government would otherwise have remained unemployed, the consequence may be an induced rise in factor purchase by business. This may come about in response to the spending of new incomes by the previously unemployed. In this case, the output of both public and private goods proves to have increased.[5]

Two aspects of factor-using governmental expenditures deserve special comment. The first is the mechanism by which the government diverts factors to its use under conditions of full employment. The second is the question whether a decline in government factor purchase would necessarily result in a rise in the volume of goods and services available to the public above the previous level.[6]

1. An increase in government factor-purchase expenditures may be financed either by increased taxes or by borrowing. When taxes are increased, or government securities are sold to savers, purchasing power in

---

Economy [New York: Prentice-Hall, 1951], p. 202). This term lumps together services provided by the factors to the government with finished products bought by the government from the private sector.

[5] This favorable result may not appear, however, if the rise in public spending is accompanied by opposition on the part of the business community to the policy. For in that case business spending may not increase despite the increased disposable income in the hands of the previously unemployed. Business investment may also fail to rise if it is believed that the increase in public spending is only temporary.

[6] The second of these points is stressed by Pigou, *op. cit.*, p. 21.

the hands of individuals is reduced. Thus the private sector can continue to consume resources only if it is in a position either to spend liquid hoards or to increase its rate of borrowing from the banking system. Individuals and firms are indeed likely to resist attempts by government to divert resources to public use during periods of full employment and high profits. For this reason it is apt to be difficult, under conditions of high-level employment and profits, for the government to increase its factor-use without causing some rise in the price level. The situation is even more inflationary, of course, if the government sells securities to the banks rather than to savers. In this case there is no pressure on the private sector to reduce either consumption or investment spending; the government simply superimposes its added spending upon the spending by the private sector until it has gained command of the desired amount of resources. Modern governments resort to this device only with respect to that portion of *emergency* spending that is in excess of that which can be taxed or borrowed from savers.

2. It is sometimes argued that a decline in government spending would increase the area of choice on the part of the individual consumer. This is certainly true with respect to a significant proportion of government spending. It is in the nature of public spending that collective consumption is substituted for individual consumption. On the other hand, many services provided by the state would presumably have to be purchased by the individual in private markets if the community did not furnish them. What the individual saved in taxes he would spend in the market. Examples are the various kinds of public protection, hospital services, and roads.

TRANSFER EXPENDITURES

Transfer expenditures differ from factor-purchase expenditures in that the recipient performs no service in return. Transfer payments fall into two general classes: subsidies to individuals who have been declared eligible by legislative act, and interest payments on the public debt. The first of these classes may be divided into two further subgroups. Some grants are pure gifts. Aid for dependent children, for example, is an outright subsidy. On the other hand a veterans' bonus implies that the recipient has provided a service to his country that was not adequately remunerated at the time it was performed.[7]

---

[7] It is not always easy in practice to distinguish between these two kinds of grants. Unemployment *relief*, for example, as contrasted with contributory unemployment *insurance*, might be considered a gift. On the other hand, even though the worker does not contribute to the unemployment relief fund, he can be regarded as having made an implied contribution if it is believed that society should pay a worker a living wage throughout his entire working life. In other words, society should pay the cost of periods of unemployment if it wishes to enjoy commodities the demand for which fluctuates.

From the point of view of the public budget, however, it is immaterial that the recipient may have contributed services in earlier budgetary periods. During the particular budget year (say the 1956 budget) the payment is unilateral. In this connection one may inquire whether interest payments on the debt should be classed as transfer or factor-purchase expenditures. When debt is sold to private savers, the government is paying for the use of savings. Therefore interest payments are made for the use of the factor capital. State and local debt, as well as part of federal debt, is backed by plant and equipment. On the other hand, the greater part of the federal debt was incurred in connection with unbalanced budgets during depressions and wars. Thus the assets purchased with the proceeds of the loans have largely disappeared. It might seem, therefore, that interest payments on this portion of the debt can no longer be regarded as payments for the use of capital. But this is not true. If real capital is destroyed or fails to yield a dollar return, whether it represents investment spending by business or government spending, this does not alter the fact that the payment is made for the use of resources. When interest payments on the debt are treated as transfer payments in public budgets rather than as factor expenditure, emphasis is being laid on the fact that interest is a unilateral payment during the budgetary period.

THE NATURE OF TRANSFER EXPENDITURES

Table 11 indicates the relative importance of different types of transfer expenditure for different years. It is of interest to note that the percentage increase in state and local transfer payments between 1929 and 1953 was about the same as the percentage increase in federal transfer payments. During the depression direct relief was primarily a state concern. The increase in federal transfer payments during the same period coincided with the introduction of social insurance. In the postwar period there has been a continuation of the rapid increase in social insurance benefits. Nevertheless the states and localities have been forced to increase their relief payments. It must not be forgotten, however, that prices have risen and that population has grown during these years.

Significance of Growth. A growth in the relative importance of transfer expenditures is in a sense an indication of government encroachment on the private sector of the economy. It may involve a substitution of public for private economic decisions. Although the government does not spend the proceeds, it has decided who shall do so. A growth in transfer spending cannot, however, be taken as an accurate measure of encroachment. One important reason for this is that many subsidy pro-

---

Again, the temptation exists to distinguish between contributory old-age pensions and old-age relief. Yet on a broad view the retired worker is entitled to old-age benefits even though his income as a worker had been inadequate to permit his making annual premium payments that would be large enough to carry him through retirement.

grams tend to expand automatically as the number of eligible recipients increases. To the extent that this is so, it is not clear that a rise in transfer payments represents a positive intention on the part of the government to extend the scope of its decision-making role.

Table 11. Government Transfer Payments Exclusive of Interest on Debt,[a]
1929, 1939, and 1953
(In millions of dollars)

	1929	1939	1953
Federal government	694	1,240	9,660
Benefits from social insurance funds[b]	44	696	5,607
Direct relief	—	22	—
Military pensions, etc.	443	462	2,720
Adjusted compensation benefits	96	36	1
Mustering-out payments	—	—	352
Readjustment payments to veterans	—	—	499
Other	111	24	481
State and local	218	1,272	3,125
Benefits from social insurance funds	72	157	610
Direct relief	71	1,024	2,357
Other	75	91	158
TOTAL	912	2,512	12,785

a Interest payments on the federal debt amounted to $6.5 billion in 1953 ($6.4 billion in 1954) as compared with $941 million in 1939 and $678 million in 1929. Interest payments on state and local debt have fluctuated, but have declined in terms of constant dollars, and as of 1953 (at $797 million) as compared with 1932 ($840 million) even in terms of current dollars.—Bureau of the Census, *Historical Statistics on State and Local Government Finances, 1902–1953.*

b Includes old-age and survivors' insurance benefits, state unemployment insurance benefits, railroad retirement insurance benefits, railroad unemployment insurance benefits, federal civilian pensions, and government life insurance benefits.

SOURCE: Department of Commerce, *Survey of Current Business, National Income Supplement,* 1954.

For example, social security benefits rise as unemployment rises, or as increasingly large numbers of workers become eligible for old-age benefits when the average age of the population increases. Again, interest payments on the public debt will increase when a decision has been made to finance public expenditures by borrowing rather than by taxation. On the other hand, when programs are initiated on a small scale, but can be counted upon to grow, a powerful device is in the hands of the government to expand the scope of its economic activities. Finally, whatever the reason for a growth in the volume of transfer payments, the additional taxes that have to be levied to finance them will reduce consumption and savings of taxpayers, and in addition may discourage private investment. If the latter should occur, the government might be disposed to increase its factor-purchase expenditures in order to reduce the danger of unemployment. Thus a further breach would be made in the private sector.

Government transfer expenditures have increased markedly as a percentage of national income since 1929. The rise was from 1.0 per cent in 1929, to 3.5 per cent in 1939, and 4.2 per cent in 1953. The inclusion of transfer expenditures in the numerator of the public expenditures/ national income ratio makes it difficult to interpret the significance of a rise in that ratio. The difficulty arises because transfer payments are not a part of national income. They are merely shifts in claims to income or wealth. A rise in transfer payments, therefore, will cause an increase in the numerator without affecting the denominator.[8] This is one of the reasons why it is for some purposes more meaningful, in measuring the importance of government spending, to use the ratio of factor income alone (i.e., factor-purchase expenditures) to national income.

Extra-Budgetary Transfer Expenditures. On the other hand, *budgetary* transfer payments by themselves do not by any means tell the whole story with respect to the role of the government in effecting a redistribution of purchasing power among the various segments of the population. Transfer payments include only those diversions of purchasing power from one part of the private sector to another which actually pass through the public treasuries. Yet enormous transfers of purchasing power are brought about between individuals by virtue of *nonfiscal* governmental acts. These do not appear in public spending statistics. The protective tariff, for example, forces consumers to pay higher prices to domestic producers. Indeed, a substantial proportion of public legislation is devoted to transferring command over resources in this fashion. Further examples are price-control legislation, utility rate fixing, minimum-wage laws, and a substantial part of public regulation in general. No estimate can be made of the magnitude of these "nonfiscal" subsidies. Their importance, however, is both great and growing; and their existence sharply reduces the significance of estimates of the magnitude of merely formal government subsidies.[9]

CONCLUSION

Both factor-purchase and transfer expenditures affect the distribution of resources between the public and the private sectors of the economy. Factor-purchase expenditures, however, do so *directly* to a much larger

---

[8] Even if transfer payments were included in national income, however, an equal absolute rise in transfer payments and national income would mean that the percentage rise of the numerator would be greater than the percentage rise in the denominator.

[9] For a brief discussion of some of the problems of evaluating the significance of subsidies, see Bureau of the Budget, "Federal Expenditures for Subsidies to Business and Farmers," April 27, 1949.

extent than do transfer payments. But indirectly, transfer expenditures affect the distribution of resources in two ways. This they do through their differential effects on spending by (1) the taxpayers and (2) the beneficiaries of the transfer payments. Our major interest in transfer payments, however, is their effect on the distribution of income. Transfer payments affect the distribution of income by income groups. They can be used to redistribute income either upward or downward. They also redistribute income among individuals in the same income brackets. This occurs, for example, when urban workers are taxed to subsidize farmers, or when beer drinkers and cigarette smokers are taxed to pay state bonuses to veterans. Our primary interest in the present chapter is in the allocation of resources rather than in the distribution of income. Therefore the discussion in the remainder of the chapter relates mostly to factor-purchase expenditures by governments.

► THE OPTIMUM RATE OF PUBLIC EXPENDITURE AT FULL EMPLOYMENT

Whenever the government increases or decreases expenditures, a collective decision has been made to change the allocation of resources between the public and the private sectors. It is important, therefore, that the public should be informed of the effect of this change on total welfare. If the factors of production are fully employed, the cost of an additional unit of public service is the sacrifice of the privately produced goods required in order to release the appropriate amount of factors of production. More generally, the cost of anything we buy is the collection of goods and services which we must do without in order to purchase it.

THE MAXIMIZATION OF SATISFACTION

In principle it is easy to say what combination of publicly and privately produced goods will maximize total satisfaction. The last dollar spent in a given use will simply have the same marginal social benefit as the last dollar spent in any alternative use. This is another way of saying that aggregate social welfare is maximized when no dollar is spent in a less desirable use so long as there exist more desirable alternative objects of expenditure. The same rule applies to both public and private expenditures.

If, for example, the public is provided more adequately with radios than automobiles, the satisfaction from a dollar spent for the latter will be greater than that from a dollar spent for the former. If, again, there is inadequate provision of some key public service, say fire protection, a dollar spent in this direction will have a much greater marginal utility than a dollar spent for an additional unit of a privately produced good. Another way of expressing this is that fire protection will be furnished up to the point at which the marginal social benefit of providing an additional dollar's worth of this public service is just balanced by the marginal disutility of the additional dollar of taxes required to finance it.

The principle enunciated above for allocating limited resources among competing uses is an example of the substitution at the margin which is the basis of all economic analysis. Its application in practice, however, is difficult. It assumes perfect knowledge of the alternatives on the part of the public. It likewise assumes that substitutions can be made in fairly small units. Unfortunately, however, the smooth curves used by the theorist do not usually exist in practice. Again, decisions made in the past may prejudice decisions that are to be made today. For example, it may be desirable to continue an expenditure because we find it too costly to leave a project unfinished that looks less urgent now than it did when it was initiated. Finally, it assumes that human decisions are actually made on the basis of a careful calculation of alternatives.

THE PROBLEM OF MEASUREMENT

In the foregoing discussion we have spoken in terms of "marginal social benefit," "marginal utility," and "sacrifice." If practical use is to be made of the principle, these magnitudes must be subject to some kind of measurement. In the private sector measurement is accomplished through the price system. It is assumed that the individual evaluates his benefits in terms of the prices he is willing to pay. The price system is in effect a rationing device for scarce goods and services. It is not, however, managed from above by a central office. On the contrary, through trial and error the private market constantly strives for an equilibrium in the supply and demand for commodities.

Consumers are in possession of purchasing power which they are at liberty to dispose of as they wish. If they are "rational" in the economist's sense, they strive to equalize their satisfaction from the last dollar spent for each alternative commodity. Producers, in turn, in the light of the demand curves for their products, extend production to the point at which marginal revenue just covers marginal cost.[10]

THE VOTING MECHANISM

In the public sector the criterion of price cannot be applied. The bulk of publicly produced goods are not sold in a market. Therefore the consumers of these goods are not in a position to use the price mechanism as a means for determining their satisfaction from varying amounts of different kinds of public services. Under the democratic process the decision is made by legislators, whose task is to interpret, however roughly, the desires of their constituents. On the one hand, the private market is equipped with a device which, under certain assumptions, provides an objective

---

[10] This may not be true under oligopoly, and is so under imperfectly competitive conditions only if the firm strives to maximize profits.

means of maximizing total welfare. In the public sector, on the other hand, voting with dollars is replaced with voting by the suffrage.

It is the representatives of the voters who decide when the production of governmental services has been pushed to the point at which their falling marginal social benefit is equal to their rising marginal social cost.[11] Legislatures operate through pressure groups, and many interests and points of view are therefore overlooked because they are not organized. Consequently it is obvious that the "market" for publicly produced goods is a highly imperfect one. It therefore follows that the alternative or "opportunity" cost of public services is evaluated only in a very crude manner. Before considering this point further, however, it is necessary to take a further look at the way in which the market for *private* goods and services allocates resources.

THE MARKET MECHANISM AND OPTIMUM OUTPUT

Basically, the principle leading to the optimum distribution of resources is the same in both the public and the private sectors of the economy. Social product is maximized in the private sector when the value of a marginal unit of resources is the same in one use as in another. A more precise statement would take account of the cost of transferring resources from employments in which marginal product is less to those in which it is greater. Quite apart from any failure to reach the optimum distribution of resources due to the presence of monopoly is the distortion that can occur because the costs and benefits of output accruing to a particular firm or individual may differ from those accruing to society in general. The nature of the difficulty will be apparent in the following examples.

There are some goods that most people would agree should not be sold in a private market; and there are others that cannot be produced on a socially desirable scale if they must be sold at a market price that covers their cost of production. Examples of the former are the general services of government, public works, and protective services. An example of the latter is education.

The marginal social benefit of education exceeds its marginal individual benefit. In other words, the social benefit of education greatly surpasses the benefit received by the individual who is being educated. The individual is enabled to play a more productive role in society. Under our present distribution of income only a small proportion of the population is able to pay for its own education. If education were sold, therefore, price would fall short of marginal cost, and under a market price system insufficient resources would be devoted to this commodity. In order to maximize welfare, then, the state must interfere in such a way as to divert a sufficient

---

[11] That is, the point beyond which another dollar spent on public goods will yield less satisfaction to the community as a whole than would a dollar spent for goods produced by the private sector.

amount of resources to institutions of learning so that the marginal social benefit of a dollar of spending on education is the same as that of a dollar devoted to the output of other publicly and privately produced goods.

The measurement of the *indirect* benefits and costs of alternative kinds of public and private expenditures is not possible on any exact basis. Yet an attempt has to be made to assess them along with direct benefits if we are to maximize aggregate welfare. In the case of education, for example, account must be taken of its effect on national efficiency. If costs are lowered because of increased efficiency resulting from education, purchasing power is released which can be devoted to supporting part of the costs of education. Of course it is not possible to identify all the indirect effects; and in any event it would be pointless to attempt to allocate the cost of education strictly on the basis of direct and indirect benefit.

The supply prices of some privately produced goods, rather than being too high to permit the maximization of welfare, may be excessively low because of the exclusion of various elements of cost that are inflicted on individuals who have no connection with the production of these commodities.[12] An often-cited example is the smoke nuisance. A producer of transparent plastic, for example, may have to incur additional costs if the atmosphere is dirtied by nearby heavy industry. Pollution of rivers by industrial waste is another example.

In these cases the obvious answer is either to introduce police control or to give subsidies to those whose costs are thus raised. A somewhat different case is that of the cost of caring for superannuated and unemployed workers in industry. In some industries, for example, superannuation occurs at an earlier age than in others. If the price of the product does not include a charge for this element of cost, the consumer is benefiting at the expense of the worker. In none of these cases, however, does it necessarily follow that these costs should be borne by the consumer. If for some reason it is socially desirable that these commodities be produced, the indirect costs might justly be borne by the taxpayer.

PUBLICLY PRODUCED GOODS FOR INDIVIDUAL USE

Although the bulk of government output consists of services that are consumed collectively rather than by individuals, in some areas it is advantageous for government to supplant, or at least compete with, private producers. This may be so on a number of grounds. (1) The cost of measuring the service may be relatively high, in which case a saving is effected if unlimited free use is allowed. Thus city streets are financed by tax revenues rather than by tolls, although tolls are enjoying increasing use on easily metered state throughways. Another reason for free use of public

---

[12] Here marginal social cost exceeds marginal private cost. That is, in addition to the added cost to the firm of producing one more unit of output is the added cost imposed on others.

highways, however, is that a highway network benefits taxpayers in general, not merely those who drive on the roads. (2) Justification for government production of electricity has been based on the desirability of providing a "yardstick" for the rates charged by private producers competing in the same market.[13] (3) In other cases government ownership of utilities has resulted in more forward-looking investment programs than have been ordinarily undertaken by private companies. (4) In some countries nationalization of industry has been supported on the ground that the worker may receive more favorable treatment (although the reverse may also be true).

The expansion of government activity in the production of commodities may be objectionable, in a free-enterprise economy, if private investment is discouraged by a fear of further government encroachment, or if government production methods are less efficient than those of private enterprise.[14] The extent to which these effects occur is difficult to determine, and we may expect a continuing debate between those who favor, and those who frown upon, a further extension of government production of individual goods.

MONOPOLY AND IDEAL OUTPUT

We have seen that even under conditions of perfect competition resources are not allocated in such a way as to maximize satisfaction if marginal social benefit exceeds marginal private benefit, or if marginal social cost exceeds marginal private cost. A case may exist for government intervention to bring about an increase in the output of a commodity which has a greater value to society at large than it does in the market, or to bring about a decrease in the output of a commodity which imposes a higher cost on society than it inflicts on its producer.

Under monopoly conditions still another reason exists that may justify either direct interference by the government in the price-output policies of the firms, or increased government expenditures to rectify the distribution of resources. Whereas a firm operating under conditions of perfect competition will produce to the point at which marginal cost equals price, a firm that enjoys any control over the market will have to consider the effect of its output on the price for which it can sell its product.

When the demand curve of the firm slopes downward to the right, marginal revenue lies below average revenue.[15] A policy of equating marginal cost with marginal revenue therefore means that marginal cost is

---

[13] A difficulty, of course, is that the yardstick itself is not absolute if the government-owned utility is provided with direct or concealed subsidies. This has been one of the issues with respect to the Tennessee Valley Authority.

[14] An important qualification to this statement arising out of the existence of monopoly is discussed below.

[15] Refer to Figure 7, page 128.

less than price. It also means that the demand for production factors by the firm is less than it would be if the firm equated marginal cost with price. Therefore the distribution of resources is likely to be different from the distribution under perfect competition. In those circumstances in which the motive of profit maximization leads to a less efficient allocation of resources under monopoly than under perfect competition, government intervention can increase social welfare. It should be noted, however, that the argument that imperfectly competitive conditions result in an output that falls short of that of perfect competition is based on static considerations. There is no technical reason why under imperfectly competitive conditions ability and willingness of firms to invest might not in the long run be superior to that under perfect competition.

It is apparent that the remedy for a misallocation of resources arising out of the type of situation described in the last paragraph would differ from that which is appropriate to the removal of the *abuse* of monopoly power. The Sherman Antitrust Act is not a suitable device for correcting a misallocation that may have nothing to do with the size of the firms in the imperfectly competitive industry, or with attitudes toward their ethical relation with the consumer or the worker. The entire economy is shot through with the kind of imperfection of competition which arises out of a greater or less degree of control over price. We cannot say that the firm is acting in an antisocial manner when it pursues the rational policy of equating marginal cost with marginal revenue. The question remains, nevertheless, whether or not the government should intervene in an effort to cause imperfectly competitive output to be the same as it would have been under conditions of perfect competition.

Any attempt to "restore" competition by breaking up firms into units so small that changes in their outputs would not affect price would be ineffectual. The most efficient size of the firm in many industries may be so large that output changes affect prices. Moreover, the aggregate impact of any distortion in the use of resources resulting from the widespread existence of monopolistic competition might be both large and difficult to deal with if a large number of relatively small firms were involved. Finally, direct government intervention on such a scale might have little advantage over centralized planning.

It has been suggested that an alternative approach might be to set maximum prices. This would remove the advantage to the monopolist of a restriction of output, since the price would be set high enough to cover marginal cost at competitive outputs. Such a course would be useless, of course, unless the price were high enough to cover all production costs, including those costs which are fixed in the short run. This device is actually in use for public utilities, whose rates are fixed by control commissions. However, the rates must include an allowance for return on invested capital. If this is not done private capital will not enter the industry, and unless the government takes over, facilities will gradually become inadequate to meet demand.

There is another possible device by means of which the firm in a monopolized industry can receive a price high enough to induce it to produce the competitive output: this device is a per unit subsidy equal to the difference between price and marginal revenue at that output. Producers would then produce at the point where marginal cost equals marginal revenue including the subsidy, and society would benefit from the greater output. The subsidized firms, however, would make higher profits. These, it has been suggested, could be recaptured by a tax unrelated to output. In other words, the tax would rest on "economic surplus," which by definition is the excess over the return that is necessary to call forth output.

A brief examination of the implications of this proposal suffices to expose its practical defects, though not everyone would regard them as necessarily fatal. Moreover, the criticisms that can be made of the plan are applicable to most attempts by government to affect the decisions of private producers on any mass scale. Since firms do not explicitly employ the marginal techniques of the economic theorist, the authorities would have to use a trial-and-error method in determining upon the size of the per unit subsidy to each firm. Again, the great administrative cost would apparently require restriction of the plan to industries regarded as having a particularly large public interest.

Another practical difficulty would be that of devising a profits tax, distinguishable from the ordinary corporate income tax, which could recapture the subsidy. Likewise on the tax side of the question, the continuing debate over the incidence of the present federal corporate income tax makes it rather unlikely that a tax could be devised that would have no long-run effect on cost of production, and therefore on output.

CONCLUSION

A case exists for government intervention, either in the form of police control or in the form of subsidies and taxes, to reduce the extent of misallocation of resources caused by the existence of imperfectly competitive conditions. However, there is no hope of achieving the allocation that would obtain under an economy-wide regime of perfect competition. The latter is merely a theorist's benchmark, designed as a point of reference for clear thinking. Control over price, in greater or smaller degree, is a nearly universal phenomenon. Moreover, it extends throughout the market for the factors of production, not merely throughout the market for commodities alone. Any sort of government intervention, whether fiscal or nonfiscal, involves indirect social costs that may prove to be much higher than anticipated by those who advocate such intervention. Therefore care should be taken to make ourselves aware of these costs in cases where the misallocation of resources is not so glaring as to make intervention obviously desirable. Government control over giant monopoly is, of course, another question.

► THE OPTIMUM RATE OF PUBLIC EXPENDITURE AT LESS THAN FULL EMPLOYMENT

In our discussion thus far of the optimum rate of public expenditure, the assumption has been made that the economy is experiencing no difficulty in maintaining full employment. Under this assumption an increase in government spending can take place only at the cost of a decrease in private spending. The diversion of resources to the public sector, therefore, is justified only if the marginal social benefit of a dollar of public spending exceeds that of the dollar of private spending that must be forgone.

If, on the other hand, there is much unemployment and excess capacity, it may be that an increment of government spending will involve no curtailment of the resources available to the private sector. All that is necessary is that the idle resources be sufficiently mobile so that they can be shifted to the public sector. Indeed, if there is reason for believing that debt-financed public works will stimulate a rise in private spending, the case is strong for deficit spending during a depression.[16] The extent to which this result can be expected in any particular depression is reserved for discussion in a later chapter.

► AN EVALUATION OF WELFARE EFFECTS OF PUBLIC SPENDING

BASIC PRINCIPLES

We have seen above that in broad terms the justification for an increase in public spending is a net increase in aggregate social benefit. The difficulties of applying this principle in practice have been indicated. There still remains to be considered the question whether a particular shift of resources from the private to the public sector of the economy is likely to increase aggregate social benefit.

No one doubts that public welfare will be increased if resources are diverted from individuals to government in order to permit adequate national defense or to guard against an epidemic. Much of public spending, however, is less clearly socially advantageous than this. In a government by pressure groups, many proposed types of expenditures help certain classes more than they do others. Indeed, they may help some while

---

[16] It may be, however, that welfare would be increased even more if taxes were lowered, with no change in public expenditures. This will be the case if the increase in public expenditures would have resulted in unwanted public services (e.g., leaf raking), whereas the increased private spending brought about by the tax reduction would have led to the production of useful commodities.

hurting others. An example is the taking of property by eminent domain in order to build a highway. Moreover, the taxes introduced to finance such expenditures bear more heavily on some groups than on others.

If public spending and taxing make some people better off and others worse off, this fact has to be taken into account in estimating the opportunity cost of a proposed item of public expenditure. Whenever it is decided to tax and spend, judgments are necessarily tacitly being made on the desirability of altering the relative welfares of different individuals. The legislature is in the position of having to make these value judgments, and one must inquire into its effectiveness in performing this function.

Every decision to perform an economic act, whether in the public or the private sector, hurts some people and helps others. A new invention, like the automobile, may lead to increased employment and a vast increase in the welfare of millions of people. On the other hand, it throws out of work those whose specialized training is suitable only to the horse-and-buggy economy. Yet only in rare instances does anyone try to halt this progress.[17] The philosophy of the private-enterprise economy holds that the collective decisions of private producers and consumers must be left to determine who shall be hurt and who shall be helped. The assumption is, of course, that aggregate welfare is thereby maximized. Yet it is only an assumption, for individuals can be found to support the view that aggregate welfare would be greater today if much of the material progress of recent decades had not occurred. It is at least partly a matter of opinion.

If the private sector can legitimately ignore the distributional effects of its economic decisions, why should not the government do likewise? The answer is partly that only within limits is the private sector allowed to ignore the hurts which it inflicts. Much of the regulatory power of government is devoted to minimizing the injurious effects of unrestrained private enterprise. Partly, also, the answer lies in the fact that when government spending accounts for a substantial proportion of total national income, decisions to alter the level of public expenditures assume great importance. As the sphere of government widens from the basic protective and regulative services, opinions are likely to become ever more divergent on the seriousness of the injuries.

CAN WE COMPARE THE BENEFITS AND INJURIES OF PUBLIC SPENDING?

If an economic act hurts some people and benefits others, or if it benefits some more than it benefits others, a decision to perform the act implies that a value judgment has been made. The spending authority

---

[17] Thoreau's detestation of the railroad that disturbed his solitude at Walden Pond exercised no visible effect on the development of transportation. But a powerful producer's interest can sometimes hold up progress, especially when it is pitted against the interest of the consumer rather than against that of another producer. The most famous example in recent years has been the fight waged by the dairy interests against oleomargarine. The interest of the low-income urban consumer was

takes it upon itself to compare the injury received by the one with the benefit received by the other. Yet there are no units in which the hurts and the helps can be measured. Moreover, it is tacitly assumed that all persons are alike.[18] In other words, interpersonal comparisons of utility are accepted as valid. In an effort to rationalize this practice of legislatures, the classical economists made the assumption that the capacity for enjoyment is comparable for all persons. Although this assumption may not be true, it may be more nearly true than any alternative working assumption. At any rate, it is one of the assumptions that is implied in the universal suffrage, since each person has one vote.[19]

► THE UNIVERSAL SUFFRAGE AND THE MAXIMIZATION OF WELFARE

What role is played by the suffrage in the maximization of economic welfare? How do the spending decisions made by the individual when he casts his ballot compare with those which he makes when deciding upon his spending out of his own, after-tax, disposable income? In view of the compulsory nature of public spending and taxing, is there anything to be gained by maintaining the fiction of "voluntary exchange" in the market for public goods and services? If the voter can be regarded as "buying" public services, does he apply as rigorous standards in the purchase of public services as he applies in the market for private goods?

CONSUMER CHOICE IN THE PRIVATE SECTOR

The question is whether in any significant sense the private individual retains any control over the disposition of resources when he designates the state to exercise the consumer function for him through the public budget. Any answer must be made in the light of the extent of consumer choice in the *private* sector of the economy.

---

never given much consideration, but the growing strength of the oil-seed producers ultimately became sufficient to put an end to the tax discrimination against oleomargarine.

[18] In the sense that the enjoyment of different individuals can be measured on the same scale. For example, the common practice in Europe of subsidizing opera assumes that capacity for enjoyment can be compared for different individuals (but not that it is necessarily equal). The loss in satisfaction of the taxpayer is being compared with the gain in satisfaction of the operagoer.

[19] In terms of welfare economics it can be argued that a given policy should be adopted by the government if the resulting increase in aggregate welfare is greater than the compensation that would be required to recompense those who are hurt by the policy. Since no basis for measuring the hurt and the required compensation exists, however, it is necessary in practice to rely on competition among pressure groups to maximize aggregate satisfaction.

One suggested solution to the problem is to ignore the effect of public policies on the distribution of income. It is argued that the hurts and helps in a dynamic society are distributed at random. In other words, a proposed policy would be accepted if it increased efficiency, *i.e.*, aggregate welfare. Obviously, however, there can be no random distribution of the losses and gains caused by economic progress.

Even in the private sector the consumer does not have the opportunity to apply close marginal techniques in assessing the relative desirability of alternative goods. Many privately produced commodities are not completely substitutable for others. From the point of view of the individual in a lower middle-income bracket, for example, a Deepfreeze may have a higher marginal utility than would be obtained from the same amount of money spent on a collection of less expensive goods, like movies, automobile trips, and beer. But the difficulty of saving for a freezer may cause the individual to dribble his money away on the less desired collection of goods. To be sure, the institution of installment selling was developed to take care of precisely this barrier to the maximization of utility by the individual. By permitting the individual to buy first and save afterward, installment selling makes durable and nondurable consumers' goods more nearly substitutable.

Still other factors, however, serve to limit the substitutability of goods in the private sector. In the first place, lack of knowledge and other market imperfections prevent a careful comparison at the margin. Frequently the individual makes little or no attempt to purchase with care.[20] Again, the consumer is often forced to buy a more extensive collection of goods than he really wants.

For example, a man might derive great satisfaction from moving to a better residential area. He might, however, prefer to dispense with servants and private schools for his children, but social pressure in the wealthier community might require him to buy these commodities as well.[21] Certainly it can be argued that if a man actually moves to the wealthier community, he believes that he is maximizing his aggregate satisfaction. Yet it is clear that the necessity for buying combinations of commodities, when only one of them is really desired, must often make difficult the close calculations at the margin needed for an accurate estimate of opportunity cost.

DOES THE VOTER MAKE RATIONAL SPENDING DECISIONS?

Clearly many individuals are not "rational" in their private finances, as the term is used by the economist. They do not always bother to weigh alternatives. Nor do they always take the trouble to gather even the readily available information about the goods they consider buying. Nevertheless, since they are spending their own money, they probably make closer calculations than they do as voters. This is only partly owing to the fact that the voter often thinks he is spending other people's money. Perhaps even more importantly it is attributable to certain difficulties inherent in the process of government. It will serve as a useful introduction to the

---

[20] This does not mean that it is necessarily irrational to fail to weigh alternatives. The consumer may be prepared to pay an extra price in order to avoid bother.

[21] Because of this kind of phenomenon it is often argued that it is not necessarily always true that the marginal utility of a dollar to a man in a higher income bracket is less than that of a dollar to a poorer man.

problem of public budgeting to devote some attention to these difficulties.

One of the obstacles to an accurate comparison of the marginal utility of a dollar's worth of public services with that of a dollar's worth of privately produced goods is inherent in the American legislative process. This is the fact that at the federal level public spending and tax legislation are enacted in separate bills. The consequence of this lack of association of public spending in the mind of the voter and legislator with the pain of paying taxes is the tendency to place an excessive valuation on the desirability of public goods.[22] Even when taxes are considered simultaneously with public spending, as in the British budget, the mass of the voters may be convinced that the taxes required to finance a given additional public service will fall primarily on someone else.

The major limitation on the ability of the voter to weigh alternatives, however, arises out of the great distance that he stands from the actual public spending decisions. In a representative political system the voter delegates to the legislature the right to determine the proportion of national output that shall take the form of publicly produced goods. Only in the town meeting, and through the use of the referendum, does the voter have the opportunity to register his preferences directly. The former is now relatively unimportant as a political institution. In the case of the referendum, although voters are asked to express their opinion directly, they are ordinarily asked to vote simply Yes or No on a proposed item of expenditure. If they must vote in favor of, or against, a bond issue to permit the spending of $1 million, they obviously have no opportunity to make very close calculations of the relative desirability of alternative types of spending. Moreover, it has been found that the vote is usually much lighter on financial measures than on other types of legislation. This may mean that the measure is not really considered. Those who do vote may be better informed than the average voter, but they also may be interested parties.

Since the great bulk of public expenditures is authorized by legislatures rather than directly by the voter, it is the behavior of the former rather than that of the latter that is of primary importance in welfare-maximizing decisions. Unless legislators are subject to frequent election they tend to get out of touch with the voter. Their well-known sensitiveness in election years has its counterpart in a somewhat greater independence from the voter in nonelection years.

One final point needs to be disposed of before we proceed to a consideration of the budgetary process. Clearly, decisions on public spending cannot be made to reflect the individual desires of every voter. Moreover, the vote is organized, and minorities frequently impose their will on the

---

[22] It should be emphasized that the argument in the text is not intended to apply in cases where the taxpayer *does* associate additional public expenditure with particular taxes. For example, it can be argued that the public places too low a valuation on the desirability of adequate school facilities. But schools are financed largely by property taxes, and the voter is immediately aware that his taxes will be heavier if new school facilities are built.

majority. In political theory this is no derogation of popular sovereignty. The democratic process requires the organization of parties. These maintain their power by making concessions to their constituent groups in proportion to their effective strengths. From a budgetary point of view this means that public expenditures are frequently made which benefit a group rather than society at large. If welfare is to be maximized, therefore, the selfish activities of pressure groups make it necessary that all groups be effectively and accurately represented.

► CONCLUSION

It is the job of the legislature to determine the level and the directions of public spending, and, apart from deficit finance, to find the revenues needed to cover these expenditures. If an intelligent performance is to be turned in, this task must be accomplished on the basis of some consistent set of principles. The economist finds the basic principle to be the careful comparison at the margin of the opportunity cost of the various items of public spending. In actual practice, of course, this rule is applied in an extremely rough way. Yet so long as there exists a large number of pressure groups, any proposed item of spending will be scrutinized in the light of the alternative types of private and public spending that must be forgone if this one is accepted. This inference, however, is subject to an important qualification. The prerequisite to an effective comparison at the margin of the satisfactions to be derived from alternative objects of expenditure is an intelligent system of budgeting. The budgetary process, however, is highly complex, and it is by no means an easy task to compare alternatives carefully. These difficulties, and how they are dealt with, are discussed in the next chapter.

► REFERENCES

BLOUGH, R. *The Federal Taxing Process.* New York: Prentice-Hall, Inc., 1952, Pt. V, "The Taxing Process and the Public Interest."

BOWEN, H. R. *Toward Social Economy.* New York: Rinehart & Company, Inc., 1948, Chap. XVIII, "Collective Choice."

BROWNLEE, O. H., and E. D. ALLEN. *Economics of Public Finance.* New York: Prentice-Hall, Inc., 1954, Chap. X, "The Role of Government Expenditure."

PECK, H. W. *Taxation and Welfare.* New York: The Macmillan Company, 1925.

PIGOU, A. C. *A Study in Public Finance.* 3d ed. London: Macmillan & Co., Ltd., 1947.

REDER, M. *Studies in the Theory of Welfare Economics.* New York: Columbia University Press, 1947.

SAMUELSON, P. *Foundations of Economic Analysis.* Cambridge, Mass.: Harvard University Press, 1953, Chap. VIII, "Welfare Economics."

4 Budgeting

▶ PURPOSE OF BUDGETING

Advance planning of expenditures and revenues is referred to as budgeting. Budgets are necessary because commodities and factors of production are scarce. A governmental budget is a device which, like the market for goods produced by the private sector of the economy, rations scarce commodities and factors of production among competing uses. The criterion for this rationing is the maximization of the total satisfaction derivable from the economic means at the disposal of society.[1]

In the market for privately produced commodities, rationing is performed by the price mechanism, in accordance with the incomes and tastes of consumers. A governmental budget modifies this rationing procedure. It does this by substituting a certain amount of collective for individual consumer choice. The limit of this substitution is the point at which the budgetary authority is convinced that a further expansion of public services will provide less community satisfaction than is sacrificed by the taxpayers in having to forgo private consumption. In deciding whether a given item of expenditure ought to be added to the budget, the budgetary authority must consider the alternative or "opportunity" cost of including it.

A satisfactory appraisal of the "opportunity" cost of a selected list of publicly financed goods and services can be made only by comparing in advance the relative satisfaction to be derived from the various items of public expenditure and the privately produced goods that must be forgone to make the production of the former possible. It follows that at the same time a similar comparison must be made between different items of *public* expenditure. The budget-making process is thus seen to be highly complex. Decisions are made simultaneously at the federal, state, and local govern-

---

[1] The present chapter is concerned with the techniques of budgeting. Economic aspects of the federal budget are discussed in Chapter 21.

mental levels, and at each of these levels the number of separate decisions is enormous.[2]

▶ DEFINITION OF A BUDGET

A budget is a comprehensive advance plan of governmental revenues and expenditures. It is intended to achieve a desired relation between planned expenditures and the taxes and other revenues required to finance them. The budget document provides the information needed by the executive, the legislature, and the public in order to evaluate the financial plan of the government in the light of the objectives of society. Thus the budget not only provides coordinated financial planning, but is also the means by which the public can determine the extent to which it is getting its money's worth from the government as producer. When the governmental unit is very large, this second budgetary function is difficult to perform satisfactorily, and constant experimentation goes on with different forms of presentation, each designed to emphasize a different aspect of budgeting.

The term "budget" is used in several senses, and some confusion may be caused by differences in usage. The chief executive, at the beginning of a session of the legislature, submits a document containing his proposed financial plan for the coming budgetary period. This document is usually accompanied by a budget message amplifying the appropriations and tax proposals, and assisting in the interpretation of the statistical tables. The document continues to be known as the budget throughout its progress in the legislature. The budget thus undergoes considerable change of form from the time of its preparation in the executive branch and in the hands of the budgetary authority, through the months required for authorization by the legislature, until it is finally executed. In addition to preparation, authorization, and execution, a fourth step, review of past performance, is needed to round out the process.

ALLOCATION OF BUDGETARY RESPONSIBILITY

Experience has shown that the major responsibility for *preparing* the budget should be placed on the executive. A legislative body is not adapted to performing the immense amount of detailed background work that must precede *authorization* of expenditures and taxes. In a democratic society, however, authorization of the budget belongs to the legislature.

Because of the large number of independent governmental units in

---

[2] The reader is reminded that if there is much unused capacity and unemployment, the utilization of idle resources by the government may cause an increase in total real output. Consequently, total satisfaction may be increased because the output of public services has risen without a corresponding decline in that of privately produced goods. This problem is reserved for discussion in later chapters.

the United States, there has been considerable variety in the distribution of power between the executive and the legislature. At the state and local levels there are instances of legislative responsibility for the preparation of the budget. At the federal level, on the other hand, the chief executive did not participate directly in the preparation of the budget until the Bureau of the Budget was created in 1921.

BUDGETARY COMPREHENSIVENESS

Effective budgeting requires that the entire financial picture of the government be presented in one comprehensive document. All receipts should be represented as flowing into a single unified treasury, and all expenditures as flowing from it. A common defect of budgeting is the practice of setting up special annexed budgets that are independent of the main budget. Budgetary authorities cannot properly perform their function of optimizing the level and distribution of public services if their hands are tied by the dedication of a large proportion of total revenues to specific purposes.

► THE STRUGGLE FOR THE CONTROL OF THE FEDERAL BUDGET

The long delay in the development of a unified budgetary procedure at the federal level was a consequence of the American political system, which was established in an age of fear of excessive concentration of power in a single branch of government. The lawmaking power was granted to Congress, and this power included budgeting. The legislature was to make the spending and taxing decisions, and the role of the President consisted of his right of veto, along with responsibility for execution of the budget. But the American system of checks and balances implies a continuous struggle for domination.

This struggle had already commenced during the Revolutionary War. The institutions of the national government were developing, between 1775 and 1791, at a time of deep suspicion on the part of free men toward the executive. It was believed that administrative work should be performed through committees, despite the recognized inefficiency of such a device. Throughout the greater part of this period the financial tasks of the government were left in the hands of a Treasury Board. In the eyes of many congressmen, even this was an unavoidable delegation of authority to the executive that might more safely be exercised by a legislative committee.

ASCENDANCY OF THE TREASURY

Despite the desire of Congress to retain responsibility for both the preparation and the authorization of the budget, the Treasury Act created a Treasury with a single head, and thus paved the way for a contest between Congress and the executive branch for dominance in budgetary matters.[3] Neither Congress nor the first Secretary of the Treasury, Alexander Hamilton, was prepared to establish a unified budgetary process. But the aggressive Hamilton acted virtually as a Minister of Finance, assuming authority to draw up plans for both revenues and expenditures. Because of the impossibility of devoting sufficient time to budgetary matters, Congress tended to accept his recommendations, referring all financial matters to him. Gradually, however, opposition began to crystallize against the secretary, and a movement toward the return of the spending authority to Congress got under way. Gallatin had spearheaded this movement, and when he became secretary in 1801 he recommended that the Committee on Ways and Means, established in 1796, be transformed into a standing committee to examine Treasury reports on all budgetary matters, including revenues, expenditures, and the debt.

BUDGETARY RESPONSIBILITY IN THE HANDS OF CONGRESS

The establishment of a responsible Ways and Means Committee assured Congress of domination in expenditure matters. In 1814, however, this committee was relieved of the burden of its appropriation function. The resulting establishment of a standing committee on appropriations caused a separation of Congressional responsibility for tax and spending matters that for a hundred years prevented unified Congressional budgetary action.

The decentralization of power over appropriations did not prove to be particularly serious in the period up to the Civil War. Federal spending had not yet become very large, and haphazard appropriations therefore caused no serious financial disturbances. The view was prevalent during the first half of the nineteenth century that the federal government should play a relatively unimportant role in the economic life of the nation. After the Civil War, however, this philosophy began to break down. Rapid growth of population, accumulation of capital, growth of monopoly power, and increasing concentration of wealth gave rise to a feeling that the federal government should exercise a somewhat tighter control over the economy. In the realm of fiscal matters this would call for a return to centralized supervision of appropriations and taxation.

During the years up to the Civil War, Congress and the Treasury

---

[3] V. J. Browne, *The Control of the Public Budget* (Washington, D. C.: Public Affairs Press, 1949). See also Lucius Wilmerding, *The Spending Power* (New Haven, Conn.: Yale University Press, 1943), *passim*. An excellent reference for the role of both national and state budgeting in the struggle for responsible democratic government in the United States is F. A. Cleveland and A. E. Buck, *The Budget and Responsible Government* (New York: Macmillan, 1920). For a wide-ranging and highly informative historical discussion of budgetary practice in many countries, see A. E. Buck, *The Budget in Governments of Today* (New York: Macmillan, 1934), Chap. I.

had constantly accused one another of the major share of responsibility for uncontrolled expenditures. But the real fault lay with the lack of financial planning by a single authority. Unfortunately, during the period of increasing federal expenditures after 1860, legislative control over appropriations collapsed completely. The Appropriations Committee was allowed to become so overloaded with work that it could not find time to make specific appropriations, and the power of appropriation became gradually dispersed among the various standing legislative committees, for example, the committees on military and naval affairs. Thus appropriations were made in a number of separate bills, and the way was opened for competition among the various departments of the executive branch for big appropriations. Logrolling and horsetrading are the inevitable result of allowing Congressional committees that are interested in particular departments to exercise the right to appropriate funds as well as to enact legislation. The only answer seemed to be a central appropriations committee, preferably with the mandate to suggest the taxes required to finance the appropriations it recommended.

► THE MOVE TOWARD A MODERN BUDGET

During the first two decades of the present century, sentiment for an integrated budget act developed both inside and outside Congress. A number of attempts after 1890 to tighten up federal fiscal procedure awakened interest in the possibility of improving the whole fiscal system.[4]

The debate set off by the Taft Commission in 1911, and the report of this commission in 1912, paved the way for the ultimate adoption of a federal budget in 1921. The Taft Commission recommended that the President be charged with preparing an annual budget for submission to Congress.[5] At the same time, it urged that the President be required to account to Congress for the manner in which the budget is executed. To buttress the fixing of responsibility on the President, the commission recommended that a high degree of central administrative control be placed over accounting and reporting.[6] The commission showed a predilection for the adoption of the executive type of budget in use in Great Britain.

Then as now Congress disliked the thought of surrendering power

---

[4] The Dockery Act of 1894 provided for centralized authority over auditing and accounts, and in 1905 the Keep Commission made a study of bookkeeping in governmental agencies. Under both Taft and Wilson, Congressional committees were established to encourage economy and efficiency, and in 1920 the House Appropriations Committee was re-established.

[5] Before 1921 the President did not possess the authority to make recommendations for a plan of federal spending, or for a program for financing it. The power of veto had been greatly limited by the growth of the device of the "rider." About all the President could do was to call for legislation and for the appropriations necessary to finance it.

[6] Browne, *op. cit.,* p. 75.

over the budgetary process, and the desire of the commission to introduce into this country a budgetary system patterned largely after the British executive budget did not gain acceptance. Despite the fact that legislative control is relevant only to policies and programs, Congress is always inclined to try to specify details as well as general lines of guidance. In the budgetary process the entire basis of the constitutional allocation of powers between the executive and the legislature is at stake, and the latter is naturally loath to go very far in transferring powers even in the interest of efficiency and centralized responsibility. The underlying issue has remained the same throughout our history.

► THE BUDGET AND ACCOUNTING ACT OF 1921

The Budget and Accounting Act of 1921 established two offices, the Bureau of the Budget, and the General Accounting Office. The first was intended to provide the federal government with a plan of expenditures and revenues that would make possible centralized control over fiscal policy. The second embodied the desire of Congress to provide itself with a check on both the preparation and the execution of the budget by the executive branch through an independent audit of federal accounts. The act directs the President to formulate a budget every year in such a way as to provide estimates of expenditures and receipts for the following fiscal year. If the President suggests any changes in tax rates, estimates of revenues are to be made on the basis of both existing rates and the proposed rates. In addition, estimates of revenues and expenditures for the current fiscal year are to be provided, as well as data for the preceding fiscal year. Such information as the amount of unexpended funds, the amount of annual and permanent appropriations, the end-of-year condition of the Treasury, the state of federal indebtedness, and the like, is also to be set forth.

In placing in one spot the responsibility for bringing together all relevant fiscal information, Congress was making some effort in the direction of introducing the true budgetary principles of planning in advance and assessing the opportunity cost of proposed expenditures. Thus the act provided that the President shall make recommendations for filling any deficit with taxes, loans, or other revenues. Obviously the primary intent here was not to force the President to present a balanced budget in the sense of an equation of expenditures and tax revenues. Rather, it merely had the effect of compelling simultaneous consideration of both the spending and the revenue sides of the budget in the executive branch.

THE BUREAU OF THE BUDGET

Differences in the views of the Senate and the House led to an awkward compromise over the role of the director of the newly formed Bureau of the Budget. Representative Good, the chairman of the House

Appropriations Committee, had urged that the bureau be placed in the Executive Office of the President. Senator McCormick, on the other hand, wished it to be in the Treasury. Under the compromise, the Bureau of the Budget was to be housed in the Treasury, and the director was to be subordinate to the Secretary of the Treasury. But he was given the power to supervise the budgets of all departments, including the Treasury. In addition, since the act charged the President with presenting the budget, the director was to work for the President, not for the Secretary of the Treasury. The Senate had wished to see the task of preparing the budget in the hands of the officer whose duty it was to make revenue recommendations to Congress, namely, the Secretary of the Treasury. In this way we would have had a Minister of Finance, and really centralized responsibility would have been achieved. Although the actual task of preparing the estimates rested with the Budget Bureau, budgetary policies had been made the province of the President. Not until 1939, however, was the Budget Bureau actually moved out of the Treasury into the Executive Office of the President.

For many years the Bureau of the Budget contented itself with a very narrow conception of its duties. Until Roosevelt took office the bureau was simply an agency that advocated economy in government. Certainly this attitude allayed any doubts that Congress may have had respecting the danger that the bureau would usurp any of its own functions. General Dawes, the first director, set the course that was followed for a dozen years. In his opinion the task before him was to convince the departments of the need for economy. Since he had close personal ties with President Harding, he was able to achieve a considerable measure of cooperation from the departments. Although subordinate to a cabinet officer, he was invited to cabinet meetings. His objective was to make the money appropriated by Congress go as far as possible. It must be emphasized that in the event that a President demonstrated little interest in the budget, this view of Dawes would have automatically resulted in the reappearance of the strictly legislative budget by default.

Another power given to the bureau (Section 209) was that of studying all departments with a view to increasing their efficiency and economical use of funds. Included in this directive was the right to recommend reassignment of activities as among departments and agencies, and the regrouping of services. This power was unused for twenty years, but continuous study of the administrative process by the Bureau of the Budget has now come to be one of its important functions.

LIMITED OBJECTIVES OF THE ACT

Since 1921 the United States has had the basis for an intelligent budget. But the battle for intelligent budgeting must be constantly fought anew. Under a political system of checks and balances the struggle between the executive and the legislature goes on continually. Another major defect still remains in the failure to combine responsibility for appropriations and tax revenues in a single executive department. The separation of tax and expenditure functions at the level of the Secretary of the Treasury and the Director of the Budget Bureau makes difficult over-all planning by the executive branch.

As we have seen, a major defect on the Congressional side is the continued attempt by legislators to perform budgetary functions that are essentially administrative. The result is that members of the appropriations committees and subcommittees are overloaded. Yet much of the work they do duplicates that performed by the Budget Bureau.

It has been argued that the mere fact of duplication is not necessarily a disadvantage. The point is that duplication, in the sense of a thrashing out of issues by separate authorities, can enhance the effectiveness of the democratic process. According to this view, the difficulty is that the legislative branch is not at present equipped with the technical staff to perform a task that is of approximately equal scope with that accomplished in the executive branch. But the implied remedy betrays a weakness in the argument. Although the legislative branch undoubtedly could do a much better job if its committees had greater staffs, the question is what use would be made of the staff. Opponents of the argument that the committees' staffs should be enlarged point out that if they are employed for purposes of supervising administration, matters would be worse rather than better. In other words, the problem would be how to avoid their use in encroaching on the functions of the executive branch.

THE GENERAL ACCOUNTING OFFICE

Prior to 1921 the functions of accounting and auditing resided in the office of the Secretary of the Treasury. The Budget and Accounting Act transferred these functions to a General Accounting Office, under the Comptroller General. This officer was to be appointed for a period of fifteen years, with the consent of the Senate, and was not removable by the President. The object of these provisions was to provide Congress with a watchdog on the executive branch. It was because of this lack of Presidential authority over the Comptroller General that President Wilson had vetoed the act, and despite its subsequent acceptance by Harding, a long line of critics outside Congress have sharply criticized this aspect of the legislation. The gist of the criticism has been that accounting and reporting are functions that belong in the executive branch, while the job of checking on the performance of the executive belongs to the legislature.[7] Yet in order to make an adequate check, Congress needs to review expenditures,

---

[7] Cf. Arthur Smithies, *The Budgetary Process in the United States* (Committee for Economic Development Research Study; New York: McGraw, 1955), p. 76.
The author has benefited greatly from this book, which appeared when the present chapter was being revised.

and to do this it needs the power to receive reports from administrative agencies in a form that it regards as satisfactory. In prescribing the form, it may restrict the scope of the agencies to make use of accounting procedures which they believe are necessary to perform their own task satisfactorily. The Budgeting and Accounting Procedures Act of 1950 sought to resolve the problem by dividing the responsibility; making agency heads responsible for their accounting systems; conferring upon the Comptroller General the power to prescribe the form of accounts, and to review the systems of accounting employed by the agencies; but at the same time requiring consultation with both the Treasury and the Bureau of the Budget. The General Accounting Office retains the function of auditing.

The auditing function of the General Accounting Office has been concerned with the task of ascertaining the adequacy of the controls of administrative agencies over their financial operations, and with the extent of their compliance with the conditions under which they have been granted public funds. Naturally this function is indispensable. Without it governmental financial operations would be in a state of chaos. Unfortunately, however, preoccupation with compliance leaves little time or energy for investigation into the ways and means whereby the *efficiency* of governmental agencies can be enhanced. As we shall see in connection with budgetary review, the fourth and last step in federal budgeting, it is difficult to provide effective means whereby a systematic review is made of government spending in the light of the intentions of Congress in enacting legislation.

► STEPS IN FEDERAL BUDGETING

The extent of the improvement brought about by the reform of the budget in 1921, as well as the changes made since that time and the improvements still to be made, can best be examined by making use of the four-stage division ordinarily applied to the budgetary process. As stated earlier, these four steps are preparation, authorization, execution, and review.[8] They involve such a complex of procedures, however, that the public as well as Congress often finds it difficult to remember to focus attention on the really fundamental questions: (1) What is the money wanted for? and (2) What do the taxpayers get for it?[9] The difficulty of obtaining clear answers to these apparently simple questions is explainable by the fact that the budget-making process is itself extraordinarily complex.

---

[8] See the excellent study by George B. Galloway, *Reform of the Federal Budget,* Legislative Reference Service, Library of Congress, *Public Affairs Bulletin* No. 80, April, 1950.

[9] The Hoover Commission (The Commission on Organization of the Executive Branch of the Government) argued in its report presented to Congress in February, 1949, that these questions "lie at the root of any fiscal system," and that the budgeting and accounting system of the federal government gave adequate answers to neither.

No single form of budget can answer all the questions to which answers are desired. And no single authority is responsible for seeing the budget through from its inception to its ultimate execution and review.

▶ THE EXECUTIVE AND THE PREPARATION OF THE BUDGET

Despite the reforms of the Budget and Accounting Act of 1921, federal budgetary practice has been the subject of constant criticism from all sides during the past thirty-five years. With the enormous growth in the economic role of the government, defects that earlier seemed tolerable have become more and more serious. Part of the reason for this deficiency in budgetary practice arises out of weaknesses in the treatment of the budget at the hands of the executive in the formulation of the budget. On the other hand, much progress has been made in recent years in improving the form of the budget as it leaves the hands of the bureau and the President. The fact that much still remains to be done is partly ascribable to the difficulty of learning how to handle, within the term of a few years, the enormous and complex financial relationships connected with the huge national defense establishment.

A wide variety of criticisms have been made with respect to the form and content of the President's budget as it is transmitted for legislative consideration. On many of these criticisms, however, there is by no means general agreement, either as to their validity or as to the proper course to take if they are valid. Therefore there is reason to believe that improvements over the years are likely to take the form of gradual adaptation to circumstances rather than of a blueprint that will satisfy all critics. The suggestions that have been made in recent years concern such matters as the timing of submission of the President's budget to Congress, segregation of capital outlays from current operating expenditures, preparation by the executive of an alternative budget showing what items have a low priority, abandonment of the principles of the annual balanced budget in favor of balance over a longer period (e.g., the business cycle, if such a cycle exists, or, if not, over a planning period), simplification and greater cohesion in the budget document, and reorganization of the Bureau of the Budget.[10]

Obviously some of these suggestions apply to the budgetary process as a whole, rather than to the role of the executive in the formulation of the budget. Therefore in the present context reference will be made only to the points which concern budgetary preparation.

TIMING

The proper timing of the presentation of the budget to Congress by the President is a rather difficult technical problem. The enormous task of gathering the estimates from all departments and the difficulty of making

---

[10] See Galloway, *op. cit.,* p. iii.

advance estimates of expenditures in a world of constant change and frequent crisis are likely to make any particular deadline for presenting the budget to Congress seem unsatisfactory. As the Hoover Commission's Task Force pointed out, however, the present required date of submission of the budget is difficult to meet.[11] In the year of inauguration, the outgoing President is required to submit his budget only two weeks before the incoming President takes office on January 20. This forces the new President immediately to present a new budget, particularly if his party is opposite to that of his predecessor. Even a postponement until April 1 would not give the incoming President much time to prepare a new budget, but it would be some improvement. Just how important the above criticism is in practice depends on the likelihood that extensive budgetary changes will be made at a late stage in the preparation of the budget.

Normally the major decisions in the preparation of the budget have been made a full year before the budget finally takes effect.[12] The budgetary process commences in the spring of the year, with the departments making preliminary estimates of their needs. However, departmental planning of programs on the basis of which these estimates are made naturally has taken place much earlier than this. At the same time, the Bureau of the Budget discusses the preliminary estimates with the agencies. At the beginning of the summer, matters have reached the stage at which the President, with the help of his advisers, is ready to establish preliminary expenditure ceilings for each department and agency. Unless unexpected events occur, these estimates establish the broad outlines of the budget, within which subsequent decisions on detail must be made. During the summer the departments revise their detailed estimates in accordance with these ceilings. During the fall and early winter, hearings are held, at which department heads justify their estimates to the Bureau of the Budget. At the same time the Treasury presents its revenue estimates for the coming year. Of course if important unforeseen circumstances arise, revisions have to be made in both appropriation and revenue estimates. Otherwise the estimates of the cost of major programs made in the previous June govern the expenditures proposed in the President's budget as it is presented to Congress in January.

In the light of the long incubation period of the federal budget before it is presented to Congress, it is apparent that any really important changes made at the last moment are more likely to result from unexpected devel-

---

[11] Task Force, *Report on Fiscal, Budgeting and Accounting Activities,* prepared for the Commission on Organization of the Executive Branch of the Government, January, 1949, App. F. The recommendations of the Task Forces must always be distinguished from those of the Hoover Commission itself.

[12] An interesting account of the timing of the steps in the preparation of the budget is given by Smithies, *op. cit.,* pp. 108 ff. He emphasizes that if unnecessary detail were dispensed with, Congress and the President combined could save as much as six months in the budgetary process, and major decisions could thus be made much nearer the time when they would be put into effect (p. 218).

opments arising out of major economic or military events than from the adoption of new policies by an incoming President. A criticism of a more serious nature is the requirement that the budgets of agencies be examined in detail throughout the fall, when the really basic budgetary decisions have already been made. Allied with this criticism is the further point that, except for agencies whose functions change little over time, detailed estimates are impossible to make with any accuracy. They depend on programs which cannot be foreseen in advance.

Among the numerous recommendations of the Taft Commission on Economy and Efficiency in 1911 was the recommendation that the budget be presented in a form which would permit Congress to evaluate the programs submitted for its consideration by the executive branch. It also recommended a classification of expenditures according to whether they were made for current outlay or for the acquisition of capital goods, which would yield their services over a period of years. In recent years a great deal of interest has attached to these recommendations. The distinction between capital and current expenditures in the budget is discussed in Chapter 21. At this point a few words will be said about performance or program budgeting.

PERFORMANCE BUDGETING

Until 1950 the budget of the federal government failed to carry a classification of expenditures based on performance, although many agencies had been formulating budgets that showed their activities. The Hoover Commission was particularly impressed with the seriousness of the lack of a federal budget that reflected programs, and recommended that the budget be based on "functions, activities, and projects." In 1949 Congress enacted a requirement that a program or performance budget be included among the budgetary classifications.

The defect of a budgetary form which excludes programs is that no conception can be obtained of the relationship between the benefits and the costs of public expenditures. Thus it was pointed out by the Hoover Commission that the Veterans' Administration had an appropriation of $1 billion for "salaries and expenses"; and that a naval hospital might be financed out of a dozen different accounts, so that very few individuals would be in a position to know how much this service was costing. Performance budgeting is designed, of course, to put into practice the true principle of budgeting, namely, to make clear what the cost of a given expenditure is in terms of goods and services that must be forgone by the public if a particular service is to be admitted to the budget. Moreover, this form of budget provides the basis for studies of efficiency within the departments, and for the correction of duplication and overlapping between agencies. Several cities and states have adopted the principle of the performance budget in greater or less degree. Los Angeles and Richmond, among the cities, may be mentioned, and Maryland among the states.

Desirable as it is to set forth the budget in terms of programs, it is obvious that a budget which used this classification only would fail to provide Congress with all the information it needs. This fact was recognized by the Taft Commission, but not by the Hoover Commission. The difficulty is that there is a limit to the number of classifications that are possible if a budget is to be used. Smithies has proposed that the two operations of programing and the achievement of economy be coordinated but actually handled under separate operations.[13] Congressmen are naturally suspicious of broad appropriations covering programs as contrasted with the detailed specifications which permit them to suggest the economies that make a good impression on the voters.

► LEGISLATIVE AUTHORIZATION OF THE BUDGET

Frequently observers have argued that because of the habit of Congress in responding to the pressures of self-interested unrepresentative pressure groups, the budgetary function should be lifted out of the hands of the legislature entirely. This view implies, however, that the United States should revise its form of government and follow the British system of making the budget a purely executive function, with responsibility to the electorate taking the form of liability to a vote of no confidence and the calling of a general election.

If it were true that Congress acted solely in response to narrow group pressures of this sort, the above complaint would be justified. But it also responds to another kind of group pressures, namely, those exerted by the major economic classes, regional interests, and groups representing different attitudes toward social and political questions. In a country with as great a diversity of opinions on these questions as is found in the United States, it is doubtful whether a purely executive federal budget is desirable, despite the admittedly serious defects of the high degree of legislative control over the budget under the present system. As a case in point may be cited the conflict between Congress and the administration with respect to the rate of militarization in the years after 1948. The danger of proceeding too rapidly and precipitating the world conflict that everyone wanted to avoid was as great as that of going too slowly and offering a

---

[13] Smithies, *op. cit.*, p. 85. He recommends that the President submit to Congress a program budget of a sufficiently general and simple form so that the Appropriation Committee as a whole can examine it, and provide directions for the more detailed examination by its subcommittees (p. 199). Incidentally, an advantage of thus providing terms of reference for the subcommittees might well be to place them in a better position to resist pressures from sectional groups interested in particular appropriations.

tempting target for aggression. The executive, in the minds of some observers, at least, represented one of these points of view, and the legislature tended to support the other. This is an illustration of the kind of issue on which the legislative branch exercises an important function in sounding out the feeling of the country on an issue of basic importance.

RELATIONS WITH THE EXECUTIVE BRANCH

The basic defect in the relation between the legislature and the executive branch is the practice on the part of Congress of exercising administrative functions, for which a legislature is not adapted. Congress should restrict itself to providing the money for carrying out its wishes in accordance with its legislation. It should assure itself that these functions are carried out, and that the appropriated funds are spent in accordance with law. But it should not itself directly supervise the administrative aspects of the budget. By making specific appropriations, Congress is in a position to exercise control over the executive. Lump-sum appropriations provide the executive with greater latitude. During periods of crisis, such as war and preparation for war, or rapid social change, Congress favors the lump-sum appropriation. On the other hand, it has in the past returned to detailed scrutiny when circumstances permitted. The events of recent years have favored lump-sum appropriations, which is to be expected in a period when the federal government has been rapidly increasing its permanent activities both at home and abroad. The requirement that agencies submit detailed estimates of expenditures limits the discretion of agency heads in shifting funds about in accordance with changes in needs that could not have been foreseen during the period when the budget was being prepared. The seriousness of this rigidity depends on the nature of the work performed by the particular agency.

Mention should also be made of the manner in which subcommittees on appropriations exercise authority over budget administration in the executive branch. Members of the appropriations committees receive assignments on subcommittees concerned with control over particular agencies and departments. They satisfy themselves that appropriations are being spent in the manner intended by Congress. While this procedure assures a highly desirable means of maintaining continuous legislative control, it is also true that a subcommittee member may find himself in a strategic position for influencing decisions that ought to be executive rather than legislative in nature. It should be noted, however, that at the border line between legislative and executive functions some frictional loss of efficiency is to be expected.

WHOSE IS THE RESPONSIBILITY TO COORDINATE REVENUES AND EXPENDITURES?

An example of the difficulty of obtaining executive and legislative cooperation is provided by the numerous attempts that have been made in the past by each branch to shift to the other the responsibility for achieving a balanced budget. (We are not concerned here with whether or not a balanced budget is desirable.) The Budget and Accounting Act thrust this responsibility onto the President, but softened the provision by including borrowing among the revenue sources at his disposal for balancing expenditures. President Roosevelt adopted the practice of simply submitting expenditure requests to Congresses that were largely under his control, and handing them the responsibility for finding the necessary revenues. More recently Congress has sought to place more of the initial responsibility on the President, while at the same time jealously preserving its own prerogatives with respect to ultimate budgetary decisions.

Congress has made a number of attempts to establish a more formal framework within which appropriations are made. A proposal in 1943 that Congress forgo its right to appropriate money in excess of anticipated tax revenues except by a vote of three fifths of each house was rejected, and in 1946 a different approach was adopted. The Legislative Reorganization Act of that year established a joint committee comprising the two appropriations and the two tax committees (or authorized subcommittees) to meet for the purpose of setting a ceiling on expenditures early in the session. The basic difficulty with this device, which caused its abandonment after two unsuccessful years, was the impracticability of trying to set an over-all limit to expenditures before Congress had had the opportunity to examine the details of the expenditure proposals. In 1949 two attempts to place more responsibility on the President were rejected. The first was a move to direct the President to order blanket reductions in total expenditures by not less than 5 per cent or more than 10 per cent. The other was a proposed requirement that the President submit an "alternative balanced budget." This was not to encroach on Congressional budgetary prerogatives, but would make available to Congress the considered judgment of the Budget Bureau as to how the budget might be balanced.

CONGRESSIONAL PROCEDURES IN BUDGETARY AUTHORIZATION

Before the passage of the Budget and Accounting Act of 1921 the *legislative* committees of Congress had received jurisdiction over a number of items of appropriation. The act restored the importance of the appropriations committees. Nevertheless, the perennial problem remained as to how the committees could get through the enormous amount of work connected with appropriations. Until recently their staffs have been small. The vast size and complexity of total annual federal appropriations require that the work be divided among a large number of experts. But the size of the committees has not kept up with the work load, although their membership has increased as more and more subcommittees have been needed. The committeemen and subcommitteemen have found that they cannot become experts on specific phases of appropriations and at the same time be able to put expenditures as a whole in their proper perspective. Yet it is the latter that is by far the more important. The subcommittees hold hearings on the parts of the budget that are entrusted to them. Thus their members become specialists on particular agencies. The Legislative Reorganization Act of 1946 permitted the committees to appoint such staff as they needed, although it was believed by the committees concerned that the fresh viewpoints gained through the temporary hiring of consultants and specialists would be preferable to permanent expansion of the committee staffs. Despite the expansion of staff the committees themselves are overloaded with work, and must remain so if Congress is to continue to concern itself with details that are better carried on by an expanded Bureau of the Budget.

An important question is what form the Congressional appropriations committees should take in order to accomplish their objectives. It is often suggested that a joint committee on appropriations, parallel with that on internal revenue taxation, could serve to reduce the burden of work on committee members.[14] If a well-staffed joint committee on appropriations were to work with the separate appropriations committees in both houses certain advantages would result. There would be a saving in time, a lightening of the burden on committee members, and an avoidance of the necessity for a conference committee to resolve the differences in the separate bills of each house. The saving of time on duplicated hearings alone would be considerable.

Another suggestion is to have one committee in each house handle both revenue and appropriations measures. An important advantage of this procedure would be that committee members would tend to think in terms of both revenues and expenditures, a view which the present separation discourages. But it would do nothing to eliminate the time-consuming duplication of effort necessitated when money bills are separately considered by each house. Presumably a single joint committee of both houses having charge of both revenue and appropriations would give us the best arrangement from all points of view. However, objections have been made to this solution on the ground that it involves excessive concentration of power in a single committee, and that the great increase in work load involved would make the committee unwieldy and probably ineffective.

A solution might be to establish a joint committee on fiscal policy, composed of a few, rather than all, of the members of the committees on revenues and appropriations in each house. As we have seen, such a committee was in fact established under the Legislative Reorganization Act of 1946. Its function, however, was to arrive at an arbitrary expenditure

---

[14] A bill has been under consideration to amend the Legislative Reorganization Act of 1946 to permit the creation of a Joint Committee on the Budget, furnished with the staff necessary to perform the functions for the legislature that the Budget Bureau performs for the President.—*Report* to accompany S. 913 (No. 576), 82d Cong., 1st Sess.. 1952.

ceiling early in the session rather than to study the over-all spending and revenue policies of the federal government from the point of view of maximizing social and private national product. A bill was introduced into the Senate early in 1950 to transform this committee into a service committee for providing information helpful to other Congressional committees for achieving a balanced budget, greater economy, and so on. No action was taken at that time. The Joint Committee on the Economic Report has authority to make fiscal policy recommendations.

The relations between the appropriations committees and the standing legislative committees have frequently been such as to weaken the effectiveness of Congress in enacting legislation in the general public interest. The problem is how to allocate power within Congress in such a way as to avoid giving undue influence to particular members or groups. There is, of course, no perfect answer. It is because of this that so many changes have been made in the responsibilities and powers of the revenue and appropriations committees. One quite serious difficulty has been the understanding in the House that the Appropriations Committee has the right to refuse to appropriate funds for carrying out activities that have been passed by the House itself. The result of this unavoidable requirement that legislation be voted upon twice is that not only does the Appropriations Committee have a veto over the acts of standing legislative committees; it also has one over the whole House. It should be noted, of course, that the ultimate determinant of budgetary legislation is the action of Congress itself in setting up activities and programs.

THE CONSOLIDATED APPROPRIATION BILL

In recent years there has been interest in both houses in a requirement that appropriations be made in an omnibus or consolidated appropriation bill. It has been thought that by consolidating numerous appropriations into one or two consolidated bills, Congress would be better able to assess the relative merits of alternative appropriations, as well as the virtues of appropriations in terms of the taxes needed to finance them. The objective here is apparent: it is hoped that by compelling simultaneous consideration of all claims on the public purse, the true objective of budgeting can be achieved, namely, a careful consideration of alternatives.

Presumably a consolidated appropriation bill would reduce the effectiveness of selfish pressure groups, although the counterargument has been made that logrolling by the more powerful interests might actually be facilitated. It has also been pointed out that acceptance of the consolidated appropriation makes the power of item veto by the President more indispensable than ever, since it would hardly be feasible to veto an entire appropriation bill because of a legislative rider. (The item veto is employed in the great majority of the states.) An objection to the item veto is that a President might be able to use it to nullify an entire bill of which he disapproved, though its use could be restricted to riders that are irrelevant to the bill. Probably the most important criticism of the omnibus appropriation bill is that its complexity would be so great that legislators would not gain significantly in their understanding of the relative merits of alternative appropriations. The consolidated appropriation might have real possibilities if significant progress could be made in the simplification of budgetary procedures, so that the appropriations committees could obtain a grasp of the budget as a whole.

DEFICIENCY APPROPRIATIONS

An important aspect of budget authorization is the practice of supplemental and deficiency appropriations. Inadequate estimates of their needs by the executive departments are not the only reason for deficiency appropriations. Congressional appropriations practices likewise play a part. Congress has not interested itself in the enforcement of the Antideficiency Act of 1905. Partial appropriations are sometimes made to convey the impression of economy, and these necessitate a deficiency appropriation later.

Another factor is the prohibition on the transfer of items of appropriation between different objects within agencies. This means that the agencies must either ask for more than they need or face the necessity of requesting a deficiency appropriation. Finally, delays in the appropriation process necessitate provisional financing which takes the form of deficiency appropriations. It must be concluded that in a world of uncertainty these appropriations are unavoidable, but that since they are a measure of our failure to budget successfully in advance, their number should be kept to a minimum.

TIMING OF CONGRESSIONAL ACTION

Congress is as much bothered by insufficient time for preparing the budget as is the executive branch. Six weeks are not enough for adequate legislative consideration, and an attempt to set an appropriations ceiling as early as February 15 proved completely abortive. The formal compliance in 1948 by Congress with the provision of the 1946 act setting an over-all ceiling on appropriations was meaningless. By the end of the session appropriations had far exceeded the ceiling accepted in February. With sufficient staff much of the difficulty caused by insufficient time could be eliminated. Basically, however, the weakness is due to the fact that Congress is trying to do a large part of the task that belongs to the administration.

▶ EXECUTION OF THE BUDGET

Once the budget has been enacted into law, its provisions must be executed. This is, of course, the immediate responsibility of the administrative agencies, acting under the President. Actually, however, a good bit of give-and-take is necessary between the executive and legislative branches in putting the budget into effect. The appropriations subcommittees carry on a continuous liaison with their respective executive departments and agencies, and various changes are authorized by them after the budget bill has become law. Inevitably, also, the agencies and departments have to possess some control over their programs in the light of changing events and information that is not available until after the budget has been passed by Congress.

A problem in the execution of the budget has been to draw a line between an adequate degree of control of the agencies by the President and Congress and sufficient freedom for the agencies so that they can perform their task properly in the light of often rapidly changing events. Unless the President and the Budget Bureau have the power of apportionment, the practice of direct Congressional appropriations to the departments and agencies facilitates their escape from Presidential control. In the past this avoidance of control has taken the form of overspending of appropriations, or of spending them at a rate during the budgetary year that makes a deficiency appropriation necessary. Congress itself has not desired to take on the responsibility for controlling the departments, but in 1950 it confirmed the authority of the President and the Budget Bureau to apportion funds. So long as departmental funds become available quarterly, the practice of direct appropriations to them is not a serious matter.

An important attribute of effective execution of the budget is an adequate degree of latitude to the agencies which have to spend the appropriations. If the executive branch is to have the responsibility for putting the budget into effect, it must be given sufficient elbow room to do the job. Congress should make broad appropriations, and should interest itself in important functional questions rather than in the details of budget execution. It should hold the chief executive responsible for accomplishing its legislative provisions, and for doing it without waste or inefficiency. A step in the right direction was taken when, in accordance with the recommendation of the Hoover Commission, the executive was granted the right to spend less than the amount appropriated by Congress if the objectives of Congress were accomplished without spending the whole appropriation.

Some authorities argue that the executive should be given the right to make horizontal cuts in Congressional appropriations. In 1949 a bipartisan group of senators attempted to obtain passage of a resolution directing the President to reduce total expenditures for the fiscal year 1950 by from 5 to 10 per cent.[15] It had to be recognized, however, that it is unworkable for Congress to delegate to the President the power to curtail

---

[15] Cf. Jesse Burkhead, "The Outlook for Federal Budget-Making," *National Tax Journal,* December, 1949, pp. 289–290.

the appropriations that Congress has itself enacted. Moreover, horizontal cuts without regard to differing needs of the various agencies are unintelligent, although circumstances are imaginable in which they are necessary in order to squeeze water out of the budget.

If the President had been given the power to make the cuts where and in the amount he thought necessary, this would have been a step in the direction of an executive budget. Since Congress had no intention of relinquishing any of its essential powers over budgeting, the resolution would have tended to shift responsibility to the President for work that Congress should itself perform. If Congress increases the appropriations asked for by the President in his budget message, there is little point in then empowering him to reduce expenditures. If, on the other hand, Congress accepts his budget without change, there would be no need to ask him to make the horizontal cut.

► BUDGETARY REVIEW

Budgetary review accomplishes two major functions. First, review of past performance is necessary in order to ascertain the extent to which budgetary intentions have been realized. This retrospective view of budgeting concerns itself with (1) the routine question whether government money has been spent in accordance with the law, and (2) the broader question of how far objectives have been attained, and how far they have been achieved efficiently. Second, review serves the useful function of providing guide lines for the future. The mistakes of the past can help us to find remedies only if time and effort are devoted to reviewing our experience.

It can be seen that budgetary review, in all its aspects, cannot easily be carried out by any single organization, but should be a joint effort. Thus in Congress review is the function of the appropriations and the expenditure committees, with the subcommittees on appropriations particularly concerned in connection with their continuous review of the operations of the agencies and departments assigned to them. Congress is also concerned with review in connection with the routine and special reports on agency operations made by the General Accounting Office. Again, the expenditure committees have occupied themselves with particular episodes rather than with carrying out continuous reviews. In the executive branch the Bureau of the Budget reviews the financial operations of the agencies. Representatives of the bureau meet with the agencies' budgetary officers and go over their estimates. Justifications of appropriations prepared by the agencies are naturally concerned with programs, however, and their emphasis is on future aspirations rather than on what they have accomplished with past appropriations.

There is widespread dissatisfaction with the effectiveness with which budgetary review has been carried out in the past. The basis of the criticism is that the system is complex, and that there is no really thorough-going review, with the consequence that comprehensive information is lacking on the ways in which the efficiency of governmental operations can be tightened up.

AUDIT

Review, in the sense of audit, is the function of the General Accounting Office under the Comptroller General. Concerned with assuring compliance with the law, the GAO is the agent of Congress in maintaining control over the departments. But because of the rather tenuous relationships between Congress and the GAO in the past, legislative control over audit has been somewhat fictitious. Unless a Congressional committee requires and carefully examines frequent and basic reports from the Comptroller General, Congress is failing to perform adequately its auditing function. Only since 1946, when the passage of the Legislative Reorganization Act assigned that function to the committees on Expenditures in the Executive Departments, has any Congressional committee undertaken to review the reports of the General Accounting Office; moreover, owing to the pressure of other work, the reviews have not been very thorough.

The suggestion has been made that a joint Congressional committee be created to receive the reports of the GAO. The argument is that only Congress can bear the ultimate responsibility for auditing. On the other hand, some observers feel that Congress is reasonably satisfied with the job of auditing that is being done, and that it might better be spending its time on the achievement of economy and efficiency.[16] The Hoover Commission Task Force argued that the role of the GAO should be to ferret out extravagance and misuse of funds, and to bring the executive to account for the execution of the budget.[17] It complained that the GAO has kept busy with "auditing and settling millions of vouchers and claims, which had already been administratively audited and paid."

THE BUREAU OF THE BUDGET

Over the years, the Bureau of the Budget has been assigned a number of functions in addition to those closely connected with budgeting. A comprehensive discussion of these functions lies outside the scope of a general study of public finance.[18] Among its main activities are its duties in connection with budgetary review. The present role of the bureau in budgetary review is the result of thirty-five years of development. Thus the bureau has received the authority to review departmental recommendations for

---

[16] Smithies, *op. cit.*, pp. 156, 182–183.

[17] Hoover Commission Task Force, *Report*, p. 81.

[18] Cf. Edward H. Hobbs, *Behind the President: A Study of Executive Office Agencies* (Washington, D. C.: Public Affairs Press, 1954), Chap. II, "The Bureau of the Budget."

legislation, whether or not they affect budgetary matters; it has the power to apportion agency appropriations (and thus to supervise the rate at which they are being spent); it checks departmental estimates and sets ceilings for their budgets. Moreover, under the Government Corporation Control Act of 1945 the bureau's reviewing function was extended to include government-owned corporations.[19] In April, 1952, an Office of Budget Review was set up, which, along with five new program divisions, took over the functions of the estimates division. The program divisions handle detailed matters of the budget estimates of the agencies and departments, check on compliance in the designated use of funds by them, and, in connection with making apportionment effective, may exercise the controversial function of impounding agency reserves.

The Office of Budget Review is in charge of general rather than detailed issues with respect to estimates of the agencies. Thus it is concerned with reviewing efficiency and performance. At the same time the budgets of the departments and agencies have placed more and more emphasis on their proposed programs. It has been argued that although clear-cut statements of future programs of the agencies are indispensable to an understanding of the budgetary process, it is a difficult task to deal in the same document with budgetary review and agency programing. The problem is for Congress, at one and the same time, to be in a position to evaluate a *program,* which often necessarily cuts across two or more agency lines, as well as the *efficiency* and *performance* of particular agencies. At the same time, the review of past performance, both as conducted by the Office of Budget Review and by the appropriations committees in Congress, provides a basis for elaborating new programs.

► STATE AND LOCAL BUDGETARY PROBLEMS

All states now have laws governing their budgets. Some states, indeed, anticipated the federal government by several years in the adoption of a budget. Moreover, many cities have inaugurated modern budgetary practices, and an attempt has been made by a number of states to regularize budgetary practice for their municipalities. A variety of devices have been developed to minimize expenditures. Some states avoid appropriations in excess of the available tax revenues. This prohibition cannot, however, be extended to fixed commitments, like the service and repayment of debt, or the support of schools. In any event, the effect of such a policy on really needed government services is obvious. In some states the governor has been given the power to alter the budget, either by a horizontal cut or on a selective basis, in order to ensure that expenditures do not exceed revenues. At the federal level Congress has usually opposed this sort of device on the ground that ultimate power resides with the legislature.

---

[19] *Ibid.,* pp. 35 ff.

Democratic government requires that the legislature have an opportunity to override executive veto of its proposed expenditures. The use of the specific veto among many of the states provides the executive with a large measure of opportunity to exercise real power with respect to budgeting. Conversely, it is common among some states to follow the procedure developed by Maryland in 1916, by virtue of which the constitution permits the legislature to eliminate or reduce items in the governor's budget. In order to restrain spending, however, *increases* in expenditures by the legislature are prohibited.

FORECASTING REVENUES AND EXPENDITURES

The states and municipalities face special problems in forecasting their revenues and expenditures. Deep-seated changes in the national economy in recent decades have forced both the states and the localities to make use of new sources of revenue. Since these revenues are more subject to fluctuation with the business cycle than is the traditional property tax, the art of budgeting has become more difficult. Many states have gone in heavily for the personal and corporate income tax, the yield from which falls substantially with declines in business activity. Some of the cities, in turning to the sales tax, have chosen a tax with a relatively stable yield. Thus they have somewhat lightened their forecasting problem, though at the cost of a regressive element in the tax system. On the expenditure side a major budgeting task is that of correctly estimating the future course of the price level.

There are three important reasons why the states and cities experience difficulty in achieving accurate budgeting. First, as with the federal government, revenue bills are often dealt with independently of appropriations. Failure to unite revenue and appropriations measures into a single bill precludes a really integrated fiscal policy. Second, also similar to federal experience, states and cities do not usually consider all appropriations in one consolidated bill. Third, the popularity of the biennial budget among the states has made much more difficult the problem of estimating expenditures and tax revenues. Naturally, when estimates must be made far in advance, devices have to be developed that will permit some elasticity within the budget. Examples are intra- and even interdepartmental transfer of funds, the governor's contingency funds, and in general less detailed specification of expenditures than is ordinarily favored by legislatures. In the extreme case, the governor may alter the appropriations of the legislature.

RELATION BETWEEN THE EXECUTIVE AND THE LEGISLATURE

In general there are three types of budget at the state level: the executive budget, subject to modification by the legislature; the board budget, formulated by department heads, including the governor ex officio and sometimes representatives from the legislature; and in one state only, the legislative budget. Most of the states have adopted the executive budget. Only a few cities retain the legislative budget. So long as the system of government is sufficiently centralized so that the executive is able to bring together the required information, the executive budget is superior; it has proved popular, for example, with cities operating under the city-manager form of government. The inherent superiority of the executive budget presupposes, of course, a lively interest on the part of the governor or the mayor in budgetary problems. Where this is not the case the board budget may actually turn out to be better. Since it cannot be expected that all incumbents of executive office will have equal ability and interest in budgeting, adoption of the executive budget requires the establishment of a good budget bureau. A defect often found at state and local governmental levels is the lack of an efficient, full-time, budgetary staff. Moreover, the fact that department heads are not responsible to the governor may reduce the effectiveness of the executive budget.

Even good executive budgeting at the state and local levels suffers from the lack of attention that the budget receives from the public at large. The citizen cannot be a specialist on all matters that affect the public interest, and it can hardly be expected that the average voter will take the time to read through details that have little meaning to him. Short budget summaries are desirable, particularly if drawn up in terms of function or performance. Some states anticipated the federal government in the development of the performance budget, and the principle needs to be extended.[20] Possibly much might be accomplished by making the voter aware of the alternative public services that must be forgone when particular expenditures are voted. A major step in that direction would be the general acceptance of a budget that includes both expenditures and the revenues required to finance them. An important obstacle to good budgeting at the state level is the earmarking of certain revenues for special uses.[21]

► BUDGETARY COMPREHENSIVENESS

GOVERNMENT CORPORATIONS

The major objective of budgeting is to provide a comprehensive view of anticipated revenues and expenditures. Owing to the complexity of modern governments, however, it is not always easy to include the details of all functions in a single budget. Moreover, many public economic activi-

---

[20] It should be constantly borne in mind that the performance budget, as understood at all levels of government, is not the same thing as the (probably unattainable) ideal budget that would evaluate all spending in terms of its social cost.

[21] The practice is also not unknown at the federal level. For example, Section 32 of the Agricultural Adjustment Act, as amended, assigned 30 per cent of annual customs receipts to schemes for stimulating domestic and foreign sales of agricultural commodities.

ties are self-contained and logically separable from the general functions of government. In the interest of efficiency it can be maintained that their budgets should be separate. Examples are agencies like the Tennessee Valley Authority and the Port of New York Authority. Naturally they have their own budgets, but since they are responsible to the nation, state, or city, their financial operations must be included in any comprehensive governmental financial plan.

One way of handling these functions is through a separate budget, "annexed" to the general budget, with only the surplus or deficit being carried to the latter. An advantage of this device is its convenience and the fact that it spares the agency what seems to be unnecessary trouble and red tape. A disadvantage is that it gives no information to the public with respect to either the use made of appropriated funds or the justification for any subsidies that may have to be made out of general revenues. Since 1945 the budgets of all government corporations have been integrated with that of the federal government.

Advocates of freedom of government corporations from the control, either of the Comptroller General or of the Bureau of the Budget, argue that all that is needed is (1) a post-audit, which any well-run business would regard as desirable, and (2) a running check on the efficiency with which the corporation is being operated. Government corporations object, on the other hand, to being required to observe the rules with respect to acceptance of bids and purchases of services (for example, printing) applied to agencies that are purely an arm of the government itself. An efficiently run business organization must have the discretion ordinarily allowed to a business enterprise.

Although a decision of the Supreme Court has exempted government corporations from the pre-audit, a device which encourages control by the comptroller over decisions that belong to the corporation itself, the area of freedom of the government corporation has been gradually whittled down. This development, despite the complaints of the corporations themselves, would seem to be inevitable if they are going to enter upon a variety of such unrelated activities as production and sale of electricity, deposit guarantee, mortgage activity and loans to business, purchase and sale of farm products, and the like.

ANNEXED BUDGETS

Another type of separate budget involves the short-circuiting of revenues into a special treasury. Examples are dedicated, revolving, and separate funds. To illustrate, if the proceeds of a state gasoline tax are "dedicated" exclusively to the maintenance of the highways, the appropriation each year is determined by the receipts of the tax. Thus, road building may be starved of funds or it may receive grants that are excessive. The use of separate revolving funds for state universities, schools, social security, highways, forest districts, and the like, permits the establishment of separate treasuries instead of forcing all revenues to be filtered through a central treasury and allocated to the various government functions as a result of open debate.

State governments have shown themselves to be excessively willing to establish separate budgets. It is easy to rationalize the practice. It may be argued that earmarking of revenues is a convenient way of limiting the amount of a particular public service that can be provided. Again, the state may desire to give a certain agency a degree of independence. Another rationalization is that the taxpayer is being made aware that he is helping to finance a popular service; for example, the Massachusetts tax on restaurant meals is used to help finance old-age assistance. In any event, state legislatures ordinarily tend to ignore the existence of separate funds unless the executive decides to make an issue in a particular case.[22]

One effect of separate budgets is to rigidify expenditures. Another is a decline in budgetary "morality" when an agency can count on certain sources of funds regardless of its performance. The main job becomes that of using them up rather than spending them efficiently. Again, agencies having access to segregated funds may tend to operate with undue freedom from political control. In general, all appropriations ought to be acted upon annually in order that a continuing test can be applied to all spending on the basis of performance. The separate fund escapes this test, and the longer it does so the more out of relation to need and efficiency the function is likely to become. Certain exceptions to this criticism of continuing appropriations should, however, be noted. Contractual payments, like interest charges and statutory debt-amortization payments, do not require annual scrutiny. And since legislatures sometimes become deadlocked on the appropriations bill, a minimum appropriation for necessary services may be advisable in the interest of public safety. Even in these cases some degree of annual supervision must be retained in order to avoid rigidities that might stifle the growth of desirable functions.

Much of the evil arising out of the earmarking of funds can be avoided if they are kept well below the level regarded as necessary to the function. In this way appropriations out of the general revenue fund serve as a balance wheel, and real budgetary consideration is possible. One way of accomplishing this is illustrated in Illinois, where earned receipts of educational institutions are set aside for their exclusive use, but are disbursed to them by appropriations from the state treasury. This permits the legislature to take account of them in making general appropriations.

A particularly dangerous aspect of the annexed budget is the lack of

---

[22] The federal grant-in-aid program may cause a similar loss of control by the states over their expenditures. When the states are required to match a federal grant, funds are likely to be appropriated for this purpose without real consideration of its relative desirability.

control over expenditures of important nationalized industries. Thus, for example, the nationalized industries of France are run at a substantial loss, which is financed out of the general revenues. Not only is inefficiency being subsidized, but the fact that losses will be made good encourages such enterprises to pay unduly high wages and social security benefits. Obviously social questions of this magnitude ought not to be decided by individual government corporations on the basis of their own self-interest. The danger is recognized to be particularly serious when account is taken of the political impracticability of abolishing the subsidies.

► CONCLUSION

The present chapter has dealt with the technique of budgeting, particularly at the federal level. It has appeared that one of the costs of a separation of the powers of government is an ambiguity in the fiscal relationships between the executive and the legislature. Much of the budgetary experience at all levels of government has been related to the effort to make these powers definite. Effective budgeting is most easily achieved under a system of government that places the greater part of the responsibility on the executive. Under the British system, for example, Parliament and the government in power ordinarily pursue a coordinated policy. A negative vote on a government proposal means an appeal to the electorate.

Although Congress has insisted on retaining the power of the purse, the Budget and Accounting Act of 1921 paved the way for the introduction of modern budgetary methods at the federal level. Under the Roosevelt administration the Bureau of the Budget greatly expanded its activities, and became an agency for evaluating programs rather than merely controlling expenditures. At the same time the vast expansion in the role of the federal government made it increasingly difficult for Congress to exercise close control over the executive branch. More and more the force of national and world events tended to dictate the size of the budget. General dissatisfaction with the high level of federal expenditures led to a disposition on the part of the legislative and executive branches to try to shift the blame on the other. But this in turn focused attention on the question of who really has the responsibility for determining the level of expenditures. The fact that this responsibility is divided, and divided in a rather uncertain and changing way, is partly responsible for the growth in spending which both the Congress and the executive branch frequently deplore.

At all levels of government the hope of the future is a fostering of a sense of the social cost of particular items of public expenditures in terms of the alternative public and private goods that must be forgone. The battle for an informative, but reasonably understandable, budgetary document will continue. In view of the rapidity of the growth of government in recent years, it is not surprising that much experimentation has been necessary with different forms of budgets.

► REFERENCES

BROWNE, V. J. *The Control of the Public Budget.* Washington, D. C.: Public Affairs Press, 1949.

BURKHEAD, J. "The Outlook for Federal Budget-Making," *National Tax Journal,* December, 1949, pp. 289–299.

COLM, G. *Essays in Public Finance and Fiscal Policy.* New York: Oxford University Press, 1955.

DOUGLAS, P. M. *Economy in Government.* Chicago: The University of Chicago Press, 1952.

GALLOWAY, G. B. *Reform of the Federal Budget.* Legislative Reference Service, Library of Congress, *Public Affairs Bulletin* No. 80, April, 1950.

MACMAHON, A. "Congressional Oversight of Administration: The Power of the Purse," *Political Science Quarterly,* June–September, 1943.

SMITHIES, A. *The Budgetary Process in the United States.* New York: McGraw-Hill Book Company, 1955.

UNITED NATIONS, DEPARTMENT OF ECONOMIC AFFAIRS. *Budgetary Structure and Classification of Government Accounts.* New York: 1951.

UNITED STATES BUREAU OF THE BUDGET. *The Federal Budget in Brief.* Annually.

5 The Nature of Governmental Receipts

► CLASSIFICATION OF GOVERNMENTAL RECEIPTS

The budget of a government is presented in such a way as to show all classes of receipts. These comprise not only income, but every kind of payment that is made to the treasury. The major types of receipts are borrowing, taxes, grants from other levels of government, charges for administrative services, and business receipts. Other sources of revenue are fines, escheats, and forfeitures; sales of government property; interest on government-owned securities; and rentals from leases. Borrowing by governments is not, of course, income in the usual sense. At the moment the loan is negotiated, however, the proceeds are cash receipts. If the government should repudiate its debt, a loan proves to have been a (highly unjust) tax. Responsible governments do not purposely repudiate their debts, and they could hardly repeat the act very often. Nevertheless, governmental monetary policies frequently result in a partial or total loss of principal, in terms of constant dollars, by the lender. Consequently the present chapter will discuss revenue aspects of borrowing as well as taxes and nontax revenues.

Grants-in-aid by another level of government differ somewhat from other governmental revenue sources in that they are not an ultimate source of revenue. If they are included along with the taxes or other revenues out of which they were financed by the grantor, the income figures for all levels of government prove to be fictitiously high. But from the point of view of the governmental jurisdiction that receives the grant they are just as much a source of income as any other item on the "Receipts" side of the budget. Administrative revenues comprise the miscellaneous receipts derived from fees, licenses, special assessments, on the one hand, and fines, penalties, and forfeitures, on the other. They are related to the control function of government. They are, therefore, ordinarily an incidental source of revenue, and they can be avoided if the individual is willing and able to disqualify himself.

Business receipts of governments, as the term implies, are akin to the revenues of a private business. Their extent is determined by the range of governmentally provided services that are paid for by the individuals and firms desiring to participate in them. Examples are postal charges; receipts from nationalized industries (e.g., in some countries, the railroads, electric power, coal, iron, and steel); income of municipally operated enterprises like public utilities or a harbor authority; investment income from governmentally owned securities, rents, and so on; tuition from state educational institutions; sales of public property (e.g., war surplus goods and the sale of public lands); and receipts from liquor and tobacco monopolies.

The wide range of types of governmental income makes it difficult, and probably pointless, to give them a completely logical classification. It is important, however, to take note of their characteristics, because the use of each particular source carries definite implications for public welfare.

► FEES, LICENSES, AND SPECIAL ASSESSMENTS

Fees are used primarily at the local level of government. The municipalities stand ready to provide a miscellaneous collection of services to individuals if and as they require them. Examples of fees are the charge for recording a deed or for public inspection of a restaurant kitchen or a barber shop. To the extent that the fee covers the cost of producing the service, the market for this type of public service is similar to a private market, and fees therefore become somewhat akin to market prices set under imperfectly competitive conditions.

Fees are rarely geared to the cost of production of the service; nor indeed can they be, since it is difficult to ascertain the various costs that are involved. The latter would include the services of the courts, police, and general government administrative machinery. The level of a fee is usually set at some convenient round number, and it is rarely altered to respond to changes in national income and the price level. Consequently the resemblance to a private market is superficial.

A fee that is larger than the cost of providing the service becomes a tax. For example, in the nineteenth century the states began to raise their corporation franchise fees to the status of taxes. Again, a fee is sometimes levied at a high or prohibitive rate in order to discourage an act. An example would be a very high charge for a hunting license. Another example would be the imposition of an extremely high liquor license on a restaurant or store.

Licenses and special assessments share with fees the characteristic that they are difficult to distinguish from taxes. A license is required where the public service in question is not divisible, but is available to a particular class of users, for example, fishermen or autoists. Special assessments against property owners for improvements that primarily benefit them alone (paving an alley) in practice may or may not be equal to the cost of performing the service. If not, either a subsidy or a tax is involved.

► RECEIPTS OF GOVERNMENT CORPORATIONS AND NATIONALIZED INDUSTRIES

The profits of government enterprise may constitute an important source of general revenues in those countries which (1) have a tradition of government-operated utilities or even stores and factories, and (2) wish to take advantage of the opportunity for levying a hidden tax on the consumer. These conditions are met when an article in highly inelastic demand may be legally produced or sold only under government monopoly. Examples are the government match and spirits monopolies so prevalent in Continental Europe.

Quite another philosophy of pricing is expressed by those government enterprises, like the Tennessee Valley Authority, whose purpose is in part to provide consumers with a service at a cost lower than that at which private initiative could produce it. The objective of such a policy may be to encourage a desirable social objective, for example, rural electrification. On the other hand, the policy may be adopted in order to break the power of a privately managed public utility. This element is involved when the rates charged by the government corporation are used by public service commissions as a yardstick for private rate making.

From the point of view of the public budget, a nationalized industry is likely to have decidedly different characteristics from the traditional government monopoly. Nationalization of industry ordinarily results from a belief that public welfare as a whole is likely to be benefited if certain strategically important industries are owned by the public rather than by stockholders. The policies of nationalized industries differ widely from country to country, and from industry to industry. Consequently no easy generalization can be made about the role of the nationalized industry in the public budget. In some instances, for example, nationalization has occurred in response to a belief on the part of labor that it will be better off under public ownership. It may be that wage rates, pension rights, and so on, are pushed so high that a subsidy is necessary out of the general tax funds. On the other hand, a subsidy may be needed to offset the excessively low prices charged to consumers; or, indeed, the nationalized industry may make a profit, which becomes a source of governmental revenue.

► GOVERNMENT BORROWING

Both private enterprise and governments derive receipts from borrowing. The private borrower invests the proceeds of the loan in plant, equipment, and inventories, which are expected to yield a return that will permit amortization of the debt. The bulk of government borrowing, on the other hand, is invested in projects that do not return an income in the form of money. The return on public investment in highways, for example, takes in part the form of satisfaction to those who use the highway for pleasure, and partly a reduction in costs to commercial users, and therefore in price to the consumer. The proceeds of government borrowing for war purposes may be swallowed up in the destruction of military equipment; and depression borrowing usually represents in part, at least, relief and other gratuitous transfer payments. Borrowing at the state and local level, however, is ordinarily undertaken to make possible investment in transportation facilities and buildings.

Limits exist, of course, to the extent to which a government can finance itself by borrowing. Since interest is compounded, these charges would gradually become extremely burdensome, provided, of course, the borrower were not relieved of part of the "real" burden through price inflation. Moreover, the lender may prefer to invest in private issues, either because of higher yield or because of a desire to hedge against a future price rise by investing in stocks. Again, since the purchaser of government securities can ordinarily place them on the market at any moment for cash, their prices may be low at a time when the government wishes to float a new issue.

One important point should be borne in mind with respect to the ability of governments to obtain financing through the issue of securities. Unless something happens to turn the saver against government securities (e.g., a threat of repudiation, or an unduly low interest rate as compared with private securities), the government as well as private enterprise can count on a relatively constant new demand for its securities. Both business and government can gradually increase their indebtedness over time. Indeed, if economic equilibrium is to be preserved, one or the other (or both) *must* do so, for there is ordinarily an annual increment to national savings which must find investment somewhere. To the extent that the public abstains from consuming the whole of its income, the resulting savings become available to either government or business, though their title is vested in the saver. In a balance sheet sense, then, business and/or government necessarily receives these savings as they are created.

GOVERNMENT ATTITUDES TOWARD DEBT REPAYMENT

Government borrowing is not always repaid, even ultimately. Not many persons suppose that the federal government will ever pay back the whole, or even a substantial part, of its huge debt ($277 billion as of June, 1955.) It is true that on a number of previous occasions part or all of the debt has been extinguished. The $2.75 billion Civil War debt had been reduced to less than $1 billion by 1893, and that of World War I by 37 per cent to $16 billion by 1930. In many countries, however, no sense of urgency has been displayed with respect to debt repayment. Not until the latter part of the nineteenth century did Britain, for example, feel the necessity of taking positive steps toward liquidating a part of the debt that resulted from the Napoleonic Wars. The interest payments were, of course, an important consideration; but when population and national income increase steadily year after year, these payments become a smaller and smaller relative burden. To state it differently, as national income rises, tax revenues at given tax rates automatically rise as well; therefore the interest payments can be financed without any increase in the tax burden.

Government attitudes toward the size of the public debt are apt to be quite different, however, if it is believed that there is a danger that population or national income will fall. It was this fear, for example, that prompted the economist Jevons to argue Prime Minister Gladstone into setting about repaying the British national debt. Jevons believed that the ultimate exhaustion of Britain's coal reserves would make impossible the maintenance of a high level of output and real national income, and therefore taxable capacity.[1] It is clear, of course that money national income, not real national income, is the magnitude that has immediate relevance to the burden of interest transfers from one segment of the economy (taxpayers) to another (bondholders). Money national income depends not only on the rate of physical output but also on the price level. If prices rise, creditors are paid back in depreciated currency. Moreover, if the interest payments were to become unduly burdensome in terms of taxes on income or commodities, a special levy could be assessed on all property, including government debt obligations.

PUBLIC BORROWING AS A FORM OF TAX

Government borrowing may involve a species of hidden tax if the bond purchaser receives less than the market rate of interest, or if the price level rises subsequent to his purchases of securities. In ordinary circumstances governments do pay the market rate of interest, since they have to compete with private borrowers wishing to obtain investment funds. Under certain conditions, however, a government may take advantage of its ability to exert pressure on the public to buy its bonds. If the lender is forced to purchase low-interest-bearing government securities rather than higher-interest-yielding private issues, he is in effect subjected to a tax. This device has not often been heavily exploited. In the United States, for example, even war bond issues have been sold without a great deal of compulsion. Yet the practice of payroll deductions and 100 per cent subscription goals indulged in during World War II did contain elements of coercion; and official policies had held down the yield of government securities. Germany used the device of compulsory loans, and the idea

---

[1] E. J. Hamilton, "Origin and Growth of the National Debt in Western Europe," *Papers and Proceedings* of the American Economic Association, May, 1947, p. 129.

was toyed with in this country as well. An additional element of compulsion is to block interest payments for the duration of the war. Unless the blocked interest is compounded, the effective rate of interest falls still lower.

If savers can be forced to accept lower than market interest rates, they might conceivably be induced to lend to the government at a zero rate of interest. A device by which this can be accomplished is the so-called fiat issue of hand-to-hand currency, or, as it was called during the Civil War, greenbacks. The government confers legal-tender power on its own issues of unbacked IOU's, and so long as these notes continue to circulate, the government does not have to redeem them. Indeed, it can in effect refuse to redeem them by merely reimbursing the holder with a similar note.

The fiat issue was formerly resorted to almost as a matter of course when the sovereign wished to undertake a foreign adventure. More recently the printing of non-interest-bearing government obligations has been largely restricted to countries facing economic or political breakdown. Since, in a currency-using nation, the only limit to the size of an issue of paper currency is the discretion of the issuing authority, it is easy to understand that overissue has frequently occurred. Prices are likely to be driven up through the excessive competition by the government for limited supplies of goods. Those who have held amounts of the paper issues have often found that they have been taxed through inflation.

THE FIAT ISSUE IN A DEPOSIT-USING ECONOMY

In a modern industrial economy, with a well-developed system of checking accounts, the price inflation associated with the prosecution of a major war comes about through the nation's taxing and debt-marketing policies rather than through its taxing and fiat-currency issues. In both cases the basic cause of inflation is failure to tax sufficiently. But when the great bulk of transactions are financed through the use of checking accounts, the scope for the issue of non-interest-bearing hand-to-hand currency is limited. The reason for this is that the currency will for the most part be quickly deposited into the checking accounts of firms and individuals at the commercial banks. Therefore it is not appropriate to say that the government finances part of the cost of the war by "printing up paper money." Rather it permits an excessive increase in deposits (which are also a form of money) by allowing an excessive amount of government debt to be bought by banks.[2]

The proportion of the paper currency issue that would return to the banks as described above would be determined by the proportion of the

---

[2] When government securities are sold to the commercial banks, the government receives a checking deposit which may not be offset by a corresponding decline in the deposits of firms and individuals. Therefore, so long as the banks have a sufficient volume of excess reserves, so that they do not have to sell private securities or call some of their private loans, the government has received new deposit money, which

public's liquid assets that it wishes to keep in the form of hand-to-hand currency. The absolute amount of such currency that the public wishes to hold is also affected, of course, by the level of national income. An increase in national income means an increase in transactions and therefore in the need for currency for transactions and precautionary purposes. It is true that the habits of the public with respect to the amount of currency it wishes to hold in relation to checking deposits may alter over time, as well as seasonally. For example, an increase in tourist travel may cause an increase in per capita currency holdings, and a corresponding decline in checking deposits. Again, the Christmas trade is associated with an increase in the demand by the public for currency, and this additional currency flows back to the banks soon after the holiday.

It is true, however, that even in a deposit-using economy a government at war could, if it seemed worth while, finance a rather small percentage of its military expenditures by the issue of non-interest-bearing currency. The government would simply pay for goods and services by the new issues. Since the newly issued currency is additional to the purchasing power already outstanding, the immediate effect, at wartime full employment, would be to push prices up. Thus money national income would rise, and there would be some additional demand for hand-to-hand currency, along with an additional demand for checking accounts to finance transactions at a higher level of income and prices. The major saving to the government, however, is not the fact that no interest is paid on paper issues. Rather it is the circumstance that when prices rise, debtors (in this case the government) pay interest and repay debt in depreciated dollars. Moreover, tax receipts rise when national income in dollar terms rises.

► TAXATION

A tax is a compulsory, nonreturnable contribution to the government. When this very general definition is made more specific we quickly encounter exceptions. Thus licenses and fees are not taxes because they are made in payment for a service enjoyed by the person or firm who makes the payment. Yet some taxes are imposed for the specific purpose of providing a service to a particular class of taxpayers. An example is the use of motor-vehicle taxes for road construction. Taxes are primarily imposed for revenue, but many taxes are not levied for revenue purposes at all. The objective of a tax may be to induce or discourage some action on the part of the public. The protective tariff, for example, is intended to discourage imports of the protected commodities.

Taxes designed to *encourage* some practice that is deemed socially

---

it can now spend in competition with the private sector of the economy. Thus, as in the case of the "printing up of new money," the result is inflation if the economy is at or near capacity output.

desirable have been more often proposed than adopted, for they may also carry adverse welfare aspects that have to be set off against their intended benefits to society. An example is the often proposed tax on currency and checking accounts during depression in order to stimulate spending. The unfavorable aspects of this tax are its great administrative difficulties, as well as its unpredictable effects on the free-enterprise system. Another case would be a special tax on spending (i.e., that part of a person's income which he does not save) in order to stimulate national saving. Here, again, the adverse effects have to be taken into account. For example, a permanent spendings tax would discourage spending during depression, when on the contrary, encouragement would be desirable.

THE BENEFIT PRINCIPLE

In the market for private goods the purchaser gets what he pays for. Private goods are rationed among purchasers in accordance with their ability to buy them. The principle is that the benefits furnished by private enterprise accrue to individuals rather than to society as a whole. Even in the private sector, however, the benefit principle is subject to qualification. Goods bought by one individual may indirectly benefit society at large. For example, a large property in a crowded suburb relieves congestion and lets in light and air.

Most publicly produced goods, on the other hand, cannot be broken up in such a way that each individual can be charged a price (cost per unit) for his share. This creates a difficulty. Since individuals do not associate the pain of paying for particular government services with the receipt of them, a strong tendency naturally arises to call for more and more government-produced goods. This in turn induces those who are tax-conscious to urge the use of the benefit principle in payment for government services wherever they are divisible, and therefore can be measured according to use by each individual.

Despite the limits on the extent to which the benefit principle can be applied in the area of publicly produced goods and services (even if it were desirable to do so), the use of this principle has been increasing in recent years. An important reason for this development is the rapidly growing complexity of economic society, and the resulting necessity for the state to undertake the production of goods and services which cannot be, or ought not to be, produced by private enterprise.

For example, state and national highways partake strongly of a public interest, and are therefore regarded as more appropriately constructed and maintained by government than by private interests. Yet, different people derive varying amounts of benefits from the highways, depending on their tastes. Moreover, charges can be related to benefits, for the use of throughways is easily metered. Consequently strong pressure has arisen to finance the construction and maintenance of highways by taxes on users. The results have been the widespread practice of segregating gasoline taxes and revenues from motor-vehicle licenses for this purpose, and the development of the toll road. Another example of the benefit principle in the public sector is the placing of payroll taxes imposed on workers in a special fund out of which benefits are paid to retired and unemployed individuals. Still another would be the restriction of the proceeds of a land tax to improvements to land.

A slightly different situation is that in which the proceeds of a tax paid by one group of taxpayers are used for the benefit of another group. An example of this form of special benefit taxation is found in the Agricultural Adjustment Act of 1933, which levied a so-called processing tax equal to the difference between the actual price of an agricultural commodity and its "fair" price.[3] The proceeds of the tax were devoted to payments to farmers for acreage reduction. In this case the consumer paid much of the tax; but instead of going into a general revenue fund it was short-circuited to the farmer. The Supreme Court declared this type of special benefit tax, which benefited a group other than those who bore the burden of the tax, to be unconstitutional.[4]

The narrowest interpretation of the benefit principle is found in those cases where there is a sale of public services that, directly at least, benefit only the taxpayer himself. Such cases are, indeed, rather difficult to find, for few public services benefit the immediate recipient alone. A dead-end private road would be an example. Another would be the use of a public snowplow to clear the driveway of a private home situated at some distance from the road. Garbage collection might appear to be another case, but the public in general benefits from the improvement in sanitation that results from denying the individual the right to make up his own mind on this delicate subject. The special tax levied in some states on fire insurance companies to help support the fire department is a somewhat more general type of benefit tax, but is perhaps better regarded as simply a supplement to the property tax.

Use of the Benefit Principle.   Progress in the public conception of the role of government in the economy has had the effect of considerably extending the use of the benefit principle of taxation. In a state that has a strongly developed conception of its function in increasing the welfare of its citizens, various groups may be taxed in order to receive benefits which as individuals they would have been unable or unwilling to provide

---

[3] The "fair" or "parity" price is, of course, a matter for legislative definition, and therefore has no absolute meaning. It is customary, in establishing this sort of standard, to regard the fair price as that which in some past year, or years, was relatively favorable to the group whose political support is being sought.

[4] On the ground that the rehabilitation of agriculture is the concern of the states; but also, as pointed out in Justice Stone's dissent, because the use to which the proceeds of the tax were put was disapproved. *United States v. Butler et al.*, 297 U. S. 1, 1936.

for themselves. An example is the substitution of government contributory social insurance for the voluntary old-age pension and unemployment relief schemes which, around the turn of the century, did not enjoy enough popularity to become generally adopted. Therefore it must not be inferred that benefit taxation owes its existence entirely, or even primarily, to the activities of special-interest groups who desire to reduce the extent to which they are taxed in the general public interest. A paternalistic government assumes the right to tell its citizens how they shall spend a portion of their income, and acts as agent for the individual in disposing of it.

The success of interested groups in inducing legislatures to segregate revenues for the benefit of particular classes of taxpayers needs some explanation. Apart from the case (mentioned above) in which the initiative comes from the government itself, the development may be explained on two grounds. The first is the fact that in a democracy, pressure groups are often able to fight successfully to get the government to sell certain services.[5] But if the principle is accepted that a public service is sold by the government, it becomes less likely that the payments will be partly diverted to cover the cost of *other* government services.

The second is the success with which interested groups have been able to convince legislatures that when certain publicly produced goods are sold to individuals, there are indirect benefits to society as a whole. If this is so, it is contended, none of the payments should be diverted to help finance other costs of government. This can also be illustrated by the example already used with respect to the dedication of gasoline and motor-vehicle taxes to the upkeep of highways. One can argue that if part of these taxes is diverted to other uses, an inferior road network will result. However, not only will this be a disadvantage to the automobilist; it will also be detrimental to commerce. It will thus reduce efficiency and raise costs. Therefore gasoline taxes should not be diverted from the upkeep of the roads.

As a practical matter this argument often has weight. If, however, it were possible to make effective use of the opportunity cost principle of budgeting, the amount spent on roads would not depend on the revenues that happen to be dedicated to them. The legislature would make a conscious decision on the proportion of resources that ought to be devoted to highway construction.

The Benefit Principle and the Distribution of Income.   The benefit principle may have a considerably wider application than that which has been discussed thus far. Certain important types of government spending primarily benefit particular income classes. If, then, the burden of the

---

[5] The tax may be a rough measure of the amount of use made of the service, or it may not. When a gasoline tax is devoted to the upkeep of the highways, those who drive a great deal pay a larger proportion of the tax than do those who drive rarely. On the other hand, if highway costs are financed by a flat motor-vehicle tax, the former group benefits at the expense of the latter.

taxes levied to finance these expenditures falls on the same income class, we have an application of the benefit principle. Under this broader interpretation we find that the benefit principle has been more extensively employed in the past than might be supposed, although not always intentionally. One or two examples will serve to illustrate this point.

Suppose that a large national debt has been incurred in connection with the financing of a war, and that this debt is exclusively owned by individuals in the $10,000 income group and above. If an income tax is levied, applicable only to incomes above $10,000 and on unearned income alone (i.e., interest on bonds, dividends, and the like), the interest paid to the owners of the debt comes from precisely the same income group in the form of taxes.

Another example would be the financing of old-age security payments exclusively out of taxes on the recipient during his working life. The vast bulk of the tax is paid by the low-income receiver, since his numbers are large, and most of the benefits are received by the same income class. A similar effect would be achieved if social security were to be financed by a general sales tax. The incidence of the tax is largely on the mass of the consumers, who in turn are approximately the same groups who in the aggregate receive the bulk of the social security benefits.[6]

TAXATION FOR REVENUE

Revenue is, of course, the primary objective of taxation. It is not possible to say precisely what proportion of total revenues at a particular moment is derived from taxes that are not levied primarily for revenue. The motives behind taxes are often mixed. The major increases in tax rates, however, have usually occurred in response to revenue needs. An exception to this statement is the reform legislation under the New Deal, when social control on occasion shared honors with revenues as the major objective of tax legislation. Even when the primary purpose of a tax is social control, revenue needs may play an important role. For example, it was recognized by the socially minded proponents of the progressive income tax, prior to 1913, that one of the prerequisites to its adoption was either a greater need by the federal government for revenue, or the elimination of the customs as the major source of federal revenue. Not until the appearance of the enormous financial demands of World War I was the opportunity presented for a test of the social effects of sharply progressive rates.

---

[6] An example of this was the advocacy by the Townsendites, during the thirties, of a turnover tax to finance $200 monthly payments to the aged. A turnover tax is a kind of sales tax, the incidence of which rests largely on the consumer. Thus the tax would be paid by the mass of the workers, to the benefit of retired workers. This mode of financing would have brought into focus the conflict between the interests of young and old workers. The conflict would, of course, have been resolved once no retired workers were receiving benefits who had not been paying sales taxes into the retirement fund over their full working life.

FUNCTIONAL FINANCE

Taxation for revenue may be looked at in two ways. The first is the traditional point of view that taxes are the source of government income required to balance public expenditures. The second is that taxes are a device for reducing the purchasing power in the hands of individuals. These are merely two ways of looking at the same phenomenon. The true function of taxation, however, is much better exposed when attention is transferred from the narrower interests of the public treasury to the economy as a whole.

On the assumption that supplies of production factors are fixed, the government can increase its use of resources only if someone in the private sector surrenders them. In a completely planned economy it would be feasible for a state planning board to issue orders diverting the required resources to the government. Once this decision was made, such tax rates could be fixed and such prices set for government-produced commodities that the correct amount of purchasing power would be taken from the private sector. Thus simultaneously the governmental budget would be kept in balance and inflation would be avoided.

In the absence of central planning it is more difficult to divert purchasing power from individuals to the public treasury in this frictionless manner. The decision is made by the legislature on the volume of public spending. Taxes are then voted to cover this spending. Unless there are direct controls, like rationing and allocation of resources to particular uses, it does not necessarily follow that private spending will therefore decline by the same amount as the rise in public spending. The fiscal system may be called truly functional, if, when resources are fully employed, private spending declines by an equal amount when public spending rises. This criterion of taxation is called "functional finance."[7]

Clearly if a tax-financed rise in public spending were to exert no distorting effects whatever on the economy, the decreases in private spending would have to occur at precisely those points at which public spending is increased. This is not possible in practice, and a more aggregative conception of functional finance is necessary. At the same time, lack of exact knowledge of the incidence and economic effects of taxation limits the applicability of functional finance as a practical tool in the hands of budget makers. If the person on whom the tax is levied is able to shift it to someone else, this has to be taken into account when the tax system is devised. If it is not known who actually bears the tax, it is not possible to use the tax instrument in a precise fashion. And if an effect of the tax is to alter

---

[7] The leading exponent of this position is Abba Lerner. See *The Economics of Control* (New York: Macmillan, 1944), p. 307: "The purpose of taxation is never to raise money but to leave less in the hands of the taxpayer." As Lerner points out, the government can print the money (create new deposits by borrowing from the banking system) if the only problem is that of obtaining purchasing power.

the level of investment and employment, a further element of uncertainty is introduced into the plans.

The functional approach therefore sheds the most light on the fiscal process when the incidence of a tax is reasonably definite. The personal income tax comes the nearest to qualifying under this condition, as well as being of great quantitative importance in the tax system. We have then, another reason for wanting to know as much as possible about the incidence and economic effects of all important taxes. We need to study the incidence of taxes in order to make the tax system accord with our concept of equity, and we cannot use the tax system as an instrument of economic control unless we have a fairly clear-cut idea of the incidence and economic effects of taxes.

► REFERENCES

See references at the end of Chapters 1 and 2.

6 The Objectives of Taxation

► INTRODUCTION

In the preceding chapter the sources of government finance were examined. The purpose of the chapter was to indicate the place of taxation in the framework of governmental revenues as a whole. We now turn our attention to the three major objectives of taxation. These are taxation for revenue, regulatory taxation, and the use of the tax instrument as one of the devices for the control of income and employment.

► TAXATION FOR REVENUE

Taxes are levied for the use of society as a whole, and many politically difficult decisions must be made in distributing the tax burden. Since there is ordinarily no particular relationship between the liability of the individual for taxes and the benefits that he receives, the essence of the process is the attempt of each group to minimize its share of the tax burden. In a modern economy, to be sure, the complexity of economic relationships tends to obscure the conflicts among the different groups. A man may be at once a highly paid worker, a property owner, a consumer, and an heir to an estate. Clearly his views on the proper objects of taxation are divided. Nevertheless it remains true that most individuals think of themselves primarily as members of a particular group: as worker, consumer, property owner, and so on.

Public interest in the equity of the tax system has always been keen. When the standard of living of a nation is low, every dollar taken in taxes noticeably curtails the family's consumption standard. Even when the productivity of the economy increases in response to technological progress, the tendency of the government to share in the increments to productivity keeps the question of tax equity to the fore. In times of stress, as the proportion of taxes to national income sharply rises, the need to evolve a tax system that corresponds to accepted standards of equity becomes more and more acute.

► THE EQUITY BASIS OF AN ACCEPTABLE TAX SYSTEM

The first and most important canon of taxation, according to Adam Smith, was that taxes should be equitable.[1] The term "equity" as used by him refers to the concept known as "reasonable classification." This means that persons or things similarly situated ought to be treated similarly under the tax laws. A flagrant characteristic of taxes under despotic and arbitrary rule has always been discrimination between individuals who ought to be treated alike. Examples are the taxes imposed on particular groups on the basis of race in Hitlerite Germany, and the confiscatory taxes levied in Russia for the purpose of liquidating the landowner.

REASONABLE CLASSIFICATION

Canons of taxation are much easier to state as principles than to apply in practice. It is difficult to translate them into concrete terms that are acceptable to all taxpayers. Moreover, the canons necessarily tend to conflict with one another in a tax system marked by any degree of complexity. For example, consider the difficulties that face a strict adherence to the principle of reasonable classification (also called tax uniformity). It is easy to say that in principle a tax should be a uniform levy on all individuals who fall within a certain class. The problem, however, is to agree on a method of classification.

Does a special license tax on a chain-store outlet constitute a violation of reasonable classification? Yes, if the outlet has no advantages which enable it to drive the individual proprietor out of business. No, if it does have such advantages, and if also public opinion happens to favor the preservation of the individually owned store. Does the exemption from the federal income tax of interest on state and local securities amount to a violation of the uniformity principle? In other words, does the question of who issued the securities constitute a relevant criterion in the definition of the base of the income tax? Most economists would argue that here is an instance of unreasonable classification.

Many instances can be found of taxes which, though based on reason-

---

[1] The others were *certainty, convenience,* and *economy* with respect to the cost of collection. The first of these is an injunction against arbitrary or haphazard assessments. The local property tax, particularly with respect to intangible property, may be criticized on this ground, since unequal enforcement penalizes the honest taxpayer who declares his bank deposits, stocks and bonds, and so on. Convenience and economy are relative matters, and other more important considerations may prevent paying too much attention to them. There is nothing very convenient to the average man in having to keep records for the sake of declaring his personal income. In two thirds of the states a separate declaration must be made for the state and federal governments. But the compliance cost is regarded as reasonable in return for the increase in equity. Similarly, sentiment can exist for favoring a tax merely because its collection costs are low, but only if it measures up to the more important standards of equity and relatively favorable economic effects.

able classification under certain assumptions, are not so based if these assumptions are rejected. One widely publicized example will suffice. During the years prior to World War I, when the adoption of a permanent progressive income tax was being hotly debated, the opponents of progressive rates cried "unreasonable classification." What they meant was that all citizens of a free-enterprise democracy ought to be regarded as falling within the same class for income tax purposes, and that the income tax should have flat rates, identical for all incomes. Advocates of the tax argued, however, that a high-income receiver is really in a different tax class from the recipient of a low income. There was agreement that taxes should be levied on the basis of reasonable classification, but disagreement over how the principle should be applied in this specific case. Even now that the public generally accepts progression as consistent with reasonable classification, an apparently permanent debate goes on as to *how much* progression is consistent with it.

Adam Smith wrote during the eighteenth century, when revenues were derived from a limited number of tax sources. Consequently if one of these taxes was subject to unreasonable classification, the damage to public welfare was clearly visible. The exemption of powerful classes in some countries created opposition that would not be stilled, and led to violent political struggles.

With the increasing complexity of modern civilization, and the multiplication of taxes, it has become correspondingly difficult for any class, however powerful, to remain exempt. When the tax system is highly complex, and a particular tax is found to bear unequally on different groups who ought to be treated alike, rough tax justice can often be achieved by changing the rates of some other tax. Even if every reasonable attempt is made to achieve equity, the complicated interrelationships of different economic groups in the modern industrial nation may make this impossible. The elimination of one inequity may give rise to another, and we are frequently faced with the necessity of choosing the less serious alternative. The problem is particularly difficult because the choice cannot often be made on an objective basis, but must be resolved by the struggle of opposing political groups.

The abuses that frequently arise as a result of arbitrary tax classification have led on occasion to a prohibition against certain types of classification. This is, of course, no complete answer to the problem, since the absence of formal classification may imply an informal one that may be still worse. Ample evidence of this appears in the constitutional or statutory provisions found in some states that forbid the practice.

If, for example, all sales within a given tax class must be treated alike, the effect may be to forbid the exemption of food, utility clothing, and subsistence rents from a general retail sales tax. The result is a serious discrimination against those whose incomes are not much above subsistence. Another example of the unfortunate effects of a rigid interpretation of the meaning of classification is a general property tax that applies similar assessments and rates to all property without regard to its use. To mention but one of the inequities caused by this rule, a home mortgaged up to 50 per cent of its value would pay half again as much property tax as one free of mortgage, since the mortgage is a form of intangible property that cannot be exempt if classification is not permitted.

THE PRINCIPLE OF ABILITY TO PAY

Taxation according to ability to pay takes account of the different taxpaying capacities of different individuals. Many factors enter into the capacity of an individual to pay taxes. A person with a large income, or with large accumulated wealth, has the power to pay a greater tax than a person who is indigent. Family obligations differ, and some types of income are more regular than others. Even in the private sector of the economy some account is taken of these differences. For example, fees of doctors and lawyers are often based in part on the individual's income, and the wealthy tend to devote a larger proportion of their incomes to private charities.

One of the obstacles to the acceptance of the principle of ability to pay in politically undeveloped economies is its conflict with the competing criterion of ease of collection. When the latter is given the preference, the basic source of revenue is apt to be either a poll tax, an excise on a basic necessity like salt or matches, or some form of general sales tax. Although one indication of ability to pay taxes is indeed consumption, the consumption of *subsistence* goods is no measure of ability to pay.

Acceptance of the principle of ability to pay requires a conscious effort on the part of the electorate. Historically this effort has been associated with a rising trend in the political power of the lower-income groups. In many countries today the higher-income and wealthy classes have retained much of their former power, and have therefore succeeded in retarding progress toward the adoption of this principle. The example of other nations, however, has tended to keep such countries in a constant state of political ferment.

The application of the principle of ability to pay can at best be made only very roughly. The reason for this is in part the great complexity in the forms of income and wealth. Some types of income, for example, have a greater taxpaying capacity than others. Income from wealth is ordinarily believed to represent greater ability to pay than income earned by one's own efforts. The income from a capital asset is net of depreciation, whereas that of an individual does not take depreciation of his physical powers into account. Another reason for the practical difficulty in applying the ability principle of taxation is that for most taxes there is disagreement and doubt as to the actual distribution of the burden.

THE SACRIFICE PRINCIPLES

The ability principle is likewise subject to conceptual difficulties. The adage "from each according to his ability" throws no light on how much from each. To ascertain the latter, appeal has often been made to the "sacrifice" principle. This doctrine traces its ancestry back to the utilitarian principle of the greatest good for the greatest number. The principle of ability to pay is a proposition in welfare economics. How can the payment of taxes be made to cause the minimum loss of satisfaction to society as a whole? Presumably by taxing in such a way as to make the aggregate sacrifice of paying taxes a minimum. But aggregate sacrifice relates to the taxpayers taken as a group. The separate sacrifices of each taxpayer are therefore added. This implies that they are comparable, and that it is possible to compare the loss of satisfaction suffered when a dollar is taken from wealthy taxpayer A with that suffered when a dollar is taken from poor taxpayer B.

Minimum Aggregate Sacrifice. The principle of minimum aggregate sacrifice states that public expenditures should be financed by taxing the highest incomes first; and if more taxes are required, proceeding from the higher to the lower incomes. It is taken for granted that the higher one's income, the less a dollar means to him. The underlying assumption is that every man's tastes and capacity for enjoying income are the same as those of all other men. This is, of course, the only assumption that can be made in a democratic society, where each citizen has one vote. Nevertheless, it may be far from being true.

Minimum sacrifice leads to the extreme form of the ability principle. If the need for revenue were very great the result could be (theoretically) the equalization of incomes. Even far short of this point, however, a tax policy that chops off the top of the income pyramid is inconsistent with the basic tenets of a society which accepts differences in personal incomes.

Quite apart from the likelihood that capacity to enjoy income differs among individuals, differences in income are acknowledged to be necessary in order to call forth maximum effort. In other words, the extreme application of the ability principle might reduce the level of national income, and therefore the tax base as well. The principle of least aggregate sacrifice could be applied, however, if the proportion of national income taken in taxes were small. For if modest taxes on the very wealthy were adequate to finance the costs of government, the disincentive effects would be infinitesimal.

Equal and Proportional Sacrifice. Two variants of the doctrine of minimum sacrifice are the principles of equal and proportional sacrifice. They are intended to avoid pursuing to their logical conclusions the implications of minimum aggregate sacrifice. If we were to believe that the top dollar of the income of a man in a higher-income bracket means more to him than does the top dollar of the income of a man in a lower bracket, then there would be no logical basis for equalizing incomes through taxation. The doctrine of equal sacrifice assumes that there can exist *some* levy on a smaller income that involves a sacrifice that is no larger than the sacrifice entailed by the levy on a greater income. It stipulates that tax rates should be such that sacrifice is equalized for all taxpayers.

The doctrine of equal sacrifice, however, throws no light on just what rates would actually equalize sacrifice. There are no units on the basis of which a comparison of utility can be made. It nevertheless calls attention to the fact that the assumption may be unwarranted that all persons have the same tastes and capacities for enjoyment.

The concept of proportional sacrifice is similar and is subject to the same type of objection. It states that the sacrifice of different taxpayers should not be equalized, but that the man with a higher income can bear a proportionately higher sacrifice. In other words, if under the principle of equal sacrifice an income tax were progressive, under the principle of proportional sacrifice it would be more so. Unfortunately in practice we are thrown back upon finding a solution through the political struggles among the various income groups.[2]

► ADEQUACY OF THE REVENUES

The general public, as well as legislatures and government officials, ordinarily judge a tax system mainly on the basis of its ability to produce needed revenues. The reason for this is that the political penalty for failure to cover expenditures with revenues is likely to be immediate and severe. The political opposition can always point to a budgetary deficit as evidence of ineptitude, even when on the basis of economic considerations a deficit might have been advisable.

Part of the reason for preoccupation with adequacy of the revenues in the narrow sense is simply the preservation of tradition. Much thinking has been devoted by economists in recent years to the scope for using public finance as an instrument of economic control. Nevertheless, a great deal of the comment in the public press and elsewhere is concerned with the prospects that the government will be able to balance the budget. This is understandable, of course. The problem of balancing treasury income and outgo is an annual or even continuous occurrence, whereas the need for conscious manipulation of the budget in the interest of economic control

---

[2] Cf. Elmer D. Fagan, "Recent and Contemporary Theories of Progressive Taxation," *Journal of Political Economy,* August, 1938; M. Slade Kendrick, "The Ability to Pay Theory of Taxation," *American Economic Review,* March, 1939; National Tax Association, *Proceedings,* 1940, pp. 368–389.

appears much less often. Yet in a more significant sense "adequate" tax revenues may on occasion imply a budgetary surplus for the purpose of lessening the rate of private spending, and thus reducing inflationary pressure.

FLEXIBILITY OF THE TAX SYSTEM

An indispensable characteristic of a modern revenue system is flexibility. By flexibility is meant a sufficient degree of freedom in changing the kinds and rates of taxes so that unexpected emergencies can be quickly and adequately met. Two major hindrances may stand in the way of the achievement of flexibility of the tax system. First, the legislature may be unable to act, or to act quickly enough, to make the changes that are required in response to dynamic economic factors. Second, the tax system may already be making use of so many taxes, at such high rates, that further *upward* changes, at any rate, may not appear advisable or even possible.

The states and the municipalities, especially the latter, often have inflexible tax structures because they are limited to certain kinds of taxes. In some states a constant struggle goes on between the localities and the state governments over the scope of the right of the former to tax. The states wish to reserve some taxes to themselves, and the use of other taxes by the municipalities may not have constitutional or customary sanction. Even in those cases where the states have enacted legislation permitting wide discretion on the part of the localities, the need of the latter for relatively stable revenue sources has caused some observers to advise the cities and towns to rely for the most part on the property tax alone. The states themselves, moreover, are limited in their choice of taxes in those instances in which the federal government has to a large extent monopolized the field, particularly in the area of income taxation.

The federal tax system possesses a large degree of flexibility, but this was not always so. For 125 years the major source of federal revenue was the customs, and at times it was virtually the only source. The use of the tariff for protection as well as for revenue made it extremely difficult to match a change in the need for revenues with a change in tariff rates. Consequently for many years periods of unwanted surpluses alternated with periods of deficits.

The adoption of the federal income tax in 1913, however, made the federal revenue system very responsive to changes in revenue needs. It proved very fortunate for the financing of World War I that this country had ready at hand a workable income tax law which could be quickly manipulated through changes in rates. The return to high exemptions and low rates after the war again gave evidence of the relatively rapid adaptability of the federal tax system.

Events after World War II have, however, shed a different light on the flexibility of the federal tax system. Enormous demands for revenues to finance militarization and foreign aid have forced the government to make considerable use of its available tax resources. Although further extension is undoubtedly possible, some observers believe that the limits to American taxable capacity are beginning to become visible.

A country will find its tax system relatively flexible if the party in power is in a position to get its tax programs quickly accepted by the legislative body. This is the case in Britain, where the government can make the acceptance of its fiscal program subject to a vote of confidence. If the ruling party has a reasonable majority, it is certain of being able to enact the desired fiscal legislation so long as the country is willing to maintain it in power. The British, of course, have been forced to make such thoroughgoing use of the tax power that little flexibility is left in the system.

Quite the opposite situation exists in relatively undeveloped regions. The flexibility of the tax systems of a number of countries is limited by what might be called a kind of fiscal immaturity. In some of the Mediterranean and Near Eastern countries the public seems to prefer hidden taxes, regardless of their incidence.[3] The absence of effective political power on the part of the lower-income groups has been an obstacle, both to the development of more progressive taxes and to the acceptance of the levies needed to assure balanced budgets. Again, in France and Italy, among other Latin countries, the administration of the personal income tax has not been effective enough to provide an adequate basis for taxing the income of businessmen. This situation is not only highly inequitable; it seriously limits the ability of the tax system to meet emergencies.

TAX RESPONSES TO INCOME CHANGES

As we have seen, tax flexibility can be achieved through the readiness and ability of the government to make use of a wide variety of taxes at varying rates. In addition, the response of a tax system with *given* taxes and rates to changes in levels of income and spending is important, from the point of view of adequate revenues and as well as that of economic control. We are at present interested, however, only in the revenue aspects.[4]

The more extensive the progressive elements in a revenue system, the more markedly tax receipts respond to fluctuations in the level of national income. As the latter rises or falls, taxpayers are thrown into income brackets that are respectively subject to higher or lower rates of tax. An elastic tax is one in which percentage changes in yield are greater than

---

[3] This point of view also received support in the United States from the conservatives around the turn of the century when the federal government was considering an income tax.

[4] The role of the tax system in the control of income and employment is discussed in later chapters.

percentage changes in the base. A particular tax can be inelastic, or even perversely elastic, to changes in the level of national income.[5] That is, a rise in income may exert virtually no effect on the yield of the tax, or the yield may actually decline.

During the nineteenth century the tariff was an example of an inelastic source of revenue. At times it was even perversely elastic. During wartime international trade and tariff receipts declined at the very moment when the level of money national income, public spending, and the need for revenue greatly rose. Conversely, during prosperous peacetime years the rise in taxable imports, despite the policy of protection, provided the country with a rising, and at times unwanted, source of revenue.

The latter situation was particularly acute during Cleveland's administration. During the 1880's, under an administration opposed to a large amount of public spending, the high tariff introduced by the Republicans brought large amounts of revenue into the Treasury. Under the prevailing spending philosophy the only thing that could be done with these revenues was to pay off the Civil War debt. This was done up to the amount that matured each year, but purchases of *unmatured* debt on the open market threatened to push government obligations up to a high premium. In fact, these circumstances, together with other factors, did cause some types of government obligations to rise to a premium of 25 per cent, which naturally raised the suspicion that Treasury policy was aimed at benefiting a special class.

Whether or not an elastic response to changes in the level of national income and spending is a desirable property of a tax system depends on the fiscal and economic objectives of the particular taxing jurisdiction. For the cities and states it is obviously a disadvantage if revenues fall off more rapidly than national income during a depression. If they cannot balance their budgets they must borrow, and their securities do not necessarily have the marketability of those of the federal government.[6] The states often prefer to rely on sales taxes rather than on income taxes. Sales taxes in turn respond more sharply to changes in the level of income than does the property tax. Relative constancy of yield is a major reason for the retention of the latter by the localities, despite the large amount of criticism on all sides.

One device sometimes employed to prevent too pronounced a decline in state tax revenues during a recession is to prescribe that taxpayers use

---

[5] On this question, and on the measurement of elasticity, see W. Vickrey, "Some Limits to the Income Elasticity of Income Tax Yields," *Review of Economics and Statistics*, May, 1949, pp. 140–144.

[6] The latter, of course, has the power to create unlimited purchasing power for its securities through the deposit of gold certificates, based on an enormous supply of gold in treasury vaults, in the federal reserve banks, which in turn purchase federal securities with the excess reserves thus created. It may be noted in passing that another restriction on state and local borrowing is debt limitation.

that alternative of two tax bases which gives the higher yield. For example, two states, New York and Massachusetts, have required corporations to pay either a corporate income tax or a capital stock tax, depending on which yields the greater tax. This assures at least some revenue in years when corporate profits are very low. Those few cities that have adopted some form of income tax during the prosperous years since 1940 have yet to experience the effect on their revenues that would be produced if a serious depression were to develop.[7]

An elastic revenue system clearly pleases state and city authorities when the level of income rises. Revenues are produced that permit either the repayment of debt or an increase in public spending, perhaps to the advantage of important projects that previously have had to be delayed because of a lack of funds. On a longer view, however, whether or not this is an advantage to the state or municipality depends on the wisdom of the use which is made of the windfall to the treasury. If, for example, the major reason for rising money incomes is rising prices, the authorities may yield to the temptation of engaging in construction programs at an excessively high price level.

► REGULATION THROUGH TAXATION

Taxation is often used to supplement the police power as an instrument of regulation. Every tax necessarily exerts some kind of effect on the ability or willingness of an individual to undertake an economic act. If he pays the tax, he has less purchasing power to use in other directions. If he avoids paying the tax by failing to perform the action which makes him subject to it, the tax has conditioned his actions.

Obviously if the regulatory effect of the tax is only incidental, the tax should be classed as a tax for revenue, not for regulation. It is not always possible to draw the line very sharply, however. In some instances the regulatory and revenue aspects, though conflicting, are of roughly equal importance. An example would be a moderate tax on the undistributed profits of corporations. The effect of such a tax might be to increase dividends, but not to eliminate undistributed profits altogether. Therefore some revenue would be collected, but at the same time revenues would be sacrificed to the extent that firms responded to the tax by declaring dividends. In many instances, of course, legislators intend that a tax shall have both revenue and regulatory effects.[8]

---

[7] A city income tax, without progression or exemptions, is not as responsive to income changes as is the federal income tax. Its yield would, however, decline in a downswing more than the yield of a sales tax, since income would decline more than consumption.

[8] An interesting historical example of a tax designed to combine revenue and coercion was the so-called Saladin tithe, used during the Third Crusade (1189–1192) to encourage enlistments and raise revenues. "A scheme of taxation—the Saladin

UNINTENDED COERCIVE EFFECTS

Attention should be called to the widespread extent to which the tax system interferes with the economic life of the people even when such interference is not consciously intended. No complete conception can be given of this phenomenon within a short space; therefore we must content ourselves with a few examples selected from various taxes.

When tax rates in the middle- and higher-income brackets become very high in response to revenue needs, the net savings of the wealthy may fall substantially.[9] If this occurs, a secondary effect may be to decrease contributions to charity. The end result may be a shift from privately sponsored hospitals to public hospitals. Yet this effect was not desired by either the public or the taxing authority.

Another example may occur under the estate tax. One consequence of this tax has been to encourage disposition of part of the estate to wives and children before death. Although in many instances this practice involves no important change in the effective control of wealth, the net effect has undoubtedly often been to speed up the rate at which the younger generation participates in the benefits of property ownership. Moreover, the enactment of a separate gift tax has not eliminated gifts.

Again, a tax on the profits of corporations may exert some effect in the direction of encouraging the proprietorship or partnership form of enterprise. Still another example is the property tax on improvements, which often results in the failure of landowners to build on vacant lots or to eliminate eyesores from residential areas. Finally may be mentioned the discouragement to the sales of fur coats and jewelry that resulted from the retention after 1945 of the wartime excises on these items. The effect was to divert consumer purchasing power toward competing articles, and to depress these industries.

THE REGULATION OF CONSUMPTION

Regulatory taxation has a long history, probably as long as taxation itself. In the distant past taxes have been levied to discourage men from growing beards, and penalty taxes were imposed on the wearer of expensive clothing in order to prevent members of the rising merchant class from displaying their wealth. Regulation of consumption through taxation (sumptuary taxation) remains an important part of tax systems to this day.

---

tithe—was imposed on all who did not take the cross; and this taxation, while on the one hand it drove many to take the cross in order to escape its incidence, on the other hand provided a necessary financial basis for military operations."—*Encyclopaedia Britannica* (Chicago: 1910), VII, 538.

[9] On the other hand, savings may not fall; and they *will* not do so if the income of these classes before tax greatly increases through a concurrent rise in government spending.

To be really effective, the tax must be levied at prohibitive rates. Thus the heavy taxes on liquor do decrease consumption by those with moderate incomes, but leave that of the more wealthy unaffected. A successful case was the heavy tax on white phosphorous matches, imposed by the federal government in order to prevent the consumption of a commodity that is injurious, not indeed to the user, but to the worker who makes the matches. A similar philosophy was expressed in the federal tax on the product of child labor (if the goods crossed state lines) imposed during World War I, but later declared unconstitutional. The classic example, of course, is a tariff that really protects domestic industries from foreign competition.

TAXATION AND THE CONTROL OF BUSINESS

The tax instrument is used extensively in the control of business and commerce. Taxes are imposed to affect the form of business enterprise, as well as methods of doing business, and the kind of business done. To protect the dairy industry, discriminatory taxes have been levied on oleomargarine. Again, in order to protect the independent grocer, special taxes have been imposed on chain stores. Moreover, the tax often becomes a subsidy (negative tax) when the intention is explicitly to encourage a course of action. The agricultural price-support program is a large-scale example. Other examples are subsidies to airlines and the merchant marine.

A variant of the subsidy is the tax reduction. An exemption of a few thousand dollars of corporate income from the corporate income tax may be granted in an effort to encourage small business. Firms engaged in favored forms of output (say war matériel) may be allowed to reduce their income tax liability for a few years by taking accelerated depreciation of plant and equipment for tax purposes. Oil and mineral producers are permitted a very generous deduction (depletion allowance) from taxable profits, presumably in order to encourage the opening up of new sources. Firms having good employment records are granted lower payroll tax rates under state unemployment insurance systems.

MONOPOLY CONTROL

Antimonopoly feeling in the United States has resulted in a number of modest attempts to supplement monopoly control, as exercised through antitrust legislation, with a tax discouragement to monopoly. A 2 per cent tax on intercorporate dividends and a 15 per cent tax on consolidated returns have been enacted by the federal government to discourage concentration of ownership. The undistributed-profits tax of 1936 was in part intended to reduce monopoly power by forcing profitable corporations to distribute dividends, and thus to have to compete in the private investment market on even terms with others. Again, one of the objectives of the advocates of a permanent peacetime excess-profits tax after World War I was to discourage monopoly through a reduction in the economic power of profitable enterprise.

In general it may be said against antimonopoly taxation that the abuse of monopoly power and the ability to make profits are not entirely synonymous. On the other hand, no single attack on the monopoly problem is likely to be adequate, and the use of a range of weapons may be necessary to achieve a reasonable measure of success.

REGULATION OF THE ECONOMIC SYSTEM

Taxation and tax exemptions have often been used to encourage a broad-gauge institutional or social development. Perhaps the most famous case of the use of the tax instrument to bring about a basic change in an important national institution was the tax imposed on the notes of state banks under the National Bank Act during the Civil War. This proved to be a successful effort to remove these notes from circulation in order to provide a uniform national currency.

Another example of this sort of tax legislation is the special tax on bachelors imposed in some countries. The reasons vary: sometimes the proceeds are earmarked for the support of indigent spinsters; but more often the tax, if its rates are high enough, is really intended to encourage population growth. The United States does not have a bachelor tax, but the same kind of effect is produced by the marital exemption under the federal income tax. The exemption of $600 a child virtually relieves from paying an income tax the worker whose income is relatively low and whose family is numerous. Again on the subsidy side, the exemption of church property inhabited by clergymen is intended to aid in the cultivation of a national religious spirit. These are, of course, only a few examples of this kind of tax policy.

The tax instrument may be used to rectify, in part at least, an inequity arising out of fundamental economic changes. Thus, for example, many of the countries of Europe emerged from World War II with excessive supplies of currency and deposits. In order to reduce the inflationary pressure from the presence of this superfluous purchasing power, a special tax was in many instances levied on bank accounts and hand-to-hand currency. Admittedly this step penalized individuals who had held their wealth in this form. On the other hand, it was argued that many owners of buildings and personal property had suffered war damage.

If all types of wealth are included in the tax base, this kind of tax becomes a capital levy. This was a popular form of tax after World War I. The capital levy is not aimed particularly at the inflation problem. Rather it is intended to reduce the seriousness of the inequity caused by the amassing of war fortunes. Finally may be mentioned the unjust-enrichment tax, which can be applied at rates in the vicinity of 100 per cent to recapture an unjustified windfall gain made by a class of individuals as a result of unexpected circumstances.[10]

► THE CONTROL OF INCOME AND EMPLOYMENT

Changes in tax rates comprise one of the instruments at the disposal of a central government for influencing the level of national income and employment. The effects of the rate variations are twofold. On the one hand, manipulation of tax rates brings about changes in the disposable income remaining in the hands of individuals and firms. On the other, effects can be exerted on the willingness of individuals and firms to consume and invest. A full discussion of the use of fiscal policy for full employment is reserved for later chapters, but the major characteristics of taxation as an instrument of economic control may be indicated here.

PURCHASING-POWER ASPECTS

If the employment problem is viewed as one of over-all purchasing-power flows, the role of taxation is simply to remove purchasing power from the income stream. If public spending is held constant, an increase in tax receipts means a reduction in the purchasing power available to the private sector; and conversely if tax receipts fall. Unless individuals and firms then counter by changing the rate at which they spend their disposable incomes after payment of taxes, the effect is a change in total spending, and therefore in the level of employment.[11]

A weakness of a policy of tax reduction in order to stimulate increased spending by individuals and firms is that they may merely hold the released purchasing power idle. This they are particularly likely to do when a downswing looks as if it will be severe and of long duration. Nevertheless this is not an overwhelming criticism of the scheme. It is difficult in any case to find a single policy that is equally effective throughout the entire business

---

[10] Congress passed such a tax in 1936. It was designed to recapture revenues refunded to processors of agricultural products (when the Agricultural Adjustment Act was declared unconstitutional), but who had passed the tax forward to consumers. Cf. P. E. Taylor, *The Economics of Public Finance* (New York: Macmillan, 1953), pp. 481-484, for a discussion of this tax.

[11] Reference may be made to the proposal of the Committee for Economic Development to take advantage of the so-called "built-in flexibility" of the fiscal system to modify fluctuations in private spending. If federal expenditure programs are held constant, and tax rates are left unchanged, a rise in national income will automatically produce added revenues. If, further, the level of expenditures and taxes is adjusted so that the federal budget is in balance at full employment, a tendency toward inflation will produce a surplus in the budget. This surplus can be held idle, and will thus discourage further inflation. On the other hand, a decline in employment will result in falling tax revenues; and with expenditure programs fixed, more money is left in the hands of firms and individuals. If they spend this money, a braking effect is felt which assists in combating depression.—Committee for Economic Development, "Taxes and the Budget," November, 1947.

cycle. The important thing is not to expect a given program to accomplish objectives for which it is not adapted. Tax reduction to stimulate private spending works best early in a recession from full employment, particularly if businessmen have felt that income and profits taxes have been too high, or if taxes on consumption have had the effect of weakening the market for consumers' goods.

If tax rates are increased in order to arrest an inflation of income and prices, purchasing power is removed from the hands of firms and individuals, and it is therefore likely that private spending will be curtailed. Under conditions of high-level employment and rising prices, it is hardly to be expected that firms and individuals will have large amounts of idle balances out of which they can maintain spending in the face of the increase in tax rates. Therefore tax policy as an instrument for controlling the economic system is apt to be quite effective in combating inflation, provided that the monetary authorities discourage any increase in commercial-bank borrowing in order directly or indirectly to maintain levels of business or consumer spending.[12]

TAXATION AND ECONOMIC INCENTIVES

Changes in tax rates are an effective means of inducing a desired reaction from consumers and investors. Taxpayers can be discouraged from consuming or hiring factors of production when rates of certain taxes are increased. On the other hand, they can be encouraged to spend if rates are reduced. A different approach is penalty taxation to stimulate a desired course of action. For example, a tax on hoarded currency or idle deposits might be expected to stimulate spending. This policy has been advocated as a depression measure, though it has not met with much favor because of its administrative difficulties as well as because of its unwanted effects on the free-enterprise system. Administratively, the problem would be how to avoid a widespread repayment of commercial-bank indebtedness by firms in order to avoid being subject to the tax. If this occurred, though the rate of spending of part of the money supply would rise, this rise would be counteracted by a decline in the volume of money. From an equity standpoint, the owners of certain types of wealth, namely currency and deposits, would be subject to a differential tax penalty as compared with owners of other types of wealth.[13]

Still another difficulty would arise to the extent that the policy was actually effective in stimulating spending. An upswing generated in this

---

[12] This is true only if the device is used with care. If budgetary surpluses are the only anti-inflationary device used, very high tax rates may be necessary. These may discourage output, reduce the flow of goods more than the flow of purchasing power, and thus actually aggravate the inflation. Cf. R. A. Musgrave, *Papers and Proceedings* of the American Economic Association, May, 1948, pp. 391–392.

[13] Penalty taxation is further discussed in Chapter 19.

fashion would not be balanced and healthy, and would run the risk of resulting in a more or less serious misallocation of resources. Penalty taxation is a synthetic substitute for the normal business incentives. It is true, however, that if for some reason the economy were on dead center, this device might provide the needed shock. The question is whether it would not be better to try to provide it in a different way.[14]

Another means of encouraging an increase in business spending is to remit or reduce taxes in exchange for a desired action by the firm. This device has been more popular in Germany and other Continental countries than in the United States. For example, a reduction in corporation taxes or other taxes on business may be granted to those firms which hire additional workers, increase inventories, or add to plant and equipment.[15] A major difficulty of a plan of this sort is that it accords preferential tax treatment to those firms which are in a position to take advantage of the scheme. Unexpected effects would surely be produced on the relative competitive positions of different firms.

When taxes are remitted or reduced in return for hiring more labor or increasing investment, it is obvious that some firms will participate in the benefits who would have performed the desired act in the absence of the bonus. It follows that tax remission is a rather clumsy and inefficient method of stimulating a rise in national income. On the other hand, it must be remembered that alternative fiscal devices for increasing investment are also likely to involve much waste motion. The policy cannot be condemned out of hand, therefore, but must be compared with its alternatives. At any rate, it seems likely that, to be effective, tax remission has to be tied to specific acts of investment. Otherwise, during time of depression, the released taxes will probably largely be held idle. Yet to make tax remission contingent on acts by the individual firms means that an extensive control arrangement must be set up, and this in turn may lead to an excessive degree of governmental influence over the actions of the private sector. The greater the extent of such interference, the less does tax remission have to recommend it over outright government planning.

In conclusion, one of the most important contributions that tax policy can make to economic stability is the avoidance of taxes that discourage investment. In order to do this, careful attention has to be paid to the

---

[14] For currency and deposit tax proposals and discussions see Irving Fisher, *Stamp Scrip* (New York: Adelphi, 1934); Arthur Dahlberg, *When Capital Goes on Strike* (New York: Harper, 1938); W. J. Shultz, "The Proposed Currency and Deposits Tax," National Tax Association, *Bulletin,* March, 1939; and A. G. Hart, *Money, Debt, and Economic Activity* (New York: Prentice-Hall, 1948), Pt. V.

[15] For the German experience with tax remission during depression, see Gerhard Colm, "Why the Papen Plan Failed," *Social Research,* 1934, pp. 83–96; and for a discussion of the problems of tying the tax reduction to specific acts of investment, K. E. Poole, "Tax Remission as a Means of Influencing Cyclical Fluctuations," *Quarterly Journal of Economics,* February, 1939, pp. 267 ff.

incidence and economic effects of taxes. Although as we shall see, these effects are often difficult to isolate in practice, the effort must be made and, so far as possible, taxes should be employed whose economic effects are relatively easy to determine.

► SIMPLICITY AND CLARITY

An important, though subsidiary, objective of taxation is simplicity and clarity in the drafting of tax laws. A continuing conflict exists between these objectives and some of the other characteristics of a good tax system discussed above. The increasing complexity of economic life makes inevitable the use of new forms of taxation and complicates the administration of old ones. Frequently when a new tax is added nothing is done to remove other taxes that have become obsolescent. There is a very substantial lag in the modernization of tax systems, and in the phraseology of tax laws.

One of the reasons for complexity of the tax system is the existence of three independent major governmental levels in the United States. No complete solution is possible so long as it is regarded as indispensable to preserve the political independence of the states and localities by allowing them to retain their own sources of tax revenues. The added cost, in terms of inefficiency, duplication, and compliance, is a price that the citizen must expect to pay in order to escape undue centralization of political power. Particularly at the federal and state levels the normal tendency of tax systems is toward greater and greater complexity. This is the combined result of the multiplication of public services at these levels, the activities of many special pressure groups, and the increasing complexity of legal verbiage due partly to attempts to remove inequities.

The voter cannot have an appreciation of the cost of public services unless he understands the taxes that he is paying. Some simplification devices obscure from the taxpayer the nature of the tax base. Simplified tax declarations, for example, reduce compliance difficulties, but they may also remove from the taxpayer all conception of what he is really doing when he computes his tax. He is led by the hand through the tax form and performs many operations in ignorance of their meaning. An example is the husband-and-wife-income-splitting calculation under the personal income tax. Another simplification device, intended to spare both the taxpayer and the Internal Revenue Service the necessity of making and checking numerous calculations, is the standard deduction of 10 per cent. This is permitted up to an income of $10,000 in lieu of detailed calculation of personal deductions. Against the admittedly great compliance advantage has to be set the fact that millions of payers of the income tax soon tend to forget the reasons why these various deductions are allowed.

The tax system also needs to be as understandable and as clear as possible so that taxpayers are made immediately aware of the effects on themselves resulting from any change in the level of public expenditures. An irreconcilable conflict exists between (1) the temptation to conceal taxes in order to extend the limits of taxable capacity, and (2) the achievement of maximum directness so that the taxpayer is kept constantly aware of his role in supporting the government.[16]

► SUMMARY

The objectives of taxation are threefold, comprising revenue, regulation, and economic control. The tax system as a whole, and even individual taxes, contains varying elements of all three of these objectives. A tax for revenue, for example, may incidentally affect business practices as well as business spending. As a result, it is ordinarily not possible to apply any simple standard for measuring the desirability of a particular tax. Only through the operation of the political process can an evaluation be made of the relative merits of a tax in terms of its possible objectives: uniformity of treatment of similar classes of taxpayers, relative sacrifice, ability to pay, revenue adequacy, flexibility, simplicity, and ease of compliance. Moreover, some of the objectives of taxation conflict with others. The goal of regulation is often inconsistent with the desire to obtain revenues; and the laudable objective of simplicity and understandability frequently has to be sacrificed in favor of the still more laudable objective of equity.

The rapidly increasing complexity of modern economic life has stimulated an equally rapid development of nonrevenue uses of taxation. The tax instrument has come to be an important adjunct to the police power in the control of both economic actions and other activities of individuals. More than this, in the hands of central governments it has been a powerful tool of intervention in the free-enterprise system. Two fundamental questions therefore arise: (1) How does the effectiveness of the tax instrument compare with that of other instruments of control? (2) Even to the extent that taxation is an *effective* instrument of social and economic control, what are the social costs of making use of it as compared with the costs of refraining from doing so? The answers to these questions are not simple, but are subject to many qualifications and assumptions. The judgment made by a particular individual is bound to be strongly colored by his own evaluation of the proper role of government in society.

---

[16] Henry Simons, writing during World War II, was an earnest advocate of directness in taxation in order to facilitate the weighing of the opportunity cost of public services by the voter. (*Federal Tax Reform* [Chicago: University of Chicago Press, 1950].) Not foreseeing, of course, the continuing need for very high revenues in a cold war, he believed that the personal income tax "could . . . (and should) . . . afford all or most" of federal financial needs (p. 5). The possibility of using the income tax as a "single tax" is discussed in Chapter 7.

► REFERENCES

GEORGE, H. *Progress and Poverty*. New York: Robert Schalkenbach Foundation, 1940.

GROVES, H. M. *Viewpoints on Public Finance*. New York: Henry Holt and Company, 1947.

HOBSON, J. A. *Taxation in the New State*. New York: Harcourt, Brace and Company, Inc., 1920.

KALVIN, H., and W. J. BLUM. *The Uneasy Case for Progressive Taxation*. Chicago: The University of Chicago Press, 1953.

LERNER, A. *The Economics of Control*. New York: The Macmillan Company, 1946, Chap. XXIV, "Functional Finance."

LUTZ, H. *Guideposts to a Free Economy*. New York: McGraw-Hill Book Company, Inc., 1945, Chap. IX, "Progressive Taxation."

SIMONS, H. C. *Personal Income Taxation*. Chicago: The University of Chicago Press, 1938.

7 The Shifting and Incidence of Taxation

► THE MEANING OF SHIFTING AND INCIDENCE

It is important to have as clear a conception as possible of who actually bears the burden of a tax. Otherwise the objectives discussed in the preceding chapter cannot be pursued intelligently. If, for example, the purpose of a tax is to produce revenues, we cannot begin to discuss its equity unless we know where the burden (or incidence) lies. If, on the other hand, its purpose is the regulation of business, we need to know whether the tax is paid by business or by someone else. For example, a holding company will not be discouraged from adding to its subsidiaries if a tax on intercorporate dividends is shiftable to the consumer.

IMPACT, INCIDENCE, AND ECONOMIC EFFECTS

Formidable difficulties may face the attempt to determine who bears the burden of a tax. The person who initially pays the tax incurs its impact. The burden or incidence of the tax is said to be on the one on whom it rests after further shifting becomes impossible. The price and output reactions to the tax, by virtue of which it may be partly or entirely shifted by the original taxpayer, induce further economic effects which affect the welfare of still other elements in the economy. Moreover, these indirect economic effects modify the process of tax shifting, so that unless they can be taken into account, an erroneous conception of the location of the burden of the tax may result. The incidence of the tax cannot be known, therefore, until all the direct and indirect effects have worked themselves out. But this may take months or even years, for among the indirect effects are such reactions as the rate of capital formation, technological advance, and the long-run trend of prices and output. The longer the time period, the more difficult it becomes to isolate the economic effects of the tax from other forces in the economy which alter prices and incomes.

The analysis of shifting and incidence, therefore, has to be related to the time period in which we are interested. The shorter the period that is under consideration, the more definite are the conclusions that can be drawn. Short-run or immediate incidence comprises the short-run effects of the tax on the supply and price of the taxed factor, commodity, or income. For example, a firm can respond by altering its output from a given size of plant, but it cannot change its scale of operations. Long-run or ultimate incidence is determined on the basis of complete adjustment to the tax. In terms of clock time this may be a very long period indeed, allowing time not only for alterations in the size of plant but also for responses in terms of changes in technological processes.

The indirect effects of taxation continue to emerge throughout the entire interval between the imposition of the tax and the final reaction in the chain of responses to it. Consequently both short-run and long-run incidence are subject to these indirect effects. We have to conclude that in a dynamic world we are not always in a position to say anything very definite about the quantitative aspects of tax incidence in its broadest possible sense. Formal analysis, therefore, is usually restricted to the conclusions that can be drawn with the aid of the tools of price theory. It is necessary to narrow the meaning of incidence, and to proceed a step at a time. Moreover, despite the complexity of the economic process, a point comes at which someone finds it impossible to shift the tax further. In the case of many taxes this point can be identified, and we can say that the burden of the tax comes to rest at a definite spot. Even so, economic effects flow from the reaction of the individual on whom the burden falls, and we may be even more interested in evaluating these than we are in the location of the tax burden itself.

THE INITIAL RESPONSE

The burden of a tax does not necessarily remain at the point at which the tax is originally levied. The taxpayer, who is the person on whom the impact of the tax falls, may find himself in a position to shift it to someone else. The latter is therefore taxed *indirectly*.[1] A tax can be shifted

---

[1] In the literature of public finance much controversy has arisen over what was actually meant by the constitutional prohibition on *direct* taxes if not apportioned among the states according to population. The economist takes a *direct* tax to be one that is borne by the individual upon whom the impact falls, whereas an *indirect* tax is one that is shifted. In other words, an indirect tax is levied in the expectation that it *will* be shifted.

Since it depends on circumstances what part of a particular tax is shifted, the distinction is not a very useful one. When the Supreme Court (in 1895) declared the personal income tax act of 1894 unconstitutional, conservative opinion held that it was contrary to the intention of the Founding Fathers that direct taxation should be part of the peacetime fiscal system. (Cf. Harold Groves, *Financing Government* [New York: Holt, 1954], p. 148.) In other words, an attempt was made to read into the Constitution that, in general, taxes should be ultimately paid by consumers.

only if there is a subsequent market transaction.[2] If someone else pays more for a product sold by the taxpayer than he would have had to pay in the absence of the tax, part or all of it is borne by the purchaser. The tax is shifted forward. If, because of the tax, someone receives less for a commodity or personal service sold to the taxpayer, part or all of the tax is borne by the seller. In this case the tax is shifted backward.

The direction in which a tax is shifted may depend in part on the reaction of the firm or individual who initially pays the tax. If a tax on the firm, for example, is regarded as an addition to cost, it may try to include the tax in the selling price, and thus if possible to shift it forward. On the other hand, it may be that the easier course is to try to pass the tax backward by paying less to the factors of production, or by reducing output.

If markets were perfect it would make no difference if the taxpayer's first reaction were to try to pass the tax forward instead of backward. The result would be determined solely by the relative strengths of resistance offered by those to whom it was attempted to shift the tax. In a world of imperfect markets, however, the effects are not so clear. Suppose a tax is imposed on the privilege of doing business, such as a business occupation tax or license. The firm expects to receive a price that covers all its costs, fixed as well as variable. It does not necessarily succeed, however; depending on the state of competition, resistance may be met with on the part of the purchaser at the next stage of production. The firm then finds that it may be able to escape the tax by forcing those who sell it goods or services to accept lower rates of return. On the other hand, it may not be possible to force down the rates of return to the factors. Part or all of the tax may come to rest on profits. Because of frictions and uncertainties, the initial reaction of the taxpayer may be significant in determining the ultimate incidence.

COMPLIANCE COSTS AND COSTS OF SHIFTING

Even if the original taxpayer succeeds in shifting the whole of the tax he may be forced to incur significant costs. The major cost effects that impinge on the person on whom the impact falls are (1) the addition to cost of production and the claims on the taxpayer's time incident to compliance with the provisions of the tax, and (2) the costs incurred by the taxpayer in attempting to shift the tax.

From the point of view of society in general, the added cost takes the form of a diversion of resources into the mechanical operation of taxpaying. No tax is free from compliance costs, but they are greater for some

---

[2] However, as we have seen, the fact that a tax must reduce the income of *someone* means that indirect effects are bound to be produced on the demand for goods and factors of production. Ultimately it is the total effect of a tax on incomes that is important, not merely the burden of the tax itself.

taxes than for others. Moreover, they can be reduced if a tax is levied upon the person who is expected to bear the burden. The costs of shifting could be entirely avoided if it were feasible to select taxes that remain at the point of impact. An example would be a universal poll tax. The payer of this form of tax is not in a position to reduce the offerings of his services or product, and thus cannot shift the burden. Some economists have recommended greater use of this type of tax for precisely this reason; but the higher the level of public spending and taxes, the more difficult it becomes to find taxes that are not at least partly shifted.

Compliance costs to the firm may be substantial. Social security payroll taxes and withholding taxes under the personal income tax, for example, require the firm to furnish services to the government. For small firms this cost can be a significant proportion of total cost; but despite numerous protests business has not got very far with ridding itself of the burden. If the firms were reimbursed, an equivalent amount of taxes would presumably have to be imposed elsewhere. Thus the matter would become a political issue. From the point of view of efficiency it would be more costly to have these taxes collected directly by the Internal Revenue Service. The firms do, of course, maintain the necessary records, and are the logical candidates for the task. Even if it is argued that these collection costs are ultimately largely shifted, it is probable that the competitive positions of the firm are affected.

INDIRECT COSTS

Whether or not a tax is shifted, someone's disposable income is reduced. Therefore if we consider the effects of the tax alone, ignoring those of the spending of the proceeds of the tax by the government, there is a negative effect on some combination of savings and consumption. In addition, the tax may have disincentive effects on willingness to put forth effort. As we shall see in subsequent chapters, the effect of an increase in taxes, when matched by an equal increase in government spending, may be to increase rather than to decrease the level of total spending. The reverse may also be true, however; and if so, the economic burden in terms of unemployment or in a changed allocation of resources may be much more significant than the actual burden of the tax itself.

Even the government does not escape the burden of the effects of taxation. If a rise in tax rates should produce a decline in the level of national income and spending, the base of the income and consumption taxes will become smaller. Therefore, less than the expected net addition to tax revenues will materialize. It must be borne in mind, however, that this is a complete picture only if the proceeds of the tax are hoarded by the government, or if tax rates have come to be so high as to discourage willingness to work and invest.

When account is taken of government spending, an offset appears to the negative effects of taxes on demand curves for consumers' and producers' goods. The positive effects of government spending and the negative effects of taxes do not, however, necessarily cancel one another out. No firm or individual can ordinarily expect to experience an increase in government demand that exactly equals the decline in the demand for product or service by the individuals on whom the burden of the tax falls. Therefore it cannot be said that the effects of taxing and government spending are neutral to the economy. Although the Treasury normally puts back into the income stream the whole of the purchasing power that it takes out, various differential effects are produced on the net income after taxes and public spending of firms and individuals. They in turn respond variously to these differential tax and spending effects. These indirect effects exerted by the fiscal system are of great importance in the evaluation of fiscal policy, but discussion of them is reserved until later chapters.

TAX AVOIDANCE

A discussion of the incidence and other effects of taxation assumes that there is a base to which the tax is applied. Under certain circumstances, however, taxes can be avoided. An individual may refuse to earn income, or to consume taxed commodities, or to own property. Nevertheless, no one can avoid taxes entirely. Moreover, apart from illegal evasion, there are some taxes that cannot be escaped by anyone. The poll tax has been cited above as an example.

To the extent that taxes are avoided, no question of shifting and incidence arises. Nevertheless there are indirect effects, and they can have great economic and social significance. A heavy excise on a particular commodity, for example, may drive it off the market in favor of untaxed competing goods. Since no tax is paid, there is no tax burden in the sense in which we have used the term, but incomes are affected, and the budget patterns of consumers are subjected to modification. Again, a window tax would tend to cause houses to be built without windows. A more modern example is the progressive income tax. A working wife is subject to the top-bracket income tax for her entire income. Consequently, if in the lower-income brackets exemptions are low and progression is steep, wives may be discouraged from working outside the home. The unfavorable effects of this on the production of military goods during time of war, for example, are obvious.

There is no point in multiplying examples of the economic and social effects of tax avoidance. Many of them will appear in connection with the discussion of particular taxes. It is apparent, however, that in order to minimize undesired effects of this sort, maximum use ought to be made of taxes that are relatively difficult to avoid. With respect to one of the examples cited above, avoidance might be reduced if the additional income received by a working wife, or for overtime work, were subject to special lower tax rates. This device has been used to encourage output in some of the countries of postwar Europe. Again, a general sales tax will be less subject to avoidance than is a selective excise, which leaves scope for a redirection of demand to untaxed commodities.

▶ PRINCIPLES OF TAX SHIFTING

In undertaking an analysis of the factors that enter into the forward and backward shifting of taxes, it may be reiterated that there is no clear distinction between incidence and other economic effects. The two interact, and a comprehensive discussion of incidence therefore requires an integration of price theory and income theory, as well as a consideration of effects on the allocation of resources, distribution of income, and production. As a practical matter, however, the first step in the analysis of shifting is to examine the price effects of the tax. These are produced via the responses in supply and demand.

BASIC ASSUMPTIONS

Broadly speaking, taxes are levied on three bases: on the consumer, on the firm, and on the owner of resources. The formal theory of incidence, like the theory of price of which it is a part, makes the same basic assumptions with respect to the reactions of each of these to the tax. The assumptions are (1) that everyone is in some sense trying to maximize his advantage, and (2) that prior to the imposition of the tax each taxed unit had reached its preferred economic position. In other words, the assumption is made that everyone is an "economizer," in the sense that through substitution at the margin, and the weighing of the alternative cost of a given course of action, he maximizes his own welfare.

On the basis of this fundamental proposition of economic rationality, it is possible to deduce, under restricted assumptions, the effects of a tax on price and output. Incidence analysis proceeds by following the successive changes in the intersection of market supply and demand curves in response to tax-induced shifts in supply and demand. It is apparent that if, under a sales tax, for example, price were to rise by the exact amount of a tax per unit of product, this rise would probably prove nothing about the incidence of the tax. Many other influences in addition to taxes operate on the intersection of supply and demand curves. A tax has at least partly been passed forward if price is higher than it would have been in the absence of the tax. But the fact that at a given moment price is higher than before tells us nothing about what it would have been if the tax had not been imposed.

THE PRINCIPLES IN PRACTICE

The economizing proclivities of consumers, firms, and resource owners are obviously not as clear-cut in practice as they are necessarily treated in a simple theoretical model. The economist's conception of rationality, for example, is narrowly restricted. Neither the consumer, the firm, nor the resource owner consistently strives to act as the economist says he does. Of course, it is true that the consumer does attempt to maximize his satisfaction in some sense. Nevertheless, this does not mean that he necessarily weighs carefully his alternatives in narrow budgetary terms. Part of his satisfaction may actually derive from failing to bother to do this. These peculiarities are reflected, however, in his demand curve, and price analysis can proceed so long as consumer demand curves can be described. In other words, there must simply be a consistent set of consumer preferences.

What does the basic economizing motivation mean with respect to the behavior of the firm? A firm is assumed to be in business to maximize profits. Therefore any influence, including taxes, which produces a shift in either its supply curve or its demand curve may affect the output of the firm through the effect on profit positions. In practice, however, maximization of profits must be interpreted broadly. A firm cannot be regarded as constantly reacting to day-to-day economic changes. It is interested in long-term as well as short-term profits. Moreover, it must preserve a position of liquidity sufficient to meet unexpected contingencies. The firm, furthermore, is interested in its relative position in the industry, both in the present and in the foreseeable future. Some companies may be prepared to forgo present profits for an assured future position; still others, satisfied with a reasonable return, may respond only sluggishly to moderate changes in supply-and-demand conditions.

All these additional considerations modify the theory of tax incidence as based on marginal analysis. Their effects can, however, be taken into account. This does not mean that it is easy to do so; at the present time we lack the necessary empirical knowledge.[3] Further work is necessary on the impact of the modern corporation in business practices, and assistance is needed from specialists in the area of business psychology.

The resource owner includes two broad categories: the owner of property, and the person who brings his own labor to market. Both these groups can be thought of as striving to maximize their economic welfare, though institutional and other circumstances modify the practical application of the principle. The owner of an income-yielding piece of property wishes to maximize his income. The worker strives for the best possible welfare position, including rates of wages, working conditions, leisure, security, and so on.

In both these cases, if the resource owner has maximized his return before the tax is applied, the application of the tax will lead to a reconsideration of his position. If, for example, a tax is levied on residential building, investable funds will tend to flow toward other untaxed types of

---

[3] For an example of the work that has been done along these lines see the series of studies on "Effects of Taxation," sponsored by the Harvard Graduate School of Business Administration.

resources. Again, an increase in the rates of the personal income tax may lead some workers to strive to increase or decrease their leisure; and an attempt by firms to shift backward to the workers a tax on a particular product will encourage the latter to seek work in other industries. These tendencies may not, of course, be strong enough in fact to bring about a substantial reduction in supply. If they do, however, the effects on supply schedules in turn affect price, and therefore the location of the burden of the tax.

▶ THE MECHANISM OF SHIFTING

COMPETITIVE CONDITIONS

The mechanism of tax shifting will be illustrated by a tax on a commodity per unit of output. The principles are the same for an ad valorem tax, under which the amount of tax depends on the price of the commodity.

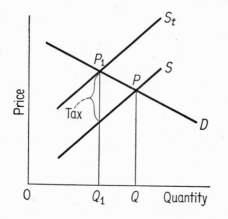

Fig. 1

MARKET SUPPLY AND PRICE AFTER TAX (COMPETITIVE INDUSTRY)

The process of shifting will differ as between conditions of perfect competition, imperfect competition, and oligopoly. Under perfect competition the firms whose product is subject to tax will be unable to shift the tax immediately forward to the consumer, for these firms have no control over price. They may, however, withhold supplies of goods from the market in response to the lower per unit price after tax. If the effect of this reaction of the firms is to cause a significant reduction in market supply, price will rise (see Figure 1).[4] This cannot occur, of course, if, as has often been the case with certain agricultural products, supplies cannot be withheld from the market. An example would be found in a situation of perishable goods or inadequate storage facilities.

When we turn from the market situation to the short run, enough

---

[4] D, S, and S_t are ordinary supply and demand curves. The tax shifts the supply curve vertically upward. Thus S and D no longer intersect at P, but at P_1. Supply has been reduced and price has risen.

time is allowed to elapse so that output can be curtailed. Thus the short-run supply curve moves up, and price will rise still further. In perfect competition all firms in the taxed industry are assumed to respond similarly to the rise in cost due to the tax. Each firm will strive to equate its now higher marginal cost with price, and the fall in output will both raise market price and result in a reduction in demand for factors of production. If this causes a fall in their price, the tax is borne partly by consumers and partly by owners of the resources, including labor, that are devoted to the

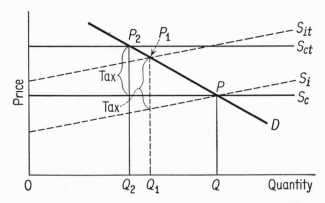

S_{ct} and S_c depict the supply situation with and without tax, respectively, under constant cost conditions, and S_{it} and S_i similarly under conditions of increasing cost.

Fig. 2
LONG-RUN SHIFTING OF A TAX PER UNIT OF OUTPUT
(COMPETITIVE INDUSTRY: CONSTANT AND INCREASING
COSTS)

production of the taxed commodity. The prices of mobile unspecialized factors, which are able to leave the industry, will not fall. Moreover, if factor markets are not competitive (for example, labor is unionized), factors may prefer unemployment to reduced rates of return. It should also be noted that in the case of a fairly heavy excise tax, applying to a widely consumed commodity, a fall in the income of resource owners could cause a leftward shift in the demand curve, thus bringing about an induced decline in price.

We have thus far considered the market and short-run reactions of supply to the imposition of the tax. Over the long run, supply can, of course, be reduced still further, as some of the firms leave the industry. Under competitive conditions firms will continue to leave the industry so long as price does not cover cost per unit including the tax. Equilibrium is restored when the departure of firms, and thus the upward shift in the supply curve of the commodity, has proceeded to the point at which normal profits are being made by the remaining firms.

The taxed commodity may be produced under conditions of long-run increasing, constant, or decreasing costs. The first and second cases are the ones commonly met. In the constant cost case the whole of the tax is shifted forward in the long run, for the supply of all factors of production is completely elastic to the industry. If, on the other hand, the long-run supply curve rises, reflecting increasing costs, price does not rise by as much as the tax. This case is illustrated in Figure 2, with price rising only to P_1, which is less than the amount of the tax.

In a reasonably perfect market for commodities and factors of pro-

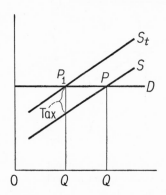

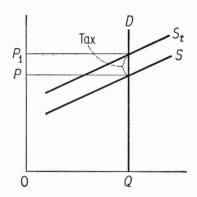

Fig. 3
CASE 1: A HORIZONTAL
DEMAND SCHEDULE

Fig. 4
CASE 2: A VERTICAL DEMAND
SCHEDULE

duction tax shifting can be analyzed with the aid of supply-and-demand curves. When continuous straight-line curves are assumed, as in Figure 2, the proportion of a tax per unit of output that is shifted forward or backward can be visualized by inspection of the diagram. Clearly, it is the relative slopes of the supply-and-demand curves of the taxed commodity which determine the extent of the reduction in output, and therefore the direction of shifting of the tax. It is evident from Figure 2 that under increasing cost conditions, the greater the slope of the supply curve (S_i) the greater the proportion of the tax that will be shifted backward. In other words, a relatively large amount of the tax can be shifted to the factors without causing a significant exodus from the industry. Under constant cost conditions, on the other hand, the reduction in supply proceeds to the point at which price has risen by the full amount of the tax.

LIMITING CASES

Figures 3–6 show the effect of rotating the supply-and-demand curves for the taxed commodity on the direction of shifting. Thus the more nearly horizontal the demand curve, the smaller will be the rise in price and the greater the reduction in the amount sold (Figure 3). If, on the other hand, demand is independent of price (a vertical demand schedule), the entire tax can be shifted forward. In this case an upward shift in the supply curve due to the inclusion of the tax in cost has no effect on the quantity taken.

When the supply curve is a vertical line, as in Figure 5, the entire tax is shifted backward. This is the situation in which the tax makes no difference to the output decisions of the firm; the pretax intersection of the supply and demand curves therefore still holds. Here all factors are completely specialized to the industry. Moreover, this is evidently the market

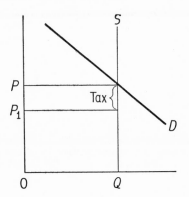

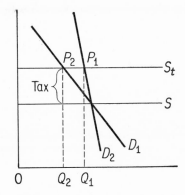

Fig. 5
CASE 3: A VERTICAL
SUPPLY SCHEDULE

Fig. 6
CASE 4: A HORIZONTAL
SUPPLY SCHEDULE

supply case, since under the assumption of perfect competition the addition of the tax raises the firms' marginal cost curves and immediately brings about a reduction in output.

Finally, the supply curve is horizontal when suppliers will bring to market any amount of product at a particular price. This is illustrated in the case of constant costs. The decline in the amount supplied does not reduce unit cost. Figure 6 indicates that under conditions of constant cost the slope of the demand curve is irrelevant to the incidence of the tax, since the whole of the tax must be passed forward. The slope of the demand curve determines the extent of the reduction in the number of units sold.

IMPERFECT COMPETITION

The analysis for firms operating under conditions other than perfect competition is basically similar. As before, the effect of the tax is to raise cost curves. If we retain the assumption of a fixed demand schedule for the taxed commodity, the intersection of the new marginal cost curve (including tax) with the marginal revenue curve is at the left of the old intersection. The situation is shown in Figure 7, which is applicable both to the case of complete monopoly and to monopolistic competition. The firm reacts by raising price and reducing output. The extent of the price rise, and therefore the proportion of the tax shifted to consumers, will depend on the shape of the demand and cost curves. In the demand and cost situation expressed in Figure 7, illustrating the reaction of a firm

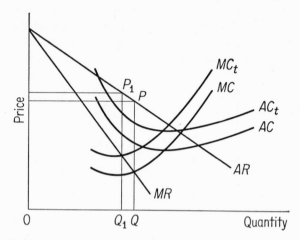

Fig. 7
REACTION OF A MONOPOLIST TO A TAX ON OUTPUT

making monopoly profits, the tax has caused the average and marginal cost curves to rise by more than the increase in price. Therefore only part of the tax has been passed forward.

Under conditions of monopolistic competition the situation is intermediate between perfect competition and perfect monopoly. Although each firm has a degree of control over price by virtue of product differentiation, demand curves are nevertheless nearly horizontal. Therefore, prices will rise only moderately, and part of the adjustment in the long run is likely to take place by virtue of the departure of some firms from the industry. If the effect of the tax is to push the average cost curve above the average revenue curve, firms will leave the industry until the share in the market of each remaining firm is large enough to permit a price that covers average cost including tax.

OLIGOPOLY

The oligopoly case, which is very common, offers the greatest difficulties to the theory of tax shifting. When sellers are few, firms are uncertain about the nature of the responses of their competitors to changes in costs. If they act entirely independently, the levying of a tax on sales is likely to affect all of them in much the same way. Conscious of the monopolistic elements in their situation, they will restrict output and raise price. If, on the other hand, each firm gears its price policy to what it expects the reaction of other firms in the industry to be, there is scope for diversity of judgment, and generalization with respect to the price reaction to the tax becomes difficult.

There is reason to believe, however, that in general members of a group of oligopolistic firms are likely to react similarly to the tax. This will be the case, for example, if one or two of the firms are larger than the rest, and price leadership prevails in the industry. It will also be so if each firm reasons that all the others are subject to the same tax addition to costs which it experiences itself.[5] Again, like a monopolist a number of oligopolists may be stimulated to maximize profits when they become subject to an output tax, even if, due to inertia, they had not been careful to equate marginal cost and marginal revenue prior to the imposition of the tax. They will not find it profitable to raise price in response to the tax, of course, if demand conditions are such that profits will no longer be maximized.

DEMAND CONSIDERATIONS

Substitution Effects.   The analysis thus far has run in terms of the response of producers of the taxed commodities. Demand schedules have been assumed given, and demand effects have been considered in terms of the slopes of the demand curves for the taxed commodities. But when a tax per unit of output is imposed on one or more commodities, demand schedules are not likely to remain unchanged. It will be shown below that demand for a taxed commodity could rise. To the extent that demand is increased for a taxed commodity, forward shifting is facilitated, and conversely if demand is decreased.

In the first place, if a sales tax is levied on a number of commodities, a reduction in total spending occurs on those commodities for which the elasticity of demand is greater than unity. Allowing for the additional tax liability, this releases purchasing power which may be directed in part toward other taxed commodities that are regarded by consumers as substitutes for the former commodities. This phenomenon is the more likely to appear in instances in which the rise in price of certain goods caused by the addition of tax occurs at a particularly elastic portion of their demand curve. Conversely, if, as a result of the tax, consumers spend

---

[5] The effects may differ significantly among different countries. Thus in France business firms are apparently especially prone to mark up all additions to cost without worrying much about reactions in sales volume. In the more aggressive business relations which characterize American industry the uncertainties of oligopoly seem to favor more complex pricing policies. Cf., for example, H. C. Eastman, "The Economic Effects of the French Minimum Wage Law," *American Economic Review,* June, 1954, pp. 369–376.

more than before (plus the additional tax due) on a taxed commodity for which the demand is highly inelastic, purchasing power may be diverted away from other taxed commodities. Thus the demand schedules of the latter shift to the left, and this effect of the shift in spending has to be considered along with effects produced by the shape of the demand curve.

Income Effects. When the tax is imposed on the product of a single industry, and that industry not a relatively important one, it may be assumed that the income effects, and therefore the effects on the position of the demand curve for the taxed product, are not of great quantitative

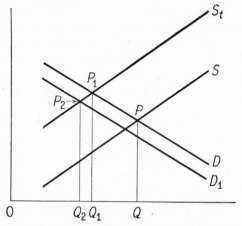

Fig. 8
INTERDEPENDENCE OF SUPPLY
AND DEMAND CURVES

importance. When, however, the tax per unit of output is applied over a wide range, as in the case of a general sales tax, and at high rates, the result is different. The decline in output may exert effects on the demand for the taxed products that make it unrealistic to assume the demand curve to be fixed. The interdependence of the supply-and-demand curves is illustrated in Figure 8.

Let it be assumed in Figure 8 that market supply decreases as a result of a per unit tax. If, as assumed in partial equilibrium analysis, the shift exerts no effect on demand, price will rise to P_1, and quantity will decline to Q_1. In fact, however, the demand for the taxed commodities may fall. For the decline in output will reduce the incomes of the factors of production, whether or not their rates of remuneration are also forced down. Therefore the demand curve may not remain at D, but may move (perhaps only slightly) to D_1. Thus price drops to D_2. Here again there are substitution effects, because the income elasticity of demand on the part of the factors whose income has fallen will differ for different commodities. It is not inconceivable that the reaction in terms of reduced spending may be so strong with respect to some of the taxed commodities that purchasing power is actually released for increased spending on others. Ordinarily, however, a much more moderate redistribution of spending would occur.

EFFECTS ON AGGREGATE SPENDING

Thus far it has been assumed that the factors of production are unable to react to any reduction in their incomes resulting from the effects of the tax by successfully demanding increased rates of remuneration. However, if the workers, for example, are able to achieve increased wage rates on the basis of an increase in cost of living, they are enabled to pass the tax on to their employers, who in turn may be able to raise price in response to the rise in wage rates. This series of events may become automatic if labor contracts contain a wage escalator clause tying wage rates to the consumer price index of the Bureau of Labor Statistics. But virtually the same effect may come about if, even without an escalator, the major criterion of labor bargaining is the cost of living. Unless price inflation is taking place on a fairly considerable scale this may not be the case, however, for labor may prefer to bargain on the basis of the firm's ability to pay, or on the basis of increases in productivity arising out of technological progress. Therefore the circumstances which favor forward shifting in this case are progressive inflation and a belief on the part of labor that it stands to gain most by adhering to the cost-of-living criterion.

GOVERNMENT SPENDING OF THE PROCEEDS OF THE TAX

An important effect on the incidence of the tax is exerted by the disposition of the proceeds of the tax by the government. This arises out of the circumstance that there must be offset against the effects on spending caused by the diversion of purchasing power from the taxpayer the effects of government spending of the proceeds.[6] The alternatives are debt repayment, holding the proceeds idle as treasury cash or deposits with the reserve banks, and government spending.

1. If the proceeds of the tax are used to repay debt, bondholders now have the purchasing power that has been surrendered by taxpayers. Since bondholders are likely to put the proceeds into some other form of saving, the result is probably a decline in consumption spending. If this is so, some unemployment may result, and employed factors may be forced to accept a reduction in rates of remuneration, thus bearing part of the tax. Conceivably a deflationary spiral might be set up, producing further unemployment effects and reduced rates of income; but this does not appear to be likely. In any event, we have considered above only the effects on relative propensities to consume. Account must also be taken of what the bondholders do with that part of the cash they receive for their bonds

---

[6] If one tax is substituted for another yielding identical revenues, however, the tax effects can be considered independently of the spending effects.

which they do not devote to consumption. Provided there is a demand for loanable funds, none of the proceeds of their bond sales to the government is held idle. Therefore there is no decline in the over-all demand for production factors. There will, of course, be a shift in the relative demand for factors producing consumers' goods and factors producing producers' goods. This may or may not involve changes in their rates of remuneration, depending on elasticities of supply of different types of factors. In conclusion, it should be pointed out that this case is rarely met; governments do not often impose sales taxes for the purpose of repaying debt.

2. The situation is quite different if the government holds the proceeds of the tax idle. The income of those who pay sales taxes has declined, but there is no offsetting rise in spending by other groups. Consequently, demand for commodities, and the factors that produce them, has fallen off. If competition is perfect, and if there is complete inelasticity of factor supplies, there is no unemployment but factor income falls, and the incidence of a general sales tax will be similar to that of a proportional income tax. In the real world competition is not likely to be perfect, however, nor are factors of production often in perfectly inelastic supply. The actual incidence, therefore, is likely to be quite different. Part of the tax will be shifted forward. Conditions are certainly not favorable to forward shifting. Part of the tax will be borne by the factors of production, and part is likely to fall on profits. Moreover, to the extent that the supply of certain factors is elastic, unemployment will appear (for nothing has occurred to increase the demand for them in untaxed industries), and the incomes of these factors are likely to fall to a greater extent than would have been the case had they remained in employment and borne the tax. Finally, if the tax were levied at high rates, and on a wide range of commodities, a policy of holding the proceeds idle might set in motion a deflationary spiral. Obviously, no government would pursue such a policy.

3. If the proceeds of the tax are spent by the government, there is a strong possibility that aggregate spending (public and private) increases. If this is so, forward shifting is encouraged. The marginal propensity of the government to spend the proceeds of the tax is one, but the marginal propensity to consume of the payers of the tax is very likely to be less than one. This occurs because to some extent the tax reduces saving, though the major effect of a sales tax is to discourage consumption. If the businessmen who had previously borrowed these savings now turn to the commercial banks, and if the banking system is willing to permit new private debt to be monetized (that is, to create new money in making the loan), government spending has increased without a corresponding decrease in private spending, and the tax will tend to be passed forward. The demand for factors of production will have increased as a result of the levying of the tax, and there may even be a rise in the rates of remuneration of some factors (i.e., those whose supply is inelastic).

Of the three cases discussed above, the third is the most likely possibility. Sales taxes are usually enacted to finance increases in expenditures or to avoid curtailment of governmental budgets. Particularly in states which have been unwilling to adopt personal income taxes, the sales tax has made possible expanded expenditures during the years subsequent to World War II. At the federal level the same point applies to the excise taxes. An exception to this argument would have been provided if, during the nineteen twenties, the substitution of a general sales tax for part of the personal income tax had been effected, a step that was strongly urged by powerful economic groups. If this had taken place, it would have been appropriate to consider only the effects of the adoption of the sales tax and the lowering of income tax rates, and to exclude from consideration the effect of the spending of the proceeds of the tax, for government spending would presumably have been the same regardless of which tax was utilized. It is not likely, however, that in the foreseeable future a general federal sales tax will be enacted in order to permit a reduction in personal income tax rates.

In conclusion, attention is directed to the importance of the role of monetary policy and the money supply in the above analysis. If the volume of transactions remains unchanged, a larger money supply is necessary if the sales tax is to be passed forward in the form of higher prices. The money supply is, as a matter of fact, quite elastic, and even if it were less so, a tendency exists for monetary devices to be developed which permit a rise in velocity, and thus avoid downward pressure on incomes and prices. In the short run, of course, the coincidence of the introduction of a sales tax and a tight monetary policy might well produce a deflationary situation that would favor backward shifting.[7] But if much unemployment developed,

---

[7] Recently there has been renewed debate over the contention that sales and excise taxes are borne by the production factors rather than by consumers. Cf., for example, H. G. Brown, "The Incidence of a General Output or Sales Tax," *Journal of Political Economy*, April, 1939, pp. 254–262; E. R. Rolph, "A Proposed Revision of Excise Tax Theory," *Journal of Political Economy*, April, 1952, pp. 102–116; and *The Theory of Fiscal Economics* (Berkeley: University of California Press, 1954), Chaps. VI and VII; John F. Due, "Toward a General Theory of Sales Tax Incidence," *Quarterly Journal of Economics*, May, 1953, pp. 253–266; and R. A. Musgrave, "On Incidence," *Journal of Political Economy*, August, 1953, pp. 306–323.

The opinion is ventured here that the correct way to ascertain the incidence of either an excise or a general sales tax is to take into consideration the circumstances in which the tax is levied. If this is done, one is not tempted to make general statements to the effect that the whole tax is shifted either forward or backward. For example, a high level of aggregate spending coupled with a ready response of the money supply to rises in cost encourage forward shifting. Conversely, under depression conditions factors of production are likely to be more ready to accept reductions in rates of remuneration than during more prosperous times, while purchasers of commodities are more likely to be sensitive to attempts to pass a sales tax forward to them. Consequently, a condition of widespread unemployment would appear to be favorable to backward shifting. But this does not mean that the supply of factors is perfectly inelastic while consumer demand is perfectly elastic. All that is involved is a shift toward a greater measure of backward shifting.

we can be sure that the federal government would eliminate it via monetary and fiscal measures.

► A TAX NOT RELATED TO OUTPUT

Thus far we have considered the shifting of a tax per unit of output. Firms are also subject to taxes that are unrelated to output. A tax of this sort does not affect marginal cost, and therefore leaves unaltered the point of intersection of marginal cost and marginal revenue. If we ignore income effects, the tax exerts no effect on output and price, and the burden of the tax remains with the firm. If income effects are taken into account, on the other hand, demand curves will be affected. If the tax is of general application, at a high rate, some firms will reduce output, while others, experiencing an increase in demand as the government spends the proceeds of the tax, will expand production. Thus the price effects will vary, and therefore also the proportion of the tax that is shifted.

A tax which does not affect output in the short run may nevertheless do so if a long enough period is under consideration for firms to alter the size of plant and equipment. For example, a tax that is an addition to fixed costs, say a business license, does not affect output or price in the short run, and it is borne by the firm. The firm will go on producing so long as variable costs are covered. Fixed costs become variable in the long run, however; therefore, in the absence of monopoly profits, disinvestment will occur in the taxed industry unless the tax can be passed either forward to the consumer or backward to the factors.

"ECONOMIC SURPLUS"

In its most general application a tax that is not related to output is a tax on "economic surplus." By definition economic surplus is a return that is in excess of what is required to call forth a given resource or factor of production. Thus a personal income tax is such a tax to the extent that it does not result in reduction of effort on the part of the taxed individual. Again, a tax on business profits is a tax on economic surplus provided the base of the tax is carefully defined to exclude elements of either short-run or long-run cost (see Figure 9). A tax on the economic rent of land also falls in this class because the supply of land is relatively fixed, and can only be slowly "reduced" through failure to maintain improvements. All these are taxes unrelated to output, and are therefore borne by the person or firm upon whom the original impact falls.

It will be readily appreciated that if a short enough time period is taken, returns to all factors are in a sense economic surplus, and a tax on them cannot be shifted. In other words, for a tax to be shifted time enough must be granted for supply to be reduced. Only if no conceivable amount of time is sufficient to permit a reduction in supply will the tax remain entirely where it is levied. This will be the case when the tax does not enter into cost even in the long run, and when the tax is so generally applied that firms or production factors cannot gain by moving to untaxed areas.

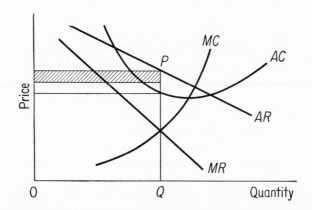

Fig. 9

A Tax Independent of Output: Monopoly Profits

Figure 9 depicts a situation of monopoly profits. If a tax is imposed as a percentage of these profits, marginal revenue and marginal costs are unaffected, and output and price remain the same as before. Therefore, none of the tax is passed forward, nor is there any pressure on the factors of production to accept lower rates of return. If the tax is to remain at the point of impact, however, long-run as well as short-run costs must be unaffected by the tax. The long-run marginal cost curve will rise, for example, if the reduction in the rate of profit makes it more difficult for the taxed firms to obtain capital. The cost of floating new issues will be higher.

THE CASE FOR RESTRICTING TAXATION TO SURPLUS

The economic waste involved in the shifting of the tax could be avoided if the tax were imposed at the point of ultimate incidence in the first place. A famous example of a proposal to avoid this waste was that advanced by the Physiocrats,[8] who suggested that taxes be levied only on agricultural owners. They believed that rents were the only income in the economy that could be regarded as a surplus, and that any taxes levied on

---

[8] French writers of the middle of the eighteenth century, including Turgot, Quesnay, Du Pont de Nemours, and others.

wages, sales, business, transport, and so on, would only be shifted ultimately to the landlord. This conclusion was based on a theory of incidence in vogue at the time, and is not acceptable today.[9]

A lesson that may be learned from the proposal of the Physiocrats is the danger inherent in recommending public policy on the basis of a theory that has not been adequately tested. To the extent that a tax on a base other than agricultural rent either could not have been shifted to some point in the economy other than to rent, acceptance of the proposal of the Physiocrats would have resulted in the imposition of much heavier taxes on the agricultural landowner than was intended. Naturally, an argument of this sort would appeal to anyone who *wished* to place the entire tax burden on the landowner.

In recent years further attempts have been made to induce the adoption of a single tax on the ground that taxpaying ability is to be found in the surpluses of the economy. Aside from the proposal of Henry George, who followed the philosophy of the Physiocrats by urging a tax on increments of land values, perhaps the best known is that of J. A. Hobson. He urged that a tax system be devised to take account of the distinction between (1) those income payments that are necessary to call forth economic effort, and (2) surplus or unnecessary payments.[10]

Hobson was impressed with the wide distribution of elements of surplus throughout the economy (thus differing with the Physiocrats and George, who thought all surplus was concentrated in land rents). Hobson recognized, however, that in practice it is ordinarily impossible to distinguish between necessary and unnecessary payments. Consequently, he concluded that, in addition to a tax on rent, the adoption of progressive income taxation would be the best practical means of taxing surplus directly. Obviously death taxes would also find a place in this "functional" approach to taxation.

The consumption of luxuries likewise involves the enjoyment of income that is not necessary to call forth economic effort. But in a highly productive economy it is difficult to draw a distinction between a necessity and a luxury. Therefore Hobson found that the personal income tax is the most logical tax for getting at surplus. Unfortunately Hobson's approach does not give us much guidance on how to recognize in practice taxes that are unrelated to output. Furthermore, when Hobson wrote, the income tax was already an accepted device for reducing "unnecessary" payments

---

[9] Wages were assumed to be at the minimum of subsistence, so that a tax on them would reduce the efficiency of labor and, by a reduction in supply, would be shifted through increased money wages. Taxes on business would discourage output and investment, thus also reducing supply and raising prices.

[10] J. A. Hobson, *Taxation in the New State* (New York: Harcourt, 1920). See the summary of Hobson's views by Harold Groves, in his *Viewpoints on Public Finance* (New York: Holt, 1947), pp. 105–106, as well as the selections from George's *Progress and Poverty,* and E. R. A. Seligman's criticisms, pp. 414–420.

to those enjoying relatively high incomes, and his book is thus largely a theoretical justification of contemporary practice. The Hobson approach is logically attractive, however, and the concept of functionalism has been extended to include both expenditure and revenue aspects of public finance.

▶ TAX CAPITALIZATION

An important instance of backward shifting is the capitalization or amortization of a tax. When a tax affects the yield of an income-earning asset, the owner who wishes to sell may find himself immediately compelled to pay the capitalized value of the tax. If he did not sell, of course, he would pay the tax in annual installments. In other words, under certain conditions a purchaser of the asset would buy permanently free of the tax. This means that if, for example, the new owner continues over the years to pay a property tax that had been introduced during the tenure of the previous owner, the former is shifting it to the latter in a single lump sum by virtue of paying him a lower price. This is, of course, an instance of backward shifting. Yet this is a very special kind of shifting, and it is somewhat more usual to say that a tax is capitalized only to the extent that it is not shifted.[11]

Tax capitalization takes place in the following manner. The imposition of a tax that has the effect of diminishing the net yield of a durable asset causes the value of the asset to fall immediately in an amount equal to the capitalized tax. As stated above, if the owner were to hold the asset, he would be subject to the tax annually. Thus he cannot escape paying, the tax whether he sells or does not sell. The reason for this is that the value of an income-earning asset is determined, as explained in the next paragraph, by capitalizing its prospective income at the current rate of yield applicable to the particular kind of asset in question. If that yield is reduced by an annual tax, say a property tax or a corporate income tax, it is the net return after tax that is capitalized. An example will illustrate the mechanism.

Suppose that A invests $100,000 in a piece of income-yielding property, say business real estate. Assume that the going rate of yield (interest) on that type of property is 5 per cent. Then A must have expected that this particular property would yield him, for an indefinite period in the future, a net return of $5,000. If he did not think so he would have invested in an asset that he believed would yield him the going rate of return.

If, on the other hand, the market thought that the net return on this

---

[11] Cf. Harold Groves, *Financing Government* (New York: Holt, 1954), p. 127. That is to say, no capitalization occurs if the property owner is able to prevent a fall in yield by restricting output in response to the tax, for in that event consumers and production factors pay the tax.

asset would prove to be *more* than $5,000, others would have bid against him until its price had risen to the point where the yield had been reduced to 5 per cent. Thus if the general consensus was that the property would yield $6,000, the price would rise to $120,000, of which $6,000 is 5 per cent. It will be noted that this assumes a perfect market, with both buyers and sellers informed and "rational," and with a sufficient number of ex-changes to establish market continuity. The essence of the capitalization mechanism is that an investor with free capital has his choice among alter-natives, and that he will choose the alternative that offers him the highest return net of risk.

Once A has bought the property he no longer has $100,000 of free capital, but a piece of property which at the moment of purchase the market believes will indefinitely yield 5 per cent. But in a dynamic world circumstances begin to change immediately. Shifts in demand for product and changes in cost of production will affect the yield of similar assets. If both are affected proportionately, the value of the asset does not change. The decline in demand is then not restricted to the commodity produced by this particular parcel of property, and potential investors have no better alternative to turn to. Consequently, since the net return on A's property has declined in the same ratio as that on all similar types of property, numerator and denominator of the capitalization formula have fallen proportionately, and there is no change in the value of A's property.

For example, suppose the net yield of A's property falls from $5,000 to $4,000. If the net yield on all comparable types of investment falls similarly, the drop is from 5 per cent to 4 per cent. The capitalized value is yield divided by interest rate, or $4,000 divided by 4 per cent. The value of the property is still $100,000.

THE CONDITIONS OF CAPITALIZATION

An annual tax that reduces net yield will cause a reduction in the capitalized value of the taxed property only if the tax is restricted in scope. A universal tax on all business income, for example, of all corporations and proprietorships alike, will not reduce capital values unless the govern-ment offers savers a bond rate of interest that is higher than the industrial yield after taxes. It should be always borne in mind that we are here ignoring the effects on demand curves of the spending of the proceeds of the tax by the government. Those firms that benefit more than others from government spending will experience a rise in net income before taxes which will, to a greater or lesser extent, offset (or even more than offset) the reduction in net income due to the tax.

In general, taxes impinge unequally on different types of income. For example, if the property tax rate is raised in a given city, potential investors in business real estate will take account of the decline in net yield after tax. Property owners will therefore find the tax capitalized against them. If the rise in rates has been deferred for many years, and is finally an extremely sharp one, the demand for real estate will fall, and current owners will suffer severe capital losses. But this rarely occurs. Tax rates are usually changed a little at a time. Consequently any loss due to capitalization of the increased tax is usually distributed among a series of successive owners. Moreover, changes in net income before tax arising out of dynamic economic forces obscure the effects of the tax alone. Finally, markets are not perfect.

The circumstances favorable to tax capitalization may be summarized as follows:

1. To the extent that the tax cannot be shifted forward or backward, net income after taxes is reduced. As we have seen, the amount of forward or backward shifting depends on the elasticity of the supply of resources and the elasticity of demand for product. The scope for such shifting differs widely among different types of capital assets. When the property is a durable consumer good, no further market exchange takes place that permits shifting through changes in price. Thus in the case of a property tax levied on owned homes, the tax remains on the home owner. It will be capitalized against him, at given interest rates, unless all residential property is similarly taxed. Again, a tax on corporate income may be capitalized, for the tax cannot be shifted if it rests on pure profits alone. To the extent that it enters long-term cost curves, however, and thus makes it more difficult to attract capital into the corporate form of enterprise, part of the tax is passed either forward or backward, and therefore does not fall on profits. Less of the tax is capitalized.

2. The smaller the area to which the tax applies, the greater the likelihood that it will be capitalized, for prospective investors in the given type of property are able to invest in alternative properties that are not subject to the tax.

3. The smaller the effect of the tax in driving down market rates of return, the greater will be the extent of capitalization. Prospective investors in the property whose income is reduced through taxation are not completely restricted to similar types of assets. Thus all market rates of return are interrelated. If alternative interest rates (i.e., rates of return) are not significantly affected by the tax, the denominator of the capitalization formula does not decline, and the extent of capitalization will be relatively great. When the Treasury and the Federal Reserve System cooperate to stabilize interest rates, declines in rates of yield of capital assets due to taxation or other causes may not be completely reflected in the denominator of the fraction, and capitalization is encouraged.

4. The more perfect the market the greater is the likelihood that capitalization will take place. The stock market is a case in point. All influ-

ences affecting net yields are quickly taken into account. On the other hand, the great complexity of the forces affecting the price of a given stock makes it difficult to isolate the precise effect of a tax that reduces the net income of a corporation.

THE CAPITALIZATION OF SUBSIDIES

The tremendous growth of subsidies in recent years has drawn attention to the fact that "negative" taxes are also capitalized, thus presenting the beneficiaries with windfall capital gains far in excess of the value of the subsidy in a particular year. Just as the entire tax loss may be borne by the current owner of a taxed asset, so the entire gain may accrue to the fortunate owner of the capital asset benefiting from a subsidy.

It is this circumstance which (among others) has militated against abolishing or sharply reducing the corporate income tax rate as advocated by those who regard this tax as discriminatory or discouraging to investment. A sudden reduction in the rate would, to the extent that the tax is actually not shifted, redound largely to the advantage of the *present* owners of stocks. Subsequent purchasers would have to pay prices that entirely discounted the rise in net yield after taxes.[12]

An example of unintended effects of subsidies brought about through the capitalization process is to be found in the agricultural price-support program. When a subsidy is not available to all, but is restricted to current owners of land, it becomes a marketable asset. Under an allotment policy that prevents freedom of entry on the part of new growers, a farmer who already has an allotment discovers that so long as the price-support policy remains in effect the net value of his crops after subsidy is enhanced.[13]

Naturally this increment is capitalized along with his other net receipts in arriving at a valuation of his property. Suppose, however, that in the course of ten years all the farms change hands. The new owners "buy free" of the subsidy. So long as it is believed that the payments will be continued, the original owner can realize a large capital gain. All foreseeable future government price-support payments are capitalized in the sale price.

---

[12] It is natural to ask why this would involve any greater inequity than was caused by the series of rises in the rate of tax since 1909. The stockholders presumably hit by the capitalization of the tax in the years of rate *increases* would be largely different from those benefiting from any rate reductions. But no one worried much about the capitalized losses during the years of increasing rates. The reason was that corporate income tax rates were raised largely during years of high war income, and high rates of corporate profits. The problem (except during the thirties) was rather how to stem an increase in stockholder income that was unjustified in view of the fact that rising corporate profits and stock yields were caused by war spending. Also, in periods when stocks frequently change hands, any given stockholder is likely to have to bear only a small part of the capitalized increases in the corporate income tax.

[13] See the interesting article on the economics of tobacco growing under price supports and allotments, *Fortune* magazine. March. 1950.

The public is then taxed year after year to reimburse the new owners. But the latter gain nothing from the subsidy, and in fact constitute a powerful pressure group for its continuation, since they would incur a loss if it were given up (unless market prices were to rise sufficiently to obviate the need for a subsidy).[14]

► APPLICATIONS OF THE PRINCIPLES OF SHIFTING

THE TAXATION OF PROPERTY

The first step in any analysis of incidence is to make certain what the tax base is. Property is a complex of types of wealth, and conclusions about the tax burden depend on which of these is under consideration. A separate analysis is required for land, improvements, personal property, and money capital.

Land and Buildings. Since the supply of land is virtually fixed, there is little scope for shifting a tax on land through a reduction in supply. Indeed, as we have seen, a differential tax on land is likely to be capitalized against the present owner. However, some scope does exist for shifting the tax in the long run. Some of the improvements made on land are akin to the construction of buildings. Thus fencing, draining, irrigation, fertilizing, and so on, will be discouraged if property tax rates are raised in a particular area. Investors with free capital will devote it to similar untaxed uses elsewhere. Therefore, output will decline and the tax will be slowly shifted through higher prices to the consumer and lower rates of return to the factors.

The shifting of a tax on building, though also slow, operates with much greater scope than does that of a tax on land. The reason is that buildings wear out. As with a tax on land, the present owner of a building cannot immediately shift the tax, for it is an added cost which diminishes his net yield, which is a rent, or economic surplus. But the return to any factor has this status only so long as its supply is fixed. If the tax is not applied universally, and therefore if alternative forms of investment become relatively more favorable than before, depreciation reserves will be slowly transferred elsewhere. Buildings will gradually run down until they become

---

[14] For many years controversy has raged over the question whether subsidies and taxes, particularly property taxes, are actually capitalized. Although the principle is generally admitted, differences of opinion exist with respect to the extent to which capitalization takes place in practice. For further references see E. R. A. Seligman, *The Shifting and Incidence of Taxation* (New York: Columbia University Press, 1926), Pt. I, Chap. IV, and Pt. II, Chap. I; R. G. Townsend, "Inequalities of Residential Property Taxation in Metropolitan Boston," *National Tax Journal,* December, 1951, pp. 361–369; A. G. Buehler, "The Capitalization of Taxes," *National Tax Journal,* December, 1950, pp. 283–297; and H. M. Somers, *Public Finance and National Income* (Philadelphia: Blakiston, 1949), especially p. 262.

unusable; thus supply decreases and rents rise. In the long run the tax will be shifted unless the owner also occupies the property. In that case there is no place to which he can shift the tax.[15]

Unless the tax is a substitute for other taxes, with spending held fixed, the true final burden of a tax on either land or improvements cannot be determined unless the effects of the spending of the proceeds of the tax have been taken into account. Conceivably these may be spent in such a way as to increase the net yield of the taxed land and buildings by an amount equal to the diminution caused by the tax. A new school, for example, may make a residential area more attractive to prospective owners. A special study would be required to ascertain the effects on property yields of the spending of the proceeds of the property tax. Such a study would be difficult to make, since repercussions of public spending on property values are mingled with other factors affecting these values.

Tangible Personal Property. Tangible personal property is of two broad types, that owned by individuals and used for consumption purposes, and that employed in business, like equipment, inventories, and raw materials. Since the former is not subject to a further price transaction, the owners cannot shift the tax. Personal property used in business, however, is part of cost of production. If it is taxed, therefore, shifting will take place in accordance with the principles that apply to a tax which becomes part of cost. Under imperfectly competitive conditions a portion of the tax may be borne by the owners of the firm if abnormal profits are being made. Otherwise the addition to cost must ultimately be covered by a rise in price or by a decline in the rates of remuneration of other productive agents.

Intangibles. Property taxes may also be levied on mortgages, capital stock, currency and deposits, and other forms of moneyed capital. The general effect of such taxes is determined by the fact that individuals with investable funds strive to obtain maximum yield with given risk. If the tax is universal it is not possible to shift into other forms of assets. If not, however, the present owners will bear the tax, while prospective investors turn to untaxed alternatives.

---

[15] A similar situation may occur under rent controls. When the general price level rises, say because of a war, public sentiment opposes allowing owners of rented properties to charge what the traffic will bear. Rent controls quite justifiably prevent the exploitation of renters, who by and large are relatively low-income receivers. If, however, rent controls are retained indefinitely, the effect may be to reduce the net returns from ownership below what can be obtained in alternative investments of equal risk. Repairs are not made, and the unused depreciation reserves are devoted to other uses. However, although supply is decreased, price cannot rise because of the controls. The same effect is gradually achieved, nevertheless, through deterioration of product. Note that in this example, the rent controls act in a fashion similar to a tax on one group, the proceeds of which are paid over directly to another, without passing through the treasury.

In time, the burden of a tax on intangible property, like that on all forms of property, tends to spread over other types of asset. Suppose that as a result of a tax on mortgage holders, investors move out of mortgages into other forms of investment. Part of the tax is shifted to home owners in the form of higher interest rates as the supply of mortgage money declines. There is still a loose end, however. The increase in the supply of funds for other, untaxed forms of investment tends to push down their yields. The net effect will depend, of course, on the circumstances of a particular case.

DEATH AND GIFT TAXATION

Property is also taxed when it is transferred at death or by gift. Since the possibilities of shifting these taxes will be discussed later, it is only necessary to say here that although the recipient of an inheritance or gift enters into no further price transaction by virtue of which the tax can be shifted, the donor may react to the knowledge that a tax will be due by restricting the supply of his services during life or before the gift is made. On the other hand, he may work harder because of the prospect of the tax. Here again, theory provides us with the framework for incidence analysis, but the circumstances of the particular case must be known if the actual incidence is to be ascertained.

SALES TAXES

The application of incidence theory to the taxation of sales is complicated by the wide variety of institutional circumstances surrounding this kind of tax. The taxation of sales may take place at the retail, wholesale, or manufacturing stages. The tax may be a general sales tax or it may be applicable only to selected commodities. Under a retail sales tax it may be that virtually nothing is exempted, or alternatively that housing, food, and clothing are removed from the tax base. In the case of excises, the tax may be limited to a very few commodities and levied at quite high rates; or so many commodities may be included that it approaches the status of a general sales tax. These already complex possibilities are still further complicated by the fact that both the federal and the state governments may make use of one or more types of sales tax. In recent years even a few cities have experimented with this form of tax.

It is necessary to indicate the manner in which the institutional characteristics of alternative methods of taxing sales affect the practical application of the theory. The following generalizations may be made.

1. The more nearly universal the tax, the fewer are the opportunities for purchasers to escape the incidence by shifting their purchases to untaxed commodities. But the same argument applies to the production factors:

there are fewer industries to which they can transfer their services. It is probable, however, that in this country, at least, the workers will be able to put up a greater resistance to backward shifting to them than the consumers are able to muster.

2. Under increasing costs, the more inelastic the demand for a particular taxed commodity, the more likely it is that the consumer will bear the incidence. Since the demand conditions for commodities vary widely, equally wide variations exist in the incidence of a general sales tax among the taxed commodities. Therefore, a newly imposed general sales tax or an extensive system of excises may result in a considerable shifting about of demand, and consequently of resource allocation among industries.

3. The higher the level of employment and incomes, the more likely it will be that consumers will bear the tax.

4. The stronger and more aggressive are trade unions, the greater the likelihood that those workers who are unionized will be able to escape the tax by obtaining higher wage rates.

5. A state sales tax is relatively difficult to pass forward to consumers if they are in a position to buy similar commodities free of tax from neighboring states or by mail. So-called "use" taxes[16] have been increasingly utilized by the taxing states to prevent avoidance.

6. Part of the incidence of both general sales taxes and excises may fall on the producer when monopoly profits are being made.

7. To the extent that firms use percentage markups, a sales tax applied at a stage preceding the retail stage may be automatically passed forward. If demand is relatively elastic, a relatively large decrease in sales will occur, the profit position of the firms will be less favorable than it would have been had account been taken of the effect on sales, and resources will tend to leave the industry.

8. In general, sales taxes tend to be borne largely by the consumer, even if they are usually imposed at an earlier stage of production than the retail stage. This conclusion, however, must be modified to the extent that output and employment are affected by the tax. Employment effects introduce the possibility of backward shifting.

INCOME AND EXCESS-PROFITS TAXES

If the base of the corporation income and excess-profits taxes were truly long-run economic profits, the incidence would remain with the stockholder. Under both these taxes, however, and particularly with respect to the excess-profits tax, profits subject to tax may be defined in various ways. Considerable differences of opinion may exist over what should be included in deductible costs. Therefore, the actual definition is likely to be

---

[16] A compensating tax applied to commodities imported from nontaxing states on the use of the commodity within the borders of the taxing state is called a use tax.

reached as a result of a compromise, and the base of the tax may include elements of cost. If so, the tax must be in part passed either forward or backward in the long run unless there are monopoly profits.

Since the rate of the excess-profits tax is likely to be virtually confiscatory (80–100 per cent), any inaccuracy in the definition of the tax base means a substantial addition to costs. Therefore, much opposition exists to the excess-profits tax as a permanent feature of the tax system. Opinion is more divided on the milder corporation profits tax, although as its rates have risen over the years, more and more concern has been expressed by businessmen over its cost aspects.

Of all the important federal taxes the personal income tax is the most difficult to shift. Most taxpayers do not enter into a further price transaction which makes shifting possible. However, when rates are very high the supply curve of certain types of labor may shift to the left. There may be greater reluctance to work overtime, and businessmen may retire from business earlier or take longer vacations. If rewards are increased to offset this discouragement to effort, part of the tax is passed on to the consumer. The debate on the incidence of a high-rate personal income tax centers around the question whether or not rewards are actually increased in response to high income tax rates. In any case, it is quite apparent that for the vast bulk of personal incomes the individual is in no position to restrict the supply of his services in response to the tax. In the few instances where a fee or salary is publicized as including the tax, all that has happened is that the amount that the employer was willing to pay in the first place is divided into two parts and stated separately.

▶ CONCLUSION

Modern governments must take account of the effect of their tax policies on the allocation of resources. Therefore, every effort must be made to be informed on the incidence of taxation. The minimum interference with resource allocation occurs when taxes are imposed so far as possible on economic surplus. But tax needs are far in excess of the revenues that can be derived from easily accessible elements of surplus. Therefore a majority of taxes are levied in the knowledge that they will be shifted.

A tax can be shifted only if the taxpayer can alter the supply of his goods or services, or his demand for some other product or factor of production. This he can do only if he is in a position to enter into a subsequent price transaction. Shifting may be forward or backward, and the extent of shifting will be determined by the resistance on the part of those to whom it is attempted to shift the tax. Thus the study of tax shifting involves an examination of the factors that determine the strength of this resistance. The less elastic the supply of the goods or factors bought by the taxed individual, the more easily the tax can be passed backward. The less elastic the demand for the goods or services sold by the taxpayer, the more easily the tax can be passed forward.[17] If the taxpayer is a firm, the tax must be shifted in the long run under conditions of perfect competition or the firm will go out of business. If there are monopoly profits, the firm may bear part or all of the tax even in the long run.

The theory of tax shifting does not end with price effects alone. Repercussions on the income of factors of production, both by the tax and by the spending of the proceeds of the tax by the government, affect the positions of the demand curves. Price is, therefore, still further affected, with further possibility of shifting. Thus the theory of tax incidence proceeds by way of partial equilibrium analysis. Price and income effects are examined separately.

If the conclusions of theory are checked against those of empirical studies, it is found that with present tools of analysis the operation of influences other than taxes cannot easily be distinguished from tax influences. Therefore, it is usually not feasible to reach conclusions with respect to tax incidence by means of such empirical studies. Consequently, despite its limitations partial equilibrium analysis remains the basis for the study of tax incidence.

► REFERENCES

BROWN, H. G. *The Economics of Taxation*. New York: Henry Holt and Company, 1924.

DUE, J. F. *The Theory of Incidence of Sales Taxation*. New York: King's Crown Press, 1942.

MERING, O. VON. *The Shifting and Incidence of Taxation*. Philadelphia: The Blakiston Company, 1942.

ROLPH, E. R. *The Theory of Fiscal Economics*. Berkeley: University of California Press, 1954, Chaps. VI and VII.

SELIGMAN, E. R. A. *The Shifting and Incidence of Taxation*. 5th ed. New York: Columbia University Press, 1926.

SILVERMAN, H. *Taxation: Its Incidence and Effects*. London: Macmillan & Co., Ltd., 1931.

VITI DE MARCO, A. DE. *First Principles of Public Finance*. New York: Harcourt, Brace and Company, 1936.

---

[17] In a constant cost industry the elasticity of demand exercises no effect on the shifting of the tax. (See Figure 6, page 127.)

8 The Personal Income Tax: I

► ORIGIN AND DEVELOPMENT

The primary reason for the introduction in 1913 of the federal personal income tax as a permanent part of the tax structure was to inject into the fiscal system an element of ability to pay. Almost immediately, however, Congress discovered the enormous revenue potentialities of personal income taxation, and the focus of interest shifted correspondingly. The personal income tax, along with the tax on corporate net income, are heavy revenue yielders, and together they form the backbone of the tax system of the federal government. The two taxes must be discussed separately, however, since the individual and the corporation are separate accounting and legal entities, and because the incidence of the two taxes is different.

The personal income tax has been discovered, in recent years, to be a useful instrument for accomplishing a number of economic and social objectives besides that of merely providing revenues. In view of the debate occasioned by these nonrevenue objectives of the income tax, it is worth while to note that its origins lie far in the past. Most of the characteristics of the tax were developed in an age when its only objective was to obtain revenues during periods of particular financial stress.[1] Thus in England, for example, a progressive income tax on certain limited types of income was introduced for a short period as early as 1435. This tax had a basic rate of 2½ per cent (on incomes between £5 and £100), rising to a maximum of 10 per cent (on incomes above £200).[2]

► MODERN BRITISH EXPERIENCE

Widespread opposition to income taxation long discouraged its use, and it was not until 1798 that Pitt, under the immediate stress of the

---

[1] This is not to say, however, that the public was ignorant of the fact that traditional taxes placed much the greater proportion of the tax burden on the lower-income groups. It was largely in order to redress this situation that income taxes were used in the nineteenth century by certain of our Southern states.

[2] S. Dowell, *History of Taxation and Taxes in England* (London: Longmans, 1888), I, 104–113, 316.

French war, was able to introduce the first modern personal income tax.[3] Its purpose was revenue, and the refinements subsequently enacted were intended to strengthen its revenue-yielding characteristics. The tax was regarded as an emergency levy for the prosecution of the war, and was not retained after 1815.

Despite the intense opposition to the British income tax, however, it was again revived in 1842, when Sir Robert Peel required a substitute revenue source for the customs when England repealed the Corn Laws. Again it was thought that the tax would be merely temporary. The prevailing attitude toward the income tax in the nineteenth century was that it should be kept at low rates, with high personal exemptions, and employed as a supplementary tax when an elastic source of revenue was needed to meet an emergency. The high exemption, however, by limiting its application to the relatively few, made it popular with the bulk of the population. Gladstone failed to enlist support for its abolition in 1874, although the widespread belief that the income tax was merely a temporary emergency device delayed the adoption of progression until the budgets of 1906 and 1909.[4] The long experience of the British with the personal income tax brought home to the lower-income groups the realization that this tax could be used to offset the regressivity of such taxes as excises and the customs. The concurrent movement toward universal suffrage and the growth of the political solidarity of the workers made it inevitable that the personal income tax would be retained, and that it would ultimately become progressive.

► AMERICAN EXPERIENCE

The development of the income tax idea in the United States shows a rather surprising similarity to that in England, with a lag of somewhat over half a century. Certain of the colonies had made use of a so-called "faculty" tax, levied on both income and property, to take account of the fact that the growing population of the cities often had income but did not own real estate. This tax ultimately became impossible to administer, with the available facilities for assessment and collection, as the urban population rapidly increased. However, eight of the fifteen states still included incomes from certain occupations in their property tax base as late as 1796.

The emergency of the Civil War led to the introduction of a temporary personal income tax, which was abolished in 1872, thus paralleling the British experience of the Napoleonic Wars. An even more striking

---

[3] From the time of the Property Tax Act of 1601, however, local tax assessors had often included the income from certain occupations for taxation at property tax rates. Therefore, the idea of using an income tax for revenue purposes had been kept alive.

[4] For British experience see F. Shehab, *Progressive Taxation* (New York: Oxford, 1953).

parallel was the fact that a large part of the campaign for the introduction of a permanent income tax was based on the program of the liberal political elements to abolish the protective tariff, and to make up the loss in revenues with an income tax. Finally, the failure of conservative elements to eliminate the personal income tax after World War I was partly due to the determination of the political representatives of the lower-income groups to retain permanently the only quantitatively important progressive element of the entire federal-state-local tax system.

This similarity of development of the personal income tax in the two countries prompted many wealthy men to complain of our propensity to ape the British on the road to "disguised socialism." It is apparent, however, that an important factor was the parallelism of underlying economic and social aspects of the two societies.

The income tax of the Civil War period owed its existence in part to the feeling that there should not be a federal tax on property, and in part to the possible constitutional barrier to direct taxation of property without apportionment among the states. The extensive use made of the taxation of property at the lower levels of government likewise militated against the introduction, even for war purposes, of death taxes that included real property. On the basis of experience in the War of 1812, however, it might be expected that the yield from the tariff would fall substantially during wartime, and the only productive alternative appeared to be the income tax. Under the 1861 tax the personal exemption was high ($800), and the rate low (3 per cent). Even in its final form the tax was only slightly progressive. In the act of 1865 the top rate was 10 per cent on incomes over $5,000.

Important lessons were learned from the Civil War experience that stimulated sentiment for acceptance of the income tax as a permanent feature of the federal tax system. The tax proved to be very productive. In 1865 it provided almost 20 per cent of federal revenues. The discovery was made that an income tax could be a very effective instrument in helping to reduce the war debt during the years of prosperity and low federal expenditures that followed the war. Although this fact did not prevent the rejection of the income tax after 1872, it played an important part in the income tax rate struggle during the crucial period after World War I.

THE BACKGROUND OF THE MODERN INCOME TAX

The temporary victory of the anti-income tax forces in 1872 had no permanent effect on the struggle for a more progressive tax system. Western Congressmen had managed to block repeal in 1870. Their argument was that without an income tax the federal tax system would have no element based on ability to pay. After repeal, two important political elements pressed for the adoption of a permanent income tax. The first group comprised the new political parties, like the Grangers and the Populists, that desired to better the position of the lower-income receivers. The nascent labor union movement likewise favored the income tax. The second was the liberal wing of the Democratic party, which opposed the protective tariff and desired to see it replaced with an income tax. Both these groups played important roles, though in different ways. It was in part the fear of the Socialist movement that prompted some representatives of the middle-income groups to come to favor the income tax as a "backfire" against the more violent proposals of left-wing extremists. But it was the widening of the left-wing segment of the Democratic party which gave the political respectability to the income tax movement that was required to overcome the heavy opposition of powerful conservative elements.

The Income Tax Act of 1894 was adopted as a climax to the struggle between the advocates and the opponents of a high tariff. It was first thought that the new lower tariffs proposed by the Democratic (Cleveland) administration would reduce revenue and thus automatically require the introduction of an income tax. Although changes in the Senate bill disappointed these expectations, an income tax act was nevertheless forced through Congress with the help of farm and labor interests. This took place despite the combined opposition of (1) those who feared adverse effects on business initiative and (2) those who viewed the income tax as an entering wedge for the equalization of incomes.

The high exemption ($4,000) gave rise to the complaint that this was really a class tax, and thus violated the rule of reasonable classification. A further objection was that since the mass of voters would not be subject to the tax, they would fail to comprehend their stake in good government. The first of these objections has now been finally rejected as erroneously assuming that persons in different income groups are really "similarly situated" persons for tax purposes. The second has some validity, though even if exemptions are very low, the withholding of the tax by the employer (which is indispensable under an income tax that comprehends the bulk of the workers) causes the average individual to think of his income as net of tax, and therefore to forget that he is paying it.

REASONABLE CLASSIFICATION

The difference of opinion with respect to "reasonable classification" was largely based on differing interpretations of the role of an income tax. Proponents of a progressive income tax were thinking of the effects of the tax on the aggregate income going to each income *group*. What rates of tax would be needed, for example, so that taxes and spending as a whole would no longer divert income from the group earning less than $3,000 a year to those earning more than this figure? The opponents of the tax were thinking of the effect of progressive taxation on a particular individual: different rates of tax were to be applied to him from those applied to his

lower-income neighbor.[5] Thus the argument resolved itself into a difference in interpretation of the meaning of "treating everyone alike under
the law."

The liberals regarded as discriminatory a federal tax system which,
before 1913, derived its entire revenues from taxes that took a greater
proportion of a poor man's income than of that of a wealthy man; or,
looking at it somewhat differently, that brought money into the Treasury
largely from the lower-income groups and paid it out again in a manner
that did not necessarily favor these groups. Indeed, during periods of debt
repayment and heavy interest payments on the debt, a large part of federal
revenues was being paid to those whose high incomes had permitted them
to save and buy government securities.

The importance of the political complexion of the courts was demonstrated in the Supreme Court decision (*Pollock v. Farmers' Loan and Trust
Co., 158 U. S. 601, 1895*) of 1895 that nullified the act of 1894 on the
ground that since the tax included rents from property in its base it was
to be regarded as a direct tax. Many authorities differed with the Court
that this was a direct tax, and a number of earlier decisions supported the
contrary view. The acceptance of this definition would have made an
income tax impossible, for the Constitution requires a direct tax to be
apportioned among the states according to population. This is not practical
under an income tax, since a very populous but poor state would be subject
to impossibly high rates in order to fulfill its quota.[6]

It was the inclusion of income from property in the tax base that
provided the opportunity for the Court to liken the income tax to the
property tax, and thus to class it as a direct tax. If property income had
to be excluded, however, an income tax would obviously be inequitable,
and the only course was either to await a change in the personnel of the
Court or to amend the Constitution. It is ordinarily agreed that in the
Pollock decision the Court was allowing its disbelief in the economic and
social justification of an income tax to influence its opinion.

---

[5] In this connection it is interesting to note that the Ways and Means Committee
in 1815 rejected a proposal of the Secretary of the Treasury that an income tax be
levied on certain salaried groups. It was argued that a tax determined by net income
would be an admission that excessive compensation had been allowed in fixing the
salaries of public officers.—P. Studenski and H. Krooss, *Financial History of the
United States* (New York: McGraw, 1952), p. 81.

[6] It was the agricultural slave states that had insisted on the apportionment of
direct taxes. A property tax would be largely paid by them. To reduce the impact of
any apportioned tax they succeeded in having slaves counted as three fifths of free
persons. The origin of the apportionment requirement indicates that the framers of
the Constitution regarded only property and capitation taxes as direct taxes. During
most of the nineteenth century the Supreme Court adhered to this narrower view. The
carriage tax of 1797 was sustained (*United States v. Hylton*) on the ground that it was
not a direct tax, but an excise, and therefore did not have to be apportioned according
to population. Again, in 1880, the Court unanimously ruled the Civil War income tax
an indirect tax, and therefore not subject to apportionment (*Springer v. United States,
102 U. S. 586, 1880*).

THE STRUGGLE RENEWED AFTER 1895

After 1895 sentiment rapidly grew for a permanent income tax, and it is probable that changes in the personnel of the Supreme Court would have resulted in a favorable decision if an income tax had been enacted again. But proponents of the tax decided to strive for a constitutional amendment that would specifically exclude the income tax from the category of direct taxes. By 1913 this amendment, the sixteenth, had been ratified by three fourths of the states.

In 1909 a corporation income tax was enacted, bearing the low rate of 1 per cent on corporate income in excess of $5,000. To avoid constitutional difficulties it was called an excise for the privilege of doing business, this privilege to be measured by corporate net income. The Supreme Court sustained this tax as an excise, and therefore not as a direct tax, as it had done in the case of the income tax of the Civil War period. A distinction was made between the subject of a tax (in this case the privilege of doing business) and its measure (corporate net income). This hairline distinction, aimed at finding a basis on which to sustain the act, reflects the change that had occurred in the complexion of the Court since the 1895 decisions.

The reasons for the delay in the enactment of a permanent income tax until 1913 are of interest for the light they throw on the type of political and constitutional obstacles that must sometimes be hurdled even when a preponderance of public opinion favors a change. An important delaying factor was the lack of need for new revenues. Recurring treasury surpluses during a relatively peaceful era favorable to the yield of the customs obviated the need for a new species of tax. Consequently a double battle had to be fought: (1) for the new tax, and (2) for the elimination of some of the importance of the tariff. But a crisis in 1907 made the excises and customs inadequate to finance the rising federal economic activities and thus paved the way for the acceptance of a new source of revenue. Another circumstance was the softening of President Taft's earlier opposition to the income tax, an opposition that had been based on the purely technical ground that he feared the adverse effects on the standing of the Supreme Court if it should again declare an income tax unconstitutional. Finally convinced of the shift to the income tax even within his own party, he recommended both the corporate income tax and a personal income tax amendment to the Constitution.

A PERMANENT FEDERAL INCOME TAX FINALLY ENACTED

As one would expect, the rates of an income tax introduced in time of peace[7] were modest and the exemptions high. A distinction was made between normal and surtax net income that persists to this day, though

---

[7] As an amendment to the Underwood Tariff Act of 1913.

the significance of the distinction has declined and the normal and surtax rates have now been combined into a single schedule. The married exemption was at the high rate of $4,000, and the normal tax rate of 1 per cent applied to net taxable income above the exemption. Above $20,000 of taxable income a surtax was levied in addition to the normal tax, starting at 1 per cent and graduated to 6 per cent on incomes over $500,000.

If one of the purposes of the backers of the income tax was the downward redistribution of income, the first income tax act did not go far toward accomplishing it. But events proved those correct who maintained that any departure from strict proportionality of rates would mean the end of objective standards, and a tendency ultimately to a steeper and steeper progression. The concept "surtax net income," particularly confusing in recent years when it has applied even to the first taxable income bracket, was adopted instead of the simpler outright progression of bracket rates. This was done in order to make possible different tax treatment of different types of income. Dividends, for example, were exempt from the normal tax. Various tax credits could be made applicable to the one and not to the other. The interest on government bonds could be made taxable under the surtax, while left exempt from the normal tax in order to encourage holdings by small savers. The effect of the distinction was, however, to make more difficult the popular understanding of a tax that has come to be the major element in the tax systems of democratic nations, and it was for this reason that the two schedules were combined in 1954.

The enactment of a federal income tax several years before it was to be put to a severe test in World War I provided much-needed time to gain the necessary experience. No new system works well. By 1919 successive changes in the act had raised the basic rate to a graduated 6 to 12 per cent, and the maximum surtax rate to 77 per cent on incomes over $1,000,000. This enormous increase in the steepness of progression was designed to produce revenue, not to reduce income equality. The bulk of the proceeds of the rise in rates would naturally come from the lower middle- and middle-income brackets, though on equity grounds still higher rates would be required on the highest incomes. The net redistribution, if any, would be small for the tax system as a whole. War always requires substantial increases in taxes on the consumer, who in the aggregate is largely synonymous with the low-income receiver. Moreover, much of war spending is converted into high personal incomes that are higher even after payment of tax than they were before the increase in government spending.

To prevent an undue increase in windfall profits, therefore, it was felt necessary to raise sharply the rate of the corporate income tax (to 12 per cent by 1918), and to impose a special tax on the profits of munitions makers and, somewhat later, on "excess" profits in general. Although the income tax did become much more progressive in World War I, incomes after tax nevertheless remained highly unequal. Yet because of the tendency of both advocates and opponents of progression to concentrate attention on a few taxes instead of on the tax system as a whole, the progressive income tax came under sharp attack during the twenties by those who deplored its equalizing tendencies. It should perhaps be added that in addition a part of the reason for the attack was the general feeling that the country ought to return to prewar "normalcy."

The decade of the twenties saw a determined effort to make the income tax less progressive. The struggle was complicated by the efforts of certain bankers and businessmen to introduce a general federal sales tax to replace the revenues lost by a reduction of surtax rates. The selfish interest was obvious, but the move went deeper than that. The wealthy believed that rapid capital formation and full employment required that a maximum amount of savings be left in the hands of those who have the responsibility for investment decisions.[8] They saw no reason to worry about the possible adverse effects on mass consumption, and therefore on business profits, that would be exerted by a sales tax in a period when personal and corporate savings were already extremely high.

Although the sales tax campaign failed because this tax was regarded as inequitable to the lower-income groups (not because of any fears concerning its possible adverse economic effects), income tax rates were reduced several times during the twenties, predominantly in the upper brackets. Thus, for example, the maximum surtax rate was cut to 50 per cent in 1921, to 40 per cent in 1924, and to 20 per cent in 1926, and the normal tax in the first bracket to 4, 2, and 1½ per cent, respectively. These reductions were made possible by persistent treasury surpluses brought about by the prosperity of the twenties, and despite annual repayments on the war debt averaging $1 billion.

REVENUE NEEDS AND PROGRESSION

Congressional policy with respect to income tax progression has continued to be guided much more by revenue requirements than by the specific intent to alter the distribution of income. It was the budgetary troubles incident to falling revenues and increased relief expenditures in the depression of the thirties that forced a return to more progressive rates.[9] By 1932 the maximum surtax rate was back up to 55 per cent. The sharp rise to 75 per cent by 1935 was, on the other hand, the result of the adoption by the administration of a more positive policy against inequality of income distribution.

As a result of the writings of John Maynard Keynes, it was gradually

---

[8] The word "investment" is used by economists to denote the acquisition of plant, equipment, and inventories, and not the exchange of money for other types of assets in the securities markets.

[9] It is not intended to imply that the policy was (or was not) correct.

coming to be realized that increased tax rates during depressed times may so discourage spending as to result in even lower tax yields. At the same time, however, sharply progressive tax rates reduce savings, and thus may stand in the way of recovery. For taxes on savings are not restricted to *hoarded* savings alone. Relatively modest effects in stimulating the rate of spending by taxing idle savings into the Treasury (which immediately pays them out) may be more than offset by the discouraging effects on the willingness of businessmen to invest the savings that are left in their hands. The Roosevelt administration solved this dilemma by combining a sharply progressive income tax with heavy public spending, counting on the latter to encourage consumption, and therefore indirectly the willingness of firms to invest despite high individual surtaxes in the middle and upper income brackets. A still more stimulating effect could have been achieved, of course, if public spending had been increased without bothering to try to tax idle savings. Advantage would thereby have been taken of the effect of liquidity on willingness to spend.

The advent of World War II obviated the necessity of drawing conclusions as to the correctness of Roosevelt's social and economic objectives. Since 1940 the economy has been almost constantly operating under forced draft, and the sharp increase in progression that resulted in a top effective rate[10] of 90 per cent in 1944 has had no discernible discouraging effect on investment.

The reduction in income tax rates under the Revenue Act of 1948 had to face the issue of how to distribute the tax reductions among the income brackets. In this connection a legitimate conflict of opinion arises. If the sole reason for increased progression is the need for revenue, it is logical to return to less steep progression when that need passes. If, on the other hand, the reason for increased progression is in part an attempt to make the distribution of income after taxes less unequal, the reduction resulting from decreased revenue needs should not benefit upper brackets more than proportionally. The 1948 act raised personal exemptions, and the percentage reduction from the tentative tax, previously a flat 5 per cent, was made greater on low than on high incomes. On the other hand, income splitting conferred an important benefit to married persons having higher incomes.

In the actual circumstances of 1941–1945 motives were mixed: war spending not only requires increased revenues but favors the creation of high incomes. Since the maintenance of a high level of federal spending continued to contribute to high personal incomes, the continuation of sharp progression could be justified. In any event, the reduction in rates in 1948 (which limited the maximum effective rate to 77 per cent) proved

---

[10] The effective tax rate is the tax divided by the taxable net income. The top marginal rate, on the other hand, is the rate that applies to the top taxable income bracket of the taxpayer.

ill-advised in view of the huge commitments of the United States government both at home and abroad. The war in Korea and the worsening
international situation reversed the downward trend of income tax rates;
moreover, it not only prevented anticipated reductions in excise taxes but
led to increases. In 1954, despite the risk of a budgetary deficit, income
tax rates were again moderated, the rates ranging from 20 to 91 per cent.

► INCIDENCE AND INCENTIVE EFFECTS

As we saw in Chapter 7, it was thought by Hobson that the personal
income tax is the nearest thing to a tax on surplus alone, and is therefore
the best means of avoiding the tax shifting that is characteristic of all
taxes that enter into cost. To the extent that the income tax affects willingness to put forth effort, however, it also affects supply, and therefore price
of product and demand for other factors of production.

Interest in the shifting and incidence of the income tax has naturally
grown as events of recent years have indicated that a high rate schedule is
likely to be the rule rather than the exception in the future. But the usual
incidence analysis based on price theory is not well adapted to the income
tax. We are concerned with the reactions of individuals rather than of
firms. Moreover, effects of the tax must include the incidence and economic
effects of the spending of the proceeds, since rises in income tax rates are
usually associated with rises in public spending. This is not the case, of
course, if a rise in income tax rates permits the reduction in the rates of
other taxes.

The more general the application of a tax, the fewer are the opportunities for those subject to tax to transfer their efforts to untaxed activities.
The federal income tax applies, of course, throughout the entire country.
Only a few people escape it by working outside its borders. State income
taxes and, to a much greater extent, city income taxes apply within a
limited jurisdiction. Therefore, there may be some incentive for individuals
to transfer their activities to jurisdictions that do not apply the tax. Since
state income tax rates do not usually exceed 6 to 8 per cent, however,
there has been no significant tendency for income receivers to migrate to
other jurisdictions.

The only avenue by which shifting can take place under the federal
income tax is through withdrawal of services from the market. Here
generalization is so difficult as to provide no definite conclusions. The basic
question is how far net income after tax is the chief motive for remaining
at work. Undoubtedly a margin of the working force is prompted to reduce
effort when the proportion of additional income taken by tax increases.
But there is at present no way of knowing how wide this margin is, or how
it responds to dynamic changes in the economy and to changes in the rate
structure. All that we can do is indicate the nature of the reactions.

INVESTMENT INCOME

So far as income from capital is concerned, the effect of high rates is to encourage the holding of earning assets in a less risky form. The higher the tax bracket of the investing individual, the greater must be the gross return on prospective investment to ensure a given return after taking account of risk. This tends to reduce the flow of capital into the riskier types of venture, and therefore raises the interest cost to them. The price of the end product is thus higher than it would otherwise be. Furthermore, if new issues of tax-exempt state and local securities are available, an effect of a high rate scale might be to encourage the holding of some savings in this form by individuals who are financially able to undertake risky investment. In this event the saver would avoid the tax by refusing to permit his capital to earn high-yield income, but the welfare of the community would suffer through a lower rate of technological process.

SALARIES AND WAGES

High income tax rates exert two types of effect on willingness to earn and to pay taxes. These effects operate in opposite directions. On the one hand, the reduction of income by the tax reduces the incentive to put forth effort. On the other hand, since income after tax is lower by the amount of the tax, the marginal utility of the income that remains in the hands of the taxpayer is higher. In any case, the effect of high income tax rates is probably to discourage entrance into occupations where training costs are high and are not deductible for tax purposes. Progressive income taxation reduces compensation differentials, and unless other reasons exist for individuals to acquire skills and education, a significant reallocation of talent is to be anticipated. This statement is subject to the qualification that a reduction in the supply of a given type of ability may produce a compensating rise in its rate of remuneration *before* tax.

Income earners react differently to the income tax, depending on their taxable bracket, type and conditions of work, age and family status, individual psychological reactions to income and to the income tax, and so on. A person in a low-income bracket may take on extra work if a rise in his bracket rate threatens his standard of living. On the other hand, married individuals in income brackets appreciably above the margin of subsistence may not find it worth while for the wife to work if the marginal rate applicable to their combined income is high. This point takes on added significance if, as has been the case under the federal income tax, the cost of employing household help is not deductible from the extra income earned by the wife.[11]

---

[11] The 1954 amendments to the Internal Revenue Code permit a $600 deduction (maximum) for expenses incurred by a working wife for the care of a child under twelve years, provided that adjusted gross income of husband and wife does not exceed $4,500. This deduction is reduced by the amount that income exceeds $4,500. Clearly

Again, it has been the experience in Britain that under very high rates of tax applicable even to the low taxable brackets, absenteeism increases substantially. Absenteeism is impossible in many occupations, of course, owing to the nature of the work. But workers may refuse overtime, since it is taxed at the top bracket to which the worker is subject, and none of it is exempt. In an effort to circumvent this effect overtime may be paid at time and a half or double time. Alternatively, special treatment may be accorded overtime income under the tax law. Thus in Germany certain overtime has recently been exempted from the tax. These measures recognize that there are circumstances in which the income tax is either shifted or causes repercussions which slow down the rate of production and capital formation.

In the upper earning brackets retirement may be hastened by the income tax, especially since a man is likely to reach his highest taxable bracket during the years when he is considering the possibility of retirement. Even if he retires, however, the effect on the supply of managerial labor, and consequently on price of product, is indeterminate. If the promotion of younger and more vigorous men is thereby encouraged, the effect on output and prices may be favorable rather than unfavorable. The man who is most likely to retire because of the tax is apt to be also the man whose interest in the success of the business is marginal. In any case, the effect of high income taxes on executives' salaries has been rather to encourage the setting up of liberal pension schemes, since salary paid directly to the pension trust is not taxable.[12] This would apparently indicate that managerial labor is in general more interested in finding ways to continue working, while effecting a reduction in the burden of the tax, than it is in retiring early.[13]

The effect of the income tax on the desire for leisure is much easier to determine after several years of operation with a given set of rates than it is during a period of rapidly rising government spending and income tax rates. Reactions on the part of workers and executives who have grown up under a high rate schedule are certain to be very different from the responses of those who remember the days of low rates. It is for this reason that proposals tentatively advanced in some quarters to tax leisure, quite apart from their undemocratic connotations, are at least premature.[14]

---

this provision is aimed at hardship cases rather than at the problem of maintaining work incentives. (The provision, without the $4,500 limit, also applies to other working women and widowers.)

[12] Tax is deferred until retirement, when the individual is ordinarily subject to a lower rate.

[13] On this subject see C. A. Hall, Jr., *Effects of Taxation: Executive Compensation and Retirement Plans* (Boston: Harvard University, Graduate School of Business Administration, 1951).

[14] This would be done by requiring an individual to include in taxable income a money equivalent of the number of hours per week worked below the standard in the industry.

During the transition period, when workers are becoming accustomed to higher rates, inducements may be necessary to encourage maximum effort. But these should take the form of the carrot, not the stick. A tax on leisure would suffer from the usual objection to direct controls, namely, that they generate still further controls. Standard working days and weeks would have to be established for all occupations, and an extensive system of administrative controls established. Even if this were done, there is no democratic device for forcing workers to put forth their best efforts, or for requiring managers to be aggressive and imaginative.

Apart from the taxation of leisure, there remains the possibility of adopting measures to reduce the impact of sharply rising marginal income tax rates at the various levels of income. Schedules could be established by means of which lower rates of tax would be made to apply to income from the types of effort that it is desired to encourage. Thus standard rates would apply to merit raises, but some fraction of standard rates to increases in income due to extra effort. There is no perfect solution, however. For to the extent that merit raises are a reward for extra effort rather than for mere longevity, considerations of both equity and the stimulation of incentives would require that a favorable rate be applied to this class of raises as well.

"EXCESS" INCOME TAXATION AND INCENTIVES

The problem of maintaining incentives becomes especially significant in the evaluation of a scheme that has been advocated in wartime, namely, a special income tax applied to so-called excess income. This is a proposal to apply a special surtax to that part of personal income that exceeds the income of a base year, with exemption allowances for seniority, raises, rise in cost of living, and the like. Interest in this proposal is attributable to the analogy of certain types of wartime personal income with the "excess" profits of munition makers and others who experience particular benefit from government war spending.

Assume that two neighbors each earned $5,000 a year before the war. The one, on a fixed income, continues to earn this amount during the war, while the other shifts to a war job and earns $7,500. It might be argued that the latter should not only pay the additional income tax applicable to the higher income, but also a special surtax designed to take account of the fact that this extra income is a windfall to him brought about by government spending.

The higher pay in war plants, however, is intended to facilitate the movement of labor into war industries. To apply a special tax to what is regarded as an inducement to mobility would be to reduce the effect of intended incentive effects of the higher pay. An excess income tax might be necessary if extraordinary conditions caused a truly excessive increase in the rate of pay of war workers. But within a rather wide range of income the use of such a tax to remedy inequities in the scale of wages as among different occupations runs counter to the more important objective of stimulating a rapid change-over to military production.[15]

▶ INCOME AS A MEASURE OF ABILITY TO PAY

Ability to pay is not determined by a man's income alone, but by his property as well. Even if property does not return a flow of taxable income in terms of dollars, ownership relieves the individual of the necessity of saving for future contingencies. In any case the use of the property is itself real income, for it reduces the owner's need to spend out of his money income for these services. To lessen this inequity it is sometimes argued that unearned income from property ought to be taxed at a higher rate than earned income. Presumably this suggestion would involve an exemption for those whose total incomes are low, and would also provide for the taxation of *imputed* income from property.[16]

The argument for higher taxation of property income rests largely on the contention that the income from property is net of depreciation, whereas income earned by the individual makes no allowance for deterioration of the human machine. One possibility is to take account of the difference through different rate schedules for earned and unearned income. Another is to rely on the fact that property income accrues primarily to the higher-income groups, and therefore to depend on a system of graduated rates.

Precisely the opposite argument is sometimes made, namely, that so long as there is a property tax no income tax should be applied to the yield of property. As a matter of fact, at the present time the federal and state income taxes do not tax the *imputed* income from property. They do, however, tax the dollar income from property that is rented or used for business purposes. Since the imputed income has a dollar equivalent, it ought to be taxed similarly to dollar income. The question is, Should either dollar or imputed income be taxed under the income tax if the property that yields it has already been subject to the property tax?

The answer to this question depends on whether or not it is possible to tax property in such a way that the tax is a function of the yield of the property. If so, it makes no difference if the tax is levied partly on income and partly on the property from which the income is derived. In practice, of course, the difficulty is that property taxes are levied by the lower governmental jurisdictions, and that the localities, which are by all odds the major users of the property tax, do not have adequate facilities for assessing

---

[15] Theoretical and administrative problems of this tax are discussed at greater length by W. W. Hewitt, "The Taxation of Increases in Personal Income," *Bulletin* of the National Tax Association, October, 1947, pp. 11–16.

[16] Nondollar income that nevertheless has a market-value equivalent in dollars, for example, the flow of satisfaction from the ownership of a home.

on the basis of capitalized dollar and imputed income. They find it easier to infer the yield of property from its assessed value than to collect information on its income. Another point should be mentioned: Unless the imputed income of an owner-occupied home is taxed under the income tax, the elimination of the property tax would mean that such residential property would escape both the income and the property tax. Thus we conclude that, granted efficient administration, it is desirable that both property and the income from property be taxed.

▶ STATE INCOME TAXATION

The states have left the income tax field pretty much to the federal government in spite of the fact that they made use of income taxes long before the federal government did so. The taxation of income by many of the states has been closely bound up with the taxation of property and property income. Some of the colonies made use of a faculty tax, basing ability to pay on income as well as property. In some cases the income feature survived. It was Wisconsin's famous income tax of 1911 which demonstrated that a state could derive substantial revenues from this source. Her experience revived state interest in the taxation of income.

The adoption of the federal income tax, and the rapid exploitation of its possibilities for progression, sharply restricted the scope for income taxation by the states. Some of them introduced the income tax primarily in an effort to tax more nearly according to ability to pay. In general, however, the states, like the federal government in 1861, regarded the income tax simply as an alternative to the property tax. When the property tax could no longer bear the load of rapidly increasing state functions, public interest began to rise in state income taxes. The sales tax was popular, however, in those states where it was not possible to enlist legislative sentiment in favor of lessened inequality of income, although some states adopted both sales and income taxes. Even in income tax states, the rates and degrees of progression were largely determined by revenue needs rather than by an interest in progression as such.

Although only two thirds of the states have income taxes, in many more the issue is subject to lively debate. The vast increase in state functions has made the problem of new revenue sources acute. During the depression the property tax collapsed. At the same time new sources of revenue were needed for relief, payments for which were stimulated in connection with matching federal grants-in-aid for old-age assistance. As the federal government continued to encourage the extension of state activities through this device, revenue needs of the states rose still further. Moreover, the states on their own initiative extended such functions as police, public institutions, and publicity and promotion.

The income tax laws of the several states differ so greatly that it is difficult to make general statements about them. The states differ, for example, in what is included in gross income. Some (e.g., Tennessee) apply the personal income tax to investment income only. The treatment of capital gains and losses varies, as well as that of interest and dividends. The states also differ in the extent to which they claim jurisdiction over income earned outside their borders, and inequitable double taxation has occurred where they have been slow in introducing reciprocal legislation. Otherwise the state income tax form is fairly similar to that of the federal income tax. In 1953 the top tax rate of any state was that of North Dakota, at 15 per cent on net income above $15,000 (reduced to 11 per cent in July of that year) but it is substantially less than this in most states. Some states (e.g., Massachusetts) make use of flat rates which differ for different types of income.

From the point of view of taxpayer compliance, it would greatly simplify matters if the states could adopt the practice of the federal government in the calculation of net income subject to tax. If this were done the state income tax return would be a duplicate of that sent to the federal government.[17] Apart from the desire of the states for independence in these matters, however, the frequent changes in federal tax law might make it difficult for the states to accept the plan. This objection would be partly removed if, as is the present practice in Virginia, the rate of tax were announced each year in the light of revenue needs and estimated income subject to tax. Thus the state would retain independence with respect to the yield of the tax.

► CITY INCOME TAXES

In recent years a few cities have introduced an income tax. Little attention is paid to equity and ability to pay in these low flat-rate taxes, which are applied to an income base from which exemptions and deductions are in general not permitted. Collection is effected by employer withholding, and unless, as is usually done, the tax is applied to commuters an obvious inequity arises between those employed and living in the city, and those who enjoy the benefits provided by its laws and institutions while residing outside its jurisdiction.

The popularity of city income taxes is likely to spread if they prove administratively feasible and sufficiently productive, but at present less than 1 per cent of local tax revenues comes from these taxes. City income tax bases often include some income in addition to wages, but none include the bulk of investment income. On the other hand, the income tax

---

[17] In 1951 Utah adopted a provision under the personal income tax which allows taxpayers using the simplified tax table of the federal income tax to pay 10 per cent of the federal tax as an alternative to calculating their tax liability under the state rules. This was subsequently abandoned, however. The Alaskan territorial tax is set at 10 per cent of the federal tax.

constitutes an important revenue source in those cities that use it. In Philadelphia, for example, nearly one third of total general revenues was derived from the income tax in 1950. The rate of 1.25 per cent, applicable to wages only, was the highest among city income taxes, the most usual rate being 1 per cent.

Local income taxes are levied in only four states. The extensive grant of tax powers by the state of Pennsylvania to its municipalities in 1947 stimulated widespread adoption of local income taxes, until over two hundred such taxes were in operation by 1950. The possibility of double taxation and the need for tax reciprocity, also a problem under state income taxation, have especially to be guarded against under the city income taxes. It frequently happens that neighboring localities impose income taxes when they find some of their residents paying a tax to a nearby city in which they work. The general rule in Pennsylvania (except for Philadelphia) is that if the tax is levied at equal rates in both localities, the community of residence gets the tax *in toto*. When the rates are not equal, the amount paid to the latter is deductible from the amount due to the community in which the taxpayer works.

▶ QUANTITATIVE IMPORTANCE OF INCOME TAXES

The personal income tax accounted for nearly one half of total federal internal revenues in fiscal 1954.[18] Out of total internal revenue collections of $69.9 billion, the personal income tax produced $32.8 billion, or nearly 47 per cent. In contrast, the corporate income tax accounted for 31 per cent, and federal taxes on consumption[19] for about 13 per cent. Although the federal income tax yield has increased tremendously since 1929 in terms of current dollars (that is, not correcting for the price level), receipts in 1929 of $1.1 billion accounted for 37 per cent of federal tax revenues. During the decade of the thirties the income tax decreased in relative importance, the percentage being about 20 in 1939. Thereafter it rose rapidly to 44 per cent in 1945, and to about 50 per cent in fiscal 1948, before the rate reductions of that year. In 1951 it was slightly less than 46 per cent.

Relatively few important changes have occurred in the rates of the state income taxes since 1939. Some states have increased their rates moderately, and others have decreased them. Most rates have remained unchanged. Nevertheless, the proportion of total state taxes accounted for by the income tax has substantially risen. This is the natural response of

---

[18] This includes employment taxes of more than 5 per cent, only half of which are appropriately treated as personal income taxes, the remainder being paid by the employer.

[19] Including the following taxes: liquor, tobacco, manufacturers' and retailers' excises, telephone and telegraph, transportation, and admissions. Forward shifting is assumed.

a relatively elastic tax to rises in personal income. In 1932 the ratio was about 4 per cent; by 1939 it had risen to 6.4 per cent; and in 1953, to 9.2 per cent,[20] when total state receipts from this tax were $969 million. Although the yield of the personal income tax exceeded that of the corporation income tax, a much more important source of state revenue was the sales and gross receipts taxes, at $6.2 billion. Licenses accounted for another $1.5 billion or 15 per cent. Oregon, New York, and Wisconsin led the states in the proportion of total tax revenues accounted for by the personal income tax. At the local level the income tax is insignificant for the municipalities as a whole.

► THE CONCEPT OF TAXABLE INCOME

Income for purposes of the federal income tax consists of "net income" minus personal exemptions. Net income is arrived at by deducting certain types of losses and expenses from gross income. The latter, in turn, is a basket concept that is built up out of "gains, profits and income derived from any source whatever." It includes gains on sales or exchanges, wages, salaries, business profits, dividends and interest received, rents and royalties, commissions, bonuses and tips, and prizes. Behind this concept of taxable net income lie assumptions as to the nature of income. In an effort to refine the concept of taxable income, revenue authorities have frequently altered the definition. It is useful to relate the federal concept of taxable income, as it exists at the present time, to other possible concepts of income.

THE ECONOMIST'S DEFINITION

Ideally, income should be regarded as the net accretion to the economic power of the individual between two dates, added to the amount spent by him on consumption during that period.[21] In practice it has not been possible to get into the tax base either the whole of an individual's

[20] Bureau of the Census, *Historical Statistics on State and Local Government, 1902–1953*.

[21] An earnest supporter of this concept of income was Henry Simons (*Personal Income Taxation* [Chicago: University of Chicago Press, 1938], p. 51), who defines it as the sum of a person's consumption and the change in his assets between two dates. Compare R. M. Haig's concept: "the money value of the net accretion to one's economic power between two points of time," in *The Federal Income Tax* (New York: Columbia University Press, 1921), p. 7, which, properly interpreted, would include consumption spending during the taxable year. Note the following illustration:

	Individual A	Individual B
1. Value of Net Assets on January 1, 1954	$100,000	$ 90,000
2. Consumption Spending in 1953	10,000	20,000
Total	110,000	110,000
3. Value of Net Assets on January 1, 1953	100,000	100,000
4. Income	10,000	10,000

consumption or the entire increase in his economic power. The reason is that (1) a portion of a person's consumption consists of goods or services consumed directly as he produces them, and (2) not all of the increase in the economic power of an individual is realized in the form of dollar income.

A part of income consumed directly can, of course, be included in the tax base. For example, a presumptive estimate can be made of the value of home-grown food on farms.[22] But to do this for all directly consumed income would be a considerable administrative task, and might be regarded as excessive government interference. The taxation of unrealized capital gains, again, presents administrative problems that make it unlikely to be adopted in practice. Moreover, part of the increase may be in a form not measurable in terms of dollars. Thus a proprietorship may accumulate not only plant and equipment but also good will. Any evaluation of the latter is arbitrary, and therefore difficult to assess equitably. Consequently, for purposes of a tax declaration, the concept "economic power" would be translated into tangible "net worth." The taxpayer would declare his assets as of the beginning of each of two successive years, and add this difference (or subtract it if negative) to the amount spent on consumption.

One reason for hesitation in the adoption of this equitable and theoretically sound basis for calculating income subject to the income tax is the greater administrative and compliance cost that it would involve. Income is calculated indirectly rather than by making a series of deductions from a gross income figure composed of the various types of taxable income. Few people keep records of consumption, and it is hard to see how they could be forced to do so on any accurate basis. Moreover, the problem of placing a value on one's assets each year would be considerable, though not insuperable.[23] Marketable stocks and bonds can be valued with reference to the market. But not all assets have a very determinate market value. Homes are difficult to value in areas where there is little turnover. Personal property consisting of durable goods is subject to a very imperfect market. Not only is it often unstandardized, but it is partly worn out. Changes in the price level likewise would complicate the task of placing a valuation on property not traded in a continuous market.

INCOME AS CONSUMPTION

Some economists have urged that only that part of a man's income should be subject to income tax that he actually consumes during the

---

[22] Certain states require farmers to include as taxable income a presumptive estimate that is standardized.

[23] There is good reason to think that the application of this device under the Treasury's proposed wartime spendings tax might have been workable. The difficulties of achieving equity would be great, however, particularly during the period when the tax was being introduced. Cf. A. G. Hart and E. C. Brown, *Financing Defense* (New York: Twentieth Century Fund, 1951), pp. 78–86.

taxable year. In other words, savings should be exempt from the income tax regardless of the source or the size of the income, so that the income tax would be a tax on spending only. Since it is a little difficult for anyone convinced of the justice of the ability-to-pay principle of taxation to understand the reasoning behind this suggestion, something should be said of its background.[24]

Economics deals with the maximization of welfare in a world of scarcities, and among the scarcities is that of capital for investment in cost-reducing roundabout production processes. It follows that so long as business firms are restricted in their ability to build new plant and equipment by lack of savings, a case can be made for encouraging, or at least not discouraging, the savings of individuals and corporations.

One obvious way to do this is to exempt part or all of the saved portion of income from income taxation. This solution relies on the smooth and uninterrupted transformation of savings into productive capital instruments, and implies that as of a particular moment of time tax equity among income groups is less important than encouragement to a rapid increase in productivity. The lower-income receivers can save little, and therefore would receive little or no benefit from the exemption of savings from taxation; it is the high-income savers that would benefit from the exemption of savings from the income tax. Since these savings themselves yield a return, the exemption of savings would contribute to a steady widening of the gap between the economic status of low- and high-income receivers.

The proposal to exempt savings from the income tax bears a resemblance to the old abstinence theory of the origin of interest, which regarded interest as a payment to savers for performing the sacrifice of refraining from spending the whole of their incomes. Actually, the higher one's income the less is likely to be the disutility in the sacrifice of consumption that is required in order to save. Thus the abstinence theory meets with no support today. But in the free-enterprise economy no escape can easily be found from the dilemma that a growth of savings and real capital may have to be associated with a relative increase in the economic power of the classes whose incomes are high enough to permit automatic saving.

Apart from the equity considerations discussed above, the restriction

---

[24] Irving Fisher was an ardent supporter of the view that only the enjoyment of consumers' goods should be called income, while savings ought to be viewed as an increase of capital. He distinguished between *earned* income and *realized* income, the former including savings. By excluding increases in a man's capital from income, he arrived at the conclusion that realized income is restricted to spending on consumption. *On this definition* it follows that to tax earned income, which includes savings, instead of realized income alone, is "double taxation to the saver and remission of taxes to the spendthrift."—Irving Fisher, *The Nature of Capital and Income* (New York: Macmillan, 1919), p. 255. John Stuart Mill also recommended the restriction of the income tax to spending.

of the income tax base to that part of income spent on consumption raises questions of major importance for the maintenance of stable, high-level employment. These will be discussed in detail in later chapters. Here it is only necessary to say that it is an advantage, from the point of view of long-term increases in productivity, to encourage savings during periods when investment demand is high. But when savings are lying idle for want of investment outlets, the restriction of the income tax to consumption spending would obviously worsen matters. Since periods of high and low investment succeed one another over the years, a permanent spendings tax would be as likely to depress as to stimulate economic activity; and if any sustained tendency toward underinvestment were to develop in the economy, acceptance of the spendings concept of income under the income tax would aggravate it. Therefore, little support exists for so restricting the income tax.[25]

In conclusion reference may be made to the Treasury's spendings tax proposal of 1942, to be discussed in Chapter 13. It differed from the Mill-Fisher type in that it was to be progressive according to the amount spent, and was regarded as an addition to the ordinary income tax, not a substitute for it. Although both these types of tax apply to spending, the emphasis is different. The Mill-Fisher version is primarily concerned with stimulating saving, and therefore investment. It simply ignores the corollary effect on consumption spending on the ground that no deficiency of total spending need be reckoned with. The Treasury's version was concerned with forcing a reduction in personal consumption at a time when a reduction was necessary during a period of inflationary war spending. The two proposals differ, therefore, in the economic contexts to which they are meant to be applied.

PSYCHOLOGICAL INCOME AND LEISURE

Before we turn, in the next chapter, to an analysis of the federal income tax, a few words may be said concerning two types of income which no one seriously argues ought to be taxed but which are nevertheless income. Psychological income and leisure would be difficult in practice to translate into dollars, and thus they could hardly be included in a tax declaration. Yet since individuals frequently make a choice between earning dollar income and, for example, enjoying leisure, these types of income are not without interest from a conceptual point of view. Pleasant working

---

[25] The enormous need for capital by the government in connection with the cold war after 1945 convinced some economists of the desirability of discriminating in favor of savings under the tax system. Sumner Slichter has argued for the application of lower income tax rates to that part of income that is saved. See "The Problem of Inflation," *Review of Economics and Statistics,* February, 1948, and the "Reply" by James Tobin, *American Economic Review,* December, 1949. Another strong advocate of the view that savings should be encouraged, even at the cost of income inequality, is D. M. Wright ("Income Redistribution Reconsidered," in *Income, Employment and Public Policy,* Essays in Honor of Alvin Hansen [New York: Norton, 1948]).

conditions and proximity to mountain and seaside resorts constitute income for which the individual is frequently willing to pay cash or sacrifice dollar income. This is evidenced whenever a worker refuses a job at a higher wage rate because he feels himself satisfied in his present position. The dollar worth of this psychological income can be measured. Obviously *some* wage will attract him, and the differential between the wage he is getting and the wage he could get in a less pleasant occupation is the dollar value of his psychic income. It is well known, for example, that certain department stores have been able to pay less than the going wage because of the valuation placed by the staff on the privilege of serving a given class of customer. Again, disagreeable occupations often, though by no means always, pay a premium intended to offset their disadvantage.

Although the taxation of psychological income lies outside the area of practical policy, the same effect is achieved if a subsidy (i.e., a negative tax) is paid out of the general revenues to workers engaged in unpopular occupations. An example would be a subsidy for the purpose of increasing the wages of coal miners, for on the assumption that a given amount of revenue is to be raised from a tax on wage and salary incomes, the subsidy makes higher tax rates necessary on incomes from more desirable occupations.

A conceptually very important exclusion from gross income subject to income tax is the imputed income of leisure and the shorter working day. Here again, no one has seriously suggested imputing a money income to the shorter workweek in order to subject such "income" to the income tax. But it is a fact that worker income subject to income tax is less than it would have been had hours of work not been reduced as much as they have over the years.[26] This statement has one important qualification, however. Worker productivity is greater when hours per week are not excessive. The optimum workweek differs in different types of work. All that one can assert is that in most instances when the workweek declines from, say, forty-eight hours, worker productivity does not increase, but the worker is preferring to take his income partly in the form of leisure.

Can the government afford under all circumstances to ignore the tendency of the working force to substitute leisure for spendable income.[27] There are two aspects to the question. (1) In terms of dollars, at a given

---

[26] It is partly because of the growth of leisure that labor's share of national income paid out has remained fairly constant in the vicinity of 60 per cent since the Civil War. See the study by S. Kuznets, *National Income: A Summary of Findings* (New York: National Bureau of Economic Research, 1946), p. 49.

[27] For an illustration of how the matter is handled in Russia the following news item from the *New York Times*, August 15, 1954, may be cited. A law was adopted in 1953 in the USSR which provides that "any family of collective farmers having a member who does not fulfill the minimum number of labor days work required must pay an income tax 50 per cent higher than the general rate for each area." The purpose is to reduce the time spent on gardening for the family's own use, thus releasing manpower for national economic goals.

price level the taxable income base is narrowed. (2) In terms of real production, the real income base, to a share of which the government asserts a claim, is likewise smaller. Moreover, to the extent that workers devote part of their leisure to producing goods that they consume directly (for example, growing their own vegetables and painting their own houses) factors of production are in a form that cannot easily be diverted to government use. A factory can be converted to war production, along with all its workers. It is less easy to draft the older worker who devotes his leisure to working around the home.

No sentiment arises for limiting the freedom of the worker to choose between leisure and work during an era of peace, and in the absence of competition with powerful national adversaries for leadership in the output of capital and military goods. The implications of permitting this freedom during periods of national emergency, however, may be serious. They are brought into focus by a consideration of the relation between trends of per capita productivity and length of workweek during past periods. Thus according to one study, per capital real income increased at the rate of 2¼ per cent a year from 1869 to 1909, while the average from 1909 to 1941 was only 1 per cent.[28] During the latter period the standard workweek outside agriculture fell from fifty-five to forty-four hours.

Great care must be used in drawing inferences from a comparison of these figures, since annual increments to productivity can be measured in various ways, and are subject to different interpretations. But changes in the length of the workweek and in the size of the labor force are major causes of variations in per capita productivity. Thus during World War II per capital real income increased tremendously. This was owing almost entirely, however, to the increase in the length of the workweek, to the inclusion in the labor force of women and other groups not normally accepting work, and to a shift toward the production of military goods, for which output per man-hour is relatively high.

The question may sometime have to be faced whether the same amount of discretion as formerly can be left to the individual in his choice between work and leisure. The enormous cost of military equipment at the present level of technological development indicates that circumstances could arise in which this problem would have to be solved if the nation were to survive. The situation might force either governmental direction of the labor market (a device that has been adopted, among the democracies, in Great Britain), or changes in the tax system designed to alter the choice between work and leisure in favor of the former. If the latter were adopted, greater public support could be enlisted by making the maximum possible

[28] R. F. Martin, *National Income in the United States, 1799–1939* (New York: National Industrial Conference Board, 1939), brought through 1941 by the NICB in its *Economic Almanac*. See J. J. Spengler, "Prospective Population and Income Growth and Fiscal Policy," *National Tax Journal*, March, 1950, p. 39.

use of subsidies as a reward to increased effort, or for moving out of less to more important lines of work. These subsidies could take the form, for example, of lower income tax rates on income derived from hours worked above a certain weekly standard. In any event, there are no present indications that this problem is likely to become critical in the foreseeable future in this country.

► REFERENCES

BLACK, D. *The Incidence of Income Taxes.* London: Macmillan & Co., Ltd., 1939.

BLAKEY, R. G., and G. C. BLAKEY. *The Federal Income Tax.* New York: Longmans, Green and Co., 1940.

BLAKEY, R. G., and V. JOHNSON. *State Income Taxes.* Chicago: Commerce Clearing House, 1942.

BREAK, G. F. "Income Taxes, Wage Rates, and the Incentive to Supply Labor Services," *National Tax Journal,* December, 1953, pp. 333–352.

BUTTERS, J. K., L. E. THOMPSON, and L. L. BOLLINGER. *Effects of Taxation: Investments by Individuals.* Boston: Harvard University, Graduate School of Business Administration, 1953.

FISHER, I., and H. FISHER. *Constructive Income Taxation.* New York: Harper & Brothers, 1942.

QUINTO, L. J. *Municipal Income Taxation in the United States.* New York: Mayor's Committee on Management. Survey of the City of New York, 1952.

SIMONS, H. *Personal Income Taxation.* Chicago: The University of Chicago Press, 1938.

VICKREY, W. *Agenda for Progressive Taxation.* New York: The Ronald Press, 1947.

9 The Personal Income Tax: II

► CONCEPT OF INCOME UNDER THE FEDERAL INCOME TAX[1]

The concept of income employed under the federal income tax necessarily differs in many respects from the ideal of income as an increase in economic power plus consumption. When the income concept is arrived at by aggregating various components of income, it is inevitable that administrative considerations and court decisions will cause the actual definition of income to differ from that of the accountant or the economist. Expediency as well as trial and error play their part. The best way to understand the problems that must be faced in striving for a logical definition of taxable income is to examine the federal income tax concept of the taxable income of the individual, along with his exemptions and deductions.

CONSTRUCTIVE RECEIPT OF INCOME

Income that is "constructively" received must be included in gross income. That is, income is taxable when, under the taxpayer's system of accounting, it is owing to him. For example, interest due the holder of a Series E bond at maturity may not actually be collected. But since it has become legally the property of the taxpayer, he must enter it in his gross income for that year.

Constructive receipt of income has come to be of significance for the average worker, since the sums withheld in connection with payroll deductions for the purchase of government bonds, group life and health insurance, employees' social security taxes, current payment of income tax, and so on, must be included in gross income. Other examples of constructive receipt are the cancellation of a debt in return for services performed

---

[1] The federal income tax is explained in an annual treasury publication: *Your Federal Income Tax*. An aid in making out income tax forms is J. K. Lasser, *Your Income Tax*, published annually (New York: Simon and Shuster). Much greater detail, coupled with convenience, may also be found in the tax manuals, for example, Prentice-Hall, Inc., *Federal Tax Handbook;* and Commerce Clearing House, *United States Master Tax Guide*. There are also a number of tax services which are invaluable for keeping current on court interpretations.

(otherwise it is a gift); profits paid to the taxpayer's agent or broker whether or not he exercises the right to receive them himself; and payments made for prior services even though the taxpayer does not wish to accept them. The taxpayer is not allowed to defer receipt of income until it is convenient, or in order to reduce the bracket rate to which he is subject in the current taxable year.

GROSS INCOME

Gross income is arrived at under the federal individual income tax return by adding up the various types of income that can accrue to the individual. Separate schedules are provided for wages; salaries; dividends; interest; profit or loss from a business, profession, or farm; net gain or loss from sales of capital assets; annuities and pensions; rents and royalties; estates and trusts; and finally the usual catchall item "other sources." In view of the comprehensiveness of this definition it would appear that all conceivable types of income are included in the concept "gross income." However, not only are there several explicit exclusions, but some types of receipts are rightly not regarded as partaking of the nature of income. An example is receipts arising from the repayment of debt.

The income tax law is silent about certain types of income that are not easily subject to measurement, and which, because they are consumed directly, do not appear in a transaction for money. Before considering the specific exclusions and deductions from gross income, it will be useful to consider the equity and economic implications of these special exclusions.

Income Consumed Directly. The treatment of *imputed* income for income tax purposes has varied in different jurisdictions and over time. Occasional attempts have been made to tax certain types of income that are consumed directly, and thus do not take the form of taxable income under ordinary definitions. In Britain, for example, a rent is imputed to the ownership of a home, and this rent is includible in the income tax base. Considerable scope exists for refining the income tax base in the interest of equity as among individuals whose real income is the same but who differ in the proportion of income that is received in the form of money. Differential tax treatment of imputed and money income results in changes in the income tax base that are quite haphazard. They arise out of the fact that services previously performed by the individual for himself may now be sold to him by others for taxable income, and conversely.

Along with the problem facing the taxpayer in finding the cash to pay the tax, the major problem with respect to the taxation of imputed income is therefore one of equity.[2] When the tax is strongly progressive, however,

---

[2] Non-money income assumes great importance with respect to studies of the distribution of income. Since these studies have not ordinarily attempted to take account of income paid in kind, as well as most other types of imputed income, it is certain that the distribution of real income (including psychological income, leisure, and so

the question of effects on incentives also arises. The problem is the more acute because the exclusion of large amounts of *imputed* income from the tax base means that the rates applicable to income received in *money* form must be higher than would otherwise be necessary. Serious disincentive effects may arise if the family's marginal (i.e., top) bracket rate is applied to the income of the working wife, and if deductions for maid service and other expenses that would not otherwise be incurred are not allowed. One way to achieve equal treatment would be to require that the imputed income of housewives be included in the income tax base. If this seemed too unpopular, the alternative course might be taken of allowing the working wife to subtract from her earned income the imputed income she would have earned as a housewife. The loss of revenue would, however, require higher bracket rates. Although the tax would be fairer, at a high level of national spending, the higher tax rates would add to the disincentive effects of the income tax.

An Owned Home.   A very significant distinction is made under the American income tax between renters and home owners. The former must pay a tax on the income out of which they pay their rent. Home owners, on the other hand, are exempt under the income tax from the imputed rent of their homes. This exemption occurs by virtue of the fact that the flow of income yielded by durable consumers' goods is not expressed in terms of dollars.

Of two men with equal incomes, one may have invested his savings in stocks, the other in his house. The former pays income tax on his dividends.[3] If the owner has a mortgage, a greater differential exists because taxes and the interest paid on a mortgage are deductible from gross income in arriving at the income tax base.[4]

---

on), is different from the distribution of money income. Therefore, proposed fiscal and other measures for redistributing income in the interest of greater equality must be judged on the basis of the extent to which they recognize the consequences of identifying money income with total real income. This problem is discussed in some detail in Chapter 23.

[3] Assume that an owner and a renter, each with a salary of $5,000 a year, occupy similar homes worth $10,000. The renter pays $500 rent, but has invested his savings of $10,000 in stocks yielding 5 per cent. Then since the owner does not include imputed rent in his taxable income his tax base is only $5,000, while that of the renter is $5,500. If homes and bonds, stocks, and savings bank deposits were perfectly substitutable forms of personal savings, the effect of this concession to the home owner would be to increase the demand for houses relative to that for rentals. This would eliminate the advantage to the home owner. But many who are able to save the amount necessary to buy a home do not live in areas in which homes can be bought. Consequently owing to market imperfections the home owner remains in possession of what amounts to a subsidy from the Treasury.

[4] However, the provision that allows a standard deduction of 10 per cent of adjusted gross income up to a maximum of $1,000 nullifies this latter advantage for the bulk of home owners. Since the man may take this standard deduction whether or not he incurs the expense, the effect is to eliminate the tax and interest deductibility for all those whose total itemized deductions do not exceed the 10 per cent standard deduction.

Although it is difficult to avoid the conclusion that the income tax law should be changed to remedy the inequity that exempts the home owner from including imputed rent in his tax base, it must not be supposed that this change would automatically bring about complete equity. The home owner is liable to many repair and maintenance expenses which the renter escapes. And if required by circumstances to move quickly to another area he may incur the capital loss incident to a partially forced sale. In any case he ordinarily pays a 5 per cent commission to the realtor. Again, the inclusion of the rent of an owned home in the income tax base still leaves unanswered the question of the rent of durable instruments other than homes, for example, automobiles, clothes, and so on. It would be difficult to know where to draw the line.

SPECIFIC EXEMPTIONS FROM GROSS INCOME

The exclusions from gross income mentioned thus far arise for the most part out of the circumstance that the income tax concept has usually been restricted to money income. In addition there are exclusions of income received in the form of cash or its equivalent that are specifically exempted from gross income. Gross income is a basket item, which under present law, includes salaries, wages, rent and royalties, tips, bonuses, business profits, interest, dividends, realized capital gains (to a limited extent), gambling winnings, and prizes won in a contest.[5]

Alimony is now taxable as income to the recipient, not to the one making the payment. The latter may deduct it from his adjusted gross income. It would be interesting to know whether and how far alimony judgments will take account of the fact that the recipient must pay an income tax. To the extent that judgments tend to become more generous the tax is shifted to the payer. But the shift in the tax liability from payer to payee has the effect of reducing the marginal income tax rate of the former. The husband's marginal bracket rate is likely to be higher than the wife's. Thus even to the extent that the tax is shifted, some concession is usually automatically being made to the payer to take account of the fact that it costs more to support a wife and children outside the home of the payer of the income tax. However, unless he remarries, he loses the benefit of income splitting.

Gifts and bequests are excluded from gross income under present law on the grounds that the income has already been taxed in the hands of the donor, and that no service is performed in return. They are taxed,

---

[5] Under the 1954 revision of the tax code all prizes and awards were subjected to tax except those made in recognition of past achievements in the nature of a public service. Court decisions had regarded prizes on giveaway programs as not to be income. The Tax Court of the United States held, in a decision in November, 1954, that grants made by foundations for research purposes are not taxable, even though the recipient is expected to perform research services in return for the grant.

however, under the federal gift and estate taxes, as well as under the parallel system of state death taxation. Interest on state and local bonds is not subject to the federal income tax, nor is interest on federal obligations taxable by the states. Some income formerly excluded from the federal income tax base is now taxable, for example, salaries of state and local employees. Before 1940 interest on federal securities was exempt from the normal federal income tax, but not from the surtax. Finally, it is a nice legal problem whether proceeds of a robbery ought to be taxed, since the possessor does not have legal title to them. The Supreme Court has ruled that embezzled funds are not taxable. This is a matter of some importance to the business that hopes to recover the money from an embezzler. A recent ruling of the Supreme Court, however, has treated money obtained by extortion as taxable.[6]

Other statutory exclusions are life insurance proceeds paid by reason of the death of the insured, part of the compensation paid members of the armed forces, payments to veterans, earned income up to $20,000 of a United States citizen living abroad more than 18 months, sickness and disability benefits, the rental value of a residence furnished to a clergyman, and other miscellaneous items. The 1954 act excluded the first $50 of dividends from tax (in addition to providing a credit against tax of 4 per cent of dividends in excess of the exclusion). This provision was intended as an answer to the objection that the federal tax system discriminates against corporate income by taxing both corporate income and the dividends paid out of it.

THE EXEMPTION OF INTEREST ON GOVERNMENT SECURITIES

Reciprocal tax exemption of the interest on federal, and state and local, securities owes its existence to the fear on the part of the Supreme Court, as expressed in a long series of opinions, that the states might use the tax instrument to the injury of the federal government. Thus federal securities may not be taxed under state and local income or property taxes. In the famous case of *McCulloch v. Maryland* (1819), Chief Justice Marshall's opinion denied the right of a state to tax the instrumentalities of the federal government.[7] By extension the argument applies also to the taxation of state and local instrumentalities by the federal government.

The operation of this principle is not unlimited, however, for govern-

---

[6] In a five-to-four decision, March 24, 1952. In his dissent Justice Black stated his disbelief that Congress intended to treat the plunder of criminals as their legitimate income.—*New York Times,* March 25, 1952.

[7] This doctrine has been used to the detriment of the states and cities in that the Court accepted the principle that, *whether or not the tax is discriminatory,* it may not be applied to federal instrumentalities. Only a discriminatory tax could cause the damage to another level of government envisaged by the Supreme Court; therefore all that was necessary was to forbid discriminatory taxation.

ment securities are taxable under the estate, inheritance, and gift taxes, and the income from tax-exempt federal securities is subject to state taxes on corporate income. Some progress was made in remedying the reciprocal tax-exemption abuse in 1939, when by virtue of Supreme Court decisions and the Public Salary Tax Act, federal and state governments were permitted to tax the salaries of one another's employees. (Cities and towns receive their powers from the states, and the latter are therefore free to tax the instrumentalities of the former.)

Because the Sixteenth Amendment empowered the federal government to tax all income, regardless of source, it would appear that constitutionally there could be no objection to removing the federal income tax exemption from interest on state bonds. This step has not been taken, partly because of a fear of the political repercussions of what would seem to many a further encroachment on the powers of the states by the federal government; and the first permanent income tax act (1913) established a precedent by specifically exempting interest on state and local bonds.

PROBLEMS IN REMOVING THE EXEMPTION

Tax exemption of interest on government securities has inevitably given rise to vested interests that make its abolition difficult even if desirable. Those who have already bought tax-exempt securities would presumably have to be recompensed if the exemption were removed. Again, the states and cities are loath to surrender the advantage of lower interest rates resulting from the market evaluation of the worth of the exemption. In competing for the supply of tax-exempts, investors drive the price up and the effective interest rate down. Proposals have been made to compensate for both of these losses. Holders of outstanding bonds could be given an appropriate tax credit, and the states and localities might receive federal subsidies geared to the increased cost of borrowing.[8]

Apart from the dislike of the lower levels of government for surren-

---

By employing the concept in too inclusive a manner, the Supreme Court has put the federal government in the position of making it difficult for states and cities to tax property within their boundaries. The principle has been carried so far as to prohibit sales taxation within military posts. The problem is particularly acute in states in which federally owned land constitutes a large proportion of the whole. The federal government has given some relief in the form of voluntary grants for the support of state and town services. But these grants suffer from being *ad hoc* and based on different principles from those which govern tax payments made by similar property not owned by the federal government.

[8] See the proposal, for example, of L. C. Fitch, *Taxing Municipal Bond Income* (Berkeley: University of California Press, 1950). An example will illustrate the interest-reducing effect of the tax exemption. The income tax saving causes the demand curve for tax-exempts to shift to the right. Their prices thus rise. Suppose a bond has been issued at $1,000 to yield $30. If the price rises to $1,100, the effective rate of interest is no longer 3 per cent, but $30/$1,100, or 2.7% (assuming a no-maturity bond).

dering what they regard as a constitutional right, considerable difficulties face any attempt to assess the value of the exemption privilege. A number of factors influence the yield of government securities, of which tax exemption is only one. Unless a mutually satisfactory formula could be found, the way would be paved for much bickering over the size of the subsidy. Moreover, there is a valid argument against multiplying federal subsidies. A tax exemption offers less scope for an extension of federal control over the states and localities than does the introduction of another subsidy.

The exemption has been attacked on several grounds: (1) To the extent that investors purchase tax-exempts instead of investing in riskier forms of enterprise, the latter may find it more difficult to obtain the funds necessary for expansion. (2) Taking all governmental jurisdictions together, aggregate revenues are reduced because of the exemption. This is connected wtih still another objection, namely (3), that high-income purchasers of tax-exempt securities are presented with a tax exemption which is in many instances greater than necessary to induce investment in the tax-exempts. Because of the progression of the income tax rate, the interest cost saving to the states and cities is less than the tax saving to the higher-income purchaser of the securities, who saves more in tax than does the lower-income purchaser. Abundant supplies of securities tend to be so priced that the higher-income purchaser gets a bargain.

Since it is *federal* taxes that the purchaser of the security saves, the states and cities are naturally not very conscious of the loss of tax revenues. Some economists have suggested that the federal government could make needed grants to the states out of the added revenue from taxing the income from municipal and state issues. The states, however, can hardly be criticized for not placing much faith in the suggestion that the resulting increase in federal tax receipts would actually be placed at their disposal. Moreover, although abolition of the exemption would tend to increase the effective progression of the federal income tax, many states and cities would be likely to turn to the regressive sales tax to finance any added interest cost.

Many states and most cities benefit from the tax-exemption privilege despite the fact that for the economy as a whole revenues are lost. Thus a minority pressure group resists its abolition. Moreover, even if a state or city does lose revenues on balance, this consideration may not necessarily outweigh its need to have available at all times a good market for its securities. The states and cities argue that they need the advantage of tax exemption if they are to compete in the capital market. They are at a disadvantage because of (1) the necessity of competing for the available supply of savings with the federal government as well as with private issuers, and (2) the fact that, unlike the federal government, they have neither unlimited tax power nor the ability to create money (via the Federal

Reserve System) if necessary in order to ensure the success of a bond issue.[9]

PENSION FUND PAYMENTS

Under "qualified" pension funds, payments made by an employer into an old-age pension fund are excluded from the employee's personal income tax, while payments made by the employee are taxed. If a plan qualifies, the employer's contributions are currently deductible as a business expense. A plan automatically qualifies if 56 per cent or more of the employees are covered, though the Commissioner of Internal Revenue may admit plans that do not meet this requirement. The purpose of requiring that the plan cover a large proportion of employees is to prevent discrimination in favor of highly paid executives. Even so, because of income tax rate progression the use of the pension plan does confer on a firm the opportunity to relieve the highly paid employee of part of his current income tax liability. When a raise takes the form of increased payments into a pension trust fund rather than an immediately taxable cash increase, a portion of income tax liability is postponed until retirement, when the executive is likely to find himself in a lower tax bracket. Compound interest on the forgone tax is also saved by the employee.

Pension payments made under qualified plans by the employer are deductible from the corporate income tax base. Therefore the advantage to the employer is partly paid for by the federal government. It must be remembered, of course, that when the pension system has reached maturity (no further excess of entries over retirements) the revenue loss will be somewhat mitigated by the tax due on retirement benefits. In an era of extremely high income tax rates, the case is quite strong for allowing tax exemption to a reasonable amount of saving for retirement and unforeseen contingencies. As the tax operates at present, however, without a ceiling to the amounts that are tax exempt in a given year, even without discrimination a result is to reduce sharply the effective progression of the income tax on very highly paid executives.

CAPITAL GAINS AND LOSSES

If capital gains are not realized they are not includible in gross income. Likewise, unrealized capital losses are excluded. When a capital

---

[9] Recently steps have been taken in some states to pass the tax-exemption privilege along to private industry in an attempt to attract business from other areas. States have permitted cities and towns to issue tax-free bonds for the purpose of building factories. These are then rented to business concerns, and the interest saving can be used as a subsidy for a period of years to a firm that will agree to move there. If this abuse, which is of course similar to property tax exemption for the same purpose, should become widespread, sentiment would grow for abolition of the exemption. In one instance the corporation that bought the securities issued by the city occupied the factory built with the proceeds of the loan.

gain or loss is realized through sale, special provisions apply. Detailed discussion of capital gains and losses is reserved for Chapter 10.

THE CONCEPT OF GROSS INCOME: SUMMARY

We have thus far been concerned solely with the problems involved in arriving at a definition of gross income for tax purposes that is equitable, and that corresponds reasonably well with the economist's concept of income. It has been shown that gross income, as the tax commissioner views it, is a basket concept. It is built up out of a large number of separate items that are declared to be income by law. Certain types of receipts of individuals that might conceivably be included in gross income are excluded. The reasons for their exclusion vary widely. Some, like leisure and psychological income, are excluded from the accepted concept of income. Other exclusions are made on administrative grounds, for example, income consumed directly. In other cases the reason is either habit or political pressure. An illustration is the exemption of the income accruing to the ownership of durable consumers' goods, particularly housing. Some exemptions have nothing to do with the concept of income. For example, the exemption of the interest on government securities by other levels of government arose out of an intergovernmental power conflict. Finally, one of the knottiest of the problems is the treatment of capital gains and losses. The next step is to proceed from gross income to taxable income.

► TAXABLE INCOME

As a further refinement intended to produce a logical definition of taxable income, federal income tax practice allows two sets of deductions from gross income. The first consists of deductible expenses incurred in connection with the production of income, together with allowable losses from a sale or an exchange of property. When these have been subtracted from gross income what is left is adjusted gross income. The second comprises the allowable deductions unconnected with business, which the taxpayer itemizes only if they exceed the 10 per cent standard deduction. Since the latter is limited to $1,000, a taxpayer actually incurring deductible expenses in excess of this amount will itemize them. (Since 1954 the personal and dependency exemptions have been converted from credits against net income to deductions from adjusted gross income.)

The standard deduction succeeded the "earned income credit." At the time this credit was repealed in 1943 it permitted a deduction of 10 per cent of income up to $14,000 for purposes of the normal tax but not the surtax. Since all income up to $3,000 was considered earned, and all over $14,000 unearned, the term "earned income credit" was not very accurate. Evidently large salaries were regarded as resembling property income. The discrimination against property income was not allowed to operate provided income was small (e.g., the case of a widow with not more than $3,000 of dividend income).

BUSINESS DEDUCTIONS

Business expenses are deductible, including depreciation, wages, taxes, interest, and the like. But they must be necessary and reasonable. The test is whether they can be construed as contributing to the income of the business or profession. It is in this area that much goes on that trespasses on the most elementary concept of ethics. This is probably inevitable when the taxpayer is required to make his own assessment, and in view of the fact that there are innumerable borderline cases that can only be decided by appeal to the courts.

A question may also arise as to how much of a particular business expense ought to be allowed under the criterion of reasonableness. For example, advertising cost is allowed as a business deduction. It would appear, however, that some limits ought to be set. Under high income tax rates there is an inducement to inflate advertising expenses on the ground that the government is footing most of the bill. Again, corporations are allowed to deduct charitable contributions up to 5 per cent of net income. In a partnership such deductions have to be made on the partner's personal return. Since businesses are under pressure to make charitable contributions in order to gain good will, the deduction encourages indirect government subsidies to charities.

Professional men may also deduct necessary expenses, but the deduction may not be taken by an employed professional man whose expenses are not directly related to the earning of his income. If he employs an assistant, the cost is not deductible unless a separate income arises (royalties) from which the assistant's salary can be deducted. The cost of attending conventions is deductible. So also are subscriptions to learned periodicals, but it should be noted that for the great majority of taxpayers employed on a salary basis the standard deduction nullifies this privilege unless this cost can be deducted from a source of income other than salary. Individuals in a position to deduct business expenses may be at an advantage, as compared with other wage and salary earners, because they derive personal satisfaction from at least a part of the expenses of running an automobile used in a business or profession, entertainment of customers, and travel expenses. Business expenses in the nature of capital expenditure must be prorated over the presumed useful life of the instrument.[10] Thus the cost of books bought by a professional man is deductible, but since books ordinarily have a useful life beyond one year, depreciation allowances are based on the estimate of useful life.

---

[10] It is not necessary that the straight-line method be used. For the 1954 accelerated depreciation provisions, see Chapter 11.

It is impossible to say what the loss in revenue is from unwarranted deductibility of business expenses, since certainly the greater part of it is a legitimate element of cost. The difficulties inherent in excluding unjustifiable deductions for business expense were highlighted in a law passed by the West German Parliament, in the summer of 1951, in an attempt to limit expense-account deductions to the amounts actually spent and allowable. It was necessary to state precisely the procedure to be followed by the businessman, even to the point of requiring the signature of the restaurateur who served the meals. Detailed provisions of this sort are generally unworkable. The Internal Revenue Service has operated through a tighter administrative policy on lavish expense accounts.

PERSONAL DEDUCTIONS

Deductions for personal expenses comprise interest paid on loans, deductible taxes, contributions (up to 20 per cent of adjusted gross income, plus another 10 per cent for specific charities), medical and dental expenses above a certain percentage of adjusted gross income (3 per cent, with a ceiling)[11] casualty losses, union dues, alimony payments by the one who makes the payment, and other miscellaneous items. Practice varies among the income tax laws of the states. Thus some states try to keep the contributions to charities within their own boundaries by restricting the deduction to "domestic" charities. Practice also varies from state to state as to deductibility of insurance premiums and federal income taxes.

The personal deductions are a hodgepodge of concessions to the taxpayer, some of which are justified and some not. Interest paid on a mortgage on an owned home ought not to be deductible if the interest indirectly paid by a renter is not. Limited contributions to charities by individuals ought probably to be deductible in order to help keep certain community enterprises financially independent of the federal government. The alimony deduction is equitable; but as we have seen, one possible effect could be to increase alimony judgments so that the recipient retains the net income intended by the court. This deduction means some loss of revenue owing to the fact that the husband is likely to be in a higher income bracket than the wife.

Practice with respect to the deductibility of sales taxes bears little relation to generally accepted analysis of the incidence of these taxes. A tax paid on sales is not deductible if, like a wholesale tax, it is not levied on the taxpayer directly. But he bears the burden just as much as if the original impact had been on him as well. Most state sales taxes, however,

---

[11] The ceiling for deductibility of medical expenses may work a hardship in cases where the payment is outside the control of the individual; but, on the other hand, it serves to discourage inflation of medical fees. The ceiling is now $2,500 per exemption, not to exceed $5,000 for a single person or separate return, and $10,000 for a joint return or head of household.

are retail taxes. Under the federal income tax, the *federal* income, estate, and gift taxes are not deductible, while customs and excises are deductible only to the extent that they are part of necessary business expense. State inheritance, estate, and gift taxes are not deductible from the federal income tax base, but state income taxes are deductible, as well as state and local property taxes and the gasoline tax. Social security taxes levied by the federal government are regarded as an income tax, and therefore are not deductible by the employee. However, they are a business expense, and are deductible by the employer.

DEDUCTIBILITY OF STATE INCOME TAXES

The significance of the deductibility from the federal income tax base of the income tax paid to a state needs particular emphasis because of its effect in encouraging uniformity among the state income tax laws.[12] Owing to the highly progressive federal rate structure, the deductibility of tax paid to the state permits the latter to make use of the income tax without causing an equal increase in total income tax liability. Indeed, at very high incomes the deductibility provision virtually obviates any increase in total liability. In such cases the deductibility provision is in effect a means of crediting the state with part of the tax paid to the federal government.

About two thirds of the states allow taxes paid to the federal government to be deducted from income subject to state tax. The effect of this provision is to reduce the total income tax liability of an individual living in an income tax state. But since state income taxes are in most cases quite low, the reduction is substantially less significant than in the case of federal deductibility of state taxes. The deductibility provision prevents the top rate on any income from exceeding 100 per cent. This is so even if the state does not permit the deduction of the federal tax from income subject to the state tax. The reason is that the state income tax is deductible from the *top* taxable bracket under the federal tax. This is illustrated in the following example.[13] Suppose the marginal (top) state bracket rate is 10 per cent, and that the federal government permits the state tax paid to be deducted from income subject to federal tax. Then the top $100.00 of income will always be subject to a deduction of $10.00 of state tax before income is arrived at for federal tax. At the lowest 1953 federal bracket rate of 22.2 per cent, for example, this means a federal tax of $19.98, which, added to the state tax of $10.00, gives a total tax of $29.98, or a combined marginal federal and state tax rate of 29.98 per cent. Let the federal marginal rate be moved up toward 100 per cent. It will be seen

---

[12] E. R. A. Seligman argued that the system of state income taxes would be improved if states levying an income tax were granted a credit equal to a percentage of the federal tax, the rate of the federal tax then being raised to compensate the national government for the loss in revenue. Cf. his article on the income tax, *Encyclopaedia of the Social Sciences* (New York: Macmillan, 1937), VII, 636.

[13] Derived from the example given in *Federal-State-Local Tax Coordination*, U. S. Treasury, Tax Advisory Staff of the Secretary, dated March 7, 1952, p. 22.

that the highest possible marginal rate is exactly 100 per cent, and that at any federal top rate below 100 per cent the combined rates must likewise remain below 100 per cent:

	(1)	(2)	(3)	(4)	(5)	(6)
Marginal income	$100	$100	$100	$100	$100	$100
State tax	10	10	10	10	99	100
Income subject to federal tax	$ 90	$ 90	$ 90	$ 90	$ 1	$ 0
Federal marginal tax rate	22.2%	92%[a]	99%	100%	100%	100%
Federal tax	$19.98	$82.8	$89.1	$ 90	$ 1	$ 0
Combined federal and state tax	$29.98	$92.8	$99.1	$100	$100	$100
Combined marginal tax rates	29.98%	92.8%	99.1%	100%	100%	100%

[a] The top federal bracket rate as of 1953 was 92 per cent.

PERSONAL EXEMPTIONS

Personal exemptions and deductions for dependents[14] are justified primarily on the ground that low-income receivers already pay a large proportion of their incomes in the form of sales and excise taxes. From the point of view of administration, exemptions are warranted by the cost of processing millions of tax returns from which little revenue can be expected. The lowering of the real value of the exemption through price inflation in recent years has, however, partly nullified this advantage of an exemption. Low exemptions have been advocated as a means of making every citizen conscious of his role as taxpayer; but this virtue is largely offset by the lulling effect of withholding the tax at the source by the employer. Support can be found for relatively high exemptions, especially in the form of a vanishing exemption,[15] on the ground that in a mass-production economy it is necessary to leave as much purchasing power as possible in the hands of the lower-income groups. This argument does not have application at all stages of the cycle. Lower exemptions help to arrest the course of inflation. It is during the depression phase that exemptions might well be increased in order to stimulate the propensity to consume. Varying exemptions operate in a fashion similar to changes in rate progression. Indeed, since exempt income may be regarded as income taxed at a zero rate, the exemption has the effect of modifying the graduation of the income tax rate schedule.

[14] The basic personal exemption is $600. Note the distinction between the personal exemption and personal deductions, discussed in the text.

[15] For the definition of a vanishing exemption, see below, page 184.

A good deal has been made of the fact that the real value of the ex-emption varies geographically, and from city to country, because of regional variations in the level of money income and prices. The exemption is worth less in Chicago and New York than in a small town in the South; yet hundreds of thousands of people are at the verge of subsistence in the great cities. The obstacle to taking account of these regional differences is the statistical difficulty of comparing costs of living in different sections of the country. Also, except at the extremes, the differences are hardly great enough to justify the added cost of administration.[16] The same kind of inequity exists, of course, with respect to a sales tax to the extent that prices vary regionally.

The size of the personal exemption (in 1956 for a single person $600; married $1,200) is regarded by some as excessively high.[17] (It is considerably lower in Great Britain, for example.) Moreover, there are additional $600 exemptions for those over sixty-five, or who are blind. Obviously the amount of the exemptions is arrived at without any accurate consideration of the need for the exemption by the taxpayer. There is no reason except legislative inertia why the exemption for a blind person should be the same as that for a dependent minor. The proper way to care for those over sixty-five, or who are incapacitated, is through social insurance and subsidies rather than through exemptions under the income tax.

The question also arises whether the personal exemption and deductions for dependents should not take the form of a vanishing exemption rather than an exemption. An exemption accrues to all taxpayers, regardless of their income bracket. The value of an exemption to the taxpayer is greater the higher his income, since it comes out of his highest tax bracket. A vanishing exemption is one that disappears as taxable net income rises above the point at which income is regarded as high enough to preclude the necessity of an exemption. It is administratively somewhat more difficult to apply than an exemption or an exclusion.[18] Another method of preventing an exemption from being worth more in dollars to a high-income receiver is for the exemption to be given the form of a credit deductible directly from the tax rather than from income. Some of the states make use of this device.

---

[16] S. Borden, "Cost of Living Variations and the Personal Exemption from the Income Tax," *National Tax Journal,* June, 1949, p. 165.

[17] The more common objection, however, is that the personal exemption is too low, particularly because of the rise in prices since this figure was selected. However, a $600 allowance for each dependent removes many families from the income tax rolls entirely.

[18] An example of an *exclusion* is provided under the city income tax of Springfield, Ohio, which exempts from tax all income up to $1,040, but taxes the *entire* income if it exceeds this. It will occur to the reader that hardship cases arise under an exclusion at levels of income just above the amount of the exclusion. A man with taxable income of $1,050 is little better off than one with an income of $1,040. This inequity can be avoided by eliminating the exclusion gradually. The size of the exclusion could be reduced by one fourth, say, for each increase in income of $250 over $1,000. This would eliminate the exclusion at an income of $2,000.

► THE TAXPAYER UNIT

A husband and wife are permitted to file a joint tax return. In addition they are allowed to split their income for tax purposes. Thus instead of filing separately, they total their gross income and deductions. Taxable income is then divided by two, the tax on one half is found, and is then multiplied by two. Because of rate progression and the nature of the structure of the income tax rates, this usually results in a lower tax on incomes above about $2,000. Half the benefits of income splitting have also been extended to heads of households, including even a dependent parent living under another roof, but receiving more than one half his support from the taxpayer. Under separate returns the exemptions of a spouse having no separate income may be wasted, and a joint return with income splitting therefore results in a tax saving. Compulsory joint returns without income splitting would (apart from the double marriage exemption) throw a married couple, each having a separate income, into the same tax bracket as a single individual having an income equal to their combined incomes. Giving the taxpayer the option, on the other hand, allows him to use to his advantage the differences in the way that joint and separate returns treat such items as capital gains and losses, charitable contributions, medical expenses, and so on.

Income splitting was introduced in 1948 as an answer to long-standing complaints of unfairness as between (1) families having identical incomes distributed differently between husband and wife, and (2) families residing in different states. Prior to 1948 the federal income tax law followed state law in the treatment of income. In the so-called community-property states[19] this meant that income earned and property acquired after marriage belonged equally to each spouse. The advantage often accruing to taxpayers in community-property states by dividing income for tax purposes was therefore extended to residents of all states. One of the effects of this extension was that some states repealed their newly enacted community-property laws. The effect of permitting income splitting when only one spouse actually receives the income has been to reduce substantially the progressivity of the income tax, although the benefit is slight in the very high brackets. Those spouses whose incomes are approximately equal likewise derive little benefit.

► SUMMARY OF CHAPTERS 8 AND 9

The personal income tax has been discussed with primary reference to the federal tax. Most of the problems are met with in much the same form in the income taxes of the states and of other countries. The personal

---

[19] Arizona, California, Idaho, Louisiana, Nevada, New Mexico, Texas, and Washington. In addition, each of these states has its own special interpretation.

income tax shares with a property tax (or more accurately, a net worth tax) the attribute of taxation according to ability to pay. On both conceptual and practical grounds, however, it is difficult to produce a definition of net taxable income that gives a precise measurement of ability to pay. A number of alternative definitions of income were examined, and the conclusion was reached that the ideal concept would be net accretion of wealth, taking account of consumption. In practice, however, strict adherence to this definition would cause hardship when income is not in the form of cash. Moreover, administrative and compliance costs would be greater, though not necessarily prohibitive.

The alternative procedure is to arrive at taxable income by way of a series of refinements of gross income. Under the federal income tax, gross income includes all sources of income except those which are specifically exempted. In addition to these exemptions, and deductions for dependents, two types of deduction are allowed. These are (1) business expenses (depreciation, travel, business losses, and the like), which are deducted to arrive at "adjusted gross income," and (2) nonbusiness expenses. The latter may be itemized or they may be taken in the form of the standard deduction.

Consideration of the history of the federal income tax, as well as that of the states, throws light on both the differences and the common features of the income tax structures of the various governmental jurisdictions. The comparison centers around the concept of ability to pay. Room for differences in the interpretation of the principle of ability to pay exists with respect to the source of income, exemptions, graduation of rates, the degree of regularity of income, deductions, and the timing of realization of income for tax purposes. Because of the great complexity of modern economic life, an equitable income tax structure requires many separate legislative and legal decisions. Moreover, rapid economic changes make it difficult for the legislatures and courts to keep the tax treatment of personal income abreast of the times. Finally, the remedying of one defect may give rise to another, and choices have to be made constantly between the sacrifices involved in adopting alternative courses of action. Despite these difficulties, however, the American public has confidence in the essential fairness of the personal income tax as the major source of federal revenue.

► A NOTE ON TAX AVOIDANCE AND TAX EVASION

TAX AVOIDANCE

The payment of a tax can be avoided legally by refraining from performing a taxable act. In the case of the income tax, avoidance can take the form of refusal to earn income. It is this type of avoidance that may threaten the tax base when rates are so high as to discourage willingness to invest or to work. Avoidance also comprises the almost numberless .

devices available in a complex economy for converting taxable into non-taxable income, or into income that is taxable at a lower bracket rate. While the ethics of the former type of avoidance are not open to question in a society based on individual consumer choice, the admissibility of the latter has sometimes been held up to question. How far is a taxpayer justified in making use of every possible legal device for reducing his tax?

Despite the apparent lack of dignity of some of the dodges that have been used, there can be no doubt that only through the use of all devices for avoidance, and the closing of loopholes either by Congress or through court decision, can the public know exactly what the law is. It is true that a readiness on the side of both the Treasury and the taxpayer to fight every issue adds greatly to the expense of collecting taxes. It is also true that in a dynamic economy many issues are left in doubt simply because they have not been subjected to court test. This adds to the uncertainties of doing business and gives rise to many hardship cases involving the payment of back taxes and interest. These difficulties are ascribable to the complexity of economic relationships in the modern industrial economy rather than to the income tax itself.

The personal holding company is so called because it is closely held, and derives its income mostly from the ownership of securities. It is, therefore, an avenue for tax avoidance, since interest, dividends, and other income can be paid into the company without subjecting the owners to personal income tax. Before the most obvious loopholes were closed in the thirties, the personal holding company provided the wealthy taxpayer with a very flexible instrument for tax avoidance. Up to 1936 dividends received by the corporation were exempt from the corporate income tax. Even that part of the corporation's income that was taxable was likely to be taxed at lower rates than the marginal income tax rate of the wealthy stockholder.

Dividends paid out by the personal holding company to its owner were taxable, of course, but their timing over the years could be controlled in such a way as to minimize the tax. In any case, only that part needed to be distributed which was required for current consumption. Thus to the extent that tax liability was incurred, the effect was similar to that of the Mill-Fisher type of spendings tax, and even this liability could be avoided by borrowing from the corporation for purposes of consumption. Still more flagrant were the incorporated yachts and racing stables, to which investment income and other types of income could be diverted, and from which the "losses" of operation (i.e., personal consumption expenditures) could be deducted for tax purposes. If the holding company was liquidated, the proceeds were subject to the lower rates of the capital gains tax.

Although these advantages do not exhaust the list, they are sufficient to make it clear that the device of the holding company would inevitably become a target for legislation under a liberal administration during a depression. An attempt in 1934, and again in 1936, to buttress the ineffective Section 102 (the penalty tax on profits retained by corporations in order to avoid tax) with graduated surtaxes on the undistributed earnings of all personal holding companies did not prove effective.

Much of the scope for avoidance was removed, however, in the Revenue Act of 1937. This act imposed a penalty tax, in addition to regular corporate income tax rates, of 75 per cent on the first $2,000 of the undistributed net income of a personal holding company, and 85 per cent on the excess over that amount. The definition of a personal holding company was taken to be a corporation, 50 per cent of whose stock is effectively owned by not more than five persons, and 80 per cent or more of whose income is from investments. Although this law has eliminated the worst abuses, a good deal of scope for avoidance by closely held corporations still remains. Although the penalty is effective against corporations that are defined as personal holding companies under the statute, the statutory definition is not strict enough to eliminate the possibilities of converting ordinary income into capital gains.

THE PROBLEM OF EVASION

The personal income tax is a self-assessed tax. The taxpayer himself is responsible for listing his sources of income. The tax collector must depend heavily on the honesty or fear of the taxpayer for accurate reporting. The greater the confidence of the taxpayer in the equity of the tax system the more likely he is to report his income accurately. When it is common knowledge that others are evading the tax the infection spreads. Much of the success depends on adequate and competent staffing of the Internal Revenue Service. Relatively low salaries, coupled with the opportunity to use experience with the Service as a steppingstone to highly paid tax work in private industry, have made it difficult for the Service to maintain high standards of performance. Furthermore, a false sense of economy on the part of Congress has prevented the hiring and training of sufficient staff. There seems to be little doubt that increased appropriations for the administration of the federal income tax would return many times their cost in additional revenues. It may be pointed out that in Germany there are state-run financial schools for training tax personnel, and that considerable dignity attaches to the position.

Until World War II the federal income tax law depended almost entirely on *information* at the source rather than *collection* at the source as a device for discouraging evasion.[20] The British, on the other hand, made use of collection at the source as early as 1803. Information at the

---

[20] Use was made of collection at the source under the Civil War income tax. Despite its success (in 1865 over one third of the tax was collected at the source), the fact that the provision applied only to salaries of federal employees and income from stocks and bonds exposed a serious weakness in this device as a limited

source is merely a threat. If the taxpayer has relatively little income outside his regular wage, he may feel that the chances of his being apprehended for failing to report such extra income are slight even though it is actually reported to the Service.

With over 60 million tax declarations, the man who pays a small tax knows that the likelihood of his return's being examined is small. Thus a considerable number of tax evaders are in the low-income groups. It was to reduce this type of petty evasion, which in the aggregate may become significant, that an attempt was made in 1951 to require corporations to deduct the tax before payment of dividends. This would have encouraged more honest reporting on the part of the stockholder, though of course only the lowest bracket tax could be withheld. The corporate income tax was originally thought of as primarily a means of collecting at the source, but rates were quickly raised to the point at which it became an independent tax. The British corporate income tax is still regarded mainly as a device for collection at the source.

Efforts to reduce evasion have taken the form of fines and jail sentences for deliberate falsification, publication of returns, and sampling of tax returns in the higher brackets. A great step forward in ensuring accuracy of returns would be accomplished if the taxpayer were required to include an annual inventory of his assets in the tax return. The most serious difficulties would arise in connection with the valuation of assets that do not have a ready market. But for purposes of control of income tax evasion, it would not be necessary to have an accurate valuation of all assets. An enumeration of shares of stock and of property held would make it difficult for the taxpayer to invest unreported income in concealed assets. The facts would have to come out at death, in any event. This device could not, of course, control income spent on consumption during the year. Reliance would continue to be placed on evidence of a scale of living beyond that which is possible on the income reported in the declaration.

▶ REFERENCES

See also references to Chapter 8.

Federal Tax Handbook. New York: Prentice-Hall, Inc., annually.
U. S. Master Tax Guide. Chicago: Commerce Clearing House, annually.
Your Federal Income Tax. Washington, D. C.: Bureau of Internal Revenue, annually.

---

measure. It discriminates against those whose income is of such a nature as to make withholding administratively easy. Consequently, if withholding is to be made use of at all, its application should be as general as possible, and the Internal Revenue Service should be granted enough funds to be able to require high standards of reporting from those professional and businessmen whose income cannot be subjected to withholding.

10 The Tax Treatment of Capital Gains and Losses

► CAPITAL GAINS AS INCOME

A special problem for the definition of gross income arises out of the existence of capital gains and losses. A capital gain or loss is a change in the value of certain types of property. Under the economist's definition of income discussed above, capital gains and losses would be fully taken into account in arriving at gross income for income tax purposes. It would not matter whether the taxpayer sold the property, and thus realized his gain or loss in terms of dollars, or refrained from selling or exchanging it. Under the federal income tax law, however, unrealized capital gains are excluded from gross income. Yet the owner of an appreciated asset has a greater ability to pay than does another individual who has kept his assets in the form of cash.

Since the opportunity to purchase assets that are subject to capital gains is not equally available to all savers, and particularly not to the very small saver, the exclusion of unrealized capital gains and losses from gross income diminishes the effectiveness of the progression of the income tax. Other factors must also be taken into consideration, however. Because of these factors, as well as on administrative grounds, it is difficult in practice to tax unrealized capital gains.

IS CAPITAL GAINS TAXATION DOUBLE TAXATION?

The principle of ability to pay would be violated if it could be established that capital gains taxation is a form of *inequitable* double taxation. We have seen that the value of a property is ascertained by capitalizing its prospective net yield at the rate appropriate to assets of comparable risk. The argument has been advanced by some economists that a capital gain occurs because of the expectation of income in the future. There is inequitable double taxation, it is asserted, if the capitalized value of this expectation is taxed, and if subsequently the income itself is also taxed.

This argument cannot be sustained, however. In the first place, not all capital gains occur because of an increase in expected future income. For example, when a corporation withholds profits, there is a tendency for this fact to be reflected in the price of the stock, for the profits may be distributed at a later time. The withheld profits are not taxed under the personal income tax, and in the absence of a capital gains tax they are not taxed at all.

Even when the capital gain results from the capitalization of expected future increases in income the tax is justified. Suppose a piece of property worth $10,000 yields a net return of $500, and because of a population influx this rent doubles. On the assumption that there is no change in the net return on comparable assets, the value of the property rises to $20,000. If the present owner sells, and is not taxed on his capital gain, tax equity and the principle of ability to pay are not satisfied merely because the buyer pays an income tax on the additional $500 of rent per year. Clearly both the capital gains tax and the tax on the added income are necessary to take account of the changes in taxpaying power arising out of the increased rent.

BASIS FOR SPECIAL TREATMENT OF CAPITAL GAINS AND LOSSES

Although capital gains ought to be taxed on the basis of ability to pay, gains and losses are nevertheless usually regarded as deserving special treatment under the income tax law. For several reasons changes in the value of capital assets are awkward to handle under the ordinary conception of income.

First, there is a question how far an increase in the value of an asset is synonymous with income. Even if unrealized it does mean an increase in economic power. On the other hand, the increase in value of a capital asset does not always represent an addition to immediately disposable purchasing power.

Second, capital losses are difficult to take into account. For example, political objections have been raised to allowing high-income receivers a reduction in their over-all income tax liability through unlimited deduction of losses from other income. Moreover, it is administratively difficult to allow unlimited deductibility of capital losses from capital gains.[1] Tax returns might, in some instances, have to be kept open for years if the taxpayer had no gains from which to deduct losses. To provide relief for

---

[1] Under federal tax law deductibility of losses is determined as follows: Aggregate short- and long-term losses are deductible from aggregate short- and long-term gains during the taxable year, plus (in the case of individuals but not corporations) $1,000 of other income. If there remain losses in excess of gains plus $1,000 of other income, these losses may be carried forward into the next five succeeding years. (Short- and long-term gains and losses are not completely mingled. Net short-term losses go against net long-term gains, and net long-term losses go against net short-term gains. Net losses in both categories are aggregated for offset against ordinary income or carry-forward.)

those who have made gains in the past, but will not make them in the future, a carry-back of losses would have to be allowed; and in some cases this might require the reopening of tax declarations for years back. Incidentally, the limitation on the deductibility of capital losses is also partly due to the fact that one effect would be a fall in revenues.

It can be argued, nevertheless, that full deductibility of capital losses should be permitted, regardless of the number of years involved. Since this would probably prove administratively unfeasible, however, the next best solution is to tax capital gains at more favorable rates than ordinary income.[2] If this is not done the effect may be to discourage investment. When losses are not fully deductible from capital gains, and if necessary from other income as well, there is an added element of investment risk. The problem is to decide the extent to which capital gains should be favored as compared with ordinary income.

A third reason for special treatment of capital gains arises out of the exemption of unrealized capital gains from taxation. An inducement exists to avoid the realization of capital gains and thus the tax.[3] Relatively favorable rates of tax on realized capital gains as compared with ordinary income reduce the tax barriers to realization, and thus reduce the illiquidity of investments.

Equitable taxation of capital gains is further complicated by a fourth consideration, namely, that the personal income tax is subject to progressive rates. The growth in the value of an asset may be spread over a decade. Realization in the tenth year may mean that the taxpayer is thrown into a higher tax bracket than would have been the case had he paid a tax on the annual increment in the value of the asset as it accrued. In the absence of taxation of unrealized capital gains, a method of handling this problem would be to divide the gain by the number of years the asset was held, and add this amount to the taxpayer's other income in the year of realization. On the basis of this income his marginal tax rate would be determined. Then the entire capital gain would be taxed at this marginal rate, which would be lower than the rate that would apply if the marginal

---

[2] It is only a next best solution because it does not help a taxpayer who has made a capital loss if another taxpayer receives favorable tax treatment on a long-term capital gain. However, the knowledge that long-term gains will be favorably treated enters into the risk calculations of the investor.

[3] Even if gains are ultimately realized, and the tax paid, an advantage may accrue to the taxpayer by deferring realization as long as possible. If he had been taxed on his unrealized capital gain in each year, he would at once have lost the use of the tax money. Thus the taxpayer gains compound interest at the expense of the Treasury, determined by the amount of the capital gain each year multiplied by the number of years until realization. This could easily be taken account of if capital gains accrued evenly. Since gains accrue unevenly, interspersed with losses, an enormous amount of bookkeeping by the taxpayer and checking by the Internal Revenue Service would be required. Without it, however, an incentive remains to avoid realization of capital gains.

rate were determined by including the whole capital gain in the income of a single year.

Finally, capital gains may not be full-fledged income in the same sense as ordinary periodic income or income from profit-seeking transactions. The making or even the realization of capital gains may be involuntary.

LONG- AND SHORT-TERM CAPITAL GAINS

The federal tax law has usually distinguished between "long-term" and "short-term" capital gains. Short-term gains have always been treated as ordinary income, partly because they are regarded as essentially speculative, and therefore deserving of no particularly favorable treatment. Another reason is that short-term gains may be more closely associated than long-term gains with ordinary income. The taxpayer who is frequently in and out of the market may be regarded as a trader. Again, long-term gains may involve a high tax bracket in the year of realization, and in the absence of a complete system of offset against losses it is usually agreed that they should receive favorable treatment. The definition of short- and long-term gains and losses and the extent of the favorable treatment to be granted to the latter have changed frequently over the years.

DEFINITION OF A CAPITAL ASSET

The distinction for tax purposes between a capital gain and ordinary income makes necessary a definition of a capital asset, for the realization of a rise in the value of property other than a capital asset is taxed as ordinary income. A capital gain or loss results from the sale or exchange of property that is defined by law as a capital asset. This definition has changed over time, but at present all property is included except specifically exempted assets. These exempted items are stock in trade, depreciable assets, real estate used for business purposes, copyrights (but not patents) and certain short-term government securities sold on a discount basis. Thus for the most part capital assets are restricted to stocks and bonds, real estate other than that used in the business, and partnership interests, patents, and so on. It is estimated that approximately three fourths of all taxable capital gains arise out of sales of stocks and bonds.

Because of the wording of the law, which includes all assets except those specifically exempt, durable consumers' goods are regarded as capital assets. Thus during World War II when the prices of used cars rose above new-car prices, profits on their sales were subject to the capital gains tax. Yet losses from the sale of durable consumers' goods are not deductible, because the law regards them as arising out of personal consumption. Definitional problems of this kind have detracted from the equity of federal capital gains taxation.

A capital gain or loss occurs when there is a change in the market value of a capital asset. The essence of the economic distinction between ordinary income and a capital gain has been said to be the fact that the former is an expected gain, while the latter is not foreseen.[4] Thus the profits of a dealer in real estate are taxable as ordinary income, while the sale of one's house at a profit involves a capital gain. One who buys and sells stocks as his regular business is regarded as earning income, while the nonprofessional makes capital gains and losses. However, the dealer, too, cannot avoid contending with the unexpected in his business. Therefore, the distinction between capital gains and ordinary income must in some instances be arbitrary. Capital gains often contain elements of ordinary income. For example, to the extent that the occasional purchaser of a stock brings to bear his experience and skill in making his selection, any resulting capital gain is partly a reward for the effort put forth.

THE "NET ACCRETION" CONCEPT

If the "net accretion" concept of income were adopted, there would be no distinction between realized and unrealized capital gains and losses. Whether or not an appreciated asset were sold, the valuation of assets at the end of each year would cause all capital gains and losses to be automatically included in taxable income. Even on the assumption that the difficulties of accurate valuation could be overcome, hardship problems would arise in the taxation of unrealized capital gains. Unless the taxpayer had liquid funds out of which to pay the tax on an unrealized capital gain, he would have to sell some of his assets. The market might be unfavorable at the time the tax must be paid. Furthermore, a person in a relatively low-income bracket would be the one most likely to find himself in this position. Thus the effect of the taxation of unrealized capital gains might be to increase the risk of this type of investment by small savers. Again, if the small saver were forced to sell shares of stock to pay the tax on an unrealized gain, his equity in the firm would be decreased. Although this would be of no importance in the case of a widely distributed stock, the effect could be to alter ownership and affect management policies in the case of a small corporation.

One difficulty with the taxation of unrealized capital gains would be mitigated if capital gains were usually associated with the distribution of dividends out of which the tax could be paid. A significant rise in stock prices would provide the occasion for the declaration of a dividend. The taxation of unrealized capital gains would probably call for a more liberal policy of profit distribution than has often been the practice in recent years, though to the extent that the higher dividends were also capitalized, a larger capital gains tax would be due. The most serious difficulties would

---

[4] L. H. Seltzer, *The Nature and Tax Treatment of Capital Gains and Losses* (New York: National Bureau of Economic Research, 1951), Chap. III.

arise with respect to unrealized capital gains on durable consumers' goods classed under the law as capital assets—for example, an owned home. In order to pay the tax a man with a low income might be forced to take out a mortgage or even sell his home. Therefore little political support could be found for including assets of this kind in the base subject to capital gains taxation.

In conclusion, it may be said that if unrealized capital gains were made subject to taxation, it is likely that a more restricted definition of capital assets would have to be adopted than at present. Moreover, to take care of hardship cases it would probably be necessary to allow an exemption from taxation of a certain percentage of gains. The fact that much revenue might be lost through the inclusion of unrealized capital *losses* in the tax base makes it doubtful whether the Treasury would care to see the criterion of realization surrendered. Unlimited deductibility of losses from other income would be imperative if unrealized capital gains were taxed. Finally, all the problems of administration, investment incentive, and equity under capital gains taxation would be accentuated.

REALIZATION AT DEATH

A serious inequity related to realization stems from the fact that under present law death does not result in the realization for tax purposes of capital gains. If all unrealized gains and losses were to be regarded as realized at death, account would be taken of them in the final income tax return. As it is, they are not taxed under the income tax. If there are net unrealized gains, the estate is, of course, larger than it otherwise would have been, and part of the lost tax revenue is recaptured under the death taxes. If estate tax rates are less than 100 per cent the lost revenue is not entirely made up.[5] This loophole results in an inequity between the very rich and the near rich. Those who are only moderately well off are less likely to be able to hold capital assets until death in order to avoid taxation. Assets have to be sold off in old age when retirement eliminates earned income.

CHANGES IN FEDERAL TAX TREATMENT OF CAPITAL GAINS AND LOSSES

The difficulty of achieving and maintaining an acceptable procedure for taxing capital gains is illustrated by the frequent changes in the federal law since 1913. Before the act of 1921, capital gains were taxed as ordinary income, and until 1916 capital losses were not deductible. The law was liberalized in 1916 to allow deduction of capital losses from capital gains. From 1918 through 1923 the closest approach ever made to equal treatment for gains and losses was achieved by allowing capital losses to be offset without limit against all taxable income. If the loss exceeded total

---

[5] It will be noted, incidentally, that state inheritance tax receipts are likely to be greater because of the sacrifice of federal income tax revenue.

income for the year, however, it could be carried forward for one year only. Therefore, even during this period gains and losses were not accorded completely equal treatment.

Since 1921 favorable treatment has been given to long-term capital gains, but the mechanics were changed on a number of occasions until 1942. From 1922 to 1933 a taxpayer was permitted to have his long-term capital gains taxed at 12½ per cent. In 1934 a ladder approach was adopted, whereby the longer an asset was held, the smaller was the percentage of the capital gain (or loss) that would be included in taxable income. On assets held more than ten years, only 30 per cent of the gain or loss was includible in taxable income. This method was found to be complicated, however, without noticeably increasing the equity of the tax, and since 1938 capital gains and losses have been treated more simply. Since 1942, capital gains and losses on assets held over six months have been included in gross income only to the extent of 50 per cent of the gain or loss; an alternative tax calculation serves to limit the top rate to 25 per cent.

As of 1956, both long- and short-term realized capital gains and losses were included in the gross income of both individuals and corporations. However, in the case of individuals, a deduction of 50 per cent is allowed from the excess of long-term capital gains over short-term capital losses. Both corporations and individuals are allowed to compute an alternative tax, such that the maximum effective tax on the excess of net long-term gains over net short-term losses shall not exceed 25 per cent. With a top marginal rate of 91 per cent this is a tremendous concession to the very high-income receiver who makes a realized capital gain, and it constitutes a powerful incentive to the conversion of ordinary income into capital gains.[6]

The history of the treatment of capital losses illustrates the frequent change of opinion on the part of Congress in its attempt to avoid a tax-loading against risky types of investment. The limitation on loss deductions, originated in 1924 in an effort to offset the low rate applied to gains, was further extended after the stock crash of 1929. It was discovered that wealthy men frequently paid no income tax as a result of deducting in full, from taxable income other than capital gains, realized losses on assets held less than two years.

In 1932 it was decided to limit the deduction of such losses from sales of stocks and bonds to gains from similar transactions, although other losses could still be deducted in full from income of any kind. Thus a breach was made in equality of treatment in order (1) to propitiate a pub-

---

[6] Analytical and historical studies of capital gains taxation are available in Seltzer, op. cit.; S. Ratner, American Taxation (New York: Norton, 1942), especially Appendix: Supplement; and United States Treasury, Federal Income Tax Treatment of Capital Gains and Losses, June, 1951.

lic outcry against a form of avoidance that often looked worse than it was, and (2) to arrest the decline in revenue that at the time was thought to threaten the solvency of the government. As of 1956, capital losses could be deducted from capital gains, plus $1,000 of other income in the year of realization and each of the next five years. At first sight this might seem to favor unduly the individual engaged in very unimportant transactions in capital assets, but it must be borne in mind that capital losses occur with greatest frequency in that group.[7]

► QUANTITATIVE IMPORTANCE OF CAPITAL GAINS TAXATION

The modest quantitative magnitude of capital gains tax receipts rather belies the economic and social importance of this form of taxation. Thus from 1926 to 1951 the net yield is estimated at $7.2 billion, and for the year 1951 alone at about $900 million, or 3.7 per cent of total yield of the individual income tax.[8] But the taxation of capital gains adds substantially to the progressivity of the income tax, since net gains are concentrated in the higher incomes. This fact has to be borne in mind when comparing the progressivity of the British personal income tax, for example, with that of the United States. The British recognize neither capital gains nor losses for income tax purposes (though it must be pointed out that they do tax as ordinary income some profits that would be taxed as capital gains in the United States). Consequently the effective rate of tax on higher-income receivers is significantly lower than the nominal rate.

► REAL VS. FICTITIOUS CAPITAL GAINS AND LOSSES

A source of contention with respect to the taxation of capital gains has been the question whether some capital gains can be regarded as fictitious, and thus ought not to be taxed. A fictitious capital gain (or loss) arises when there is no change in the real net worth of the taxpayer, but merely in the nominal (dollar) value of his asset. This will occur when the prices of other goods also rise or fall proportionately. In practice it is difficult to distinguish real from fictitious capital gains. The multiplicity of factors affecting the prices of assets complicates the picture.

The prospective earnings of a capital asset may be affected by a

---

[7] This is in part due to the fact that small savers have not in the past had the necessary access to sources of information with respect to the course of market prices, and also to the fact that small investors frequently do not have an adequate margin of savings to be able to avoid selling when the prices of assets are low.

It should be noted that since the realization of capital losses reduces taxable income and the realization of capital gains increases it, a false impression is created of the distribution of gains and losses among the different income brackets. The extent to which losses are concentrated in lower incomes, and gains in higher incomes, is exaggerated.

[8] United States Treasury, *op. cit.*, p. 3.

variety of causes, among them the reinvestment of corporate earnings;[9] increases in earning power as a result of population growth, innovations, and aggressive management; changes in price of product; and changes in the price level and the interest rate. All these factors also affect the rate at which prospective income is capitalized. But rarely are the numerator and denominator of the capitalization formula affected in the same way. In a dynamic world changes in the value of capital assets are ordinarily the result of a complex of factors, and combine fictitious and real capital gains and losses. There is no possibility of separating these out in order to purify the capital gains tax. A comparison of fictitious and real elements will provide the basis for deciding whether capital gains should be taxed as income.

Although some capital gains and losses are in a sense illusory, it does not necessarily follow that they should be subject to favorable treatment. Certain types of changes in ordinary taxable income are likewise illusory. Yet revenue considerations have thus far prevented Congress from according them favorable treatment. For example, a rise in the general price level means that a greater proportion of a man's income is taken by a progressive income tax. Capital gains attributable to rising general prices likewise give rise to tax liability without a corresponding increase in real ability to pay. Since the inequity is similar in both cases, differential treatment should be granted only if the effects are significantly more serious in the one case than in the other.

A clear-cut instance in which an income increase is illusory occurs when a rise in money income is accompanied by a rise in prices which is in the same proportion, so that income in real terms does not rise. In such a case income tax receipts automatically rise, and unless there is agreement that additional revenues are needed, income tax rates should be reduced. Because of lags in the receipts of certain kinds of taxes under inflationary conditions, it may be that an automatic increase in revenues is needed in order to permit the government to maintain its previous level of real expenditures.

In practice, a rise in incomes and the price level is always accompanied by a change in relative prices. Consequently, the real incomes of some individuals will rise relatively to those of others. Therefore, to such individuals the rise in income, whether in ordinary or capitalized income, is not fictitious but real. Their *relative* taxpaying ability has increased.

The argument of the previous paragraph may be supported with an illustration. Suppose the interest rate is 5 per cent, and a no-maturity bond

---

[9] The withholding of profits from distribution tends to cause a rise in stock values for two reasons. First, the corporation is in possession of assets equivalent to the undistributed profits. Second, the reinvestment of corporate earnings creates the presumption of greater earnings in the future. Other stock market influences may prevent an actual rise in the value of the stock, but on the assumption of a perfect market there will be a *relative* rise in its price.

has been issued at 100 to yield $5. Then a fall in the market rate of interest to 4 per cent means that a potential purchaser would be willing to pay a price for it that yields the new lower market rate of interest. Five dollars is 4 per cent of X dollars, or $125. Competition by purchasers should drive the price up to this point.

Although the original bondholder has made a capital gain of $25, it is often argued that the capital gain is illusory. If he sells the bond, and is taxed on the gain, the net proceeds are insufficient to buy securities that yield as much as before, and his economic position is therefore worsened. But his *relative* position is better than that of individuals who did not possess such a bond. Only if we suppose that he is entitled to continue to receive his higher income when the market rate of interest has declined, should we be willing to exempt his relatively higher income from taxation.

A particularly striking instance of a fictitious capital gain occurring when the price level changes is that of the home owner. Suppose the value of a man's house rises from $15,000 to $20,000 solely because of price inflation. If he is forced to take a job in another city he needs the entire $20,000 to buy a similar house. If he is taxed on the realized capital gain he is unable to do so. This is obviously, therefore, a fictitious capital gain as compared with that of the man who is not required by circumstances to move. However, there is nothing fictitious about it as compared with the smaller capital gain made by the owner of a capital asset the price of which has risen less. Compare the situation of a young couple in the market for a home after prices have risen. They would not regard the capital gain of a middle-aged home owner as fictitious.

In 1951 the capital gains provision was altered to exempt the seller of a home from the capital gains tax provided he buys a home within a year at a price at least as high as that for which he sold. This provision, though further liberalized in 1954, does not encourage the man whose children have grown up and left home to reduce his claims on scarce national housing by moving to smaller or to rented quarters.

▶ THE EFFECT OF THE TAX ON THE MARKET
FOR CAPITAL ASSETS

A major problem of capital gains taxation is how to tax gains without discouraging exchanges of capital assets. A vigorous stock market is necessary in order to encourage present holders of seasoned securities to sell and reinvest the proceeds in securities of promising new and relatively risky undertakings. But unwillingness to realize capital gains because of liability to tax makes the stock market a less than perfect market for newly seasoned issues. Moreover, the higher prices have risen, the greater the tax liability resulting from realization. At the same time, the taxation of the capital gains that are realized cuts down the supply of investable funds. A thin market means that fluctuations in stock prices tend to be more violent. This reduces the efficiency of the stock market as an institution for directing savings into productive channels; and it increases the risk of loss by the smaller saver, who is apt to possess little expert information. On the other hand, higher stock prices may mean more favorable financing terms for new issues.

The existence of a capital gains tax not only affects willingness to sell capital assets, and thus their supply, but also willingness to buy them. The purchaser of a capital asset knows he will be liable for a tax if and when he ultimately sells it. However, a man who has already made a capital gain is more conscious of the tax he must pay if he realizes his gain than is a man who is contemplating the purchase of stock and is not even certain he will make and realize a capital gain. Therefore, one would expect that a capital gains tax would reduce the offerings of capital assets on the market more than it would reduce demand.

So many psychological factors are at work here that not much can be said about the effects on stock prices attributable to the capital gains tax alone, and therefore on the cost of raising capital. Under conditions of a general expectation of moderately rising stock prices, as we have seen above, the effect of the capital gains tax on both supply and demand is negative. Consequently, the effect of the tax under these conditions is to reduce stock transactions. Since a thin market is likely to be unfavorable to new issues, the interest cost tends to increase.

The situation is different in a falling market, when losses may be offset against gains for tax purposes. It is then an advantage to realize a capital loss, and this factor contributes to the supply, thus forcing stock prices down still further.[10] The effect of the taxation of realized capital gains is therefore to accentuate fluctuations in stock prices. If unrealized as well as realized capital gains were subject to tax, this reluctance to take capital gains during upswings and desire to do so during downswings would be eliminated. Again, if capital gains were treated as realizable when a transfer is made by gift or at death, one important discouragement to exchanges would be removed.

► THE CONVERSION OF INCOME INTO CAPITAL GAINS[11]

An important role in risky investment is played by those who undertake the task of organizing a business and establishing a market for its product, and then sell the good will to conservative investors who are more interested in stability of yield than in quick gains. This method of convert-

---

[10] See the interesting discussion in Harold Somers, *Public Finance and National Income* (Philadelphia: Blakiston, 1949), pp. 198–202.

[11] See the chapter on "Tax Avoidance through Capital Gains" in Seltzer, *op. cit*

ing ordinary income into capital gains is available only to limited types of personal service. For those who can qualify, it makes possible a reduction in marginal income tax rates from a maximum of 91 per cent to the 25 per cent maximum rate applicable under long-term capital gains taxation.

Favorable treatment of capital gains naturally results in attempts to convert ordinary income into capital gains. The incentive to do so is stronger the more sharply progressive the rates of the personal income tax and the more generous the tax treatment of capital gains. The wide variety of legal avoidance techniques puts a premium on the ingenuity of the taxpayer. It likewise focuses attention on the seriousness of the inequities that arise out of the necessity of making hairline distinctions between cases that to the layman appear virtually identical. More important, it points up the fact that the complexity of modern financial arrangements of business may render a completely equitable tax system virtually impossible.

An effective avoidance device has been the "collapsible" or "Hollywood" corporation, by means of which the excess of liquidation value over the original amounts invested takes the form of a capital gain. Thus a corporation is established, with a merely nominal capital, to make a moving picture that will take more than six months to produce. When the picture is completed the corporation is liquidated, and the stockholders' capital gains for income tax purposes are based on the estimated earnings of the picture minus the insignificant original cost of their stock. Moreover, since the corporation is liquidated before any income is realized, no corporate tax liability is incurred.

Cognizance was taken of this means of avoidance in the Revenue Act of 1939, which taxed the shareholder at ordinary rates if the corporation was deliberately availed of for avoidance purposes, if the shareholder held 10 per cent or more of stock, and if 20 per cent or more of the gain was attributable to property of the inventory type. In 1950 and again in 1954 the law was made somewhat more stringent, including a provision reducing the 10 per cent ownership test to 5 per cent. The courts have held that if the reason for liquidation has nothing to do with tax avoidance, the proceeds are to be taxed as a long-term capital gain.

Ordinary income can also be converted into a capital gain in cases where it is possible to satisfy the Internal Revenue Service that the individual is selling an asset rather than his personal services. For example, according to newspaper reports in 1948, the owners of the Jack Benny Show wished to convert ordinary income into capital gains by selling the show to the radio network. The attempt failed because Jack Benny was regarded by the Internal Revenue Service as indispensable to the performance, and therefore was selling his personal services. A similar attempt by Amos n' Andy succeeded because it was believed that other actors could be substituted, and the show was therefore salable. Evidently a tightening up of the law is necessary in order to avoid having to make such hairline distinctions.[12] Finally must be mentioned the withholding of profits from distribution in the expectation of their being converted into a rise in the value of the stock. It is of interest to note that, depending on the reaction of the market, *either* the distribution or the retention of profits can cause a rise in stock prices, since either circumstance can be interpreted as implying that the corporation is in a strong position.

▶ SUMMARY

Much controversy has been waged over the taxation of capital gains, and the treatment that should be accorded to capital losses. The difficulties arise basically out of the relation of property values to the income from property. Certain types of capital gain are similar to ordinary income, while others differ substantially from income in the ordinary tax sense. Consequently, proposals for the tax treatment of capital gains and losses have ranged from complete exemption to treatment that is identical with that given to ordinary income. The difficulty of taking full account of capital losses constitutes an argument for favorable tax treatment of capital gains. But it provides no criteria for just how favorable that treatment should be. Moreover, the distribution of capital gains and losses is such that favorable treatment to capital gains does not offset the unfavorable effects experienced by those who have capital losses but no capital gains.

The differential tax treatment of realized and unrealized capital gains leads to inequities, as well as to the discouragement of sales and exchanges of property. Under the net accretion concept of income, both would be taxed, and the problem would disappear. Administrative difficulties, however, as well as the likelihood of undue hardship in certain instances, are obstacles to the adoption of the net accretion concept of income. Moreover, a difficulty exists in the differentiation between real and fictitious capital gains and losses. Failure to regard all assets as realized at the taxpayer's death discourages sales and exchanges of property, and thus creates inequities.

Finally, if special rates are applied to capital gains, an incentive is created to convert ordinary income into capital gains. Distinctions between conversion that is admissible and that which is not necessarily rest on legal points that often result in drastically different treatment for individuals who ought to be treated alike.

---

[12] Other devices, equally interesting, cannot be discussed at length. Among them are the conversion of investment income into capital gains through the device of the personal holding company; partnership liquidations; deferred compensation, pension, and certain lump-sum payments to employees; stock purchase options. Although the regulations have been tightened, and are likely to be further tightened in the future, considerable scope remains for this kind of avoidance. For a detailed discussion, see Seltzer, *op. cit.*

► REFERENCES

GROVES, H. M. *Production, Jobs and Taxes.* New York: McGraw-Hill Book Company, Inc., 1944, Chap. VIII, "Capital Gains and Losses."

SELTZER, L. H. *The Nature and Tax Treatment of Capital Gains and Losses.* New York: National Bureau of Economic Research, 1951.

SOMERS, H. M. "An Economic Analysis of the Capital Gains Tax," *National Tax Journal,* September, 1948, pp. 226–232.

UNITED STATES TREASURY DEPARTMENT. *Federal Income Tax Treatment of Capital Gains and Losses.* Washington, D. C., 1951.

11 The Taxation of Corporate Income: I

▶ INTRODUCTION

Regardless of the point at which a tax is levied, it is ultimately paid by individuals. For this reason it can be argued that the proper way to tax income is to impose the levy at the point at which income is paid out to the factors of production. The tax system is simplified, and incidence is easier to establish.

Governments have not taken very kindly to this advice. The typical modern tax system taxes personal and corporate income separately. When business was done exclusively by proprietorships and partnerships, no occasion existed for this separate treatment. The income would be taxed once, in the hands of the owners. The corporation, however, has a legal existence that is separate from that of the owners. The separate taxation of corporate income means that income is taxed once in the hands of the corporation, and a second time when dividends are distributed to the stockholders.

A number of difficult problems are created when business income is subject to special taxation. These problems concern administration, economic effects, and equity. They are made even more difficult by the fact that income of corporations may be taxed in more than one way. In addition to the taxation of corporation income, taxes may be applied to excess profits and to profits that are not distributed in the form of dividends. On the other hand, a special tax is sometimes applied to profits which *are* distributed.

It is the purpose of this and the following chapter to study the effects of the taxation of business income. The characteristics of the corporate income and undistributed- and excess-profits taxes will be examined, and their incidence and economic effects appraised. Administrative and equity aspects will also be considered, and issues relating to the integration of the corporate and personal income taxes will be discussed. We shall commence with a description of the federal corporate income tax in its present form, together with the historical background of the federal tax.

► THE FEDERAL CORPORATE INCOME TAX

All taxable corporations are required to file an annual declaration of income. As under the personal income tax, the base of the corporation income tax is determined by first aggregating the various types of taxable income, then deducting various allowable expenses and losses, and finally deducting certain credits, or special deductions. The base of the tax is then separated into two parts. One is subject to the normal tax, and the other to the surtax. Under the Revenue Act of 1951, which still held through 1955, the normal rate was 30 per cent, and the rate on surtax net income (i.e., corporate net income above $25,000) was 22 per cent. Therefore the total corporate income tax on net incomes below $25,000 was 30 per cent, and on incomes above $25,000, 52 per cent. Partially taxable interest on federal securities received by the corporation is taxed under the surtax but not under the normal tax.

Gross income of corporations may include any or all of the following: profits from sales, interest and dividends received, rents and royalties, receipts from services, and capital gains or losses. Deductions from gross income include payments of wages, salaries, rent, interest, taxes, casualty losses, repairs, bad debts, depreciation and depletion, amortization of emergency facilities, advertising, pension and profit-sharing plans, and contributions to charities up to 5 per cent of net income. A net operating loss deduction can be taken from profits in other years. Losses in a given year may be carried back two years and forward five years, for a total spread of eight years. In addition, there is a deduction of 85 per cent against dividends received by a corporation.[1]

ORIGIN AND OBJECTIVES OF THE CORPORATE INCOME TAX

The first permanent federal corporate income tax was introduced in 1909 at the rate of 1 per cent.[2] The reason for its introduction was partly the fear that another attempt to introduce a personal income tax would meet the same fate at the hands of the Supreme Court as did that of 1894.[3] Pending the enactment of a personal income tax amendment to the Constitution, which would remove this danger, the corporate income tax

---

[1] The tax on intercorporate dividends was intended partly as a discouragement to the use of holding companies. It has also been supported as a device for restricting the opportunity for tax avoidance under graduated corporate rates, whereby corporations are split up to qualify for lower corporate income tax rates.

[2] State corporate income taxes came into being as part of a general expansion of state revenue sources after the Civil War. Rapid industrialization forced the states to provide many more services than could be financed by the property tax.

[3] The income tax of 1894 applied alike to corporate and individual income. Consequently, dividend income was not taxed to the individual, since it had already

was also wanted for its own sake in order to make a breach in the virtually exclusive dependence of the federal government on the customs. This development contrasted with the experience in Britain, where no constitutional bar existed to a personal income tax. In that country, moreover, business income taxation was regarded primarily as a means of collecting part of the personal income tax on dividends rather than as an independent source of revenue.

In the United States, therefore, a tradition of federal corporate income taxation was established largely on the basis of purely fortuitous circumstances. In order to decrease the likelihood that the corporate income tax would also be declared unconstitutional, Congress resorted to the legal fiction that it was an excise tax measured by corporate net income. The tax was sustained by the Supreme Court on the ground that it was not a direct tax (which would have had to be apportioned among the states according to population), but an excise on the privilege of doing business in the corporate form.[4]

YIELD

Once the revenue-yielding possibilities of the corporate income tax were fully appreciated, both the states and the federal government began

Table 12. Recent Trends in Corporate Income Tax Yields
(In millions of dollars)

	Federal			State		
Year	(1) Total Federal Taxes	(2) Corporate Income Tax	(3) Column (2) as % of Column (1)	(4) Total State[c] Tax Revenue	(5) Corporate Income Tax	(6) Column (5) as % of Column (4)
1931	2,807	1,026	36.5	2,042	115	5.6
1939	5,481	1,122	20.5	3,085	134	4.3
1945	44,155	4,879[a]	11.1[a]	4,349	454	10.4
1951	51,076	14,388[b]	28.2[b]	8,934	687	7.7
1954	69,920	21,546[b]	31.0[b]	11,089	772	7.0

[a] If excess-profits tax is included, $16,027,000,000, or 36 per cent.
[b] Including excess-profits tax, formerly shown separately.
[c] Excluding unemployment compensation taxes.
SOURCES: Bureau of the Census, *Historical Review of State and Local Government Finances,* June, 1948; *Summary of State Government Finances,* annually; *Annual Reports* of the Secretary of the Treasury.

been taxed as corporate income. The passage of a separate corporate income tax in 1909, four years before the permanent personal income tax, provided a basis for the separate taxation of corporate and dividend income that has persisted to this day.

   [4] *Flint v. Stone Tracy Co.,* 1911. Since corporations are created under the laws of the states it is, strictly speaking, the states, not the federal government, who are entitled to tax corporations on their privileges.

to exploit them heavily. Corporate profits are particularly responsive to changes in the level of national income. In addition there have been many rate changes. Another reason for changes in the relative importance of this tax is that substantial changes have also occurred in the use made of other taxes. Again, the statistical picture is complicated by the frequently changing importance of the federal excess-profits tax, which plays a major role during wartime, and even during some peacetime years, because of back collections.

FEDERAL CORPORATE INCOME TAX RATES

Because the revenue needs of the federal government have varied widely under the impact of wars and depressions, the rates of the federal corporate income tax have been frequently changed. Also, an element in the numerous changes has been the variable public attitude toward the taxation of corporate income. The high national income and relatively low federal expenditures of the twenties might have made possible a return to lower corporate income tax rates after World War I. Nevertheless, in 1921 the rate was increased from 10 per cent to 12½ per cent in order to compensate for the repeal of the excess-profits tax. The permanent retention of higher rates was also part of the price paid by high-income stockholders for the concession made to them through the great reduction in the rates of the personal income tax in the middle and higher brackets during the twenties.

Owing to declining tax yields in the depression the maximum rate was increased to 13¾ per cent in 1932, and to 15 per cent in 1935. In World War II corporate income tax rates were again raised in order to produce more revenue. Under the Revenue Act of 1942, the first $5,000 of corporate income was taxed at a rate of 23 per cent, with a maximum rate of 40 per cent applying to the entire corporate net income in excess of $50,000.[5] An excess-profits tax was also enacted, which yielded $11 billion in 1945.[6] After the war the latter was repealed, but the corporate income tax remained virtually unchanged at 38 per cent. The war in Korea necessitated still further increases in revenue, and the top rate of the corporate income tax was increased to 45 per cent.

In the fall of 1950, the debate centered around whether Congress should grant the administration's request for a reintroduction of the excess-profits tax, or whether it should again sharply raise the rates on corporate

---

[5] The enormous increases in tax rates that have occurred under the federal corporate income tax since 1909 raise the question whether stockholders were not subject to great losses of capital through capitalization of the tax. That this was not so, except with respect to the increase in rates that occurred during the depression years, is argued in Chapter 7, page 140, footnote 12. A sudden repeal of the tax would, however, give present owners of stocks substantial windfall gains.

[6] This is, of course, the nominal yield. An excess profits tax reduces the base and yield of the personal income tax.

net income. Ultimately both these steps were taken. Further changes in the Revenue Act of 1951 raised the maximum corporate profits tax rate to 52 per cent. With the excess-profits tax left at the 1950 level of 30 per cent, the combined taxes were levied at the marginal rate of 82 per cent. A limit of 70 per cent, however, was established on the proportion of the income of a corporation that could be taken by the combined taxes. The excess-profits tax was repealed in 1954.

► STATE CORPORATE INCOME TAXES

The marked cyclical fluctuations in the yield of the corporate income tax are a disadvantage from the point of view of the states, whose limited borrowing capacity requires fairly stable revenues. Nevertheless, two thirds of the states levy a corporate income tax. Though sometimes known as license or franchise taxes, they are based on net income. Some states make use of progressive rates; for example, the 1955 Idaho tax was graduated from 1.5 per cent on the first $1,000 to 8 per cent on corporate net income above $50,000 (with a 7½ per cent surtax on total liability). The typical rate is 4 per cent. There is, of course, a jurisdictional problem among the states under the corporate income tax. A state is constitutionally required to permit out-of-state corporations to declare only income earned within its boundaries, and although it may tax domestic (i.e., intrastate) corporations as it pleases, the usual practice is to allow them also to allocate their income. In general the definition of corporate net income among the states follows that of the federal tax, though a large number of minor differences do exist.[7]

► ARGUMENTS IN FAVOR OF A CORPORATE INCOME TAX

The corporate income tax is a highly lucrative tax. Once it has been accepted, the tax becomes very difficult to do without. There are, however, a number of other reasons that have been advanced in favor of the taxation of corporate income. The Supreme Court's acceptance of the constitutionality of the corporation income tax was based on the view that a tax measured by net income is justified by the advantages of doing business in the corporate form. These advantages are (1) the limited liability of stockholders, (2) liquidity of ownership through marketability of shares, and (3) continuity of ownership and management. In a word, it is less risky to do business in the corporate form than as a partnership, and this advantage, conferred on corporations by government, should be paid for. Thus the benefit principle is one of the arguments in favor of a corporate

---

[7] Among the most important of these variations are the treatment of capital gains and losses, interest on securities of the federal government, and dividends received.

income tax. Other arguments that will be considered are monopoly control and ability to pay.

THE BENEFIT ARGUMENT

The benefit principle as a basis for the taxation of corporate net income suffers from the difficulty that the privileges and advantages of incorporation are also enjoyed by corporations making no taxable profits. Moreover, the volume of profits is no measure of the benefit. For example, stockholders in a firm that is making no profits, or is even making losses, are likely to be deriving particular advantage from the protection against personal loss conferred by the laws under which corporations do business. It is purely arbitrary to measure the benefit by net income.[8]

The benefit theory does indeed provide an argument in favor of other kinds of business taxes, for example, business license and occupation taxes. It is reasonable to include the cost of benefits provided by the state in the costs that must be covered by the price paid by the consumer. Unless these taxes can be shifted, firms on the border line of making losses may have to go out of business. If the tax really measured the benefit received by the corporation this would be a reasonable result, just as any rise in cost that cannot be covered in selling price may put marginal firms out of business. Since, however, the benefit cannot be measured, it is difficult to regard the benefit principle as having any practical application. Moreover, benefit does not justify the imposition of the tax at a rate high enough to yield revenues in excess of the cost of the benefit. Not only is the benefit not measurable, but the use of the corporate income tax at very high rates to finance the general costs of government makes it obvious that the benefit principle is a fiction intended to justify a tax that in good times is highly productive. The case is stronger, of course, at the state level. Incorporation takes place under state laws.

MONOPOLY CONTROL

Some economists have advocated the corporation income tax as an antimonopoly weapon. The corporate profits tax does reduce the net profits of monopolistic firms enjoying advantages arising out of restriction of entry. Therefore its effect would be to make more difficult the strengthening of the monopoly position by profitable corporations. A corporate income tax would be ineffective, however, as an antimonopoly device with respect to monopolies that are not making large monopoly profits. Yet they might be engaging in practices associated with the abuse of monopoly power. Again, not all firms subject to the corporate income tax are

---

[8] Cf. R. Goode, *The Corporation Income Tax* (New York: Wiley, 1951), p. 29. The same argument would give support to considering the personal income tax a benefit tax. Taxable personal net income could, of course, be taken as a measure of the value of the opportunity provided the individual by the state to earn income. But this would be a very special sense of the term "benefit."

monopolies. The definition of taxable corporate income under the federal tax is not identical with monopoly profits. Indeed, no legislature can define taxable profits precisely as the economist defines monopoly profits. Even competitive firms make profits that are normal to the industry. Again, dynamic changes in the level and distribution of national income give rise to profits and losses in competitive industry. Finally, a corporate income tax may hinder new rivals from financing expansion out of undistributed earnings. Yet with all these qualifications, the fact remains that a high corporate income tax can be part of the armory of antimonopoly weapons at the disposal of the government.

ABILITY TO PAY

Ability to pay has no meaning except with respect to the individuals on whom the ultimate tax burden falls. Therefore it provides no justification for a tax on corporate income. It is worth while, however, to note why this is so. We have seen in Chapter 7 that in the short run the incidence of the corporate income tax is primarily on the stockholder, but that in the long run the possibility of shifting is greater. Most of the shifting that takes place is in the direction of the consumer. Stockholders are likely to be in higher income brackets than either the general consumer or the wage earner. Therefore, the greater the extent to which the tax is shifted, the less clearly is the corporate income tax an ability tax.

Even if none of the tax is shifted, so that the stockholders bear the whole of it, the fact must be recognized that not all stockholders have the same ability to pay taxes. Yet the share of each in the income of the corporation is subject to the same rate of tax. In order to tax stockholders according to ability to pay it would be necessary to regard each stockholder as a partner. The tax would then not be levied on corporate income as such, but on the share of each stockholder in the total profits, whether or not distributed, and at a rate that takes account of his other income.

Still another difficulty in taxing according to ability under the corporate income tax arises out of the application of exemptions and rate graduation. If a lower rate is applied to the profits of a corporation making small profits than is applied to the profits of one that makes large profits, the implication is that stockholders of corporations making small profits are relatively poor, and conversely for stockholders of those making large profits. As a matter of fact, the opposite may be true. The stock of many large public corporations is widely distributed, whereas that of the smaller private corporation making smaller profits may be held by a few wealthy individuals.

A special element of ability to pay would be found in the corporate income tax if it could be shown that dividend income has a greater tax-paying capacity than the same amount of earned income. Income from physical property undoubtedly has a greater taxpaying capacity than does income from individual effort, even when both types of income are very large. This is because the latter takes no account of the depreciation of the human body as the years pass. Income from property, of course, is taxed net of depreciation. No single generalization can be made, however, to cover all ranges of personal and property income. The wealthy stockholder is in a very different position from that of the person who is able to own only a few shares of stock; and the possessor of rare earning power is apt to receive rewards in excess of those necessary to assure an adequate supply of the type of services which he is able to provide.

Despite the special taxpaying capacity of dividend income, the low-income stockholder may be entitled to favorable treatment. It is true that a person receiving a small amount of dividend income is in a superior position to a worker receiving an equivalent amount of wages. On the other hand, social policy may call for the encouragement of the extension of participation in the ownership of industry to the lower middle-income groups. Therefore, even if it is believed that unearned income has a greater taxpaying ability than earned income, the same rates might be applied to both up to some relatively small amount of interest and dividend income.

▶ INCIDENCE

It is apparent that the incidence of a tax on corporate income will differ from that of a tax on the income of a proprietorship. The latter is taxed under the personal income tax. We have seen that under certain conditions the personal income tax may be partly shiftable. If the supply of a given type of personal service is reduced because of high income tax rates, its remuneration may increase. On the other hand, the personal income tax is difficult to shift, and its incidence ordinarily remains for the most part on the proprietor or partners. Businessmen have argued strongly that the corporate income tax, however, is largely shifted forward to the consumer. They base this contention on their interpretation of the price and output response of the corporation to the imposition of the tax.

The argument that the corporate income tax is shifted deserves careful analysis. The incidence of this tax is usually believed by its advocates to fall on the stockholder. Their objective is not to tax the consumer or the worker. They urge the continuance of the corporate income tax on social grounds, and evidently do not believe that an equal amount of progression could be obtained if we were to rely on the personal income tax alone for what is at present accomplished by the corporate and personal income tax combined. The case is weakened, however, to the extent that the tax is shifted.

Before considering the probable incidence of a tax on corporate net income we may note that even if the corporate income tax is partially shifted there might well be a justification for retaining it. Limits of taxable capacity can be extended by use of hidden taxes when all possible use has been made of taxes whose incidence is more certain. Some doubt with respect to tax incidence might conceivably serve to lessen the violence of the struggle over tax progression between different income classes. On the other hand, it would seem to be a count against the tax if workers favored it under the illusion that it was borne by the stockholders alone.

THE STANDARD SHORT-RUN ANALYSIS

The standard short-run analysis of the corporate income tax is based on the view that only the firm that makes "economic" profits pays a tax. Taxable profits as defined by the legislature are presumed to be identical with the concept of profits as used by the economist.[9] In other words, the tax does not enter into the short-run cost curve, and since spending of the proceeds of the tax by the government is ignored, it is assumed that the tax is also independent of demand. Both marginal cost and marginal revenue are therefore regarded as unchanged. Consequently, the point of intersection of these curves is likewise unchanged, output and price remain as before the tax, and none of the tax is passed forward to the consumer in the form of higher prices. Similarly, since optimum output has not changed, demand for labor and other factors of production is unaltered, and no part of the tax is passed backward to these factors.

If all firms in a competitive industry are identical, there can be no yield from a corporate income tax that is levied on economic profits alone. Average cost will equal average revenue for each firm, and price will merely cover all costs including normal profits. If, however, some firms are making above-normal profits, they will pay a tax. This might happen, for example, because of dynamic changes in demand conditions.

The analysis is the same for industries operating under conditions of monopolistic competition. Under oligopoly or monopoly, with entry restricted, firms making monopoly profits also have no incentive to alter output after imposition of the tax provided they were previously maximizing profits. The intersection of the marginal revenue and marginal cost curves is unaffected. If, however, they had not exploited to the full their monopoly position, either through moderation or because they had been maximizing some combination of return in addition to and including profits (for example, good will or liquidity), the imposition of the tax might prompt them to pay greater attention to profits alone. If the tax were high enough to overcome inertia, oligopolists would be likely to agree among themselves to raise prices up to the point indicated by the intersection of the marginal cost and marginal revenue curves.

The analysis thus far has related to the short run only. It assumes that plant and equipment are fixed. Under the assumptions of partial equilibrium analysis supply schedules are not altered. Moreover, it is assumed

---

[9] See the diagrammatic analysis in Chapter 7, Figure 9.

that there is no change in market demand resulting either from the imposition of the tax or from the spending of its proceeds by the government. Prices, therefore, remain unchanged and the tax is not shifted. However, account must now be taken of the possibility that businessmen will not react in the fashion assumed by equilibrium theory.

QUALIFICATIONS: SHORT-RUN INCIDENCE

The possibility exists that the businessman might regard the corporate income tax as itself a cost. If it were really a cost, the average and marginal cost curves would shift upward, the intersection between marginal revenue and marginal cost would move to the left, supply would be curtailed, and prices would rise. Moreover, the demand for the factors of production would likewise decrease, and part of the tax might be shifted backward.

It is not certain, however, that businessmen actually consider the tax to be a cost of production.[10] Even if they do so, it has to be remembered that this tax "cost" is greater the larger the profits of the firm. Therefore, firms find themselves in unequal positions with respect to the extent to which they wish to respond by raising prices. A firm may be making high profits, and therefore paying a high corporate profits tax per unit of commodity sold. If this firm attempts to base price on average cost including tax, it is likely to lose sales to those firms that are making lower profits. Therefore it is more probable that firms realizing high profits will continue to equate additional revenue with additional cost excluding tax, and price their product accordingly.

A more serious limitation on the inference that the intersection of marginal cost and marginal revenue is unchanged arises out of the assumption that none of the short-run economic profits are really a payment for the risk of adverse price changes incident to producing for inventory or for a market subject to fluctuations. Under these circumstances the effect of the tax even in the short run might be to cause a curtailment of output, and a shifting of part of the tax.

SHORT-RUN BACKWARD SHIFTING

The corporation might attempt to pass the tax backward to labor in the form of reduced wage rates. Under the assumption of the marginal productivity theory, the corporate income tax cannot affect wage rates in the short run. No corporate income tax is payable with respect to the marginal unit of labor hired, so that the point of optimum output is arrived at independently of the tax. Therefore no pressure is exerted on wage rates by way of reduced output.

The above conclusion may need to be qualified, however, if account is taken of the modifications in theory introduced by wage bargaining practices. Unions may bargain on the basis of corporate profits either

---

[10] See the very lucid discussion of incidence by Goode, *op. cit.,* Chap. IV.

before or after tax. If they base their wage demands on corporate profits *after* tax, the greater the reduction in profits caused by the tax, the weaker is the bargaining position of labor. It is possible that part of an increase in corporate income tax rates may therefore be shifted to labor. This would take the form of a more moderate rise in wage rates than would have been obtained had labor succeeded in forcing collective bargaining to center around profits *before* tax. If we take cognizance of the bargaining theory of wage determination, therefore, it becomes apparent that generalization is difficult even with respect to short-run incidence of the corporate income tax. There may be a substantial range of indeterminacy associated with bilateral monopoly.[11]

LONG-RUN INCIDENCE

The corporate income tax is more likely to be shifted in the long run than in the short run. One reason for this is that economic profits are apt to be primarily a short-run phenomenon. In the long run it is more difficult to restrict freedom of entry of new firms, and the rate of return therefore tends to remain closer to normal profits. So far as this is so, the tax tends to be part of the cost of production.

Another point is that to the extent that the tax discourages private investment, the long-run trend of real costs is likely to be less rapidly downward than would be the case in the absence of the tax. Therefore, prices tend to be relatively higher because of the tax.[12] This is based on the assumption, however, that the taxed corporate savings would have found a ready outlet for investment. It also assumes that the use made by the government of the proceeds will be less cost-reducing than is the same amount of investment in the hands of the corporations. This may not always be true (for example, transportation subsidies in order to open up new areas, the development of atomic energy). However, it certainly holds for a large part of government spending, which is primarily directed toward public consumption rather than toward investment.

The corporate income tax, levied at high rates, may be suspected of discouraging risky investment in the long run. There must be some rate of tax high enough so that for each type of undertaking the prospect is reduced that profits after tax will be great enough to cover all costs including risk of loss of part of capital. No one knows exactly what rate this

---

[11] See the Hearings before the Joint Committee on the Economic Report December, 1948, *Corporate Profits*, for the views of representatives of both corporations and labor unions on the economic role of corporate profits. For a discussion of incidence, see Goode, *op. cit.*, pp. 62 ff., and the *Final Report* of the Committee on the Federal Corporate Net Income Tax, *Proceedings* of the National Tax Association, 1950, pp. 54 ff.

[12] This assumes that there is no decline in aggregate demand, including consumption spending. Otherwise, of course, the price level may decline in response to secular stagnation. In any event, the cost of goods in terms of hours of work required to buy them will be higher.

will be for a given type of enterprise, because the tax is only one of many influences on net profits. Therefore, some observers believe that the corporate income tax is partly shifted forward in the form of higher prices because savings are thought to be gradually redirected from investment in plant and equipment to seek the safety of government securities and cash. There is little evidence, however, that this has occurred in recent years of high-level demand and relatively sure profits. At any rate, the tax may equally well be shifted backward to labor and other factors of production as demand for their services falls with the decline in investment.

▶ ECONOMIC EFFECTS

Thus far attention has been concentrated on the short-run and long-run incidence of the corporate income tax. The ultimate economic effects of the tax are determined not only by the long-term investment responses of the taxed corporations but also by the income and spending effects resulting from such changes in investment. These are likely to be so complex that they cannot be isolated. They take much time to work themselves out. Moreover, they become inextricably mingled with the many dynamic changes that are constantly taking place in the economy. Both the long-run direct and indirect effects commence to make themselves felt immediately, however. The moment the tax is imposed some corporations will be in the act of deciding whether to change their scale of plant or whether to introduce some improvement in technology. If the tax affects their decisions, supply schedules are immediately affected, as well as incomes paid to factors of production.

In considering the final incidence of the corporate income tax, especially as it has developed under federal experience in the past four decades, it is important to take account of the spending of the proceeds of the tax. Increases in rates have usually been accompanied by increased government spending. Demand curves of the taxed corporations are therefore affected, and an offset is provided to the discouraging effects of the tax itself on investment and the supply curves of the corporations. If, in addition, rate rises are accompanied by inflationary government borrowing (as in time of war), the net effect may well be to increase rather than reduce corporate profits. Thus it would be misleading to consider merely the incidence of the tax itself.

Wide variations exist, however, in the effects on different corporations. If, for example, a rise in the rate of tax is accompanied by heavy war spending, the net effect in many instances will be to encourage an expansion of investment in plant and equipment despite the tax. In wartime the great majority of corporations benefit, either directly or indirectly, from government spending. The situation is entirely different, of course, if during time of peace a decision is made to increase corporate income tax rates in order to permit a reduction in the rates of some other tax. In this case the rate of spending remains the same, and the tax effects alone are under consideration.

► A SPECIAL CASE: PUBLIC UTILITIES

When prices are controlled by public regulation, as in the case of public utilities, the extent to which the corporate income tax can be shifted to the consumer in the form of higher prices differs from the case where prices are not subject to control. The courts have decided that such businesses are entitled to a "fair" return, and that income taxes are to be regarded as operating costs. In other words, the corporate income tax may be explicitly passed forward to the consumer.

Whether this is possible in fact as well as in law, however, depends on what happens to sales if prices are raised. Demand may indeed be almost completely inelastic over a wide range of price. Examples are the demands for electricity, heating, and local telephone service, as contrasted with that for railroad transportation, which has to compete with other forms of transport. When demand for a regulated public service is very inelastic it is likely that less than the full monopoly price had been previously charged, and the tax can probably be passed forward. Public-utility commissions, however, facing public opinion, are slow to allow rate increases, and the evidence in the thirties and the forties was that utility rises did not often follow increases in corporate income tax rates.[13]

Over the long run the corporate income tax on public-utility income may cause a downward revision in conceptions of what constitutes a fair return on capital. If this occurs, the tax is less likely to be shifted. On the other hand, cost-reducing technological progress may take place. If public-utility commissions are slow to permit rate rises, forward shifting may then take the form of a failure to reduce rates as costs fall. Furthermore, even when demand conditions do not permit a rate rise granted by the public-service commission actually to become effective, the standard of service may gradually decline without any drop in sales. In effect, then, the tax is shifted forward.

► ACCELERATED AMORTIZATION

In the long run if the corporate income tax is not to rest on costs rather than on pure profits, the firm must be permitted to deduct each year an amount from gross income that corresponds to the wearing out of plant and equipment.[14] The tax laws require certain procedures to be followed

---

[13] Goode, *op. cit.*, p. 52.

[14] For gas and oil wells and mineral properties, depreciation is taken in the form of depletion. Basically, the method is to estimate the amount of the deposit, allocate cost to the depletable reserves, and on the basis of the amount extracted

in making annual deductions for depreciation and obsolescence. The size of the annual deduction is related to the life of the kind of equipment being depreciated. Under certain circumstances, however, equipment may have to be junked before it is worn out. It may become obsolescent, or demand for its end product may decline. Unless the corporation is allowed to accelerate the rate at which it depreciates the property for tax purposes, the whole of its cost has not been taken into account. In other words, the corporate income tax then becomes partly a tax on costs. This situation may be met with during time of war as well as during a period of militarization. It may also occur when, for reasons of national policy, firms need to be encouraged to accelerate the rate at which they install new equipment. For example, if the rate of technological progress is high, a rapid write-off of the nation's plant and equipment could contribute to an increase in efficiency.

Suppose that it is expected that a war will last five years, and that the life of certain equipment installed to produce military goods is twenty years. Suppose further that the equipment has no value for the production of civilian goods. Then the firm might be allowed to accelerate the amortization of such equipment. This it would do by including one fifth of its cost in the deduction from gross corporate income in each of the five years.[15] Thus the profits tax base would be reduced in each year. This procedure would not necessarily reduce the tax, however, if the war lasted more than five years, for in the sixth year there would be no deduction from gross income on account of amortization. The firm could, however, junk the plant and install new, more efficient facilities. It would derive part of the funds for this purpose out of its lower tax during the five years. Therefore, accelerated amortization can be a stimulus to the introduction of new and more efficient equipment. If public welfare demanded a continuation of the accelerated investment policy, the newly installed equipment could likewise qualify for accelerated amortization. Otherwise the standard regulations could be brought back into force.[16]

---

each year, reduce gross income by "deductible cost depletion." An alternative method is to deduct a percentage of gross income each year as the depletion deduction. The percentage for gas and oil wells, for example, is 27½ per cent. Partly because of political reasons, and in part in order to stimulate discovery of mineral resources, depletion allowances have been very generous, and have provided the occasion for vigorous debate in Congress and in the press.

[15] Accelerated amortization includes obsolescence as well as depreciation.

[16] Federal law does not prescribe a particular method of taking depreciation. The straight-line method was the one most often used prior to 1954. Changes in the revenue code made in 1954 have been designed to encourage a businessman to recover about two thirds of the cost of equipment in the first half of its life. This change takes account of the fact that actual depreciation is likely to be greatest during the early years. Under the straight-line method one tenth of the cost of the equipment is a deductible expense in each year (for example) of a presumed life of ten years. Under the declining-balance method, 20 per cent of the cost may be taken into account the first year, 20 per cent of the remainder in the next, and so on. A variation on the declining-balance method is the sum-of-the-years-digits method. For details see Commerce Clearing House, *Master Tax Guide*, 1955 edition.

The advantages to the firm of accelerated amortization during wartime are severalfold. (1) It cushions the impact of a decline in the peacetime demand for the end product. (2) The write-off is concentrated in years of high profits. Even though the equipment is still used after the period of militarization is past, there may be no profits against which to charge the depreciation after the expiration of the five-year period. (3) If there is ground for believing that the corporate income tax rate may fall again, it is desirable for the firm to incur as little profits tax liability during the emergency period as possible. (4) If a firm desires to expand operations it is an advantage to recover its investment quickly. By investing the proceeds in new plant, corporations can get the benefit of still further accelerated amortization. Results similar to those of accelerated amortization can be achieved by requiring *deferred* depreciation for that investment which is regarded as *immaterial* to the war effort. Thus Canada, in 1951, introduced this device as an incentive to conversion to military production.

► DEDUCTIBILITY OF INTEREST ON INDEBTEDNESS

A special difficulty created by the corporate income tax arises out of the fact that whereas dividends are a part of profits, and are therefore taxable, interest paid on corporate debt is deductible from taxable profits. The result is that a corporation can reduce its tax liability by substituting bonded indebtedness for stock issues. The line between these two varieties of financing is often hard to draw, and to a large extent they compete for similar types of savings.

The alternatives to present practice would be either to require interest paid to be included in taxable corporate profits, or to exempt dividends from the tax. The former procedure, by increasing costs, would tend to increase bankruptcies among unprofitable corporations unless and until the tax could be shifted. The transition would have to be made gradually. The latter course would be similar to a tax on undistributed profits, but would greatly narrow the tax base. Logically the inclusion of interest would also require the inclusion of rents paid by the corporation, since rents and interest are economically similar. The administrative difficulties of such a procedure would be great, however, and the bankruptcy rate would probably be still further increased.

► INTEGRATION OF THE CORPORATE AND PERSONAL INCOME TAXES

The fact that the corporation has a legal identity that is distinct from that of its owners makes it difficult to tax the personal income of stockholders on the same basis as that of proprietors and partners. The latter are taxable on their entire net business income, whereas stockholders are taxable on only that part of corporate profits that is distributed to them. If a corporation were to withhold all profits from distribution, only the corporate income tax would be paid. If all profits were distributed, both corporate and personal income taxes would apply to every dollar of profits. The argument has frequently been made that stockholders are subject to an inequity because of double taxation. That is, distributed profits are taxed first under the corporate income tax and again under the personal income tax. But it can be seen at once that to the extent that profits are withheld from distribution, invested in the business, and become the basis for unrealized, nontaxable capital gains, the stockholder has a decided advantage over the proprietor or partner.

From the point of view particularly of the internal financing of a small growing business, there seems to be little doubt that the partnership form is at a disadvantage as compared with a corporation. The partner and proprietor are subject to the individual income tax rate at whatever rate is appropriate to their taxable brackets, whether or not they withdraw profits for personal consumption or saving. Consequently, if they are in a high income bracket, they may find it difficult to accumulate capital out of profits in order to expand business operations. Because of this disadvantage to noncorporate enterprise, proposals have been made to exempt individual savings from the income tax. Irving Fisher was a well-known advocate of the exclusion of both individual and corporate saving from the concept of income.[17] Thus both the stockholder and the proprietor would be taxed on their consumption spending only. Fisher's views have received support in recent years from those who regard the encouragement of saving as an indispensable basis for rapid economic progress. But the proposal is no answer to the problem of equity. The exempted savers would, of course, be those who are in the higher-income brackets, and the distribution of income would become more unequal.

Corporations, within certain limits, can remove their profits from liability to the personal income tax by reinvesting them in the business. If the owners of a closely held corporation[18] are all subject to a very high personal income tax rate, there is an advantage over the partnership because profits can be withheld from distribution, and thus be taxed at the lower corporate income tax rate. Thus there is an incentive to withhold profits from distribution. This has, in addition to the effects on the distribution of income, important economic effects hinging on the self-financing of corporate business expansion out of internal funds. This advantage to corporations has indeed declined as corporate income tax rates have been increased. At a rate of 52 per cent stockholders must be in a very high-

---

[17] Irving and Herbert Fisher, *Constructive Income Taxation* (New York: Harper, 1942).

[18] A closely held corporation, owned by a small number of stockholders, is usually also managed by them. It is therefore similar in important respects to a partnership.

income bracket if they are to be liable for a greater personal than corporate income tax. An excess-profits tax may also have to be taken into account, since this applies only to corporations.

THE PARTNERSHIP METHOD

The only complete integration of corporate and personal taxation is achieved through the partnership method, which treats stockholders as partners for tax purposes.[19] This would permit the abolition of the corporate income tax. Personal income tax rates might then be adjusted so that the same revenue would be yielded as under the corporate and personal income taxes combined.

The method would in principle be simple. Each stockholder would receive an information certificate with respect to his share of corporate profits. He would then be required to include in his taxable personal income both distributed and undistributed profits. This device would be workable for the bulk of the half million corporations which, because of their small size, are closely akin to partnerships. It would not be as easily applicable, however, to the large public corporations, whose stocks may be distributed among thousands of stockholders, and whose capital structures may be complex. The former point is much less serious than the latter, however, since it is no more difficult to mail out information certificates than dividend checks.

If a stockholder is taxed on his share of both distributed and undistributed profits, he may not have the funds out of which to pay the tax if the firm withholds profits for reinvestment. The problem raised by the taxation of individuals not in control of a business, on earnings of which they cannot get possession, is a serious one. This is true despite certain mitigating circumstances which may operate in some cases. In most small corporations a satisfactory agreement on distribution policy can be reached. Even when the stockholder has no voice in the proportion of net profits distributed as dividends, he may have other income out of which he can pay the tax. In many instances, moreover, some profits will be distributed. Finally, the stockholder can sell part of his stock. The disadvantage of the latter procedure, of course, is that he is at the mercy of the market at the time when he must sell stock in order to pay the tax. Again, the sale of stock dilutes the stockholder's equity in the corporation; but this is of no importance in a large corporation, where this equity is very small and carries no power to participate in management decisions.[20]

---

[19] This method was adopted during the Civil War, but the growth in the complexity of ownership of corporations since that time has made its use more and more difficult. Also, there is some doubt whether the partnership method would be upheld by the Supreme Court if it were made compulsory. The 1954 revenue code permitted *unincorporated* businesses to elect to be taxed as *corporations*.

[20] One solution that has been proposed is to collect the tax at the source. In effect the corporation would be distributing enough profits so that each stockholder could pay his tax.

REPEAL OF THE CORPORATE INCOME TAX

The elimination of the problems connected with the existence of separate corporate and personal taxes on income cannot be effected merely by repealing the corporate income tax. Such a step would confer an important advantage on those who are in a position to save indirectly through the accumulation of undistributed profits, taking their savings in the form of capital gains. The latter are not taxable until realized, and even then are taxed at favorable rates. As stated above, in order to obtain the same amount of revenue from the personal income tax as from the combined personal and corporate income taxes, personal income tax rates would probably have to be raised.[21]

The repeal of the corporate income tax would, of course, be a very poor solution to the equity problem unless undistributed profits were taxed under the personal income tax. Otherwise, only if undistributed profits were completely reflected in the form of capital gains, and if capital gains were taxed whether realized or not, would this method be identical with the partnership method.

DEVICES FOR PARTIAL INTEGRATION

Three devices are at hand by means of which the corporate and individual income taxes may be more closely integrated.[22] (1) A dividend credit can be given to the corporation for distributed profits; or, conversely, undistributed profits might be subjected to a special tax in addition to the corporate income tax. (2) The corporate income tax could be regarded merely as a withholding tax for the personal income tax. This has been at least in part the British philosophy, and was the intention of those who originally regarded the federal tax on corporate income merely as a prelude to the adoption of a permanent personal income tax. (3) A credit might be given the personal income taxpayer for the tax paid by the corporation.

1. The Credit for Dividends Paid. Under this method of coordination, corporations would be allowed a deduction from taxable income for dividends paid. In its pure form this device would result in the taxation of undistributed profits solely under the corporate income tax, and of distributed profits only under the tax on personal income. A possible modification would be to allow only a partial deduction for dividends paid. A credit for dividends paid, it will be noted, provides a tax inducement to corporations to distribute profits, and one's approval of the credit will

---

[21] The effect of repeal of the corporate income tax on the revenues would depend on the relation between the corporate income tax rate and the schedule of personal income tax rates, together with the proportion of corporate profits withheld from distribution.

[22] For an excellent discussion, see United States Treasury, *The Postwar Corporation Tax Structure* (by R. B. Goode), December 6, 1946, reprinted in *Hearings on Revenue Revision*, House of Representatives, 1948, pp. 1136 ff. See also Goode, *The Corporation Income Tax*, pp. 190 ff.

depend largely on his assessment of the economic implications of bringing about a rise in the proportion of distributed to total profits.

The credit for dividends paid does not provide a complete answer to the problem of coordinating the corporate and personal income taxes, because personal income tax liability on the profits distributed to the stockholder depends on his tax bracket. Despite the credit for dividends paid, the retention of profits would still benefit wealthy stockholders, because, above a certain income, personal income tax liability would exceed the corporate income tax on profits withheld from distribution.

2. *The Withholding Method.* "Double taxation" of distributed profits could be eliminated if a withholding tax were levied on corporate profits. The tax paid by the corporation could be deducted from the tax due from the stockholder. One advantage of this method would be to assure payment by thousands of widely dispersed stockholders of personal income taxes due on dividends received. Under this method, the stockholder would include in his personal income tax return his dividends plus his share of the tax paid by the corporation,[23] and would subtract the withholding tax paid by the corporation from his income tax.

This approach regards the withholding tax on corporate profits as a means of enlisting the services of the corporation to collect the tax from the stockholder. However, stockholders subject to tax-bracket rates greater than the withholding tax rate would have a further tax to pay, while stockholders with incomes small enough to be subject to no tax, or to a rate lower than that of the withholding tax, would get a refund.

3. *The Credit for Dividends Received.* A version of the withholding approach is the credit for dividends received, which was a feature of the federal law up to 1936. Although subject to the surtax, dividends were not taxed under the normal tax rate. As under the withholding method, the credit for dividends received tacitly assumes that the incidence of the corporate income tax is on the stockholder. To the extent, however, that the tax is passed forward to the consumer, or backward to production factors, the credit represents a windfall to the stockholder. If the tax is not shifted there still remains the problem of reimbursing stockholders whose incomes are too low to be taxable under the personal income tax. Moreover, there is an inequity when taxable stockholders are not required to declare as income their share of the tax paid by the corporation.[24]

Incentives to Distribute Profits. These three plans for partial integra-

---

[23] Just as a taxpayer in any case figures his federal income tax on his income without deducting his tax.

[24] In 1954 a provision was enacted permitting individual income taxpayers to exclude from gross income the first $50 of dividends received from qualified domestic corporations. In addition, a credit was provided amounting to 4 per cent of dividends above the $50 exclusion, and included in gross income. It is apparent that the credit for dividends received is construed by Congress more as a concession to dividend income than as a device for complete integration. As stated in the text, only the partnership method can accomplish the latter.

tion are inferior to the partnership method of taxing corporate profits, which eliminates entirely the distinction between the corporation and the stockholder for tax purposes. They would, however, provide an incentive to the distribution of profits, and thus augment the proportion of corporate profits subject to the personal income tax.[25] Indeed, one of the plans, the dividends-paid method, is similar to a penalty tax on undistributed profits. The difference is merely that attention is focused on the fact that lower rates are to be paid on distributed profits, rather than on the higher rates on undistributed profits.

Since the credit-for-dividends-paid approach would tend to convert the corporate income tax into a tax on undistributed profits, there is the danger that it might be regarded as primarily a penalty tax on retained earnings, rather than, as intended, a method for partially integrating the corporation and personal income taxes. A tax on undistributed profits is, in fact, intended to do both these things, and both objectives were included in the proposal of the Roosevelt administration in the thirties for an undistributed-profits tax. But emphasis of the tax as finally enacted proved to be on the penalty aspects rather than on integration. We turn now to a consideration of the undistributed-profits tax of 1936.

► REFERENCES

BROWN, E. C. "Accelerated Depreciation: A Neglected Chapter in War Taxation," *Quarterly Journal of Economics,* August, 1943.

CONGRESS OF THE UNITED STATES, JOINT COMMITTEE ON THE ECONOMIC REPORT. *Corporate Profits.* December, 1948.

GOODE, R. *The Corporation Income Tax.* New York: John Wiley & Sons, Inc., 1951.

NATIONAL TAX ASSOCIATION, COMMITTEE ON THE FEDERAL CORPORATE NET INCOME TAX. *Final Report.* Published in the *Proceedings* of the National Tax Association, 1950, pp. 54 ff.

SMITH, D. T. *Effects of Taxation: Corporate Financial Policy.* Boston: Harvard University, Graduate School of Business Administration, 1951.

STUDENSKI, P. "Toward a Theory of Business Taxation," *Journal of Political Economy,* October, 1940, pp. 621–654.

TAX INSTITUTE. *How Should Corporations Be Taxed?* New York: The Tax Institute, 1947.

UNITED STATES TREASURY DEPARTMENT, DIVISION OF TAX RESEARCH. *The Postwar Corporation Tax Structure* (December 6, 1948), reprinted in the *Hearings* on Revenue Revision, House of Representatives, 1948, pp. 1136 ff.

[25] Goode, *The Corporation Income Tax,* p. 195.

12 The Taxation of
Corporate Income: II

A special tax on undistributed profits arouses particular interest because of the experiment made in this direction by the Roosevelt administration from 1936 to 1938. A tax on undistributed profits, applied at progressive rates to various proportions of total profits not paid out in dividends, could make it prohibitive to withhold more than a permitted amount of profits. Thus any desired fraction of corporate profits could be forced into the hands of the stockholder for taxation under the personal income tax. President Roosevelt had recommended the replacement of the corporate income tax with a tax on undistributed profits, but Congress enacted the latter without abolishing the former.

Attempts were made to justify the 1936 undistributed-profits tax on a number of grounds other than that of integration alone. Underconsumptionists thought that forced distribution of corporate profits would increase total spending. They assumed (1) that corporations would not reinvest the undistributed profits, but would hold them in the form of idle cash, and (2) that dividends are largely paid to individuals who will spend rather than save them. The fact that a large proportion of undistributed profits is not in the form of cash made the first assumption doubtful even during depression. Again, although dividends to small stockholders are undoubtedly largely spent on consumption, a large proportion is saved.[1]

---

[1] By contrast, it is interesting to note the British official attitude toward undistributed profits during an inflationary period. A distinction has been made between the inflationary power of a given amount of spending by consumers and the same amount of spending by producers. In 1947 the standard rate of the corporate income tax was 45%, plus a 5% profits tax. Chancellor of the Exchequer Dalton requested a tax of 12.5% on *distributed* profits. Later he asked that both the 5% tax on undistributed profits and the 12.5% tax on distributed profits be doubled. His reasoning was that dividends are spent on consumption, while undistributed profits contribute to the modernization of plant and equipment, and thus serve to increase the flow of commodities.

When personal income tax rates are extremely high the likelihood is increased

Another argument in favor of the tax was made by those who thought that the stock market is in a better position to make decisions on the proper allocation of capital than is the individual corporation that happens to have made the profits. In other words, if a progressive undistributed-profits tax compelled distribution, the corporation would be forced into the capital market instead of being able to rely on withheld profits. Something may be conceded to this argument, but it must be pointed out that many corporations, particularly small and new corporations, suffer by being forced to distribute profits. Because they do not have access to the stock market they may depend heavily on undistributed profits for new investment. Again the stock market is far from a perfect market, and therefore does not itself do a perfect job of rationing capital among competing uses. Moreover, the cost of a stock issue is not small,[2] and the effect of the tax may be to discourage investment.

THE UNDISTRIBUTED-PROFITS TAX OF 1936

Because of its hampering effect on corporate financial policy, the undistributed-profits tax of 1936 proved to be extremely unpopular with businessmen.[3] Its rates were not sufficiently progressive, however, to make retention of profits impossible. The range was from 7 to 27 per cent of undistributed net income:

Adjusted Net Income, Percentage Retained	Rate of Tax
Up to 10%	7%
10–20	12
20–40	17
40–60	22
Over 60	27

It has been estimated that the surtax on undistributed profits caused an increase in dividends of about $1 billion in each of the years 1936 and 1937.[4] This represents an increase in dividends of about one third as

that dividends have to be devoted to consumption. On the other hand, even a modernization program designed to lower costs may set in motion an inflationary spiral during the period before the flow of goods is actually increased. Cf. M. Beck, "The British Anti-Inflationary Tax on Distributed Corporate Profits," *National Tax Journal,* September, 1948. The tax on distributed profits was raised to 27½ per cent in October, 1955.

[2] Cf. Securities and Exchange Commission, *Cost of Flotation for Registered Securities, 1938–1939* (Washington, D. C., 1941). This cost may absorb as much as 20% of the proceeds of the issue.

[3] Among the studies of the effects of this tax on dividends and business policies may be mentioned G. E. Lent, *The Impact of the Undistributed Profits Tax, 1936–1937* (New York: Columbia University Press, 1948). See also S. P. Dobrovolsky, *Corporate Income Retention: 1915–1943* (New York: National Bureau of Economic Research, 1951).

[4] Lentz, *op. cit.,* p. 175.

compared with what they would presumably have been in the absence of the tax.

Other effects of the tax, particularly on small and medium-sized corporations, were to encourage the payment of higher salaries and bonuses; and, in common with a tax on excess profits, to cause an increase in advertising budgets and other miscellaneous expenses that reduce profits subject to tax. The influence of the tax on the policy of dividend distribution varied greatly according to the particular circumstances of the corporation. Corporations having heavy indebtedness, or needing to maintain a high level of assets, tended to distribute a relatively smaller proportion of profits.

On two counts the undistributed-profits tax had the effect of decreasing the level of saving. First, corporate savings were reduced to the extent that withholding of profits from distribution involved a corporation in payment of tax. Second, part of the dividends distributed because of the tax was spent on consumption.[5]

ACCUMULATED-EARNINGS TAX

Although the 1936 undistributed-profits tax was finally repealed in 1939, undistributed profits are still subject to a special penalty provision when the purpose is to avoid personal income taxation by the stockholders of closely held corporations.[6] This provision or a similar one has operated since the passage of the income tax act in 1913. It is directed, however, only at "unreasonable" withholding of profits. If the burden of proof lies with the corporation, the effect is likely to be to cause some corporations to distribute profits when the interests of the stockholders and the corporation would be better served by a greater amount of reinvestment. In 1954 the burden of proof was shifted from the corporation to the government.

"Improperly" withheld income has been taxed since 1942 at the rate of 27½ per cent on retained income up to $100,000 and at 38½ per cent above this amount. Income is regarded as *properly* withheld if it is invested in ways that are relevant to the regular business of the corporation, like investment in plant or inventories, or repayment of debt. Income is not properly withheld, for example, if devoted to the purchase of stock in a corporation in an industry that is unrelated to that of the corporation withholding profits. The Internal Revenue Service has instructed its agents to give close attention to the returns of corporations which have not distributed at least 70 per cent of their earnings as taxable dividends. The enormous variations in the need for liquidity from industry to industry, and from firm to firm, make it difficult to determine in many instances

---

[5] Lent (*ibid.*, p. 188) states that consumer expenditures were increased by about half a billion dollars more "than would probably have been realized from the most logical alternative form of tax."

[6] As we have seen, a special provision applies if the corporation is a personal holding company, which is one 50 per cent of whose stock is owned by not more than five persons, and 80 per cent of whose income is from investments.

whether or not corporate income is being improperly withheld. The 1954 revision allows all corporations a minimum accumulation, free of tax, of $60,000.

AVOIDANCE OF CASH DISTRIBUTION

The ability of a corporation to finance expansion is enhanced to the extent that it can avoid the distribution of dividends in cash. Dividends may be declared in the form of the corporation's own stock (stock dividends). This obviates the necessity of meeting the test of the market, which the firm has to do if it wishes to finance expansion after having distributed cash. From the point of view of a tax on undistributed profits, however, effective distribution has not been made unless the dividends are taxable in the hands of the stockholder. A purpose of an accumulated-earnings or undistributed-profits tax is to encourage the taxation under the personal income tax of stockholders' shares of corporate profits.

THE SUPREME COURT ON THE TAXATION OF STOCK DIVIDENDS

The Supreme Court has long been concerned with the problem of the separate existence of the corporation from that of its owners. The questions are, What constitutes taxable income in the hands of the stockholders, and at precisely what point are profits of corporations to be regarded as taxable individual income? From the standpoint of the legal concept of the corporation, dividends have not been declared unless there is a separation of assets. The way in which this might ordinarily be expected to take place is through the distribution of cash, which is, of course, a corporate asset.

A definition of income widely accepted by economists is increase in economic power. It will be recalled that the income of an individual between two points of time is regarded, under this concept, as consumption plus the net change (positive or negative) in a person's wealth. Even if the courts were so disposed, however, they would encounter difficulty in applying this entirely logical definition. Since the stockholder is one of the owners of the corporation, his income has increased proportionately at the moment the latter is in receipt of income. Yet unless this income is immediately distributed to him he has no more cash than before with which to pay income tax.

In other words, because the corporation has a legal existence separate from that of its owners, it may not be practicable to insist on the application of the pure economic definition of income. If the stock market reflected precisely all amounts of undistributed income, the stockholder would be able to obtain the cash necessary for payment of tax by selling part of his stock. Since this is not even approximately the case, some other criterion of income must be found.

The Supreme Court first stated its position in 1920 on the taxation of stock dividends in *Eisner v. Macomber* (252 U. S. 189, 1920), when it held that a dividend in the common stock of a corporation paid to the common stockholders is not income within the meaning of the Sixteenth Amendment.[7] The reasons advanced were (1) there had been no severance of the corporation's assets, and (2) no change had been made in the pre-existing proportionate interests of the stockholders. When common stock is paid to holders of common stock, relative shares of ownership are unchanged. Therefore it is possible to take the position that stockholders have nothing that they did not have before.

In implementing the Court's decision, the Treasury went still further. It issued regulations exempting from income tax all income in the form of stock dividends, whether or not the shares issued as dividends were of the same class as that previously held by the stockholder. In 1921 Congress specifically exempted stock dividends from the income tax, thus confirming the Treasury's interpretation. In a later case, however (*Koshland v. Helvering*, 298 U. S. 441, 1936), the Supreme Court held that stock dividends are taxable if they change the previous ratio of stockownership, and the statute was changed to provide for the taxation of whatever stock dividends were declared by the Supreme Court to be taxable. The 1936 decision implied that preferred stock issued to holders of common stock, if preferred was already outstanding, and common stock issued to holders of preferred stock, gave stockholders an interest in the corporation that differed from the previous interest, and the income was therefore taxable. This decision set in motion a series of Court decisions that attempted to decide just when a stock dividend does or does not change the relative interest of stockholders. Because of the confusion engendered, Congress decided in 1954 to exempt all stock dividends from the income tax, except those received in lieu of cash dividends on preferred stock currently owing, or where there is an option to receive property or money.[8] Thus in general the situation is back where it stood in 1921.

► EXCESS-PROFITS TAXATION

A special form of corporate profits tax is the levy on excess profits. The taxation of "excess" corporate profits has traditionally been restricted to wartime. Public opinion has always favored special war profits taxation of firms that benefit from military spending. A large proportion of war

---

[7] A stock dividend is to be distinguished from a "dividend in stock." The latter involves a dividend in the form of the stock of another corporation, ordinarily a subsidiary. Thus in this case it is an *asset* of the dividend-declaring corporation that is being distributed. Clearly part of the assets of the corporation are being separated, exactly as in the case of a cash dividend. Therefore a dividend in stock is taxable.

[8] The practical effect of the 1954 rule is to exempt from taxation a preferred stock dividend to common stock shareholders in the case where preferred stock is already outstanding and not held pro rata by the holders of common stock.

profits is a windfall, and therefore is believed to have a special ability to pay. It is, however, not merely firms producing directly for the military effort that benefit from deficit spending in time of war. Workers in those industries have more money to spend, and a large segment of the economy therefore benefits indirectly.

These indirect effects have not always been recognized in the federal tax system. For example, in 1916 Congress enacted a special tax on the profits of munitions manufacturers alone, following the precedent of most of the belligerents.[9] The rate of this tax was 12½ per cent, and it applied to the net profits of partnerships as well as corporations. Events quickly required further tax revision, however, and in March, 1917, the United States followed the lead of the other warring nations by enacting a full-scale excess-profits tax. This tax likewise applied to partnerships as well as to corporations, but not to proprietorships or individuals. It recognized that all forms of business enterprise, in all types of industry, may benefit from war spending. The revised excess-profits tax enacted on October 3, 1917, applied (at a low rate) to the income of individuals as well as to that of partnerships and corporations. This extension of the scope of the concept of "excess" income quickly brought to a head some of the administrative and equity difficulties inherent in this form of taxation. The tax did not apply to income from rents, dividends, and interest, and it was therefore regarded as discriminating against earned income.

Instead of attempting to extend the concept to cover all types of "excess" income, Congress in 1918 limited the excess-profits tax to the income of corporations only. The extension of an excess-profits tax beyond the corporate form introduces the difficult problem of drawing the line between business partnerships and the self-employed professions. Moreover, the earnings of individuals and partnerships are subject to the progressive rates of the personal income tax, and the entire earnings are taxable. Congress has continued to follow the precedent set in 1918 of limiting the excess-profits tax to corporations.

THE CONCEPT OF "EXCESS PROFITS"

There are three senses in which profits may be regarded as excessive. (1) Some part of the profits from the sale of munitions may be deemed excessive even when they are no greater than the profits of corporations engaged in nonmilitary output. This view may be based on the circumstance that firms benefiting from military demand are, during the period of hostilities, exempt from some of the ordinary risks of business. Alter-

---

[9] Cf. Sidney Ratner, *American Taxation* (New York: Norton, 1942), pp. 358–359. On the other hand, as early as 1863 the state of Georgia had enacted an excess-profits tax on earnings in excess of 8 per cent of the capital stock of corporations. Anita Wells, "Legislative History of Excess Profits Taxation in the United States in World Wars I and II," *National Tax Journal,* September, 1951, p. 237.

natively, it may stem from a feeling that there is something tainted about profits from the production of munitions. (2) Profits attributable to the general increase in demand for most commodities during time of war ("war profits") may be defined as "excess profits." (3) Profits may be regarded as too high in relation to a "normal" or "reasonable" return on invested capital.

The Revenue Act of March 3, 1917, employed the reasonable-return approach. The rate of the tax was 8 per cent of net income in excess of (1) an exemption of $5,000, and (2) 8 per cent of invested capital. In other words, if a firm made profits of less than $5,000, they were not regarded as excessive even if they exceeded 8 per cent of capital. Above the exemption, only the difference between 8 per cent and the actual profit rate was defined as excess profit. Under this act, invested capital was defined as the cash value of assets, including paid-in surplus, earned surplus, and undivided profits. Borrowed capital was excluded. The treatment of borrowed capital has been subject to much debate, since a given amount of corporate income may be a much larger percentage of capital when, for excess-profits tax purposes, the latter is restricted to equity capital.

A PERMANENT VS. A WARTIME EXCESS-PROFITS TAX

One of the hotly debated issues in World War I was whether the excess-profits tax should apply to war profits only, or to a broader concept of profits that would apply in peacetime as well. This debate turned largely on administrative considerations, but also of importance was the question whether the excess-profits tax should become a permanent feature of the federal tax system.[10] The adoption of a permanent excess-profits tax carries implications with respect to what is the proper distribution of income among the factors of production.

Public opinion has given little support to the acceptance of a permanent peacetime excess-profits tax in this country. In general, the view has been held that the health of a free-enterprise economy depends on the possibility of large profits on successful ventures. Admittedly profits of 20 or 30 per cent are high, but a new firm does not know that it will make large profits when it undertakes risky investment. Consequently, the high profits of successful businesses are required to offset the low profits or losses of the unsuccessful ones. If all profits above 8 or 10 per cent were to be cut off by a high-rate excess-profits tax, the dice would be heavily loaded against forward-looking risky ventures.

---

[10] Ratner (*op. cit.*, p. 409) states that businessmen were afraid that a permanent excess-profits tax would be the first step toward socialism. Professor R. M. Haig, however, saw in the excess-profits tax simply a chance to reduce monopoly profits.— "The Taxation of Excess Profits in Great Britain," *American Economic Review*, December, 1920, cited by Ratner, p. 410.

THE TWO APPROACHES TO EXCESS-PROFITS TAXATION

In all three periods of hostilities since 1917 the excess-profits tax in this country has provided for two alternative approaches to the calculation of excess profits. These are the earnings standard and the invested-capital standard. The former accepts as normal the level of profits in an earlier period; the latter treats some percentage of capital as a reasonable rate of return. For example, the Revenue Act of 1918 imposed a (supplementary) *war-profits* tax on all earnings exceeding average net income during the years 1911–1913 (with an exemption of $3,000). The invested-capital feature of the 1917 act was retained, and the choice between the two was determined on the basis of which method would yield the higher tax. Under the excess-profits tax of World War II, both bases were again included, but the corporation was instructed to employ the method that would involve the smaller tax. This meant that to be liable for the tax, not only must a company have experienced during the taxable year an increase in profits over average profits of the base years, but the profits must be high in relation to capital. A firm having both a low capitalization and low earnings in the base period is discriminated against under both methods. Consequently, a complicated system of relief provisions had to be worked out.

THE EARNINGS STANDARD

The base period approach is useful only for a temporary excess-profits tax. With the passage of time, profits in the base period become less and less appropriate as a standard of normality. It becomes necessary to take account of the fact that even in the absence of war many firms would have grown, so that base period earnings do not reflect capacity to make profits in later years if there had been no war.

Another difficulty with the earnings standard is the assumption that the profits of the firm during the base period were "normal." At any given moment, there are thousands of firms that have not yet reached their optimum profit position, and there are thousands more making profits that are greater than those they will enjoy in the future. Again, concepts of what are normal profits change over time in response to the relative scarcity of capital and to changes in productivity. In other words, the earnings standard assumes that the economy is free from trend movements. This assumption is essentially true only for relatively brief periods of time.

Under the average-earnings method provision has to be made for a rise in profits due to an increase in the size of the firm. This occurs automatically when the invested-capital basis is used. If the earnings basis is used, the same objective can be accomplished by adjusting the credit for increases or decreases in capital. In the second 1940 act, for example, an increase was allowed in the credit by 8 per cent of additions to capital (and a decrease by 6 per cent of net reductions in capital). In effect this permitted the use of the invested-capital method for the computation of part of the tax.

THE INVESTED-CAPITAL STANDARD[11]

In assuming that some proportion of earnings to capital is normal, the invested-capital method has the advantage of allowing for growth. If capital and dollar earnings rise proportionally, no change occurs in the percentage return. Again, the invested-capital method offers an opportunity to depressed industries, when national income is high, to regain their position in the economy. For example, through the use of the invested-capital base the railroads were able to retire much debt during World War II, as well as to build up reserves to do some of the modernizing that was necessary in order to meet increased competition from trucks and planes after the war. The invested-capital method is also used by firms that have come into existence since the base period.

This method has some problems of its own, however. A major difficulty is the measurement of invested capital. The alternatives are original cost, replacement cost, cost to present owners, and value as a going concern. Each of these measures yields a different valuation. There is, of course, no completely satisfactory answer to the valuation problem.

The Treatment of Borrowed Capital. Under the invested-capital approach the treatment of borrowed capital is crucial, for practice varies greatly among business firms with respect to the proportion of equity financing to bond financing. If bonded indebtedness is included in the base, its inclusion increases the exemption and reduces the yield. Moreover, its inclusion encourages corporations to borrow in order to increase the exemption, although the necessity of paying interest on such borrowing is usually a deterrent to this method of avoidance. If borrowed capital is excluded from the base, however, corporations that are forced to borrow because of lack of access to the equity capital market are penalized. It is typically the small and growing corporation that must borrow.

Under the World War II excess-profits tax this difficulty was met with a compromise. Half of borrowed capital could be included in the invested-capital base, but only half of the interest payments on the borrowed capital might be excluded from earnings subject to the excess-profits tax. This principle was retained in modified form under the excess-profits tax of 1950. Exclusion of interest payments favors those less financially stable firms that are forced to pay high interest rates. Consequently a division of opinion exists among businessmen over the question of the base. The financially stable, older firms prefer to have the whole of borrowed capital

---

[11] Cf. D. T. Smith, "Role of Invested Capital Base in Excess Profits Taxation," *National Tax Journal,* September, 1951, pp. 208–218.

included, with no allowance for interest deductions. The inclusion of borrowed capital favors firms that have expanded largely through borrowing, as well as those which, like the railroads and public utilities, customarily have a high proportion of bonded indebtedness.

Losses of Capital.   Although the invested-capital method automatically allows for *increases* in capital, losses have not been treated in parallel fashion, and corporations that have suffered losses have thus received favorable treatment. When losses are not required to be deducted from capital, the invested-capital base is increased and the excess-profits tax correspondingly reduced. The fact that World War II succeeded a long period of depression meant that certain industries, for example the railroads, benefited substantially from the provision that net deficits did not have to be offset against paid-in capital and surplus. This feature of the invested-capital method tends to become less important after a long period of prosperity.

ALLOWABLE RATES OF RETURN

Except during a period of assured demand, as in an all-out war, provision must be made to prevent the excess-profits tax from discouraging investment incentives as well as from impeding the accumulation of capital. The 1950 excess-profits tax made the allowable rates of return under the invested-capital credit higher than those of World War II. On the first $5 million of invested capital a rate of 12 per cent was permitted; on the next $5 million, 10 per cent; and on all amounts over $10 million, 8 per cent. Under a new provision of the 1950 act, a rate of 12 per cent was allowed also on *new* capital accumulated during the tax year. This provision was designed to assist "normal" business expansion, but did not, of course, benefit the smaller corporations already allowed the 12 per cent rate of return. Although these rates seem high enough, it has been pointed out by economists that many business ventures need to promise a return higher than 12 per cent to compensate for the risk of failure and to be able to compete in the capital market.

COMPARISON OF THE TWO METHODS

The majority of corporations were entitled to a higher excess-profits credit under the invested-capital method during World War II than under the earnings approach.[12] The reason was that for most corporations earnings from 1936 to 1939 were low. The problem of reconciling equity with productivity of yield arose again in connection with the reintroduction of the excess-profits tax in 1950. An excess-profits tax that made use of a period of high earnings as a base (for example, 1946–1949) would encourage the corporation to select the base period method. However, this

---

[12] Statement of Secretary Snyder before the Committee on Ways and Means, November 15, 1950.

loss of revenue could be reduced by exempting only a percentage of base year profits. In World War II the exemption was 95 per cent of the average annual profits over the four years 1936 through 1939. Under the excess-profits tax enacted in 1950, corporations were allowed to take the best three years out of the four years 1946 through 1949 as their base, but only 85 per cent of earnings in the selected period was used for the earnings standard. This was reduced to 83 per cent in the following year. These provisions were intended to provide relief for the firm that may have had one year of low profits or losses, while taking cognizance of the fact that 1946 through 1949 were years of very high corporate income.

THE EXCESS-PROFITS TAX AND ECONOMIC SURPLUS

From the standpoint of its effects on investment incentives, an excess-profits tax, carefully defined, should be neutral. The objective is to tax part, or conceivably all, of that portion of corporate income which is greater than necessary to call forth the desired level of output and investment. Presumably profits in excess of those in the base period, or a rate of return on capital in excess of that generally conceded to be normal to the industry, can be regarded as falling within the meaning of "economic surplus." As a corollary, the incidence of an excess-profits tax should be on the stockholder.

In practice, however, the excess-profits tax does exert an effect on costs and on willingness to put forth effort. Consequently, some part of the tax may be shifted. When the rates of tax are high, either under an excess-profits tax or a corporate income tax, the incentive to hold down costs is weakened. Economic decisions are made with the tax in mind. It follows that the tax can therefore affect output decisions. It can be admitted that firms will continue to strive for increased efficiency despite high taxes on profits. But expenditures on advertising and for good will are likely to be influenced by the fact that the government is paying 80 or 90 cents on the dollar. Thus the incidence and economic effects of the excess-profits tax depend to a large extent on the rates of the tax.

EXCESS-PROFITS TAX RATES

The problem of selecting an appropriate tax rate under an excess-profits tax is a difficult one. If the profits are really "excess" it might be argued that the rate should be 100 per cent. The argument would be weak, however, unless all elements of "excess" income were similarly taxed. Under the World War II tax, the rate, after 1943, stood at 95 per cent. There was deducted, however, a postwar credit to the corporation of 10 per cent. Thus the act contained an element of compulsory saving. This credit brought the rate down to 85.5 per cent. Another provision limited the total tax liability of any corporation under the combined corporate income and excess-profits taxes to 80 per cent. The British rate was

100 per cent, with 20 per cent returnable after the war. The rate under the 1950 federal excess profits tax was 30 per cent.

These extremely high rates were adopted largely in order to make wage controls and increased rates of personal income and excise taxes palatable to the worker. The use of the adjective "excess" may be said to have backfired, since it is hard to convince the layman that an excess return ought not to be virtually confiscated. The purpose of the postwar credit under the excess-profits tax was to give the impression that very high rates were being applied, while avoiding too great disincentive effects on the war effort of the taxed corporations. Unfortunately, labor leaders kept themselves aware of the refund aspect, so that most of the expected psychological benefit was lost. The use of the refund for reconversion during 1945 and 1946 added to the postwar inflationary potential, though it is not possible to say that businesses would not have invested at just as high a rate even if they had had to borrow or sell new stock. Again, rapid reconversion advanced the date when a disinflationary supply of civilian goods would appear on the market.

ATTITUDE OF BUSINESSMEN TOWARD EXCESS-PROFITS TAXATION

Sharp criticism has been leveled at the excess-profits tax by businessmen. Part of the objection is directed at excess-profits taxation in general, and part at the methods employed to determine the base of the tax. Large differences exist in the "normal" return on capital invested in different industries. A satisfactory return in one industry is often inadequate to attract capital to another. The problem is to allow a return sufficient to cover varying degrees of risk, while avoiding such liberal provisions that significant amounts of unduly high profits escape tax.

Congress has not been able to meet this test very well. On the one hand, rates have been set high in order to assure the public, and labor in particular, that there is a serious intention to obviate windfall gains to corporations during periods of heavy government spending. On the other hand, the administration of the law has been liberal. The result has been that some profits escape taxation that ought to be taxed; but some are taxed at high rates that ought to be exempt. The attempt to reduce the number of hardship cases through increasing complexity of the law has, moreover, led to another difficulty. This is the vast amount of litigation that necessarily attends a highly complex tax law, and which may continue for years after the law has been repealed.

RENEGOTIATION OF CONTRACTS

Renegotiation of contracts was intended to recapture excessive payments in those cases where accurate estimates of costs could not be made in the hurry of all-out mobilization, and where time was lacking for an adequate perusal of the details of contracts. The knowledge that contracts will be renegotiated has a very desirable, stimulating effect on the accuracy and honesty of bids. In addition, it restores to the government large amounts of excessive payments on war contracts. These overpayments are to a considerable extent unavoidable in any event, since complete cost data are not at hand when the bids must be made.

During and after World War II, over $11 billion was recovered through renegotiation.[13] Nevertheless, the major purpose of renegotiation is not necessarily revenue. Although the practice did not apply to all types of government contracts, it did extend the post-audit to large numbers of contracts, and contributed to a general atmosphere of care and honesty in the drawing up of contracts.

Data on the sums recaptured by renegotiation may, however, be rather misleading. Contracts may be drawn somewhat more carelessly because of the knowledge that they will be renegotiated. Renegotiation also introduces an element of uncertainty into business decisions. The practice is, of course, to be regarded as only one element in the complex of instruments designed to maintain a politically acceptable distribution of income among different groups during wartime. It is not perfectly adaptable, for example, for rectifying contracts between a businessman and his suppliers. Moreover, under a complex system of subcontracting it is difficult to prevent padding and waste all along the line.

► THE TAXATION OF THE INCOME OF NEW
AND SMALL BUSINESS[14]

In recent years there has been growing sentiment in Congress for special tax treatment of small business. This interest has been reflected in the establishment of the House and Senate committees on small business. Two questions are involved so far as taxes are concerned. First, does federal tax practice discriminate against small or new business? Second, should federal business taxation try to compensate by means of favorable tax treatment for the disadvantages under which small or new business operates?

In a number of respects federal taxation of business income discriminates among firms on the basis of size. It also does so between new and old business. But the direction and degree of discrimination are not entirely clear. Small firms are favored by exempting the first $25,000 of

[13] Commerce Clearing House, *News Bureau Report,* July 14, 1952.

[14] There is a growing literature on this subject. See, for example, K. Butters and J. Lintner, *Effect of Federal Taxes on Growing Enterprises* (Cambridge, Mass.: Harvard University, Division of Research, 1945); A. D. H. Kaplan, "Small Business: Its Place and Problems," Committee for Economic Development, 1948; C. Schmidt, D. Smith, and H. Dougall, "Government Financial Aid to Small Business," *Journal of Finance,* June, 1951, pp. 143–160; and *Hearings* and *Reports,* House of Representatives, Select Committee on Small Business.

income from profits taxes. The 2 per cent corporate income tax on consolidated surtax net income and the 15 per cent tax on intercorporate
dividends are conscious attempts to reduce the tax advantage of larger
corporations arising out of their ability to offset losses of one subsidiary
against gains of another.[15]

On the other hand, the federal corporate income tax may discriminate
against small or new corporations. To some extent there may be some
discouragement to the withholding of profits from distribution because of
a fear that firms may subsequently find themselves subject to the penalty
tax on "improperly" accumulated surplus. As a result, their growth through
reinvestment of earnings may be discouraged. Again, any business tax that
reduces capacity to save strikes harder at the corporation that needs to
reinvest in order to reach its optimum size. A new corporation may need
capital for expansion, whereas an older corporation (whether large or
small) may not wish to do more than maintain output.

Policy with respect to deductible losses is of particular importance
to the new corporation. It has no past profits from which current losses
can be deducted. Therefore, even if a generous carry-back is allowed when
the corporation does begin to make profits, this is of no help during the
early years when its existence may be at stake.[16] Small corporations may
be subject to a greater year-to-year fluctuation in profits, with periods of
profits alternating with periods of losses. Consequently, they are discriminated against unless all losses may be deducted from profits. The Revenue
Act of 1950 provided for an extension of the period over which losses can
be carried forward against profits from two years to five, while retaining
the carry-back of one year. In 1954 the carry-back was extended to two
years; thus operating losses can now be spread over an eight-year period.

Discriminations are often found in unexpected places. For example,
under the federal unemployment insurance law a firm must be subject to
payroll taxes for three years before becoming eligible to the favorable
lower rates that apply to firms with good employment records. Quite
unintentionally this provision places a handicap on new firms.[17]

SHOULD SMALL OR NEW BUSINESS BE FAVORED?

The second question to which an answer is needed is whether or not
the tax system should actually *favor* the small or new corporation. This
opens up the whole question of the desirability of government intervention

---

[15] An argument that has been made against the proposed constitutional amendment to limit federal income taxes is that most of the reduction in the corporate
income tax would accrue to the larger companies, thus weakening the competitive
position of small firms. See the Joint Committee on the Economic Report and House
Select Committee on Small Business, *Constitutional Limitation on Federal Income,
Estate and Gift Tax Rates,* 82d Cong., 2d Sess., 1952.

[16] It usually requires at least three years for a successful new business to
establish a solid position in the industry.

[17] Experience rating is discussed in Chapter 24.

in an attempt to affect the allocation of resources. If this is assumed to be justified, the further question arises as to what instruments are best adapted to accomplish this.

Over-all tax measures are blunt instruments, and their cost in terms of windfall benefits to those firms that do not need the subsidy may be great. In any case, the proper objective would be to limit the granting of tax advantages or subsidies to the small corporation that desires to expand, or needs to gain a foothold. On the basis of this test, the exemption and surtax under the federal corporate income tax prove to be an inefficient instrument. All corporations with small profits benefit, regardless of their capital needs. The same criticism applies to the (at present limited) graduation of corporate net income tax rates in effect in a few of the states, which was introduced in order to encourage small business.

Because of the lack of precision of purely general tax measures, proposals have been made for restricting the scope of tax advantages to those firms that it is desired to encourage. Thus a small corporation might be allowed to take accelerated depreciation on part or all of its capital assets. This would avoid giving an advantage to those small corporations which do not desire to expand. The latter would not wish to accelerate, since taxable profits would be greater after all depreciation had been deducted than would have been the case had normal depreciation been taken. On the other hand, the new corporation intending to expand would benefit, for it would be constantly adding new plant and equipment, thus extending the number of years in which depreciation could be taken.

TAX EXEMPTION FOR PRIVATE SECURITIES

Accelerated depreciation, however, does not help the new corporation that is not yet making profits from which to deduct depreciation. It has been suggested that income from securities issued by new or small corporations be exempted partly or entirely from the personal income tax. The resulting competition for their securities would tend to drive down their interest charges, thus giving them the advantages of tax exemption that have been enjoyed by the states and cities. The criticism could be made, however, that the individual in a high-income bracket benefits more from such an exemption than does the lower-income receiver.

Since few small new corporations have access to the stock market, this device might encourage an excessive amount of debt financing. Moreover, it would be administratively difficult to phrase the law so that the advantage did not accrue to those small or new corporations already making adequate profits.

Another difficult problem would be to decide when a small corporation had become large, and therefore no longer entitled to the exemption. There would be a temptation to keep reorganizing in order to remain "new." Furthermore, when the firm was no longer new, and it was time to make the transition to tax the income from its securities, adverse effects might be produced on the firm's financial arrangements. The fall in the prices of its securities might damage the marketability of new issues. An alternative to this approach would be to allow small or new corporations to retain a greater proportion of earnings without being subject to an undistributed-profits tax.

The conclusion seems inescapable that special tax assistance to small firms should ordinarily be restricted to avoiding discrimination against them rather than encouraging their growth. In a study of the problem in 1947, the Treasury concluded that the best way to encourage small business is "through general tax revisions that improve the equity of the system and minimize any adverse effects on investment and consumer demand."[18] During good times the bankruptcy rate declines. Discriminatory taxation always results in socially wasteful attempts to qualify for the favorable rates. Once subsidies or favorable tax rates have been granted they are extremely difficult to remove. Moreover, if determined steps are taken to avoid conferring tax advantages where they are not required, the need for government interference may lead to excessive bureaucracy.

Much scope for removing tax disabilities on new and small business exists in the area of special business taxation, which comprises the complex system of occupation taxes levied by the states and municipalities for the privilege of doing business. These taxes are usually arbitrary and haphazard. They lend themselves to political pressure, and therefore tend to penalize the small business, which is unlikely to enjoy much political power.

► CONCLUSION

Business income to partnerships is taxed under the personal income tax, and to corporations under the corporate profits tax, the tax on un-distributed profits, and the excess-profits tax. Businessmen have been strongly opposed to both the undistributed- and the excess-profits taxes. After the short-lived experiment with a progressive rate undistributed-profits tax from 1936 to 1939, the federal tax system preserved only the Section 102 penalty against "improper" accumulation of profits to avoid the personal income tax. With respect to the excess-profits tax, despite widespread agreement on the wastefulness and administrative cost of this tax, wartime revenue needs have made this tax difficult to do without.

The incidence of the corporate income tax in the short run is largely on the stockholder, but it is less clearly so in the long run. To the extent that the base of the tax contains elements of cost, the tax is shifted. Because it is not easy to determine the precise effects of the corporate income tax on the availability of capital to corporations, room exists for debate over the incidence of the tax. To the extent that the tax is not

---

[18] United States Treasury, *The Taxation of Small Business,* October, 1947, p. 3.

shifted it is borne by the stockholders. It becomes, therefore, an income tax; but it is not adapted to take account of differences in the income brackets of different stockholders. A number of devices have been suggested for integrating the personal and corporate income taxes. A basic requirement for integration is the inclusion of undistributed profits in the tax base. This involves administrative difficulties, though they are not insuperable. This requirement would also have to be satisfied if the corporate income tax were abolished. The abolition of a corporate income tax at high rates would be likely to result in a loss of revenue. However, an important effect would be to raise the level of income subject to the personal income tax, and a substantial proportion would be recaptured.

► REFERENCES

DOBROVOLSKY, S. P. *Corporate Income Retention: 1915–1943*. New York: National Bureau of Economic Research, 1951.

GILLIM, M. H. *The Incidence of Excess Profits Taxation*. New York: Columbia University Press, 1945.

GROVES, H. *Postwar Taxation and Economic Progress*. New York: McGraw-Hill Book Company, Inc., 1946.

KEITH, E. G. "Repercussions of the Tax System on Business," Chapter VII in K. E. Poole, ed., *Fiscal Policies and the American Economy*. New York: Prentice-Hall, Inc., 1951.

LENT, G. E. *The Impact of the Undistributed Profits Tax, 1936–1937*. New York: Columbia University Press, 1948.

SYMPOSIUM ON THE EXCESS PROFITS TAX. *National Tax Journal*, September, 1951, pp. 193–207.

UNITED STATES TREASURY DEPARTMENT. *The Taxation of Small Business*, October, 1947.

13 The Taxation of Consumption

► THE MEANING OF CONSUMPTION TAXATION

A consumption tax is a tax that rests on the consumer. It may be levied directly on the consumer, or it may be shifted to him in the price of the product that he buys. Therefore it is not always immediately apparent whether or not a particular levy is a consumption tax. The definition depends on the incidence. When, as in the case of the retail gasoline tax, the tax is stated separately from the price of the commodity, the intention is evidently to place the burden on the consumer. A license tax imposed on a liquor store, again, though ostensibly a business tax, is likely in large part to be shifted forward to the consumer.

Because many taxes are shifted to the consumer, a consumption tax may be defined as either a tax that is measured by consumption or one that is actually borne by the consumer. A tax on telephone calls is measured by the consumption of telephone service. A manufacturers' excise, on the other hand, is levied in the expectation that it will be shifted to the consumer. Indirectly, of course, this tax, also, is measured by consumption. However, a flat business license, if shifted, is a consumption tax that is measured neither directly nor indirectly by consumption. Ordinarily consumption taxes are thought of as sales taxes and excises, customs, and the often proposed spending tax.

In one sense it might be argued that most taxes are at least in part consumption taxes. The two sources of ability to pay are income and property. Whenever a tax reduces disposable income, it is probable that the sacrifice of income will be allocated by the taxpayer between his savings and his consumption. The income tax paid by the low-income receiver, for example, will represent almost entirely a burden on his consumption. That of the high-income receiver may or may not curtail solely his savings. Nevertheless, an income tax is not measured by consumption, nor is it imposed with the specific intention of placing a tax burden on consumption. Its effect on consumption depends on the rate schedule, the distribution of income, and the reaction of the taxpayer.

241

Many individuals have considerable scope in the extent to which they may choose between a reduction of their savings or their consumption in response to the income tax.

The accepted definition of consumption taxation suffers from a certain awkwardness. A tax on consumption does not necessarily reduce the rate at which all individuals consume. The higher the income bracket of the taxpayer the more likely he will be to maintain consumption and allow his savings to decline by the amount of the tax. In this respect a consumption tax is no different from an income tax. Therefore, whether we have in mind a tax measured by consumption, or one that is shifted to the consumer in the form of a higher price of product, we do not necessarily mean by a consumption tax a levy which curtails personal consumption. Only under very rigid assumptions will any tax accomplish this exclusively. To qualify, the tax would have to make it prohibitive for all income groups, from the lowest to the highest, to spend more than a permitted amount on consumption. As we shall see below, an extremely progressive spendings tax would accomplish this.

► OBJECTIVES

Traditionally the two objectives of consumption taxation have been revenues and social control. These objectives are as important as ever in the minds of legislators. In recent years, however, economists have paid increasing attention to consumption taxation as a means of reducing the consumption spending of the population as a whole. The great practical impetus to this approach has been the need to divert resources away from consumers during time of war. From the point of view of economic theory, as we have seen, the stimulus has come from the functional approach to taxation, and the concentration of attention on a national economic budget rather than merely on the narrower concept of the budget of the Treasury. Each of these objectives needs to be considered.

► REVENUES FROM SALES TAXES, EXCISES, AND CUSTOMS

Until the advent of the personal and corporate income taxes, by far the greater proportion of federal taxes was derived from excises and the customs. In 1913, when the corporate income tax was in its infancy, and the personal income tax had not yet gone into effect, customs and excises provided 95 per cent of the total federal tax revenues. By 1954 the combined taxes produced only 13.9 per cent of the total (Table 7, page 25).

With the states, on the other hand, the trend has been in the opposite direction. The major reason has been the decline in the reliance of the states on the property tax. In 1915, the latter tax accounted for slightly over 50 per cent of state tax revenues. By 1954 the ratio had dropped to 3.5 per cent, while taxes on general sales, tobacco, liquor, and motor-vehicle fuels stood at over 50 per cent (Table 8, page 30).

The localities, in contrast with the states and the federal government, have never made great use of sales taxation. Despite the introduction of sales taxes by some cities, sales and gross receipts taxes accounted for only 6.9 per cent of total municipal tax revenues in 1953 (Table 9, page 32). Licenses and permits, "and other," however, which are largely shifted to the consumer, were another 5.0 per cent. Moreover, the 87.1 per cent of total municipal tax revenues accounted for by the property tax was derived in large part from business properties and therefore largely shifted to the consumer. To a considerable extent, the local property tax must be regarded, therefore, as a tax on consumption.

From the point of view of productivity and stability of yield, sales taxes possess great appeal. The level of consumption spending fluctuates in narrower cycles than does national income.[1] This is largely because the bulk of the population are at the level commonly regarded as the "minimum acceptable" standard of living. Although much of their consumption is not what could be characterized as subsistence spending, they strive to maintain their rate of spending even during downswings. Moreover, receipts from the personal income tax are subject to relatively violent fluctuations because of progressive rates. As recently as 1932 Congress considered an attempt to combat a decline in the revenues by enacting a federal sales tax. This step was not taken. It was beginning to be realized that stability of revenues may have to be purchased at the cost of a deflationary fall in consumption spending.[2]

EARLIER FEDERAL EXPERIENCE WITH CONSUMPTION TAXES

The constitutional basis for federal commodity taxation, together with a brief historical sketch, will indicate the traditional importance attributed to the taxation of consumption in the United States. Congress was given the power to levy and collect taxes, duties, imposts, and excises "to pay the debts and provide for the common defence and general welfare of the United States." But no export duties could be levied by the federal government. The states, incidentally, were given independent taxing power, except that they could not levy either export or import duties. Congress

---

[1] Under conditions of stable, high-level national income this advantage disappears, of course. Thus it is pointed out on page 65A of the 67th Budget of the State of Illinois that beginning in 1947 "the amount of the Retailers' Occupation [i.e., sales] tax in Illinois collected in any one year has never varied more than 3 per cent from the amount calculated on the basis of disposable income data." It is recognized, of course, that rationing and shortages would alter these conclusions.

[2] On the other hand, the federal government made use of regressive taxes to finance agricultural relief payments (the processing tax, which was partly shifted forward). The social security payroll tax on workers, introduced in 1936, also constitutes a burden on consumption.

at once recognized the possibilities of the tariff on imports as a source of revenue. On the other hand, the desire to stimulate industrialization immediately injected the principle of protection of domestic manufactures.

Because the federal government, at Hamilton's insistence, had assumed the debt obligations of the states, the customs alone did not promise sufficient revenues. Consequently, Congress enacted excises in 1791 and 1794. The best known of these was the whisky tax (1791), which led to the Whisky Rebellion in western Pennsylvania in 1794. Imposts were also levied on the manufacture of salt and snuff, on the ownership of carriages, on auction sales, and on sugar refining. The levy of carriages was clearly an attempt to inject some degree of progressivity into a regressive tax system. Except for this item, however, the excises were regarded as taxes on the low-income groups. On the other hand, the bulk of imports at this time consisted of luxury goods consumed by the wealthier classes. As a result, the tariff enjoyed a popularity that did not apply to excises.

The excises were abolished under Jefferson's administration, when rapidly increasing foreign trade lifted the revenues from import duties to a level high enough to finance federal expenditures. Nevertheless, the Federalists called attention to the fact that excises would prove more stable than customs in the event of a decline in imports during war or depression.

In the War of 1812 the excises were reintroduced. As soon as the arrival of peace restored the yield from the tariff, however, they were again abolished. At the same time the complexion of imports began to change from primarily luxury goods to semifinished goods that ended up in the form of commodities bought by the population at large. The result was to lessen somewhat the popularity of a tariff for revenue, and to encourage further a shift in emphasis to protection that accompanied the industrialization of the nation. On the other hand, a rapidly rising trend in national income kept the tariff a heavy revenue producer despite the growth in sentiment for protection.

THE STATES AND MUNICIPALITIES

At the level of the states and municipalities the need for stable revenue sources makes it important to utilize relatively inelastic tax sources. Consequently, there has been a great movement toward the sales tax by the states, particularly during the depression. As we have seen, however, the cities and towns have not done much with this tax. It is sometimes argued that even a sales tax is too elastic for the municipalities, and they should rely almost exclusively on the property tax. It must be remembered, however, that a property tax is ordinarily paid out of income, and the gain in revenue stability must be paid for in terms of an inequity to property owners. This is especially serious for the lower-income receivers. Although there may be a substantial lag before rents respond to the tax, low-income home owners with heavy mortgages are placed in a difficult financial position if property tax liability does not fall with income during a downswing.

It might well be argued that instead of relying on inelastic tax sources during depression, the localities should be given temporary subsidies by the federal government. In this connection it should be noted that increased grants-in-aid by the *states* to the localities might encourage greater use of sales taxation at the state level.

► CONTROL OF CONSUMPTION

The taxation of consumption is frequently justified as an instrument for controlling (1) the level , and (2) the direction of consumption. This is the broadest sense of the term "sumptuary taxation." Commodity taxation, as usually practiced, is not a good device for controlling the *level* of consumption. Unless the tax is applied to every commodity and service, the effect may be largely to divert spending from those items that are taxed to those that are not. Total consumption may remain the same. The devices appropriate to the limitation of consumption spending are the graduated spendings tax, expenditure rationing, compulsory savings, compulsory purchase of government securities, and a low-exemption, high-base-rate personal income tax. Sumptuary taxation in the usual sense, however, is the narrower concept of control over the direction of consumption.

LUXURY SPENDING

A sense of guilt has often attached to those types of personal consumption that are regarded by a particular society as luxury spending. In earlier times autocrats sought to convince the public that only the chief of state should indulge in luxury. Whenever the nobility was powerful the line was drawn to permit their luxury spending as well. In more modern times, the display of the rising merchant and warrior classes produced a reaction in favor of a cult of simplicity. Thus society, like the individual, suffers from complexes that are rooted in the experience of the past. Of course, the condemnation of undue luxury spending is based on firmer grounds than this. If income is unequally distributed, the public conscience cannot remain unaffected by the coexistence of poverty and great luxury.

It is difficult to develop a system of luxury taxation that has the merit of consistency. No very clear-cut definition of a luxury exists, and only relatively few commodities would be designated as luxuries by virtually everyone.[3] Obviously we are involved again in the problem of interpersonal comparisons of utility. Is aggregate welfare increased if luxury consumption

---

[3] Groves distinguishes three definitions: (1) goods bought mainly by the rich, (2) those for which demand is elastic, and (3) goods that could be forgone without "loss of health or the requisites of good citizenship."—Harold Groves, *Financing Government* (4th ed.; Holt, 1954), pp. 246–247.

is permitted? Would it be greater, on the other hand, if the same amount of resources were devoted instead to the production of nonluxuries? Consumers of expensive luxuries are fond of pointing to the fact that specialized workers would be left without employment if luxury consumption were prohibited. Witness the effect on the hunter of the musk deer, or the sea otter.[4]

While this argument is hardly convincing when applied to commodities bought only by the rich, a very high proportion of total employment is actually accounted for in the production and distribution of goods that are not necessary to maintain health and efficiency. If there is anything in the view that underconsumption is a cause of depression, effective luxury taxation in this broad sense could wreck the economy.

A major objection to luxury taxation for sumptuary, as opposed to revenue, purposes is that in effect it tells the man with a low or moderate income that while a wealthy person may enjoy a commodity, he may not. This argument applies, of course, only to commodities within his reach before the tax is applied, and not afterward. It may or may not be desirable to impose high excise rates on goods (e.g., oceangoing yachts) that are bought only by the wealthy. It is very doubtful, however, if the attempted prohibition should be extended beyond articles of extremely conspicuous consumption. The history of a modern industrial economy can be written in terms of a constantly rising living standard for the mass of the population. The luxury of today is the necessity of tomorrow. Sumptuary taxation of this kind would only serve to arrest material progress.

THE SELECTIVE EXCISE AND CONSUMPTION CONTROL

Regulation of consumption by taxation has usually been effected by means of special, high-rate excises. The history of public finance provides a long and varied list of such taxes, for conceptions as to what is harmful or socially undesirable vary greatly from country to country and from one age to another. Special taxes have been levied, sometimes at graduated rates, on a range of luxury articles from mansions and carriages to expensive clothing and jewelry. In the United States the major excise of a sumptuary nature has been the liquor tax. High taxes have also been levied on articles the possession of which is illegal, like machine guns and narcotics. This practice amounts to an admission that the police power may at times need to be supplemented by the tax power.

The taxation of tobacco and liquor deserves special mention. These taxes have often been rationalized on the ground that consumption is harmful. In fact, however, the very high rates of these taxes both here and abroad merely reflect a desire to take advantage of inelastic demand for

---

[4] The pelt of the sea otter brings $1,000. It is said that deer musk would sell for $40,000 a pound if it could be had in unadulterated form. Prizes of this magnitude create powerful vested producer interests.

revenue purposes. Rates must be extremely high before demand is noticeably affected, and short of this point an injustice is done to the lower-income groups, who in the aggregate pay the bulk of the tax. Moreover, once tax rates have been raised to a level high enough to discourage sales, the problem of evasion, particularly under the liquor tax, becomes acute. This effect became noticeable after the substantial increase in the federal liquor tax incident to the war in Korea.

The great defect of a sumptuary tax that does not virtually prohibit consumption of the taxed article is that demand is likely to be diverted from socially more desirable commodities in order to maintain consumption of the taxed commodity. This result is especially serious for the very low-income groups, who frequently forgo consumption that is necessary for the maintenance of health in order to enjoy the highly taxed commodity.

Taxes are also levied to control consumption by affecting the form and nature of business enterprise. Often this is done at the instigation of rival interests, though the narrow producer interest is not always paramount. Thus in 1912 a prohibitive tax was finally levied on white phosphorous matches in a successful effort to eliminate the occupational disease caused by phosphorous poisoning, and in 1914 a tax of $300 a pound was levied on manufacturers of opium for nonmedicinal purposes.

In other cases public interest does not receive much consideration. The oleomargarine tax, in the form of both a heavy license tax and a tax of 2 cents a pound, was levied in 1886 at the behest of the dairy interests in order to prevent inroads on the butter market. Consumer interests, representing the lowest-income groups, were never able to get the federal tax removed. The consumers finally benefited when the cottonseed-producing states united with the margarine manufacturers to push a repeal bill through Congress in 1950. The rate at which the states repealed their own discriminatory measures depended on the balance of power of their dairy interests and their urban populations.

THE PROTECTIVE TARIFF

The protective tariff is in essence a system of selective excises on imports that compete with the output of strongly organized producers. There are, in fact, two tariff systems. The one is a general system of tariffs at high rates traditionally designed to yield revenue. The other comprises the special tariffs enacted as a result of the pressures put on Congress by special interests to restrict the importation of competing products. Thus, although protection and revenue are inconsistent objectives, revenues can be maintained by applying moderate tariffs to imports of articles that do not face domestic competition, while protection can be reserved for those commodities which, for one reason or another, it is preferred should be produced domestically.

From the point of view of efficiency it is generally admitted that free trade and international specialization would maximize economic satisfaction on a world basis. The consumer pays higher prices for protected goods. Efficiency may suffer because the producer is spared the necessity of striving to reduce his costs. There is a good deal of public support for protection, however, because the individual regards himself as having primarily a producer's rather than a consumer's interest. He is therefore more concerned about the possibility of losing profits or becoming unemployed because of foreign competition than he is about being able to buy the imported commodity at a lower price.

The standard argument of free traders has been that if Country A would permit the unrestricted entry of commodities in which it has a comparative disadvantage,[5] purchasing power would be spread to foreign producers and workers. They, in turn, would then buy a greater amount of other goods produced by Country A. Thus total employment would tend to rise. Temporarily, of course, some workers would become unemployed because they would have to move to other industries. It is exactly this movement of resources that protectionists wish to avoid. A particular businessman or worker is specialized to his industry, and since it does him little good if demand rises for some other commodity, he can be counted upon to use his energies to try to keep out imports that compete with his own product.

A noneconomic argument in favor of protection is the necessity of maintaining equipment and skills in industries that are indispensable in time of war. This argument goes well beyond tariffs alone. It explains, for example, the existence of an American merchant marine, which can only be maintained through extensive subsidies; again for military reasons, all countries subsidize their airlines. As a general proposition the military preparedness argument in favor of protection cannot be refuted. On the other hand, it can easily be understood that many businessmen are likely to try to obtain high tariffs and other forms of protection on the basis of a very tenuous relationship with national defense.

Finally may be mentioned the infant industries argument. This justification for protection is likely to be found mainly in small countries that are attempting to industrialize. Large areas of the world are in the process of trying to rid themselves of the role of "hewers of wood and drawers of water" that has been the lot of nations that export primarily raw materials and agricultural products. Their feeling of grievance against long-continued real or imagined exploitation by the highly industrialized countries leads them to insist on a high rate of industrialization. They tend to do this even in those instances where location, the kinds and distribution of their resources, and national skills may make this extremely difficult or even impossible. In many instances, of course, the infant industry argument is

---

[5] For present purposes this term is simply used to describe the market situation of commodities that are produced domestically and that cannot compete with imports.

completely justified. Powerful foreign producers may purposely or otherwise drive the new industry from the domestic market.

CONTROL OF THE LEVEL OF CONSUMPTION

The existence of economic fluctuations makes it imperative that the tax system be an effective instrument for drawing off purchasing power when the level of national spending threatens the economy with price inflation. A tax on consumption has an important role to play in this connection. If we consider the tax effects alone, a tax that reduces personal spending power contributes to reducing the competition of the public for scarce goods and factors. Its effectiveness is reduced, however, if the introduction of the tax serves as an incentive to the granting of higher rates of remuneration to the production factors. Those who stress the anti-inflationary rather than the revenue characteristics of taxation, therefore, may raise the question whether all forms of consumption taxes are equally desirable in all circumstances. Specifically, doubts rise particularly with respect to the various forms of sales taxes. A tax on an individual's total spending, as well as the income tax in so far as it rests on consumption, is less likely to stimulate increases in wages and farm price-support levels.

Sales Taxation and Price Inflation.   When income and employment are increasing, it is relatively easy for labor to win increases in wage rates. Even though these wage rises may not keep pace with the rise in the consumers' price index, they are part of the process that propagates inflation. In considering the possible inflationary effects of sales taxes it is necessary to divide the problem into two parts.

In the first place, sales taxes imposed at stages earlier than that at which goods are sold to consumers become inextricably bound up with other costs of production. They play the same role, therefore, as other costs in the determination of prices. Second, retail sales taxes imposed at the moment when the good is sold to the consumer, and, stated separately in the price of the article, are not part of costs. Neither are they part of the retailer's markup. Therefore, they are not includible in a cost-of-living index unless somehow labor unions are able to induce employers to write such a stipulation into their contracts with the unions.

If the latter were done, the wage earner, as such, would escape the tax. In that case the employer would try to cover the additional cost in the price of the product, and he could do this in a period of high-level total spending. To a minor extent the tax might be borne by other cooperating factors of production, the supply of which is inelastic. Much of the tax would, in fact, be borne by labor, however, since the wage earner is also a consumer. Nevertheless, consumers and wage earners are by no means entirely identical groups.

Under what circumstances is it likely that labor will find it possible to make a sales tax the occasion for a compensating rise in wage rates? So long as an official cost-of-living or consumption good price index is used as the basis of wage contracts, retail sales taxes quoted separately from the price of the product are not taken account of in wage agreements. If, in general, sales taxes are shifted to the consumer it might be argued that all sales taxes ought to be included in the cost-of-living index. On the other hand, it is difficult to find a moral justification for explicitly making a tax the basis for an increase in wage rates. In the case of hidden sales taxes, imposed before the final stage, it is simply impossible as a practical matter to separate taxes from other costs. In what follows we shall be concerned only with sales taxes which are automatically included in the Bureau of Labor price index of consumption goods bought by the average family.

Price Escalators. A price escalator is an automatic relationship between a factor's rate of income and the prices it has to pay for commodities. Only a proportion of wage contracts are rigidly tied to the cost-of-living index.[6] In most instances a rise in the price level of consumers' goods, whether caused by the imposition of a sales tax or otherwise, simply increases the pressure on unions for a revision of the contract. In the absence of inflationary business or government spending, these increases are not always easy to obtain. The firm must consider the effects of rising prices on its sales. Even if the rise is granted, a drop in sales may force the dismissal of part of the labor force. If the firm has been making monopoly profits, however, it may be able to absorb the burden of the tax.

The situation is likely to be quite different, however, during wartime. It can then be assumed that there is repressed inflation, both business and the government having increased their rate of borrowing from the commercial banks. If a wage-stabilization agreement has been entered into between business and labor, any rise in prices, whether caused by a sales tax or otherwise, that entered into the consumers' price index would put pressure on labor to seek a rectification of the agreement.

Suppose, on the other hand, that for some reason a sales tax happens to be imposed during a peacetime boom generated by increased business borrowing from the banks. In that case there would probably have been no wage-stabilization agreement. On the contrary, businessmen may be hiring labor away from one another, so that wage rates are rising rapidly. The effect may be that real wages are actually increasing; in other words, wages are rising more rapidly than the prices of consumers' goods, includ-

---

[6] As of September, 1952, it was estimated that 3.5 million workers (6 per cent of the labor force) were covered by formal escalator contracts, mostly in automobiles and railroads.—H. M. Douty, "The Growth, Status, and Implications of Wage Escalation," *Monthly Labor Review,* February, 1953, pp. 126–129. It is not known how many workers are actually, as well as formally, under the escalator clause. Also, it should be noted that wages of other workers are often influenced by the rates received by workers subject to escalation.

ing the sales tax.[7] In this case it is not the sales tax that is propagating the inflation.

In the past there has been a marked tendency for wage rates to lag behind the prices of consumers' goods during an ordinary business upswing. Institutional developments during recent years, however, have contributed to a reduction in this lag. After 1948 the use of wage escalators became more widespread, though it looks as if they would be less popular in the absence of fears of inflation.

Wage contracts of the General Motors type give the worker an automatic claim to a rise in wage rates when the cost-of-living index rises. Conversely, of course, wage escalators extend the area of deflation when prices are falling.[8] So long as an easy monetary policy permits demand curves to rise, the effect of a wage escalator is to put pressure on other workers to try to participate in the benefits of this device. Otherwise, their real wages fall in response to the rise in the prices of consumer goods caused by the escalator. In these circumstances the imposition of a general sales tax, at fairly high rates, is particularly likely to contribute to the propagation of the inflation.

When two or more escalators, each of them representing broad segments of the economy, react on one another the effect could be very inflationary. Thus a rise in wage rates due to rising prices caused by the sales tax adversely affects the purchasing power of farmers, since prices rise a second time in response to the increase in the wage rate. But the farm price parity formula provides that farm prices be supported when the ratio of prices paid by farmers to prices received by farmers becomes less favorable than it was in a base period.[9] Consequently, farm prices automatically increase. They in turn, however, enter into the cost-of-living index of the workers, and the wage escalator comes into play again.

Theoretically, this process could go on until brought to a halt either by an inelastic money supply or by a crisis and depression resulting from a general situation of price-cost and output dislocations. In practice, however, even when excessive purchasing power has been created by the banking system, the escalators do not necessarily operate as rigidly as this. Moreover, a sales tax alone is not likely to set the chain of events in motion. For example, the circumstances that are here assumed to have led to the necessity for the imposition of the sales tax, namely, heavy business as well as private spending, may at the same time push up farm prices. This moves them "off the peg," and only the wage escalator oper-

---

[7] If, as is more likely, money wages are rising but price rises are leading wage rises, it would still be true that the impetus to inflation comes from the demand side.

[8] Unless the firms and the unions agree to set limits on the extent to which wages can fall. This has actually been the case, though wage rates may fall substantially if a wage *rise* has first taken place after the signing of a contract.

[9] The support level may be at a percentage of parity rather than at 100 per cent.

ates. On the other hand, wage rates could conceivably rise faster than the cost of living, in which case it would be the wage escalator that is inactive. This does not mean that the extent of inflation is necessarily less, but merely that the course of inflation is by a route other than that of the escalators.

► SALES TAXES FOR REVENUE

A wide variety of commodity, sales, and spending taxes lies at the disposal of the tax authorities. The breadth of selection has resulted primarily from the ingenuity of hard-pressed governments in seeking out taxes that are at the same time productive, easy to collect, and not discouraging to economic incentives. In recent years new forms of commodity taxes have been developed in an effort to escape some of the inequities of the traditional types and to cope with special situations.

The following list of sales taxes indicates the wide scope of commodity taxation: general manufacturers, wholesale and retail sales taxes; turnover, gross income, and transactions taxes;[10] selected excises on manufacturers, wholesalers, and retailers; the tariff; the purchase tax; the use tax, and business taxes based on sales or number of outlets, like the special tax on chain stores.

The primary goal of a tax on consumption is to tax *all* consumption except that which it is intended specifically to exempt. No tax applied to particular commodities, or even to all tangible goods, can pass this test. For to the extent that certain commodities and services consumed by the public are exempt from taxation, consumers of the taxed goods are discriminated against. Excises levied at high rates on particular commodities are especially subject to criticism on this score, unless the discrimination is based on a desire either to conserve scarce raw materials or to impose differentially high rates on goods whose consumption it is wished to discourage. During World War II, for example, federal excises were levied on long-distance communications in order to discourage civilian use of overburdened long lines. Again, the excises imposed on furs and jewelry were intended primarily to inject some measure of progressivity into an inherently regressive tax. The normal peacetime excise, however, cannot be defended on these grounds.

► PRICE-DISTORTING EFFECTS OF EXCISE TAXES

Selective excises, applied at high rates to widely consumed commodities, are heavy revenue yielders. For this reason excises play an important role in the federal tax system. An objection that has been made

---

[10] A *turnover* tax is a tax applied at every stage in the production process at which goods are exchanged for money. It is a form of *gross income* tax, which taxes exchanges at all levels. If personal services are excluded it is known as a *gross*

against them, however, is their alleged distorting effect on resource use. The objection is valid only if the distorting effect is greater than would be exerted if the same amount of revenue weré to be raised by some other tax.

Classical economists argued that a selective excise, by distorting the price relationships among commodities, forces the consumer to shoulder two burdens. Not only does he pay the tax (forward shifting was assumed), but he will consume a different combination of commodities from that which he would have selected in the absence of the excise. This has been called the "excess burden" of the excise. A general coverage tax like the income tax, it was contended, can be made to yield the same amount of revenue without distorting consumer choice. A general sales tax, while producing some distorting effects by virtue of differing elasticities of demand for different taxed commodities, would be regarded, nevertheless, as superior to the selective excise.

Evidently the pattern of resource use is altered by the excise, and if the distribution of resources in the absence of the tax is taken to be ideal, a separate additional burden is added to that of paying the tax. The original distribution may not have been ideal, however, in which case an excess benefit rather than burden might be involved. For example, if an effect of the tax were to force resources into monopolized industries, output would be increased and prices would tend to be pushed down in these industries. The net effect might, or might not, be a better distribution of resources than that which obtained before the excise was imposed.

The notion that an excise tax imposes a greater excess burden than do alternative taxes has been attacked on the ground that all taxes exert effects on economic incentives.[11] A personal income tax, for example, affects the exchange relationship between leisure and income. In other words, when income tax rates are high, individuals may prefer to earn less taxable income and enjoy more leisure than they would have done in the absence of the tax. The effect is a distortion similar to that produced by the excise. Most workers have no choice with respect to the number of hours they will work, but high rates of income tax can encourage absenteeism; and businessmen are in a position to vary the amount of effort they put forth. Moreover, high income tax rates may encourage early retirement.

---

receipts tax. A purchase tax is a form of excise levied at high rates on articles that compete for scarce resources, and a use tax is a tax levied by a state in order to prevent evasion by purchasing outside the tax jurisdiction.

[11] The modern analysis runs in terms of indifference curves. The interested reader is referred to the following: J. R. Hicks, Value and Capital (New York: Oxford, 1939), pp. 40–41; M. F. W. Joseph, "The Excess Burden of Indirect Taxation," Review of Economic Studies, June, 1939, pp. 226–231; H. Wald, "The Classical Indictment of Indirect Taxation," Quarterly Journal of Economics, August, 1945, pp. 577–596; A. Henderson, "The Case for Indirect Taxation," Economic Journal, December, 1948, pp. 538–553; and O. H. Brownlee and E. D. Allen, Economics of Public Finance (New York: Prentice-Hall, 1954), pp. 287–290.

Although all taxes produce distorting effects that are separate from the burden of surrendering purchasing power to the government,[12] it remains true that some cause greater distortion than others. A general sales tax may alter the relative desirability of purchasing goods and holding assets. Any effect would depend on whether the tax was expected to be permanent or temporary. If the former, it seems probable that the effect on the decision to spend or not to spend would not be very great. Again, a personal income tax will not affect willingness to earn unless rates are very high. Thus we must conclude that the high-rate selective excises that have from time to time characterized the federal tax system do exert distorting effects on resource allocation that would not be caused by an income tax yielding the same amount of revenue. However, if the system of excises were abolished, and the same revenues were derived from a considerably more progressive income tax than we have at present, it seems possible that the adverse effects on willingness to work might be so large as to result in greater distorting effects than are caused by our present system of combined excises and income taxes.

► UNIFORMITY IN CONSUMPTION TAXATION

Once the decision has been made on the kinds of sales that ought to be exempt from a consumption tax, all other sales should be subject to the tax, and should be taxed uniformly. In other words, in order to avoid unintended economic and equity effects, the tax should be uniformly applied. Only one consumption tax satisfies the condition of full coverage. This is the spendings tax, which is not, of course, a sales tax. It is an annual tax on the consumption spending of the individual. If the spendings tax base is defined properly, no consumption whatever remains outside the tax base except that which is specifically exempted.

When we turn to the conventional sales taxes, we discover that none of them completely satisfies the test of uniform coverage. The retail sales tax, however, comes the closest. Manufacturers' and wholesale sales taxes, which are applied to sales of commodities at the manufacturing and whole- sale stages, do not result in uniformity at the consumer stage. Profit mark- ups vary from industry to industry, with the result that even if the tax is

---

[12] Even a poll tax can produce distorting effects. Although there is nothing the taxpayer can do to avoid paying the tax, he has less spending power after paying it. The tax is unrelated to his income, but it diminishes his wealth. Consequently, he will reconsider the allocation of his income among the different objects of spending, and the distribution of resources in the economy will be changed. It must be borne in mind that we are considering here a very high-rate poll tax which can be con- sidered as an alternative to the excise, sales taxes, and income tax in producing large amounts of revenue. A five-dollar annual poll tax will not significantly affect consumption decisions, but neither will a 2 per cent excise.

uniform at the time it is applied, it varies from industry to industry as a percentage of the retail price.[13]

► THE RETAIL SALES TAX

In practice, the retail sales tax falls short of achieving uniformity because it exempts services.[14] Critics of this exemption point out that this is a regressive element in the retail sales tax, for the purchase of services constitutes a larger proportion of a wealthy man's income than it does of a poor man's. While this undoubtedly provides an argument for the inclusion of certain services in the retail sales tax base, it is evident that others not only are purchased by the relatively poor, but also cannot be avoided by them.

Examples are plumbing, electrical, and other household repairs, all of which are at present notoriously expensive.[15] The average householder has to buy these whether he wants to or not. Considerations of equity demand that they be included along with tangible goods, but their inclusion would not contribute much to tax progressivity. The cost of hiring help when a wife works, and of nursing and other assistance during illness and childbirth, would appropriately be exempt.

An administrative difficulty caused by the present practice of excluding services from the retail sales tax is the ambiguity of the definition of a taxable sale. Where the sale of a commodity is accompanied by a service, state practice ranges from requiring the inclusion of both the good and the service to (in some instances) exempting both.

EFFECTS ON DISTRIBUTION OF INCOME

It is quite as important under retail sales taxation to provide the desired exemptions as it is that its coverage should be complete and uni-

---

[13] This was one of the major factors in the preference for a retail sales tax shown by the Division of Tax Research of the United States Treasury in its report: *Considerations Respecting a Federal Retail Sales Tax*, printed in the Hearings before the Committee on Ways and Means, House of Representatives, 78th Congress, 1st Session, October 4–20, 1943. The following example was used to illustrate the effect of the difference in markup on the percentage of retail price accounted for by the tax (p. 1119):

  Suppose that the retail price of each of two commodities is $1.00.
  Let the manufacturer's price for A be 50 cents and for B, 90 cents.
  Then a 20 per cent manufacturers' excise will be 10 cents for A and
    18 cents for B.
  Thus the tax amounts to 10 per cent of the retail price of A, and 18
    per cent of the retail price of B.

[14] This is not always so, however. In many states various types of services are taxed.

[15] The reason for their high cost is not only aggressive union policy; it is also accounted for by the comparative disadvantage of small service jobs in a highly mechanized economy.

form. Consumption taxation is regressive. Moreover, it discriminates against large families. Food, the major expense of large poor families, is often included in the base. It is estimated that about one fifth of the tax base is lost if food is exempted.[16] On the other hand, the elimination of food from the base has been shown to convert the sales tax from a regressive tax to one that is fairly proportional.[17] Other articles regarded by lower-income receivers as virtually as necessary as food must in any case be included or the tax base will suffer severely. Tobacco and clothing are examples.

There are some objections to the elimination of food from the base, but if food is included, the problem is how to make the sales tax progressive, or at least not regressive. The objections that have been advanced to excluding food are (1) other expenditures of low-income receivers may be as entitled to exemption as food,[18] (2) the exemption of food is likely to cause some shift in demand from taxed commodities to food, and (3) those in the medium- and higher-income brackets share in the exemption.

The effect of progression could be obtained by including food in the tax base, while refunding part of the tax in relation to size of family and size of income.[19] The refund would be made on the basis of information reported on the federal income tax form. Another device would be to provide each individual with sales tax receipts in the amount of the desired exemption. Thus no tax would be paid until purchases exceeded the exemption, which would vary according to the size of the family but not according to its income.

Many proposals of this sort have been made in order to increase the equity of consumption taxation. Legislators have never responded very favorably, however, apparently preferring to rely on the slow process of shifting through rising wage rates when taxes are levied on those with low incomes. If tax changes were infrequent, something might be said for rely-

---

[16] J. F. Due, "Retail Sales Taxation in Theory and Practice," *National Tax Journal*, December, 1950, p. 317.

[17] D. C. Miller, "Sales Tax Progressivity Attributable to a Food Exemption," *National Tax Journal*, June, 1951, pp. 148–159. Miller's findings were confirmed in a Canadian study of the Canadian manufacturers' sales tax. See J. F. Due, "The Sales Tax as an Anti-Inflationary Measure," *Public Finance*, December, 1951, p. 391. The Canadian Minister of Finance maintained that the Canadian manufacturers' excise is regressive only on incomes above $7,000 a year, and that the exemption of food, fuel, and building materials makes the tax actually progressive for incomes up to $6,000 a year.—Joint Committee on Internal Revenue Taxation, Congress of the United States, *Summary of the Budget of the Dominion of Canada* (presented April 10, 1951), and *National Tax Journal*, June, 1951, p. 188.

[18] This objection lacks much force, however, because even if other necessities are taxed, a food exemption nevertheless reduces the burden on the poor. A better way to put it would be to argue that to select food alone out of the entire range of necessities is to cause the exemption to the poor to be too low.

[19] Cf. W. A. Morton, "A Progressive Consumption Tax," *National Tax Journal*, June, 1951, pp. 160–166. If the credit is inverse to the size of income it is a diminishing exemption; the credit disappears when income reaches a given level.

ing on this "diffusion." Frequent changes in tax rates, however, place large burdens on those least able to bear them.

COMMODITIES FOR RESALE

An advantage of a retail sales tax over sales taxes applied at prior stages of production is that the frictions caused by shifting of the tax can be avoided. Consumption can be taxed directly. In practice, however, a minor difficulty arises out of the fact that producers as well as consumers buy many final goods. If the former are taxed, they will, of course, try to shift the tax to the consumer. Most state retail sales taxes include in their base all tangible personal property "for purposes of use or consumption." Commodities are not taxed, therefore, if the firm intends to resell them; but to merit the exemption the goods have to become *physical ingredients* of the commodity they contribute to making. This does not hold for machines, equipment, fuel, and building materials, and they are therefore usually taxed. The result is an inequity against consumers of goods made with much plant and equipment. This lack of uniformity is similar to that illustrated in the example cited above in criticism of the manufacturers' and wholesale sales tax.[20]

PROBLEMS OF ADMINISTRATION

The cost and effectiveness of administration is an important, though not necessarily determining, factor in the choice of tax. Administration is easier the more definite the tax base, and the more readily the tax liability can be ascertained. In general, the record of the retail sales tax with respect to prevention of evasion is fairly good. It does operate under the disadvantage, however, that the number of retailers is much larger than that of wholesalers and manufacturers. Moreover, many small retailers keep no records.

The Treasury has estimated that with given exemptions there are about seventeen times as many taxpayers under a retail tax as under a manufacturers' tax, and over nine times as many as under a wholesale tax.[21] Moreover, the fact that many farmers sell only occasionally at retail adds to the difficulty of defining the tax base. On the other hand, the problem of ascertaining the base and determining the valuation of the article subject to tax is less acute at the retail level. There are two reasons: (1) under the retail sales tax the quoted price is more often the actual commercial price than is the practice with wholesale and manufacturers' sales taxes, and (2) there is less variation in distribution practices at the retail stage.

The effectiveness of administration also depends on the governmental jurisdiction that is to administer the tax. The federal government, for

---

[20] See footnote 13, page 255.
[21] United States Treasury Division of Tax Research, *op. cit.*, p. 1120.

example, has had much experience with manufacturers' excises, and very little with taxes on retail sales. On the other hand, the states have had considerable experience with the latter. This tax is more adaptable to state use than are the manufacturers' and wholesale sales taxes. Retail sales are more likely to be made within the borders of the state. The exceptions to this statement are, however, of considerable importance, as the volume of sales by mail-order houses and sales of cigarettes through the mails will testify.

Sales across state lines pose the problem of the role of the states with respect to interstate commerce. They do not have the right to tax interstate sales, but ambiguity arises out of the difficulty of defining interstate commerce. A workable solution is necessary, however, because untaxed sales across state lines not only diminish the sales tax revenues of the taxing state but offer unfair competition to merchants in that state. Under present Supreme Court interpretation, interstate sales are taxable if the seller also has a place of business in the taxing state. This leaves the whole matter in a rather chaotic condition. In any event, the taxing state cannot apply the tax unless it is aware that the sale has taken place.[22]

The Use Tax.   A device introduced in a number of states, which has been upheld by the Supreme Court, is the *use tax*. This is a tax on the use of a commodity on which no sales tax has been paid because it was bought outside the state. No use tax can be collected, of course, unless the state tax authorities have the necessary information. The postal authorities have not reacted favorably to violating the secrecy of the mails in order to inform state authorities of shipments of taxable goods into the state. Police inspection of automobiles at state borders makes a poor impression in a country that is proud of its absence of internal customs barriers. Furthermore, the use tax is not very practicable when applied to a long list of commodities because inspection offices become swamped with work. If applied to *all* commodities, however, the task becomes easier. A good deal can be done through information supplied by the shippers or the carriers. However, the effectiveness of this type of control depends largely on the extent to which taxpayers are frightened by the knowledge that this information is in the hands of the state tax authorities.

The complexities of commodity tax relations among the states might lead to the view that they ought to surrender this source of revenue to the federal government. This raises the whole question of intergovernmental fiscal relations, which is discussed in Chapter 17. An alternative would, of course, be for the states to agree on a standard form of sales tax. This,

---

[22] Progress toward administrative cooperation has been made. Thus the (federal) Jenkins Act of 1949 requires that persons shipping cigarettes across state lines to other than licensed distributors forward monthly information to tax administrators in states levying sales or use taxes.

however, is an unlikely possibility because of the wide variations in the economic structures and financial requirements of the different states and the consequent obstacles to cooperation. A third possibility would be the entry of the federal government into the area of retail sales taxation, accompanied by a sufficient de-emphasis by the states on sales taxation so that lack of uniformity of state sales tax practice would have unimportant consequences.

Attitude of the Taxpayer.   An important consideration in the effective administration of a tax is the attitude both of the taxpayer and of those who are responsible for administering the tax. An advantage of the retail sales tax is that since it applies to the final stage, where the value of the commodity is highest, a given amount of revenue can be raised with lower rates of tax than is the case with the wholesale and manufacturers' sales taxes. Therefore taxpayer resistance arising out of an objection to high rates is likely to be less in the case of the retail sales tax.

On the other hand, the attitudes of various groups toward a particular form of sales tax depends on how it affects them as producers as well as on the incidence of the tax. Large retailers have opposed the retail sales tax, whereas certain financial interests have in the past favored such a tax at the federal level as a device for reducing the degree of progression of the personal income tax. The National Association of Manufacturers prefers a manufacturers' sales tax to a retail sales tax, largely on the ground that the great number of small retailers complicates the task of collection.

Many businessmen, who wish to make sure that the tax will actually be borne by the consumer, have expressed a preference for the retail sales tax. They believe that a greater percentage of a tax imposed at the end of the production process will be shifted forward than is the case with a tax imposed at an earlier stage. The consumer is naturally much more conscious of a retail sales tax, especially if it is separately quoted. The great diversity of interests among taxpayers, coupled with the likelihood that it would not take long to become accustomed to a given type of sales tax, makes it doubtful that an attitude of opposition would develop that would seriously affect administration.

► SHOULD THE FEDERAL GOVERNMENT ADOPT A RETAIL SALES TAX?

A perennial fiscal issue in the United States is the question whether or not the federal government should enter the sales tax field. If the substitution of a general retail sales tax for the present system of federal excises were to yield greater revenue, the contribution of the federal tax system to income equality would be reduced. This would be justified, of course, if mass consumption had to be curtailed in order to permit militarization or an increase in the national economic potential. Wage controls might at the same time be required in order to prevent any resulting rise in the cost of living from becoming the occasion for increases in income.

If a retail sales tax became a permanent part of the federal fiscal system, the inflationary impetus caused by the tax should gradually disappear. Even if the monetary authority acquiesces in the passing on of a sales tax in the form of higher prices, thus providing an elastic money supply, the existence of lags in the recapture of real purchasing power by the various groups in the economy means that the inflationary movement tends to be damped. Under our present assumptions, the price level would be generally higher because of the tax, but there would not be an inflationary spiral.

Neither the states nor the United States Treasury has in the past looked with favor on the entrance of the federal government into the sales tax field. An exception to this statement was the request for a sales tax by Secretary Mills when federal revenues declined in 1932–1933. But apart from times of acute revenue need during a depression, the Treasury's representatives have preferred an extension of the selective excises, on the ground that these can distinguish between necessities and luxuries. The states have feared that entry by the federal government into the realm of general sales taxation would circumscribe their freedom to use it. It is likely that a realization of the need for revenues by the states has tended to stay the hand of Congress in entering a tax field which it would probably never again surrender.

An influence operating to encourage the adoption of the general sales tax in some form (retail, wholesale, or manufacturers') by the federal government is the fact that many foreign central governments make use of this tax.[23] In most instances, however, it was introduced during depressions, and for political reasons could not be eliminated even when economic recovery made it feasible to do so. Foreign experience with sales taxation does not provide an appropriate model for federal fiscal policy. In some countries sales taxes have been retained because of apathy on the part of politically powerful groups toward inequality in the distribution of income. From the point of view of tax policy, the Congress of the United States has shown itself to be more concerned with the problem of inequality than is the case in some of the countries of Western Europe.

THE BRITISH PURCHASE TAX

Since the central government must assume responsibility for any coordinated fiscal policy aimed at the control of private spending, a strong

---

[23] The National Association of Manufacturers in 1953 urged the adoption of a federal manufacturers' sales tax of approximately 5 per cent on all finished products except foods (and tobacco and liquor, already taxed at higher rates). A major objective of this proposal was to eliminate the discrimination of a system of selective

argument exists in favor of restricting federal sales taxation during wartime to excises (and possibly the graduated spendings tax). This accounts for the growth in the popularity of the British purchase tax with some fiscal economists in recent years. This tax was used during World War II mainly for the purpose of discouraging the purchase of commodities using scarce resources. Persistence of scarcities into the postwar period necessitated retention of the tax, and under the 1950 amendments, four classes of commodities were established. The first class (necessities) was exempt, the others being taxed (at the wholesale stage) at rates of 33⅓, 66⅔, and 100 per cent, respectively.

It is of interest to note that although motives were somewhat mixed in the British purchase tax, the purpose was not primarily to discourage luxury consumption, but to conserve resources. To a considerable extent, it is true, these two objectives are identical. Revenue considerations were, of course, by no means absent. The purchase tax yielded about £300 million in 1951, or nearly 3.5 per cent of domestic consumer spending. But this revenue was derived to a large extent from spending on articles that are not part of cost of living. Consequently, the purchase tax, through careful selection of commodities and rates, can be kept relatively non-inflationary.

That the British were striving for this goal can be seen by inspecting the articles subject to the different rates under the statute as it stood prior to 1952. Thus, utility clothing and utility furniture, which not only use a minimum of labor and materials but are prominent in a consumer's price index, were entirely exempt. Domestic cooking and heating appliances were likewise exempt, as well as food, drugs, and simple household equipment.[24] On the other hand, nonutility garments, carpeting, radios, cutlery, nonessential drugs, and lighting fixtures were included among the articles taxed at the 33⅓ per cent rate. The fact that some element of luxury taxation was present is evidenced by the inclusion of musical instruments, garden furniture and gas space heaters in the group taxed at 66⅔ per cent, and of jewelry, cosmetics, leather luggage, and electric space heaters in the 100 per cent group. On the other hand, in view of Britain's tight foreign exchange position, it can be maintained that with respect to these articles, too, the major objective was to conserve a scarce "resource," for the very high rate of tax served to release these commodities for export.

The attempt to minimize the inflationary effects of the purchase tax by exempting utility goods, however, gave rise to a number of undesirable economic effects. These induced the government to steer the purchase tax

---

excises. The Ways and Means Committee, however, chose the alternative of reducing the rates of excise to 10 per cent on all commodities and services (except liquor and tobacco).

[24] Tobacco and liquor are not taxed under the purchase tax because they are already subject to special taxation, which is much heavier than the same taxes in the United States.

back more in the direction of a general sales tax.[25] An investigating committee had found that the wartime objective of encouraging standardization and efficiency by exempting utility goods from the tax was no longer being achieved. Specifications for each type of good had enormously multiplied. Moreover, British manufacturers found it impracticable to produce the higher-quality goods demanded abroad because the high purchase tax on these goods meant that producers could not count on an alternative market at home. Finally, Britain was being accused of hindering imports, because few foreign goods could qualify for the tax-free utility designation.

In response to these complaints a new scheme was established which, for clothing, shoes, and textiles, substituted for the former system of utility classifications and maximum utility prices a new criterion called the "D" level. Where wholesale prices exceeded the new tax-free level (established for each good), tax was to apply to the excess only. This change removed the sharp discrimination against better-quality goods selling at prices not much above utility prices. Unfortunately, in order to keep up the revenues, the government had in some instances set the tax-free limit below the old utility price. This subjected certain commodities to tax that had previously been exempt. In response to complaints, the rate scale of the purchase tax was, in April, 1953, reduced from 100, 66⅔, and 33⅓ per cent to 75, 50, and 25 per cent. This step encouraged consumer demand, and thus provided a weapon against deflationary forces that were beginning to gather at the time.[26]

Selective excise taxation for the purpose of economic control is more adapted to the British form of government than to that of the United States. In Britain, changes in the rates can be made relatively easily, since with a reasonable majority the government can be certain that its proposal for changes in rates will be accepted by Parliament. An equally flexible instrument of control could be used in this country only if Congress were to grant the executive the right to vary rates of tax within certain prescribed limits. This will be recognized as similar to the power already granted the President with respect to the tariff. Congress was none too sure of its willingness to yield this much of its power, however, and even a limited surrender of the vital tax power to the executive in the interest of economic control does not appear imminent.

FEDERAL CONSUMPTION TAXATION: CONCLUSION

We conclude that important objections can be made to an extension of sales taxation by the federal government in the form either of a general

[25] For informative discussions of the British purchase tax, see Arnold Soloway, "Economic Aspects of the British Purchase Tax," *Journal of Finance*, May, 1954, pp. 188–208, and John Due, "The British Purchase Tax," *Canadian Tax Journal*, March–April, 1955, pp. 97–112.

[26] Soloway, "Economic Aspects . . . ," *loc. cit.*, p. 207. In 1955, however, the rates were again raised (to 90, 60, and 30 per cent) in an effort to combat inflation.

sales tax or of selected excises. It is likely to represent a backward step with respect to the progression of the tax system as a whole. Although it is admitted that this might be necessary if consumption has to be restricted, the likelihood is great that the tax would be retained after the scarcities had been eliminated. The states and cities depend heavily on sales taxation, and their problems would be complicated by the presence of the federal government in this tax area.

The major justifications for selected excises or a purchase tax are (1) the need to conserve strategic resources, and (2) a willingness to vary the rates of tax in accordance with changes in relative scarcities. During World War II the first of these conditions did obtain, and temporary excises were justified. But the failure to repeal them after the war made it clear that the major objective had become revenue rather than economic control. With the present very wide coverage of the personal income tax, there is scope for increasing taxes on the lower-income groups by lowering exemptions and raising the first bracket rate rather than taxing the same income groups by means of an addition to the already extensive sales tax structure. The possibility of adverse effects of the income tax on incentives is recognized, but considerably higher rates in the lower brackets in England have apparently not had a significant discouraging effect.

Finally, however, it must be admitted that substantial further increases in the need for revenue by the federal government might create enough sentiment for a retail sales tax or a great extension in the excises. Each type of tax has its particular disadvantages, and this fact would argue in favor of opening up new tax sources rather than relying entirely on increases in the rates of taxes that are already in use.

► THE INCIDENCE OF SALES TAXES[27]

The incidence of sales and excise taxes is ordinarily believed to be primarily on the consumer. This is the traditional conclusion of incidence theorists, though, as we saw in Chapter 7, it has recently been subjected to re-examination, and is denied by Brown and Rolph. It is also the view that is evidently held by legislatures. The existence of a wide variety of types of sales taxes, levied at various stages of production, probably bears witness to the confidence of tax legislators that no matter where sales taxes are originally imposed, they are ultimately shifted to the consumer.

Perhaps it would be more accurate to say that legislators are not greatly concerned over whether or not the taxes are shifted, for the major objective has been to produce revenues with a minimum of effort. In any event, sales taxes are often defended on the ground that they are consumption taxes which are justified despite their regressiveness. It is argued that exemptions and family deductions under the income tax relieve many per-

---

[27] The general principles have been discussed in Chapter 7.

sons from paying that tax, but that persons who frequently change their residence find sales taxes more difficult to escape than state income and property taxes.

Under the conditions of perfect competition average cost is just covered by price, and the sales tax cannot in the long run be borne by the firm. Because of the wide extent of monopoly profits throughout the economy, however, considerable scope may exist for absorption of some part of a sales tax by sellers. Obviously the extent to which absorption takes place depends in part on the type of sales tax under consideration. The narrower the scope of the tax, the more numerous are the opportunities to avoid it through the transfer of resources to untaxed uses.

It is a frequent practice to require a sales tax imposed at the consumer stage to be stated separately from the price of the commodity. One of the reasons for this is to discourage the retailer from advertising that he is absorbing the tax. Despite this legislative attempt to put the burden of the tax definitely on the consumer, there is nothing to prevent the seller from reducing his percentage markup and thus in effect absorbing the tax. The same practice can, of course, be indulged in by manufacturers and wholesalers with respect to sales taxes applied at earlier stages of production.

More precise knowledge of the incidence of sales taxes depends upon the making of factual studies of the responses of firms selling in imperfectly competitive markets.[28] Under certain conditions firms may indeed find it worth while to absorb the tax in order to attract business. On the other hand, it is common for sellers to publish an entirely new price schedule in response to the imposition of a general sales tax. Suppose that firms respond by raising prices by the amount of the tax. Can we conclude that the incidence is therefore entirely on the consumer?

The sales tax is for the most part shifted forward if certain assumptions are satisfied. It is probable that these conditions are indeed largely met and that the tax tends to be passed forward. One of the assumptions is that there is no decline in aggregate demand for the factors of production. This will be the case if the decline in factor demand by consumers in response to the tax is matched by the rise in demand on the part of the government.[29] Consumers find that their money does not go as far as before. Assuming that they spend the same amount, they receive fewer goods. The income of the government has increased by the amount of the tax, and the government receives the goods that are yielded up by the consumers. The demand for production factors is therefore unchanged, and in the aggregate

---

[28] Cf. J. F. Due, "Toward a General Theory of Sales Tax Incidence," *Quarterly Journal of Economics,* May, 1953, pp. 253–266.

[29] This statement abstracts from indirect effects on the demand for factors. More properly, the aggregate demand for factors remains the same if, taking account of both immediate and subsequent effects, any change in private demand is just offset by an opposite change in the demand by the government. Aggregate demand includes both consumption and investment demand.

none of the tax will be shifted to them. Since prices are higher than before, the consumer bears the tax.

Prices can be higher, however, only if the money supply is elastic. Otherwise the same amount of transactions as before must be carried on at higher prices with an unchanged money supply. This will drive up interest rates and discourage investment. Therefore unemployment will appear and production factors will be forced to bear some of the tax through reduced rates of remuneration. It is likely, however, that, unless there is fear of a dangerously rapid inflation, there will be no obstacle placed by the monetary authorities to the expansion of the money supply, and little of the tax will be passed backward.

► PYRAMIDING

It is probably safe to assume that some part of a multistage sales tax is covered out of profits and reduced payments to factors at various stages of production. On the other hand, in the aggregate, this phenomenon may be more than offset by pyramiding. At any given stage of production the tax base is the price of the product. Price includes cost plus markup. But all taxes paid at earlier stages are included in this cost. The inclusion of the tax in the base of a subsequent cost markup is called pyramiding.[30] Pyramiding can occur, however, only when the money supply is elastic, and when the level of aggregate demand is such that all transactions can be covered at a price inclusive of tax plus the markups.

Even when merchants believe that they are applying an automatic percentage markup, they may be forced to take account of an elastic demand through bargain sales, special discounts, and the like. If demand is elastic, pressure is greater for producers at each stage to absorb part of the tax, or to try to shift it back to producers at earlier stages and to factors of production. Clearly the situation most favorable to pyramiding is rising money incomes. Automatic markups are then possible, and another escalator is added to the collection of forces that propagate inflation.

Pyramiding is more serious under a multistage general sales tax than it is under a single-stage manufacturers' or wholesale sales tax. If a production process involves a number of stages, and the tax is applied at each stage, a nominal tax of, say, 2 per cent may amount to 10 or 15 per cent of the price of the end product. Under a system of price markups, even a single-stage tax, applied at the manufacturers' level, will comprise a larger proportion of the value of the final product than its nominal rate would imply, because at subsequent production stages the tax forms part of the

---

[30] The discussion of pyramiding should be read in the light of the role of the effect of the tax on the aggregate demand for factors of production discussed in the preceding section. *All* the repercussions on demand have to be considered if we are to obtain an accurate conception of the extent of pyramiding.

base to which the markup is applied. Pyramiding is apt to be quantitatively unimportant, however, except in the case of a general sales tax used in conjunction with a number of stages of production. The worst offender among the sales taxes in respect to pyramiding is the turnover tax, which is the popular source of revenue in some European countries. Its pyramiding characteristics can be avoided by substituting for it another tax applied at successive stages of production, namely, the value-added tax. Both these taxes may be briefly considered.[31]

THE TURNOVER TAX

Under the turnover tax, commodities are taxed at each stage of production. For many years the normal rate of this tax in Germany,[32] for example, was 2 per cent, but it was later raised to the extremely high rate of 4 per cent. Although the German turnover tax applies substantially lower rates to sales at the earlier stages of production, the pyramiding effect is considerable, and a high degree of distortion is injected into the allocation of resources. There are two reasons. First, more than any other type of sales tax, the turnover tax enters into cost of production and therefore affects economic decisions. Its incidence is, of course, largely on the ultimate consumer. Second, the tax is discriminatory against industries characterized by a relatively small amount of vertical integration, with a correspondingly large number of taxable sales. The Germans have made some effort to reduce this discrimination through the imposition of a supplementary tax on integrated firms, but the corrective has actually been applied only to the textile industry.

Administrative and political considerations, coupled with the fact that

---

[31] Particular interest in this country attaches to the turnover tax because of the advocacy by Dr. Townsend of a 2 per cent turnover tax to finance his proposed old-age pension plan. He saw the problem solely in terms of finding a tax that would be sufficiently productive to finance the extremely generous benefits (at the price level of the thirties) of $200 a month to persons over sixty-five years of age. Since the turnover tax is a highly productive tax, with a relatively stable yield, it seemed to him an appropriate device.

What he overlooked was that the bulk of the tax would be paid by the same income groups that would later receive the benefits. The aged themselves would lose part of the real value of their pensions through the rise in consumer goods prices. Most of the rest would be paid by the generation of active workers. In effect, therefore, there would be a substantial shift of purchasing power from younger to retired workers. The political impact of a plan of this sort can easily be imagined. The turnover tax feature made the Townsend plan perhaps unique among income redistribution schemes.

[32] The turnover tax has also been used in Japan and France. The Japanese tax, which was modeled after the French turnover tax, has accounted for about 7 per cent of total revenues. (Carl Shoup, "Tax Reform in Japan," *Proceedings* of the National Tax Association, 1949, p. 411.) The French turnover tax was introduced in 1920, but because of its discrimination against vertically unintegrated industries a single-payment tax was authorized for many products. Though the latter principle was extended in the legislation of 1936, the turnover tax has been in part retained. Because of its productivity a turnover tax is hard to do away with, but recently the French have moved toward a value-added tax.

the number of production stages varies widely from industry to industry, have made it impracticable to improve the turnover tax. Economists have rightly placed this tax low in their scale of preference. It should be remembered, however, that when a given set of rates has been in operation for many years, a considerable measure of adaptation to the tax has gradually taken place. If the tax encourages vertical integration, its effects will ultimately become widely diffused through shifting and capitalization.

Perhaps the heaviest count against a palpably inequitable and capricious tax like the turnover tax is that, once established, it does not easily lend itself to rate changes. Increases in the rate of the turnover tax cause much more serious economic dislocations than are produced when it is found necessary to alter the rates of those taxes whose distorting effects are less pronounced. Conversely, a turnover tax causes similar, though opposite, disturbances when it is repealed.

Exemptions under the turnover tax have little to do with the income bracket of the consumer who ultimately bears the tax. They ordinarily comprise imports of raw materials important to the economic and military capacity of the nation, sales of services by public utilities, and the like.[33]

THE VALUE-ADDED TAX

A tax that is designed to avoid the defect of pyramiding, while at the same time taking advantage of the fact that it is administratively easier to collect a tax at an early production stage, is the value-added tax. This is a tax on the value added by manufacture; in other words, it is a tax on wages, interest and profits, rent, and depreciation incurred at each stage of production. Consequently, taxes and profit markups at earlier stages do not become the basis for the tax at a later stage. Since wages comprise most of value added, the value-added tax is largely a payroll tax. Labor leaders have therefore frequently opposed this tax on the ground that it is borne by the worker.[34] It is probable, however, that the bulk of the tax is passed forward to the consumer, as with other forms of sales taxes.

As under the turnover tax, exemptions under the value-added tax are

---

[33] The Russian turnover tax bears no resemblance to the turnover tax discussed in the text. This is an arbitrary markup, applied at every stage of production, to absorb the excess purchasing power of consumers. The production plans of the central government provide that a given amount of goods be made available to consumers annually. On the other hand, in order to maintain incentives, and partly because of errors in planning, consumers may receive more purchasing power than can be absorbed by the goods available to them at the controlled prices. This excess purchasing power is siphoned off by a "turnover" tax applied at the various production stages. Thus the Russian turnover tax is not a fixed-rate tax, with the yield a dependent variable. On the contrary, the desired yield determines the rate, which also varies in response to particular demand and production conditions.

[34] The first experiment with a value-added tax in the United States was the measure adopted by Michigan in July, 1953. (A lucid discussion of this tax can be found in an address by Alan L. Gornick to the University of Michigan Law School Institute, July 30, 1953, entitled "The Michigan Business Receipts Tax.") The lack of opposition to it is probably attributable to the low four-mill (now six-and-one-half

unrelated to considerations of income distribution. An exemption may take the form of an exclusion of a part of wages, rent, interest, and profits, and, particularly, depreciation. Evidently the exemption under this tax is peculiarly adapted to favoring particular classes of industry, say small or new business, cooperatives, exceptionally risky enterprise, and the like. The exemption would be likely, therefore, to stimulate certain favored types of business savings and investment. The effect of this on the distribution of income would depend on circumstances. The consumer would benefit if the effect were a fall in prices. Under imperfect market conditions, however, prices might not fall, and the gain would go to stockholders, who are in a higher-income bracket than are consumers. It should be noted that the rate of the value-added tax would have to be considerably higher than the rate of a turnover tax designed to yield the same revenue, since in effect a value-added tax is intended to provide a tax base of the same order of magnitude as that of the retail sales tax.

► A NOTE ON THE TREASURY SPENDINGS TAX
PROPOSAL OF 1942[35]

The economic aspects of a tax on spending as a permanent feature of the federal tax system have been discussed in Chapter 8. The spendings tax has usually been proposed as a substitute for the personal income tax, by the expedient of defining income for tax purposes as identical with spending on consumption. As we have seen, the Mill-Fisher version of the spendings tax is subject to the criticism that the principle of ability to pay is surrendered, and that savings are favored at the expense of consumption. Even if the spendings tax is treated as an additional tax, so that the principle of ability to pay is preserved, the effect is to discourage consumption during a depression, when it needs to be kept as high as possible in order to cushion the effects of a decline in investment spending. Therefore, a permanent spendings tax has favorable economic effects only during periods of excessively high personal consumption, as in time of war. Except during periods when the national interest requires personal spending to be reduced, a modern high-income type of economy requires a high propensity to consume.

Because of this defect of a *permanent* spendings tax, the Treasury proposed during World War II that a spendings tax be adopted that was

mill) rate, and to the high exemption of $10,000 plus the 50 per cent deduction feature. These provisions exempted the small farmer and small service establishment from the tax, and thus made the tax a popular one. One condition of successful administration, as was learned in France, is the absence of numerous exemptions. For a discussion of technical difficulties of the value-added tax, see M. Bronfenbrenner, "The Japanese Value-Added Sales Tax," *National Tax Journal,* December, 1950, pp. 303–308.

[35] For the details of the proposal see *Annual Report* of the Secretary of the Treasury, 1943, Exhibits 81 and 82.

based on a different philosophy. Instead of a permanent tax, a special wartime spendings tax should be enacted that would be designed to discourage consumption, and thus release factors of production to the war effort. The measure of success of the tax would be the extent to which it did *not* yield revenue, for this would indicate a high level of personal saving.

The Treasury's proposal was actually a combination of compulsory savings and a progressive tax on personal spending. It provided for a dual set of rates; (1) a normal tax of 10 per cent, refundable after the war, on all personal spending above a basic exclusion of $500 per person ($1,000 for a married couple, and $250 for a dependent), and (2) a nonrefundable graduated surtax. Thus the tax would have a double-barreled effect. The mass of the population would be forced to reduce spending by virtue of the absorption of their purchasing power by the normal tax. Persons receiving higher incomes would be discouraged from excessive spending by the graduation of the surtax rates. Nothing would prevent the rates from going above 100 per cent. If, for example, a man with large amounts of liquid savings insisted on maintaining a high standard of living despite the war, the only way to discourage him would be to make him pay prohibitively high taxes on his spending.[36]

From the point of view of public morale the graduated spendings tax would perhaps play its most important role in preventing the high-income groups from maintaining excessive rates of "conspicuous consumption." Since the vast bulk of the consumption spending is done by individuals subject to the low rates, the spendings tax would in large measure amount merely to an addition to the basic rate of the income tax. It was chiefly because of this fact that Congress showed no disposition to give the new proposal serious consideration. The graduated portion of the spendings tax would not become effective until those levels of personal spending had been reached at which the individual has the choice whether to spend or save.

In other words, the economic control aspects of the tax, as distinguished from its purely purchasing-power characteristics, would be restricted to the middle- and higher-income groups. Moreover, the longer the period of time over which a progressive spendings tax operates, the greater its effect in stimulating savings by those groups that are able to save. The distribution of wealth therefore becomes more unequal. Because of this the Treasury proposed the tax only as a means of controlling consumption

---

[36] It is pointed out by C. L. Harriss ("Revenue Implications of a Progressive-Rate Tax on Expenditures," *Review of Economic Statistics,* August, 1943, p. 187) that rates over 100 per cent would not really be a novel device, because when effective income tax rates go above 50 per cent the amount left, even if the whole of it is spent, is less than the tax. Suppose that a man's income is $100,000, and his income tax is $60,000. Then if he saves nothing he has only $40,000 to spend. In the absence of an income tax it would require a spendings tax rate of 150 per cent to yield the same amount of tax.

spending during the war, and as an addition to a sharply progressive income tax that already rested heavily on savings.

The spendings tax form submitted for the consideration of Congress was similar to the income tax blank, and not much more complicated. The taxpayer was to be required to aggregate the funds at his disposal, from which he would deduct the total of his nontaxable uses of funds. The tax rate would be applied to the difference. "Funds at the disposal of the taxpayer" comprised his gross income as reported in his income tax blank, plus receipts from gifts, bequests and insurance policies, sales of capital assets, repayment of loans, and new borrowing, plus cash and bank balances on hand at the beginning of the year. For completeness an item entitled "Other Receipts" was included. Deductions consisted of all the nontaxable uses of the individual's funds; his cash and bank balances on hand at the end of the year, gifts and contributions, interest and taxes paid (except on owner occupied homes, which was an attempt to remove part of the advantage that a home owner has over the renter under the personal income tax),[37] purchase of capital assets, premiums paid on life insurance, annuities, and pensions, debt repayment by the taxpayer, and loans made by him. Thus spending on consumption was to be arrived at indirectly, through a statement of income and a comparison of net assets at the beginning and the end of the taxable year.

There was nothing in the mechanics of the spendings tax declaration that would have made the tax impossible to administer. The major difficulties would be those of the transition period, namely, anticipatory buying in advance of the effective date of the tax, and the detection of hoarded cash. A permanent problem would be to take account of direct consumption by those whose incomes are partly received in kind, for example, home owners and farmers.

▶ CONCLUSION

The taxation of consumption is usually associated in people's minds with sales taxation. The incidence of sales taxes is generally assumed to be on the consumer, though under certain assumptions backward shifting is possible. While this conclusion is broadly true, other taxes besides sales taxes affect consumption; on the other hand, sales and excise taxes not only affect consumption but may reduce savings. Even though a tax is measured by consumption, individuals in income brackets substantially above subsistence are more likely to curtail savings than consumption whether the tax is measured by income, property, or consumption. Moreover, except under conditions of perfect competition a portion of the tax may not be shifted. In this event profits are reduced, and either corporate

---

[37] Cf. K. E. Poole, "The Spendings Tax: Problems of Administration and Equity," *American Economic Review*, March, 1943, pp. 69–73.

savings are smaller or dividends are curtailed. Whatever the proportion in which the direct incidence of sales taxes is distributed among production factors, the firm, and consumers, there are indirect effects on income, saving, and the inducement to invest; and these in turn affect still further the ultimate burden of the tax.

Agreement is general that consumption may have to be forcibly reduced in a war boom, and that in the absence of expenditure rationing some form of sales taxation is likely to be necessary. But there is sharp disagreement over the proper role of sales taxation during peacetime. One view is that savings and capital formation, and thus national productivity in the future, need to be stimulated by relatively heavy consumption taxes. Opposing this view is the contention that a high level of consumption spending is necessary to assure full employment, and therefore in turn a high level of saving and investment. Political authorities tend to approve of sales taxes because of their heavy revenue-yielding capacity and their role in extending the limits of taxable capacity. So long as a political balance exists between higher- and lower-income receivers, the use of both the progressive personal income tax and the regressive sales taxes will continue to reflect the will of the people.

► REFERENCES

BRONFENBRENNER, M. "The Japanese Value-Added Sales Tax," *National Tax Journal,* December, 1950, pp. 298–313.

BROWN, H. G. "The Incidence of a General Output or Sales Tax," *Journal of Political Economy,* April, 1939, pp. 254–262.

DUE, J. F. *The Theory of Incidence of Sales Taxation.* New York: King's Crown Press, 1942.

FISHER, I., and H. FISHER. *Constructive Income Taxation.* New York: Harper & Brothers, 1942.

FRIEDMAN, M. "The Spendings Tax as a Wartime Fiscal Measure," *American Economic Review,* March, 1943, pp. 50–62.

JACOBY, N. H. *Retail Sales Taxation.* Chicago: Commerce Clearing House, 1938.

NATIONAL INDUSTRIAL CONFERENCE BOARD (Symposium). *Consumption Taxes and Tax Reform.* New York: The Board, 1953.

POOLE, K. E. "The Spendings Tax: Problems of Administration and Equity," *American Economic Review,* March, 1943, pp. 62–73.

ROLPH, E. R. *The Theory of Fiscal Economics.* Berkeley: University of California Press, 1954, Chaps. VI and VII.

SOLOWAY, A. M. "Economic Aspects of the British Purchase Tax," *Journal of Finance,* May, 1954, pp. 188–208.

UNITED STATES TREASURY DIVISION OF TAX RESEARCH. *Considerations Respecting a Federal Retail Sales Tax,* Ways and Means Committee, *Hearings,* Revenue Revision, 1943, pp. 1095–1272.

14 The Taxation of Property: I

► THE OBJECTIVES OF PROPERTY TAXATION

A property tax is an annual tax levied on the possessions of the tax-payer. Although property is the basis of assessment, the tax is actually intended to be paid out of income, for the property itself is expected to remain intact. Thus a property tax differs from a capital levy, which is a nonrecurrent tax based on property, usually levied after a major war, that may be expected to reduce the amount of property in the possession of the taxpayer.

There are two types of property tax, the general and the specific. The former aims at obtaining a measure of the total economic wealth of the individual. Together with the general income tax, the general property tax provides a means of taxing the two sources of ability to pay, namely, wealth and income. The specific property tax, on the other hand, aims at taxing particular items of property, and is therefore not a personal tax. Thus one individual may have a large part of his wealth in a form that is subject to a specific property tax, and another may not; yet both may possess the same aggregate amount of property.

► THE TAXATION OF NET WORTH

Neither income nor property, taken alone, is an adequate measure of ability to pay taxes. A person who possesses property is spared the necessity of saving further against ill-health and old age, and therefore has an advantage over a propertyless individual in the same income group. On the other hand, if property alone were accepted as the measure of ability, a high-income spendthrift who avoided accumulating wealth would find himself exempt from taxes. The problem is how to strike a satisfactory compromise between the use of property and the use of income as measures of taxpaying ability. This is true despite the fact that in both cases the tax is actually paid out of income.

If it is granted that ability to pay depends on ownership of property

272

as well as on income, the tax base must take account of the whole of the property of the individual. Moreover, his debts must be subtracted from the tax base. A net worth tax, therefore, would require an annual declaration of all kinds of property, minus debts. A tax on net worth is not intended to be shifted. Like the general income tax it is personal. It is not the separate parcels of property that are being taxed, but rather the wealth of the individual as evidenced by ownership.

A net worth tax, as ordinarily conceived, would not include the capital invested in a man's training, and to that extent would fall short of including total "wealth." The individual makes a choice among (1) consumption, (2) the acquisition of wealth, and (3) educational investment in himself. Only to the extent that he selects the second choice does he subject himself to a net worth tax.

ADVANTAGES OF A NET WORTH TAX

A net worth tax has been recommended on a number of grounds,[1] although ability to pay is the most important of them. Another is that, as a supplement to the personal income tax, the net worth tax may permit an extension of the limits to taxable capacity. This is most important when rates of the income tax are so high as to threaten investment incentives. A tax levied on wealth is more independent of willingness to put forth effort than is a personal income tax. It is true that the knowledge that savings will be subject to a net worth tax may exert some discouraging effect on saving itself. The tax will be substantially less likely to discourage willingness to earn, however, since it can be avoided by consuming instead of saving.

An argument that some might make in favor of net worth taxation is that it can be used to discourage the undue accumulation of wealth. Whereas with death taxes, for example, the individual remains in possession of his property throughout his lifetime, an annual progressive net worth tax could be designed to help reduce the concentration of wealth. There is no sentiment for this kind of tax in the United States. More moderately progressive net worth taxes have been used abroad, for example, in the Scandinavian countries.

An administrative advantage of a net worth tax would be the assistance it would provide in tightening up the administration of the personal income tax, as well as the estate and gift taxes. One of the major sources of evasion under these taxes is the failure to require the individual to declare his assets as of each taxable year. Therefore, a valuable check on the accuracy of the declaration of income and gifts during the year is lost. Considerable

---

[1] See the discussion of the net worth tax (proposed as a supplement to the Japanese income tax) by the Shoup Mission, *Report on Japanese Taxation* (Tokyo: Supreme Commander for the Allied Powers, 1949), I, p. 81 ff. Also W. Vickrey, *Agenda for Progressive Taxation* (New York: Ronald, 1947), p. 9.

risk would attend the failure to declare income if assets and liabilities of individuals had to be listed annually. For unless savings were converted to consumption they would ultimately show up in the estate at death, at which time back taxes and penalties would be collected. Prior to death the individual would constantly face the possibility of discovery. Thus it might conceivably be argued that the administrative difficulties of a net worth tax ought in any event to be incurred in the interest of effective administration of the income and the estate and gift taxes.

Finally, a net worth tax helps to diminish the inequity that is produced under the personal income tax between property income that is relatively stable and that which fluctuates. To the extent that stability of income is reflected in a higher market price of the property, a greater tax would be paid if the net worth tax were adopted as a supplement to the personal income tax.

OBJECTIONS TO A NET WORTH TAX

The net worth tax is subject to a number of objections that have made it unpopular in many countries. It is perhaps a short step from the use of such a tax, as an aid to the adequate measurement of ability to pay, to its employment for the more radical goal of the equalization of income and wealth. Public sentiment in most countries is likely to regard the personal income tax and progressive death taxes as sufficient obstacles to the undue accumulation of wealth and economic power. For that reason the experiment has usually been made only by socialist-inclined governments (for example, Germany after World War I).

A number of other objections are closely associated with this one. To many people the prospect of having to list their assets and liabilities is an unpleasant extension of the inquisitiveness of the personal income tax authorities. The objection is much less strong when only a part of a person's wealth has to be declared, as under the specific property tax. In that case nothing is revealed about a man's over-all economic position. Those whose activities are complex, though not necessarily dishonest, are not receptive to the idea of having their affairs anatomized in the tax collector's office. Again, even if the tax is not used directly to reduce inequality of wealth, legislatures may be tempted for revenue reasons to increase rates in the middle and upper brackets, and thus create the impression that the tax system is unduly weighted with redistributive taxes.

A more remote possibility is that the tax might be used to increase the economic power of the central government in relation to that of the private sector. This might be accomplished without intent, through the gradual adoption of such stiff rate scales that savings hitherto available for private investment were increasingly diverted to the government. Even if the process were not carried this far, the public might question whether the use made of savings by the government would maximize the rate of capital formation. In brief, a net worth tax might prove to be *too* effective an instrument for nationalizing savings.

Finally, the administrative difficulties cannot be ignored, despite the fact that the adoption of a net worth tax would have important by-products in the form of more effective administration of the income and death taxes. It might be argued that the problems of valuation, and of checking on taxpayer honesty and accuracy, are so great that the income and estate tax might be better administered without an annual declaration of assets. However, the administrative difficulties would be greatly minimized if a fairly high exemption were admitted. On the other hand, the greater the exemption the less would be the resemblance of the impost to a net worth tax.[2]

► THE GENERAL PROPERTY TAX

The general property tax is so called because the base is intended to include all property having exchange value that is not exempted. Thus it is usually provided in the constitutions of the states that all real and personal property is to be included in the base of the property tax. Taxable personal property, in turn, consists of both tangible and intangible property. The latter represents claims to wealth. Evidently it is the intent of a general property tax to treat all property alike.

The state constitutional provisions with respect to the comprehensiveness of the property tax represent a trend in the taxation of property that had been developing in the United States throughout the nineteenth century. Originally the property tax was thought of primarily as a tax on land. In an agricultural society, in the days before mechanization, land was the main index of wealth, and a land tax was essentially a tax on an individual's total property. But even in rural areas the invention of new types of agricultural machinery began to make the land tax obsolescent. In the cities the rising standard of living increased the proportion of personal property to real estate, and therefore diminished the value of real property as an index of wealth. Items of personal property were added only gradually, however, and administrative difficulties ultimately reversed the trend to greater comprehensiveness.

As new types of property were added to the tax rolls, the states began to substitute the general property tax for incomplete lists of taxable items of property. The opposite course had been followed in Continental Europe. One of the grievances of the people in prerevolutionary France was the exemption from the property tax of the wealth of the nobility and the

---

[2] A net worth tax at the federal level in the United States would be in the same position constitutionally as a federal property tax. As a "direct" tax it would have to be apportioned among the states according to population, and inequities that would therefore be caused among states would prevent its adoption.

clergy, and the general property tax grew less general as personal property and intangibles came to be excluded from the base. In some European countries the property tax has tended to be restricted to land.

The difficulty of administering a general property tax equitably arises largely out of the fact that it is "general." When a variety of different types of property are included in the tax base, the problem arises of achieving an equitable and logical valuation procedure. Administration of the property tax is easiest when taxable property is relatively simple and uniform. Thus the land tax, with assessments based on location, yield, and other relevant data prepared on the assumption of "prudent management," can be administered fairly equitably. This limited type of property tax is in use in certain European countries.

Attention should be directed to the phrase "having exchange value" in the definition of the property tax. Obviously a property tax can be levied only on property that has a value in exchange. This limitation, however, leads to what might appear to be a potential inequity in the tax. During the past fifty years or more there has been a rapid increase in the proportion of the property of the professionally trained man that takes the form of intellectual "capital." In colonial times the "faculty" tax was intended to take account of the property value of a man's capacity to earn income. At present, however, this phase of a man's wealth is taxed under the income tax rather than the property tax. By way of illustration, the education of a doctor may involve an investment in personal capital of $30,000 or more, none of which is taxed as property.

There are, however, important differences between personal capital and property of the usual kind, and these differences militate against taxing them in the same way. There is the risk of demise or illness, which, in contrast with the destruction of tangible property, may be prohibitively expensive to insure against. Another point is that the property tax, as it exists today, is not a personal tax, whereas personal capital is inseparable from the individual. The taxation of personal capital would be, therefore, a more relevant issue with respect to the net worth tax than to the general property tax.

HISTORICAL DEVELOPMENT

The taxation of property has been subjected to more criticism than has any other tax. Most of the widespread resentment against this tax arises out of the unequal treatment of taxpayers caused by archaic state constitutional limitations and poorly drafted laws, as well as by inferior administration.

The fact that in the United States the property tax is the basic source of tax revenues for the localities greatly enhances the practical seriousness of its defects. Despite the development in recent years of new types of local taxes, the rapidly growing revenue needs of the towns and cities have preserved the great relative importance of the property tax as a source of tax revenue.[3] Table 13 provides a general view of the trend in the relative importance of the property tax at the state and local levels since the turn of the century. (During this period there has been no federal general property tax.)

Table 13. State and Local Property Tax Revenues, Selected Years
(In millions of dollars)

Year	Property Tax Receipts		Total Tax Receipts		Property Tax Receipts as a Percentage of Total Tax Receipts	
	State	Local	State	Local	State	Local
1902	82	624	156	704	52.6	88.5
1913	140	1,192	301	1,308	46.5	91.1
1932	328	4,159	1,890	4,274	17.3	97.4
1946	249	4,737	4,937	5,157	5.1	91.7
1953	365	9,010	10,552	10,356	3.5	87.1

SOURCE: Bureau of the Census, *Historical Statistics on State and Local Government Finances, 1902–1953*.

The most striking feature of Table 13 is the stability of the relative importance of the property tax as a source of tax revenue to the localities in the past fifty years. The ratio of property taxes to total taxes was virtually identical in the two years 1902 and 1953. This constancy is the more extraordinary in view of the vast increase in the types and quality of public services that the localities have been called upon to provide during the period. The table illustrates, incidentally, a significant characteristic of the relative importance of the property tax to the municipalities. In 1932, the ratio of local property taxes to total local taxes rose to 97.4 per cent. This rise indicates the tardiness with which the property tax responds to cyclical swings in the level of income, and explains both its popularity with the localities and its inequity and discouraging economic effects during a depression.

Equally striking, in percentage terms, is the great decrease in the use made of the property tax by the states during the same period. This partly reflects an actual movement away from this tax at the state level. For the most part, the great decline in the percentage has been caused by the expansion of other, more elastic, forms of tax. They have furnished the added revenues necessitated by the revolution in the concept of the functions of the states during the past half century.

Taking the states and localities together, property tax receipts in

[3] The increasing use of the grant-in-aid has, of course, reduced the relative importance of local taxes in comparison with *total* local revenues.

uncorrected dollar terms have increased about thirteenfold over the period, while total tax receipts have increased about twenty-four times. Although the property tax now accounts for not much more than half as great a proportion of total state and local taxes as it did at the turn of the century, the fact that this ratio is still over 40 per cent makes obvious the seriousness of the inequities and poor administration of this tax.

REAL PROPERTY

General property consists of real and personal property. Although borderline cases blur the distinction, real and personal property differ in that the latter is movable and the former is not. For example, buildings, though sometimes moved, are classed as real property. Real property consists of land and the improvements made on it. These improvements take the form of drainage, fertilization, and the like, as well as buildings.

The distinction between land and its improvements is an important one. For the supply of land is fixed, or virtually so, while the making of improvements is contingent upon the expected realization of net income in the form of money or personal satisfaction. The step is taken, therefore, only after a comparison with the net return that would be derived from alternative investments. A tax on increments of land value rests on economic surplus (i.e., rent), and cannot be shifted by a reduction in supply. A tax on improvements, on the other hand, may discourage owners from making them. If so, supply is restricted, and the tax may be passed forward to renters.[4]

PERSONAL PROPERTY

Personal property consists of two classes, tangible and intangible property. Tangible personal property, as the term implies, can be "touched"; it has body and occupies space. It, in turn, is divisible into two main classes; tangible business property, and tangible property of individuals. The former includes the machinery, equipment, and inventories of business firms. It also includes agricultural machinery and inventories (i.e., harvested crops). Examples of tangible personal property of individuals are clothing, jewelry, house furnishings, automobiles, and so on.

Thus the tax on tangible personal property has two quite different effects. To the extent that it applies to personal possessions, the tax remains where it is imposed. No further price transactions are likely to occur by means of which the tax can be shifted. On the other hand, to the extent that it rests on business inventories and equipment it becomes part of cost. A large part of it, therefore, is likely to be ultimately shifted. We have here

---

[4] Advocates of the single tax on land rent base themselves on this distinction. They would exempt improvements, on the ground that the owners are entitled to the reward for effort, but land rents are regarded as arising solely out of a rising demand for a fixed factor. Therefore the increment in land value is regarded as unearned and taxable.

an indication of the amorphousness of the property tax as an instrument of economic control. It does not lend itself well to "functional" concepts of public finance.

In most of the countries of Europe, including Great Britain, home furnishings and personal property of individuals are not now taxed. Although such property certainly represents ability to pay, the great difficulties involved in setting a value upon articles of varying age and degree of obsolescence make the administrative task too great to bring about equitable assessments. Moreover, the cost of collection is excessive. Evasion is easy, and since for the vast bulk of families the value of depreciated household effects does not greatly differ, the benefits in terms of tax equity and recognition of the principle of ability to pay are not worth the cost of separate assessment. Similarly, in some states either local tax assessors have given up attempting to collect the tax on household effects owned by moderate- and low-income families, or, by assuming some low value for such property, they have in effect converted the tax on personal and household effects into a flat-rate poll tax.

INTANGIBLE PERSONAL PROPERTY

Intangible personal property consists of legally enforceable titles to real and tangible personal property. These are in turn classifiable into representative and nonrepresentative intangibles. The former "represent" the real and tangible property which they describe. Examples are mortgages and bonds. The test of a representative intangible is that its value is derivative from the property that it represents. If an uninsured house burns down, a mortgage on it becomes worthless. If both the representative intangible and the property itself are taxed, the same base is in effect being taxed twice. This opens up the possibility of inequitable double taxation.

Nonrepresentative intangible property differs from representative in that it is not a kind of warehouse receipt for real or tangible personal property, but possesses an independent value. Examples are patents, copyrights, and corporate excess.[5] When nonrepresentative intangible property is taxed there is no question of double taxation. Some intangibles contain elements of both representative and nonrepresentative value, and thus pose a difficult problem for tax administration. The value of the stock of a corporation, for example, may be expected to reflect corporate excess and good will as well as plant, equipment, and inventories.

The existence of an enormous volume of intangible property subject to tax greatly complicates the task of administration. Intangible property is easy to conceal. Moreover, it can be moved in and out of given tax jurisdictions around assessment dates.[6] The extent to which intangible property is included in the tax base varies tremendously from one juris-

---

[5] Corporate excess is the value of a corporation in excess of its physical property.
[6] Illegally, of course; but the tax authorities may look the other way.

diction to another. Taxpayer morale depends on enforcement as well as on the public's opinion of the reasonableness of the rates applied to intangibles.

DOUBLE TAXATION OF INTANGIBLES

Since representative intangible property is merely a paper title to an equivalent value of real or personal property, one of the main weaknesses of the general property tax is inequitable double taxation. If a piece of property carries a mortgage, the total tax is greater than that on similar unencumbered property.[7] Under a net worth tax this defect would not exist, for debts are subtracted from the base.

The application of the tax to representative intangible property has been justified, however, on the argument that a man who invests his savings in a mortgage should pay a tax, as well as the man who buys a house. The difficulty is that, whereas the owner of a home does not enter into any further transaction by virtue of which he can shift the tax, the owner of a mortgage may be in a position to shift the tax. The home owner will have to bear it if his demand for housing is inelastic. Therefore it is probable that some portion of the tax on intangible property will be shifted to the owner of the tangible property it represents. To this extent the purpose of the tax on intangibles is defeated.

► CLASSIFICATION OF PROPERTY

Property is classified for purposes of administrative convenience as well as to provide the basis for differential tax rates. Classification may be applied to real property and to both tangible and intangible personal property. The exemption of certain classes of property is a form of classification, since the tax is technically being applied at a zero rate.

REAL PROPERTY

The major classification of real property is, as we have seen, the distinction between land and improvements. In addition it may be classified according to use, e.g., business, agricultural, residential, mining, forest, and the like. Both of these classifications may provide the basis for differential tax treatment. Practice varies in the different states. In a few cases improvements are taxed at a lower rate. The reason may be to encourage building; again it may be related to the idea that land rents are in the nature of an unearned increment. Differential rates may be applied on social or economic grounds to real property that is used for different purposes. Often the distinction is arrived at through political pressures. Thus agricultural

---

[7] The differences between tangible and intangible property with respect to tax-paying capacity, as well as the different administrative problems involved, have given rise to much discussion of the desirability of retaining the tax on intangibles. Cf., for example, P. H. Cornick, "Should Taxes on Intangible Personalty Be Abolished?" Tax Institute, *Tax Policy,* May, 1950.

real estate may receive favorable treatment.[8] Again, lower rates may be necessary to encourage the exploitation of resources. For example, the opening up of mining properties, a risky business venture, may be fostered by favorable tax treatment.

INTANGIBLE PROPERTY

The methods of classifying intangible property vary widely among the states. In over half of them it is exempt. Intangible property is taxed in over a quarter of the states at lower rates than those on real estate, a common rate being $5 per thousand. Another method of favoring intangibles is to enter them at only a fraction of their face value. For example, bank deposits may be counted at the rate of only 4 per cent, and then taxed at general property tax rates. Different kinds of intangible property may be taxed at different rates; and some states tax only the income from intangibles.

Intangible property may have to be accorded favorable treatment because of the difficulty facing the tax assessor in locating it. Taxpayers are less likely to conceal their intangible assets if the rates are low, and higher revenue yields may result from a drop in the rate. Another argument commonly made for favorable rates is that full assessment, coupled with standard property tax rates, would seriously reduce the net yield of an intangible asset. A tax rate of $30 per thousand, or 3 per cent, would eliminate the yield on a 3 per cent bond.

TANGIBLE PROPERTY

With respect to tangible personal property, classification may be made according to whether the property is for business or personal use, and as between urban and rural property. The former classification is of particular importance for incidence, and the latter for the balance of political power between agricultural and industrial areas. Farmers have at times been able to obtain relatively favorable treatment for both their real property and their household effects.

Under the constitutions of some states classification is forbidden by the so-called "uniformity clause."[9] Although the observance of this rule closes the door to much political manipulation, in some circumstances it can prevent the use of the tax laws to achieve desired public goals.

CONCLUSION

Classification of property for purposes of applying differential burdens has strongly modified the concept of the general taxation of property. The reasons for classification are severalfold, and may be related to economic

---

[8] On the other hand, it must be stated that the reason for the lower taxes on agricultural real estate is usually that the cost of rural government is lower.

[9] Despite constitutional or legal prohibitions, classification may be actually carried out informally by local assessors.

incentives, equity, and effectiveness of administration. Classification has taken place gradually, usually on a piecemeal basis. Consequently, a logical system has been lacking. Moreover, some forms of classification lend themselves easily to pressure politics. An important reason for classification has arisen in connection with the attempt to get all property listed in the tax base. Lower rates may be applied to intangibles in order to get them listed. Although improvement has been noted, much property still escapes listing. A great deal depends on the ability and industry of the assessors.[10]

► EXEMPTIONS

The general property tax, as we have seen, covers all property that is not specifically exempted. Therefore, as technological progress takes place, newly developed types of property are automatically included unless a case is made with the assessor or the legislature for their exclusion. Exemptions from the property tax are a mixture of logic and historical accident, coupled with inertia. Exemptions granted in former years tend to remain on the books long after their justification has passed. Political pressures play a prominent part, and the cumulative effect, over the years, of ad hoc measures enacted to provide exemptions is to complicate greatly the base of the property tax.

Broadly speaking, property tax exemptions occur (1) in order to simplify administration, (2) to encourage a class of individuals that needs, and is felt to deserve, public support, (3) to make a subsidy to a particular group of individuals, (4) to recognize lack of tax jurisdiction,[11] and (5) to encourage a particular kind of economic activity that is expected to benefit business or the public in the taxing jurisdiction. Each of these objectives may be briefly considered.

1. EXEMPTIONS TO SIMPLIFY ADMINISTRATION

Exemptions may be granted from the property tax when the cost of forcing the taxpayer to include certain items is excessive. This is one of the arguments in favor of exempting house furnishings and the personal property of individuals. An alternative approach would be to assess each person or family a standard amount to cover these items. This, however, would convert the tax into a poll tax. To avoid this the amount of the tax might be related to the size of the residence, perhaps also taking account of its location. The effect in this case, however, would simply be to take a person's real property as a measure of his personal property. In other words, for home owners the tax would in fact be restricted to real property.

In both Europe and this country it is increasingly the practice to

---

[10] For a discussion of the problem of classification see S. E. Leland, *The Classified Property Tax in the United States* (Boston: Houghton, 1928).

[11] Strictly speaking, of course, this does not involve an exemption.

ignore furnishings and personal effects. In some states the assessor makes a low flat assessment, while assessing the family automobile on the basis of its make and year. In this case the personal property tax becomes mainly a tax on automobiles. When a declaration is required of the taxpayer, savings accounts, cash, expensive furnishings, and personal effects must be included. But little attempt is ordinarily made to check on the taxpayer. The tax thus tends to become a penalty on honesty.

2. EXEMPTIONS TO BENEFIT A PARTICULAR GROUP OR SOCIAL ACTIVITY

Tax exemption and subsidies to foster the development of a socially desirable activity are firmly based in tax policy. There have been occasions when this was the only feasible method of accomplishing an important objective. The device suffers, however, from two defects. It encourages competition for these advantages among the groups that may appear to have a claim; and once the exemption or subsidy has been granted, it is very difficult to remove it if this should seem desirable.

When the nation was struggling to establish a system of higher education, one state exempted the real and personal property of college professors. The purpose was, of course, to permit the struggling colleges to pay lower salaries than would otherwise have been necessary. Evidently it was easier to ask the legislature for lower appropriations, and to allocate the smaller appropriation among fewer payers of the property tax than to seek higher appropriations, and to allocate the burden among all taxpayers. The basic objection to this kind of exemption became apparent, however, as time passed. The exemption amounted, of course, to a subsidy; but it was a subsidy that was not subject to annual legislative review, and therefore violated one of the fundamental principles of good budgeting.

Still another difficulty was that the value to the recipient of an unlimited property tax exemption depends on the amount of property he owns, as well as on the proportion of total taxes accounted for by the property tax. Different individuals possess different amounts of property, and there is no way that their salaries can be kept lower in proportion to the tax benefit.[12] The secular rise in property tax rates, as well as the rise in per capita wealth, steadily increased the value of the exemption until it ultimately bore virtually no relation to its original purpose.

A similar objection exists with respect to the exemption of the housing of clergymen; and, indeed, to the exemptions of property devoted to educational, religious, and charitable purposes in general.[13] Accepting the principle that the state should come to the aid of private charities, we may

---

[12] Another serious objection arises out of the tacit assumption that payers of the property tax in the locality in which the exempted persons have their residence benefit more from the presence of the college than do taxpayers in localities more remotely situated.

[13] In some instances charitable institutions (e.g., a university) make special contributions for fire and police protection.

still question the advisability of doing this through tax exemption rather than by way of carefully considered subsidies accompanied by removal of all tax concessions. Against this, however, it may be argued that the government is less likely to increase its control over the policies of the exempt charities if the aid takes the form of tax exemption than would be the case with an outright subsidy.[14] In an age when the government is encroaching on the freedom of activity of the individual on all fronts, the importance of the latter argument should not be minimized. The price of whatever freedom is thereby preserved, however, is the inefficiency of a very capricious method of giving grants-in-aid.

Another example of an exemption, the effects of which were hardly thought through by its protagonists, is the homestead exemption. During the depression the newspapers frequently carried reports of embattled home owners resorting to force against foreclosure. Had they not been liable for property tax, their chances of keeping up their mortgage payments during a period of falling incomes would have at least been increased. Largely as a result of this experience, about one fourth of the states enacted legislation granting varying amounts of exemption to urban and rural land and buildings occupied by home owners.

The homestead exemption offers an instructive example of the weakness in such legislation, without consideration of the competing claims of other needy groups, and perhaps with an undue admixture of sentiment. Unless the taxing jurisdiction intends to reduce the relative importance of the property tax, the effect of such an exemption is, as we have seen, to increase the burden on other types of property. Thus all the defects of the property tax are concentrated in the form of higher rates on fewer taxpayers. If, on the other hand, the effect is to reduce property tax receipts, the municipality must resort to other taxes. Since the tax most likely to be selected is the sales tax, a large part of the advantage of the exemption to low-income home owners is lost, and the low-income renters are hit even harder.

Another argument often made in favor of the homestead exemption is that it encourages home ownership. Obviously, however, it cannot do this in congested urban areas, where everyone lives in tenements and apartments. Furthermore, the lowest-income groups are not likely to find that partial exemption from the property tax is going to reduce their expenses enough to enable them to make monthly payments on a home.

On the other hand, a homestead exemption (of, say, $2,000) does make the property tax less regressive as between those with moderately low incomes and those with somewhat higher incomes. Individuals in both these groups are in a position to buy homes. Against this advantage, however, must be set the fact that the lowest-income receivers, who are likely to have to rent, get no benefit from the exemption. If the forgone revenues

---

[14] This point is not very important, of course, if it is the *locality* that administers the tax.

are made up with a sales tax without a food exemption, those in the lowest-income groups actually pay part of the cost of the exemption to those in somewhat higher-income brackets. Again, the amount of the exemption varies widely among the states that have introduced it, which, from the point of view of the country as a whole, makes haphazard whatever value it has in encouraging home ownership. Finally, even if the practice is adopted, the exemption should take the form of a diminishing exemption or an exclusion. Higher-valued properties are already underassessed by local tax assessors.

3. EXEMPTIONS TO REWARD A PARTICULAR GROUP

Tax exemptions have offered one means by which the states have rewarded their veterans. In some states veterans have been granted an exemption of the first few thousands of dollars in the property tax base. Although in the first instance the generosity of the state appears to be at the expense of the localities, an effect is to increase the pressure for state grants-in-aid. There is no doubt, however, that the exemption has complicated the financial problems of the localities.

Here again the value of the exemption depends on the role played by the property tax. Every change in property tax rates changes the effective amount of the exemption in the same direction. Moreover, this sort of tax concession is likely to place a special burden on other payers of the property tax. When veterans are given subsidies out of the general tax revenues, all taxpayers contribute. But when the subsidy takes the form of partial exemption from real-estate taxes, payers of the property tax alone may have to bear the burden. This will not be true, of course, if the decline in the property tax base prompts the state or municipality to make greater use of other types of tax, or to curtail expenditures.

The discrimination against payers of the property tax becomes less serious when a subsidy is financed in a combination of several different ways. Thus if veterans, for example, receive part of their compensation in the form of a cash bonus that is paid for out of sales tax revenues earmarked for the purpose, consumers join payers of the property tax in paying for the bonus. Indeed, the veterans themselves pay a substantial part of their own bonus through taxes on their purchases.[15]

4. EXEMPTIONS TO ACKNOWLEDGE LACK OF JURISDICTION

The constitutional prohibition on the taxation of federally owned property by the localities and states means a steady narrowing of the tax base as the federal government acquires land for national forests, parks,

---

[15] On veterans' and homestead exemptions the following references may be consulted. D. W. Burch, "Rural Homestead and Veterans' Exemptions in Property Taxation," *Agricultural Finance Review,* November, 1950; W. B. Aycock, "Homestead Exemptions in North Carolina," *North Carolina Law Review,* February, 1951; and R. Barlowe, "Homestead Tax Exemption," *Journal of Land and Public Utility Economics,* November, 1947.

military installations, and the like. In some instances, it is true, voluntary payments are made. The federal government has taken steps in this direction by making payments in lieu of taxes. The fact that the initiative often comes from the hard-pressed municipality, however, creates a presumption that these payments do not necessarily equal the lost taxes. The multiplication of public services and the resulting acquisition of land and buildings by the taxing jurisdiction itself also causes some diminution of the tax base, since there is no point in a town's taxing its own property.

5. EXEMPTIONS TO ATTRACT NEW BUSINESS

Quite a different type of exemption is that which many states permit their localities to grant to manufacturers for a term of years in order to attract new business. They hope to make up the difference through resulting increases in the yield of other taxes. This practice often leads to a loss of revenue, however, since some firms keep moving from one town to another in order to make their exemption permanent. But the greatest objection to the practice is that what one town gains another loses. Moreover, the advantage goes largely to those firms whose operations are financially so marginal that the relatively small advantage of five years of property tax exemption makes a significant difference.[16]

To the small extent that plant location is affected by tax considerations, the geographical distribution of resources is distorted from the economic optimum, and this causes a loss of national efficiency. This exemption should be considered in connection with the practice, permitted to the localities in some states, of passing on the advantage of the exemption from federal income tax of the interest on local obligations to manufacturing concerns in the form of reduced rentals on factories built by the town. The saving takes the form of a lower interest rate payable on tax-exempt securities. If the town cares to combine the two exemptions, only one of which is at the expense of its own revenues, a somewhat more significant inducement is created.

CONCLUSION

The necessity for granting exemptions from the general property tax has converted this tax into a tax on particular types of property. The proportion of real property alone that is exempt from taxation in this country is on the order of one fifth. The proportion of intangible property that escapes taxation varies enormously from state to state. Exemption provisions differ greatly, but even more significant is the variation in enforcement.

---

[16] Since local property taxes reduce the corporate income tax base, the exemption is worth less to a profitable corporation. Therefore, the exemption can be more easily justified with respect to a *new* firm, which may need a few years to break even, than to an old firm that contemplates moving. The exemption should be restricted to new firms. This is difficult to do, however, in view of the possibility of reorganization in order to make a firm look new.

A good case can be made for many, though by no means all, of the exemptions from the property tax. The difficulty is that an exemption is usually granted without any consideration whatever of its cost to the community. An exemption means that someone else pays a higher tax. Ideally the claims of all should be entertained at once. This is obviously impossible, and such over-all equity as is achieved comes about through the mutually opposed activities of pressure groups.

► THE REAL PROPERTY TAX BASE

AMERICAN PRACTICE

The theoretical base of the property tax in the United States is fair market value as agreed upon between a willing buyer and a willing seller. The objective of property tax statutes is to establish the "normal" value of property as it would be determined in a well-balanced market. By "normal" the tax statutes mean a long-term standard that abstracts from short-term changes in the price level. This means in practice that there is a strong tendency to regard values over recent years as the standard. The consequence is that assessments lag both in the upswing and in the downswing of the business cycle. Therefore, even if markets were perfect, this retrospective approach to valuation would result in a divergence between assessed valuation and true value.

The fact that markets for property are far from perfect greatly complicates the work of the tax assessor. Certain types of improvements to property are highly specialized, and there may be no market for them whatever. An example is a factory specially built to house certain dangerous chemical processes. In any case, many properties are never offered for sale, and there may be no comparable properties sold in the market that could serve as a standard of comparison. Moreover, many sales in depression are forced, and therefore may not reflect the true market value.

These problems have led to demands on the part of many tax administrators that market valuation be supplemented with a criterion of value based on the capitalization of income. An alternative would be, of course, to base the property tax on income directly, thus avoiding the difficulties incident to the selection of the correct capitalization rate. The difficulty with this approach, which is the one that has been adopted in Britain, is that not all property yields income in the form of money. In order to arrive at a money income to capitalize, therefore, arbitrary assumptions may have to be made about the value of the property. For this reason it may be as easy to start with the valuation approach in the first place. The difficulties of the capitalization method are discussed elsewhere.[17] At this point we may take note of the differences between the British and American approaches to property taxation.

---

[17] Chapter 7.

BRITISH PRACTICE

The British property tax is levied on occupiers of real estate, whether they are owners or tenants. The rate is uniform, and the base is the "hypothetical annual net rent" of the property. Therefore, there is no property tax on vacant properties. Moreover, the tax is automatically reduced if the property is not used in a way that yields the maximum income. The failure to impute income to vacant property, or property that is not being employed in its most productive use, detracts from the usefulness of the rental approach. The British system, therefore, does not in practice come very close to the ideal. The proper method would seem to be to set up standards of income from various types of property as the basis of tax, whether or not this yield was achieved in a particular instance. Of course, allowance would have to be made for special circumstances. In the case of property such as railroads and natural resources, the net income of which may be difficult to establish accurately, this method may have no advantages over the market value approach.

The annual rental method of property taxation is at its best when a relatively large proportion of properties is rented, and in the absence of rent controls, or when the income from property can be fairly easily estimated. This method is also particularly useful for older properties. It is easier to ascertain their present value by capitalization of income than by way of either cost minus depreciation or replacement cost. Older properties may have been largely depreciated even though they are still capable of yielding income, and because they are not likely to be very comparable with newer properties used for similar purposes.

Despite the influence of the British tax system on early American tax practice, at the time of Secretary Wolcott's report in 1796 only a few of the states were using annual value as the basis for the real-estate tax.[18] Most of the residential property at that time was owner-occupied, and the fact that considerable property was bought and sold made it easy to ascertain market value. This encouraged the use of capital value as the basis of the property tax.

As time passed, however, this situation changed. With increasing urbanization, and with a higher proportion of properties rented, a defect of basing the tax on capital value began to appear. This was the lack of awareness on the part of the renter that he was paying a property tax. If the tax were levied on the annual rental value, the occupier would be aware that he was paying the tax, and would thus be conscious of the need for economy in local government.

The annual-income approach also poses other problems. This method would be inequitable, of course, if it failed to take account of increases in

---

[18] P. H. Cornick, "Alternative Methods of Taxing Real Property," *Proceedings* of the National Tax Association, 1946, p. 150.

taxpaying ability arising out of increments of land value.[19] These increases are likely to take place in anticipation of future increases in yield. Therefore the market value of a property may rise in expectation of a rise in yield that has not yet taken place. From the point of view of the general property tax, the base should therefore now be larger. If valuation is according to rents actually being paid by occupiers, however, the tax will remain the same as before. Therefore it follows that the valuation of the property ought to be based on the capitalization of potential yield rather than on actual yield.

Again, under the rental approach, the yield of the property tax is likely to be much more sensitive to cyclical changes in national income than is the case under the market-value approach. Acceptance of the rental approach would create serious problems for the localities; since their borrowing powers are limited, they would have to depend on increased federal and state grants during depression. Property owners, however, would welcome the prompt downward revision of assessments in the depression.

▶ PROPERTY TAX RATES

The property tax is levied at flat rates on the assessed valuation of property. Although the rates are often classified according to the kind of property, they are uniform for each class within a given tax jurisdiction. The general property tax rate is calculated by dividing the amount of local expenditures to be financed out of this tax by total assessed valuation. In New England, expenditures include the locality's share in those county and state expenditures that are to be defrayed by the property tax. In the South and West, the rates applied by each tax jurisdiction are summed to give the total rate.[20] The lower the total assessed property of the locality, the higher must be the tax rate in order to produce a given amount of revenue.

Much of the criticism, as well as the approval, of the property tax arises out of this method of determining the tax rate. The local property tax is the only American tax under which the amount of taxes to be raised is taken as given.[21] The yields of the sales tax, the personal income tax, and the tax on corporate income, for example, are determined by the size of the base after the rate has been established by law. Therefore once the rate has been set, fluctuations in yield are determined by fluctuations in the base.

---

[19] The assessed-valuation method accomplishes this, though usually with a marked time lag.

[20] Examples of separate local tax districts are town, school, forest, lighting, drainage, and water districts.

[21] A tax designed to siphon off purchasing power in order to arrest inflation would also take the base rather than the rate as given, for example, the Russian turnover tax.

The derivative nature of the rate of the property tax encourages property owners to contest proposals for increased local expenditures, for the effect of higher spending is immediately felt in rising rates of the tax, which is almost the sole source of local tax revenues. It is this aspect of the property tax that bears much of the responsibility for the drive for property tax limitation.[22] From the point of view of the municipality, the fluctuating rate of the property tax is an advantage. Short of depression, accompanied by a collapse of property values and tax defaults, property tax yields are kept relatively stable through the flexibility of rates. It is for this reason that the property tax is regarded by many as the bulwark against loss of political autonomy by the localities.[23]

Over the long run the property tax rate is subject to a flexibility which results from the struggle between those who desire increased local services and the property owners, who believe that they will be the ones to pay for them. The tax rate is determined as the result of a race between (1) the assessed valuation of taxable property in the locality, which depends on exemptions and on the alertness of the tax assessors, and (2) the volume of needed public services in response to the growth of population, urbanization, and changing concepts of the role of the municipality in local economic and social life.

NOMINAL VS. TRUE RATES

It has been pointed out above that the property tax is levied on the assessed valuation of property. Unless it is possible to enforce constitutional or statutory provisions requiring full valuation of property, the ratio of property tax assessments to full value fluctuates over time. This enforcement is difficult to accomplish, and the attempt is rarely made to insist on full valuation. In addition, there is apt to be a lag in revising assessments during periods of rapid change in the general price level. Therefore nothing can be said about property tax rates by looking at nominal rates alone. Comparisons of tax burdens among localities must be made in terms of the true rate. This rate is ascertained by multiplying the nominal tax rate by the ratio of the assessment to full value. For example, if the tax rate in a certain city is $25 per thousand, and the percentage assessment is 50, the true rate is $12.50 per thousand (or, as often expressed, 12.5 mills per dollar).

---

[22] Property tax limitation is discussed below. The close relation between expenditures and tax rates is an illustration of the advantage of unconcealed rather than concealed taxes. The public weighs the satisfaction of increased spending against the dissatisfaction of paying higher taxes.

[23] In those countries of Northern Europe where the property tax is a traditional revenue source of the municipalities, local self-government is likewise a strong tradition. On the other hand, in Southern and Eastern Europe, where this has not been the case, the localities are simply administrative units.

Care must also be taken, in making interregional comparisons of property tax burdens, to select comparable property tax rates. The nominal tax rate of a particular city may be considerably higher than that of another city with which it is being compared. Yet in the one case all municipal functions may be performed by the city as a single local unit, whereas in the other a comparable rate can be achieved only by adding to the city tax rate the additional rates imposed by school and sanitary districts, county governments, and the like.[24]

PROGRESSION AND REGRESSION

Although the property tax is at present levied at flat rates, early in the nation's history attempts were made to introduce some degree of progression into the tax system by way of the property tax. Under the apportioned federal property tax of 1798, houses were taxed on an ad valorem graduated basis. The carriage tax had been levied a few years earlier on the assumption that its incidence would be restricted to the wealthy because poor men did not own carriages. In recent years the effect of graduation has been sought through the exemption of commodities that are important to the lower-income groups. This has been said to be an objective of the workers in securing a limited exemption of the personal property of householders in California, and is one of the effects, though not the original objective, of the homestead exemption. An exemption confers progressivity on the rate schedule by virtue of the jump from a zero rate of tax on the first (exempted) bracket to the standard rate on all the brackets above this one.

Residential Property.   The degree of progression of the tax is affected, of course, by the size of the exemption. The tax is more progressive if the exemption takes the form of an exclusion, thus not applying at all to properties valued at more than a few thousands of dollars.[25] Again, a diminishing exemption could be used. A full exemption of $2,000 might be allowed to properties valued up to, say, $5,000. No exemption at all might be granted to properties worth $10,000 and more. Between $5,000 and $10,000 the exemption would be reduced by $400 for each $1,000 increase in valuation. The effect of this device, for properties valued somewhat above the level that is eligible for the exemption, would be to make

---

[24] It is on the ground of a failure to take adequate account of this correction that two well-known studies of the New England area have been subjected to some criticism. See the review by L. C. Fitch of S. E. Harris, *The Economics of New England* (Cambridge, Mass.: Harvard University Press, 1952), and Council of Economic Advisors, Committee on the New England Economy, *The New England Economy* (Washington, D. C.: Superintendent of Documents, 1951), printed in the *American Economic Review,* December, 1952, especially p. 999.

[25] For example, the California veteran's exemption of $1,000, applicable only when his total property is valued at $5,000 or less.

the tax less progressive than would be the case with an outright exclusion.[26]

Despite the nominal proportionality of the property tax rate, an important element of regression enters by way of the propensity of tax assessors to assess more valuable properties at a lower percentage of full valuation than they do less valuable ones. A strict interpretation of full valuation would eliminate this practice. It is a product largely of lack of knowledge and experience on the part of the local assessor, and appears with respect to both business and residential properties.

The reverse effect could be achieved if we specified that a lower percentage of assessed valuation should be subject to tax in the case of lower-valued than higher-valued properties. This device would be appropriate only to residential properties, for progression has no meaning except with respect to individuals. Since housing usually takes a larger proportion of a poor man's income than of the income of a wealthier person, a proportional real property tax is in fact regressive. This is not a peculiarity of the property tax alone, however; the sales tax also bears more heavily on the lower-income groups unless expenditures on food, housing, and other commodities bought by them are exempt.

Business Property. The real and personal property taxes as applied to business are part of cost of production,[27] and therefore must be borne to a large extent by the consumer. Some scope exists for absorption of the tax by firms making monopoly or windfall profits, and a part of it may be shifted backward to those factors of production whose supply is inelastic. Since the bulk of the tax is passed forward to the consumer, the incidence is approximately the same as that of a sales tax. However, as with the sales tax, depression or restrictive monetary policy would encourage backward shifting. To the extent that property is differentially taxed by different

---

[26] The difference in progression, in terms of the percentage of assessed value that would be subject to tax, is as follows:

| | | | Percentage of Assessed Value Subject to Tax | |
Assessed Value	Diminishing Exemption	Exclusion	Diminishing Exemption	Exclusion
$2,000	2,000	2,000	0	0
3,000	2,000	2,000	33	33
4,000	2,000	2,000	50	50
5,000	2,000	2,000	60	60
6,000	1,600	0	73	100
7,000	1,200	0	83	100
8,000	800	0	90	100
9,000	400	0	96	100
10,000	0	0	100	100

[27] Except to the extent that the rate of return on investment can be depressed without reducing investment. In the short run there is considerable scope for this, and even in the long run a part of the tax may remain on capital.

jurisdictions, the effects on supply and factor incomes are apt to become too complex to follow.

The difficulty of ascertaining the effect of the tax on business property on the distribution of income is illustrated by the tax on inventories. This tax is probably largely passed forward to consumers. Since the bulk of the consumers are in the lower- and lower middle-income brackets, it follows that the tax is regressive. The extent of its regressiveness, however, may be affected by circumstances. If, for example, an effect of the tax is to promote efficient merchandising through its discouragement to the holding of excessively high average inventories, it is possible that at least some portion of the tax will be neutralized by lower costs. The tax may still be regressive, but its quantitative effect may be less significant than would appear from a glance at the tax collections. On the other hand, a decline in efficiency of distribution may result in a rise in costs if, in order to reduce stocks of goods on shelves on assessment dates, merchants temporarily reduce purchases from earlier production stages.

CONCLUSION

Because of the heterogeneity of the property tax base and rates, no simple statement can be made with respect to its regressivity or progressivity in general. There seems to be no doubt, however, that on balance it is a regressive tax. Assessment practice favors the higher-valued properties. Housing is a larger proportion of a poor man's income than that of a wealthy man. The bulk of the tax on real and personal business property is passed on to the consumer, who in the aggregate comprises the lower-income group. The objective of the general property tax is, therefore, quite different from that of the tax on net worth. The major consideration has been to obtain revenue, not to tax according to ability to pay.

▶ TRENDS IN THE BURDEN OF THE PROPERTY TAX

Pronounced differences of opinion have arisen in recent years over the question whether the relative importance of the property tax in terms of average real rates has increased or decreased. The reason that such differences in opinion are possible is that both nominal rates and assessment ratios fluctuate. Therefore it is often difficult to know what the true rate actually is. On the one hand it is argued that greater and greater use has been made of the property tax,[28] while on the other it is asserted that

---

[28] For example, Harold Somers, *Public Finance and National Income* (Philadelphia: Blakiston, 1949), p. 431. Increases in both assessed valuations and property tax rates continued through 1949, leveled off in 1950, but continued their upward trend in 1951. It must be remembered, however, that unless property tax liabilities increase at the same rate as the income of property owners when there is a rise in the general price level, the burden of the property tax is decreasing.

in terms of true rates the localities were using the property tax less intensively in the 1940's than in the 1920's.[29]

The kind of comparison that is made determines whether or not one believes this burden to be increasing. Therefore, it seems likely that considerable disagreement will continue to exist over the quantitative importance of property taxation. The debate must be judged in the light of the fact that the ratio of total taxes of all levels of government to national income has greatly risen since before World War I. In these circumstances a struggle inevitably takes place among different taxpaying groups to place as much of the burden as possible on others. Therefore, as expenditures of the localities have risen, a constant pressure has been maintained by those who do not own property to place most of the burden of increased expenditures on the property tax; and conversely, property owners try to obtain acceptance of the proposition that the limits of capacity of the property tax have already been reached. As in all arguments of this sort, each side chooses the comparisons that best suit its purpose.

Whether or not true property tax rates have risen depends on what years are taken for comparison. It has been argued that true rates declined during the 1940's, and that municipalities were therefore using the property tax less intensively.[30] They lagged behind the rising price level in raising assessments and nominal tax rates. Any home owner who compares his property tax with his other expenditures in recent years can testify to this fact. This lag may be temporary, however.[31] The unavailability of manpower and materials to the towns and cities during World War II forced postponement of the construction of many facilities that are ordinarily financed out of revenues from the property tax. The subsequent filling of this gap puts pressure on them to raise assessments as well as rates. Thus purely *postwar* observations of true property tax rates are likely to suggest that the localities are increasing their use of the property tax to an extent that increases the real burden on property. But *average* true rate over the war and postwar period taken together gives a different impression. Temporary fluctuations in true rates are not apt to be very meaningful. Another point is that the rapid inflation after the removal of price controls in 1946 was associated with an inevitable lag in the increasing of assessments. Thus a comparison of the ratio in 1946 and 1947 with later years would give the false impression that recently more intensive use has been made of the property tax.

---

[29] C. D. Campbell, "Are Property Tax Rates Increasing?" *Journal of Political Economy*, October, 1951, p. 441. As Campbell shows, part of the reason for disagreement over the trend of the burden of the property tax is attributable to the statistical difficulties involved in ascertaining true property tax rates. For a discussion of the role of exemptions in reversing the pre–1929 upward trend in the ratio of property taxes to wealth, see Mabel Newcomer, "The Growth of Property Tax Exemptions," *National Tax Journal*, June, 1953, pp. 116–128.

[30] Campbell, "Are Property Tax Rates Increasing?" *loc. cit.*, pp. 438 ff.

[31] It would probably be permanent under secular inflationary conditions.

► THE TAXABLE CAPACITY OF PROPERTY

No fixed limits to the expansibility of a particular tax exist. Consequently, it is not easy to evaluate the contention that as of a given moment the limits are being approached. It might be argued that at some point it would be inequitable to increase property tax rates further, or that undesirable economic or social consequences would follow upon further increases in rates. The same argument, however, can be applied to increases in rates of other taxes as well. In any case, we have seen that local property taxes as a percentage of total local taxes have remained surprisingly constant in the last fifty years, and that the proportion with respect to state taxes has greatly fallen.

On the other hand, it may be that the capacity of property owners to pay taxes has not risen in correspondence with that of income or spending. Whether this is the case, however, is a matter that is difficult to determine. There appears to be no evidence that property taxes have discouraged the accumulation of taxable property. Moreover, the rise in the grant-in-aid by the federal and state governments to the localities, financed out of taxes other than the property tax, has contributed to an increase in the taxpaying ability of property owners. These grants are made in part directly to the locality, and in part to individuals living within its boundaries. Their effect is to cause an increasing in spending within the locality which affects property values. When the latter rise there is an automatic increase in property tax receipts. Consequently, nothing can be said about the secular trend in the burden of the property tax by examining solely the ratio of property tax collections to total taxes.

PROPERTY TAX LIMITATION

The possibility of holding down taxes by means of constitutional or statutory provisions has always had considerable public appeal. Pressure for it is to be found at all levels of government.[32] In contrast to the federal system, state and local budgets are drawn up to include not only expenditures but also the taxes to finance them. Attention can therefore be focused on the tax implications of decisions to appropriate money for public services. Limitations can be applied where they belong, namely, at the spending stage. On the other hand, spending may be hard to stop, even with effective budgeting.

The limitation of the rates of a particular tax differs from general tax

---

[32] In recent years a concerted attempt has been made to extend tax limitation to the federal government. Cf. *Constitutional Limitation on Federal Income, Estate, and Gift Tax Rates,* Joint Committee on the Economic Report and House Committee on Small Business, Washington, 1952. Like the property tax limitation, this device is intended to accomplish by indirection what cannot be accomplished directly, namely, curtailment of public expenditures.

limitation. The objective of a property tax limitation, for example, is to reduce property taxes, or to prevent them from rising. Therefore the property tax limitation is not primarily intended to be an indirect means of holding down expenditures, although this is, of course, one of the virtues claimed for it. There are important alternatives other than a reduction of spending. Other taxes may be introduced, particularly the sales tax, or greater reliance may be placed on grants-in-aid from the states to the localities, or debt may be incurred.

TYPES OF RATE LIMITATION

Two types of property tax limitation have been employed. The first, and more general, is a limit on the rate that may be applied by each tax jurisdiction. This might be 2 per cent of the assessed valuation of the locality, or, in the case of a state, one half of 1 per cent. The second is an over-all maximum rate that may be levied on a given class of property by all jurisdictions combined. Only about a quarter of the states have constitutional or statutory provisions limiting their own property tax rates, but in the majority of the states there are limits on the rates that may be levied by the localities. There is a rather better case for the limitation in the case of the localities. They do not have sovereign powers, and they may need to be controlled by the state. There remains, nevertheless, an inconsistency between the tax rate limit and local fiscal autonomy.

EFFECTIVENESS OF RATE LIMITATION

Both of these types of tax limitation have been rather easily circumvented. Those who deplore such ceilings would, of course, regard this as a virtue. Escape clauses have on occasion been written into the statute to avoid the danger that essential services might have to be curtailed. For example, taxes to cover educational expenditures have often been exempted. Again, provision has been made for lifting the rate limit by way of the referendum,[33] and state tax boards have been given the power to act on the application of a locality to permit a rise in the property tax rate.

The most effective avenue of escape has been by the exemption from limitation of those taxes that are levied for the purpose of financing debt. This encourages municipal borrowing in order to finance current expenditure in excess of that which can be financed within the tax limit. Thus in effect deficiency taxes are levied each year to liquidate the previous year's expenditures. Still another means of avoidance of the limitation is the multiplication of tax districts, all with separate taxing powers. Each new district adds its rate to the total. In addition to defeating the tax limit, this

---

[33] It should be noted that the voter is usually exceptionally ill-informed on financial issues, and the vote on the referendum is apt to be so light as to reflect doubt on the wisdom of this procedure.

development operates to complicate local government, with adverse effects on efficiency.

The property tax limitation also stimulates the use of the special assessment; in other words, an encouragement is given to excessive reliance on the benefit principle. The practice of allowing a higher rate limitation where assessment values and population are high also provides flexibiilty as well as an incentive to raise valuations. In some states the maximum is not fixed in terms of an absolute rate. It is related to the rate of the previous year, or, alternatively, to revenue from other taxes. Both these methods are means of introducing flexibility.

The second type of tax limitation (the over-all maximum) has been somewhat more successful in achieving its objective. By the same token, however, it has pointed up sharply the dangers of setting a rigid ceiling without providing a safety valve. The comprehensive-rate limitation lacks some of the possibilities of avoidance that can be used under the fixed-rate limitation. When maximum rates are fixed, avoidance through the formation of special districts is not possible. However, there is no bar to the making of temporary excess levies, or to special assessments for servicing bonds issued to construct school buildings.

In some states the effect of the comprehensive tax limit has been to delay for months the payment of salaries of public servants, as well as to halt the provision of essential public services. Obviously, any ceiling merely diverts pressure. Consequently, the introduction of a ceiling is sure to set up side effects that were neither anticipated nor desired. A rigid element is placed in a dynamic process. In those states, like Ohio and West Virginia, in which a rigid interpretation of the limit was made, severe financial crises necessitated the provision of escape clauses.

When a ceiling is placed on the major source of municipal revenue, the true function of budgeting is severely circumscribed. The purpose of a budget is to permit the expression of the collective desires of the voters with respect to public services in terms of the types of revenues chosen to finance them. A property tax limitation, to the extent that it is effective, permits constitution makers and legislators to place limitations on the freedom of action of their successors. Since they cannot foresee the future, this is a violation of the true principle of budgeting, the essence of which, as we saw in Chapter 4, is advance fiscal planning and a weighing of alternatives. It is hard to avoid the comparison between rate limitation and an autoist who, to avoid going into a ditch, drives down a crowded highway with his steering wheel locked.

CURRENT PRACTICE

The over-all type of tax limitation is in effect in nine states. An early example of this kind of provision is to be found in the amendment to the West Virginia Constitution in 1932. The tax commissioner at that time convinced the voters of the state that an effect of the depression had been to shift an unduly large proportion of the fiscal burden onto the property owner and the farmer.[34]

The West Virginia amendment provides for four classes of property, for each of which a maximum rate limit is set. The classes of property and their maximum rates as of 1952 were as follows: (1) farm equipment and intangibles, one half of the 1 per cent; (2) owner-occupied homes and farms, 1 per cent; (3) business property and personal property of individuals situated outside municipalities, 1.5 per cent; and (4) similar property situated within municipalities, 2 per cent. The statutes in turn break the rate down for each class of property into maximum rates for each level of government, namely, the state, the municipalities, the counties, and the school districts. Even in the absence of the specification of maximum rates for each jurisdiction, the over-all limit may make it impossible for one jurisdiction to expand its use of the tax unless another reduces its rate. Therefore interjurisdictional functions are apt to become frozen. This can prove to be a serious defect during periods of rapid expansion of public functions.

AN ALTERNATIVE TO RATE LIMITATION

Means other than property tax limitation can be employed to reduce the relative importance of this tax. Whenever there is an increase in federal or state provision of public services that would otherwise be furnished by the municipalities, there is an automatic shift away from the property tax. An increase in grants-in-aid to the localities will have the same effect. If the state relies primarily on a sales or personal income tax, an increase in state grants may permit a reduction of local property tax rates. The wealthier the municipality the more likely will it be that property tax rates can be reduced, for the wealthy locality may already have been providing the service contemplated in the granting of the subsidy by the state. This constitutes one argument against the flat grant-in-aid. The proceeds of this type of grant can be used to reduce tax rates. On the other hand, subsidies might be made to the localities only in return for the provision of additional locally financed services. Thus they could not be used as a device for reducing the burden of the local property tax.

CONCLUSION

Since the severest forms of property tax limitation were introduced during and because of depression, the original reasons for setting a ceiling to property tax rates no longer exist. Where other taxes have been de-

---

[34] See the study by H. J. Shamberger and J. H. Thompson entitled *Operation of the Tax Limitation Amendment in West Virginia* (Morgantown: Bureau of Business Research and Bureau for Governmental Research of West Virginia University, November, 1950); and the article by J. H. Thompson, "Effects of Property Tax Limitation in West Virginia," *National Tax Journal,* June, 1951, pp. 129–138.

veloped to take the place of the property tax, however, the decline in the relative role of the latter is probably permanent. Even so, it would be desirable to remove the limitation. More revenues may be needed in the future, and it may be necessary to exploit further the potentialities of the property tax.

▶ A SPECIAL CASE: THE CITY AND ITS SUBURBS

The property tax confronts the rapidly growing city with a special problem. As population moves out into the suburbs, more and more of the cost of urban services rests on the property owners who remain within the city. The commuters pay their property tax in the suburb, while enjoying police and fire protection and other services provided them during the working day by the city. The problem has become acute with the development of more rapid transportation; but cities have always been faced with the loss of property tax revenue as a result of the emigration of the more wealthy to suburban "tax colonies."[35]

Studies indicate that the true property tax rates within the city is apt to be substantially higher than that in the suburbs.[36] This is an inequity that places an additional tax burden on those classes which are least able to bear it. Alternatively, the effect is to force the city either to lower its standards of public service or to make greater use of other taxes. In the crowded urban area the cost of government is higher than in the wealthier suburbs. Prosperous suburban residents often prefer to purchase for themselves such services as schools and various forms of entertainment. Moreover, the tax base is larger when the average home is both new and relatively high priced.[37] With the passage of time, of course, greater and greater pressure builds up against the suburbs to become incorporated into the city. But by then the wealthier families may have moved still farther out into the country.

---

[35] A tax colony is an area with high per capita wealth, fairly evenly distributed, so that the well-to-do are not paying taxes to support expenditure programs from which persons of little wealth benefit. Thus a high level of services is provided with low tax rates, since the tax base is high relative to expenditure requirements.

It is to the interest of the tax colony to remain politically distinct from surrounding areas that are not only less wealthy but may have to provide a greater variety of protective services. If the poorer area, lying between the wealthy suburb and the city proper, is well provided with police, the suburb does not need as large a police force as would otherwise be the case.

[36] For example, R. G. Townsend, "Inequalities of Residential Property Taxation in Metropolitan Boston," *National Tax Journal*, December, 1951, pp. 361–369.

[37] It has been observed, however, that it is not always the case that the metropolitan area has a higher effective tax rate than do the surrounding suburbs. Residential suburbs tend to have higher rates when they are so new that they have a larger than average number of school-age children, particularly if there are few industrial or commercial properties in the tax base.—G. W. Mitchell, "Property Taxation in Relation to Investment in Urban Areas," *Journal of Finance*, June, 1951, p. 205.

ANNEXATION

Although the annexation of suburban towns provides a solution for the financial difficulties caused to the city by a large daytime population living in dormitory towns, a cautious policy has to be pursued. If annexation is indiscriminate it may turn out that true tax rates do not fall. The absorption of incompletely developed areas, containing much waste land, is likely to force the city into a high level of expenditures. This spending may be greater than the property tax revenues that the annexed areas are capable of yielding for many years to come. The difficulty is serious if undeveloped areas lie between the city and the tax colony which it desires to engulf. On the other hand, the city benefits considerably on balance from the annexation of industrial districts growing up on the fringes, whose working force live within the city.[38]

CAPITALIZATION EFFECTS

When a suburb is annexed to the city, equalization of tax rates has to be accomplished simultaneously for all properties in the annexed area. Moreover, the effect of equalization may also be to change (probably to reduce) tax rates within the city. These extensive tax rate changes introduce the possibility of capitalization. If equalization results in a decline in urban tax rates, a windfall gain is quite likely to accrue to urban property owners. By causing windfall gains to some and losses to others, capitalization may result in dissatisfaction with the equity of the whole proceeding.[39] Consequently, equalization may not always be desirable. Since over the course of time many properties will be bought and sold, much capitalization will ultimately take place. The seriousness of this inequitable windfall is reduced, however, to the extent that the process is spread over considerable time. The change in tax rate is not the only factor that affects property values, and the longer the period the greater the relative importance of the other factors.

▶ REFERENCES

JENSEN, J. P. *Property Taxation in the United States.* Chicago: The University of Chicago Press, 1931.

[38] R. C. Schmitt, "Fringe Growth and Tax Rates," *National Tax Journal,* December, 1951, pp. 370–371. See also the articles "Changing Character of the City," *Tax Policy,* February–March 1952, and "Fiscal Difficulties Caused by Urban Decentralization," *Tax Policy,* September, 1951.

[39] An analysis of the possibilities of capitalization is given by Townsend, "Inequalities of Residential Property Taxation . . . ," *loc. cit.,* in his evaluation of the argument of H. A. Simon (*Fiscal Aspects of Metropolitan Consolidation* [Berkeley: University of California Bureau of Public Administration, 1943]) that in general tax differentials are capitalized.

LELAND, S. E. *The Classified Property Tax in the United States.* Boston: Houghton Mifflin Company, 1928.

NATIONAL TAX ASSOCIATION. *Annual Proceedings and Journal,* (Current articles on various phases of property taxation).

NEWCOMER, M. "The Decline of the General Property Tax," *National Tax Journal,* March, 1953.

TAX POLICY LEAGUE (Symposium). *Property Taxes.* New York: 1940.

15 The Taxation of Property: II

► ASSESSMENT PROCEDURE

The key to the successful administration of the property tax is to be found in assessment. The problem of achieving equitable assessment is twofold. First, an inequity may result from improper assessment within a particular tax jurisdiction, such as the state, the county, the city, or the school district. Second, assessment may vary as between districts, so that if property is also taxed by a higher level of government, the property owners in one tax jurisdiction pay higher taxes than those in another.[1]

The assessment of property has traditionally been left in the hands of the local assessors because the property tax has usually been primarily a local tax. Moreover, so long as the major constituent of the property tax is residential property and farm real estate, local assessors are in a good position to accumulate the experience necessary to make reasonably accurate comparisons of the properties within their jurisdictions. Local assessment, however, begins to break down with the progress of industrialization and the development of transportation and communications. Factories are built that contain equipment which local part-time assessors cannot possibly evaluate. Again, not only are the properties of railroads, airlines, and telephone companies difficult to value, but the question arises what proportion of total revenues rightly belongs to each jurisdiction through which the line passes. Local assessors are not, however, rendered entirely obsolete by industrial progress. It is recognized that much property, even at the present time, can best be valued by those who are conversant with local conditions.

► LOCAL ASSESSMENT

The job of the assessor is to set a value on each parcel of taxable property in his district. This is done as of a particular date each year,

---

[1] For a recent discussion of this problem, cf. E. C. Lee, "State Equalization of Local Assessments," *National Tax Journal,* June, 1953, pp. 176–187.

and an independent assessment ought to be made every year. The office of the tax assessor is the repository of the assessment roll, which lists and values each taxable item. The taxpayer has the right to question his assessment, and the usual practice is for an agency other than the assessor to pass on his protest. This step is known as review.

Since the localities are the creatures of the states, the latter technically have the power to intervene in the original assessment. If the state exercises the right of initiating the revision of local assessment, the latter is in effect replaced by central assessment. State intervention rarely takes the form of dictation, however, but is usually limited to instruction and advice. Through this means some of the states have made progress in raising standards of local assessments. A few states provide training for local tax assessors, and in some states the state tax board can initiate removal measures against incompetent tax assessors.

A number of ways are at the disposal of the states by means of which they can improve local assessment standards through cooperative measures. An example of this sort of assistance is offered by the experience of Kentucky.[2] The legislature has shortened the tax calendar and simplified the appeal process; the county tax commissioners have been provided with assessing manuals, maps, and other equipment useful in raising the standard of assessment; and the Department of Revenue has cooperated in county-wide reappraisals at the request of the county boards. It is noteworthy that the state has restricted itself to technical assistance, leaving the localities in possession of their traditional autonomy. It should be pointed out, however, that were the states to provide their tax boards with adequate funds, the latter might well seek to expand their activities, and a trend could thus arise in the direction of curtailment of more substantive local powers.

The penalty of relying on inferior assessment personnel could be the disappearance of the function at the local level. The depths to which the caliber of assessment can descend are seen in those instances in which the assessor merely copies the tax roll of his predecessor, or in which a new assessment is made only if property changes hands. The resulting inequities are seriously adverse to taxpayer morale. When property values are changing, the effect is to give lower assessments to older properties and to those that change hands infrequently. A frequent experience of those who have bought new homes since the war has been assessments that are high as compared with comparable older homes.

Part of the answer to inferior local assessment is to make the term of the assessor long enough so that the locality benefits from his accumulated experience. Preferably he should be appointed, not only to relieve him

---

[2] F. J. Shannon, "Assessment Improvement Program in Kentucky," *National Tax Journal,* September, 1950, p. 241. For the experience of California, Illinois, and Minnesota see the articles in *Tax Policy,* May and June, 1950.

of pressure from the voters, but because the job is a technical one. It is true, of course, that politics also enter into appointments. In either case, certain educational and training qualifications are required. Standards of pay should be brought in line with other types of work that require similar abilities.

FULL-VALUE ASSESSMENT

A fundamental problem has to be solved if local assessments are to be equitable. Assessments have to be consistent and accurate. This means that all assessments must be made either at full value or at a constant percentage of full value. The difficulties facing attempts to require full-value assessment are very great. Some states have enacted amendments to their constitutions providing that assessments must be made at 100 per cent of true value. They recognize that any compromise with this principle must result in chaos. Not only is assessment inequitable, but taxpayers exert constant pressure for the reduction of the ratio of assessment to full value. These provisions, however, are difficult to enforce. Tax assessors evolve informal classification procedures of their own which, though they would not stand up in the courts, are not often actually challenged.

Frequently, the existence of some other statutory provision induces the assessor to violate the full-assessment requirement. For example, in Louisiana the homestead exemption amounting to the first $2,000 of assessed valuation has put the parish assessor under pressure from home owners to make the assessment as close as posible to $2,000.[3] The average assessment is only 25 per cent of full value.

Fractional assessments would merely result in a higher tax rate, of course, if all property were subject to the same fractional assessment ratio. No inequity occurs if every parcel of property pays a higher rate of tax on a lower valuation, but fractional assessment opens the door to informal classification of property for assessment purposes. The result is that inequities may be created among different classes of property.

An inequity which could be avoided by publicity is the long-standing tendency for local assessors to place lower valuations on property owned by residents than on that owned by nonresidents, particularly public-utility corporations. Finally, the frequent practice of the states of setting statutory limits to property tax rates encourages the municipalities to adjust assessment ratios when more revenues are needed.

EQUALIZATION

When the property tax is also relied upon by governmental jurisdictions above the locality, they must either do their own job of assessment

---

[3] E. J. Davies, "The Louisiana Property Tax Relief Fund," *National Tax Journal,* September, 1948, p. 271. Reduced assessments are encouraged by the operation of the relief fund established by the state to recompense the localities for revenue losses

or make use of the assessment rolls of the latter. It would, of course, be very expensive for the states and the counties to duplicate the work of the municipalities. Yet they should not use the local assessments as they stand. Variations in the ratio of assessments to full value among the localities would result in higher contributions to the state or county property tax by those localities whose assessment ratios were high. The increasing interest on the part of the states in the property tax in the last century therefore made inevitable the introduction of state property tax equalization boards.

Basic economic and institutional changes have made the drive for equalization increasingly powerful in recent years. The great mobility of the population has brought to a focus the tax inequities between different geographical areas. The rise in the public's consumption of state and local services has brought with it an ever-tighter fiscal relationship between the states and the municipalities.

The growth of state grants-in-aid to the localities, moreover, has been an important factor in the recognition of the need for equalization. The reason is that if an element of the grant-in-aid formula is the assessed valuation of property, assessment ought to be uniform as among the localities. Again, when statutory limitations on tax rates and debt limits of the localities are based on assessed valuations, equalization is necessary to make them uniformly effective.

A valuable by-product of the equalization boards has been, as one might expect, a tightening up of administration all along the line so that the municipality itself has benefited from their work. In recent years, however, the states have retired more and more from the property tax field. Consequently their direct interest in equalization has sometimes reached the vanishing point. Nevertheless, if the property tax is to remain the most important single source of the tax revenues of the municipalities, the state boards of equalization must be retained. For that reason many experts argue that the states ought not to give up the property tax entirely, but should derive sufficient revenue from that source to retain a selfish interest in its administration.

When performing the function of equalization the states or the counties raise the varying assessment ratios of the communities to full value by applying an equalization factor.[4] The assessed valuation of the total property within the locality is multiplied by the reciprocal of its ratio to true value. "True value" is, of course, the value arrived at by the state or county

---

from the homestead exemption. The homestead exemption of $2,000 of the state of Georgia contributed to "a calamitous decrease" in the property tax base.—P. Brooks, *The Georgia Property Tax* (*Monograph No. 7*; Athens: Bulletin of the University of Georgia, January, 1950), p. 11.

[4] The discussion in the text refers to the "uniform ratio" method of equalization as used, for example, in Illinois. See R. B. Welch, "A New Multiple-Purpose Equalization Program," *Proceedings* of the National Tax Association, 1949, p. 262.

board of assessors on a basis that is uniform for the entire state. For example, suppose that the property in a city has a "true value" of $100,000,000, but is assessed at only $50,000,000, or one half. Then the reciprocal of this ratio is multiplied by the assessment, which gives $100,000,000. If the assessment were $90,000,000, the same true value would be reached by multiplying 10/9 by the assessed valuation of $90,-000,000. If the equalization factor is applied merely to the total property of the locality, not to particular parcels, it does not change the assessments within the locality.[5] Consequently, equalization does nothing *directly* to improve relative assessments of particular properties.[6]

SHORTCOMINGS OF EQUALIZATION

Not only are there inequities that equalization is not adapted to correct; the actual practice of equalization frequently fails to realize its own possibilities. Equalization is sometimes carried out on the basis of an across-the-table discussion with the representatives of the local units. This procedure implies a departure from the use of an impartial formula, for assessments are raised or lowered more or less arbitrarily. Again there is a tendency to continue equalization ratios, once established, over a period of years; but the ratios of assessed to full valuation do not remain constant in the counties or the municipalities, and the equalization factor may therefore become meaningless.

If equalization factors are left unchanged for a number of years the likelihood is increased that the changes, when they are finally made, will be fairly substantial. Thus the chances are great that unexpected increases or decreases in tax rates will be capitalized against the present owners.[7] Finally, the fact that assessments are equalized by the state tax commission may have some effect in causing the public to overlook the existence of inequitable assessments *within* the county or locality, which central assessment is not designed to remedy. On the other hand, it has been argued that state equalization stimulates interest in exposing inequities.

In some states there exists no real equalization or central assessment;

---

[5] The full-value assessment program enacted in 1945 by Illinois has been one of the most determined efforts to equalize assessments among the counties in order to make assessments in all cases equal to "full, fair cash value." Assessment ratios of the counties in 1945 varied from 14 to 68 per cent. (Cf. L. A. Stiles, "Full-Value Assessment in Illinois," *Proceedings* of the National Tax Association, 1946, p. 159.) The Department of Revenue has the power to order reassessments but not to revise individual assessments of local assessors. For a comparison of methods of property tax equalization used in a number of different states see E. A. Myers and R. S. Stout, "Recent Trends in Property Tax Equalization," *National Tax Journal,* June, 1950, pp. 179–186.

[6] In some cases, however, equalization agencies may order changes by class of property or by geographical subdivisions. This presumably results in an improvement in relative assessments, since the device contains aspects of both assessment review and equalization.

[7] H. A. Simon, *Fiscal Aspects of Metropolitan Consolidation* (Berkeley: University of California Bureau of Public Administration, 1943), p. 77.

in others the attempt is made by the state board to rectify inaccurate local assessments, a task for which it is not likely to be equipped. It is true, of course, that some state agency has to perform this task. The standards of central assessment and equalization are in general so low that one authority has stated that they "are probably the weakest stage in the property tax procedure of most states."[8]

► THE TAXATION OF MINES

The taxation of subsurface natural resources constitutes a special case under the property tax. Should depletable resources be taxed as property, or is some other form of taxation more appropriate? The problem has a number of facets. If the property tax is believed to be the most feasible method of taxing natural resources, the localities are likely to play an important role in the administration of the tax. At the same time, difficult problems of valuation will arise, and these will call for participation of the state tax board in assessment. Yet regardless of the efficiency of assessment, the difficulty cannot be avoided that no precise information is likely to be available on either the amount of natural resources lying beneath the soil, or the probable cost of raising them to the surface. The question of the proper method of taxation is also closely bound up with that of economy in the use of depletable natural resources.

THE TAX JURISDICTION

For a number of reasons the states are concerned with the taxation of natural resources: (1) They have an interest in the subsurface rights within their borders. (2) Their rapidly increasing revenue needs force them to take advantage of all possible sources. (3) In some instances mines located within the state are owned by nonresidents, and this fact furnishes a temptation to levy special taxes. (4) Since a large proportion of the output is usually sent out of the state, an opportunity is presented to tax citizens of other states. (5) The localities do not usually possess the facilities for valuing mine and oil properties. Therefore administration may logically belong to the state, whether or not the whole of the revenues do. Finally, (6) the state is interested because a strong case exists for permitting localities, other than those which happen to lie over mineral deposits, to share in the revenues.

Most states, therefore, levy some form of tax on mineral resources. Ad valorem taxation of mineral deposits is the most general form, while some of the states in addition levy a *severance* tax on the removal of deposits from the ground. In 1951 Texas derived nearly 28 per cent of its tax

[8] Harold M. Groves, *Financing Government* (4th ed.; New York: Holt, 1954), p. 77. It should be noted that authorities do not uniformly agree with this view. In any event, some of the difficulties are inherent in any attempt to combine local responsibility with central supervision.

revenue from this source; Louisiana, 22 per cent; Oklahoma, 14 per cent; and Minnesota, 10 per cent.[9] In most states, however, the lack of important mineral deposits eliminates this form of taxation as a significant source of state revenues.

The municipality, too, has an interest in taxing mining properties. A town that has been built up because of the existence of minerals has a natural claim to revenues based on them. The value of local property apart from subsurface resources is, of course, automatically subject to the local general property tax. Moreover, the value of the property, and therefore the tax base, is probably greater because of the influx of capital and labor to exploit the mines. On the other hand, the mines may attract a relatively poor group of workers, who are forced to live crowded into property having little taxable value. At the same time, families may be large, and the town may be forced to provide extensive educational and protective facilities. Therefore, it might work an injustice to assess the mining property at the same value as property in the vicinity that has no subsurface resources. A case exists for additional taxation by the locality.

Even though a good argument can be made for permitting the locality to derive substantial revenues from mines operating within its boundaries, the property tax may not be the single best means of tapping these revenues. If there is only a single mine in the area, and no possibility of making further strikes, the revenue from a property tax is greatest in the first year, when the resources are intact. As the mine is worked, the property tax base declines. Unless the local authorities are foresighted, they may succumb to the temptation to inaugurate a standard of public service that cannot possibly be maintained. This difficulty is avoided, however, if no attempt is made initially to assess the mining property on the basis of its entire value. In practice, since it ordinarily takes time to ascertain the full value of newly discovered mineral resources, it would appear that the localities have for the most part avoided this pitfall.

Valuation of mine and oil properties often cannot be made with any pretense of accuracy, and for this reason there is a strong argument in favor of removing them entirely from the base of the property tax. Despite the traditional use of ad valorem taxation of other types of property by the states, the experience thus gained is likely to be of little use in this specialized field. Excessive assessments discourage the search for new mineral resources, while unduly small valuations rob the localities and states of revenues to which they are entitled.

The sharp decrease in the use of the property tax by the states in recent decades means that the states have relied on other means of taxing natural resources. The severance tax is relatively easy to administer, and its burden is often largely borne by individuals outside the state. The best solution to the division of revenues between the states and the localities would seem to be that the state should reserve to itself most of the revenue

---

[9] Bureau of the Census, *State Tax Collections in 1951*, p. 5.

from the severance tax. The locality, in turn, should be allowed a sufficient yield from the property tax to defray the additional cost of providing municipal services to the new population, as well as a reasonable share of its ordinary expenses.[10]

TAXATION AND RATE OF USE

An important test of the basis for choosing a tax on natural resources is its effect on their rate of use. Natural resources, once exhausted, are gone forever. The question arises, therefore, whether tax policy should not be so devised as to slow down the rate at which they are consumed. In some cases, on the other hand, it may best serve the national interest to hasten exploitation rather than to retard it. This would be true if there were arguments in favor of a rapid rate of industrialization. It would seem that no general answer can be given, since there are far too many variables to permit clear-cut inferences. Some natural resources are irreplaceable; there are at least partial substitutes for others; in the case of still others, future inventions may well demonstrate that economy had been unnecessary. It has been reasonably argued, however, that the present generation has no right to assume that new supplies of minerals will automatically appear when needed by subsequent generations.

Resource allocation between this generation and the future is not subject to any simple analysis. It is not likely that the supply of a particular mineral will become completely exhausted. What will happen is that costs will rise as supplies gradually become restricted, and the less economically important uses will therefore not be satisfied. There is, moreover, a favorable offsetting consideration. So long as resources have not been wantonly wasted in the past, they have contributed to industrial progress from which future generations are the major beneficiaries. A slower rate of use would have retarded the rate of increase in national productivity. This point is irrelevant, of course, in the comparatively rare cases where the supply of a resource is fixed and there are no substitutes.

The role of tax policy in the rate at which resources are exploited must be kept in perspective. Other factors often play a much more important part. The most rapid rate of exhaustion of strategic resources comes about during periods of heavy armament. Even during peacetime, however, not much effect can be exerted on the rate of use if demand is inelastic. Such will be the case, for example, when the consumer has little or no choice in his rate of consumption. As example is the use of natural gas for residential space-heating. Once he has installed gas heat, and assuming that he desires a given temperature, the home owner's use of gas is governed by the thermostat, not by the rate he must pay. Within a substantial

---

[10] See the discussion by E. C. Crockett, "Some Policy Questions Relating to the Taxation of Mineral Resources," *Proceedings* of the National Tax Association, 1948, pp. 223 ff., and H. K. Allen, "Ad Valorem versus Severance Taxation of Minerals," *Proceedings* of the National Tax Association, 1952, pp. 574 ff.

price range a rise in price, whether due to a tax or otherwise, merely forces him to divert spending from other goods and services. Alternatively, if the consumer of coal or natural gas has an annual margin of savings, he is likely to allow his savings to decline when price rises. In any event, little evidence exists to show that the rates of tax that have been imposed on the products of mines have been levied in order to discourage consumption, or have had that effect in practice. The tax authorities do not find it easy to be interested at once in obtaining revenue and in conserving natural resources.

If mining properties are taxed under the general property tax on the basis of assessed valuations that are much above what they would be if the property were left unused, there is an incentive to exploit the mine as rapidly as possible. Moreover, mineowners are encouraged to work only the richer ores, and then leave the mine idle, for the tax is the same whether or not the mine is worked. There is an offset, however. Rapid exploitation may require extra equipment. This might raise average costs and thus nullify a part of the tax saving.

If, on the other hand, the mine is taxed on the basis of physical output, the effect is to slow down the rate of exploitation. The reason for this is that high-cost producers tend to leave the industry. A tax based on the tonnage of ore removed is a higher percentage of the cost of production of a unit of low-grade than of high-grade ore. The effect may be likened to that of a flat (specific) tax per package on both low- and high-grade cigarettes, which encourages a shift to the higher-priced cigarette. There is an inducement to restrict production to the richer ores and those that lie nearer the surface.

An ad valorem severance tax based on gross income also tends to reduce output. The costs of various producers differ, and the higher the tax the more likely it will be that some producers are forced out of production. For this reason it has been urged that the tax be graduated on the basis of differences in the cost of extraction, so that higher taxes would be paid by the low-cost mines and wells.[11] The advantage would be that the relative rate of exploitation of the richer mines would be slowed down.

Although a very high severance tax based on value of output would tend to restrict output to the more productive mines, it does not necessarily follow that a tax applied at a moderate rate would have that result. The effect would, in fact, depend on the nature of the mining operations, and no generalization can easily be made that would justify the general use of a graduated tax. Indeed, it seems probable that any subsidy to encourage output from poorer mines ought to take the form of an outright grant

---

[11] M. S. Kendrick, *Public Finance* (Boston: Houghton, 1951), p. 278. Kendrick's interest is in conservation, with the objective of leaving at least part of the richer ores for future generations. Probably not everyone would agree that this is necessarily a desirable objective, or that, even if so, tax policies should be directed toward this end.

rather than a differential tax advantage. The cost of a grant is easier to ascertain than is the cost of a tax advantage, and it can be more easily altered in response to changing economic conditions.[12]

► FORESTRY TAXATION

The property tax is particularly inappropriate for the taxation of forests and the land devoted to them. A major objective of forest policy has come to be conservation. Unfortunately, neither private owners nor can the localities always ignore their own interest and thus assure the nation of the constant replacement of its forests. Even a *state* may not be in a position to incur the cost necessary to maintain the forests in prime condition, and the federal government may have to intervene. Because of the way in which forest land is distributed, however, there is a practical limit to the proportion of the total forest area that can either be nationalized or be taken over by the states. This means that in the foreseeable future much forest land is likely to remain in private ownership. Therefore the problem of how this property shall be taxed has to be faced.

Tax policy alone cannot solve the problem of forest conservation. Taxes do add to the many risks involved in growing timber, and these risks should be minimized so far as possible. But the social benefits of having a large proportion of total land area covered with forests greatly transcend the net return to private owners. These benefits take the form of favorable effects on climate and weather, flood control, and recreation. The owner cannot be expected to take them into account. It follows that the case for public ownership of a large proportion of forest land is strong.

EFFECTS OF THE PROPERTY TAX

Taxation under the property tax at full rates puts a premium on early cutting, just as property taxation of mines stimulates rapid exploitation. The tax has to be paid whether or not any timber is being sold. For this reason many states have made special provision for the taxation of forests. The logical way to tax them is on the basis of the value of the timber cut and sold. A forest takes fifty to one hundred years from time of planting to the harvest. During this period the owner is making a capital gain which he can realize only by selling to someone else. Thus there is no dollar income out of which the tax can be paid. The owner therefore not only has had to tie up his capital and defer compound interest on it, but he must pay an annual property tax.[13] On this tax he likewise loses interest, compounded from the date the tax is due each year until the forest is cut.

---

[12] For views on the taxation of natural resources see D. H. Eldridge, "Tax Incentives for Mineral Enterprise," *Journal of Political Economy,* June, 1950, pp. 222–240; United States Department of the Interior, "Mining Taxation: Changes in Federal Tax Laws Needed to Encourage Mining Enterprise" (February, 1950).

[13] However, it must be remembered that these facts are taken into account in the determination of the purchase price of immature timber.

Against these expenses, moreover, there have to be set a number of particularly unpredictable risks. These risks cannot be avoided in an investment that does not yield its return for decades; and they may become intolerable if they are augmented by a property tax which has to be paid out of an income that may never be realized.

One of these risks is the possibility that the rates of the property tax will be raised at some time in the future. The capitalization of the reduction in potential yield will involve the owner in substantial losses if circumstances should force him to sell. Another risk is that the interest rate will rise, thus also involving the owner in a capital loss. The major risk, however, is the loss of timber through wind damage, fire, or disease. Under the property tax, he is being asked to pay his tax annually before there is any assurance that he has any product to be taxed.

In addition to the problem of risk there is also that of timing. It will be recalled that in the discussion of the taxation of capital gains (Chapter 10) it was argued that in the case of a rise in the value of shares of stock, a few shares can be sold in order to pay the tax on the gain. But a forest is not divisible like shares of stock. It is true, however, that under a proper system of rotation, enough could be cut each year to provide both an annual income and the ready cash to pay the tax. One difficulty with this solution, however, is that market conditions may change from year to year. If so, an incentive is provided to alternate overcutting and undercutting. This prevents the achievement of a steady flow of income.

A common solution of this problem has been to combine a relatively low property tax with a tax on the yield when the forest is cut.[14] In some states the trees are exempt up to a certain age; in others they are entirely exempt; and in still others the land is exempt as well. Some argue that the property tax should be abolished entirely, since there is no sense in which the private owner, as contrasted with the public as a whole, derives any income before harvesting.

REVENUE ASPECTS

Forestry taxation must also be examined from the point of view of the taxing jurisdictions. Substantial differences exist in their attitudes toward forests as a source of revenue. The national government may find

---

[14] A typical method is that of Oregon, under whose 1939 statute land is classified by the State Forestry Board as to its eligibility for special yield taxation. The state may contract with the owner to give special tax treatment if the land is used primarily for timber production, and if it is provided the protection required by law. The tax on the timber takes the form of a yield tax of 12½ per cent of the value before cutting, and the land is taxed at the specific rate of 5 cents an acre west of the Cascades (otherwise 2½ cents). The Washington law is similar, except that the yield tax is at the rate of 1 per cent of market value during each year of classification, with a maximum of 12½ per cent. The land tax is considerably higher: $1 and 50 cents, respectively.—C. A. Newport, "A Summary of Forest Taxation Laws by States," *Journal of Forestry*, March, 1951, pp. 196–200.

it desirable to subsidize forests in the interest of flood control and other public benefits. The states, counties, and localities, on the other hand, have to consider forest land as a potential source of revenue.[15]

A locality whose economy is based on the surrounding forest is virtually dependent on the property taxation of the forest for its tax revenues. Yet this is an unsatisfactory revenue source. Revenues cannot be counted upon to be steady, for once an area is cut over the greater part of the value of the property is gone. At this stage the owner may decide that it is better to let the property go on a delinquency lien than to see his capital eaten up by an annual property tax payment. This result may be made more certain by the prevailing tendency to overassess harvested areas. Some of these difficulties could be minimized by adopting the common European practice of requiring that cut timber be replaced with equivalent new planting. This would, of course, affect the demand for forest property by potential risk takers, and might discourage investment in this form. The conclusion seems inescapable, however, that retention of the property tax on forests can be justified only when market and other conditions favor rotational cutting on an annual basis.

CONCLUSION

Ideally, forests ought to be taxed solely by means of a yield tax. From the point of view of the locality, forestry taxation is a very uncertain source of revenue. Grants-in-aid from the state are likely to be necessary to supplement local taxes. This is particularly likely to be the case if the town has incurred the expense of building roads and other facilities that involve a permanent upkeep even after a large part of the forest has been removed. The state, not the locality, should administer a yield tax. Only the state can provide the assurance of constant or predictable rates that is needed to reduce the uncertainty of an extremely risky business. Only the state, again, has the research facilities to make possible the selection of a rate for the yield tax that is consistent with taxes on alternative types of enterprise, and that takes into account the cost equivalents of the risks that are peculiar to this particular type of investment. In conclusion it should be repeated that no perfect solution to forestry taxation can be expected. Moreover, many of the difficulties would remain, short of nationalization, under any system of taxation.

► PUBLIC CARRIERS AND UTILITIES

A difficult special case in the application of the property tax is met with in the taxation of the natural monopolies that do business across local and state lines. Included in this category are the railroads, bus and truck

---

[15] Cf. R. W. Marquis, *Forest Tax Yields* (Washington, D. C.: U. S. Department of Agriculture, April, 1952).

lines, airlines, gas and oil pipelines, electric light and power companies, gas utilities, and telegraph and telephone communications.

Except for bus lines and trucking concerns, these activities require a very large amount of expensive plant and equipment, rights of way, terminal facilities, and the like. These provide a property tax base which the localities, as well as those states that make use of the property tax, cannot ignore. Each of these types of activity has special problems of its own, however, that make it inappropriate to adopt the assessment and allocation procedures that have become standard in the taxation of ordinary business and private property. Consequently, within the space of the few pages that can be devoted to the subject here, no adequate treatment can be given of the complex issues involved.[16] The major problems, particularly those which are common to all types of public-utility, transport, and communications enterprises, can be indicated.

VALUATION

The most difficult of the problems facing the localities and the states in the assessment of the property of these types of enterprises is that of valuation. It is at once clear that the task of assessment should not be undertaken by the localities.[17] Local assessors have no idea of the value of operating properties of a railroad or a pipeline, since only a minute proportion of the whole system lies within their local boundaries. The small part of the total that comes within their jurisdiction can only be valued independently of the remainder on the unsatisfactory basis of original cost, or of some concept of replacement cost. Yet the localities in a number of states assess not only the nonoperating property of railroads and public utilities, such as hotels and ordinary real estate owned by them and rented to others, but the operating properties as well.

The problem of assessment goes beyond the merely technical question whether a given level of government can be adequately staffed to make proper assessments. The major difficulty is the selection of a meaningful method of valuation. The standard method of valuing property by local tax assessors is to estimate the market value of particular pieces of real and personal property. But this method has no place in the valuation of prop-

---

[16] For a somewhat more extended treatment than is found in most public finance texts, see M. S. Kendrick, *Public Finance* (Boston: Houghton, 1951), Chap. XII. More detailed discussions are available in R. B. Welch, *Carrier Taxation,* House Document No. 160, 79th Cong., 1st Sess., 1944; E. W. Williams, Jr., "An Evaluation of Public Policy toward the Railroad Industry," *Papers and Proceedings* of the American Economic Association, May, 1951, pp. 506–518; H. G. Guthmann, "Competition from Tax Exempt Business," *Journal of Finance,* June, 1951, pp. 173 ff.; Federation of Tax Administrators, *Multiple Taxation of Amusements and Selected Utility Services,* Research Report No. 27, January, 1950.

[17] Nevertheless, in four states and the District of Columbia local or county assessors have this responsibility. In the rest of the states assessment is performed variously by the department of revenue, the state tax commission, the public-service commission, the corporation tax bureau, the state board of equalization, and other agencies.—Commerce Clearing House, *Tax Systems,* 1952.

erty that is not placed on the market (except rarely, and then often for its junk value). Even in the exceptional instance when a railroad is sold, the buyer pays for the line as a going concern; he does not buy a mere collection of rolling stock, track, and repair facilities. Moreover, most of the property of railroads, pipelines, and similar enterprises, is so highly specialized that once installed it may have no market value whatsoever. Its value is derivative from the enterprise as a whole and may fall greatly if the company fails to make money.

If, on the other hand, there is net income that can be capitalized, the securities of the concern have a value which reflects the possession of both physical property and intangible property like good will and patents. The allocation of this total value among the different sorts of tangible property must be done on the basis of a formula. Consequently, the share of the total property tax base lying within the boundaries of a given locality or state must likewise be largely arbitrary. Once the impracticability of direct market valuation of property is admitted, there remains the problem of arriving at a satisfactory allocation formula that is acceptable to the competing tax jurisdictions.

APPORTIONMENT

The apportionment of revenues yielded by the property tax on public utilities, transport, and communications among the jurisdictions that are entitled to share in the tax cannot be accomplished in a very logical fashion. Under the unit rule the entire property has to be valued as an integrated whole, and no independent value can be attached to particular items of specialized property lying within the several tax jurisdictions.

The problem of allocation is the more complicated because both interlocal and interstate relations are involved. Moreover, allocation cannot be avoided by the device of having the higher jurisdiction take over the administration and collection of the tax. So long as the property tax is retained as the major source of tax revenue for the localities, the allocation of revenues to them by the states must take account of the extent of the property lying within the jurisdiction of the various states or localities. Otherwise, what is really happening is that the higher level of government has in fact taken over the property tax with respect to this type of enterprise, and has substituted for it a system of grants-in-aid.

When left to itself, naturally each state through which a railroad or airline route passes does all it can to increase its share in the total proceeds of the tax. The states adopt apportionment formulas that weight most heavily the factors that favor themselves.[18] Thus under railroad taxation a thinly populated "bridge" state, with long lines of track but no need for terminal facilities, favors the ratio of mileage within the state to total

---

[18] In the case of railroad taxation the elements generally used, variously combined, are gross and net income; car-, locomotive-, and train-miles; road- and track-miles; cost; and "traffic units" (passenger-miles plus ton-miles).

mileage. Another state with relatively little trackage, but in which travel density is especially high, will wish to weight the latter factor more heavily.

The Supreme Court has declared invalid the use of a single criterion that grossly favors a state which merely provides a passage between terminals located in other states. Provided a formula gives weight to all the relevant factors, it is unlikely, however, that it will result in a flagrant bias in favor of the state that applies it. In 1947 the National Association of Tax Administrators found that each state employing the unit rule made use of a different formula. In any case, there is no objective basis on which the various elements can be assigned weights that have significance. Clearly, however, an important step forward would be taken if all states were to make use of the same formula.

The National Association of Tax Administrators has recommended that three factors be taken into consideration, namely, the tonnage passing through the terminals, investment, and ton-miles and passenger-miles carried within the state. The use of an excessive number of factors lends itself to attempts at meaningless weighting or bias.

METHODS OF ASSESSMENT

Four methods of assessment are available for the valuation of the property of public carriers and utilities. These are original cost minus depreciation, replacement cost (also net of depreciation), the value of outstanding stocks and bonds, and the capitalization of net earnings. The first method is generally condemned by experts in the field of valuation, though in some states it is included as one among several other criteria in a combined formula. The relation between the original cost of a railroad, for example, and its present value is likely to be extremely tenuous. Much of the equipment is obsolete, and changes in public taste often force the disuse of equipment that is still in good working condition. In many instances the competition of trucks, busses, and pipelines has reduced the present value of what was originally a costly investment.[19]

Replacement Cost. Replacement cost less depreciation, the second method of assessment, is an improvement over original cost in that the data are brought up to date. This method, however, like original cost, takes no account of the fact that the earning power and capitalized value of an undertaking have no particular relation to either the original or the reproduction cost of equipment. The method of replacement cost less

---

[19] The rapid growth in population and national income, however, and geographical shifts in population and directions of spending, have served to maintain the value of many railroad properties. Cf. W. E. Deaton, "Investment Costs as a Criterion of Value," *Proceedings* of the National Tax Association, 1949, pp. 425–426.

The relation between original cost and value of electric and telephone properties is closer. This is due to the fact that in recent years utility commissions have tended to use original cost as the rate base, thus supporting the capitalized value of the property.

depreciation is ordinarily used by local tax assessors, who lack the facilities for using more meaningful methods. Since they are apt to rely on the data provided them by the taxpayer, the local assessors are not really assessing the property. Even state tax commissions often lack personnel trained in the specialized problems of valuation.

Market Value of Securities. The third method of property valuation is the market value of outstanding stocks and bonds. Opinions differ on the trustworthiness of this method of assessment. Certain difficulties are immediately apparent, though authorities differ on their seriousness. The stock market is far from perfect, and the value of securities therefore fluctuates with changes in stock market conditions that have nothing to do with the value of the firm's plant and equipment, or its earning power. Therefore the property may be alternately over- and underassessed.

A tax base that fluctuates with the stock market has a number of disadvantages. It is a poor source of revenues for the states and municipalities. Year-to-year fluctuations can indeed be reduced by a moving average, but this device does nothing to eliminate the effects of longer-term swings. Again, if future tax liabilities are to be affected by the course of the stock market, the riskiness of investment is increased. Another obstacle to the use of the value of securities as a basis for assessment is the problem of double counting. The value of nonoperating as well as operating property is reflected in the price of outstanding securities. Nonoperating property, however, is already assessed by the municipalities along with other similar properties, and thus its value must be deducted from the stock and debt value if double counting is to be avoided. Finally, the prices of a company's securities may be affected by its particular financial arrangements, and thus may fluctuate independently of the value of its taxable property. For example, if a firm guarantees the interest on the securities of a subsidiary, the effect is to support their price. The solution here is to include parent and subsidiary in the unit for which a value is to be obtained.

As in the case of assessment on the basis of original investment and reproduction cost less depreciation, the stock-and-bond method is often used as one element in a combined formula. Appraisers are hesitant to surrender this approach entirely, particularly when it is diluted by other terms in the formula used to determine assessed valuation. Some authorities prefer it to alternative methods.[20]

Capitalization of Earnings. The fourth method, the capitalization of net earnings, has considerable theoretical attraction as an approach to the problem of assessment. It is a logical basis for the valuation of the property as a whole (the so-called "unit rule"), without regard to the situs of the earning power of particular items. Usually when valuation is made accord-

---

[20] Cf. L. A. Stiles, "Railroad Assessment and Allocation," *Proceedings* of the National Tax Association, 1949, p. 421.

ing to the unit rule, the capitalization of net income is given substantial weight. It cannot ordinarily be given the sole weight, however. The capitalization approach implies that if the company is expected to earn nothing in the indefinite future, the value of its property is zero. This would mean that if, owing either to declining demand for product or to inefficiency, prospective income were to decline, property tax liability would decline with it. There might be a case for this, provided it could be ascertained that inefficiency had nothing to do with falling income. In practice, however, it would be difficult to arrive at market value by capitalizing the net income of a hypothetical, efficiently run enterprise. In any event, if this method were applied to public utilities and carriers, it ought, in theory, at least, to be extended to all types of income-yielding property.[21]

Present value has no relation to past income unless that income is expected to continue in the future at the same level as in the past. State tax boards cannot predict the future, however, and it has therefore been the custom to capitalize past earnings. The boards recognize that earnings in the past year alone have no significance, and therefore they try to take a long enough period of time so that past earnings may be taken as an indication of probable future earnings.

The seriousness of this difficulty is reduced if assessments are revised annually. In some cases, particularly with respect to gas and electric utilities, this procedure has some merit. Rates are subject to public control, and with demand relatively inelastic and fairly predictable, some of the more important elements leading to wide variations in net income are absent. Even so, periods of rising or falling prices affect costs, and therefore net income. The capitalization method is also subject to the practical difficulty of ascertaining true net income. Any errors are magnified by the process of capitalization.

Another problem is to select the proper rate at which to capitalize net income. In theory this rate is the one that could be earned in an equally risky alternative enterprise. In practice the states frequently select that rate of return which has in the past been regarded as a "fair" rate of interest, without regard to differences in risk among alternative forms of investment. The rate of 6 per cent has so often been chosen as the rate of capitalization that it has been said to look like a habit. Again the rate has been taken to be the ratio between the market value of the securities to "earnings available for securities" for the concern whose property is being valued.[22]

---

[21] As a practical matter it is much more important that the income-capitalization approach be used for some types of property than for others. It is particularly useful for obsolete properties, whereas for ordinary business and residential property the results should not differ greatly from those obtained by the replacement-cost-less-depreciation approach.

[22] For a discussion of the market determination of capitalization rates see W. K. Bush, "The Proper Rate of Capitalization to Be Applied to Railroad Earnings in the Unit Valuation Process," *Proceedings* of the National Tax Association, 1949, pp. 430 ff.

PROBLEMS OF EQUITY

A number of difficult equity problems exist with respect to the taxation of carriers and public utilities. In general, the relationships to be considered are those between the stockholders of the company whose property is being taxed with (1) stockholders of competing companies, (2) owners of other types of taxable property, (3) other types of taxpayers, and (4) consumers of the product of the taxed firm.

With respect to the first of these four classes, the greatest difficulties appear to be faced by the railroads. Their stockholders have regarded the property tax as particularly burdensome. The railroads have to make use of far greater amounts of physical property than do the bus lines, trucking concerns, and airlines. State legislatures have indeed recognized the need for taking account of this problem. The taxation of bus and truck lines relies more heavily on other forms of taxation than the property tax.[23] Special license taxes have been levied in order to force them to pay their share of new construction and depreciation of highways. The question still remains whether in addition they should not contribute to the general revenues. The railroads do so.

The airlines have received substantial subsidies from all levels of government, particularly for the construction of airports and terminal facilities. This encouragement to an economically and militarily strategic industry has a precedent, of course, in the treatment accorded some of the railroads a century ago. Land grants were sometimes made, not only to provide rights of way but to furnish capital for construction. Moreover, until after the Civil War some states continued to exempt railroads from the property tax.

From the point of view of the railroads, the difficulty is that the airlines are receiving similar subsidies, made largely in the interest of the national defense, at a time when the railroads are struggling against the competition of the private auto, the airline, trucks and busses, and subsidized waterway traffic. Quite apart from the question of taxation, the railroads are having to fight a rearguard action against this formidable coalition of alternative forms of transportation. The spokesmen for the railroads argue that at least some of the pressure would be taken off if property assessments of little-traveled roads were reduced in accordance with their low capitalized value.

---

[23] Not all the states employ the property tax for taxing railroads. Some tax the railroads on a percentage of intrastate, plus prorated interstate, gross revenues. See the discussion by W. K. Bush: "The Impact of State and Local Taxation on Railroads," *Proceedings* of the National Tax Association, 1947. This form of tax does not take account of the earnings condition of the railroads. Bush believes that the railroad taxes in states using the gross earnings method are probably greater than in the states using the property tax (p. 266). Other forms of railroad taxes are taxes on capital stock and bonded indebtedness, mileage taxes, as well as other special bases. All of them are unrelated to whether or not the road is profitable, except franchise taxes measured by net income.

Under certain conditions the stockholders of privately owned public utilities might be adversely affected through the tax exemption of the property of government-owned utilities. It is not the custom of governments to tax the public utilities which they themselves own. The reasoning is that this would merely be taking money out of one pocket and putting it in another. If, however, the rates charged by public utilities were to be used as a yardstick in the determination of the rates that the privately owned utilities are allowed to charge, the effect would be to force down rates of return.

The interest of the federal government in providing electric power to rural areas, for example, has led to the erection of huge hydroelectric installations whose functions are closely bound up with flood control and military potential.[24] Consequently government corporations like the Tennessee Valley Authority have received subsidies that permit them to finance costs which private producers must be prepared to meet out of revenues. The issue of using the rates charged by a subsidized public authority as a yardstick for private companies has been an acute one for years.

The major aspects of the second point, namely, the achievement of equity with the generality of those who pay property taxes, have been discussed in connection with valuation. A further point remains, however. Once the assessment has been made, equalization is necessary to take account of the fact that other types of property are assessed at less than full value. Local assessors tend to apply higher assessment ratios to absentee corporate owners, who are not in a position to exert the same pressure that can be applied by the home owner and the local businessman.[25] In the short run, at least, property taxes tend to remain on the stockholder. Prices are subject to official control, and compensating rate increases take time. In any case, the nature of the process of production makes it unfeasible to affect price through changes in supply. On the other hand, the effect may be to hasten the ultimate cessation of the service (in the case of railroads), to the disadvantage of consumers in general.

The circumstances of shifting of the property tax on public utilities determine its impact on consumers and on other types of taxpayers. To the extent that the property tax on public utilities is borne by the stockholders, the tax burden is lessened on other payers of the property tax, and possibly on other types of taxpayers. This will be the case if no rate rises are permitted. In practice, however, the tax ultimately, if not immediately, tends to be passed forward to the consumer. It is customary, in the case of public-utility rate making, for taxes to be taken into consideration

---

[24] These multiple-purpose projects are typically subsidized, and even single-purpose projects often receive subsidies through tax exemption.

[25] On the other hand, local assessors are apt to be ignorant of the full value of expensive installations belonging to absentee corporate owners. Another source of discrepancy can arise because of the assessment of utilities by state agencies, and other property by local assessors.

in determining a fair rate of return on capital. Considerable delay usually occurs, however, between a rise in costs and the granting of permission by the regulatory commission for a rise in rates. Special difficulties face the passing forward of the tax by the railroads, because of the competition offered by other forms of transportation. A trend toward more substantial taxes on gasoline, license fees, and other taxes on competing forms of transport would facilitate some measure of forward shifting.

▶ THE GENERAL PROPERTY TAX: CONCLUSIONS

We have seen that the general property tax is subject to a long list of criticisms. These complaints may be summarized.

1. Probably the worst fault of the property tax is that the base is very largely a matter of the judgment of the assessor. The consequence is that the taxpayer has little or no recourse from an arbitrary or inequitable assessment. There is often nothing with which to compare one's assessment except full-value assessment, which does no good when the average actual assessment is far below full value. The taxpayer is beaten before he starts. Comparison with assessments on similar properties is not usually possible, for they may be located in quite different parts of the locality.

2. The base of the tax is not capable of logical definition in practice. The inclusion of intangible property leads to inequitable double taxation. Constant pressure exists for the multiplication of exemptions. The reasons for the exemptions vary from case to case, with the result that it becomes impossible to define the tax with any accuracy. Some exemptions are granted on the grounds of lack of ability to pay taxes. Others are based on the desire to give subsidies to charitable or religious organizations, educational institutions, groups within society that have made a particular contribution to national welfare, groups that have been exposed to hardships, and so on.

3. The classification of property for tax purposes supposedly reflects differences in the taxpaying capacity of different kinds of property. Do such differences actually exist? If markets were perfect, all differences in net income from property due to taxes would be reflected in capitalized values. But the capitalization process does not work perfectly, and differences in taxpaying capacity do exist. Since, however, there are no clear-cut measures of such differences, classification in practice is likely to be based on rule of thumb, expediency, and political pressures.

4. Assessments are extremely inaccurate, and equalization at the state level cannot remedy inequities among taxpayers. On the other hand, a full program of centralized assessment, or mandatory state power to revise local assessments, might threaten the independent powers of the localities. Consequently, these inequalities may be part of the price that has to be paid for the administrative independence of local officials. Assess-

ments are also difficult to make, even by well-staffed state tax boards, on railroad and other properties put to highly specialized uses and spread over more than one tax jurisdiction.

5. The property tax is not geared to changes in the income of the taxpayer. Only in the case of business property is the tax paid out of income from the property itself. When unemployment rises, many home owners lack income out of which to pay the tax. In an acute deflation like that of the thirties the tax becomes so great a real burden that (temporarily) delinquency is widespread and social unrest becomes serious.

6. Assessments lag behind changes in property values caused by fluctuations in the level of national income. Therefore, the burden is excessive during depression, but is relatively light when incomes are rising.

7. If the property tax is recommended on the ground that it is one measure of ability to pay, the answer must be given that this can be properly accomplished only by a tax on personal net worth. A marked improvement, of course, would be to exempt debt from the property tax. Wherever, as in the taxation of business property, the tax is likely to be shifted, it cannot be justified on the ground of ability.

If the property tax is subject to these criticisms, why does it remain a part of our local tax system? The answer is that the property tax is the only important tax available to the localities. The only feasible alternatives, the income tax and the retail sales tax, cannot be successfully administered by any but the large municipalities. Any substantial development of the already extensive system of federal and state grants-in-aid to localities, and to the individuals living in the localities, will tend to encourage the decline in local initiative to a point that is dangerous for their independence from central authority. Therefore, the property tax will probably have to be retained. But every effort must be made to improve its administration. Although the nature of the defects that need to be remedied is clear, improvement can come about only by the painful method of independent effort on the part of thousands of separate local governments.

▶ REFERENCES

See references to Chapter 14.

16 Estate, Inheritance, and Gift Taxation

THE NATURE OF DEATH AND GIFT TAXES

► THE NATURE OF DEATH AND GIFT TAXES

Death and gift taxes partake of characteristics of both the income tax and the property tax. To the recipient of a bequest the addition to his property is income in the sense of being an accretion to his wealth. Conceivably it might therefore be taxed under the personal income tax. In practice, however, gratuitous income is excluded from income tax.[1] The inheritance tax bears a certain similarity to the income tax in that it is assessed to the recipient of the inheritance, and thus is a tax on one form of "income" to him, levied at the time the bequest is received. The estate and gift taxes are levied on the estate of the deceased and on the donor, respectively. They are, therefore, in a sense akin to a property tax. But they are taxes on the transfer of property rather than annual taxes. Other differences may be mentioned briefly. The property tax is levied at flat rates, and the tax is proportional, whereas the rates of death and gift taxes are ordinarily progressive. The property tax is impersonal, levied without regard to the particular ability to pay of the person who happens to own the property. Death and gift taxes, on the other hand, are personal, and the rates are graduated according to the size of the estate or gift, or to the size of the inheritance and degree of relationship of the heir to the deceased.

The estate tax is imposed on the entire property left by the decedent after deductions for funeral and administrative expenses and charitable bequests, after the marital deduction, and after the exemption. This is the form of death tax used exclusively by the federal government and seven of the states (including New York). Inheritance taxes are imposed on the share of the estate received by the beneficiary, and exemptions and graduation of rates are usually based on degree of relationship to the decedent

---

[1] Since a bequest is a very irregular form of income, it could not be taxed at income tax rates, and a form of averaging would be necessary.

as well as on the size of the bequest. Every state except Nevada levies some form of death tax. Three states tax inheritances only. The rest tax both estates and inheritances.[2]

► THE RATIONALE OF DEATH TAXATION

The taxation of the transfer of property at death has long been recognized as a justifiable source of revenue. The grounds on which this justification has been based, however, have greatly changed with the development of political and social institutions over the centuries. Under the feudal system the nobleman's estate paid a sum to the king in return for the recognition of the right of succession. Originally the payment was not primarily a tax, but a means of formalizing the political relationship between the vassal and his lord. One of the functions of death taxes was to force the return of the estate by the sovereign to the heir. Chapters VII and VIII of Magna Charta were aimed at assuring the prompt transfer of the estate to the widow, and at preventing the sovereign from gaining control over it by forcing her to marry a court favorite. On the other hand, death taxes, along with other feudal dues, enabled the sovereign to meet such extraordinary expenses as knighting his eldest son, providing his daughter with a dowry, or extending his military power.

In more recent times death taxes have been justified on the ground that the state, by granting the protection of its laws, becomes a silent partner in the accumulation of property. This contention has a good deal of force, but it provides no clue to how much the state should be paid for this protection. It is not easy to justify graduation of rates if the partnership argument is the main justification for death taxes. The position would be much stronger if society, rather than the state, were regarded as the partner of the individual who succeeds in amassing a fortune. It can be argued that it is easier in some societies than in others to collect a large amount of property. Therefore graduated rates can be justified on the ground that great fortunes are more a product of the economic and other circumstances of society than of the activities of the individual.[3]

During the past century death taxes have been justified primarily on the basis of ability to pay. Some proponents have gone further than this, advocating them as a means of reducing inequality of wealth and increasing equality of opportunity. The growth of this sentiment was hastened by the extension of the franchise to the lower-income groups through the elimination of the property qualification for voting.

---

[2] Most of the state estate duties are imposed primarily in order to take advantage of the federal credit provision. This is discussed below, pages 339–340.

[3] For example, the high real income of the American workman probably had as much to do with the Ford fortune as did the ability of a particular businessman.

Another rationalization of succession taxes owes its origin to the fact that high-income receivers are in a position to avoid part of their income tax through special capital gains taxation, deductible business expense, and the like. Thus death taxes are sometimes regarded as a sort of deferred income tax. Since the estate tax is graduated, it does tend to correct for loopholes in the income tax, though the connection is, of course, imperfect.

Finally, it has often been pointed out that the reason for the introduction of permanent death and gift taxes in the last generation or two has been the increasing need for revenue. This factor undoubtedly carried weight with those who pressed for their introduction, but at neither the federal nor the state level have death and gift taxes proved to be among the major taxes.

► THE FEDERAL ESTATE TAX

Temporary death duties had been accepted by Congress as early as 1798, and again in the Civil War and the Spanish-American War. The first permanent federal estate tax, however, was not enacted until 1916, after years of agitation by the same liberal groups that had fought for the progressive income tax.

Graduation of the federal estate tax was at first quite limited, the range of rates under the 1916 tax rising from 1 per cent on net taxable estates over $50,000 to 10 per cent of estates over $5,000,000. The advent of war, however, induced Congress to pay greater attention to revenue considerations. The Revenue Act of October, 1917, increased the range of rates from a minimum of 2 to a maximum of 25 per cent, although the maximum rate was now applied only to estates above $10,000,000. Receipts were only $6,000,000 in 1916, but reached $82,000,000 in 1919. The latter was still less than 2 per cent of total federal revenues.[4]

Since federal death taxes had always been regarded as an emergency measure only, opponents of this form of taxation sought its elimination immediately after the war. The retention of the tax was confirmed in 1924, however, and again in 1926, although in the latter year the maximum rate was reduced from the 25 per cent established in 1917 to 20 per cent, and the exemption was raised to $100,000.

The onset of the depression sharply stimulated the interest of the federal government in the estate tax. The maximum rate was raised from 20 to 45 per cent in 1932, to 60 per cent in 1934, and to 70 per cent in 1935. The 70 per cent rate was applied, however, only to estates above $50,000,000. In the same year the exemption was lowered to $40,000,

---

[4] Sidney Ratner, *American Taxation* (New York: Norton, 1942), pp. 380–381; P. Studenski and H. Kross, *Financial History of the United States* (New York: McGraw, 1952), p. 297.

and the minimum rate was raised from 1 to 2 per cent. Thereafter there was no change until 1941. At that time a so-called *supplementary* federal estate tax was enacted. As of 1953 the two taxes were subject to a separate scale of rates, both progressive.[5] The exemption under the basic tax was $100,000, as under the 1926 tax. Since 1942, that under the supplementary tax has been $60,000. The significance of the distinction between the two components of the federal estate tax is that the credit for state inheritance and estate taxes, to be discussed below, was applied to the basic tax only. The necessity for computing the basic tax separately was eliminated in 1954, but no change was made in tax liability or in the credit for state death taxes.

► STATE DEATH TAXES

Death taxation by the states was introduced primarily in order to obtain revenues. The states had made an abortive attempt to introduce death taxes in the first half of the last century. After 1825 several states adopted them, following Pennsylvania's example. These taxes were not successfully administered, however, and they had been largely abandoned by 1885, when the effective New York state tax initiated a reversal of the trend which was confirmed by the Wisconsin inheritance tax of 1903. By the time the federal government got around to permanent death taxation in 1916, all but five states had adopted some form of death duties. The reason for the popularity of state death taxes was their effectiveness in producing revenue when soundly conceived and legislated. A new feature, added around the turn of the century, was the grouping of heirs into different classes based on degree of relationship to the decedent, the rates being lower for those in the direct line.

Although an effect of the federal credit provision (discussed below) has been to promote uniformity in state taxation of estates, the inheritance taxes differ greatly from one state to another. Each state makes its own decisions with respect to exemptions, rate schedules, and what is to be included in the base of the tax. Exemptions vary widely. Thus in 1952, for example, the exemption for a spouse in Maryland was $150. In Illinois it was $20,000. The exemption for parents is ordinarily the same as that

---

[5] The graduation of the basic estate tax rate was from 1 per cent on the first $50,000 of taxable estate to 20 per cent on that part of the estate which is over $10,000,000. The rates of the additional tax ran from 3 per cent on the first $5,000 of taxable estate to 77 per cent on the excess over $10,000,000. The final tax liability was the tax as computed under the additional tax, minus 80 per cent of the tax as computed under the basic estate tax, or minus the amount of state tax, whichever was smaller.

The complexities of the federal estate tax can be properly understood only by studying one or two examples. Sample calculations may be found in the annual publication of the Commerce Clearing House, *U. S. Master Tax Guide,*

for children, and here again the range is wide among the states. Exemptions are smaller for brothers and sisters, and for other collateral heirs are almost invariably under $1,000.

In most states the rates are graduated according to the size of the inheritance. Maximum rates applied to inheritances of spouse and lineal heirs are rarely above 10 to 12 per cent; and in most states the maximum rate applies to inheritances of from $500,000 to $1,500,000. The impact of state inheritance taxes is often lessened by virtue of exclusions from the tax base. Thus in Pennsylvania, for example, some important items are exempt. These are insurance that is not part of the estate, homesteads, and joint bank accounts. This liberal treatment accounts in part for the low exemption of $750 for a widow (but not for a husband), and the lack of any exemption for children, parents, or other heirs.[6]

▶ FEDERAL AND STATE GIFT TAXES

The enactment of an estate tax implies as a corollary the passage of a gift tax as well. This truth was recognized by Congress at the time of the Civil War, in the act of June 30, 1864. But the need for a gift tax in order to discourage avoidance of death taxes was not as keenly felt at the time of the enactment of the federal estate tax of 1916. A gift tax was not passed by Congress until 1924, and it was repealed two years later. The gift tax did not become a permanent feature of the federal tax system until 1932.

The federal gift tax is levied on gifts that are not made in contemplation of death or to take effect at death (in these cases the estate tax is applicable), at rates three fourths as high as those of the estate tax. Exemptions are generous. The amount of $3,000 tax-free may be given by an individual to each recipient without limit. In addition, he may make further gifts up to a lifetime total of $30,000. For married couples these exemptions are doubled, to $6,000 and $60,000, respectively. This provision is analogous to the marital deduction under the estate tax (introduced in 1948), which allows the decedent to leave up to one half of the estate to his spouse free of tax. In the case of the gift tax, the gift is regarded as being made to the extent of one half by each spouse.

Some of the states have also adopted gift taxes, and, as with the federal gift tax, the purpose has been primarily to discourage avoidance of death taxes. The nature of the exemption and the rate schedules differ among the states, and in some instances the tax is assessed to the recipient rather than to the donor. Revenues from state gift taxes, like those from the federal tax, are small.

---

[6] See the excellent *Report* of the Tax Study Committee, May, 1953, Alfred C. Buehler, chairman. The basis for favorable treatment for relatives in the direct line is discussed below.

▶ REVENUE IMPORTANCE OF DEATH TAXES

TRENDS

The trend in the relative importance of death taxes at the federal and state levels since 1929 is indicated in Table 14. During the depression years the federal government made significant use of the estate tax as a source of revenue. The act of 1932 was careful to exempt the additional tax from the operation of the federal credit for death taxes paid to the states. Since 1939 the vast increase in revenues from the income taxes and excises has again reduced the relative importance of the federal estate tax. By comparison, in Great Britain the succession duties accounted in 1951, for example, for £185 million out of total tax revenues of £3,730 million, or 5 per cent.

Table 14. Receipts from Death and Gift Taxes
(Dollar amounts in millions)

	Federal			State		
Fiscal Year	Total Internal Revenue Receipts	Estate and Gift Taxes	Percentage of Total	Total State Taxes	Death and Gift Taxes	Percentage of Total
1929	2,939	62	2.1	1,951	149	7.6
1939	5,182	361	7.0	3,085	133	4.3
1954	69,920	935	1.3	11,089	247	2.2

SOURCES: *Annual Reports* of the Commissioner of Internal Revenue; Bureau of the Census, *Historical Review of State and Local Government Finances,* June, 1948; *Summary of State Government Finances in 1954.*

The relative importance of death taxes in state tax systems has declined. The yield has not kept pace with the rise in prices and the level of national wealth since 1939. The states would like to obtain more revenue from this source, and to that end their spokesmen frequently urge the liberalization of the credit against the federal tax for death taxes paid to the state. It is argued that this tax ought to be the sole prerogative of the states. The transfer of property at death is governed by state law. Moreover, the states pioneered the estate and inheritance taxes as permanent peacetime imposts. The major argument is, however, that the states are more limited in their revenue sources than the federal government, and that the latter should get out of this field except to ensure uniformity in the state taxes. There is no immediate prospect that the federal government will do so. However, the high federal exemption was introduced, and has been retained, in order that the states might tap the broad base of the moderate-sized estates and inheritances.

PRODUCTIVITY

Although death taxes appear to be relatively unimportant in the tax structures of the federal and state governments as a whole, it cannot be denied that the revenue interest in these taxes is definitely present. Evidence of this is to be found in the demands by the states that the federal government leave the field to them, and possibly also in the retention of the estate tax by the national and some state governments when the much more equitable inheritance tax is at hand. Because the estate tax takes no account of the different taxpaying capacities of different heirs, it is considerably more productive of revenue than is the inheritance tax. The great bulk of all estates pass to very close relatives, who are subject to the lowest rates under the inheritance tax. An estate tax ignores their special claims.[7] One reason for the popularity of the estate tax is, of course, that it is more easy to administer than the inheritance tax. A tax that is relatively easy to administer is also likely to be somewhat more productive, since a given amount of effort will result in greater revenues.

► THE EQUITY PROBLEMS

DEATH DUTIES AND ABILITY TO PAY

Death and gift taxes are, par excellence, taxes geared to ability to pay. So long as exemptions are generous, particularly to the spouse and dependents, that which remains and is subject to tax has a high degree of taxpaying ability. Since, however, legacies and gifts are taxed on the transfer, the interesting question is raised as to whose ability to pay is under consideration, that of the decedent or that of the heir. The ambiguity arises under the estate tax.

Assume two net taxable estates of equal size, the first left entirely to one legatee, and the other split among five children. If each estate is worth $100,000, and the effective tax rate is 50 per cent, then the single heir receives $50,000, or five times the bequest net of tax received by each of the heirs to the other estate. His ability to pay based on the bequest, however, is obviously much greater than that of the others. If the principle of progression is to be accepted, therefore, his tax should be greater than their combined taxes. An inheritance tax is necessary to accomplish this objective. If the estate is not taxed at all, but progressive rates are assessed

---

[7] It is pointed out by W. J. Shultz that this was the reason for the insistence by the Socialists in France and Germany after World War 1 on estate duties rather than inheritance taxes. Under the latter no substantial revenues could be derived from estates passing to close relatives.—*The Taxation of Inheritance* (Boston: Houghton, 1926), Chap. XIII. An excerpt from this chapter is reprinted in Harold Groves, *Viewpoints on Public Finance* (New York: Holt, 1948), §40, "The Estate Duty vs. the Inheritance Tax," pp. 220–225.

against the inheritance of each legatee, any desired degree of progression can be achieved. The question still remains, however, whether a separate schedule of progressive rates ought to be levied on the estate itself.

There is one argument in favor of applying progressive rates to the estate, without taking into account the shares going to different legatees. The possession of some property makes it easier to accumulate still more property. Therefore, it can be argued that in lieu of the failure to offset this advantage through adequate income taxation during the years when the estate was being accumulated, progressive rates ought to be applied at death to the estate itself.

Because of our failure to apply the income tax to large amounts of unrealized capital gains it might be argued that a deferred income tax ought to be paid at the time the estate passes. This point gains particular weight when it is remembered that one of the most potent arguments set forth by businessmen in favor of exemption from taxation of capital gains is the need of a growing business to retain capital in order to be able to expand. If we grant the desirability of making this concession to the individual who builds the business, we are by no means constrained to continue the favor to his heirs.

ABILITY TO PAY AND THE INHERITANCE TAX

The graduation of inheritance tax rates according to the size of the bequest constitutes an effort to tax according to ability. How far does it achieve the purpose? One defect is immediately apparent. If a particular individual were to receive a $50,000 bequest from each of several aunts and uncles, it is inadequate to graduate his tax on the basis of each of these bequests separately. If the principle of progression is granted at all, he has more than five times the taxable capacity of another person who receives a single bequest of this amount. For this reason it has been proposed that the inheritance tax be made an *accessions* tax. Under this version of the inheritance tax, as each new bequest is received, the tax liability of the legatee is recalculated on the basis of the cumulated amounts.[8]

It will occur to the reader at once, however, that although an accessions tax would indeed improve the equity of death taxation from the point of view of ability to pay, much would remain to be done before all differences in the taxable capacity of differently situated legatees were eliminated. Some might argue that an equitable inheritance tax should also be expected to take account of the wealth already in the possession of the legatees. If a millionaire receives a bequest of $50,000 (retaining the assumption that the principle of progression is valid), this sum represents a greater ability to pay taxes than does an equal amount received by a

---

[8] For a discussion of the accessions of tax, cf. H. J. Rudick, "A Proposal for an Accessions Tax," *Proceedings* of the National Tax Association, 1946, pp. 179 ff.

poor man. But have we gone far enough? Should we not allow for differences in the earning power, or even the prospective earning power, of the legatee?

For example, is there no difference between the taxpaying capacities of two persons, each previously indigent, but one having the training of a physician and the other functioning as a day laborer? The question is, of course, how far we are willing to go. The logic of this kind of thought would lead inevitably to equalization, not only of property but of income as well. Like the personal income tax, the inheritance tax is faced with an insoluble logical problem as soon as the principle of progression is admitted.

Certain European governments of socialist leanings have experimented with basing the progression of an inheritance tax not only on the amount of the inheritance but also on the amount of property already in the possession of the legatee. Such a provision was included in the new German death taxes introduced after World War I under the Weimar Republic.[9] Suppose that A receives a bequest of $100,000, while B receives one of $25,000. If the tax were made progressive on the basis of the inheritance tax alone A would pay not only a higher tax but a higher effective rate of tax. If, however, B already had property worth $75,000, while A had nothing, a case might be made for collecting the same tax from each.

Suppose, however, that B had acquired his $75,000 estate through hard work and abstinence from consumption, while A had always lived for the moment. The inequity of including this property is obvious. Even more serious would be the adverse effects on willingness to work and save. The knowledge that all one's own savings would be taxed *at the top tax bracket* applicable to the sum of these savings and the inheritance would be a serious deterrent to the saving, and possibly to the willingness to work, of any person having an expectation of an inheritance. In view of the multiple tax discouragements to work and invest, it is questionable if this device would be viable, even if we were sure that it increased equity.

THE RIGHT TO INHERIT

It is not immediately obvious that a man has the right to dispose of his estate entirely as he sees fit. Other rights than those of the decedent alone are involved. Society has the duty to decide on the rights of beneficiaries to receive gifts and inheritances. Two cases may be distinguished. The heirs may or may not have performed services which the bequest may be regarded as compensating. If not, account must be taken of the extent of the right of the individual to receive an addition to his wealth that is in the nature of a windfall. Considerations of both equity and economic incentives are involved.

---

[9] Shultz, *op. cit.,* pp. 87 ff.

The Spouse.   The wife or husband of the deceased is obviously in a special position in the right to inheritance. Where community property laws apply, the acquisition of property since marriage is regarded as due to the joint efforts of both spouses. Indeed, the emphasis often placed by the business corporation on the social graces of the wife in determining its personnel promotion policy stresses her role in the earning of the family income. It could be argued that no tax whatever should be imposed on direct heirs unless the property passes either forward to the next generation or backward to the parents. If this view were accepted, however, a limit on the age differential between spouses would have to be established (say fifteen to twenty years) to prevent tax avoidance by marriages between very old and very young persons. A major justification for lower rates on the widow's or widower's share stems from the fact that since they are usually fairly close in age, the estate is likely soon to be transferred again, and therefore be subject to another tax.[10]

Other special considerations that apply in the case of the widow are (1) she is burdened with the inheritance tax at the moment she loses her husband's earning power, and (2) as she grows older her earning power is likely to become progressively less, owing both to advancing age and to the passage of time since she has been in the labor market, if, indeed, she had ever worked at all. On the other hand, it must be borne in mind that exemptions are usually sufficiently generous to reduce the seriousness of these inequities for moderate estates. When estates are more than large enough to support the widow there is a strong case for taxing the excess heavily.

It is sometimes argued that the widow should be entitled to live on the same scale that she enjoyed during her husband's life. The acceptability of this view is limited by the fact that the vast majority of families in any case have insufficient property to make this possible. Therefore why favor the few? Basic needs should be taken care of through social security. To refrain from taxing merely on the ground that the standard of living will suffer is a policy that takes no account of the fact that different people with the same wealth customarily have wide differences in their living standards. The tax system should not be expected to assist in the preservation of a high scale of expenditure.

Children.   Another interesting question is whether and how far children should be allowed to receive inheritances. There would appear to be no doubt that for minor children, at least, equity requires an adequate exemption from death taxes. If there is no property, however, the tax exemption does no good, and equity is therefore impossible to achieve

---

[10] That rapid succession has not been the reason why legislators have taxed inheritances of widows relatively lightly, however, is evidenced by the fact that inheritances of parents are usually taxed as heavily as those of children, who will presumably die at a much later date.—William Vickrey, *Agenda for Progressive Taxation* (New York: Ronald, 1947), p. 214.

between a rich and a poor family. Why worry about one inequity if we can do nothing about the other? The answer is, of course, implicit in a society that recognizes the right to own and transmit property. The usual question arises with respect to how far society is willing to go in redistribution by taxation.

Complete equality of treatment would be achieved only if the state undertook the care and rearing of all children from birth. This would, of course, assume a society that is quite different from the one we are examining. Therefore, the best we can do is to provide generous exemptions for estates passing to minor children and those unable to work for a living. The courts have broadened their earlier conceptions of the "subsistence" that society recognizes as the right of a dependent child. In a recent alimony case the court approved the inclusion of a college education as part of this subsistence. By parity of reasoning this finding strengthens the argument for a liberal exemption for inheritances received by minor children. By the same token, however, the case is strengthened for redistributive taxation to finance equality of opportunity for all children.

The case for permitting adult offspring to receive inheritances is quite different from that for minor children. The inheritance is a windfall. Yet it may serve merely to preserve living standards established during childhood. Some adverse effect on national output might be caused if the right to transmit property were abolished. This right is one of the incentives to hard work. No one can pretend to know what the effect would be, however. The desire to become wealthy in one's own lifetime is in itself a powerful incentive. Finally, against the incentive to work provided by the right to bequeath property to children must be set whatever disincentives to work result from the receipt of the bequest by the children. No quantitative data are available, of course.

Collateral Heirs. Is there any reason to permit the transmission of an estate to any person outside the immediate family, or not dependent upon it? If the decedent had no responsibility for the welfare of these persons during life, why should the law permit him to take on such responsibility after death? The receipt of income is normally a reward to the individual for putting forth effort. A bequest may relieve him of the necessity to do so. Therefore we must ask whether or not this right contributes to social welfare. The ultimate answer to this sort of question will have to be decided by society.

In any case, it must be conceded that not all extrafamily inheritances are uncompensated. Many bequests are made in return for value received, as in the case of faithful servants. In some instances, however, servants are rewarded out of all proportion to their services. It might be argued that nothing should be left to deathbed caprice. A better means of assuring the social security of household servants is to require joint contributions to a pension plan, as indeed is now the case under federal law.

► DEATH TAXES AND THE REDISTRIBUTION OF INCOME

Proposals have been made for successions taxes that are far more powerful in their redistributive effects than any at present in effect in capitalistic societies. The Italian economist Eugenio Rignano advocated that a higher schedule of rates be applied to that part of the estate which the decedent had inherited or received as gifts than to that which he had accumulated himself. The purpose of this device was to apply a brake on the accumulation of property over a number of generations.

It is probably no coincidence that this proposal was made by a native of a country famous for its family dynasties. Although perhaps not many families do succeed in maintaining their wealth for more than one or two generations, it is possible that those which do so tend to become unduly powerful even in relation to their wealth. Over generations they may be able to bring their economic power to bear politically in ways not possible to the man who makes a fortune during his own lifetime. Thus the Rignano plan may be judged in large measure as a device against concentration of power as well as a means of redistributing wealth.

Even if the Rignano plan were socially attractive to the legislature of a capitalistic nation, it would be extremely difficult to administer. Except for landholdings and tangible property it is impossible to distinguish between the part that a man brings together himself and that which he has inherited. For example, suppose that a man inherits $100,000, loses the whole of it in a disastrous venture, but then borrows enough to start over. If he dies leaving $100,000, should his heir be taxed under the lower or the higher schedule of rates? One might be tempted to choose the lower level, for otherwise the incentive to recover the fortune in order to leave it to wife and children is lessened. On the other hand, this means a lower tax than that which must be paid by the man who was lucky or smart enough not to lose his inheritance in the first place.

The simple distinction made by Rignano between earned and inherited portions of an estate does not exhaust the inequities that he is attacking. The man who inherits $100,000 has the use of it through life. Even if such high rates are applied to it that his son receives little or nothing, the possession of this capital has facilitated the accumulation of more property, and at his death this is taxed at the lower rate. Furthermore, the son receives a better education and makes better contacts than a man of equal ability who was born with nothing. Finally, unless the higher tax schedule applies to the interest accumulation he has received throughout life on the sum inherited from his father, a significant loophole has been left in the scheme.

In conclusion it must be said that quite apart from the administrative difficulties, the Rignano plan would not accomplish the objective of giving individuals of equal ability and ambition the same starting point in the race. It would, of course, slow down the ability of those who have property to use that property to increase their wealth further.

The English economist Hugh Dalton has offered another plan to narrow the spread between the opportunities of the propertied and the propertyless classes, and to reduce the discouragement of inheritors to put forth effort and earn incomes. He proposed that part of every estate passing at death (in excess of an exemption) be "compulsorily exchanged for terminable annuities." These annuities would run for the life of the inheritor, or alternatively, for twenty years, and their annual income would be equal to the annual return on the property that had been turned in to the Treasury in exchange for them.[11] Thus the property would eventually pass to the government.

▶ INCIDENCE AND ECONOMIC EFFECTS

The incidence of the estate and inheritance taxes is almost entirely on the beneficiaries. The estate tax reduces the size of the estate which is to be divided, and the inheritance tax reduces the share of each legatee. There is no price transaction by means of which the beneficiaries can shift the immediate burden of the tax. Death taxes are to a large extent, therefore, taxes on economic surplus.

It may be possible for a particular beneficiary, however, to escape the burden of the tax. The testator may provide that the legacy of some one or more of the heirs shall be free of tax. In other words, the bequest may be made larger, by the amount of the death taxes, than it would otherwise have been. If this is done the other heirs have only a residual claim after this amount of property has been set aside. Thus the tax burden is shifted to them. It may be noted that the person who is thus benefited is not necessarily the principal heir. Indeed, he is more likely to be an invalid or a faithful servant, for whom it is desired to establish a subsistence annuity.

One important qualification must be made to the statement that the incidence of death taxes is on the legatees as a group. Although they are in no position to react to the tax by reducing the supply of their services, the decedent himself may already have responded in some way to the knowledge that the tax would be imposed. This response may take one or both of two forms. The first is concerned with avoidance of the tax, and therefore is related to economic effects rather than to shifting and incidence.

---

[11] Hugh Dalton, *Public Finance* (9th ed.; London: Headley, 1936), p. 117, and his evidence before the Colwyn Committee (1927), pp. 317–318 of the *Report*. A somewhat similar idea was set forth by Jeremy Bentham as early as 1795. Cf. *Jeremy Bentham's Economic Writings*, Vol. I (edited by W. Stark), Burt Franklin, 1953. For views on the inheritance tax see Shultz, *op. cit.*, and Josiah Wedgwood, *The Economics of Inheritance* (London: Routledge, 1929).

The second, however, involves the possibility of an attempt by the decedent himself to assume the burden of the tax in anticipation of his death.

AVOIDANCE

In the first place, a man may limit his own efforts if he feels that an unduly large proportion of his estate will be taken in taxes. In the aggregate, and under very high rates of tax, the repercussions of this reaction on national income might be significant. The effects cannot be traced with present techniques, however. No one knows how much effort he would have actually put forth in the absence of the tax.

Estates are usually accumulated while a man is still relatively young. Death taxes do not loom as large in calculations as will be the case later on. Moreover, it is not usual to know beforehand that the estate will ultimately be so large that taxes will take a substantial part of it. Most of the adverse commentary on estate taxes comes from those who are already wealthy. A man on the way up is not likely to diminish his activity in anticipation of taxes, for it is dangerous to adopt a passive attitude towards one's business.

Again, the disincentive effects on personal effort exerted by a particular tax cannot be considered apart from those of alternative taxes. Ordinarily tax rates are increased in response to a need for revenue. Therefore only the *net* disincentive effects of death taxes must be considered. These may actually be negative, if, for example, the alternative is to raise *income* tax rates to the point at which disincentive effects are substantial.

Thus far we have considered the effects on the incentive to work. In addition account must be taken of the effects of death taxes on willingness and ability to save. Death taxes reduce the capacity of the community to save by taking property out of the hands of those whose average propensity to save is relatively high. This in turn reduces their interest income, a large proportion of which would probably have been saved. The effects on *willingness* to save, on the other hand, are not easy to judge. The impact on both willingness to put forth effort and to save is likely to be significantly different in the early years of high rates from what it will be after a generation or so. Those who grew up under a system of higher death taxes would probably be less influenced by the tax than would the older persons who remembered the days of lower taxes.

ASSUMPTION OF THE TAX BY THE DECEDENT

The second way in which the decedent may have responded in advance to the tax is by striving to build up a larger estate. He may do this by taking out life insurance policies in an amount sufficient to cover the tax liability.[12] If all that is involved is a transfer of assets from one

---

[12] Life insurance may be taken out also in order that a large enough proportion of the estate may be liquid so that funds are available to pay the tax.

form to another, there is nothing in this action that will relieve the beneficiaries of the burden of the tax.[13] More may be involved than this, however. The decedent may have worked harder during his life in order to earn the premiums required to carry the insurance that is to pay the estate tax, or even the inheritance taxes. If it could be asserted, for example, that as a consequence of this reaction on the part of executives in general the supply of the executive function increased and its price declined, part of the burden of the tax would be voluntarily assumed by them. This is not, of course, a consequence of any practical importance.

EFFECTS ON SAVING AND INVESTMENT

Since death taxes impinge directly on property, it is often argued that they constitute a particularly heavy burden on saving. It is then inferred that if estate or inheritance tax rates are much increased, investment will not be adequate to provide the accustomed rate of increase in productivity. Furthermore, a low rate of capital formation will be insufficient to absorb the annual increment to the labor force as population grows. Therefore the downward redistribution effects of the tax will be nullified through unemployment.

This argument of the classical economists accepts the view that savings are always invested without difficulty. Experience has taught us, however, that a poor business outlook can cause savings to be left idle. The argument also gratuitously assumes that the government will not use the proceeds of the tax as effectively as would the private sector in building up the nation's capital. This assumption may indeed be borne out by the facts, but it must at least be subjected to scrutiny. State enterprises may be as effective in creating capital instruments as private enterprise. Moreover, the government may see to it that a proportion of tax revenues is devoted to capital formation.

There is no doubt that the classical view corresponds to a possible sequence of events. The question, however, is, To what extent is this result actually likely to occur? Again, even if it does, how far is this a valid criticism of death taxes as such, rather than a general characteristic of government taxing and spending? Finally, the quantitative importance of the argument must be kept in mind. In the United States, as we have seen, death taxation accounts for a very modest proportion of total taxes. Therefore, acceptance of the view that death taxes create a deficiency of savings would imply a belief that the particular savings tapped by the estate and inheritance taxes are of *strategic* importance to the maintenance of a high annual increment of national productivity.

---

[13] This statement must be qualified. To the extent that insurance receives favorable treatment under the estate tax, total tax liability is reduced if part of the estate is in the form of insurance. Some of the states do exempt insurance paid directly to the heir. Moreover, in 1954 Congress made it possible to exclude from the taxable estate the proceeds of life insurance built up to pay the estate tax.

The mere act of taxation does not destroy any existing real savings. Title simply changes hands from individuals to the government. If the government uses these savings for purposes that can be truly called investment (construction of highways, power projects, development of natural resources, and so on) there is no question of a destruction of national savings. It is true, however, that savings available for types of projects normally undertaken only by private investors are discriminated against in favor of public investment projects. Thus it can be argued that the availability of savings to business is reduced by any tax that impinges on savings. In any event, it is immaterial whether the transfer of the savings from private to public hands is accomplished by way of death taxes or by any other tax that rests on savings.[14]

Since 1929 few economists can be found who would argue that the private sector is invariably willing to invest the entire annual increment of national savings. If some savers' balances are idle, the taxation and investment of these balances by the government would not divert any investment funds away from the private sector. On the contrary, the effect might be a rise in national income, and therefore in the size of the flow of savings. After a time business might actually find it easier to borrow than before.

Magnitude of Impact on Saving. As pointed out above, the contention that death taxes discourage saving has little importance if a very small proportion of total national savings is affected. In fiscal 1953, for example, federal and state inheritance, estate, and gift taxes accounted for about $1.1 billion out of total federal internal revenue collections and state tax revenues of $80 billion.[15] This does not look very important. Moreover, not the whole of the $1.1 billion would have been saved. According to the Department of Commerce, total gross private domestic investment in *calendar* 1953 was $51.4 billion, a figure which by comparison does not give the impression that death and gift taxes are doing much to hold down the rate of investment.

Comparison with Income Taxes. The personal and corporate income taxes are much more effective in reducing the amount of savings available to private industry than are death taxes. Among the reasons for the relatively small yield of death taxes is that the large amounts of undistributed corporate profits are not part of individual estates, since, owing to stock market imperfections, they are not always completely reflected in the stock price. The corporate income tax, on the other hand, directly reduces the volume of net profits; and the personal income tax further curtails savings by reducing net dividends after tax. In 1953, once again,

---

[14] There are, of course, differential effects on willingness to earn the income out of which savings are made. But, as we have seen, these disincentive effects are relatively small under the estate and inheritance taxes.

[15] *Annual Reports* of the Secretary of the Treasury; Bureau of the Census, *Summary of State Government Finances,* published annually.

these two taxes at the federal level accounted for $54.1 billion of revenue, while at the state level they took $1.8 billion. Therefore, even though a large proportion of the total of $56 billion would have been spent on consumption, the effect on savings available to private investment was far greater than that of death taxes.

A further point is that the personal income tax, like the corporate income tax, takes savings from those who are likely to be actively engaged in business. Death taxes, on the other hand, rest largely on savings that would otherwise have been left to a considerable extent in the safe form of government securities or real property. Thus a given amount of savings diverted to the government by the corporate and personal income taxes is likely to have greater disincentive effects on risk investment than does the same amount tapped off by the estate and inheritance taxes. Admittedly this generalization must be scrutinized carefully, for corporate profits are also distributed to widows and orphans, and by no means the whole of savings in the form of estates and inheritances is invested in bonds and real estate. It is nevertheless true that after an estate passes out of the hands of the person who engaged actively in its accumulation, the odds are that a change-over will be made to more conservative forms of investment.

► PROBLEMS IN ESTATE AND GIFT TAXES

THE FEDERAL CREDIT

Competition among the states for the residence of wealthy individuals for a time threatened to vitiate the use of state death taxes. A state in which few wealthy people lived would stand to gain if it offered to refrain from enacting inheritance or estate taxes. Little revenue would be lost, and the state would be able to collect compensating revenues each year in the form of increased income, property, and sales taxes. Moreover, local industry would benefit from the spending of wealthy individuals and their retainers. This situation was brought about by the concentration of the great estates in a few states like New York and Illinois.

In order to protect the states from competition among themselves, Congress in 1924 provided for a credit of 25 per cent against the federal estate tax. The effect of the credit was to allow full deduction of state estate and inheritance taxes up to a maximum of 25 per cent of the federal estate tax. If the state levied no tax, the estate would pay the full federal tax. In 1926 the federal credit was increased to 80 per cent.

The enactment of the federal credit provision was a kind of benevolent coercion of the states by the national government in an area specifically reserved to them under the Constitution. The states have independent taxing powers. Yet the federal estate tax credit was putting pressure on the states to enact tax legislation which some of them would not otherwise have put on their books. Consequently, the federal credit provision was attacked in the courts. Florida, which had repealed its inheritance tax law in 1924 in an effort to attract wealthy residents, fought the case through to the Supreme Court. The provision was upheld, however, and has remained a feature of federal law.[16] The court in effect held that state fiscal sovereignty does not extend to an interstate rivalry that may injure the states as a group.

As a result of the federal credit, several states enacted estate taxes, and almost all the states that had relied exclusively on inheritance taxes passed estate taxes in order to take advantage of the credit.[17] Therefore death taxation at the state level has become very complex. Four types are now in use. These are the inheritance tax, the estate tax independent of the federal estate tax, the estate tax levied in order to take advantage of the federal credit,[18] and the estate tax based on the federal levy.

Very few states have limited their estate taxes to 80 per cent of the 1926 federal rates. Moreover, although a substantial part of their revenue comes from estates in the $50,000–$100,000 brackets, these taxes are not eligible for the credit. In the 1926 federal act, the exemption was $100,000, and it has been $60,000 since 1942. The 1926 exemption was retained, however, as the basis for the credit. The result was that an estate of $80,000, say, would be taxable, under the federal law, on $20,000. Yet no state taxes paid on this amount would be deductible because the credit would not apply until an estate was larger than the 1926 exemption of $100,000.

The sharp rise in federal estate tax rates beginning in 1932 likewise reduced the relative importance of the credit. The consequence was that between 1931 and 1948 there was a decline from 76 to 10 per cent in the percentage of federal estate tax liability that was offset by taxes due to the states.[19] The credit varies greatly between states (in 1948, for example, from 2.4 per cent in Wyoming to 15.3 per cent in Michigan).

---

[16] *Florida vs. Mellon*, 273 U. S. 12, 1927.

[17] The federal credit provision is a kind of shared tax, under which the federal government determines how large the tax shall be, and turns part of the revenue over to the states. In this sense it has to be judged in the light of political and fiscal relations between the national and state governments. This device does nothing to equalize the financial power of rich and poor states, nor is it intended to do so. The greater the amount of taxable wealth in the state, the greater its estate tax revenues under the federal credit provision.

[18] The states levy a differential tax that is intended to make the inheritance or estate taxes imposed by them as great as the federal credit. This is done by means of a supplementary tax schedule with graduated rates. If the tax liability under the ordinary inheritance or estate tax falls short of the federal credit, the supplementary estate tax is imposed. The federal government foots the bill, of course, by forgoing this amount under its own estate tax.

[19] United States Treasury Department, *Federal-State Tax Coordination*, revised March 7, 1952, p. 44.

STATE JURISDICTIONAL PROBLEMS

Since death taxes are imposed by the states, a jurisdictional problem arises that is similar in nature to that under the property tax on railroads and airlines. It is not always clear what part of an estate should be subject to the estate and inheritance taxes of a particular state. Decedent and heirs may be residents of different states. The real property, as well as the tangible and intangible personal property, of the estate may be located in several states. The complexity of interstate death tax relationships arises out of the contention that if any contribution is made to the transfer of property rights at death, a state has the right to share in death taxes. The consequence is, of course, the danger of multiple taxation.

In general, no controversy has attended the taxation of real property or tangible property at death. The right to tax resides in the state in which the property is located. Intangible property, on the other hand, is taxable by the state of domicile. Domicile differs from mere residence in that the former is the place where a person declares his intention of making his home. Unfortunately, the states have not always been able to agree on which of a wealthy man's several residences is his domicile. This has resulted in attempts of two or more states to tax the intangible property.

The Supreme Court has shown an unwillingness to impose a judgment on the determination of the state of domicile. Despite the hardship that this interpretation can produce by way of multiple taxation of the same estate, the Court has held that the proper remedy for this inequity is through interstate fiscal cooperation. It has been willing to assume responsibility only when the estate is insufficient to satisfy both the claims of the federal government and those of the states claiming jurisdiction. This attitude of the Court, which was formed gradually during the decade of the thirties, reversed a trend toward the elimination of multiple taxation that had reached its climax in a number of well-known decisions at the beginning of the decade.[20]

Practice with respect to the taxation of intangibles is characterized by much complexity and vagueness. The shares of stock in a corporation owned by an estate might conceivably be taxed by several states. The state of domicile has given the protection of its laws to the decedent during his lifetime. The state in which the stock certificates have been kept for safe-

---

[20] E.g., *Farmers' Loan and Trust Co. v. Minnesota*, 280 U. S. 204, 1930; *First National Bank of Boston v. Maine*, 284 U. S. 312, 1932. A consequence of the Supreme Court rulings permitting double taxation could be the passage of laws by the states authorizing taxation also on the basis of the domicile of the *heir*. They could base their move on the contention that the incidence of death taxation is on the heir, or that the heir is one of the parties to the transference. Moreover, precedent exists under Canadian law, which places jurisdiction with the province in which the heir is domiciled. G. R. Hawkes, "Death Duties and Double Taxation," *National Tax Journal*, June, 1952, pp. 145–154.

keeping has likewise provided a service. But states also incorporate the firms which issue shares of stock. Therefore it can be argued that the incorporating state has the right to impose a tax when the shares change hands at death.

By extension, it might even be held that a state has a right to tax stock shares if any of the property of the corporation is located within its borders, or if it does business in the state. The effect of the acceptance of this kind of contention can be imagined in the case of a corporation owning property or doing business in many states. Finally, when the intangible is in the form of a debt rather than a share of stock, the state of residence of the debtor, as well as that of the creditor, can be shown to have an interest.

The taxation of intangibles has gone through three phases since the early twenties. During the period up to 1925 intangibles were increasingly subject to multiple taxation, as the states sought reasons whereby they might extend their own tax coverage. At the same time, however, a number of states were leading the way toward ending the abuse. They were making reciprocal agreements not to tax intangibles located within their borders but owned by nonresidents. Again, the Supreme Court contributed by restricting the taxability of intangible property. Thus gradually it came to be accepted that in general moneyed property should be taxed only in the state of domicile of the decedent.

Recently, however, the Court's decisions have taken quite a different direction. In decisions commencing in 1942 it has held that intangibles may be taxed by the state of the decedent's domicile, by the state of the situs of the intangible property, and by the state that incorporated the firm that issued the stock.[21] In other words, the Court now holds with the earlier view that intangible property can receive the protection of the laws of more than one state. This new development again puts pressure on the states to make reciprocal agreements. Indeed, it was in part intended to do so. The effects of multiple taxation are mitigated, of course, by the fact that account can be taken of it prior to death. Consequently the problem, though serious, is not as serious as might at first appear.

THE MARITAL DEDUCTION

In eight community-property states earned and unearned income of either spouse is in principle held to be the property of both. If one spouse dies, only one half of the property can be regarded as being transferred. Therefore the tax base is halved, though the rest of the estate is taxed, of course, on the death of the relict. Under a system of progressive rates, the tax liability on two separate transfers is smaller than that on a single transfer. Clearly this situation makes possible an inequity between residents of community- and noncommunity-property (common-law) states, and

---

[21] Cf. United States Treasury Department, *op. cit.*, pp. 47–49.

remedial legislation was required. The Revenue Act of 1942 sought to include the whole of the property in the estate of the spouse who died first, with the exception of the earnings that could be specifically attributed to the survivor. In 1948 Congress restored to the community-property states the privilege they had enjoyed prior to 1942; but by making available to all states a marital deduction of up to one half the estate, Congress removed a discrimination against common-law states that had existed before 1942.

The marital deduction under the estate tax has been subjected to a considerable amount of criticism.[22] In the first place, the provision has naturally resulted in a substantial reduction in revenues. By dividing the tax base an estate can be subjected to a lower rate of tax. Second, under the marital deduction a gift from one spouse to the other is taxable on half the amount of the gift, whereas in community-property states a spouse obtains, without any tax, title to half the income received by the other. In other words, geographical inequality of tax treatment still exists in spite of the amendment of 1948. Third, the marital deduction may encourage the disposition of an estate in a manner that differs from that which would have been adopted in the absence of the deduction, and which may produce undesirable results. The transfer must be absolute in order that the exempt half of the estate can be taxed when the surviving spouse dies. This may create problems of management of the estate.

EXEMPTION OF CHARITABLE BEQUESTS

Bequests to charitable institutions are exempt from the federal estate tax. The states, too, provide for such an exemption, although in some instances they restrict it to charities located within their borders. This exemption has greatly stimulated the establishment of charitable trusts, e.g., the Rockefeller and the Ford foundations. An important reason for their popularity is that the stock made over to them may be nonvoting. The danger of control over the business passing into other hands is therefore removed.

When death taxes are avoided by this device, the fact that high rates of tax apply to large estates means that the government (i.e., other taxpayers) is actually providing most of the funds for the selected charities. At the same time the government is conferring on a group of private citizens the right to determine the directions that charity should take. Some might question whether individuals should be allowed to retain this right. A man may have been extraordinarily successful in amassing property, but does this type of ability and experience qualify him to make a better judgment on the use to which property should be put after his own death than the judgment that the public as a whole can make acting through

---

[22] Cf. Adrian Dewind, "The Approaching Crisis in Federal, Estate, and Gift Taxation," *California Law Review,* March, 1950, pp. 79–116.

Congress? On general grounds the answer must be negative if we accept the concept of voter sovereignty implicit in modern democratic society. On the other hand, experience with reputable charitable foundations in the United States has in general been good. The administrators of a charitable trust rely on the advice of individuals and groups who are expert in searching out the deficiencies in our society that need to be remedied. Therefore they can be instrumental in filling gaps that may seem unimportant to congressmen, who are at the mercy of the pressures of the moment in their support of public spending programs.

For example, governmental agencies demonstrate far more interest in applied research and other programs promising immediate results than they do in the highly theoretical studies that will not produce results easily appreciated by congressmen and their public. Yet pioneering research, it is well known, has been responsible for enormous strides in the advancement of human welfare. So long as the government demonstrates a critical, but understanding, interest in the results of the efforts of charitable organizations, a justification can be made for exemption of bequests to charitable trusts. This is not to imply that the nation should not take a lively interest in their work, however. In any event, members of the family should certainly not act as paid directors of charitable trusts.

INTERRELATIONSHIPS BETWEEN DEATH AND GIFT TAXES

A separate gift tax is not a satisfactory way to make death taxes effective, for the two taxes are subject to separate exemptions and separate rate schedules. Thus a gift of $10,000 would have been subject to the top-bracket rate if left to be taxed under the estate tax, but it might be entirely exempt under the gift tax.

So long as gift and estate taxes are treated as two separate taxes, provisions intended to effect partial integration have little chance of any real success. A case in point is the provision under the act of 1932, and subsequent acts, which provides that the federal gift tax schedule be three fourths that of the estate tax schedule.[23] This concession was made because gift tax liability arises earlier than estate tax liability. Therefore the man who pays a tax on a gift loses compound interest as compared with the man who retains his estate intact until death.[24] This is a crude device, however, for purposes of equalization. If a gift is made late in life, little interest is lost. In any event, a person who makes a gift that is taxable under the gift tax does so in order to escape a still higher estate tax.

---

[23] Gifts are cumulated, of course, since otherwise it would not be possible to apply progressive rates. The rate applicable to the latest taxable gift is determined in the light of previous gifts.

[24] Note that it is the loss of compound interest on the *tax* that is under consideration. There is, of course, no case for arguing that the donor should be recompensed for the loss of interest on the gift itself. The gift of a property implies the right of the recipient to receive the income from it.

Another advantage under the gift tax, which at the least argues against a lower rate schedule, is that an estate tax applies to the entire taxable estate, whereas the gift tax applies to the gift only. Suppose that the question is to be decided whether an estate of $60,000 is to be transferred by gift or succession. Suppose further that the two taxes are both levied at the rate of 50 per cent. Then a gift of $40,000 could be made, the amount of $20,000 being taken in tax. But if the estate tax were applicable, the tax would be $30,000, leaving only $30,000 to be transferred to the heirs.

The separate taxation of gifts under the federal tax system works out to be unduly favorable to the very wealthy as compared with those who are moderately wealthy, for a man with a relatively small estate of, say, $200,000 cannot afford to give away his property to his children during his lifetime. Even when two estates are of equal size, one person may be in a position to make greater use of the gift device than the other.

Another factor that favors the owner of a large estate is his greater ability to pay for expert legal advice, and therefore his greater awareness of economic and other circumstances that bear on the question whether or not to distribute property before death. Of course the very wealthy and the moderately wealthy alike take the risk that they may be predeceased by the donee, in which case the estate may be taxed twice. Another inequity is that a man who lives long has more time to dispose of part of his estate. Again, some estates must be kept intact because they consist solely of the family business. In this case gifts made for the purpose of avoiding death taxes might weaken the control of the owner of the business over policy decisions.

Gifts in Contemplation of Death.   So long as gifts are taxed under a separate schedule the question is bound to arise whether a particular gift was made in contemplation of death. If so, it is taxed as part of the estate, since the intent to avoid the estate tax is obvious. It is not always clear, however, whether a gift is made in anticipation of death. Deathbed gifts, or, in certain circumstances, gifts to take effect at death, offer no problem; they are included in the taxable estate. It is tempting, when a large gift is made by a man who obviously has not many years to live, to require the gift to be included in the estate on grounds of "conclusive presumption" that it was made in contemplation of death. A gift made within, say, three or five years before actual demise might be grounds for taxing it as part of the estate. The Supreme Court has refused to uphold conclusive presumption, even when the period has been as short as two years. Some lawyers believe, however, that the Court might change its position if the question were to arise again. Again, the burden of proof can be put on the estate when death occurs within a specified period after the making of a gift. Under the federal tax this period is three years.

In general the federal government has not been conspicuously successful in convincing the courts that gifts were made in contemplation of death. It should be noted, however, that the proportion of victories and defeats for the government may not be adequate evidence of the success of the "contemplation" criterion. Much depends on how far the government is willing to go in challenging the taxpayer. If many cases are challenged, one would expect the proportion of decisions favorable to the government to be low, while at the same time, fewer taxpayers would use the gift device in doubtful circumstances.

Gifts and the Income Tax. Gifts can be made in order to reduce the joint income tax liability of donor and donee. If the former is in a sufficiently high tax bracket relative to the latter, it may be worth while for him to make a gift even though it is subject to the gift tax. The income from the gift will be taxed at lower income rates.

Another problem relative to the relation of gifts to the personal income tax is whether gifts should be included in the income of the donor, the donee, or both. A gift is a form of income to the donee. Under the accretion-of-income concept of income taxation, gifts would be income to the donee, and they would be subtracted from the income of the donor. Administratively, it would be difficult to make sure that donees included all their receipts for tax purposes. Aside from this, however, the Treasury would lose revenue; the donor usually has the higher income, and a lower income tax rate would be substituted for a higher.

From the standpoint of logic there seems to be no good reason to remove gifts from the income of the donor. In making the gift he exercises the same rights over his income that another man exercises when he decides to spend on consumption or to save. In other words, the donor derives a satisfaction in making the gift. Because of this, some economists have advocated the inclusion of gifts in the incomes of both donor and donee.[25] At present there appears to be no prospect of a change in the practice of exempting the donee, but not allowing the gift as a deduction from the taxable income of the donor.

INTEGRATION OF DEATH AND GIFT TAXES

The failure of the gift tax to make the estate tax completely effective argues strongly for the integration of the two taxes.[26] The simplest way of accomplishing this would be through an extension of the principle already in use by the federal government under the gift tax alone, which requires gifts to be aggregated over the years in order to determine the appropriate bracket rate. This could be done by treating the transfer of the estate as the final gift in a series. As each gift was made, a tax would be collected on it at the new bracket rate.

---

[25] Cf. Henry Simons, *Personal Income Taxation* (Chicago: University of Chicago Press, 1938), pp. 125 ff. In his later work (*Federal Tax Reform* [Chicago: University of Chicago Press, 1950]) he moderated the severity of his views.

[26] A proposal for complete integration of gift and death taxes is made by William Vickrey, *op. cit.,* pp. 198–273.

AVOIDANCE THROUGH FAILURE TO TAX EACH TRANSFER

Another major loophole in the federal estate tax law is the failure to tax the estate at each death. Since deaths may succeed each other rapidly, it is not contended that estates should necessarily be taxed at full rates at each succession. Whether or not a tax is applied, however, should not be allowed to depend on the ingenuity of tax lawyers. Through the devices of power of appointment, life interest and remainderman, and the trust, it is possible to avoid the application of death taxes to one or more successive transmissions.

A man may give successive life interests in his property to his son and grandson, leaving the remainder to his great-grandson.[27] Through this device three successions are taxed only once because under American law remainders are not subject to tax. The British do not exempt remainders, and estates are consequently subject to tax at each succession.

Alternatively, property may be left to one's child, and at the same time the latter may be given a power of appointment to name his children as beneficiaries. Although the property is taxed on the first transfer, it is not taxed on the second.

Another method is to give or bequeath the property to a trust fund, the income of which is paid to the beneficiary.[28] A trust fund is established by the settlor, vesting legal title in a trustee, who administers the fund for the benefit of a third person. If a trust is revocable, the settlor is not regarded as having made a definitive transfer, and it is taxable. Even an irrevocable trust fund is taxable if the settlor reserves rights to himself. This naturally poses problems to the creator of the fund where the heir has to be held to certain standards of behavior or competence. Scope still exists for avoidance by this means, however, because of the legal difficulty of determining whether or not a given trust fund is revocable.

The difficulty of writing a satisfactory provision for taxing life estates, and their consequent exemption, provides much opportunity for avoidance. At high rates of tax the financial difference to an estate in being liable or not liable to the tax is enormous. The extremely large number of variations in the possible forms of powers of appointment, life interests, and other avoidance devices has made it possible for the great majority of large estates to reduce the number of taxable transmissions. The rule against perpetuities prevents these devices from being used indefinitely. The usual

---

[27] See the excellent discussion in Harold Groves, *Postwar Taxation and Economic Progress* (New York: McGraw, 1946), pp. 265 ff. The reason that the second life interest and the remainder are not taxed is that the law regards the son and grandson as having used up their bequests during life, and therefore as having nothing to bequeath.

[28] It has been proposed that a privilege tax might be levied on the use of trusts and powers of appointment for prolonging control over property after death. This might take the form of an additional tax on the income of property subject to the control of the decedent.—Vickrey, *op. cit.*, p. 273.

restriction is to limit the power to name successive beneficiaries to persons still living, plus twenty-one years.

RAPID SUCCESSION

If avoidance through the use of the life estate were to be prevented by making remainders taxable, it would be even more necessary than it is at present to give relief for rapid succession. The federal government and some states allow the first tax as a credit against the second if two deaths occur within a short time. Under federal law prior to 1954 this period was five years, but in that year the provision was changed, as noted below. An arbitrary dividing line accentuates the inequity facing an estate when one death follows another by slightly more than the designated number of years. Moreover, the Internal Revenue Service had tended to insist that the exemption applies only when, at each succession, it is the same property that is passed on. This obviously works hardship when a man's business is marked by complex and frequently changing property relationships. Consequently sentiment developed in favor of liberalization of the five-year rule.

One proposal was to take a given number of years as the normal interval between deaths, including the whole estate in the tax base when deaths actually occur at this interval. If the actual interval is shorter than the normal, only the prorated amount of the estate would be included. Logic would seem to require that *more* than the whole estate be included in the tax base when the interval between deaths exceeds the normal. But this could cause undue hardship. An alternative proposal was to include a greater proportion of the estate in the tax base the greater the age differential between the decedent and the heir. In 1954 Congress replaced the five-year rule with a provision which allows a full credit for two years only, but eliminates the inequities of a sharp dividing line by reducing the credit by 20 per cent every two years, until no credit is allowed after the tenth year.

LIQUIDITY

The taxation of estates may exert an adverse effect on the volume of savings available for risky investment. This will occur if the effect is to encourage individuals to convert their assets into relatively liquid form considerably in advance of death in order to make certain that resources are available out of which to pay the tax. If large numbers of persons were to react in this way, the yield on safe investments might be driven down slightly, and the cost of borrowing to engage in risky enterprise increased.

A number of considerations, however, raise doubts as to the quantitative significance of the discouragement to risky investment caused by the payment of death taxes. In important instances it is difficult or unfeasible to convert property to liquid form. This is the case, for example, with agricultural property. It is true, of course, that the tax may cause the breakup of estates as parcels of land are sold for cash to pay the tax. Again, a family-owned factory cannot conveniently be converted into cash. When, moreover, the estate takes the form of shares of stock, all that happens is a change of ownership. This is so whether the stocks are sold in anticipation of death, or to pay the tax after death. The sale of stock will have no effect on the investment policy of a public corporation, though it may do so when a corporation is closely held. To be sure, the new ownership may be less efficient and aggressive than the old. This possibility would have to be faced, however, even in the absence of death taxes, as advancing age forced the major stockholders to release control.

If large blocks of stock must be put on the market quickly in order to pay the tax, stock prices may be depressed. This not only reduces the value of the estate but may increase the difficulties of firms in raising funds from the stock market. Provision is usually made to avoid this contingency. The Internal Revenue Service may give the estate up to ten years to pay the tax (with accrued interest, of course). Also, in order to reduce the burden on illiquid estates, stock in closely held corporations may under certain restrictions be redeemed for the purpose of paying estate taxes without being subject to the income tax.

A proprietorship may obviate the need for liquidity in anticipation of the owner's death by paying insurance premiums.[29] In effect, this diverts some of the savings of the small firm to the insurance companies. Whether the net effect is a bias against risky investment or not depends on what the insurance companies do with the funds. Although they have widened the scope of their activities in recent years, their investment interest obviously differs from that of the small, new firm.

▶ CONCLUSION

Death taxation derives its justification from ability to pay. The ability that is relevant is that of the heir. Under the assumptions of the Western democratic type of society the right of inheritance is maintained. This right, however, is subject to modification by the state in response to changing concepts of the rights of decedents and heirs as measured against those of society as a whole.

Because of an interest in revenues that is greater than appears to be justified by the quantitative importance of death taxes, governments have tended to favor the estate tax over the inheritance tax. Yet the latter is the more equitable tax. The fact that the inheritance tax can be graduated

---

[29] It is of some interest to consider whether this procedure would convert death taxes into an annual tax similar to the income tax. From the point of view of the businessman, the premiums are the equivalent of a tax. The Treasury, however, does not come into possession of these sums until the estate passes; consequently, it loses compound interest as compared with the situation under an income tax paid annually.

both by size of bequest and by degree of relationship with the decedent has led some economists to argue that account should be taken of the wealth of the heir. Still others would go further and discourage the transmission of property. The present make-up of most Western governments has remained unfavorable to the latter view.

It is generally recognized that, in the interest of equity, improvements are in order. The gift tax should be integrated with the estate tax. Again, account should be taken of the fact that death is unpredictable, and that estates which happen to be transferred often are at present penalized. On the other hand, through the use of trusts and life interests a form of avoidance is possible that sharply reduces the effectiveness of death taxation in this country. Another important issue is raised by the exemption of charitable bequests. On the one hand, exemptions help support charities and research which would probably not receive government support. On the other hand, the exemption means that these good works are actually supported by other taxpayers. The social issue here is a complex one. Finally, a difficulty peculiar to the federal form of government is the inequity caused by jurisdictional conflicts among the states.

► REFERENCES

HARRISS, C. L. *Gift Taxation in the United States.* Washington, D. C.: American Council on Public Affairs, 1940.

OAKES, E. E. "The Federal Offset and the American Death Tax System," *Quarterly Journal of Economics,* August, 1940.

RIGNANO, E. *The Social Significance of the Inheritance Tax.* Translated by W. J. Shultz. New York: Alfred A. Knopf, Inc., 1924.

SHULTZ, W. J. *The Taxation of Inheritance.* Boston: Houghton Mifflin Company, 1926.

VICKREY, W. *Agenda for Progressive Taxation.* New York: The Ronald Press, 1947, pp. 198–273.

17 Intergovernmental Fiscal Relations

► THE NATURE OF THE PROBLEM

So long as the various levels of government possess independent tax and spending powers there must be a problem of intergovernmental fiscal relations. If stable political relationships are to be maintained among governmental jurisdictions, an understanding must be reached on the allocation of expenditures and revenues. Political power follows control of the purse.

The impact of the problem of maintaining satisfactory intergovernmental fiscal relations is felt most keenly under the federal form of government.[1] Under the constitutions of federal unions like Canada, Australia, and the United States, the states and the provinces are not merely creatures of the central government. They are equipped with independent fiscal powers. A constitutional guarantee of independent powers, however, does not mean that in practice they can be preserved without a struggle. The Constitution of the United States did not bar the use of a particular tax by more than one level of government. Therefore one level of government may encroach on the tax base depended upon by another.

For a long time the federal, state, and local governments indeed tended to restrict themselves to particular taxes. But the rapid development in the complexity of economic relationships after the Civil War led to intergovernmental competition for revenues. Thus overlapping of the sources of revenue became a major fiscal problem. Moreover, short of complete absorption of one level of government by another, a constant struggle must go on as each jurisdiction strives to maintain or increase its share in the responsibility for spending and taxing. No stable equilibrium

---

[1] Although emphasis is placed here on the greater difficulty faced in solving the fiscal problems of federal countries, the line between federal and unitary countries is not a sharp one. Even in a federal country one school of thought is constantly pressing for greater centralization of power. It is argued that decentralization cannot easily keep pace with the problems of modern society, in particular, industrial capitalism. Cf. J. A. Maxwell, *The Fiscal Impact of Federalism* (Cambridge, Mass.: Harvard University Press, 1946), Chap. II, "Fiscal Problems of Federalism."

is possible in modern society, for economic and political developments occur rapidly. Any jurisdiction that consistently refrained from taking on new functions might soon find itself in possession merely of duties that had become obsolete.

► THE DISTRIBUTION OF FISCAL FUNCTIONS

In a federal democracy it appears that the distribution of public spending and taxing among the levels of government ought to do the following four things. First, and most important, it should contribute to the maintenance of the political independence of each level of government, within the limits provided by the constitution. Second, by giving to each level of government the fiscal responsibilities for which it is best adapted, it should encourage maximum efficiency in the performance of public functions. Third, it should respond quickly to changes in the economic, social, and political relations among the various levels of government. Fourth, the fiscal policies of all levels of government should, so far as possible, be coordinated in the interest of economic stability.

1. THE MAINTENANCE OF THE POLITICAL INDEPENDENCE OF EACH LEVEL OF GOVERNMENT

History teaches us that fundamental effects can be produced on the locus of governmental power through the decisions that are made with respect to the distribution of tax and spending functions. Ordinarily these decisions are made gradually, and the effects are not revolutionary. For this very reason a trend may be established that is difficult to halt or reverse. On occasion, moreover, conscious attempts have been made to utilize a redistribution of fiscal powers in order to accelerate a trend either to centralization or to decentralization of political power. An interesting example of this is offered by the experience of Germany since 1815. This example is the more striking because to a substantial degree the struggle for fiscal supremacy between the central and the state governments is still going on.

The German Case. After 1815 German politics largely centered around the attempt to federate the separatist-minded states into a single country. Up to and during World War I, however, progress toward centralization of power in Berlin was slow, largely because the states had the political strength to retain for themselves the major lucrative taxes. The central government, on the other hand, was restricted to the customs. As we have seen, the tariff is a poor source of revenue when a nation goes to war. In being forced to resort to the states for grants of money, the Reich was naturally compelled to give greater attention to their political demands than would otherwise have been necessary. The inability of the Kaiser to centralize Germany's fiscal system was an important factor in the inflation of World War I.

This lesson was well learned by Hitler, who, under the policy of intergovernmental coordination during the thirties, reduced both the fiscal and the political powers of the states to insignificance. At the conclusion of military action in 1945, however, the pendulum swung again. The Basic Law of the West German Republic was so drawn that the Länder (the states) received the revenue from the most productive tax sources. Here again was a fiscal measure that was really political, this time with the benediction of the Allied powers, who feared a resurgence of German aggression.

As an illustration of its operation in the realm of finance the role of the income tax may be cited. Under the Basic Law the Bund (the central government) could lay claim to a portion of the receipts of this tax. It could not, however, divert more than approximately one fourth of the proceeds away from the states without the approval of the upper house (Bundesrat). But the upper house is essentially an organ of representation of the states. Therefore the Bundesrat has been extremely loath to relinquish any substantial amounts of income tax revenues to the Bund. The desire to prevent the return of the supercentralized governmental system of the Nazis is evident in this arrangement, which is contrary to the trend in all modern nations.[2]

The Problem in the United States. The problem of fiscal independence by level of government in the United States is twofold. First is the distribution of fiscal powers between the federal and the state governments; and second, the distribution between state and local governments. Direct federal grants to citizens, it is true, do involve the municipalities, since local relief and certain other services can be cut down if veterans and others receive federal subsidies. But the struggle for fiscal and political power is not between the federal government and the localities.

The tendency in this country has been toward a centralization of fiscal powers. Through grants-in-aid and increased spending on the factors of production, the federal government has increased its power relative to the states. By a similar process the states have expanded their fiscal functions in comparison with those of the municipalities.

Obstacles to Fiscal Equilibrium. In addition to the centralizing effects of wars, and apart from changing political philosophies, two major factors may serve to whittle away the fiscal independence of the lower

---

[2] It should be noted, however, that whereas the states were asked to hand over to the federal government only 17 per cent of their revenues in 1949, this proportion had risen to 38 per cent by 1953, and in his budget of March, 1954, Finance Minister Schaeffer asked that the figure be raised to 40 per cent.

levels of government. This development is observable in the majority of federal countries under present-day conditions. These factors are (1) the vulnerability of the states and municipalities to cyclical and secular forces that tend to undermine their political and fiscal independence, and (2) the tendency of budget makers at a lower level of government to accept with a sense of relief the offers of financial assistance from higher levels.

The first of the above factors is likely to be a particularly serious problem for the states in their role as politically independent middlemen between the federal and the local governments. A depression could bring on a collapse of both state and local revenues. The result might then be an increase in the number of "direct national-local programs," and the states would emerge from the depression with their political as well as their fiscal powers reduced.[3]

So long as the states are in an intermediate position between the federal and the local governments, they preserve a significant measure of independence in setting standards for the localities. This they can do by prescribing conditions for that part of municipal revenues which takes the form of grants. They are more than mere agents for transferring funds from the federal to the local governments. Thus in 1954 the states paid out in intergovernmental subsidies $5.7 billion, receiving less than half that amount, or $2.7 billion from the federal government.[4] If they are to retain this position they must have a reasonably assured source of revenues in depression as well as in prosperity.

Much less tangible is the role of the attitude of mind of state budgetary officials and legislatures. A conscious effort must be made not to allow immediate fiscal problems to undermine the long-term advantages that accrue from a high degree of financial independence. It is sometimes possible to detect a note of satisfaction on the part of state officials when the federal government increases its share of the burden of financing some service. Thus, for example, the sixty-seventh budget of the state of Illinois[5] stated:

Increases in coverage and benefits under the Social Security insurance programs can be expected to decrease loads materially. The 1950 amendments to the Federal Social Security Act which increased Old Age and Survivors' Insurance benefits have already begun to reduce the rolls. . . . the Public Aid Commission was able to drop more than 4,000 cases and reduce assistance payments to more than 12,000 other cases.

The relief of state budget makers at seeing their responsibility for the aged

---

[3] Cf. M. Grodzins, "State-Municipal Fiscal Relations," *National Tax Journal,* March, 1950, pp. 16–17.

[4] Bureau of the Census, *Compendium of State Government Finances in 1954.* The states received $215 million from the local governments.

[5] State of Illinois, *67th Budget,* for the Biennium July 1, 1951 to June 30, 1953, p. 44A.

and indigent disappear is readily understandable.[6] If, however, this sense of relief is indulged every time the opportunity presents itself, the states are going to risk losing their resistance to further encroachment on their fiscal functions by the federal government.

2. THE CRITERION OF EFFICIENCY

The requirement that the fiscal system give to each level of government the functions for which it is best adapted seems to be of less importance than the distribution of fiscal power. Excessive centralization of the fiscal function encourages similar centralization of political power. If this power were to get out of control, regional influences on national policy might become seriously attenuated. But the waste and inefficiency that results from a misallocation of fiscal functions among the various governmental levels might itself encourage a drive for centralization of fiscal authority. Consequently, great care needs to be devoted to allocating these functions properly.

Efficiency of Taxing vs. Efficiency of Spending. Unfortunately, a choice must be made between the most efficient distribution of revenue functions and the most efficient distribution of spending functions. Because of their nearness to local problems, the states and the localities are in a position to perform many types of spending much more efficiently than the national government can do it. The chiefs of bureaus sit in Washington, and the bureaucratic point of view is apt to become somewhat remote from that of the men in the field.

On the other hand, there is no basis for assuming that the states, and more especially the localities, have at their disposal precisely the taxes necessary to finance the spending functions that they are best able to perform. In general terms, it can be said that the administrative ability of the localities to spend greatly surpasses their capacity to raise revenues. On the other hand, the federal government can tax much more effectively than it can spend.[7] The states stand somewhere in between these two extremes.

Suppose, for example, that a state should decide that the localities ought to increase the level of their educational standards. It may be impossible, however, for the localities to accomplish this out of their own resources. They may already be at the limits of their taxable capacity. Nevertheless, public opinion might insist that education is properly the function of the locality.

If this is so, the only escape from the dilemma is the grant-in-aid. The state performs the tax function, the locality supervises the spending,

---

[6] Under the federal social security program it is contemplated that in time the receipt of assistance granted as a sort of *favor* to indigent individuals by the states will be superseded by the *right* of the individual to social security according to the standards of the federal government.

[7] Cf. Maxwell, *op. cit.,* p. 36.

and the difference is made up through a grant to the locality by the state. Thus each level of government takes on the function for which it is held to be most suited. But there is a loose end. If the state provides part of the money, it is likely to insist on "minimum standards." Here is the lever by means of which the independent powers of the localities may come to be gradually curtailed. The problem is to develop a system of grants that will minimize the tendency toward centralization of fiscal power.[8] Obviously the issue is even more serious as between the federal government and the states.

Attitude of State Officials.   As one might expect, differences of opinion exist among the various levels of government over the allocation of fiscal powers that will maximize economic welfare. Representatives of the state governments and state and local tax administrators have argued that each level should support its activities from its own revenues. The government responsible for the taxes ought to control the expenditures which it makes possible. At the same time, federal grants ought to be held down to the point at which the states and cities are left with a sufficient tax base so that they can levy taxes of their own.[9] The larger the federal grants the more money is drained out of each state and each locality into the federal Treasury; consequently, state and local tax bases are narrowed.

The Treasury, on the other hand, tends to reflect the favorable attitude of the federal government toward grants-in-aid. Regardless of opinions on the matter, the tendency has been sharply in the direction of grants-in-aid from higher to lower levels of government. The view has been widely accepted that it is more important, as well as more feasible, to leave with the lower levels a greater responsibility for spending than for taxing. The present indications are that as pressure for rising standards of public service continues, the intergovernmental subsidy is likely to assume even greater importance in the future than it has enjoyed in the past.

3. FLEXIBILITY OF FEDERAL, STATE, AND LOCAL FISCAL RELATIONS

It is important that the intergovernmental distribution of taxing and spending responsibilities should be able to respond quickly to the changes in their functional relationships. Unless the response is fairly rapid, the system becomes less and less efficient, and the danger arises that it may break down. Under a highly centralized form of government, though there may be technical obstacles to this adaptation, there are no constitutional or statutory rigidities that cannot quickly be swept aside.

---

[8] Grants-in-aid are discussed below.

[9] Cf. the Joint Committee of the American Bar Association, the National Tax Association, and the National Association of Tax Administrators, *The Coordination of Federal, State, and Local Taxation.* Also United States Treasury, Tax Advisory Staff of the Secretary, *Federal-State-Local Tax Coordination,* dated March 7, 1952. For developments up to 1943 see Senate Document No. 69, 78th Cong., 1st Sess., 1943. See also A. G. Buehler, "Federal Grant-in-Aid versus Separate Revenue Sources," *Proceedings* of the National Tax Association, 1949, pp. 384 ff.

Under a federal system of government, on the other hand, where quick adaptation is especially desirable, these rigidities form a real barrier. In addition to the carefully prescribed constitutional power relationships among the different levels of government are the self-denying ordinances sometimes applied to itself by each jurisdiction.[10] Again, the courts may lag in their interpretations of the meaning of the constitutional limitations on the taxing powers of the various levels. For example, because of the prohibition on direct taxes levied by the national government, unless apportioned among the states according to population, it took the United States twenty years to obtain a federal income tax that would stand up constitutionally.

4. FISCAL COORDINATION AND ECONOMIC STABILITY

The integration of federal, state, and local tax and spending policies in the interest of economic equilibrium is believed by some economists to be the most important of the four criteria. In this view the fiscal autonomy of the lower levels of government is, within limits, to be subordinated to what is regarded as a more important goal. This goal is the coordinated fiscal policy for economic stability that is necessary in order to preserve the free-enterprise economy.

The fiscal approach to the maintenance of stability contends that fluctuations in the level of private investment and consumption spending ought to be compensated for by opposite changes in the level of government spending. This is known as "compensatory" fiscal policy. An inflationary rise in national income should be offset by a deflationary rise in the ratio of tax receipts to government spending, so that a budget surplus is created or a deficit is reduced. The purchasing power represented by the surplus is removed from the income stream if it is held idle in the form of treasury cash or deposits with the federal reserve banks. A reduction in the deficit is likewise deflationary to the extent that government borrowing from the banks is reduced. Conversely, if the rate of private spending falls below the level which corresponds to full employment, the Treasury should collect less in taxes than it pays out into the income stream for commodities and factors of production. This policy contributes to a rise in the level of income and employment.[11]

Obviously this policy is difficult to carry out if the tax and spending policies of the state and local governments (1) are independent of federal fiscal policy, and (2) comprise a quantitatively significant proportion of total government spending and taxing. In addition to being independent and quantitatively important, however, state and local fiscal policies are

---

[10] For example, a prohibition on tax classification, or on the use of a particular kind of tax.

[11] The economics of this problem is discussed in subsequent chapters. Here the problem is merely stated.

apt to be the opposite from what is needed during a depression.[12] Since the states and localities do not have the unlimited borrowing powers (from the federal reserve banks) enjoyed by the national government, they necessarily strive to curtail expenditures during a business downswing. Again, in order to reduce their deficits, they are under pressure to raise tax rates when compensatory fiscal policy would call for a reduction in taxes. For this reason some economists have deplored the recent tendency for the lower levels of government to work toward financial self-sufficiency. Thus we find a potent economic argument in favor of centralization of fiscal powers.[13] Added to this argument are the facts that both a reduction in state and local services and a rise in tax rates are highly undesirable aspects of a depression.

▶ INTERGOVERNMENTAL TAX RELATIONSHIPS

The fundamental question to which an answer is needed with respect to the fiscal interrelationships of the three levels of government is this: What taxes are most suitable to each? This question raises the further issue whether it is desirable or possible to effect a separation of tax sources as among the national, state, and local governments.

DUPLICATE TAXATION

There is, of course, no reason why certain taxes may not appropriately be used by more than one level of government. If this occurs, more than one set of rates is applied to a particular tax base. This is not in itself inequitable. It does, however, open the door to the possibility of inequitable multiple taxation. If, for example, the federal government and the states both tax incomes without regard to the rates imposed by the other, it is possible that the combined rates may take more than 100 per cent of very high incomes. Thus equitable multiple taxation implies a recognition by each jurisdiction of the claims of the other, as well as of the rights of the taxpayer.

---

[12] For an excellent discussion of these problems see A. H. Hansen and H. S. Perloff, *State and Local Finance in the National Economy* (New York: Norton, 1944), Chap. IV.

[13] It is of interest to note that treasury officials sometimes appear to be more interested in this aspect of federal-state-local fiscal coordination than in the problems that most disturb the states and cities and that form the core of the discussion of the present chapter. In an address before the National Tax Association on September 21, 1949, Thomas Lynch, Treasury General Counsel, listed the "achievement of a coordinated national policy of economic stability" as the first of the three major issues of intergovernmental fiscal relations.

This attitude is natural. From their own point of view federal agencies are being altruistic in cooperating with the lower levels of government in order to help them maintain their fiscal independence. These agencies are conscious of the possibility that the federal government may be held responsible by the public for preventing serious fluctuations in the level of income and employment.

A similar problem exists between horizontal jurisdictions. If one state taxes a corporation on the basis of its income, another on its gross sales, and another on its property, inequities are bound to arise. Moreover, when two sets of administrative machinery are used, compliance costs to the taxpayer are raised, as well as cost of administration. The states have made increasing use of reciprocal tax agreements to prevent double taxation of the incomes of individuals who work in one state while maintaining residence in another.

Duplicate taxation is no answer to the problem of the state or city with a low level of income, spending, or property values. Just as the federal government cannot raise substantial amounts of revenues within the borders of such a locality or state, neither can the lower jurisdiction itself do so. In this instance the only solution is the grant-in-aid.

SEPARATION OF REVENUE SOURCES

If each governmental level is guaranteed exclusive reliance on certain taxes, the possibility of encroachment by other levels of government is removed. The major point of conflict is, of course, the rivalry between the states and the federal government. Separation of sources is not practicable, however, if a particular selection of taxes awarded to a given jurisdiction does not possess the taxable capacity to provide it with adequate revenues. Conversely, separation is not to be recommended if it furnishes a given level of government a volume of revenues that is more than adequate to fulfill its expenditure functions. The importance of this point is apparent when it is remembered that wide differences in wealth and income exist among the states. There is no reason why the whole of the revenues from an income tax, for example, should remain within the borders of a state which happens to be populated with individuals whose average income is high. Because of this kind of problem, officials of the national government, taking the over-all view, are prone to argue for the grant-in-aid as opposed to separation of tax sources.[14]

Historical Background. Only since the turn of the century have either the states or the national government given much attention to the possibility of separation of tax sources. The aggregate revenue needs of all levels of government had previously been too small a proportion of national income, except in time of war, to make this a serious matter. A brief review of the historical background from the point of view of competition for revenue sources will be useful in providing a setting for the problem.

During the early part of the nineteenth century the states began to take on new functions that made necessary a regular source of revenue. Sporadic fund gathering through land sales and lotteries became more and more unsatisfactory. By mid-century the property tax had become the

---

[14] Tax Advisory Staff of the Secretary of the Treasury, *op. cit.,* p. 9.

major state revenue source. Property taxation was, therefore, no longer the sole prerogative of the localities. This tax was not sufficiently productive, however, to finance the whole of the rapidly increasing expenditures of the states.

The federal government, as we have seen, was committed to a low level of expenditures. It therefore discovered that the customs and the sales of public lands were more than sufficient to finance its needs. This combination of circumstances paved the way for the acceptance of the principle of the federal grant-in-aid. The distribution of surplus revenues that was made in 1837 took the form of a loan to the states. Since it was not intended that this loan should be repaid, the effect was an outright subsidy. This early type of grant differed substantially, of course, from the modern variety. It was not made for a specific purpose, or even because the states needed assistance. Nevertheless, a precedent was established in federal-state fiscal relations.

During this same period the localities made a constantly heavier use of the property tax, by way of both rising rates and increasing valuations. The demand for protective and other services supplied by the cities stemmed from the increasing density of population and the spread of popular representation. It was likewise a period of growth in separate local taxing authorities. The most important of these was the self-governing school district, equipped with the power to levy taxes.

Developments after the Civil War. The rapid development of communications and transportation after the Civil War, coupled with increasing complexity of economic and financial relationships, brought about a search for new revenue sources by the states and cities. Again, although the federal government was still plagued by surpluses, the growing realization of the need for greater federal control over economic life was beginning to make it apparent that new revenue sources would ultimately be needed by the federal government. For the time being, however, the search for new revenues was restricted to the lower levels of government. The struggle for the federal income tax, it will be remembered, did not hinge primarily on revenue needs.

The states found that however desirable it was to modernize the property tax, through improved administration and equalization of assessments from one community to another, other taxes would be necessary to finance their rapidly growing expenditures. During this period they introduced the inheritance tax, taxes on rail transport and public utilities, business taxes, and liquor taxes. By 1880, revenues from state taxation of banks in Massachusetts, for example, had outstripped those from the property tax. Owing to the wide diversity in the underlying economic basis of taxation in the various states, considerable differences arose in the complexion of state tax systems.

The localities likewise became responsible during this period for large additional expenditures. A constantly growing movement of population to the cities, both from abroad and from the rural areas, hastened the need for increased public services. Standards of education were rapidly raised, and the mingling of heterogeneous national populations in the large cities made necessary the creation of many new types of public services. As yet, however, the localities made no use of new kinds of taxes. The property tax remained the major source of local revenue. The result was that the state grant-in-aid now took its place along with the federal subsidy to the states. Both developments occurred in response to a growth in functions at lower levels of government that exceeded their taxable capacity. For example, states began to make larger and larger grants-in-aid for education, which had become increasingly democratized after the Civil War.

The Move for Separation of Sources.   The movement for separation of state and local revenue sources gained momentum in the early 1900's. Pennsylvania had adopted the policy as early as 1885, and a number of other states quickly followed suit. Several factors contributed to the trend. Advocates believed that if the state superimposes a property tax on that of the localities, an incentive is given for competitive undervaluation by local assessors in order to minimize the locality's share in state taxes. In this connection, it was also thought that the rural-urban tax conflict might be alleviated by separation of sources. In part the movement was based on a desire for a greater measure of home rule by the municipalities. Some economists recommended separation on the ground that if the states renounced the property tax they would be forced to make use of higher taxes on banks and public utilities, which it was thought were undertaxed. As is frequently the case in controversies of this kind, the reform was regarded as a panacea for everything that was wrong with the state-local tax system. Advocates of separation tended to forget that any device which removes one set of problems is likely to introduce another collection of its own.

The major objection to state-local separation of sources proved to be the withdrawal on the part of some states from the exercise of their constitutional responsibility for the supervision and fiscal welfare of the localities. Furthermore, separation of sources may leave the assessment of property entirely in the hands of the localities;[15] the states must guard against surrendering their interest in equitable assessment even if they themselves derive no revenue from the tax. An interesting recent development has stimulated state interest, however, in effective local use of the property tax. The financial difficulties of the states, enhanced by demands

---

[15] J. W. Martin and C. M. Stephenson, "Aspects of the Movement toward Separation of Sources of State and Local Revenue," *Tax Magazine,* January–February, 1933, p. 14.

by school districts and other local governmental units for increased grants-in aid, have prompted many states to expand the local property tax base and improve administration.

In recent years a movement has gained momentum toward a greater measure of home rule for the localities. A leader in this field has again been Pennsylvania. In 1947 she granted extremely wide scope to the localities to tax whatever objects the Commonwealth did not tax. The result was a rapid spread in the development of the city income tax, as well as of admissions, business, severance, and poll taxes. Although this power was somewhat curtailed two years later, Pennsylvania's step has accelerated a trend toward increased local taxing powers that had already become marked during the war. Many other states have extended the powers of the localities with respect to one or more taxes.[16] For the states as a whole, however, the trend has been slowed down by the action of some of them in restricting the tax powers of the localities.

Some important objections stand in the way of excessive state generosity in extending the tax powers of the municipalities. Although it is certainly desirable to do everything possible to encourage local initiative and independence from the states, the locality is usually too narrow a jurisdiction for effective administration. Evasion of local taxes is relatively easy, and cost of collection is high. On the other hand, the force of these objections has been decreasing somewhat in recent years, in part because of the failure of state tax systems to become substantially less regressive. No state has adopted an income tax since 1937, and few have raised income tax rates. Moreover, many states have adopted cigarette and sales taxes, and have raised the rates of existing sales taxes. In contrast, the municipal gross income tax is a proportional levy, and is therefore less regressive than the sales tax, which is the largest state revenue producer.

Priority.   An argument sometimes made by spokesmen for the states in favor of separation of tax sources is that if a particular level of government first made permanent use of a given tax, no other jurisdiction should encroach upon it. It is true that once a fiscal system has become geared to a certain group of taxes, a decision by another level of government to make use of the same taxes is likely to restrict scope for any further extension. Indeed, instances can be cited where excessive use of a tax by one level of government has caused a reduction in the receipts of another.[17]

---

[16] Although Pennsylvania is exceptional in its grant of wide fiscal powers to the localities, similar results elsewhere have tended to follow from piecemeal legislation. Thus in 1951 at least fourteen states extended new taxing powers to their municipalities, covering such disparate taxes as a 10 per cent tax on beer (Tennessee), a use tax on liquor (California), and a 1 per cent tax on real-estate sales (Washington).

[17] The extensive use of a tax by one level of government may actually cause a reduction in the receipts from a tax applied to the same base by another level. But the facts may be difficult to establish. In 1952 the liquor industry contended that high federal liquor excise rates had hurt sales, and had therefore caused a reduction

In general, a certain amount of interest does attach to temporal priority in the use of particular taxes by a given jurisdiction. It takes time to develop an efficient administration for a new tax. Therefore, a higher jurisdiction should not be cavalier in encroaching on the major tax sources of lower ones. Nevertheless, other considerations are often likely to be more significant. In the first place, as we have seen, the fact that a lower level of government may have been first in the field does not mean that it is necessarily the most efficient administrator of the tax. It may be desirable for the higher level to take over certain taxes. On the other hand, this argument must not be pushed too far, for it might leave the localities, if not the states, with few sources of revenue. The federal government is in the best situation to administer most types of taxes. Efficiency, however, can be bought at an excessive price in terms of state and local autonomy.

Second, the fact that the states, or some of the states, happened to be quicker to adopt a given tax than the federal government is likely to have been a historical accident. Merely because the public demand for some of the types of services provided by the federal government came into being subsequently to the increase in demand for those ordinarily furnished by the states and localities is no reason to handicap the national government when circumstances have changed. Moreover, a given level of government, though technically first in the field, may have made only nominal use of the tax.

In an effort to assist in the preservation of the political and fiscal autonomy of the lower levels of government the national government has in certain instances paid some attention to the fact that the states were there first. Thus as a result of the objections raised by the states after the enactment of the first permanent federal estate tax in 1916, Congress introduced the estate tax credit in 1924.[18] Moreover, the federal exemption has always been kept high so that the states could exploit the tax on moderate-sized estates. Other examples are the repeated refusal of Congress to enact a general sales tax, and the decision not to raise the federal gasoline tax to a still higher level during World War II. Such instances of abnegation on the part of the federal government are rare, however.

Examples of Separation. Although separation of sources is not feasible for all taxes, a certain amount exists despite the avid search for new sources of revenues by all levels of government during the past fifty years. Business licenses have been left very largely to the states and localities. The property tax is at present a prerogative solely of the states

---

in state and local liquor tax receipts. Although this argument received wide attention, the fact seems to be that the drop in liquor sales in 1952 was a logical corollary of the rush to stock up on liquor as a result of the outbreak of fighting in Korea. State liquor tax receipts rose to record highs in many states despite the high federal tax rate of $10.50 a gallon.

[18] As we have seen, however, the credit was not applied to the higher federal rates after 1932.

and the municipalities; indeed, some states have allotted the property tax to the localities alone. The customs are reserved to the federal government. On the other hand, the federal government, up to the present time at least, has remained outside the area of general sales taxation. It is true, however, that the broad coverage of the federal excises represents a considerable approach to a general sales tax.

The suggestion has frequently been made that the federal government might keep the personal and corporate income taxes, while leaving excise, sales, and business license taxes to the states. The localities would be given exclusive dominion over the property tax. Moreover, the states would allow the localities to share in the proceeds of their taxes, thus sparing them the task of administration.

Certain difficulties would make the desirability of the proposed course of action rather doubtful. A major count against this rigid separation of revenue sources is that the federal government would be deprived of potential instruments in the struggle for economic stability. The states could not be expected to pursue the integrated policy required in order to make effective use of sales and excise taxation for inflation control. Whereas the cure for depression calls, among other things, for a reduction in tax rates, and conversely in an inflationary boom, the financial difficulties of the states would tend to force rate rises during depression. On the other hand, if prosperous times were to give rise to budgetary surpluses, the political pressure for rate reductions would be very great.

Another possible difficulty with the proposal is that the states might not impose as heavy sales and excise taxes as the combined federal and state governments do at present. This would, of course, be regarded as an advantage by those who desire a more equal distribution of income. If, however, the level of federal spending continued to be determined by forces largely outside Congressional control, the national government would be forced to make up the difference through increased personal and corporate income tax rates. The result might be a seriously adverse effect on incentives.

Compensating Revenues. A special case for the separation of revenue sources may be made for taxes which a lower level of government is not in a position to administer efficiently. An example that is often cited is the tobacco tax, which might be restricted to the federal government. The federal tax is levied on a relatively small number of manufacturers, while state and local tobacco taxes are collected from the much more numerous wholesalers and retailers. The cost of collection of a tax requiring the affixing of revenue stamps is high, and the states and cities have not found an entirely satisfactory means of preventing evasion of the tax through over-the-border purchases by residents of jurisdictions imposing higher rates of tax. If the states and cities were to withdraw entirely from tobacco taxation, they might be given *compensating revenues* by the federal government.

This compensatory device is, however, not a popular one with the states. The amount of revenue received in compensation by the states and localities would presumably bear a relation to the taxes originally levied. If so, this would penalize those which had imposed relatively low taxes on tobacco. Again, revenue needs may change radically after the tax has been surrendered. The states are then powerless, however, to derive revenue from the tax unless the federal government is willing to increase the amount of revenues that it transfers to them.

In Australia a similar question arose out of the announced intention of the central government to make permanent its wartime pre-emption of the income tax. The problem has been met by relating national grants-in-aid to changes in the age distribution and density of the population of the states. In Canada a somewhat similar formula was adopted for the income tax and succession duties surrendered to the national government by the provinces. A major difficulty with the compensation grant is that, as time passes, it takes on more and more the appearance of a federal subsidy. It therefore tends to add its weight to the complex of grants-in-aid that undermine the fiscal independence of the states.[19]

Conclusion.   It is not to be expected that a solution to the problem of intergovernmental distribution of revenues can be found in some sort of "ideal" allocation of tax sources to each level of government. The solution must be found, on the contrary, in a combination of separate and shared revenues, coupled with an extensive system of grants-in-aid. We now turn to a discussion of these alternatives.

THE SHARED TAX

A possible solution to the allocation of revenues by governmental level is the shared tax. Under this scheme the tax is administered by one level of government, the revenues being shared with another. The administrative advantages arise out of single assessment and collection. Not only is cost of collection reduced, but compliance cost to the taxpayer is diminished as well. Against these advantages have to be set the difficulties that would face the mutually satisfactory allocation of revenues.

If the federal government did the collecting it would presumably have to evolve a formula satisfactory to all the states. But state financial requirements vary greatly and the achievement of an agreed formula would be difficult. The states, in turn, would have a similar problem with respect to the localities. The ideal time to introduce revenue sharing is when a thorough revision is being made of the entire fiscal system, as in the case of Japan and Germany after World War II. A more limited opportunity was offered in the United States on the occasion of the repeal, in 1934, of the prohibition amendment. At that time sentiment favored the administration of the liquor tax by the federal government, with the revenue

---

[19] This is true, of course, only if compensating revenues constitute a net addition to the total of grants-in-aid.

shared by the states. The plan was not adopted, however, and in the interim state and local taxation of liquor has become extremely complex. A change now would be quite difficult.

The principle of the shared tax has a greater justification when applied to one tax than if it is extended to a number of taxes. The generalization of the practice would tend to involve a loss of fiscal independence by the sharing jurisdiction. Again, since the revenue needs of two or more levels of government do not vary together over time, provision would have to be made for permitting periodic revision of the shares going to each level. This would involve a constant political struggle. The struggle would, nevertheless, be well worth the cost in terms of the preservation of independence of one level of government from another.

In conclusion, the shared tax may prove to be a useful device, particularly when the possibilities of avoidance make a tax more difficult to administer at the lower level of government. For example, a local sales tax might take the form of an addition to the state sales tax, with the state assuming responsibility for collection. This would not prevent individuals from transferring part of their purchases out of the city, unless localities in general imposed a similar tax.

THE SUPPLEMENTAL TAX

Similar to the shared tax is the supplemental tax. Here the state tax is a percentage of the federal tax. The advantage of this device is the scope it offers for administrative simplification, and the resulting saving in cost to the lower political level. An example is the state amusement tax levied by Connecticut in 1921. This tax was assessed at the rate of 50 per cent of the federal amusement tax due. Recent experience, however, does not indicate that the states find the supplemental tax a very satisfactory device. Utah adopted a provision in 1951 which allowed the taxpayer who uses the simplified form the option of paying to the state an amount equal to 10 per cent of his federal tax liability. But the provision was repealed in 1953. The New Mexico State Bureau of Revenue recommended the repeal of a similar law adopted in 1953. Inequities arose out of the variations in personal exemptions and dependency allowances between federal and state laws.

UNIFORMITY OF THE TAX BASE

One avenue toward federal-state tax coordination would be through uniformity of the tax base. The states would simply accept the federal definition of the base of the taxes in question. It is a great advantage to the taxpayer if the federal and state taxes have the same base; it would be especially helpful under the corporate and personal income taxes. Vermont's income tax has given the taxpayer the option of using the federal concept of taxable personal income (either the federal definition as of the date of adoption of the statute by Vermont in 1947, or the definition as of the present time), and some states have accepted the federal definition of corporate income. With forty-eight states, however, progress is necessarily slow. Moreover, the states have been wary of enacting legislation which accepts federal tax practice.[20]

Apart from grants from the national government, the capacity of a state to spend and provide public services is determined by its own tax system. If federal concepts of the tax base and exemptions were accepted, a change in the federal definition might force a revision of state spending decisions. Even though the states would merely be following the lead of the federal government in statute making, and would retain the power to change their tax statutes as they wished, any lags in state legislation behind changes in federal law might cause undesired changes in state tax revenues. This fact was discovered by Connecticut when, during the decade of the twenties, increases were enacted in federal income tax exemptions. In conclusion, an important reason for acceptance by the states of federal practice has been the stimulating effect on taxpayer compliance when direct reference to the federal law is made in the state's own statutes. The administration of the law, and the collection of the taxes, remains within the province of the states.

THE FEDERAL CREDIT

The federal credit for estate and inheritance taxes paid to the states has been discussed in Chapter 16.[21] It was pointed out that the credit provision makes the federal estate tax a kind of shared tax. In effect, the federal government sets the maximum amount of tax which it is prepared to return to the states. The states, in turn, ordinarily levy additional death taxes. At the same time they urge that the federal government return the entire tax to the states.

It will be recalled that the purpose of the federal credit is to prevent competition among the states for the residence of wealthy individuals. From time to time sentiment has arisen for the extension of the federal credit idea to some other taxes. Thus those states which have so far rejected the personal income tax would be encouraged to introduce one if by doing so they could share in the revenues now collected from their citizens by the federal government.

The suggestion that the credit device be extended in this fashion raises

[20] State constitutional provisions which prohibit the delegation of state taxing powers are said to be a major obstacle to the adoption by states of income tax laws making direct reference to federal income tax law. Vermont's option to taxpayers was intended to sidestep the issue of constitutionality.

[21] This device has also been used in social security taxation. A similar crediting device has been suggested by the American Municipal Association for the coordination of federal-state-local admission taxes. In some instances the *states* have used this arrangement to encourage the use of a particular tax by the localities. For example, in 1949 Florida in effect made the cigarette tax a local tax by introducing the tax credit. The cities levy a tax of 5 cents a package, which is collected by the state and returned to them.

fundamental issues with respect to the fiscal independence of the states. In the case of the estate tax credit, it was obvious to everyone that interstate competition was injuring the states themselves. When this is not the case, the use of the credit to force the states into the adoption of a tax thought to be salutary by the federal government is a very different sort of thing. While no state can entirely insulate itself from social and political progress in other states or at the national level, there is room for differences of opinion over the extent to which the federal government should accelerate the pace through such devices as the federal credit.

ADMINISTRATIVE COOPERATION

Each of the devices that have been employed or suggested for allocating tax revenues among the governmental levels suffers from specific difficulties of its own. Moreover, since each of the forty-eight states possesses freedom of action as to what it will accept and reject, a really comprehensive program is extremely difficult to develop. For this reason most of the progress toward integration in recent years has been limited to administrative cooperation. Although some progress has been made in this country, there is a discernible lag as compared with a number of other countries. In Australia, for example, the national and state income taxes have been placed under a single administration.[22] In West Germany both the Bund and the states participate in the choice of certain tax officials. Moreover, the Basic Law has a number of provisions for making administration uniform in the several states.

In the United States the progress made thus far has been most marked in the income tax field, both as between the federal government and the states, and among the states themselves. The states are allowed to inspect federal income tax returns, and through a transcript service that keeps the states up to date the latter receive the benefit of federal enforcement and audit. The single audit spares the taxpayer visits from two sets of officials. Progress is being made in the exchange of information between the states, though much remains to be done.

RECIPROCAL TAX DEDUCTIBILITY

The reciprocal deductibility of a tax imposed by two governmental jurisdictions contributes a large measure of integration to the tax system. State income taxes, for example, are deductible from income subject to the federal tax. Some, though not all, states levying income taxes permit the deduction of the federal tax from the base subject to the state tax. Deductibility not only reduces the total tax burden as well as the relative disadvantage of taxpayers in states that levy income taxes; it also avoids

---

[22] Except in one instance the national government administers the tax for the states. One state administers the income tax within its borders for itself and for the national government.

the possibility that total taxes in the higher brackets will closely approach or exceed 100 per cent of income. The deductibility of the tax paid to the state operates similarly to the federal credit under the estate and social security taxes, except that the tax is deductible from income only, rather than, as in the latter cases, from the tax itself.[23] Since the federal income tax greatly exceeds that paid to any state, mutual deductibility would cause a much more serious reduction in state revenues. Another difficulty from the point of view of the states is that any change in the federal income tax rates affects the income tax revenues due the state. Thus the same objection applies as in the case of the supplemental revenue device discussed above.

One point should be noted with respect to deductibility from the state tax base of taxes paid the federal government. Individuals who are in high-income brackets pay a large proportion of their incomes to the federal government. If deductibility is permitted, the reduction in the state tax base is correspondingly large. Therefore, in order to derive the same revenue the state would have to apply higher rates.

THE TAXATION OF ONE JURISDICTION BY ANOTHER

Another source of intergovernmental tax conflict is the taxation of one jurisdiction or its instrumentalities by another. The Constitution grants the national and state governments independent, though limited, tax powers. Conceivably if this independence were exercised vigorously enough, either the state or the national government might use the tax instrument to hamper the activities of the other.[24]

The key Supreme Court case on this matter is *McCulloch v. Maryland*.[25] In this case, Chief Justice Marshall contended that "the power to tax is the power to destroy," and thus denied the right of a state or locality

---

[23] The effect of this provision would not, of course, be great enough to lead to the universal adoption of state income taxes. The standard deduction under the federal income tax nullifies deductibility for the mass of payers of the income tax having taxable incomes below $10,000 (the limit for the standard deduction), because the taxpayer qualifies for the deduction whether or not his deductible taxes and other expenses are actually as great as the standard deduction. For incomes greater than $10,000 the imposition of a state income tax would represent a net addition to the total federal plus state income tax burden of most individuals, despite the partial offset of a lower federal income tax.

[24] One jurisdiction can tax another, of course, if it levies a tax that is certain to be largely shifted to it. For example, if coal that has paid a state severance tax is bought for heating purposes by the federal government (or by another state), the former has in effect levied a tax on the latter.

[25] 4 Wheaton 316 (1819). Maryland had enacted a tax in 1818 on the notes of all banks not chartered by the state. The issue was twofold: whether Congress had the right to incorporate a bank, and whether a state tax on the bank was constitutional. The Court stated that "the States have no power, by taxation or otherwise, to retard, impede, burden, or in any manner control, the operations of the constitutional laws enacted by Congress to carry into execution the powers vested in the general government."

to tax federal property, agents, or instrumentalities whether or not the tax is discriminatory. The concept of federal "instrumentalities" has received varying interpretation by the Court, at first in the direction of a very liberal construction, and subsequently toward a narrower definition. By extension, the lower levels of government and their instrumentalities are exempt from federal taxation. An exception to the reciprocal immunity, however, is the specific requirement that the states pay import duties as well as certain of the federal excise taxes.

The exemption of the federal government and its instrumentalities from taxation by the states and localities has in some instances produced rather absurd results. In addition, it has often severely handicapped the lower governmental jurisdictions in the exercise of their legitimate functions. Thus, up to 1940, employees of the federal government were exempt from state income taxes, and state employees were likewise exempt from the federal tax. By no stretch of the imagination can an income tax, applied to all workers alike, be construed as an instrument for the control of another level of government.

Clearly what is needed is a prohibition on *discriminatory* taxation of federal instrumentalities. Congress could pass a law permitting taxation whenever it is nondiscriminatory. Instead of doing this it has dealt with each issue separately. Thus in 1940 the favored position of federal and state employees under the income tax was eliminated. On the other hand, the interest paid on government securities is still exempt from the income taxes of other governmental jurisdictions.

Federally Owned Property. In recent years the exemption of federally owned property from state and local property taxes has been a source of increasing concern on the part of the states and cities. These often find their tax revenues inconveniently diminished whenever it suits the federal government to take possession of more land. The seriousness of this source of complaint is brought home by the fact that during World War II the federal government took over an area said to be equal in size to the whole of New England. In a number of the Western states vast areas are owned by the federal government. The importance of this problem for federal-state fiscal relations is evidenced by the fact that it was one of the three major issues discussed in the meeting between treasury personnel and representatives of state and local governments in April, 1949,[26] when the ineffectiveness of the chaotic and often inadequate methods of reimbursing state and local governments was recognized.

Considerable variation exists in the extent to which federal property contributes to the support of local governments. In some cases no pay-

---

[26] The two other issues were how to coordinate the fiscal policies of all levels of government in the interest of economic stability, and plans for reducing conflicts in taxes and administrative duplication between the Federal government and the states.

ments at all are authorized by the federal government. At the opposite extreme, Congress has permitted taxation, either completely or in part, on the same basis as private property. In the case of federal operating properties, a part of the revenues accruing to the government is paid in lieu of property taxes, and in still other cases tax-equivalent payments are voluntarily made.[27]

Criteria for Federal Payments. It is by no means easy to arrive at an equitable formula for the taxation of federal real estate. Much of the property taken over by the federal government had previously lain virtually idle, and hence paid little taxes. Again, the presence of a large government installation means new local business and increases in sales tax and other revenues. The activities pursued on some federal property are actually intended to benefit economically the area in which it is located. In these cases payments in lieu of property taxes should be correspondingly smaller.

On the other hand, the influx of new workers requires additional local services in the form of schools, road repair, and the like. An inequity that gives an undue advantage to federal workers on such property has been their exemption from state and local personal property taxes, as well as freedom from sales taxation of goods bought at post exchanges. Since this exemption is an important perquisite of the members of the armed forces, which is tacitly part of the attraction in the recruitment of volunteers, it is not likely that this provision will be substantially changed. Another point, however, is that the standard of local services provided to workers on government reservations is not always as high as that enjoyed by the local public.

► GRANTS-IN-AID

The federal grant-in-aid to the states, as well as the grant by the states to the localities, finds its justification in several ways. In the first place, the state governments, and to a greater extent the localities, as we have seen, can spend more effectively than they can tax. They know the local conditions, and thus ought to have a hand in many types of public spending that are too costly for their own tax resources. Their relatively limited capacity to administer some of the more productive taxes, however, may argue against extending their tax systems to finance the whole of the expenditures that they are entitled to administer.

Another justification for grants-in-aid is that in a geographically varied federal country, wide differences exist in the needs of different areas for public services as well as in their capacity to finance them. The func-

---

[27] *Report on Federal Contributions to States and Local Governmental Units with Respect to Federally Owned Real Estate,* House Document No. 216, 78th Cong., 1st Sess., 1943. See also *Proceedings* of the National Tax Association, 1948 Fifth Round Table, "Tax Status of Federal Government Real Estate."

tion of the grant may be, therefore, to equalize these differences in needs and the capacity to satisfy them. Complete equalization may be both impossible and unnecessary. The objective of the grant is, rather, to assure that minimum standards of public service are met in all areas.

The justification of the subsidy from the point of view of the superior jurisdiction also needs to be emphasized. It is socially desirable that certain public services be available throughout the nation or the state. A grant-in-aid is made by one governmental jurisdiction to another when they have a common interest in the performance of a particular service. Indeed, a wealthy area may actually favor grants to aid a poor area. With the development of transportation and the increasing mobility of the population, it has become more and more apparent that wealthier areas may suffer if certain types of public services are not enjoyed by poorer ones. An example is education. Workers who migrate to other areas are more efficient and likely to be better citizens if they have had a good education. The same argument holds in varying degree for other types of public service as well. A school milk or chest X-ray program is socially rewarding to the country as a whole, not merely to the locality or state whose citizens immediately benefit from it.

The grant is not always made by the superior governmental jurisdiction. In some instances the states or provinces have greater tax powers than the central government. In Germany, as we have seen, grants have been made by the states to the central government, both prior to World War I and since 1945.

HISTORICAL BACKGROUND

As we saw earlier, the federal grant of the nineteenth century differed rather fundamentally from that of today. It often took the form of the distribution of surplus revenues, or of grants of land for the purposes of opening up the continent. Although the principle of the occasional money grant was established as early as 1836, systematic annual money grants did not become a feature of federal-state fiscal relations until after the Civil War.

With the systematic grant was born the idea of the subsidy to make possible socially desirable objectives. The first such grant was made in 1879 for the education of the blind. Similar subsidies for other special purposes were added until total federal grants to the states had reached $8 million in 1914.[28] After World War I their magnitude rose rapidly until they reached $100 million by 1930. This development took place despite the avowed opposition of successive Republican administrations to a growth in federal spending.

Since the depression, federal grants to the states have risen almost

---

[28] Paul Studenski, "Federal Grants-in-Aid," *National Tax Journal,* September, 1949, pp. 194–195.

continuously. In 1951 payments to state and local governments were $2.3 billion, while "payments to individuals within states" stood at $2.6 billion, for a total of $4.9 billion. The peak figure, $5.55 billion, was reached in 1948, when payments to veterans were at their maximum. State and local revenues from the federal government have been rising steadily, having reached $2.9 billion by 1953.[29]

Because of the fact that federal subsidies take the form of payments both to governments and to individuals, a considerable amount of arbitrariness attends any estimates of federal subsidies to the states. If payments are made directly to individuals within the states (for example, to veterans, to recipients of various forms of relief, to doctors for medical services provided to those on relief, and to farmers), they are not, strictly speaking, grants-in-aid. Yet payments made directly to lower levels of government may amount to the same thing, for they may be passed on to individuals who reside within the state or locality.

For example, although direct payments to the states dropped substantially in 1935, the drop was due simply to a shift from relief programs in which the states took part to projects financed directly by the federal government.[30] During the period from 1934 to the present time, the largest federal subsidies made directly to the states and localities have been for highways, public assistance, and public health. Direct payments to individuals within states, however, were mainly for relief until World War II; for agriculture, training, war housing, and public works during the war; and thereafter for veterans, agriculture, public health, and National Guard programs.[31]

THE MATCHING GRANT

A grant-in-aid may be made in return for a similar appropriation by the level of government which receives the subsidy. By this device a part of the responsibility is left in the hands of the state or locality. The matching grant exercises a double stimulus to action. The grant itself provides funds to the jurisdiction that is to administer the spending. Again, the governmental jurisdiction that receives the grant is encouraged to furnish financial support for a service that it would presumably otherwise leave unperformed. Even if matching grants are provided only *temporarily,* the lower governmental level may be induced to initiate and continue new programs.

The matching grant bears a family relationship to the federal credit

[29] Bureau of the Census, *Historical Statistics on State and Local Government Finances, 1902–1953.*

[30] For detailed statistics of federal grants to the states, see Joint Congressional Committee on Reduction of Nonessential Federal Expenditures, *Federal Grants-in-Aid to States,* 82d Cong., 2d Sess., Senate Document No. 101, 1952, and the earlier Senate Document No. 13, March, 1947.

[31] *Ibid.,* p. 3.

under the estate and social security taxes. Both rely for their effectiveness on distaste on the part of the states at seeing funds go to other jurisdictions.[32] The advantages in terms of improving public services are clear. The reverse of the medal is, however, the weakening of local initiative and morale that is inevitable when fiscal decisions of the states and localities are conditioned by their desire to participate in federal grants.

The matching grant suffers from the defect that it takes no account of differences in the taxpaying ability of different states. A federal grant does no good if a state is so poor that it cannot levy taxes adequate to match it. Moreover, it is not an undiluted benefit to a state to alter its expenditure pattern in order to receive federal grants. When the grants are few and small, the problem is not difficult even for a poor state. As grants multiply, however, the state with limited taxable capacity has to make the decision whether to sacrifice the subsidy or to curtail some other function in order to divert revenues to match the grant. If the latter occurs, the decisions of the national government take preference over those of the state. Yet there is no presumption that the views of the central government should always prevail if the federal system of government is accepted.

Under a federal political system the states are presumed to have a better idea of the relative priority of public services within their boundaries than does the federal government. This is, of course, precisely the issue. Political balance requires that the opinions of both the central and the state governments should be given weight. The matched grant is a device that tips the balance of political power in favor of the central government, without producing the animosity that would result from more direct political methods. Therein lie its advantages and its dangers for the federal system. The disadvantages of the matched grant can be avoided, of course, by restricting its use to the more obvious cases in which the states or the localities need prodding.

THE DIFFERENTIAL GRANT

The differential grant takes account of the differences in taxable capacity of the recipients. A differential grant can also be based on their differing needs. Rather surprisingly, not much use of this type of grant has been made by the federal government. The states, however, have striven to distinguish in their subsidies among the economic capacities of the localities. The differential or equalization grant makes it unnecessary for the recipient jurisdiction to curtail important services in order to match grants

---

[32] The disadvantage of the federal credit provision under the estate tax when there are wide geographical variations in the distribution of wealth has been strongly stressed by Vickrey: "There is probably no basis for a distribution of federal grants to the states that is less likely to meet the real needs of the various states than a grant based on federal collections from succession taxes in the various states."— William Vickrey, *Agenda for Progressive Taxation* (New York: Ronald, 1947), p. 268.

for purposes favored by the higher jurisdiction. Thus there is less tendency to a distortion of their expenditures than occurs with the matching grant.

The equalization grant can be used to assure that political subdivisions possessed of varying degrees of wealth are in a position to meet minimum standards of service common to all. It should be borne in mind, however, that some areas are basically poorer in natural resources or geographical location than others. It is therefore a matter of opinion how far the fiscal system should go in trying to compensate for these differences.

Compensation through grants-in-aid retards population movement out of the less favored areas, with consequent adverse effects on national productivity. The question may fairly be asked, How far ought the central government to subsidize poor areas without at the same time having some power to redistribute population geographically? The question is not easily answered. As stated above, at least a part of the public services thus transferred from richer to poorer states indirectly benefit the former, since their immigrants from the poorer states will be healthier and better educated.

THE EQUALIZATION FORMULA

From a technical standpoint, an obstacle to the smooth operation of the equalization grant is the selection of the formula on which to base the subsidy. The problem is to take account of a sufficient number of factors so that substantive differences in the economic positions of the states are properly reflected. The selection of the formula is also determined by the objective of the program.

For example, the major objective may be to assure a minimum standard of service, while it is nevertheless held to be desirable that a higher standard be met where possible. In this case the federal government may provide most of the benefit up to the minimum, but above that contribute a smaller proportion.[33] The effect is that if a state provides a benefit in excess of the minimum, the federal government contributes a smaller proportion of the benefit, although it pays a larger number of dollars than it does to the state that provides only the minimum benefit.

There is no reason why, under a nationally sponsored program, the citizens of a wealthy state should receive greater benefits than those in a poor state. The inequity is unavoidable, however, if the federal subsidy is to have the effect of encouraging a state to provide more than the minimum relief payment. It is open to question, on the other hand, whether the federal government should concern itself with anything above the minimum if the effect is to give greater subsidies to the wealthier states.

Equalization is usually geared to per capita income payments within the state. The federal government may decide that the state should devote a certain percentage of income to a given service. It will be noted that if

---

[33] This is the type of formula used for federal grants to the states for old-age assistance.

this principle is observed, as the number of subsidized services grows, a larger and larger proportion of the states' income is dedicated to them; in many instances this takes place at the expense of other types of public service. Thus what appears to be merely a technical equalization formula proves, when all the separate programs are aggregated, to involve an important policy determination.

It is likely that once a formula has been accepted, it will tend to become more complex as account is taken of a larger number of factors indicating differences in fiscal capacity. Critics of equalization formulas have pointed out that they involve much arbitrariness and introduce excessive rigidity. The needs and taxable capacities of the states and localities may change rapidly.

Moreover, some of the elements that are included in the formula may fail to accomplish what is intended. For example, the requirement that the states devote a certain proportion of annual income to educational purposes in order to receive anything above the minimum grant makes assumptions about taxable capacity that in certain circumstances are unwarranted. The stimulus of the formula may be nil simply because the poorer state cannot qualify.

Equalization formulas, in providing for the geographical redistribution of income, also redistribute income from wealthier to poorer groups. Consequently, the same objections have been made to the use of such formulas as were formerly directed against the adoption of a progression formula under the personal income and estate taxes. It has been argued that once the principle is adopted there is no logical stopping place. In view of the many economic and fiscal forces that operate to make the distribution of income unequal, however, there is little reason to believe that this tendency is likely to become very pronounced. Nevertheless, the critics are right in arguing that a constant incentive exists to widen the extent of equalization. No matter how much equalization is effected, there always seems to be a further margin of equalization that appears desirable and attainable.

THE CONDITIONAL GRANT

Whether or not a grant must be matched, it is natural for the jurisdiction which makes the grant to tie some strings to it. In a federal country, characterized by great differences in wealth, local standards, and needs, there is a strong argument for the imposition of minimum standards of performance on the recipient of the grant. Therefore, both here and abroad, and at both the federal and the state levels, considerable use has been made of conditional grants. On the other hand, excessive specifications imposed by the federal government, for example, on the use of the proceeds of grants to the states, freeze the social programs of the latter into a mold that is likely to fail to take account of their individual needs.

A major cause of the proliferation of detailed specifications accompanying federal grants to the states has been the popularity of separate programs and piecemeal legislation. The effect of the grant for a separate program is to assure a minimum supply of each type of desired service, for example, education, roads, health, social services, and the like. When the grants for these various purposes are aggregated, however, it becomes apparent that a large amount of detailed control is exercised over the lower jurisdiction from above. But if carried too far, this is incompatible with the concept of the federal form of government.

THE UNCONDITIONAL GRANT

If the sole purpose of a grant is entirely or partially to equalize the financial resources of the states or localities, it may take the form of an unconditional grant. The cost of complete equalization would, of course, be very great. Indeed, it would probably be impossible to equalize on this scale. A more realistic approach would be merely to reduce the inequality in the resources of the states or localities; the object would be to make it possible for each unit to provide the minimum standard of each desired public service.

So long as the grant is free of all strings, however, a particular state or municipality would have scope to provide more than the minimum in some cases, and less in others. This would not, of course, satisfy fully the objectives of the subsidizing jurisdiction. Again, the lower level might even use the unconditional grant as an occasion for a reduction in taxes. There might, of course, be a good case for this, if excessively high state or local taxes were believed to be hindering economic development, and therefore limiting taxable capacity. Another aspect of the unconditional grant is the scope it offers to state and local administrators to introduce political considerations into the use of the funds. From an administrative point of view, on the other hand, the higher jurisdiction would be relieved of the task of selecting and supervising the projects of the lower.[34]

Fiscal administrators in general entertain a rather widespread dislike of the completely unconditional grant. One solution might be to retain the principle of attaching strings to grants, but making them as general as is consistent with the achievement of basic aims. As much allowance as possible should be made for regional differences in means and needs. An important step would be to consolidate the rapidly growing number of separate programs into unified grants.[35] Within each category more freedom could be allowed to the administering jurisdiction. This is the position adopted by the Hoover Commission's *Report on Federal-State Relations,* which illustrated its point with reference to health services. These have grown up piecemeal, with new categories added as public interest has been

---

[34] J. A. Maxwell, *op. cit.,* p. 407.
[35] Studenski, "Federal Grants-in-Aid," *loc. cit.,* p. 211.

aroused. The result has been that grants have been made for highly detailed purposes, whereas the wide differences in the needs of the states argue for greater discretion on the part of state health authorities.[36]

► CONCLUSION

Intergovernmental fiscal relations group themselves into two general classes. The first is the relation between coordinate jurisdictions, that is, between separate units at the same level of government. The other is the vertical relationship by level of government. In a federal political system the major problem is to maintain the political and fiscal independence of the states or provinces. A similar problem exists, of course, as between the latter and the localities. Important objectives also are the allocation of tax and spending powers so far as possible in accordance with the capacity of particular governmental jurisdictions to administer them. These latter objectives, however, may conflict with the first. For this reason state and local tax administrators often argue that the expenditure of each level of government ought to be determined by its power to tax. The alternative is the grant-in-aid, with strings attached which reduce the fiscal and political independence of the recipient.

The integration of fiscal relationships, both horizontally and vertically, must come about gradually. It cannot be superimposed from above without the sacrifice of a healthy decentralization of power. For this reason progress has been slow in the elimination of inequitable multiple taxation. Moreover, fiscal coordination is likely to remain incomplete. Dynamic economic changes make it impossible to keep abreast of the times in remedying inequities. Because the lower governmental jurisdictions are in a position to spend more effectively than they can tax, grants-in-aid from higher levels are a necessary, and increasingly important, part of public financial policy. Under a system of conditional grants-in-aid, however, the lower levels of government are not being given full scope to make use of their knowledge of local needs. The states have recognized the desirability of allowing the localities some discretion in their use of state grants. The federal government, on the other hand, has used its superior taxing powers and the grant-in-aid to induce the states to undertake federally sponsored programs. Different regions, however, have different needs, and excessive direction from superior governmental levels should be avoided.

► REFERENCES

COMMITTEE ON INTERGOVERNMENTAL FISCAL RELATIONS. *Federal, State and Local Government Fiscal Relations.* 78th Congress, 1st Session, Senate Document No. 69, 1943.

---

[36] Cf. Task Force, *Report on Public Welfare,* prepared for the Commission on Organization of the Executive Branch of the Government, January, 1949, p. 53.

COMMONWEALTH OF PENNSYLVANIA COMMISSION ON INTERGOVERNMENTAL RELATIONS. *Reports,* September, 1954, and January, 1955.

COUNCIL OF STATE GOVERNMENTS, COMMITTEE ON FEDERAL GRANTS-IN-AID. *Federal Grants in Aid.* Chicago; 1949.

HANSEN, A. H., and H. PERLOFF. *State and Local Finance in the National Economy.* New York: W. W. Norton & Company, 1944.

MAXWELL, J. A. *Federal Grants and the Business Cycle.* New York: National Bureau of Economic Research, 1952.

————. *The Fiscal Impact of Federalism in the United States.* Cambridge, Mass.: Harvard University Press, 1946.

UNITED STATES TREASURY DEPARTMENT, Tax Advisory Staff of the Secretary. *Federal-State-Local Tax Coordination,* March 7, 1952.

18 Economic Equilibrium

► PUBLIC FINANCE AND ECONOMIC STABILITY

As we have learned in courses in economic principles, public finance may either contribute to or detract from the attainment of a stable and maximum level of employment and output. On the one hand, the disincentive effects of taxes may discourage private investment or consumption spending. On the other, public spending may encourage increased spending in the private sector. In addition to the incentive effects are the purchasing-power effects. Taxes reduce income available for consumption and saving, and government spending raises income. Both taxes and public spending, therefore, may have unintended destabilizing effects on the level of national income. But they may also be consciously used as instruments for inflation control or the reduction of unemployment.

The use of fiscal policy as an instrument for the control of the level of employment implies that a decision has been made on the level at which employment and income are to be stabilized. Obviously, the employment goal is the nearest possible approach to the utilization of the entire labor force that is consistent with other economic objectives, particularly, price stability. For some types of unemployment, however, tax and public spending measures are not appropriate. Voluntary unemployment (refusal to work at the going wage) and frictional unemployment[1] (time lost in changing jobs) are matters for settlement by arbitration and by the labor exchanges. Again, unemployment caused when wage rates are high in particular firms or industries is properly rectified by dealing with the specific cause. Similarly, the unemployment suffered in a depressed industry is best cured by shifts in the geographical disposition of labor and capital, though the pains of transition may in particular instances be alleviated through tax reductions or subsidies designed to slow down the process.

---

[1] It should be added that there is a question how much employment can be regarded as frictional. Fiscal policy can reduce frictional unemployment by stimulating the demand for labor. Naturally, a point is gradually reached, however, at which the social cost of using fiscal measures to diminish this type of unemployment becomes greater than that of alternative devices, for example, the expense incurred in operating labor exchanges.

380

▶ THE OVER-ALL VS. THE SPECIFIC APPROACH
TO ECONOMIC EQUILIBRIUM

We wish to inquire into the potentialities of the fiscal instrument for economic stabilization. Two possible approaches might be used in this analysis. The first is the over-all or aggregative approach. This treats the flow of purchasing power as if it were a homogeneous aggregate, in which the incentive effects of taxes and public spending on private spending are the same regardless of the point of impact. The second is the specific approach. Here the effects of all changes in tax rates and public spending are carefully related to the point in the economy at which they occur. The aggregative approach implies that quantitatively it makes little difference at what point purchasing power is injected into, or removed from, the private sector. Therefore specific maladjustments are regarded as being of relatively minor importance in comparison with sufficiently decisive fiscal measures.

Public finance is interested in the specific as well as the over-all approach. An immense amount of discussion is constantly going on with respect to the nature of the disincentive effects of various taxes. For example, the undistributed-profits tax of 1936 provided the occasion for a widespread public discussion of the specific economic effects of this tax. Again, the impact of high corporate income tax rates is continuously debated. And probably more has been written about the economic effects of the excess-profits tax than has been written about any other tax. This interest in the specific effects of taxation should be kept in mind when examining the economics of *fiscal policy* for economic stability. The latter, in the past, at least, has been concerned primarily with the aggregative effects on income and employment of changes in the rates of public spending and taxation. In recent years, however, much progress has been made in the disaggregation of fiscal theory.

▶ THE MEANING OF FISCAL POLICY

In the hands of its early proponents, fiscal policy and fiscal theory placed emphasis on flows of purchasing power. Interest centered in over-all magnitudes, like national income, aggregate consumption, saving, and investment. It was recognized, of course, that all these magnitudes are the resultant of millions of separate economic decisions, made under widely varying circumstances. But one might emphasize either the aggregative or the specific aspects of the economic process, and fiscal theorists chose the former. This step was taken consciously. The term "fiscal policy" was used by John Maynard Keynes and his followers to draw attention to his view that the financing of central governments should not be merely the technical matter of finding the taxes that are needed to cover expenditures. Rather, the rates of public spending and taxing should be varied in order to compensate for unwanted fluctuations in private investment and consumption spending.

We are concerned, in this and the next four chapters, with fiscal policy for economic stability. The emphasis, particularly at first, will be on aggregative economics. Fiscal policy has made its major contribution in this area. At the same time, much of the future progress in fiscal theory is likely to be made by way of the disaggregation of over-all concepts that conceal important economic variables. It is natural in any science to commence with broad generalizations, and subsequently to refine and sharpen them. Therefore, the objective of the student who is interested in fiscal policy for economic stability must be to integrate his grasp of fiscal theory with his knowledge of the specific economic effects of various taxes and types of public spending.

One further point should be noted. Fiscal policy is not the only weapon at the disposal of the central government for controlling economic fluctuations. Direct controls aimed at eliminating cost-price dislocations, monopolistic restrictions, and bottlenecks may also be of great importance. Moreover, as we shall see below, when fiscal measures are used to eliminate or cancel out a particular unwanted change in private spending, they may themselves produce other maladjustments. Therefore, in practice, a good deal of art[2] must be used in deciding on the mixture of fiscal and other control policies that is counted upon to stabilize income and employment.

► EQUILIBRIUM IN THE AGGREGATIVE SENSE

So long as we are not concerned with specific maladjustments, the concept of economic equilibrium can be stated in terms of over-all flows of purchasing power and commodities. The conditions of equilibrium are met when *at the current price level* the flow of dollars to the market matches the flow of goods and services. This means that there is neither upward nor downward pressure on prices. Notice that nothing was said above about full employment. The price level may be stable even though the economy is at substantially less than full employment. Obviously, fiscal policy is interested in achieving that particular one of the many possible equalities in the rates of flow of money and goods which corresponds to full employment.

The price level is, of course, a very general concept. A stable average price level is consistent with all sorts of maladjustments that may make stability in employment and income, as well as in prices, impossible in a subsequent time period. Consequently, although equality in the flows of money and goods to market is a *necessary* condition for economic stability,

---

[2] Thus the title of Chapter 22, "The Art of Fiscal Policy."

it is not a *sufficient* condition. The difficulty of achieving this necessary condition, however, makes it worth while to discuss the nature of the money and goods flows.

THE CONCEPT OF THE CIRCULAR FLOW: ORIGIN

The analogy of the flow of money through the economic system with the flow of liquid through a closed system of pipes was noticed early in the history of economic thought. A strong impetus to thinking along these lines in economics was given by Harvey's discovery of the circulation of the blood (1616). If the blood is pumped by the heart out through the arteries and back through the veins, might not this equilibrium be similar to what happens in the economic system?

If so, it would be fruitful to think of the market place as the meeting point of two circular flows, money and commodities. A flow of money payments originates at the point where goods are produced, in return for the services of the factors of production in cooperating to produce the flow of goods and services. So long as these two flows are equated at a given price level, the system is in over-all equilibrium. Total payments to the factors of production exactly suffice to purchase total output, covering all costs including normal profits (which, it will be recalled, are part of cost of production). By studying the system in equilibrium, it might be possible to diagnose the causes of the divergences from equilibrium so familiar in a capitalistic economy.

Thus an increase in the flow of money to the market place would cause a rise in prices unless an equal increase simultaneously took place in the flow of goods. The initial impulse might originate either on the side of the money stream or on that of the goods-and-services stream, and the movement might be either upward or downward.

A disturbance of the system from a given level of real and money income is in itself neither bad nor good. For example, a rise in the money income flow (MV) might have the beneficial effect of encouraging increased output under conditions of unemployment, while under boom conditions the effect might be an undesirable rise in prices. Clearly an analysis of the causes and effects of these initiating factors should throw light on some of the reasons for booms and depressions, and might lead to the development of instruments for reducing or eliminating depressions and inflationary booms.

LIMITATIONS OF THE CONCEPT OF CIRCULAR FLOW

A limitation of this approach must be mentioned at once. An analysis that looks only at two over-all flows, one of goods and the other of money, obviously starts by ignoring everything else that may be causing an increase or a decrease in the rate of economic activity. If we were not to go beyond the over-all flows, we would always prescribe an injection of money into the economy when it was desired to increase the flow of goods or to raise prices;[3] and we would recommend a siphoning off of purchasing power into idle pools if it was desired to reduce inflationary pressure.

Yet it is clear that some other remedy might under certain circumstances be more appropriate to the difficulty. Returning to the analogy with the circulation of the blood, we can see that if a slowing down in the rate of flow is caused by a clogging of some of the capillaries or veins, the proper remedy may be to remove the obstruction rather than to increase the pressure in the system. There may be cases in which either or both of these methods would succeed. But the delicacy of the mechanism might make the use of the former much more preferable.

In the economic system, too, a reduction in the flow of purchasing power which results in lower production and reduced employment might appropriately be remedied by increasing the flow of money in the system (we shall see later that this may be difficult to achieve in practice); but an obvious alternative is to ascertain the reason for the diminution in the flow of purchasing power, and, if there is an obstruction, remove it. The latter is the so-called *micro* approach to the solution of problems of economic disequilibrium, as contrasted with the *macro* approach, which ignores specific maladjustments on the ground that they can be washed away by injections of new purchasing power or by siphoning off any excess.

The micro approach is bound to appeal to those who like to go directly to the removal of disturbing causes. The macro approach, on the other hand, is appropriate to an analysis of economic disequilibria that lays stress on the monetary aspects and flows of purchasing power rather than on distortions in the cost structure and in the relations among economic units.[4]

There is, however, more to be said for the macro approach than this. However desirable it may be to search out the precise causes of economic disequilibria, the enormous complexity of the economic system makes this impracticable in many, if not most, instances. Suppose that the cause of a fall in production is the appearance of monopoly in a segment of industry. If this monopoly can be eliminated, or if the output policies of the monopolist can be made identical with those of the competitor, the disequilibrium is eliminated directly, with a minimum of unpredictable aftereffects. But if not, the need to remedy the maladjustment may be great enough to call for the use of an injection of purchasing power to stimulate output elsewhere. This may make the maladjustment "permanent," and, conceivably, if enough maladjustments were frozen in this way, it might

---

[3] Assuming that a significant part of the additional money would have a velocity of circulation greater than zero. Nothing would be accomplished, of course, if the new money were held idle.

[4] We are not at present concerned with the further question of whether a rise in aggregate spending is better brought about through an attempt at increasing the money supply or by measures designed to increase willingness to invest and consume.

lead to a large and increasing amount of government intervention. Nevertheless, if specific causes of unemployment cannot practicably be removed by means of specific measures, the purchasing power (macro) approach may be the only route by which to avoid the social and political stress arising out of this type of unemployment.

DISAGGREGATION

The over-all approach can be made somewhat less general by dividing the stream of purchasing power and the flow of goods into two or more parts, thus taking at least a step or two in the direction of micro analysis[5] without becoming involved in the endless complexities of the economic system. It is important to stress, however, that even if a much more thoroughgoing breakdown were made than is possible in practice, we should be a long way from having a complete picture of the details of the economic process. But (to change the metaphor) if we separate out a few threads from the skein, the nature of economic relationships may become sufficiently clear to make possible an improvement in our understanding of the nature of economic disequilibrium.

The conclusion of this section is that since, in the light of present-day knowledge, it is not possible to cure economic dislocations by removing the numberless specific maladjustments from the system, it may be necessary to compromise on the easier task of studying the relationships among certain aggregative flows of purchasing power and commodities, breaking these down so far as possible in an effort to make the cure sufficiently specific to give results.

▶ THE EQUATION OF EXCHANGE AND THE CIRCULAR FLOW

Several equations have been evolved for indicating the conditions of equilibrium between the flow of goods and the flow of money. These equations have usually regarded the general price level as the balance wheel relating these two flows.

THE FISHER EQUATION

Thus in his well-known equation of exchange,

$$P = \frac{MV}{T},$$

Irving Fisher states that an increase in the flow of money (that is, MV,

---

[5] In a sense it can be argued that no amount of breakdown in the flows of commodities and money leads in the direction of micro analysis because the two approaches are fundamentally different. It is nevertheless true, as stated above, that the more attention income theorists devote to breaking up aggregative flows into their components, the greater is likely to be the extent to which they find themselves concerned with the kinds of disequilibria that are sought out by the micro theorists.

the quantity of money multiplied by the number of times a year the representative dollar is spent) relative to the number of transactions carried out with the use of money (T) causes an increase in the price level (P).

In this equation P is the *general* price level. It is the average price of all transactions during a period of time. Not only is current output included in the concept T (and therefore in P), but also exchanges of assets already produced, as well as exchanges of stocks and bonds. The term P is therefore a basket concept having little analytical value. The only justification for such an all-inclusive concept of the price level, and it is a weak one, is that by recognizing that money is actually spent for all these things, it avoids the practically impossible task of separating out the cash balances of the public held for different purposes. Therefore the Fisher equation has the virtues and the vices of all-inclusiveness.

The quantity equation is a truism; that is, the two sides of the equation are equal by definition. Transforming the equation, we have $MV = PT$. The two sides of this equation are two different ways of saying the same thing. Over a period of time, say a year, the total quantity of money (say $100 billion) is exchanged for goods and services several times. The average dollar, in other words, turns over a certain number of times a year. For example, if each dollar is spent ten times during the year, then M multiplied by V is $100 billion multiplied by 10, or $1,000 billion. This is the total flow of money reaching the market during the year. But this is identical with PT, which is the average price at which each transaction takes place, multiplied by the number of transactions. If there were one billion transactions during the year, then it follows that the average price at which each transaction took place was $1,000.

It is important to note that the quantity equation tells us nothing about what causes what. We cannot say, for example, that even if V and T do not change, a doubling of the money supply *causes* a doubling of the price level. Unless we have evidence external to the equation itself, for all we know the reverse may be true, i.e., that a doubling of the price level causes a doubling of the money supply. Thus the mere existence of formal equality between the two sides of the equation tells us nothing about the direction of causation.

THE CAMBRIDGE EQUATION

The quantity equation can be expressed in another form, which, though algebraically identical with the Fisher equation, concentrates attention on factors that are more significant for a study of the causes of economic fluctuations. The Cambridge version has been employed by British economists to emphasize the desire of the public to hold money. One way of expressing the equation is as follows:

$$M = KPT \text{ or } P = \frac{M}{KT}.$$

Here K is the reciprocal of the velocity of money, or of V in the Fisher equation. It may be defined as the proportion of a year's income (say) that the public desires to hold in the form of money.[6]

Since K equals $1/V$, the two equations are identical so long as reference is to the same price level, and so long as the same transactions are included in T of each equation. But whereas the concept V lends itself to an examination of the statistics of check clearings and to speculation over the probable rate of turnover of currency, K is designed to focus attention on changes in the attitude of the public toward liquidity. Since these changes are one form of evidence on the rate of spending (what money is not held idle is spent either on consumption or on investment goods), this approach assists in an examination of the various motives for holding money.

Both equations suffer from the practical difficulty of separating out money spent (or held) for different purposes. In other words, little knowledge is gained of the factors that make for economic disequilibrium unless the equations of exchange can be subdivided into a sufficiently large number of subsidiary equations so that all significant factors can be examined separately.[7] This is, of course, precisely the same difficulty that is experienced when the equation of exchange is expressed diagrammatically in the form of a circular flow.

THE INCOME EQUATION

For analytical purposes one difficulty with the quantity equation is that it is too inclusive. If we are interested in the relation between the flow of goods currently being produced and the flow of purchasing power directed at them in the market, we need to define T with reference to currently produced final goods and services only. We are merely concerned with the velocity of the money actually exchanged for those goods and services. Although, as stated above, it is difficult to separate out these magnitudes statistically, from a conceptual standpoint the more narrowly defined equation of exchange is superior. Defined in this way it becomes formally identical with another type of equation, namely, the *income equation*. The name most closely associated with this equation is that of the Swedish economist of the turn of the century, Knut Wicksell. This form of the equation of exchange was made explicit by Albert Aftalion (and others), who regarded the price level of currently produced producers' and

---

[6] In the Fisher equation, if the total volume of money is $25 billion, and each dollar is spent on the average four times a year, total spending during the year is $100 billion. In the Cambridge form, if total income is $100 billion and the public wishes to hold $25 billion in currency and demand deposits, then K is one fourth.

[7] Economists differ on the usefulness of the equation of exchange. To some it is a "useless façade," while to others it summarizes "an infinity of forces into major variables." Cf. Howard Ellis's review of Joseph Schumpeter's book, *Ten Great Economists*, in *Journal of Political Economy*, October, 1952, p. 435. The view of the present writer is that the equation of exchange and the circular-flow analysis are useful tools. It is not argued that they are the *only* useful tools.

consumers' goods as the quotient of the flow of money income (Y) and the flow of real goods and services (O) on which this income is spent; that is,

$$P = \frac{Y}{O}.$$

The only difference between the income equation and the Fisher equation when restricted to current output is that the latter explicitly includes the velocity of money, whereas the former lumps quantity and velocity of money together in a single income concept, Y. Ordinarily it is preferable to break down general concepts into more specific components in order to gain a clearer insight into the relative movements of the parts. But in the hands of the classical economists, velocity in the Fisher equation tended to be treated as a constant, at least as between two points fairly close in time. The result was that changes in the rate of flow of purchasing power emanating from velocity, as contrasted with those arising out of the quantity of money, were usually overlooked. If, in the equation $MV = PT$, velocity of money is regarded as fairly fixed, and if (as quantity theorists argued) transactions and velocity tend to move together, it is apparent that M and P also tend to move together. It is an easy step from this observation to the view that it is changes in the quantity of money that lead to changes (in the same direction) in the price level, and to conclude that the price level can be controlled by controlling the quantity of money through the operations of a central bank. Yet central banks have not been very successful in controlling the price level.

Experience in the depression of the thirties convinced economists that an increase in the quantity of money does not always cause a rise in prices, let alone a rise in prices proportionate to the increase in the quantity of money. To the extent that unemployed factors of production exist in the economy, the increase in the quantity of money may cause an increase in output. Therefore prices may or may not rise, depending on how many bottlenecks there are and how they happen to be distributed. Furthermore, an increase in the money supply may be counteracted by a decrease in velocity, so that neither prices nor output increases.[8] Thus, although the equation holds in a formal sense, if we concentrate our attention on the

---

[8] If the new money is spent on securities instead of on commodities, the prices of securities may rise and the rate of interest therefore be driven down. (For if a no-maturity bond is sold at $100 with a fixed yield of $5, a rise in the price of the bond to $105 means that the yield has fallen to $5/105$, or 4.75 per cent.) It has been argued that this fall in the interest rate can stimulate investment, and therefore cause a rise in the general price level. Clearly these tendencies are likely to be much too weak to justify the inference that a rise in the quantity of money will necessarily be accompanied by a proportionate rise in the price level, or, indeed, in any rise in the price level. Moreover, if the liquidity preference function is infinitely elastic, an increase in the money supply does not lower the rate of interest. All newly created money is simply held idle.

role of the quantity of money alone we find ourselves at a dead end so far as recommendations for recovery policies are concerned.

▶ THE INCOME APPROACH

Dissatisfaction with the sterility of the quantity equation led to a de-emphasis of the importance of the role of money alone, in favor of the income approach. The income equation circumvents the difficulties caused by variations in velocity by going directly to the flow of expenditures. Moreover, while avoiding overemphasis on money itself, it directs attention to the forces that affect the flow of goods and services.

If money income rises, assuming that prices and costs do not rise proportionately, output rises. Under this assumption all that is necessary is to establish the existence of a change in the level of money income in order to infer an equal change in the same direction in employment and output. Thus emphasis is placed on changes in income and expenditure as a causal factor in the economic process. In having fewer terms the income equation actually says less, explicitly, than does the quantity equation. The role of the money supply becomes subordinate. The quantity and velocity of money are explained by the flow of expenditures, rather than conversely, as contended by the quantity theory.[9]

The income equation is directly translatable into a diagrammatic model useful for demonstrating the nature of some of the forces that lead to disequilibrium in the economic system. Before proceeding to this analysis it is important to point out once more the limitation inherent in an over-all analysis of this sort.

Equality between money income (Y) and output (O) at a given price level is a prerequisite to equilibrium but does not ensure it. The income equation, like the quantity equation, is merely a truism. It conveys no information whatever about those forces in the economy that may be operating to make disequilibrium inevitable in the future. It is merely a photograph taken at an instant of time. If, as of this instant, Y and O are equal, the most that can be said is that at the moment there is nothing in the relation between the rates of flow of money and goods tending to push prices up or down. In other words, the price level is that which equates Y and O. This process is going on continually, and a change in either Y or O results in a change in the price level of current output, so that the equation holds in a formal sense at all times.

ADVANTAGE OF THE INCOME APPROACH

The particular service of the income equation lies in the fact that, like other equations, it focuses the attention of the analyst on certain forces

9 Cf. the discussion in Alvin Hansen, *Monetary Theory and Fiscal Policy* (New York: McGraw, 1949), pp. 83–85.

that are believed to be fundamental. The income approach emphasizes the importance of demand rather than money alone. *Under equilibrium conditions,* the flow of money income *is* the demand for goods and services, and a rise in the level of income means a rise in the level of the demand curves for the products of individual firms, and therefore a rise in the demand for labor.

In the hands of Wicksell the income approach performed one more service. Wicksell was interested in the economic interrelationships between two broad categories of production, namely, producers' goods and consumers' goods. He distinguished between income (i.e., demand) directed at producers' goods and that spent on consumers' goods.[10] This permitted subsequent progress toward a more refined business-cycle theory, by allowing attention to be focused on changes in the *direction* as well as the *level* of spending. Moreover, by breaking up total spending into consumer and producer spending, it made possible a closer examination of the reasons for investment decisions, and led to an analysis of the relations among costs, employment, and prices.

THE INCOME APPROACH AND INCOME THEORY

The contribution of the income equation has been the light it throws on the mechanics of cumulative movements of income and spending around an equilibrium level. It provides a useful framework for an explanation of the forces that may lead to disequilibrium, and by the same token it assists us in thinking about possible remedies. The analysis in the remainder of the present chapter makes use of this framework. The circular flows of money and goods will be analyzed, the equation of exchange will be presented in diagrammatic form, and the causes of disequilibrium will be examined in the light of the fact that the predictions of businessmen with respect to future levels of spending on consumption and investment goods are subject to error. Finally, the analysis will be illustrated with respect to the kind of disequilibrium which can arise out of a lack of balance between exports and imports, and the relation of this case to fiscal economics will be indicated.

Before proceeding to this step, however, it is necessary to emphasize the limited nature of the objective of this chapter. We are concerned solely with mechanical aspects of oscillations and their illustration by means of

---

[10] It will be noted that by making income and demand identical we ignore the possibility of hoarding by income receivers. Therefore it is clear that in the hands of the earlier income theorists the treatment of velocity was no more satisfactory than under the quantity equation. But by making a distinction between demand for consumers' goods and demand for producers' goods, the early income theorists paved the way for a recognition of the fact that savings can remain uninvested in the sense that a reduction in the demand for consumers' goods does not necessarily result in a corresponding increase in the desire to invest in inventories and equipment. In other words, a part of income may be hoarded, and therefore not be returned to the circular flow of income. When this occurs output and employment fall.

the income equation. The income equation provides no theory of the determination of the level of income. It is the latter that is the contribution of Keynes, in his *General Theory,* and involves not merely a treatment of aggregate income and demand, but also of supply and costs. Crucial aspects of income theory which are excluded from the aggregate-money-and-goods-flow analysis are such matters as liquidity preference and the rate of interest, the consumption function and the multiplier, relations between the interest rate and the marginal efficiency of investment, and the interaction of wages and other costs with prices.[11]

► THE COMPONENTS OF THE CIRCULAR FLOW

The equations of exchange can be translated into diagrammatic terms. Whenever money is spent for factors of production and goods, the process can be thought of in reverse. That is, goods and factor services are simultaneously being "spent" for money. There must be two elements in an exchange. When we speak of two over-all flows in this way, we are by implication assuming that spending by all consumers and all business firms is aggregated.

Let us assume that all production is carried on in one stage. In other words, firms sell to consumers only, not to other firms. The consumers obtain their purchasing power through their services as factors of production. They sell these services to the firms for money. The firms, in their turn, sell the finished product to the consumers. Thus we can think of two flows, going in opposite directions. The first is the flow of money, from firms to factors of production and back to the firms again. The second is the flow of "goods." The firm sells goods to the factors of production. The factors, however, do not sell goods to the firms; they sell their services. Of course, the services performed by a worker are in a sense goods. They are part of the flow of real output on which money income is spent. Under static equilibrium conditions this flow continues indefinitely, without any change in size or rate.

These two flows are illustrated in Figure 10. The ultimate purpose of production is to provide goods that can be consumed. Those who participate in the production process receive incomes which are rights to consume (or to reserve for later consumption) a share in national output. This participation may take the form of the sale of one's personal services, of the rental of a person's property, and of the loan of capital. Under

---

[11] Schumpeter, in pointing out that the use of simultaneous equations is the more rigorous way of "representing the pure logic of the economic process," nevertheless calls attention to an advantage of the use of the tableau method (circular flow diagrams). It is able to bring out the fact of sequences in the economic system that cannot be handled as well in systems of simultaneous equations.—J. A. Schumpeter, *History of Economic Analysis,* Oxford University Press, 1954, p. 243. A practical advantage in exposition, of course, is that treatment in nonmathematical form extends the range of readers.

conditions of perfect competition, and under the assumption that secular and cyclical dynamic factors are absent, these shares exhaust the national product. Otherwise there is also a fourth share, namely, economic profits (i.e., profits in excess of normal profits).

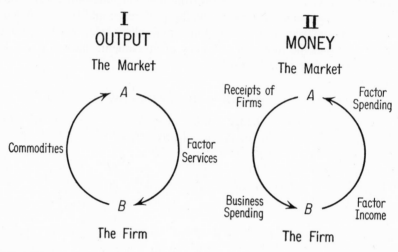

Fig. 10
THE FLOWS OF OUTPUT AND MONEY

The left-hand diagram of Figure 10 depicts the flow of factor services and commodities which are sold for money. We imagine a static closed economy (that is, a single nation economically isolated), with the factors of production selling their services to the business firms at B, and the firms in turn selling their output of goods to consumers or households at the market A. In this generalized diagram, all firms are treated as one giant firm, and all households likewise as a single unit. Since in this model the object of all production is consumption, the size of the flow of factor services is equal to that of the flow of commodities. In the absence of the institution of money, the factors would be receiving their incomes in kind, and the shares of each of the millions of contributors to total national output would add up to exact equality with the latter.

Actually, of course, we live in a money economy. Therefore, we must imagine a flow of money spending that is opposite in direction to the flow of factor services and industrial output. This is depicted in the right half of the diagram. Here we start at B, the point at which the firms remunerate the factors for their services. On receipt of their income the factors must make up their minds how to dispose of it. In the diagram as drawn it is assumed that they decide to spend the whole of it on consumers' goods. On the assumption (later to be removed) that they save nothing, factor income is equal to factor spending. Thus the same amount is spent at the market (A) on the output of the firms as was received by the factors in return for producing that output. In terms of our diagram, this is recognized to be an equilibrium situation. The firms are now in possession of income that is equal to the amount that they had previously paid out to the factors. They are therefore in a position to repeat their previous performance. Thus business spending, at B, takes the form of payments to the factors of production in return for a new batch of services.

► DIAGRAMMING THE EQUATION OF EXCHANGE

The two diagrams used above to illustrate the flow of money payments and the flow of produced goods can be consolidated into one. If this is done, we have a convenient means of diagramming the equation of exchange. In Figure 11 we are concerned with the general price level of all

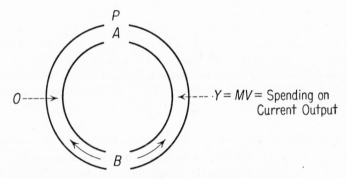

A is the market, and B is the firm.
P is the price level of *currently produced* output, established at the market.
O is the flow of goods and services from producer to market.
Y is money income, paid by the businessmen to the factors of production, which then flows to the market.

$$P = \frac{Y}{O} = \frac{MV}{O}.$$

Fig. 11
OVER-ALL EQUILIBRIUM IN THE MARKET FOR GOODS
SOLD TO HOUSEHOLDS

commodities *sold to households*.[12] No distinction is made, in this general case, among different kinds of goods, or among different factors or subfactors of production.

---

[12] The same diagram can be used to illustrate the equilibrating mechanism for the general price level of all goods, producers' as well as consumers'. In this case not only households but firms purchase the commodities sold in the market.

The substitution of the conduits of Figure 11 for the directional arrows of Figure 10 means that in the right-hand side of Figure 11 we are concentrating attention on the flow of money, and in the left-hand side, on the flow of finished goods. Thus the right-hand side is the MV of the Fisher quantity equation *as applied to current output only*. Again, it is the Y of the income equation,[13] which is defined as relating solely to current output. The reason for the substitution of pipelines for arrows is that the former provide a means of illustrating the changes in the size and rates of flow that give rise to disequilibria in the flows of output and money, and therefore in price levels and the levels of income and employment.

WHAT THE GENERAL CASE SHOWS

As we have seen, the income equation states that in equilibrium all the money paid to land, labor, capital, and entrepreneurship in connection with the production of national product flows at an even rate to the market, where it meets the stream of goods flowing at the same rate in the opposite direction. Thus we are concerned with the rate of flow of both money income and goods per unit of time, say a year. The flow of money income (Y) per unit of time, divided by the flow of real income (O) per unit of time, gives a quotient, the price level (P). If for any reason the flow of money spending increases relatively to the flow of goods,[14] an inflationary pressure arises which may take the form of a price rise, or increased output (O), or both. The price level can remain unchanged only so long as the two flows are equal. If the flow of goods changes immediately in response to a change in the rate of spending, no pressure is exerted on the price level. If the spending flow increases relatively to the flow of goods, prices must rise.

EVALUATION

Obviously this over-all diagram is of little use in explaining the causes of disequilibrium. It throws no light on reasons for changes in income, consumer spending, or output. All that it does is to focus attention on the implications of a divergence in the rates of flow of output and of spending. Nevertheless, elementary as this step is, it is an important one to take, for it provides the basis for the more sophisticated analysis that is needed in order to trace out the causes of economic disequilibrium.

The use of the income equation, and of the diagrammatic representa-

---

[13] It is also M/K of the Cambridge equation. It will be remembered that $K = 1/V$. The terms of the Cambridge equation, like those of the Fisher equation, can be defined either with respect to all transactions, or to current output only. As with the latter equation, reference here is solely to the flow of currently produced output and to the money that is spent on currently produced output.

[14] Consumer spending will increase if, for example, currency hoarded at home is released into the money stream. Again, increased bank lending to merchants, who in turn allow consumers to increase their installment purchases, will have this effect.

tion based upon it, conceals important information, and thus can easily lead to erroneous inferences. In Figure 11 it is tacitly assumed that the entire income paid to the factors of production is spent, without delay, on the very product that the factors have cooperated in producing. Moreover, it is assumed that the factors buy this output at the rate at which it comes off the production lines. In other words, income and outlay are regarded as identical. Hoarding is treated as nonexistent, and of no importance in the analysis of business fluctuations.

SAY'S LAW OF MARKETS

What this means is that "production creates its own consumption"; in other words, that there is no danger that households (i.e., factors of production) will fail to spend their entire incomes on consumption goods. If all goods were consumers' goods, and if there were no point whatever in delaying consumption, this is what would actually happen. No modern society, however, consumes the whole of its annual output. A part is saved. If the saved portion is continuously lent to businessmen, who then invest it in plant, equipment, and inventories, there is no break in the circular flow. As we shall see below, equilibrium is possible even when account is taken of the fact that part of national income is saved. The condition is merely that no savings be held idle, i.e., that they be paid out to purchase the factors of production that cooperate in the production of goods other than consumers' goods.

If it were inevitable that all savings were made available to firms and immediately paid back into the income stream we should have a condition known as Say's law of markets. Say's law insists that "we all take in each other's wash" in the sense that the incomes paid to A, B, C, and others, constitute the demand for the goods produced by D, E, F, and the rest, and conversely.[15] Malthus preceded Keynes in pointing out the fallacy in this assumption, but this fallacy cannot be appreciated so long as one relies on the over-all income equation.

DYNAMICS VS. STATICS

It has been pointed out above that an analysis of the economic system which conceives of balance as being achieved when the money flow and the goods flow are equal is merely to take a snapshot as of a moment of time. Therefore, nothing is revealed of the movement of the system either before or after this moment. We do not know whether the equation of the two flows is a coincidence or represents an equilibrium situation; and if it is the former, we do not know which stream is increasing relatively to the other.

---

[15] Thus, according to Say, "a product is no sooner created, than it, from that instant, affords a market for other products to the full extent of its own value." This is true, however, only if the factors are able to lend their savings to those who will put them back into the income stream.

Thus the analysis as represented by the various forms of the income equation, as well as the diagrams derived from them, are static, and tell us nothing of the path, through time, of the forces that affect the level of income and employment. This defect continues to apply, of course, no matter how far we go in breaking down the over-all flows into their components. It is necessary to carry the analysis further by introducing elements that will make the system dynamic.

EQUILIBRIUM AS AN ECONOMIC OBJECTIVE

One characteristic of the circular flow diagram must be re-emphasized in terms of the diagrammatic analysis. It will be noted that if Y and O are equal, with no tendency to divergence over time, the system is in equilibrium. That is, both inflationary and deflationary pressures are apparently absent (they may, of course, be simply neutralizing one another). But, as we have seen, an equilibrium situation is not always desirable.

If Y is less than the annual money income required to provide full employment, or, alternatively, if O is an annual real output insufficient to provide the desired average standard of living, disequilibrium in the upward direction of income will be preferable to a maintenance of an equilibrium situation. If steps were taken to increase O and Y up to their full-employment levels, the problem of braking the rise in real and money income as full employment was approached would, of course, have to be faced. For once full employment is approached, price rises occur which may effect an undesired redistribution of income, and may even make inevitable a subsequent crisis and depression.

In brief, analysis based on the circular flow diagram takes equality between the two flows as the standard of reference; but there is an infinite number of such possible positions of equality from zero employment and zero national income all the way up to full employment. Only one of these, the level that is as near as practicable to full employment, is the one to be taken as the goal.

► THE RELATION BETWEEN CONSUMPTION AND SAVING

The circular flow analysis, as we have seen, is concerned with income received and spent in a unit of time. Equilibrium in the receipt and spending of income requires that there be no breaks or stoppages in the circular flows. That is, money receipts must not be held idle, but must be used to buy production factors, goods, and services. In a high-saving economy a correspondingly low proportion of national income goes directly upon receipt to purchases of goods and services. Again, in an economy characterized by a high level of plant and equipment, annual depreciation charges are high. Provided savings are willingly invested, and provided depreciation charges do not exceed replacement requirements, there is no break in the circular flow. But if these conditions are not fulfilled, a downward movement may develop in the level of income and employment. In other words, gross *intended* saving may exceed gross *intended* investment. For the economy as a whole, it can happen that a decision is made to withhold a larger proportion of income from consumption than it is decided to devote to investment in plant and inventories. The resulting fall in the level of income preserves the equality between *realized* saving and *realized* investment.

By far the larger part of disposable personal income is devoted to consumption, even in a highly productive, high-savings economy like the United States. Thus in 1954, out of a disposable personal income of $253.5 billion, personal consumption expenditures were $234 billion, or about 92 per cent. In addition to personal savings of $19.5 billion, however, were undistributed profits of corporations of $8 billion. Depreciation and amortization allowances were another $12.5 billion. We conclude that despite the high proportion of personal incomes devoted to consumption in a modern industrial economy, considerable scope remains for intended investment to fall short of intended saving. The conditions under which this is likely to take place have to be examined.

THE EQUILIBRIUM CASE

In Figure 12, national income paid out by firms to the factors is divided into two flows, one representing consumption and the other savings. The consumption flow ought to be about ten times the size of the savings flow, but for illustrative purposes it will suffice merely to make this the larger of the two. Corresponding to these two flows, Cy and Sy, are the two flows (C and I) of consumers' goods and producers' or investment goods to market, where they are purchased by consumers and businessmen, respectively. In equilibrium the size of the flow of savings is the same as that of the flow of producers' (or investment) goods, and the same is true of the relation between consumer spending and the flow of consumers' goods.

Of course, workers in the consumers' goods industries do not spend their whole incomes on consumers' goods, while leaving the workers in investment goods industries to save their entire incomes. Consequently, in the lower right-hand part of the diagram the money payments of the two types of firms to the factors of production must be thought of as mingled before being separated into the savings and consumption streams. But under equilibrium conditions the effect is the same as if the consumer goods' industries and the producer goods industries paid out exactly the amount of money required to take the entire production off the market at their respective price levels. How is it that in Figure 12 the factors of production happen to divide their incomes into precisely that ratio of consumption and saving that corresponds to the output of consumers' and producers' goods?

THE DETERMINATION OF THE RATIO OF CONSUMERS' AND PRODUCERS' GOODS

The answer is that, since we are assuming that income receivers are entirely independent, in their decisions to spend and save, from the investment decisions of businessmen, the direction of causation is the other way around.[16] The proportion of national income saved depends on the saving and consumption habits of individuals, and on the policies of corporations

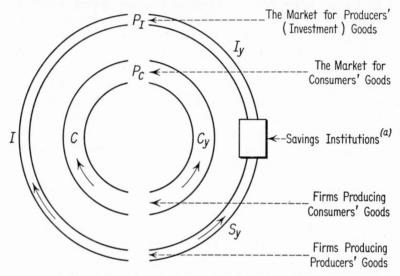

^{a} Savings institutions include the stock and bond markets, savings banks, investment banks, building and loan associations, life insurance companies, and the like.

P_I and P_C are the price levels of investment or producers' goods, and consumers' goods respectively.

I and C are the flows of producers' goods and consumers' goods.

C_y is consumption spending.

S_y is intended saving. Since in equilibrium intended saving equals intended investment, intended investment I_y is equal to S_y in the diagram, which depicts equilibrium in the flows.

In the equilibrium case, firms are producing the ratio of producers' to consumers' goods that corresponds to the ratio of factor income saved and consumed.

Fig. 12

OVER-ALL EQUILIBRIUM IN THE MARKETS FOR
CONSUMERS' AND PRODUCERS' GOODS

---

[16] Note that we are considering here only the equilibrium case. Therefore, we are not concerned with the effects of bank credit to businessmen on incomes and prices. The passivity of businessmen illustrated in the diagram is relevant only when the level of income and output remains the same period after period. In the real world, of course, business decisions do affect the ratio of consumption to saving. Indeed, investment demand in a growing and dynamic economy is probably dominant. Firms couple plans for expanded output with advertising campaigns designed to affect the savings-consumption ratio.

with respect to the proportion of profits paid out to stockholders. It is the job of the producers of consumers' and investment goods to predict both the level of national money income and the proportion that will be devoted respectively to consumers and producers' goods. Further, it is the task of the individual producer to ascertain as well as he can what part of national spending will be directed to the product of his industry, and the share of this which will come to him. Optimistic and pessimistic errors are inevitable, but provided they are quickly corrected by appropriate increases or decreases in output, no serious dislocation occurs. Cumulative errors will throw the whole system out of adjustment. In this event inflation or deflation may result.

In summary, under the assumptions of the diagram, when the level of national income is assumed constant, businessmen as a group endeavor to preserve equilibrium by adapting the ratio of the output of producers' goods and consumers' goods to the proportion of national income that the public elects to invest and consume. And so long as the equilibrium is maintained, all savings are willingly invested; therefore, in equilibrium, businessmen are dividing total production into the ratio of consumers' to producers' goods which corresponds to the proportion of national income consumed and saved.

► A DIVERGENCE BETWEEN INTENDED SAVING
AND INTENDED INVESTMENT

The potential gap between intended saving and investment is illustrated by the break in the saving-investment stream. The point at which this gap occurs may be designated the savings institutions. Very few individuals actually invest their own savings in the sense in which the term is used here. They lend them to a savings institution, which in turn acts as a market to bring lender and borrower together.[17] The latter, who is the business-man, will continue to borrow exactly the annual increment of savings at the rate they arrive at the savings institutions so long as the system remains in equilibrium.

During an upswing, however, the businessmen may wish to buy more producers' goods than can be financed out of the proportion of national savings that is available to them for borrowing.[18] With a fractional reserve banking system, like that of the United States, they can then resort to

---

[17] As stated earlier, among the savings institutions to be included are investment bankers, the stock and bond markets, savings banks, insurance companies, building and loan associations, time and demand deposit departments of commercial banks (this does not refer, of course, to the creation of new money by the commercial banks), and all other institutions that participate in the complex function of matching borrowers with the many different types of savers.

[18] Under certain circumstances a large proportion of annual savings may be borrowed by the federal government. When business is prosperous the businessman and the stock market may fear that the government is "robbing" the private sector of the economy of savings needed for investment, thus endangering the maintenance

borrowing new money on the basis of the excess reserves of the commercial banks. On the other hand, prospects may be such that businessmen do not wish to borrow the whole of the annual increment of savings available to them. In this case part of the saved portion of national income lies idle[19] in the savings institutions (and if the depression is long continued, may not even be accepted by the savings institutions from the saver, unless the latter is content with a zero rate of interest). The effect of these two sets of circumstances on the spending side of the circular flow is illustrated in Figure 13.

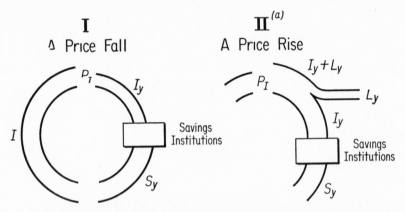

^{a} L_y is commercial bank loans to firms purchasing producers' goods.
$I_y + L_y$ is the demand for producers' goods. Bank loans to firms for increasing their purchases of the factors of production exert their effect through an increase in factor income. If factor supply is less than perfectly elastic, rates of remuneration rise, and this is reflected in the general price index. Dishoarding will have the same effect.

Fig. 13
DIVERGENCES BETWEEN INTENDED SAVING AND
INTENDED INVESTMENT

In the left half of Figure 13, a part of saving is not borrowed; the result is that unless producers of investment goods have anticipated this situation, the flow of these goods exceeds the rate of spending on them. Therefore, prices (P_I) fall, costs of production are not covered, and the

---

of the previous rate of increase in productivity. Their fears are justified, however, only if a dollar of public investment is less productive than a dollar of forgone private investment would have been. It is a separate issue if a segment of public opinion opposes an expansion of public investment even in those cases where public investment can be demonstrated to be more productive than an equal amount of private investment.

[19] From the point of view of the economy as a whole, these savings do not lie idle, but disappear. As pointed out later in the text, when intended investment falls below intended saving, income, consumption, and saving all decline, and equilibrium is not reached until intended saving and investment are equal.

normal profits required to maintain output are no longer made. Investment goods producers could reduce these losses, *at least in the first instance,* by restricting output to match the decline in spending by businessmen. If they did so, however, they would release factors of production, whose reduced incomes would mean not only lower saving in the next time period but also decreased spending on consumers' goods. This situation, which is not illustrated in the diagram, would entail reduced output in the consumers' goods industries, a further decrease in employment and incomes, and a still further reduction in spending on both consumers' goods and producers' goods. It is one of the tasks of business-cycle theory to demonstrate if and how this deflationary spiral is ultimately brought to an end. We are concerned here merely with the mechanics of changes in the relations between intended saving and intended investment.

▶ THE ROLE OF FISCAL POLICY

The possible role of the Treasury in remedying these two situations may be mentioned here, although detailed discussion of it is left to the chapters on fiscal policy. It is obvious that at least from a mechanical standpoint there is one way in which the diminished intended investment flow can be raised to equal the intended saving flow, and therefore to equal the flow of producers' goods at the current price level. If the government were either to borrow the savings, or to borrow new money from the commercial banks in an amount equal to the savings, and spend the proceeds on producers' goods, the system would again be in balance.[20]

This is, in fact, one form of fiscal policy for full employment. The federal government borrows during depression, spending the proceeds on the output of producers' goods industries. An obvious alternative would be for the government not to spend the proceeds of its borrowing on the output of the producers' goods industries (as the businessmen would have done if they had actually borrowed the savings), but to spend them on the output of consumers' goods industries, or, more likely, to put the money into the hands of the unemployed and others who will do so. If this method is used (and it is the inevitable effect of consumer subsidies or government spending directed toward the unemployed), the producers' goods industries have to be content to benefit only indirectly, as a result of orders for equipment and inventories on the part of the consumers' goods industries. During a deep depression, however, the latter may wish to hold their added incomes idle, thus not passing the purchasing power on to the producers' goods industries.

The right half of Figure 13 shows the situation when businessmen (or

---

[20] The same effect can be produced even if the additional public expenditure is covered by additional taxes. The way in which this might occur is left for later discussion.

the government) are, and remain, so optimistic as to wish to invest in an amount greater than intended saving. If the commercial banks have excess reserves, and are willing to increase their rate of lending, the demand for producers' goods rises above its previous level by the increase in the amount of lending, L. If supplies of labor and materials are available, output in the producers' goods industries will then increase (if not, prices will rise), and the increased income payments incident to the rise in employment will, in the next time period, mean that both saving and consumption are higher. The rise in saving permits a higher level of borrowing by businessmen, and the rise in consumption spreads the prosperity to the consumers' goods industries, which in turn hire more labor and buy more materials. Once this spiral is under way it continues upward until forces develop that bring about its end, and even reversal. As before, the discussion of the nature of these forces belongs in the province of business-cycle theory.

▶ DISEQUILIBRIA ARISING IN THE FLOW OF REAL OUTPUT

It must not be supposed that the only disturbing effects on economic equilibrium originate out of changes in the rate of spending. Obviously, a change in the rate of flow of goods, with the flow of spending remaining unchanged, is likewise a situation of disequilibrium. When part of national output is devoted to filling pipelines, or is directed into warehouses, incomes are paid out to the cooperating factors of production, but not the whole of the output reaches the market. Thus the goods stream (either producers' goods or consumers' goods, or both) becomes smaller than the the spending stream, and the effect is inflationary.[21] Of course, if there are much unused capacity and unemployed labor, the effect is to stimulate production rather than a rise in prices; but ordinarily some combination of both is to be expected.

AN ILLUSTRATION: INVENTORIES

During and after 1946, when a large proportion of national output had to go to fill pipelines (i.e., build up stocks at the various stages of the production process), the paying out of large amounts of income incident to the production of commodities that did not reach the market contributed to the difficulties of controlling inflation. Although the public continued to hold idle a good part of the balances accumulated during the war, the inevitable tardiness with which the new civilian output appeared on the

---

[21] An argument often made is that because investment spending gives rise to the output of a greater volume of consumers' goods, it is less inflationary than consumption spending. This is another way of saying that a high proportion of national income saved and invested enhances the rate of increase in the productivity of the economy. New investment does not, however, necessarily result immediately in a rise in the flow of goods to market to match the increased income payments and spending. During this interim, the relation between the spending stream and the goods flow is the same as it would be for a similar amount of consumption spending.

market made it difficult to keep the price situation under control. The task was made no easier by the abandonment of price controls in 1946. This was a period when the logic of events called for higher taxes. But the political situation did not permit a tax rise, the public preferring to run the risk of price inflation.

The reverse occurs when a release of goods from inventories causes a bulge in the flow of goods reaching the market. The increase in the flow of goods, not compensated for by increased factor payments, forces prices down. The so-called ever-normal granary seeks to stabilize markets by operating through variations in the flow of goods. Commodities are diverted to warehouses when demand is insufficient to allow them to be sold at given prices, and when prices rise above this point commodities are allowed to flow out of warehouses, thus adding to the current flow of goods reaching the market. The same principle is in operation when the public makes use of food lockers for leveling out seasonal fluctuations in prices of perishable foods.

ANOTHER ILLUSTRATION: IMPORTS AND EXPORTS

One more very important source of economic fluctuations arises on the goods side of the circular flow. Thus far we have operated under the assumption of a closed economy. The possibility of exports and imports has been ignored. If we relax this assumption, it appears that an excess of exports over imports (a "favorable" balance of trade) may be similar to the case where goods are diverted to stockpiles, and an excess of imports over exports is equivalent to a release from stocks.

Two cases interesting for fiscal policy may be briefly examined. One is the possibility of raising employment and prices by maintaining a favorable balance of trade. The other is the difficulties faced by countries which, during time of war, are able to export large amounts of goods at high prices, but are unable to import sufficient finished goods and raw materials to absorb the increased spending out of the high incomes of the domestic labor force at high-level employment.[22]

"Exporting" Unemployment. With respect to the first of these cases, it may appear desirable to a country to increase its export surplus in order to relieve unemployment. If, by increasing its tariff barriers (assuming that it is in a position to do this without reprisal) or depreciating its currency abroad,[23] a country can increase the ratio of exports to imports, incomes

---

[22] These two examples are, of course, on the border line between international trade and public finance. They are included for two reasons. First, they provide an exercise in the circular flow analysis which is the subject of the present chapter. Second, they are illustrations of problems, the solutions of which are to be found in fiscal policy as well as in other instruments in the hands of central governments.

[23] If the dollar is devalued in terms of other currencies, foreigners holding their own currencies can buy more dollars, and therefore more American goods. The effect is similar to a decline in prices in the United States. The *initial* effect, unless an embargo is placed on American goods, is a more favorable balance of trade. The intermediate and ultimate effects are more complex.

are paid out at home without a corresponding increase in the flow of goods reaching the domestic market.[24] As we have seen, the effect is a stimulus to output, employment, incomes, and, to some extent, prices.

The difficulty with this program is, of course, the unfavorable impression on opinion abroad. If depression is not confined to one country, the effect in other countries of a rise in the goods stream without a corresponding rise in the money income stream is a worsening of the already bad employment situation. In other words, a country pursuing this policy can justly be accused of trying to "export" unemployment.

Unfortunately, it is easy to accuse a country of striving to attain a higher level of employment at the expense of other countries even when this is not so. The mechanism is the same when the reason for the export surplus is to assist other countries to rebuild their economies after a war. Owing to the existence in Western Europe of unemployment due to lack of plant and equipment (which is an entirely different kind of unemployment from that caused by an import surplus), it was possible for opponents of American policies in the early postwar years wrongly to accuse the United States of trying to export unemployment.

So long as inflationary forces in the United States kept employment at a high level, the charge was palpably ridiculous. Moreover, countries receiving aid were grateful for assistance in rebuilding their economies. But the situation was delicate. Even a slight depression (for example, that of 1948–1949) would furnish hostile critics with ammunition for charging the United States with using its foreign-aid export surplus for bolstering employment at home. Also, the insistence for many years by important interests in the United States on an export surplus made this country politically vulnerable to the charge even when the objective had become quite different; and the experience of the great depression had made the world very sensitive to the possibility of a spread of depression originating in a large country like the United States.

An Involuntary Surplus of Exports.   The case of an involuntary surplus of exports is equally interesting. This may occur during wartime, when nonbelligerents are under pressure to export greatly increased amounts of war materials and food, and when the warring nations are unable to pay for them with an equivalent amount of goods and services. A similar situation also arises when a nation, as in the case of the United States under the Marshall Plan and other forms of foreign aid, attempts to bolster the economies of other nations.

In both these sets of circumstances, Country A with the surplus of exports ships goods abroad, and the import surplus nations B merely credit the account of the Treasury or central bank of the exporting country with an amount of the importing country's currency sufficient to pay for

---

[24] Foreigners would pay for these additional imports (i.e., exports from the country with the export surplus) out of foreign exchange holdings previously accumulated, gold, or loans and gifts from the country with the export surplus.

the import surplus. But this currency cannot be spent during the war, for the importing countries need all their resources for the war effort. Similarly, if Country B is a Marshall Plan or Point IV nation, its capacity to export only increases slowly.[25]

Thus Country A finds itself in the following inflationary situation. Even though Country B cannot immediately pay for the commodities by making available the proper amounts of its currency for spending on her goods, the exporters in Country A have to be paid or they must go out of business. Exporters need their own currency (Country A's currency) if they are to purchase another batch of goods for export in the next time period. For they must pay their labor and purchase their materials in their own (that is, A's) currency. Therefore, the central bank of Country A establishes accounts for A's exporters in their own currency. When goods are shipped abroad the exporters receive a deposit in their accounts with the central bank, and the latter accepts payment from Country B in the form of a blocked account in B's currency located in B's central bank.

From a monetary standpoint, what is happening is that the central bank in Country A is creating new money to be placed at the disposal of A's exporters. This is inflationary, for the money should come from the income stream in A; but the only way it can be prevented is to reduce or eliminate the export surplus. In a global war a neutral might find it difficult to impose an embargo on exports and still stay neutral. Again, in the circumstances obtaining after 1945, a country like the United States cannot refuse to send vast quantities of goods abroad even though they are not paid for with commodities.

The Solution.   The only way, so long as imports cannot be increased, for Country A to alleviate inflationary pressure is to reduce domestic spending. In terms of the circular flow, since goods are flowing out of the economy, an equivalent amount of spending must be diverted away from the domestic market. Ordinarily, if a country were to do this, however, the effect would be to retard the rise in prices and thus slow down the desired decline in the export surplus. Under present assumptions, foreign demand for goods is completely inelastic, so that even if prices were rising the external demand for A's products would not decline.

In the war case, for example, regardless of what happens to A's price level, the belligerent country must have the goods, the effect simply being

---

[25] During World War II among the nations that were in the position of having to combat domestic inflation for this reason were Switzerland; India; Egypt, and other nations of the Near and Middle East; Argentina, and other Latin-American countries. Stockpiling by the United States before and after the beginning of the Korean conflict created similar prosperity in the countries able to supply strategic materials. Thus in 1950, Malaya experienced very high domestic money incomes owing to the great increase in sales of rubber, coupled with sharply rising prices; but since other nations were not able to sell equivalent values of goods needed by Malaya, these high incomes proved to be an unstabilizing influence in her economy. The political dangers inherent in this situation for a country with high money incomes and insufficient goods to satisfy the increased spending ability of the workers are apparent.

a more rapid increase in the amounts of B's currency deposited (i.e., blocked) in B's central bank to the credit of A's central bank. This is what caused the immense rise in blocked sterling accounts during World War II. Of course, B's debt to A rises more rapidly when A's prices rise, but at the time there is no effect on the ratio of exports to imports in the trading countries. Therefore, in order to minimize inflation, Country A can curtail domestic purchasing power without any fear that slowing down the rise in her price level will retard the restoration of a balance of exports and imports.[26]

The Role of Public Finance.   One way to accomplish this curtailment of spending in Country A is through heavier taxes on domestic incomes and consumption. In effect, what this means is that A's citizens are forced to curtail their consumption in order that goods may be released for export. The political difficulties facing a policy of this kind, particularly when the bulk of the population may now have high money incomes for the first time, are obvious. The reason for the inflation is likely to be quite clearly the export surplus, and it may prove difficult to convince the public that money incomes or spending should be held down to correspond to the limited flow of goods and services available to the domestic consumer in view of the export surplus.

It is important to remember that the problem is made the more difficult because the high money incomes in Country A are likely to be widely distributed among the income brackets because high levels of employment may favor high wage rates. Consequently, labor is likely to succeed in actually raising its living standards despite the fact that for the country as a whole no more goods are available than before, and in fact, total real income may have to decline. For example, one effect of the high war demand for Argentine goods was to strengthen the political power of labor. Among the appeals by the government for labor support was encouragement to the urban worker to consume more beef. Thus less Argentine beef was available for export.

▶ EVALUATION OF THE ANALYSIS THUS FAR

We have attempted to translate the equation of exchange into terms of flows of purchasing power and of goods and services. The income equation can be diagrammed so as to illustrate these flows. Disequilibria can arise as a result of changes in the size or rate of both of these flows.

---

[26] Whether or not the exporting country can do this in practice is quite another thing. Wartime neutrals and other exporting nations do not like to force a reduction in living standards in order to increase the export of war goods. Moreover, the neutrals that produce raw materials often do not have an up-to-date tax system or monetary controls. Again, some inflation is inevitable at high levels of employment. Thus, inflation in India (not a neutral, of course) and other countries inflated the blocked sterling balances, and thus further complicated Britain's exchange difficulties after the war.

The analysis thus far, however, has been couched in very general terms. We have taken merely the first step in disaggregating the flows. A distinction has been made between consumption and investment spending, and a parallel distinction has been made between the flow of consumers' goods and that of producers' goods.

► THE MULTIPLICITY OF THE STAGES OF PRODUCTION

Serious disequilibria can occur in the economic system that are concealed in a purely general analysis. The breakdown of the economic process into two stages, namely, producers' goods and consumers' goods, though still a vast oversimplification, does perform the function of directing attention toward sources of disequilibrium which can be fully understood only by a further breakdown.

There are, of course, many stages of production from the raw-material stage to that at which the final product is sold to the consumer. At each step value is added to the product, and payments are made to the factors of production which have cooperated at that stage. Under perfectly competitive stationary conditions, the existence of many stages of production is no source of disequilibrium. The flows of money and commodities have adapted themselves to the economic structure. Disequilibria appear, however, when account is taken of the existence of changes in the levels of output, income, spending, and prices. Disequilibria are also caused by changes in the number of production stages.

THE NATURE OF THE DISEQUILIBRIA

The disequilibria that arise out of the multiplicity of production stages may be summarized in terms of the failure of the flows of purchasing power and output to match at the various stages. Wherever they diverge, pressure is put on prices at that stage to rise or fall. Adjustments must be made in output and in the payments of incomes to factors. The salient characteristics of the reaction are observable in the simple distinction between producers' and consumers' goods industries. Thus greater cyclical swings in output occur in the producers' goods industries than in the consumers' goods industries. This sort of evidence indicates the need to go still further in taking account of the existence of multiple stages of production. For example, the reaction of the production of durable consumers' goods to changes in income and spending will differ from that of the output of nondurables. If the breakdown is carried far enough, this approach tends to merge with the micro approach to the study of economic fluctuations.

THE ABSORPTION OF MONEY AT EACH STAGE

Distortions in the relation between prices and costs, and in directions and rates of spending, at the various stages of production may be cumulative. They do not necessarily cancel one another out. Therefore, an analysis is likely to be rewarding which examines the nature of these effects on the flows of commodities and of money, and consequently on prices, output, investment incentives, and employment. Much thought has been devoted by economists both to the nature of the demand for money at different stages of production, and to the leads and lags which may result in a lack of synchronization between the goods flow and the money flow. The inferences drawn from theoretical and factual studies are of importance for the control policies of the central government, and therefore for fiscal policy.

If the number of stages at which goods exchange for money is increased, the demand for money for precautionary and transactions purposes must rise. There are simply more business firms now holding money idle in checking accounts pending the drawing of checks. Unless the monetary authority responds by playing its part in the creation of additional money, upward pressure on interest rates will tend to cause the flow of money spending to shrink. This is deflationary. The phenomenon would not be important, of course, in the short run. It is only *changes* in the number of stages or in checking habits that are of significance. An increase in precautionary balances has the same quantitative effect on the money stream as does an increase in balances due to hoarding. On the other hand, the psychological effects on others are obviously far less.

Other possible reasons exist for the immobilization of purchasing power at earlier stages of production, with resulting deflationary effects on the economy. During the twenties economists with an underconsumptionist approach to the causes of economic fluctuations thought they saw a technical reason why money failed to flow to consumers' goods markets as rapidly as the commodities arrived there. Money was said to flow "twice into production and only once into consumption."[27] Another view was that intense stock market activity locked up funds that would otherwise have been used to buy goods and services.

A more modern version of the same approach is the doubt that is entertained by some economists with respect to the advisability of the direct investment of undistributed profits by corporations. It is feared that output capacity may thereby outrun the capacity of consumers to purchase the product of industry. Pay out more in dividends, it is argued, and the chances of economic balance are improved. Alternatively, new money may need to be created, and put at the disposal of consumers. We are not concerned here to evaluate these arguments. They are indicated simply to emphasize the importance of taking account of the role of multiple production stages in absorbing purchasing power.

Another factor which under dynamic cyclical or secular conditions affects the rate of spending of cash balances is the phenomenon of leads

---

[27] Cf. W. T. Foster and W. Catchings, *Profits* (Boston: Houghton, 1925).

and lags. There are many reasons why the recipient of cash may either delay or hasten the rate at which he returns it to the income stream. The greater the number of stages of production, the greater the possibility that these leads and lags may be quantitatively important, and that they may give rise to cumulative effects. A lag in spending exerts the same quantitative effect on velocity of circulation as does a determination to hoard. Therefore, there may be no statistical differentiation possible between the two cases, although in terms of expectations and the determination to spend or not spend, the differences may be very great.

► CONCLUSION

In this chapter we have taken the first step toward the location of the role of fiscal policy in the maintenance of economic equilibrium. The fiscal approach derives from the emphasis placed on the strategic role of money income and spending in economic dynamics. Therefore, fiscal policy and monetary policy are at once rivals and partners in the task of maintaining economic stability. In the next chapter the nature of their relationship will be worked out.

► REFERENCES

See references for Chapter 19.

19 Monetary and Fiscal Approaches to Economic Stability

► THE CHANGING EMPHASIS

The events of the nineteen thirties turned the attention of economists from monetary to fiscal policy as the major instrument at the disposal of the control authorities for stabilizing economic conditions. The purpose of this chapter is to analyze the reasons for this change of opinion, and to attempt an evaluation of the extent to which monetary policy still finds a place, along with fiscal and other measures, in the armory of weapons for combating inflation and depression. As a preface to this discussion it is desirable to fix upon a definition of money.

► WHAT IS "MONEY"?

Money is ordinarily taken to consist of the volume of adjusted demand deposits (i.e., checking accounts) plus currency in circulation. As of January, 1954, adjusted demand deposits accounted for $102 billion out of a total of currency plus demand deposits of $129 billion, or 79 per cent. If time deposits, which are not subject to check, but which can be quickly converted into either demand deposits or hand-to-hand currency, are regarded as a form of money,[1] the relative importance of demand deposits would at first sight appear to be much less. With time deposits at the above date standing at $70.5 billion, demand deposits adjusted comprised 51 per cent of total deposits and currency. It must be remembered, however, that the rate at which time deposits are converted into deposits subject to check is ordinarily much lower than the velocity of circulation of demand deposits. It is sometimes useful to distinguish between the

---

[1] Since time deposits must be converted into demand deposits or cash in order to be spent, it is not suggested that time deposits should be regarded as money. Nevertheless the concept "total deposits adjusted plus currency in circulation" includes time deposits, and in some contexts is taken to be the measure of the money supply.

supply of money, which refers to both quantity and rate of turnover, and the *quantity* of money alone, although in ordinary parlance "supply" is used to mean quantity alone.

TIME DEPOSITS

The fact that time deposits may or may not be treated as money exposes an important ambiguity in the concept of money. Under the narrow definition, which, as we have seen, includes only hand-to-hand currency and demand deposits, the concept of money is restricted to those forms of purchasing power that can be spent *directly*. Time deposits cannot be spent directly. Since they cannot be checked against, they must be converted either to checking deposits or to currency before they can be regarded as money in the narrow sense. Once this is done, however, they no longer exist; in their place has appeared either demand deposits or currency. Yet to exclude time deposits from the concept of money obscures a very important fact. Over $70 billion of *potential* or "near" money exists which, *if the public so desired,* could almost at once be converted into money. Therefore the narrow definition fails to take account of an element of instability and unpredictability in the quantity of money that under certain circumstances might be of major importance in the maintenance of economic stability.

Once time deposits are admitted as potential money, it immediately becomes apparent that still other types of assets can be converted into demand deposits or hand-to-hand currency. Examples are short- and long-term government securities, as well as other forms of debt obligations. These vary, of course, in liquidity; and the less liquid they are, the more remote is their resemblance to money. The line between money and not money is not always sharply defined.[2]

OTHER FORMS OF NEAR MONEY

Nonmonetary assets that can be easily converted into demand deposits or cash are called "near money." Since these assets confer liquidity on the holder, they are regarded as the equivalent of money. If they are to be considered a perfect equivalent of money, the holder must be able to convert them into money immediately, and without any loss in their face value. Assets in the form of plant, equipment, and inventories would not qualify as money under the most liberal definition. Stocks, though quite a different species of asset from real capital, fluctuate too greatly in price to be regarded as near money. Government securities, however, can easily be converted into money, and therefore may constitute part of the potential

---

[2] It must be noted that the possession of assets, both liquid and nonliquid, can affect the rate at which money is spent. (For an important contribution to recent thinking on the role of financial assets, see J. G. Gurley and E. S. Shaw, "Financial Aspects of Economic Development," *American Economic Review,* September, 1955, especially page 527.)

money supply. They *will* do so provided that the banking system stands ready to purchase any that the market will not absorb at prevailing prices.

Except under extremely abnormal circumstances no very large proportion of total government securities outstanding is resold during any reasonably short period of time. Large amount of securities are owned by institutions which can be counted upon to continue to hold them. For example, as of December, 1954, United States government investment accounts held $49.5 billion, and insurance companies another $15 billion. The federal reserve banks accounted for $25 billion.[3] Holdings by individuals, corporations, and commercial banks, however, are less firmly lodged. Changes in interest rates, investment opportunities, or in the price level of consumers' goods might result at any time in the release of substantial amounts of these securities into the market in return for cash. Indeed, this process goes on constantly, but it does not lead to an increase in the quantity of money if the bonds are bought by private individuals and firms. The money held by the latter is merely put into the hands of the individual or firm that wishes to exchange a bond for cash. Under what circumstances, then, are these securities likely to be exchanged for *new* purchasing power, and thus cause a rise in the quantity of money?

MONETIZATION OF DEBT

Near money (for example, a government bond) is converted into spendable money (M in the quantity equation) when the seller of the security is paid with newly created money rather than with money that was previously in the hands of another individual. This process, known as debt monetization, occurs when the security is sold to a bank rather than to an individual. The bank purchases the security by drawing on its excess reserves.

When the bank purchases the security, it credits the seller of the bond with a demand deposit, against which he may draw a check. Thus the bank's earning assets have increased by the value of the security (say $100), and its liability to the seller of the bond has increased by the same amount. Against this new demand deposit liability the bank must hold a required reserve (say 20 per cent). Therefore the bank's excess reserves decline by $20, while its required reserves increase by $20.[4]

Assume that the seller of the bond now draws a check to the amount of his new deposit. With the disappearance of the deposit, the $20 of required reserves is released to be added to $80 of excess reserves, so that the check is covered when it clears at the local federal reserve bank. The net result of the entire operation is, so far as this bank is concerned, that excess reserves have declined by $100, while another asset, government securities, has risen by the same amount. Its deposits remain unchanged.

---

[3] *Treasury Bulletin.*

[4] Shifts between required and excess reserves do not, of course, involve any change in the total assets of the bank, but only in the earmarking of reserves.

Step 1. Bank A purchases a government bond, crediting the seller with a demand deposit.

Assets		*Liabilities*	
Government securities	+100	Demand deposits	+100
Required reserves	+ 20		
Excess reserves	− 20		

Step 2. The seller of the bond draws a check in the amount of his deposit in favor of a depositor of another bank.

Required reserves	− 20	Demand deposits	−100
Excess reserves	− 80		

Net change in balance sheet:

Government securities	+100
Excess reserves	−100

We have now to consider the monetary effects throughout the banking system as a whole.

If the seller of the security withdraws his deposit in the form of currency, the quantity of money has increased by $100, and that is the end of the matter so long as this currency is not returned to a commercial bank. The government security bought by the bank has been "monetized"; it is being held by a bank, and the latter has paid for it by putting into circulation $100 of new money. In place of $100 of excess reserves, which are not money, there is now circulating in the economic system $100 of money that previously did not exist.

On the other hand, if the seller of the security checked on his new deposit to pay a bill, a depositor in Bank B would receive an additional deposit of $100, and matching this new liability of Bank B would be an equal addition to its assets in the form of excess plus required reserves. If reserve requirements against demand deposits are 20 per cent, this leaves Bank B with $80 which can either be lent out or used to buy more securities. Provided that all banks lend out or buy securities with their additional reserves, this process can go on indefinitely throughout the banking system. Thus potentially the new demand deposits created by Bank A, when it bought the original security with additional reserves, R, can become $500 throughout the banking system as a whole. The formula, applicable only if each bank makes available the whole of its additional reserves, is as follows if r is the 20 per cent reserve requirement, and $\triangle D$ the new deposits:

$$\triangle D = R \left[1 + (1 - r) + (1 - r)^2 + (1 - r)^3 + \cdots (1 - r)^n\right].$$

This can be reduced to

$$\triangle D = R \left(\frac{1}{r}\right);$$

or, in the example given,

$$\triangle D = \$100 \left(\frac{1}{0.20}\right) = \$500.$$

► MONEY AND ECONOMIC STABILITY

Changes in the quantity of money may affect the relationship between the rate of aggregate spending and the rate of flow of goods and services. Thus the quantity of money may be deficient in relation to the demand for it, so that there is pressure for a rising rate of interest. Given the marginal efficiency of capital, investment spending will tend to decline. If the money supply is perfectly elastic, on the other hand, there is no tendency toward rising interest rates. In a deposit-using economy a perfectly elastic money supply means that a sufficient amount of debt is monetized so that interest rates are held down. This can occur if the banking system is in possession of adequate reserves so that, if it is willing to do so, it can freely purchase all newly issued government securities or eligible private debt. In this case, the prices of debt obligations do not tend to fall, and therefore the interest rate does not rise.

If a rise in the volume of demand deposits (quantity of money) has occurred concurrently with a rise in output, the rise in aggregate spending may have been matched by a corresponding rise in the flow of goods to market. In this case, output and the quantity of money have increased equally (velocity assumed constant), and no price inflation has taken place. (During the forced-draft circumstances of war spending, output does not usually rise as fast as spending, and price rises do occur.) We cannot be sure that the rate of checking against these new deposits will not suddenly rise, putting upward pressure on the price level. Thus, as World War II drew to a close, it was feared by the control authorities that the public would take advantage of the vast rise in checking accounts to try to rush into durable goods faster than they would become available. To some observers the situation seemed to call for a reversal of the original action of the monetary authorities that had created the new deposits. That is, *sales* of government securities by the reserve banks in the open market would force the purchasers to draw down their checking accounts. This would have depleted member-bank reserves, and a deflationary upward movement of interest rates would have resulted. As it turned out, the public realized the futility of trying to draw checks for goods that did not yet exist, and the feared inflation did not materialize.

Two aspects of the above relation of the quantity of money to economic stability should be noted. (1) It is the reserve bank purchases of government securities that have tended to force down the rate of interest. Reserve bank purchases of securities make excess reserves available to the commercial banks. (2) The rise in the volume of demand deposits (money) incident to the rise in dollar national income may or may not exert an impact on the price level. On the one hand, the public may compensate for the rise in checking deposits by reducing its rate of checking, so that the additional demand deposits have no effect either on the prices of commodities or, through purchases of debt obligations, on the interest rate. But the existence of these highly liquid savings may at any time prompt a higher level of individual and business spending. To the extent that ownership of demand deposits causes the public to spend at a higher rate than it would spend on the basis of ownership of a corresponding amount of less liquid savings, the existence of the demand deposits will have an inflationary effect on spending and, under conditions of inelastic supply of goods, on the price level. But the connection between the rise in the money supply itself and the rate of consumption and investment is tenuous. Account must be taken of the factors influencing velocity of circulation.

In certain circumstances unwanted fluctuations in real income and employment can be reduced or eliminated through counteracting monetary policy. The monetary authority may wish to bring about a reduction in the reserves of the banks in order to reduce their power to lend and thus force a rise in the interest rate. During a depression it will want to facilitate bank lending, so that firms on the margin between investing or not investing will be stimulated to do so by virtue of lower interest rates. It is generally agreed that the second of these is much the more difficult to accomplish through monetary policy alone.

► LIMITATIONS OF MONETARY POLICY

Obviously there are potential gaps in the chain of events on which the monetary authorities must depend when attempting to increase or reduce the flow of money income in the interest of economic stability. Even if success is attained in augmenting the quantity of money during depression, and if the new money is not held idle, it may not be spent on commodities, but may go to the purchase of intangible assets, tending to raise their prices, and driving down the interest rates of certain types of securities. But the decline in interest rates may not be sufficient, or properly distributed, to encourage businessmen to undertake new investment. The trick is to force the new money into the income stream, not merely into the market for capital assets.

There are, however, other difficulties as well. The banking system is able to exercise influence only on the quantity of money. It cannot directly affect the rate of spending. It is true that the Federal Reserve System might be able, under certain circumstances, to stimulate a change in the velocity of circulation of money by threatening a radical change in monetary policy. The reaction of the public, however, would be impossible to estimate in advance, and except in very unusual circumstances control of the rate of spending therefore lies outside the power of the banking authorities.

If new money is created during a depression in the hope that it will enter the income stream at a velocity equal to that of the average dollar already circulating, this hope may be disappointed because the new money may stop circulating after, say, one spending. Whenever a dollar gets into the hands of a person who prefers liquidity to spending, its velocity of circulation drops to zero. Conversely, if in order to check a boom the reserve authorities sell government securities and raise the rediscount rate, and do succeed in reducing the volume of demand deposits, the effectiveness of the program may be limited because the velocity of money still remaining in circulation may increase. Indeed, increasing monetary use may be made of various forms of near money, thus reducing the braking effect of a tighter federal reserve policy.[5]

If the control of money income is the key to control over output and employment, and if banking policy can exercise a significant influence over the level of money income, monetary policy offers a positive weapon for attacking depression and inflation. It is then not relegated to the merely passive role of providing the appropriate framework for other instruments of economic control. Many economists contend, however, that a further step must be taken. In the depression case, assurance must be provided that the new money will be spent. This assurance is forthcoming if the new money is created in favor of the Treasury, which proceeds to spend it on public works or relief projects. Again, a tight monetary policy may not be sufficient to arrest a boom, and added effects can be obtained through budgetary surpluses, the proceeds of which are held in the form of idle cash. In other words, it is argued that monetary policy has to be supplemented by fiscal policy.[6] Fiscal policy is discussed in subsequent chapters. In the present chapter we are concerned with the scope of monetary policy.

► THE INCOME VS. THE PRICE RIGIDITY APPROACH

Both the advocates of a positive role for monetary policy, and those who believe that the authorities must go a step further and control MV by authorizing the necessary amount of government taxing and spending, reject the view held by some economists that cyclical fluctuations are

---

[5] This is not to say that if the Federal Reserve System uses all the weapons at its disposal it cannot reduce MV as well as merely M. If reserve requirements are increased, or banks are forced to hold a reserve of government securities in addition to their regularly required reserves, any given reduction can be forced in commercial loans. Therefore, an increase in the use of near money can be offset. But these stronger weapons are not always appropriate to the delicate task of controlling the flow of money income in the economy.

[6] Fiscal policy also includes the creation of deficits and surpluses through changes in tax rates, with the level of government spending held constant. This form of fiscal policy may fail to produce a rise in spending during a depression, for the forgone taxes may be simply hoarded.

solely the product of distortions in relative price and output arising out of varying degrees of price rigidity and monopoly power. Although these monetary and fiscal economists admit the existence of distortions, they do not assign them major causal significance, but regard them mainly as effects of economic change. Even though opponents of their position might demonstrate that on occasion price rigidities do actually contribute to instability, monetary and fiscal theorists feel that too much flexibility in the short run, at least, might be as likely to produce greater fluctuations as greater stability.[7] Moreover, they believe that distortions in relative prices can be made comparatively unimportant if a sufficient increase is brought about in the level of money income. They point out that, given an adequate incentive to a high rate of public spending, there is no difficulty in maintaining money income at the level corresponding to full employment. This occurs during a period of war or military preparedness; the trick is to achieve similar results during periods of peace. Conversely, any serious inflationary pressures can be obviated by an appropriate tax policy.

Thus monetary and fiscal theorists agree that the proper avenue for approaching economic stability is through the control of the rate of spending rather than through a direct attack on rigidities and price distortions. But here their agreement ceases. The basis of the disagreement, as we have seen, arises out of their differing interpretations of the impact of monetary measures on spending, particularly during the period of a deep depression before a preponderance of opinion foresees an upswing in business prospects.

THE CLASSICAL VIEW

The classical theory of employment attributed deviations from full employment to distortions in relative prices. As we shall see, however, stress was laid on one particular price, namely, wage rates. Changes in the price of labor in relation to its productivity were regarded as the major cause of cyclical fluctuations. The classical economists, however, thought there was a mechanism inherent in the economic process that would prevent these fluctuations from being of long duration, or of great amplitude. If this view were correct it would mean that, provided the money supply was kept appropriate to the volume of transactions at a given price level, no reason would exist for any degree of unemployment in excess of that caused by frictional lags in adjustment to dynamic changes. Moreover, the major friction was considered to be the failure of wage rates to adapt themselves quickly to changes in the marginal productivity of labor. It will be noted that the classical approach did not

---

[7] See Alvin Hansen, *Fiscal Policy and Business Cycles* (New York: Norton, 1941), Chap. XV, "Price Flexibility and Full Employment of Resources," and Henry Simons's criticism of Hansen's position in *Economic Policy for a Free Society* (Chicago: University of Chicago Press, 1948), Chap. VIII, "Hansen on Fiscal Policy."

feel the need for a *theory* to explain the causes of persistent unemployment. Persistent unemployment was thought to be due to the failure of wages to adjust to the marginal product of labor at full employment.

Under the assumptions of the classical theory, equilibrium exists when the rate of return paid to a productive agent is equal to its marginal product.[8] The addition of successive units of a variable factor (say labor) to a fixed amount of another factor (land or capital) results at first in an addition to output more than in proportion to the additional variable factor employed. After a time, however, diminishing returns set in; that is, the additions to total product, though still positive, become successively smaller. Under the theory of equilibrium of the individual firm, it will pay the businessman to continue to add to his labor force until the net addition to total product, expressed in dollar terms, is just equal to the addition to the wage bill. Short of this point it will pay him to increase his labor force, because each additional worker returns more than the wage that he must be paid. Beyond this point the marginal product begins to fall short of the wage. If the wage is independent of the amount of labor hired (as will be the case with a firm operating under perfect competition in factor markets), the marginal wage cost is constant.

THE CLASSICAL EQUILIBRIUM

Assuming perfect competition, the foregoing analysis for the firm can be applied to the economy as a whole to indicate the equilibrium conditions for total employment. Figure 14 is drawn to show the relation between a real wage rate that is fixed irrespective of the level of output, and the marginal physical productivity of labor. Since real wage rates are regarded as fixed, the wage line is horizontal. But marginal product declines throughout the relevant range of output $OQ - OQ_1$, because the total amount of capital is assumed to be fixed, so that at some point diminishing physical returns set in.

Under the assumptions of the classical theory, the major reason for unemployment is the existence of a real wage rate that is greater than the marginal physical product of labor at full employment. Thus in Figure 14, Q_1P_1 is the real wage rate that is equal to the marginal physical product of labor at full employment, OQ_1.[9] If the physical product of labor is equal

---

[8] The marginal product must, of course, be expressed in money terms. If competition is not perfect, the demand curve facing the firm slopes downward. Therefore, marginal value product declines more rapidly as output is increased than does marginal physical product. This is the general case, reflecting the prevalence of market imperfections. Under conditions of perfect competition the horizontal demand curve facing the firm means that as output is increased, changes in the value of the marginal product are due to changes in the marginal physical product only.

[9] There are several definitions of full employment. It may be taken here as meaning a situation in which all those desiring to work at the current wage are employed.

to the real wage rate at point P_1, any demand for a wage higher than Q_1P_1 must result in unemployment.

If the real wage rate is QP, it exceeds the marginal physical product at full employment, and employment declines to OQ. But this is not a

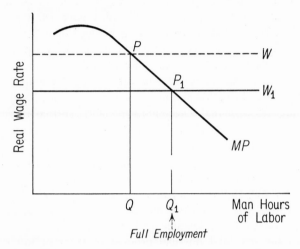

Fig. 14
THE CLASSICAL EQUILIBRIUM CASE

position of equilibrium. The unemployed, QQ_1, will not be content to remain idle merely to assure a real wage rate in excess of marginal physical product to those fortunate enough to remain employed. The "reserve army" (to use the Marxian term) will offer itself at lower wage rates until employment is driven back up to QQ_1, and the real wage rate back down to Q_1P_1.

It will be noted that the concept of the reserve army is not inconsistent with the possibility of unionization. Unions might permit some workers to remain unemployed in order that the marginal productivity of those remaining on the job would be driven up to the desired higher wage, QP. Classical equilibrium does, in fact, assume perfect competition in the labor market. Thus unemployment due to monopoly practices of labor would not be inconsistent with the classical view that the economic system tends to full employment.

Conversely, if the real wage rate were to drop below the marginal physical productivity of labor, competition by firms to take advantage of this bargain would drive the real wage rate back up to equality with the marginal physical product of labor. Thus the classical economist believed that a mechanism exists which, except for the frictions undoubtedly to be met with in the real world, can be counted upon to preserve economic stability. It is this view that is challenged by J. M. Keynes in his revolutionary work, *The General Theory of Interest Employment and Money*.[10]

KEYNES'S CRITICISM OF THE CLASSICAL THEORY

Suppose that the real wage rate and the marginal physical product of labor are equated at the wage rate PQ. In Figure 14, this means that employment is OQ, which is assumed to be less than full employment. The classical theory did not regard this as an equilibrium position, for the unemployed would offer themselves at lower real wage rates, thus driving them down to Q_1P_1 and employment up to the full employment level, OQ_1. In other words, classical theory viewed it as within the power of labor to reduce its own real wage rate sufficiently so that the whole labor force could be employed. Thus the responsibility for unemployment was laid at the door of labor itself.

Keynes argued, however, that it is here that the error of identifying the economics of the single firm with the economy as a whole leads the analysis astray. For suppose that in order to increase employment, labor consents to a wage cut intended to reduce real wages to Q_1P_1, and increase employment to the full-employment level OQ_1. Can the real wage rate be equated with the marginal physical product of labor at full employment by this route?

When *money* wage rates are reduced, the first thing that happens, before another worker is hired, is a decline in the aggregate money income of labor. This decline equals the product of the wage cut and the number of workers initially employed. Workers in the aggregate therefore have less money to spend. Unless something happens to counteract the resulting decline in their spending, demand curves for commodities shift to the left and prices fall. Is the total spending on commodities likely to rise or fall as a result of the wage cut?

An immediate effect of a decline in money wage rates is a reduced

---

[10] J. M. Keynes, *The General Theory of Interest Employment and Money* (New York: Harcourt, 1936). Keynes's position may be summarized as follows: From the point of view of national income determination, the fruitlessness of wage cuts to restore full employment can be demonstrated in terms of the relation of investment and consumption to national income. If equilibrium in the national economy is to be maintained, the aggregate demand for goods and services must equal the aggregate cost of producing them. Say's law states in effect that this will be so at all levels of output, by virtue of the fact that total payments to factors suffice to take the entire product off the market at factor cost. Competition and profit maximization will ensure the rise of output to its maximum or full-employment level. But aggregate demand consists of two parts, demand for consumers' goods and demand for investment goods. Keynes argued that an increase in income is associated with an increase in consumption, but that not the whole of the increase in income will be spent on consumption. Consequently the slack must be taken up by an increase in the demand for investment goods. Investment, however, is determined by a separate group of factors, and the slack may not be taken up. If this occurs, unemployment may develop that cannot be cured by reductions in wage or other costs. Cf. Alvin Hansen, *A Guide to Keynes* (New York: McGraw, 1953), pp. 20–35.

wage bill. But firms do not, as a consequence, have more money to spend on equipment and inventories, and to hire additional labor, unless the volume and prices of sales remain unchanged. An important element in the Keynesian analysis is, indeed, that since wages constitute the bulk of marginal prime costs, firms will cut prices in proportion to the wage cut. Even if firms were to experience a temporary addition to net receipts, it would be highly unlikely that they would put this purchasing power back into circulation. The decline in worker spending is an unfavorable sign, and firms are likely to prefer to remain liquid. They will probably not hire additional workers if, for example, they feel that the reason for depression and unemployment is that output has been excessive in relation to prospective market demand.

According to the Keynesian analysis, a money wage cut during a depression, then, is not likely to result in additional demand for labor. Demand curves for commodities tend to shift to the left, prices fall, and corresponding to the decline in money wage rates is a decline in prices. Real wage rates, therefore, may not decline at all; indeed, particularly during early stages of a downswing, they may rise. Consequently reductions in wage rates cannot be regarded as a promising route to increased employment. The view that full-employment equilibrium can be re-established through wage cuts overlooks the fact that supply and demand curves are related through income. It is not a matter of simply moving along given curves until full employment is reached. The curves themselves shift position.

The foregoing criticism of the classical concept of equilibrium does not prove, it should be repeated, that money wage cuts cannot result in increased employment. It merely shows that this effect cannot be demonstrated by using supply and demand curves which are independent of one another. Under certain conditions the effect of the acceptance of money wage cuts by the unions might be to encourage businessmen to undertake a program of investment.[11] If this occurred, workers might momentarily have less money to spend on consumers' goods than before; but the increase in the demand for producers' goods might outstrip the decline in the demand for consumers' goods, the net effect being a rise rather than a fall in employment.

It was no accident that Keynes, an adherent of the income approach to economic fluctuations, exposed the flaw in the classical analysis. The latter ignored the income effects of changing wage rates and changing levels of employment. Keynes agreed with the classical writers that the real wage rate equals the marginal product of labor, but he argued that

---

[11] The unions frequently argue the reverse; namely, that wage *increases* will result in increased demand for consumers' goods and, indirectly, for producers' goods. They assume that businessmen will either activate idle balances or increase their bank borrowing. Businessmen disagree.

employers would not keep the entire labor force at work unless effective demand were adequate to purchase aggregate output at full employment.

It is sometimes argued that there is no difference between the Keynesian and the classical analysis that cannot be accounted for by different assumptions regarding frictions and distortions. This is true only in a formal sense. The Keynesian approach focuses attention on the underlying factors relating to willingness to consume and invest that cannot be explained solely in terms of distortions in the price system. From the point of view of remedial policy, there is a world of difference between money wage cuts on the one hand, and increased business or government spending on the other, as a means of raising the level of employment.

THE ROLE OF FACTORS OF PRODUCTION OTHER THAN LABOR

Marginal productivity theory has meaning only when it is recognized that there are other factors of production besides labor, and that land, labor, capital, and entrepreneurship can all be varied with respect to one another. Thus it is not true that if demand for a product falls off, the only factor whose price ought to be reduced is labor. If the rate of interest remains above the marginal efficiency of capital that corresponds to full employment, obviously investment will be adversely affected and unemployment will develop.

Keynes's challenge to the classical school in the selection of the price of labor as the key element in situations of less than full employment was taken up by Professor Pigou, whom Keynes had singled out as the major exponent of the classical position.[12] Pigou recognized that merely to reduce money wages would not necessarily bring the economy back to full employment, unless the real wage rate were reduced as well. More could be expected in the way of equilibrating forces from a downswing than this, however. A depression reduces the rewards of all factors, not wage rates alone. If, then, there is a reduction in the general price level, the real value of cash balances rises.[13] A sufficiently violent decline in the price level might have the effect of making the owners of cash balances feel rich enough to be willing to increase their spending.[14] This effect might be

---

[12] See the discussion by D. Patinkin, "Price Flexibility and Full Employment," *American Economic Review*, September, 1948, pp. 551–552.

[13] "Cash balances" are defined to include government interest-bearing and non-interest-bearing debt, and to exclude demand deposits. This unusual definition of money serves the purpose of taking into consideration the facts that a fall in prices increases the real value of the government debt and that corresponding to the gains of private debtors from a fall in prices are the losses of private creditors. Thus the "Pigou effect," as described in the text, depends on the willingness of the government to be a heavy debtor to the private sector, and to allow the public to be richer when a price fall enhances the real value of this debt. For a demonstration that the relevant cash balance is made up of "the net obligation of the government to the private sector of the economy," see Patinkin, "Price Flexibility and Full Employment," *loc. cit.*, pp. 530–551.

[14] Pigou's case is evaluated below in connection with the comparison of monetary and fiscal policy as antidepression weapons.

great enough to halt or even reverse the downswing. The impetus for recovery might come, in other words, from the increase in the rate of spending on the part of those whose accumulated liquid assets are now in excess of their requirements.

RELATION OF THE CLASSICAL TO THE NEOCLASSICAL VIEW

This revision of the classical analysis, though styled the *neoclassical* approach, in reality has little in common with the former. To argue that the cause of unemployment is a price level that is too high in relation to the supply of liquid assets is a very different thing from arguing that the cause of unemployment is that money wage rates, or any particular set of prices, have become too high in comparison with other prices. The neoclassical explanation is, in fact, a variant of the monetary approach to full employment. Thus it must be discussed in relation to the debate between the advocates of the monetary approach and those of the fiscal approach to economic stability.

► THE MONETARY APPROACH

The monetary approach to economic stabilization is based on the quantity theory of money. In its most sophisticated form the quantity theory simply states that though variations in velocity of money are possible, velocity nevertheless tends to remain fairly stable, and that variations in MV are caused primarily by variations in M. Therefore if monetary policy is to be effective in raising the level of employment, even if the velocity of the new money is not necessarily as high as that of the average of the money already in the circular flow, it will have to be large enough so that a significant increase occurs in money income, for MV is regarded as the determinant of the level of employment. As stated earlier, the monetary approach views the level of income as the causative force, but believes that this level can be increased by operating on M alone, under the assumption that the velocity of the new money will be significant.

LIQUIDITY PREFERENCE

The fiscal approach, in the hands of Keynes and his followers, denies the assumption of the monetary school that the velocity of the newly created money will necessarily be significant. Even if velocity is not zero, a depression may be so severe that the velocity of the new money will be too low to effect an important addition to the flow of purchasing power, and therefore to total output and employment. This situation can be made clear by making use of a concept that is the inverse of velocity of circulation, namely, the demand for money to hold idle. This concept is K of the Cambridge quantity equation ($M = KPT$). As we have seen in Chapter 18, if $1/V$ is substituted for K in this equation, it is found to be identical with the Fisher version of the quantity equation, $MV = PT$.

Suppose the monetary authority desired to create $10 billion of new demand deposits, but that the public as a whole did not wish to increase its rate of spending or purchases of interest-bearing assets. This would mean that even if on balance a rise in the volume of money occurred, velocity of circulation might decline sufficiently to neutralize the effects of the rise. The banking system would be unsuccessful in stimulating a rise in national income by simply creating additional money. Our task is to determine whether any monetary policy is conceivable in these circumstances that could bring about a sufficient decline in liquidity preference so that a significant increase in national income (and therefore output and employment) could be effected. If this cannot be done through monetary policy alone, stronger measures must be adopted, and this opens up the question of fiscal policy.

EFFECT OF A CHANGE IN K

When it is said that the public increases its demand for money to hold idle, it is apparent that this can have no effect on the amount that it is actually holding. For the public cannot hold more money than there is, and the quantity of money is determined by the banking system, in conjunction with public and private borrowers. The total quantity of money must be held by somebody, and if the public decides to increase the ratio of cash holdings to national income, it is national income that must change, not the quantity of money.[15] This can be shown in an example.

Suppose that the quantity of money is $10 billion, and that K is $1/10$. Since K is the proportion of national income the public wishes to hold in the form of money, then annual income must be $100 billion. If now the public decides to hold $1/5$ instead of $1/10$ of national income in the form of money, individuals refrain from spending money. But thus far nothing has happened. In the aggregate the public holds as much as before and no more. The reason is that if every person attempts to build up his cash balance from say, $20 to $40, he necessarily fails. Everyone else has similarly reduced his rate of spending in an effort to double his cash balance, including the employers, who pay the factors of production.

This reduction in spending is itself a decline in national income, and a fixed quantity of money becomes a greater proportion of a lower national income. Thus the public fails to increase its aggregate cash holdings, but it does succeed in doubling K. In the present example, national income must drop from $100 billion to $50 billion, of which the quantity of money ($10 billion) is one fifth.[16]

The example in the preceding paragraph illustrates the difference

---

[15] Once national income has changed, of course, any resulting changes in indebtedness to the commercial banks will in turn affect the quantity of money.

[16] The reduction in spending means that prices fall, including bond prices. Therefore, the interest rate tends to rise.

between the concepts K and KPT in the Cambridge equation. At all times *realized* demand for money must equal the quantity of money. This is merely the truism expressed by the equation $M = KPT$. This has no meaning, however, for the analysis of causal factors. It is K that is of significance in the analysis of the reasons for increasing or decreasing rates of spending. By an increase in the demand for money is meant an increase in K, changes in which will be followed by changes in income unless counteracted by corresponding changes in the quantity of money. Demand in the sense of KPT is merely another way of expressing changes in the *supply* of money. Apart from central-bank open-market operations, an increase in the supply of money can come about only because either business or the government is willing to borrow from the banking system. But such an increase will not occur merely so that the money can be held idle.[17]

► MONETARY POLICY AND THE TEST OF THE THIRTIES

The immediate response of the Federal Reserve System to the crisis and business collapse of 1929 was to reverse the tight monetary policy of 1928–1929. A highly vocal school of thought argued that if depressions are caused by a decline in investment in response to unfavorable profit prospects, the right course is to effect a great enough reduction in the cost of borrowing to entice businessmen to commence investing again. It is commonly believed, however, that declining interest rates were not effective in producing a politically satisfactory rate of recovery. Yet from about the middle of 1933, both output and prices did commence the long ascent out of the depths of depression. How far was monetary policy responsible for the recovery between 1933 and 1937?

It is not easy to answer this question, partly because the Roosevelt administration during these years initiated a complex of policies aimed simultaneously at recovery and at a different concept of social justice. The specific effects of monetary policy cannot be segregated. Consequently, ample scope remains for debate between advocates of monetary policy and of fiscal policy over the proper course to be adopted in the event of another depression.

It is believed by most economists that monetary policy alone could not have brought the country out of the depression, even though an elastic money supply was surely a precondition for recovery. The monetary school has always argued, however, that not enough money was created,

---

[17] One qualification must be mentioned. Business or government may borrow from the banks in order to make payment *at a later date* for goods or services. During the interim the deposits are held idle and K increases as much as M, so that there is for the time being no effect on national income. Statistically this "precautionary" demand for money is indistinguishable from an increase in the demand for money to hoard, but the motives are very different, and the cases must be carefully separated for purposes of analysis.

and that there would have been no need to resort to fiscal policy if the administration had been prepared to cooperate with the banking system in assuring the creation of sufficient additional demand deposits.[18] After all, it is pointed out, the President did not even take advantage of the enabling legislation placed at his disposal under the Thomas amendment to the Agricultural Adjustment Act in 1933, which permitted the printing of $3 billion of new currency, as well as sales of up to $3 billion of securities by the Treasury to the federal reserve banks.[19]

THE QUANTITY OF MONEY AND THE RATE OF SPENDING

An increase in the quantity of money can stimulate increased spending by one or both of two routes. The new deposits may be spent by businessmen on the factors of production in connection with an expansion of investment. In this case a large proportion finds its way into the consumption spending stream in the succeeding time period. Again, the newly created deposits may be spent for securities, raising their price and thus tending to force down the interest rate. If, then, businessmen respond to declining interest rates by increasing their borrowing, the original increase in the quantity of money has resulted in an increase in investment spending.

In practice, both of these routes might be followed, in varying degree, and the increased consumption spending and investment reinforce one another. This result is predicated on a sufficiently strong initial impetus so that the prospect for profits is markedly improved, and an upward spiral is actually set in motion. It is necessary to consider whether an increase in the quantity of money, traveling one or both of these routes, can reverse a downswing.

AN INCREASE IN *M* TO REVERSE A DOWNSWING

Many economists argue that since the causes of depression are known to be complex, no depression can be attributed to monetary causes alone, and that it is therefore not sensible to suppose that monetary policy can

---

[18] This would be no effective answer, of course, if the new money were held idle. If the liquidity preference schedule with respect to the newly created deposits during a depression is infinitely interest-elastic, the interest rate does not fall. Furthermore, even if the rate is driven very low, the marginal efficiency of capital schedule may be very inelastic. Thus investment and income do not rise significantly.

[19] A lively debate has gone on in the journals over whether or not the money supply actually rose between the years 1933 and 1937 (the peak recovery year of the thirties before World War II). While Alvin Hansen has argued that the quantity of money rose rapidly between these years, Clark Warburton contends that although the quantity of money did increase more rapidly than the previous trend, the cessation of growth in the second quarter of 1928 had produced a deficiency in the volume of money that was not made up in the years 1934–1937. (Cf. C. Warburton, "Hansen and Fellner on Full Employment Policies," *American Economic Review,* March, 1948, pp. 128–134.)

by itself remedy the situation. On the other hand, it may be said that if the causes of depression are complex, we can hardly insist on a recovery policy that reverses all these causes. A much simpler recipe appears to be necessary, and one possibility is monetary policy. There is some support for the view that even though monetary policy alone is not likely to be effective once a depression has become severe, more liberal credit conditions can serve to prevent a recession from gathering momentum and becoming a deflationary spiral. The evidence, however, is not conclusive. Examples of unemployment situations in which monetary policy appears to have been an appropriate instrument are the 1948–1949 and 1954 recessions in this country, and the moderate decline in domestic demand in Germany in the second half of 1951.[20]

THE PIGOU EFFECT[21]

In the reference that was made earlier to the neoclassical approach to the full-employment problem at the hands of Pigou, it was pointed out that the reduction of costs and prices that is a characteristic of the downswing increases the real value of cash balances. The latter were defined as consisting of the interest-bearing and non-interest-bearing government debt. The possibility exists that the owners of these assets will, if the price level is low enough, place a higher valuation on an increase in consumption than on a further increase in real savings. Each individual may be thought of as comparing the marginal utility of a rise in his real wealth with that of an increase in consumption spending. It can be argued that if the price level is low enough, and if it is expected to continue at that level, consumption will be at a rate which will assure full employment. This argument rests on the assumption that individuals actually do respond to a rise in the real value of their cash balances by increasing consumption sufficiently so that desired savings and desired investment will be equated at full employment. They might, of course, simply prefer to grow richer.

It will be noted that the fall in prices was accompanied by a fall in money wage rates, which are a price. But if all prices fall together, real wages do not decline. Even though real wages remain the same, it will pay the worker who is on the margin between spending and saving to spend a portion of his savings, or at least to increase the proportion which he spends out of current income. For if the price level declines far enough, a small portion of the cash balances of even a relatively poor man may prove sufficient for his future requirements.

---

[20] Cf. "Recent Financial Changes in Western Germany," Federal Reserve *Bulletin,* October, 1954.

[21] Because Pigou was concerned with static considerations (i.e., the effects of a low price level, not one that is expected to go still lower), and with a rather abstract economic model, his arguments are not intended to be translated directly into policy recommendations. However, they have stimulated a great deal of discussion by those who are seeking means of avoiding depressions.

A Managed Price Cut. From the view that an automatic decline in prices during a downswing will increase the value of money assets, and therefore tend to decrease liquidity preference, it is a short step to advocate across-the-board price cuts to hasten a return to full employment.[22] If a country were to take this step, however, particular attention would have to be paid to other effects which would tend to offset this one.[23] These other effects may be important.

It has been observed above that the favorable effects on creditors and holders of liquid assets are offset by the unfavorable effects on debtors. But the debtor is by and large the businessman, who is the key person in investment decisions. If a businessman were to borrow while prices were falling, he would have to pay back more, in real terms, than he borrowed. In other words, he would incur windfall losses, which would make investment precarious, if not prohibitive. Any businessman who had borrowed before the price reduction would be severely penalized.

There is no reason to think that the increased spending of the passive saving public would be adequate to more than offset the decreased spending of those who are directly responsible for investment and employment. Moreover, in view of the fact that wealthy individuals have large amounts of liquid savings, while the bulk of the population possesses only small amounts, the former would find that they had claims to all the national product for years to come before the latter began to feel wealthy enough to increase spending out of previous saving. It would be necessary to make billionaires out of many rich people before *mass* spending began to appear.

This approach suffers from the disadvantage that it tries to increase first the spending of those individuals with the highest marginal propensity to save. Although there is reason to doubt that the marginal propensity to consume out of increased *income* is any less for the wealthy than for the less wealthy, it would nevertheless seem likely that the propensity of

---

[22] It is pointed out by Haberler that Pigou, contrary to a prevailing impression, is concerned merely with the price decline associated with the downswing. G. Haberler, "The Pigou Effect Once More," *Journal of Political Economy,* June, 1952, pp. 240–246. In view of the interest of the classical economists in automatic adjustment ("rules" rather than "authorities"), this conclusion is reasonable. By logical extension, however, Pigou's reasoning might be translated into a conscious public policy if a depression were severe and persistent.

[23] A horizontal price cut was once actually a part of the German government's antidepression policy. Its intent was to bring about an increase in spending, though by a different route. The Bruening government, in the fourth emergency decree of December, 1931, ordered a reduction of 10 per cent in all prices. The purpose of this decree was to bring the German price level down in relation to the price levels of Germany's competitors and customers in order to improve the balance of trade. By selling more abroad and buying less from other countries, it was hoped to raise the level of domestic employment. In effect it was an attempt to increase foreign investment at a time when there seemed to be no hope of inducing domestic producers to spend more to provide employment. The plan failed, and in any event countermeasures would have been taken by other countries even if it had proved administratively possible to enforce a horizontal price reduction of this kind.

the wealthy to consume more on the occasion of an increase in *wealth* of the sort under discussion here would be less than that of the less wealthy. Therefore, if we are trying to stimulate spending, it is desirable to get purchasing power into the hands of those most likely to spend it. These are the lower-income groups (consumption spending) and businessmen (investment spending).

The Effect of a Changing Price Level.   So long as the public thought that prices were going to continue downward, it would be foolish to convert liquid savings into goods regardless of how far prices had fallen already. Therefore, any attempt to restore full employment by, say, a legislative enactment of general price cuts, would not be likely to succeed unless there were a single massive cut in the price level, with assurance that no further cuts would be made in the foreseeable future. Consequently, if the plan were to succeed (quite apart from the doubts raised in the previous paragraph), the initial price reduction would have to suffice to accomplish the goal of raising the level of spending. If it failed, nothing would have been accomplished whatever. Furthermore, if the cut were much greater than necessary it might so upset debtor-creditor relationships that much harm would be done to the economy. Since, therefore, this instrument could not be applied gradually and on the basis of rational calculations with respect to probable effects, it would not prove to be a very practicable weapon against hoarding.

► PENALTY TAXATION: A HYBRID MONETARY-
  FISCAL DEVICE

The discussion thus far has led to the conclusion that monetary policy cannot be counted upon to provide the impetus to recovery from a depression. Under certain conditions it may succeed in doing so; the forces making for expansion and those which discourage spending may be so delicately balanced that a reduction in the interest rate will tip the scales in the direction of an upswing. But unemployment is too serious a matter to permit reliance on uncertain recovery measures. Consequently, proposals have been made to influence the rate of spending directly by making it expensive to *fail* to spend.

Penalty taxation is aimed at improving on the doubtful results of monetary policy to eliminate depression. It is a velocity approach rather than a quantity approach to the problem of increasing the volume of spending. Despite its appearance of being a form of fiscal policy, penalty taxation is really more nearly akin to monetary policy. Under this scheme idle currency and deposits would be subject to a tax that is designed to make it expensive to hoard money. The measure of its success would be its *lack* of revenue yield. If deposits and currency were turning over at a rate that corresponded to full employment, no tax liability would be incurred. If, on the other hand, spending were at such a low rate that significant amounts of tax were collected, the objective of the plan would not have been attained. It may be noted in passing that penalty taxation of deposits and currency bears a kinship to a progressive tax on spending. The mechanisms of the devices are similar, though their objectives are diametrically opposite. The spendings tax is intended to discourage consumption spending.

If the money supply were absolutely fixed, it would be impossible for all individuals as a group to escape both the penalty tax and the requirement that they spend their money in order to avoid the tax. The money that one person or firm got rid of would have to be held by someone else. Thus he would also have to spend it. But the money supply is not fixed, and one might expect a certain amount of debt repayment to the commercial banks by individuals and firms anxious to avoid the tax.

Suppose that each dollar held, in the form of currency or as demand deposits, were to depreciate by one cent a month unless it could be shown that its holder had received it from someone else during the month. People would attempt to reduce their holdings of cash to an amount such that they would hold no dollar longer than a month. In doing this they would have to pay it to someone else, so that thus far the objective would seem attained. Whenever a dollar got into the hands of someone who had borrowed from a bank (e.g., a businessman), however, he could avoid the tax by repaying his debt. In the absence of the tax, businessmen would have been slower to repay bank loans; and, moreover, would have tended to carry somewhat higher lines of credit at their banks. Thus, although the velocity of the money still in existence would undoubtedly be stimulated by the tax, at least a part of the money supply would be destroyed, and the net effect on MV would be problematical. Of course, a tax might also be levied on the repayment of bank debt, but it would be necessary and difficult to distinguish between repayment to avoid tax and repayment in the ordinary course of business.

▶ THE COMPARATIVE ROLES OF MONETARY AND
FISCAL POLICY

In assessing the place of monetary policy among the instruments of economic control, it must be remembered that no single approach is equally effective at all stages of the cycle. In one way or another, however, monetary policy should play an important part at all times. Although we must conclude that monetary policy alone is unlikely to prove effective in stimulating recovery from a serious depression, it does have an important function to perform both during depression and during other phases of the cycle.

Differences of opinion continue to exist over the combination of monetary and fiscal policy that is most appropriate for combating the disequilibria characteristic of different phases of the cycle. In general, monetary policy would seem to yield its most significant results during a period of high-level income and employment. This phase may be subdivided into two further phases, namely, the period during which a boom is approaching a climax, and the period when income, employment, and prices have commenced to decline.

THE BOOM

If rising federal reserve rediscount rates, sales of government securities, and warnings to the public have the effect of slowing down the expansion of bank borrowing, we can assign an independent effect to monetary policy in reducing the dimensions of a boom.[24] Experience in the late twenties, when the Federal Reserve System issued repeated warnings, and pursued a tight monetary policy, indicates that a sufficiently vigorous policy may be expected to have such an effect. At the same time, however, it was learned that the monetary measures that are likely to be used may not take hold until the situation is already out of hand. Businessmen may not pay much attention to the rise in interest rates in the early stages of a boom; and when credit policies finally become effective, the economy may already have been plunged into a deflationary spiral.

If the reserve authorities have reason to believe that monetary policy, applied at a reasonably early stage of the boom, will not be effective in curtailing investment, consideration can be given to fiscal policy. This may take the form of either a decrease in federal spending or increases in the rates of certain taxes.[25] The resulting decrease in the treasury deficit, or increase in the surplus, will be deflationary. A surplus is certainly deflationary if the proceeds are held idle in the form of treasury cash or deposits with the federal reserve banks, and probably so if used to repurchase government securities.

There is no reason why either monetary or fiscal policy, if pursued resolutely enough, should not be ultimately effective in bringing a boom to an end. The comparison of the two policies, therefore, rests primarily on such matters as relative political feasibility, the extent to which each may be expected to produce undesirable subsidiary effects, and administrative considerations.

On the first of these points, it is probable that the political reaction to changes in open-market and rediscount policy of the Federal Reserve System will be less violent than the public response to the enactment of a

---

[24] Monetary policy during a boom would also be effective if the opposite policy of *lowering* the rate of interest prevented a collapse. For qualified support of this course see Keynes, *op. cit.*, Chap. XXII, "Notes on the Trade Cycle," pp. 320 ff.

[25] There is another possibility. If both government spending and taxing are curtailed, inflationary pressure may be reduced. This approach, which does not rely on budgetary surpluses, will be discussed in a later chapter.

new tax bill.[26] This is especially likely to be the case if the public is asked to bear more taxes at a time when there seems to be no need for added revenues for purposes of financing government. On the other hand, it must be admitted that, in the past, sharp political reactions have occurred in response to federal reserve policies.

With respect to possible undesirable subsidiary effects of monetary or fiscal measures undertaken to control a boom, no general statements can be made. Everything depends on the circumstances surrounding a particular case. Both policies may conceivably not only halt the boom but also convert an upswing into a downswing. The cumulative nature of recessions means that the effects of the original policy may quickly become inextricably bound up with other dynamic factors.

From an administrative standpoint, monetary policy is much easier to apply under our present institutions. Fiscal measures have to go through Congress. Although it has been suggested that Congress delegate to an executive agency a limited power to vary rates of taxing and spending, no evidence exists at present that Congress is willing to take this step. Even if it did so, it is difficult to see how the agency would avoid the impact of group pressures which are now concentrated on Congress. The agency would report to the President, who has to keep in mind the next elections.

THE EARLY STAGE OF A DOWNSWING

As stated earlier, the belief is entertained by many economists that active monetary policy finds its most fruitful use immediately after a period of high-level employment. A more liberal credit policy can have significant effects on willingness to borrow during a period when, although investment is declining, cumulative depression forces have not yet got under way. Periods of suspended animation in economic activity, when expansive and contractive forces are roughly in balance, are actually of quite frequent occurrence. The lowering of discount rates and a stated policy of increasing commercial-bank reserves may slow down the recession sufficiently to give nonmonetary forces the time required for reversing the recession.

Monetary policy may retard a downswing. It is more questionable, however, whether it can reverse it. The role of monetary policy during a slight recession should be carefully noted. Some recessions are largely technical in nature. Certain maladjustments have developed which may cure themselves if granted the time, but which may set in motion a cumulative downswing if no action is taken. This is the point at which an easy money policy may prove highly rewarding. If, in spite of it, the downswing continues, the time has come to turn to fiscal policy. For whereas, as

---

[26] Changes in tax *rates* would not be required if fluctuations in national income and spending produced a sufficient response in the form of changes in tax receipts and public spending (the so-called built-in flexibility of the fiscal system). This possibility is discussed in Chapter 21.

stated above, an immediate increase in government spending, for example, might have aggravated the very distortions that are a possible cause of a minor recession, this defect of deficit spending has to be ignored if a really serious depression develops.

► CONCLUSION

The present chapter has attempted to indicate the boundaries of monetary policy for economic stability. In order to do this it was first necessary to recognize a distinction between monetary and nonmonetary causes of economic stability. Disequilibrium may come about through price-cost distortions due to the exercise of monopoly power, frictions, and other market imperfections. These causes of disequilibrium may or may not be removable. If they are not, and this is likely to be the typical situation, the remedy may be to neutralize them rather than try to eliminate them. Once this decision is made the choice is between monetary policy and fiscal policy, or a combination of both.

An appropriate monetary policy is a necessary but not always a sufficient condition for stable, high-level income and employment. During the periods immediately prior and subsequent to the peak of a cycle, monetary policy is likely to be at its greatest effectiveness. Federal reserve policy then not only may prove effective in retarding or stimulating business borrowing from the banks, but in addition may affect the rate of spending. When the business world is doubtful whether a given trend in the rate of business activity will be maintained, particular attention is likely to be paid to the actions of the monetary authorities.

The situation is different when the public is convinced that a boom or a depression will continue indefinitely. If it is desired to slow down a boom, monetary policy may be effective even if used by itself; but it may also be risky, since it may be applied too late and too vigorously. And it is generally agreed that monetary policy alone is not an adequate defense against a severe depression. It is at these times that fiscal policy comes into consideration. Any desired change in the level of income can be effected by way of changes in the federal budget. The major questions here, however, are whether there is a political support for an adequate use of fiscal policy, and whether the price that has to be paid in terms of effects on social welfare is greater or less than that of alternative policies.

► REFERENCES

BAUMOL, W. J. *Economic Dynamics*. New York: The Macmillan Company, 1951, Chap. VI, "Price Flexibility and the Equilibrium of the Economy."
HALM, G. N. *Monetary Theory*. Philadelphia: The Blakiston Company, 1946, Pt. III.

HANSEN, A. *Business Cycles and National Income.* New York: W. W. Norton & Company, 1951, Chap. XXIX, "Wage-Price-Profit Policy."

———. *Fiscal Policy and Business Cycles.* New York: W. W. Norton & Company, 1941, Chaps. XIV and XV (on the circular flow and price flexibility).

———. *A Guide to Keynes.* New York: McGraw-Hill Book Company, Inc., 1953.

———. *Monetary Theory and Fiscal Policy.* New York: McGraw-Hill Book Company, Inc., 1949, Chaps. III–VII.

JOINT COMMITTEE ON THE ECONOMIC REPORT, SUBCOMMITTEE ON ECONOMIC STABILIZATION. *Hearings,* December 6 and 7, 1954 on United States Monetary Policy, Recent Thinking and Experience.

OXFORD UNIVERSITY, INSTITUTE OF STATISTICS. *The Economics of Full Employment.* Oxford: Basil Blackwell & Mott, Ltd., 1944.

PATINKIN, D. "Price Flexibility and Full Employment," *American Economic Review,* September, 1948.

SIMONS, H. C. *Economic Policy for a Free Society.* Chicago: The University of Chicago Press, 1948, Chap. VIII, "Hansen on Fiscal Policy."

WEILER, E. T. *The Economic System.* New York: The Macmillan Company, 1952, Chap. II, "A Preliminary View of the Economy."

20 Fiscal Policy and National Income

► INTRODUCTION

In the conclusion of the previous chapter it was stated that through changes in the rate of federal spending and taxing, any desired effect can be produced in the level of national income. This statement calls for support in the form of a discussion of the role of the federal budget in the achievement of economic stability. Before this is undertaken, however, it is necessary to give some consideration to the mechanism of changes in national income. This will be done with respect to both an ordinary business recovery and a rise in national income engendered by a deficit in the federal budget. Account will also be taken of the situation in which national income rises as a result of an increase in federal spending that is covered by increased taxes.

This discussion will lead into a consideration of the role of federal deficits and surpluses in the achievement of economic stability. Since the interaction of consumption and investment is crucial to changes in the level of national income, the mechanisms of the multiplier and the accelerator must be explained. We shall then be in a position, in the following chapter, to consider the problem of budgetary balance in relation to economic stability.

► PRIVATE AND PUBLIC SPENDING

The size of the flow of money income is, of course, affected by both public and private spending. Again, it is affected by the payments made by taxpayers and purchasers of goods and services to governments and to businessmen. Business and government alike may cause changes in the magnitude of the circular flow of income payments. On the one hand they may fail to pay out the whole of their receipts. On the other they may borrow either idle or new money, and inject it into the income stream.

In a free-enterprise economy these changes in the rate at which income is paid out are ordinarily not the result of over-all planning in the interest of stable employment. Each firm makes its own output decisions, and therefore exercises independence in the rate at which it pays out income to the factors of production. In an unplanned society, public spending is likewise subject to considerable fluctuations at all levels of government. Consequently, there is no reason to expect that the sum of public and private spending is likely to remain long at levels which correspond to full employment. A large part of federal spending and taxing is not subject to fiscal planning for economic stability. For example, pork-barrel legislation cannot be done away with easily, even if economic considerations call for a reduction in federal spending. Military expenditures likewise cannot be greatly modified by considerations of economic stability. At the state and local level, fiscal systems are quite as independent of central control as are the spending policies of business firms.

► THE MECHANISM OF AN INCREASE IN THE MONEY FLOW DURING A BUSINESS RECOVERY

Let us assume that considerable unemployment exists. Suppose that a measure of recovery is achieved by way of increased spending in the private sector of the economy, public finance remaining passive.[1] This recovery may first take the form of a rise in investment spending, which means that demand curves in the producers' goods industries tend to rise throughout the economy. The demand for factors of production will likewise increase.

This rise in business spending will be financed through a combination of increased business borrowing and a rise in the velocity of circulation of business deposits. If the recovery is expected to continue, businessmen will respond to the rise in their demand curves by increasing either prices or output. So long as unemployment and idle capacity are very large, however, it may be assumed that most producers will prefer to expand output rather than to raise prices. Consequently, the level of employment rises, and individuals are in a position to save and consume at a greater rate than before. To the extent that the public consumes its increased income, demand curves in consumers' goods industries also rise, and the resulting increased output of consumers' goods tends to strengthen the demand for plant and equipment. These effects spread gradually as idle plant and equipment are activated, and inventories are drawn down.

The rise in MV is permanent provided that the new or dishoarded money is not subsequently held idle, or is not used to pay off bank loans by businessmen. What happens in a sustained upswing is that new borrowing and a rising rate of spending by those who are optimistic about recovery more than counterbalance debt repayment and hoarding of receipts by those who are not convinced that the recovery is permanent.

---

[1] It cannot remain *neutral,* since changes in the levels of investment and consumer spending affect both tax receipts (with tax rates unchanged) and certain types of public spending (e.g., public relief expenditures).

The role of velocity of circulation during a business recovery should be noted. The rate of spending of business and personal deposits increases during this phase of the cycle. Therefore, a part of the increased monetary circulation required to sustain the upswing is furnished by a rise in V. A further contribution arises out of the decline in unit cost of output that is associated with technological progress. Even during the relatively brief period of a business upswing the effects of increasing productivity may be felt. This will be reflected in lower prices, however, only if the agents of production refrain from requiring that all increments to national productivity be translated into higher rates of remuneration. To the extent that prices do follow the decline in costs caused by technological progress, a portion (relatively minor) of the increase in output can be financed without a rise in MV.

The contributions to the financing of an upswing in business activity made by an increase in velocity of circulation and the decreased costs and prices associated with increased productivity do not constitute a very great qualification to the statement that an increase in the quantity of money is necessary during a period of recovery. In other words, a normal upswing in business activity requires that businesses become increasingly indebted to the banking system.

BUSINESS RECOVERY AND THE ROLE OF SAVING

Another phenomenon associated with the upswing is the rise in saving. Business and personal incomes rise, and this means that business and personal saving likewise does so. If we ignore the impact on tax receipts, we must conclude that this new saving is destined to be invested in new plant, equipment, and inventories. A large part of the saving will consist of the undistributed profits of corporations.[2] The remainder is personal saving. A part of the new saving will be loaned in the market for consumer credit and thus for the economy as a whole is not saving at all. The rest will be lent to firms which desire to add to plant, equipment, or inventories. However, unless businessmen foresee a sustained recovery they may be hesitant to borrow. To the extent that this is so a brake is applied to the recovery. If the recovery is to continue, then, business firms *must* borrow a part of the newly created savings.

BUSINESS BORROWING IN A RECOVERY

In an ordinary business recovery, therefore, firms borrow from both the banks and savers. In other words, business has never hesitated to finance increased investment and output by "unbalancing its budget." The merchant and the manufacturer are not worried that their lines of credit with the banks rise as their scale of operations increases. Nor are they

---

[2] Reinvestment of undistributed profits comprises an important segment of business borrowing from savers, for undivided profits are a liability of the corporation to the stockholder.

surprised that sizable expansions in plant and equipment have to be financed by sales of securities to savers via the stock and bond markets, or through direct participation of the lender in the business. The normal expectation in an upswing from a fairly deep depression would be that in the first instance business would borrow from the banks, that the resulting increase in effective purchasing power in the hands of the agents of production would cause a rise both in demand for commodities and in savings, and that business would then commence to tap this saving.

► THE FEDERAL BUDGET IN A NORMAL RECOVERY

In a successful business upswing it is not necessary to give much attention to the problem of assuring that current saving is borrowed. Once recovery is fairly under way, the idle balances that characterized the early stages of the downswing have been largely dissipated. Incomes have been low for some time, and increments to savings have been correspondingly small. Firms now not only borrow current savings, but increase their borrowing from the banks.

Unless something happens to retard the upswing, then, business can be counted upon to borrow the increments to savings. It is not necessary for the federal government to step in to make sure that the recovery is not arrested through a failure of the economy to borrow current savings. The question whether or not the government enters the market as a borrower of savings will be decided on grounds other than those relating to the objective of economic recovery. If the government does borrow, it is competing with private individuals and firms for the definite, and therefore limited, annual increments of saving. Obviously a central government acts cautiously in the course of its ordinary borrowing activities during a normal upswing in private spending. The Treasury takes care to avoid driving up the interest rate to private borrowers. If need be, it will sell securities to the central bank.

► GOVERNMENT BORROWING TO ASSIST RECOVERY

The situation is different when difficulties are encountered in emerging from a depression. So long as prices are expected to decline further, businesses will be hesitant to invest. Even when there is general agreement that the low point of the depression has been reached, there may be a long period during which firms do not believe that it will be profitable to borrow to replenish stocks, or to buy new plant and equipment. Yet the persistence of unemployment requires that steps be taken to raise the level of national income and employment.

The possibility arises, therefore, that the federal government should make an effort to rectify the deficiency in spending. This it would do by borrowing and injecting the proceeds into the income stream by way of public works spending. Alternatively it would lower tax rates. The budgetary cash deficit thus created would have its counterpart in a greater income after taxes in the hands of business firms and individuals. To the extent that they spent this additional purchasing power they, too, would be contributing to a rise in income and employment.

COMPONENTS OF GOVERNMENT BORROWING

The government borrowing would consist of two elements. First, securities would be sold to the Federal Reserve System in return for newly created deposits; in other words, for new money. Second, as national income and saving rose in response to the government spending program, some of the newly issued government securities would be likely to find their way into the hands of savers. It would be necessary, of course, to take care that a large increase in the supply of government securities did not have the effect of driving up the interest rate to potential business borrowers. This would delay, or even prevent, the rise in private investment that is the necessary ingredient of recovery in a free-enterprise economy. This adverse effect could easily be avoided, however, by being sure to sell the bulk of the government securities to the reserve banks.

An important similarity exists, then, between the roles of business and the government during the course of a rise in national income and employment from their low depression levels. To the extent that each participates in the rise in spending, each borrows both new money from the banking system and new savings that are generated as incomes rise. Clearly, the larger the proportion of this borrowing that is done by businesses, the greater will be the assurance that an effect of depressions and their aftermath will not be an encroachment by government on the private sector. Equally clear, however, is the fact that the depression may be so severe, and so persistent, that the government must take steps to hasten recovery.

The conclusion that the government may have to increase its rate of spending and borrowing during a depression is of interest in connection with a view generally held by economists as well as politicians prior to the appearance of the *General Theory,* namely, that the budget of the federal government should be constantly kept in balance. This view meant that when national income and spending declined, tax *rates* would have to be increased in order to maintain tax *receipts* at a level that would keep the budget in balance. The bases of the several taxes decline during a business recession; and on the spending side a partial offset to a decline in normal public expenditures as prices decline is the rise in expenditures on relief.[3]

---

[3] It will occur to the reader that even if tax rates are increased it may be impossible to keep the budget in balance. For income and spending may be declining so rapidly that tax rates cannot be increased quickly enough to compensate for the decline in the base. More important than this, however, is the likelihood that increases in tax rates will themselves contribute to a further fall in spending, particularly investment spending.

The view that the federal budget should be balanced on an annual basis made a distinction between the financial practices that are proper to the business firm and those that ought to govern the actions of the federal government. It was all right for the former to borrow from the banks and from savers in order to increase investment, but the government ought not to borrow to increase its spending. It would appear, therefore, that the government was being asked to display a greater measure of caution in its financial methods than was expected of business firms.[4]

TREASURY DEFICITS AND MV

Our argument thus far has stated that a rise in the level of national income and employment requires a corresponding rise in the flow of money that is needed to finance the higher level of transactions. It was further contended that only a small part of the needed rise in MV is likely to be accounted for by an increase in the rate of spending, and that therefore economic recovery requires an increase in borrowing from the banking system. This borrowing may be undertaken by either business or the government, and it was argued that if business does not do it, the government must. Nevertheless, in order to preserve so far as possible the relative importance of the private sector, care should be taken to see to it that governmental recovery measures, as well as other functions of government, do not discourage private initiative.

An implication of the above statement of the recovery problem would at first sight appear to be that no contribution would be made to recovery if the federal government were to take steps to increase both its spending and its tax receipts equally. No budgetary cash deficit would occur, and no borrowing would be necessary. Therefore there would be no increase in the quantity of money. Does this mean that for this reason MV cannot increase, and that consequently recovery via this route is impossible? In other words, if the federal government diverts the same amount of purchasing power out of the income stream through taxation that it puts back into it by way of public spending, does this mean that increases and decreases in the size of the federal budget are neutral in their effects on national income?

The answer to this question depends on two things. The first is the effect of changes in the size of the budget on the rate of spending. The second is the effect of these changes on the volume of bank borrowing in the private sector of the economy. During the thirties most economists accepted the view that the size of the budgetary cash deficit or surplus determines the size of the change in the money supply. An increase in the quantity of active money during an upswing, for example, was taken to be

---

[4] It must be noted, however, that opponents of budgetary deficits based their objection also in large part on the view that government spending is wasteful. Historical aspects of the question have been discussed in Chapter 1.

determined by the amount of government debt that was either monetized through sales of securities to the banking system, or sold to those who were unable to find borrowers for their savings. In the one case it was M that would increase, and in the other, V. The possibility that changes in tax rates, and in the rates and direction of government spending, might have effects on the rate of private spending was recognized, but usually ignored.

► ALTERNATIVE BALANCED BUDGETS AND
NATIONAL INCOME

THE TREASURY AND THE CIRCULAR FLOW

The circular flow analysis presented in Chapter 18 does not indicate explicitly how money national income and national product can increase in response to a rise in government spending balanced by taxes. One may visualize the Treasury interposed in the money income stream in a position similar to that of the savings institutions in Figure 12 (page 398). Taxes on consumption and saving divert purchasing power out of the consumption and saving streams into the Treasury. This purchasing power is then poured back into the income stream by the government in the form of public expenditures.

From this diagram it would appear that an increase in public spending, balanced by an equal increase in tax receipts, would leave national income at the same level as before. The only difference, it would seem, would be that the proportion of national income taking the form of government services would be higher. Nevertheless, it can be shown that it is very likely that an increase in government spending, financed solely out of increased taxes, will cause an increase in dollar national income.

Evidently this conclusion can have great practical consequences for public policy. It means that it may lie within the power of the government to raise the level of national income without incurring a deficit. Before indicating the reasoning upon which the conclusion is based, the consequences for public policy may be set forth.

First, if there are widespread unemployed resources, a recovery can be generated through government spending without an increase in the public debt. A great political advantage would be gained if any initial borrowing designed to accelerate the upswing could be subsequently repaid, for this would remove an important objection to the use of fiscal policy for full employment. It remains true, however, that recovery would be more rapid if the government brought about an increase in MV by borrowing from banks.

Second, if the economy is at full employment (so defined that no increase in physical output is possible), the avoidance of inflation requires that any increase in public spending, even if entirely tax-financed, must be accompanied by an equal decrease in private spending. It follows that if military or other circumstances necessitate increased government spending, it may be insufficient, in order to avoid inflation, merely to levy additional taxes adequate to finance the new spending. Despite the additional taxes, individuals and firms may fail to curtail spending by an amount that is as great as the increase in public spending. This statement requires further explanation.

When tax receipts and government spending rise by an equal amount, the multiplier chain resulting from the spending exceeds that which results from the taxing by one.[5] For example, suppose that the marginal propensity to consume of the taxpayers is on the average 0.9. Then the series of positive multiplier effects resulting from the government expenditure is
$$1 + 0.90 + 0.81 + \cdots,$$
while the series of negative multiplier effects resulting from the taxes is
$$- 0.90 - 0.81 - \cdots.$$
The reason for this is that taxes enter net national product only on the second round. Thus regardless of the value of the marginal propensity to consume, the tax-financed additional public expenditure is subject to a net multiplier of one, and under the assumption that we are concerned with multiplier effects only, the effect is a rise in money national income.

It is necessary, however, to take account of the implications of the fact that taxpayers have reduced their saving by 0.1 in the above example. The marginal propensity to *spend* of the government is unity.[6] We are comparing this with a marginal propensity to *consume* on the part of the taxpayer of 0.9. Since part of the tax falls on saving, the increase in government *spending* is greater than the decrease in taxpayer *consumption*. If we take account of the repercussions on saving and investment, we may have to modify our conclusions.

A QUALIFICATION

The balanced budget theorem is subject to a number of qualifications, of which one is of particular interest in the present context. The fact that taxpayers react to the additional taxes by reducing saving as well as consumption is likely to have effects on the supply of credit and the rate of interest. Unless the banking system responds by permitting a rise in the supply of money, the tendency toward rising interest rates will discourage those firms from investing which were on the margin of investing or not

---

[5] Refer to Paul Samuelson, "The Simple Mathematics of Income Determination," in *Income, Employment and Public Policy: Essays in Honor of Alvin Hansen* (New York: Norton, 1948), especially pp. 140 ff. The discussion in the text assumes an elementary knowledge of the consumption function and the multiplier. The period multiplier is discussed below, pages 453–461.

[6] No distinction is made here between government consumption and government investment.

investing. Thus aggregate private investment will tend to fall slightly, and there will be a partial offset to the inflationary effect of the balanced budget multiplier. This qualification need not be an important one in practice, however, since it is within the power of the monetary authority to prevent the rise in the rate of interest.

A consideration of the mechanics of the financing of an upswing, therefore, indicates that the level of national income can be increased even if the government covers additional spending with an equivalent amount of additional taxes. Furthermore, it indicates that if the economy is already operating at full employment, an increase in government spending, financed by an equal amount of taxes, is likely to cause a rise in prices. The question remains to be considered whether or not in all circumstances a larger balanced budget is likely to be inflationary. The answer to this question depends largely on monetary policy.

It can be assumed that under conditions of substantial unemployment the monetary authority will wish to encourage a rise in national income. Consequently, the commercial banks will be provided with ample excess reserves, in order that the rise in the transactions demand for money associated with a rise in national income will not cause a rise in interest rates. In these circumstances the effect of an increase in the size of a balanced budget is inflationary with respect to income, although not with respect to prices. Incidentally, there will be a further rise in national income if the rise attributable to the larger balanced budget should stimulate some induced private investment.

During a boom period, on the other hand, monetary policy may have to be restrictive. Assume a situation like that which existed at the time of the Korean conflict. In anticipation of future government orders firms are likely to strive to maintain, indeed to increase, the level of their borrowing. It will probably be impracticable to tighten the money supply, and thus drive up the rate of interest, sufficiently to discourage new borrowing entirely. To the extent that firms do succeed in borrowing new money from the banks, they are able to continue to compete for goods and factors. Under conditions of high-level employment this causes a rise in the price level. What this means is that if the government really intends to increase its command over goods and factors, taxes must be raised still more. They must, indeed, be raised by more than the increase in public spending, and the difference must be great enough to cause a decline in private spending that is equal to the increase in public spending.[7]

---

[7] The private sector will resist a reduction in spending if businessmen anticipate a continued high level of demand that justifies further expansion of plant and equipment. It will do so also if, in response to price inflation, individuals attempt to preserve their normal standard of living in the face of higher prices. See the discussion in F. Gehrels, "Inflationary Effects of a Balanced Budget," *American Economic Review,* December, 1949.

► THE ROLE OF DEFICITS AND SURPLUSES IN
ECONOMIC STABILIZATION

EARLIER EXPERIENCE

Recognition of. the effect of treasury surpluses and deficits on the stability of the economy appeared surprisingly early in the history of this country. Alexander Hamilton perceived that the establishment of a sinking fund for the retirement of the national debt would exercise an effect on private spending, particularly if the proceeds of the taxes levied in order to build up the sinking fund were held idle in a treasury fund.[8] Secretaries of the Treasury again became acutely conscious of the economic role of federal surpluses with the establishment of the Independent Treasury in 1846. Under this system the Treasury kept its cash in its own vaults rather than in the commercial banks. This change resulted in a net withdrawal of cash from circulation by the Treasury whenever federal revenues exceeded expenditures. So long as the Treasury had deposited its surpluses with the commercial banks, the latter could continue to make discounts to business. Thus under the earlier practice treasury surpluses had no deflationary monetary effects.

By the decade of the 1850's, and again in the 1880's, the relationship between revenues and expenditures was again such as to produce recurrent surpluses. Since these surpluses were large, the effects of the cash drain out of circulation were felt in the form of a monetary stringency. In neither of these periods was there enough outstanding and maturing federal debt so that the annual surpluses might be put back into circulation by buying back securities from the bondholder. A high tariff brought in unneeded revenues, and an administration policy opposed to a high level of federal spending made inevitable, during prosperous years, surpluses that under the Independent Treasury could not be returned to circulation by being deposited in the commercial banks.[9]

Conversely, federal deficits incurred during time of war, and financed

---

[8] Cf. P. Studenski and H. Krooss, *Financial History of the United States* (New York: McGraw, 1952), pp. 53 ff. The authors point out that Hamilton could reduce the volume of money by borrowing from the banks and holding the proceeds idle, and could increase the purchasing power available to the private sector by having the treasury fund buy back government securities. If the taxes devoted to the repayment of the debt were immediately transferred to bondholders other than banks, the only effect on the income stream would, of course, be any differences in the rate at which the bondholder would spend the money as compared with the rate at which the taxpayer would have done so. The effect of repurchases of government securities from the banks would depend on whether, and when, the banks lent the cash to the private sector.

[9] E. R. Taus, *Central Banking Functions of the United States Treasury, 1789–1941* (New York: Columbia University Press, 1943). See also David Kinley, *The Independent Treasury of the United States* (Washington, D. C.: National Monetary Commission, 1910), pp. 68–70.

by bank purchases of government securities, have given rise to increased flows of purchasing power that were unmatched by corresponding increases in the flows of goods to market. Prior to World War I a large part of such deficits had been financed by the issue of paper currency, and people therefore tended to think of the inflation as caused by overissue rather than by deficit finance. But whether the deficit was financed by new currency, or by sales of government securities to the banks, the effect was the same in causing a rise in the quantity of money and spending. In the later stages of an upswing this rise was also accompanied by a noticeable increase in velocity.

THE THEORY OF DEFICITS AND SURPLUSES

It was not until the appearance in 1936 of the *General Theory* of John Maynard Keynes that the economics of government surpluses and deficits was organized into an integrated body of theory. As a result of the interest in the effect of fiscal policy on economic stability stimulated by the work of Keynes and his disciples, and by the need to find a solution to the great depression, the relationships between surpluses and deficits and the flow of money and real income have been worked over by a large number of economists.

As we have seen, one might suppose that the increase in the rate of flow of purchasing power brought about when expenditures exceed revenues is contingent solely on the size of the government cash deficit.[10] Conversely, it might appear that the diminution in the size of the income stream when tax receipts exceed revenues is likewise related solely to the cash surplus. Actually, however, both government spending and taxes exert still further effects on private spending. If we have an infinite number of different budgets, each balanced at different levels of spending and taxing, each will have a different potential effect on the rate of private spending. Given the level of national income, the larger the budget the more likely it becomes that taxes will have a restrictive effect on private spending. At the same time, the effects of government spending in encouraging induced private investment may decline, or even become negative, if the proportion of total spending accounted for by public spending becomes very large. One possible reason for this effect is the discouragement to private investment as government investment expands into areas hitherto regarded as the private domain. Evidently a size of budget can be imagined for which the expansive effects of government spending just

---

[10] It is only the *cash* deficit that is relevant, because we are concerned with the effects of the injection of money into the income stream by the Treasury, and of diversions of money out of it into idle treasury cash or treasury deposits at the federal reserve banks. Thus we are likewise concerned here with the federal *cash* budget, that is, the budget as set up in terms of cash receipts and cash disbursements during the budgetary period. For the distinction between cash and accrual accounting, see Chapter 21.

balance the restrictive effects of taxes. This has been called the "neutral balanced budget."[11] The net effects of budgets smaller than this would be expansive, while those of larger budgets would be restrictive. In a dynamic world it would be impossible, of course, to ascertain the data that would be needed for knowing which size of budget to choose in order to achieve a given effect on the level of total spending. The virtue of the approach, however, is that it focuses attention on the indirect effects on private spending exerted by government budgetary practice.

► THE INTERACTION BETWEEN CONSUMPTION
  AND INVESTMENT

The relation between changes in the levels of investment and consumption spending is fundamental to the analysis of economic fluctuations, and therefore to the success or failure of fiscal policy for economic stability. It is through the interaction of these two magnitudes that depressions and booms are propagated. Since public spending and taxing affect both private investment and consumption spending, public finance can exert quantitatively important effects on the rate at which an upswing or a downswing develops. Indeed, if the levels of taxing and spending can be altered quickly enough, national income can be stabilized.

► DERIVED DEMAND: THE UPSWING AND THE DOWNSWING

Not only do changes in the rate of investment affect the rate of income and consumption, but changes in consumption spending react back on investment. Increased production of consumers' goods can come about only through more intensive use of existing capital instruments or through additions to plant, equipment, and semifinished goods. There is, therefore, a *derived* demand for producers' goods. In the absence of excess capacity, increases in consumption spending may require new investment. Conversely, a decrease in consumption means that plant and equipment are worked less intensively, and inventories are allowed to decline. If the decline in consumption is great enough, worn-out equipment will not be replaced. Therefore, the principle of derived demand operates in the downswing as well as in the upswing.

---

[11] See the discussion of this and related concepts in Harold Somers, *Public Finance and National Income* (Philadelphia: Blakiston, 1949), pp. 507 ff.

It should be noted that the conclusion reached above is based on assumptions with respect to the responses of businessmen that might not hold if the extent of the rise in spending and taxes were so great as to make the government the real entrepreneur, and business merely the marionette to national economic policies. In this event rates of return might be guaranteed net of taxes, so that tax discouragement to investment decisions would not come in question. Similarly, once it was apparent that the government was to be the dominant force in the economy, there would be no reason why a further increase in government spending would exert an adverse psychological effect on business spending decisions.   •

The reaction in the output of producers' goods to a change in consumption spending, however, differs as between an upswing and a downswing. When consumption declines, the induced decline in the output of producers' goods is limited by the impossibility (except for disinvestment in producers' goods inventories) of a fall of output of producers' goods to less than zero. The limitations that apply in the upswing are of a different sort, and the principle of derived demand therefore does not operate in a parallel manner. The only physical limitation to increased investment in response to increased consumer demand is the availability of labor and materials and the time required for putting new investment plans into action. Below a certain level of output there are ample supplies of both labor and materials. As full utilization of capacity and full employment are approached, however, the rate of increase in new *real* investment must decline. This limit does not, of course, apply to *money* investment. Businessmen may compete with one another for limited supplies of the factors of production, simply driving up wages and prices. Here a limit, if the monetary authority causes it to operate, is found in the increasing difficulty of obtaining credit as the level of excess bank reserves begins to decline. Other limits are to be found in rigidities and lags, and changing price expectations.

In recent years attempts have been made to relate theories of economic fluctuations to the interaction of the production of producers' goods with that of consumers' goods.[12] It may be that the business cycle can be partly explained by the mutual reinforcement of changes in the rate of investment and consumption, although debate on this question lies outside the scope of the present volume. Whether or not any observed periodicity in economic fluctuations can be explained on the basis of the interaction in the output of producers' and consumers' goods, the fact that economic changes may be propagated by way of the interaction is of importance for fiscal policy for economic stability.

A distinction must be made between *autonomous* and *induced* investment. Induced investment is undertaken in response to changes in the output of finished goods. The demand for durable investment goods is derived from the demand for the goods and services they produce. We have spoken above of an interaction between the demand for producers' goods and the demand for *consumers'* goods. But the relationship is more complex than this. Induced investment responds to changes in total output (consumption plus investment), not to changes in consumption alone. Thus during an upswing, for example, an increase in investment in a particular industry may be due to an increase in investment in another

---

[12] Cf. R. F. Harrod, *Towards a Dynamic Economics* (London: Macmillan, 1949); J. R. Hicks, *A Contribution to the Theory of the Trade Cycle* (Oxford: Clarendon, 1950). The extension of the principle of derived demand to the status of an analytical tool for the diagnosis of economic fluctuations is discussed below as the *acceleration principle*.

industry rather than to an increase in the production of consumers' goods and services. Replacement investment, also, is affected by the rate of output of finished goods.

Autonomous investment is not directly related to changes in the level of consumer and investment output. An example of autonomous investment would be the introduction on a commercial scale of a new invention for which previously no demand had existed. It is expected that the demand will be forthcoming once the product has appeared on the market. For example, the development of rail transport in the nineteenth century did not count on an already existing demand, but depended on a reflux of demand for transport from the new commercial centers that the railroads themselves would open up. In this example a large part of the new demand was created directly and indirectly by the new form of investment itself. The more common form of autonomous investment may rely on economic growth to justify itself. In terms of a more comprehensive economic model including growth as one of the terms, therefore, this form of "autonomous" investment may be regarded as induced.

The interaction between investment and consumption may give rise to *cumulative* upward or downward movements in output. These movements may be either long term (associated with the growth of an industry) or cyclical. In the present context we are concerned with the latter, for we wish to lay the basis for a discussion of the use of fiscal policy to reduce or eliminate cyclical fluctuations in national income and employment. It can be shown that a change in the level of net investment produces a multiplied change in the level of income by way of the effects produced on consumption. Again, changes in the level of consumption may produce magnified effects on investment. These phenomena form the basis, respectively, of the theories of the multiplier and the accelerator. They will be discussed in turn.[13]

► ROLE OF THE CIRCULAR FLOW CONCEPT

In our discussion of the circular flow in Chapter 18, it appeared that so long as total income paid to the factors is entirely spent, either on consumption or on investment, equilibrium is possible in the economic system. This was the case of static equilibrium. Assuming constancy in population, productivity, plant and equipment, and tastes, national income paid out all returns again to the producers in payment for the goods produced during the period. The process is repeated indefinitely. We saw also that a difficulty would develop if that part of national income that is devoted to saving should not find willing borrowers who would invest this saving in plant, equipment, and inventories.

---

[13] For an excellent discussion of these concepts in the framework of the study of business fluctuations, see R. A. Gordon, *Business Fluctuations* (New York: Harper, 1952), Chaps. IV and V.

Advocates of fiscal policy for full employment contend that if it does not prove feasible to stimulate private firms to borrow and invest these savings, the government should see to it that national income is brought to the full-employment level. Although it is in practice difficult, or perhaps impossible, for the government to do this without unbalancing the budget, it is nevertheless politically desirable to accomplish the objective with a minimum deficit. Also, because it is important to have some idea of how much government spending will be required to accomplish the objective, we wish to know what becomes of the money that the government injects into the income stream.

► THE MARGINAL PROPENSITY TO CONSUME

Suppose that under conditions of considerable unemployment the government decides to increase its deficit-financed investment.[14] This means that new incomes will be paid out to the extent, let us say, of $1 billion in a year. The incomes of all those who sell goods or services to the government will increase, in different degree; each individual will spend a portion of the increase in his income, and will save the rest. Although this proportion will differ from one individual to the next, there will be for the economy as a whole some typical marginal propensity to consume out of this *new* income. In other words, we may say that when the income of the country increases, in general a certain proportion of the increase will be spent on consumption.

If the whole of the additional spending of $1 billion gets immediately into the hands of previously unemployed workers, the marginal propensity to consume is close to 100 per cent.[15] If, on the other hand, the additional investment spending was in the first instance received by high-income manufacturers and merchants, who might conceivably save the whole of it, the marginal propensity to consume would be zero. Again, part of the new investment spending will find its way into the receipts of corporations. To the extent that these fail to distribute profits to stockholders, the whole of such additional income is saved. Thus with respect to this part of additional income the marginal propensity to consume is also zero.

In practice, new money injected into the income stream enters it at many different points, so that for the economy as a whole the marginal propensity to consume is never likely to vary in anything like this degree. It is probable, however, that if the new investment spending results in the employment of a large amount of labor relative to capital, the marginal propensity to consume will be considerably higher than otherwise.

When national income remains at the same level for period after

---

[14] The same analysis applies, of course, if there is an increase in net *private* investment.

[15] Part of their new income will, of course, be devoted to the repayment of debt. This reduces their marginal propensity to consume to less than unity.

period (the static equilibrium case), it makes no difference whether the *average* propensity to consume is high or low, provided that there is no difficulty in getting all savings borrowed. That part of national income that is saved and invested contributes just as much to the maintenance of income in the following period as does that part of national income that is consumed. But the situation is different during a depression. If the prospects for profits are unfavorable, it is difficult to find investment outlets for new savings. Therefore, the greater the proportion of new income that the factors of production spend on consumers' goods rather than save, the more effective the new investment will be in causing a rise in income.[16]

► THE MULTIPLIER

By how much will national income rise in response to an increase in investment? The net increase in investment must, of course, be matched by an equal increase in saving. The latter, however, can come only from the increase in national income generated by the investment. Therefore, the amount of income created must be such that the saving made out of the increment to national income is equal to the increase in net investment. It follows that the smaller the proportion of the new income that is saved, the larger the additional income must be in order to assure that the required amount of saving is forthcoming. This case can be illustrated as follows.

Suppose that there is net additional investment (either private or public) of $1 billion. Clearly, income must rise by more than this amount if savings of $1 billion are to be generated (unless, of course, the entire addition to income is saved). For illustrative purposes let us assume that 9/10 of the additional income would be spent on consumption, and 1/10 saved. In that case additional income of $10 billion would be required in order to generate the additional saving of $1 billion. Thus, whenever there is net[17] additional investment a "multiplier" operates that relates the resulting additional income[18] to the investment. We have, of course, said nothing as yet about how much time this operation will require.

---

[16] One way in which equilibrium can be maintained when not all new savings are being borrowed is for the government to convert the excess savings to consumption by taxing savings and subsidizing the poor. This may, however, discourage investment, and thus increase the magnitude of the problem.

[17] The word "net" is crucial here. If the effect of additional public investment is to discourage private investment, there is, of course, an offset to the increase. If the decline in private investment is exactly equal to the rise in public investment, the positive and negative multiplier effects cancel each other out.

[18] Saving and investment are defined as equal in Keynesian multiplier analysis. Thus whenever net new investment is made, an equal amount of savings is brought into being. But the other side of "investment spending" is "income of sellers of productive agents." The proportion of this new income that is devoted to consumption and saving determines the increase in income that must occur in response to a given act of net investment.

Other "multipliers" can be imagined. For example, the multiplier might be taken to be the ratio of employment created by the rise in total income to the employment created by the original investment. This "employment multiplier" would be of interest primarily when an attempt

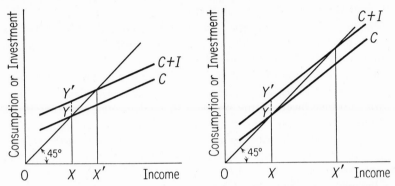

In Figures 15 and 16 a line drawn from the origin at an angle of 45° indicates that at each level of income, say OX, the whole of income is consumed. The slope of the consumption schedule, C, indicates that below income OX consumption exceeds income, and above it, is smaller than income. At incomes greater than OX the distance vertically from the consumption schedule to the 45° line represents saving (= investment).

Suppose that the government or industry increases investment. This causes an increase in income in the investment goods industries, and that part of the increased income which is spent on consumption goods propagates further the rise in incomes. If investment is YY', the increase in income is XX'. In the second diagram the steeper slope of the C line indicates a high marginal propensity to consume. Consequently, a given amount of investment, YY', has a greater multiplied effect on income, XX'. Multiplier effects are not restricted to the investment multiplier considered in the diagram; an upward shift in the consumption schedule would have a similar multiplied effect on income. Cf. A. Hansen, *Business Cycles and National Income* (New York: Norton, 1951), Chap. XII.

Fig. 15

CASE 1: THE MULTIPLIER

Fig. 16

CASE 2: THE MULTIPLIER

was being made to eliminate unemployment through increased public investment. But if the increase in investment took place at close to full employment, the employment multiplier would not be very great because not many workers could be found who were unemployed. The ordinary multiplier would not be affected by the absence of unemployment, however,

Consider the relations among income (Y), consumption (C), saving (S), and investment (I), during the time period t.

$$S_t \equiv Y_t - C_t$$
$$Y_t \equiv C_t + I_t$$

Therefore, $S_t \equiv I_t$.

That is, saving and investment are necessarily equal because they are defined as identical.

because if the net new investment were undertaken at close to full employment, prices would be driven up. The multiplier effect would be reflected in terms of dollar incomes. The rise in investment and national income would simply be partly fictitious, since it would be composed in part of a rise in prices only. The employment multiplier, therefore, throws more light than does the standard multiplier on the real effects of changes in investment, just as the concept "real national income" tells us more about national productivity than does "money national income," which says nothing about changes in the price level.

If the definition of the multiplier is made too broad, the concept loses part of its analytical usefulness, though it is true that light may be thrown on other facets of the problem that might otherwise remain invisible. Thus the multiplier might be defined as the ratio of total additional investment in all industries, or even total additional national income, to the original net increment of investment. This includes in the multiplier concept not only the effect of new investment on national income, but also the effect of the induced rise in national income on investment in still other industries. If, however, more can be learned by separating these two effects, there is no point in thus extending the coverage of the multiplier concept, although for certain purposes it may have its own particular usefulness.[19]

THE PERIOD MULTIPLIER VS. THE MULTIPLIER FORMULA

Let us go back to the case in which a single act of new investment is undertaken amounting to $1 billion. As stated above, if the factors of production which receive the payments from businessmen or the government save a portion, say $100 million, only one tenth of the savings has been generated that will be required to make possible $1 billion of investment. In Keynesian multiplier analysis, saving and investment are always equal. Therefore, the problem arises of reconciling the fact that $1 billion is invested in the first period, while only $100 million is saved by the recipients of the proceeds of the investment. Clearly, there must be an offset in the form of disinvestment of $900 million in the first period. Ultimately, when enough income will have been generated to permit saving equal to investment of $1 billion, the disinvestment offset will have disappeared. This disinvestment can be handled by taking account of the depletion of stocks of inventories that occurs when that portion of the new income that is not saved is devoted to the purchase of consumers' goods. Thus if, in the above example, $900 million is spent on consumers' goods, disinvestment in inventories of consumers' goods amounting to $900 million takes place, so that net investment is only $100 million, which is equal to saving. The value of the multiplier, then, is $1 billion

---

[19] For a generalized version of the multiplier, related to long-term growth of the economy, refer to Hicks's concept of the "supermultiplier."—Hicks, *op. cit.*, p. 62. See also page 465, footnote 32.

(the addition to income) divided by net investment ($100 million), or 10. It has been shown that by taking account of inventory disinvestment in this way, period after period, the value of the multiplier remains invariant, while it is the multiplicand (investment) that varies, reaching its equilibrium value (in our example, $1 billion) only after an infinite number of periods.[20]

THE PERIOD MULTIPLIER

The point has been made above that if new investment, financed out of bank loans or by sales of securities to savers, is undertaken during a depression, the savings that are made out of the resulting increased incomes are likely to remain partly or entirely idle. To the extent that this is so, only that part of new income which is spent on consumption will become income in the hands of businessmen in each successive time period.

Let us assume that businessmen do not hoard any of their receipts. Then on the (very restricted) assumption that a constant proportion of income is spent on consumption, period after period, the total multiplier effect can be calculated. It is important to notice that we are speaking here only of consumption out of additional income resulting from the increase in investment. If $1 billion is invested by either businessmen or the government (still assuming that all savings are hoarded), and if 90 per cent of the income thus paid to the factors is consumed and 10 per cent saved, $900,000 is spent on consumers' goods and nothing on producers' goods.

If the consumers' goods industries do not hoard their additional receipts[21] but, in order to maintain their inventories, pay the whole $900,000 out to workers and other factors in these industries, 9/10 of the original additional investment is paid out again in the second period. If we retain the assumption that 9/10 of additional income is spent on consumers' goods, then in the second period $810,000 is spent on consumers' goods, and $90,000 is saved. If we continue to assume that nothing has changed the outlook of businessmen with respect to the advisability of increasing investment, these savings again remain idle. Clearly so long as our assumptions are left unchanged, this chain goes on indefinitely, always at a diminishing rate.[22]

---

[20] Cf. Robert Eisner, "The Invariant Multiplier," *Review of Economic Studies,* XVII (3), No. 44 (1949–1950), 198–202.

[21] Which they are likely to do early in the depression at least, before they have reduced inventories to the lower level that they regard as appropriate to a low national income.

[22] The reader may detect an apparent inconsistency between the assumption (1) that no investment is induced and (2) that producers of consumers' goods are willing to reorder from wholesalers, and thus permit the multiplier effects to operate from period to period. The fact is that, particularly in the early stages of a depression, when inventories are too high for the low depression level of spending, producers may not all reorder, and to that extent the multiplier effects are stopped dead. However, no depression is likely to be so deep that *no* induced investment

The diminishing series, by means of which the so-called "period" multiplier may be calculated, is as follows:

Period	I	II	III	IV	. . .	N
Income paid out						

in $ billion...... $1 + 0.900 + 0.810 + 0.729 + \ldots \quad 1/\infty = 10.$

or $\qquad 1 + C + C^2 + C^3 + \ldots + C^n = 1/1-C.$

If the marginal propensity to consume (*MPC*), period after period, is assumed to be 5/10, the series is as follows (Example 2):

Period	I	II	III	IV	. . .	N
Income paid out						

in $ billion...... $1 + 0.500 + 0.250 + 0.125 + \ldots + 1/\infty = 2.$

Thus the multiplier is the reciprocal of the marginal propensity to save:

$$\frac{1}{\triangle s/\triangle y} \quad \text{or} \quad \frac{1}{1 - \dfrac{\triangle c}{\triangle y}} \left(\text{i.e.,} \quad \frac{1}{1 - MPC} \right)$$

where $\triangle s/\triangle y$ is the addition to saving (*S*) incident to an increase in income (*Y*), and $\triangle c/\triangle y$ is the addition to consumption. Thus in Example 1, with a marginal propensity to consume of 9/10, the formula reads

$$K = \frac{1}{1 - 9/10} = 10;$$

and in Example 2,

$$K = \frac{1}{1 - 1/2} = 2.$$

The significance of the multiplier in terms of time periods can perhaps be best appreciated by considering what would occur if all increments of income were spent on consumption. In this case the series would appear as follows:

Period	I	II	III	IV	V	VI	VII	. . .	N
Additional income									

in $ billion........ $1 + 1 + 1 + 1 + 1 + 1 + 1 + \ldots$ approaches $\infty.$

Here the multiplier is infinite. Also, the additional income, over an infinitely long period of time, is infinite. But *as of any "moment" of time,* say Period VII, or Period *N,* income has risen by only $1 billion. It is therefore important to note that only if the multiplier were infinite would

---

occurs in consequence of the rise in income. But multiplier theory may treat induced investment as an addition to the original increase in net investment; in other words, as an increase in the *multiplicand* to which the multiplier is applied. In brief, the effects of a net increase in investment are enhanced to the extent that investment is induced by the rise in income; but they are diminished to the extent that not all of the money spent by consumers is passed on by retailers and producers of consumers' goods.

a *single* act of investment of $1 billion necessarily cause a permanent increase in the level of national income of $1 billion.[23] If the multiplier is anything less than infinity, in other words, if the marginal propensity to consume out of new income is less than 1, then national income will not necessarily remain permanently at the higher level. It will do so only if all the savings made out of the new income are borrowed as rapidly as they are made. How does multiplier analysis deal with induced investment (i.e., investment which is induced by the rise in income resulting from the original act of investment)? Earlier we suggested that this might be handled by a change in the multiplicand. Another way of handling it is by redefining the multiplier according to the following formula:

$$\frac{1}{1 - (MPC + MPI)}$$

where *MPI* is the marginal propensity to invest, or $\frac{\Delta I}{\Delta Y}$.

In order to demonstrate the way in which income gradually falls back again to the level at which it stood prior to the new act of spontaneous investment, the foregoing discussion has concerned itself with a single act of net additional investment. In this case the full multiplier effects are experienced only after an infinite number of periods, although the bulk of the effects of a diminishing series are felt after relatively few periods. If instead of a single act of investment in the first period, we assume that this amount of investment is made in each time period, the full multiplier effects are ultimately experienced.[24] This is shown in the following example (assuming a marginal propensity to consume of five tenths, and thus a multiplier of 2), in which new investment of $1 billion in each period is shown as initiating a diminishing series of consumption spending in each succeeding period.

It is apparent that if a given increment of investment is repeated in each successive period, the increase in income approaches the product of the investment in each period and the multiplier. The higher the marginal propensity to consume, and therefore the larger the multiplier, the larger will be the rise in income resulting from the continuous investment of a given amount in each successive period. In period *N* the addition to income would approach $10 billion if the multiplier were 10, and so long as the investment continued to be made in each time period income would remain at this level.

---

[23] If the multiplier is infinite, and if $1 billion is invested *in each time period*, income would rise gradually to and beyond the full-employment level. That is, there would be a progressive inflation.

[24] Cf. Fritz Machlup, "Period Analysis and Multiplier Theory," *Quarterly Journal of Economics,* November, 1939, pp. 1–27 (reprinted in American Economic Association, *Readings in Business Cycle Theory* [Philadelphia: Blakiston, 1944], pp. 203–234) for an extended discussion of multiplier period analysis.

Period	I	II	III	IV	V	VI	VII	VIII
TOTAL INCOME[a]	101.0	101.5	101.75	101.875	101.9375	101.9688	101.9845	101.9924
Assumed original level of national income	100.0	100.0	100.0	100.0	100.0	100.0	100.0	100.0
Net new investment	1.0	1.0	1.0	1.0	1.0	1.0	1.0	1.0
Effects on income in each period								
	1.0	0.5	0.25	0.125	0.0625	0.0313	0.0157	0.0079
		1.0	0.5	0.25	0.125	0.0625	0.0313	0.0157
			1.0	0.5	0.25	0.125	0.0625	0.0313
				1.0	0.5	0.25	0.125	0.0625
					1.0	0.5	0.25	0.125
						1.0	0.5	0.25
							1.0	0.5
								1.0

[a] In billions of dollars.

THE ROLE OF THE SIZE OF THE MULTIPLIER

Clearly account can be taken of differences in the marginal propensity to consume from period to period only if we use the time-period approach to the multiplier.[25] Another interesting point can be appreciated through this form of the multiplier. Most of the multiplier effects are quickly achieved even with a large multiplier, but a greater proportion of the total effect has been reached as of a given period with a small than with a large multiplier.[26] Thus with a large multiplier (say 10), 34.4 per cent of the total multiplier effects have been achieved by the fourth income period:

$$1 \times 9/10 \times 81/100 \times 729/1000 = 3.439/10 = 34.4\%,$$

while with a smaller multiplier a greater proportion of the total effect has been reached by the fourth period:

$$1 \times 1/2 \times 1/4 \times 1/8 = 1.875/2 = 93.8\%.$$

It must not be inferred, of course, that this fact means that a small multiplier is more effective than a large one in stimulating a rise in national income and employment. The *absolute* effects achieved by the fourth time period are greater in the case of the larger multiplier.

We are interested, of course, in the length of these periods in terms of calendar time. It makes a great deal of difference whether a given multiplier effect is achieved at the expiration of four periods of one month each or four periods of one year each. In order to know the length of a multiplier period, we must know what a multiplier period is.

The multiplier period is closely related to income velocity, but is not identical with it. The former is the average period of time between successive spendings on consumption. The concept of income velocity, on the other hand, relates to the length of time between successive income payments. Although the two concepts differ, it is probable that both periods are, under reasonably stable economic conditions, of the order of one fourth to one third of a year. Statistical difficulties, and the lack of certain data, make exact calculations of the multiplier period difficult. Moreover, in a depression and during periods like booms and impending scarcities of goods the multiplier period may differ greatly in length from what it would be in more normal times. The period multiplier analysis, therefore, is primarily of use as a conceptual device. It would be highly misleading to assume any particular value for the multiplier period and to apply it blindly regardless of circumstances.

---

[25] The multiplier formula is a "mere arithmetic multiplier" which tells us nothing about the consumption responses, over time, of the recipients of additional income. Cf Alvin Hansen, *A Guide to Keynes* (New York: McGraw, 1953), p. 111.

[26] Machlup, *op. cit.*, p. 220.

► THE MULTIPLIER AS A TOOL IN THE ANALYSIS OF ECONOMIC FLUCTUATIONS

The discussion thus far has concerned itself primarily with formal aspects of the multiplier. The multiplier is merely a mode of expressing the propensity of the public as a whole to devote *additional* income to consumption. The limitations of the concept are implicit in its nature and objectives. One of these limitations, it appears from the foregoing discussion, is its neglect of investment. Yet investment is regarded in most business-cycle theories as the key to economic fluctuations.[27] Consequently it is clear that other tools are necessary as well if we are to search for a complete explanation of the causes of economic fluctuations and for cures by way of fiscal policy. But we also need to inquire into the reliability of the multiplier itself. Does the value of the mutliplier remain constant for periods long enough to permit its effective use as a tool of analysis? Is it possible, by studying consumption habits in the past, to draw inferences with respect to the probable multiplier effects of a change in the rate of investment?

FLUCTUATIONS IN THE VALUE OF THE MULTIPLIER

The concept of the multiplier would be of use even if we had no idea of its arithmetical value, or whether or not it remained fairly constant from period to period. It is worth something to know that the inflationary effects of net new investment are not exhausted at the end of the period in which the new money has been injected into the economy. If, however, the multiplier is to be used as a device to help predict the future course of income in order to determine what role fiscal policy should play in economic stabilization, its value must be predictable even if not stable. Otherwise, it can only be said retrospectively that although the multiplier probably had a certain value, this value cannot be known beforehand.

The fact that some proportion of national income is normally saved means that the *average* propensity to consume out of income is less than unity. Keynes stated as a conviction the view that when income rises, the public will increase the level of consumption, but not by as much as the increase in income. This he called the psychological propensity to con-

---

[27] A number of cycle theories have, of course, stressed underconsumption as the key to depression, and overproduction in the consumption goods industries as the cause of a crisis in the investment goods industries during the prosperity phase. The majority of economists believe, however, that although these factors serve to exaggerate the amplitude and duration of fluctuations, they are not the major cause of business cycles. Nevertheless, it must be pointed out that there have been a number of attempts in recent years to develop theories of the cycle based on the *interaction* of consumption and investment. This problem will be discussed briefly below, in connection with the relations between the accelerator and the multiplier.

sume.[28] To the extent that individuals do not gear their spending solely to increases and decreases in current income, the marginal propensity to consume and, therefore, the value of the multiplier are subject to doubt. It may, however, prove to be possible on the basis of statistical surveys to estimate the probable marginal propensity to consume in a given country, under given economic conditions, despite the fact that changes in consumption are not related solely to changes in income. One difficulty with attempts to evaluate the multiplier on the basis of statistics of income and consumption is that historical data are *realized* data, and therefore do not reveal future relationships between consumption and income.

OTHER FUNCTIONAL RELATIONSHIPS

When an individual receives an addition to income, the factors that determine the percentage of this income that he will spend on consumption may be quite complex. Among the most important of these are the following: the speed with which the individual responds to changes in income by altering the level of his consumption, anticipated future increases in income, the rate of change of income in the past and the expected rate of change in the future, the amount of savings he possesses, the degree of liquidity of these savings, and his former and anticipated standards of living. Finally, a separate question is whether the responses are symmetrical when the change in income is in the upward or the downward direction. Each of these cases will be briefly discussed.

Income in Earlier Periods.   The simplicity of the multiplier formula can easily lead to an exaggeration of the amount of instability in the economy when the rate of investment increases or decreases. The multiplier formula assumes that consumption is a function of income in one period only. In fact, however, consumption may also depend on income in the past. In other words, it may be necessary to take account of distributed lags. These lags tend to damp the magnitude of the multiplier effects. Thus if income has sharply risen in period $t,$ the lower incomes received in periods $t - 1,$ $t - 2,$ and so forth, would affect consumption because consumption is only in part a function of income received in the current period. Thus the marginal propensity to consume and the multiplier would be reduced. The same considerations apply in reverse, though not necessarily symmetrically, when there is a fall in investment and income.

---

[28] Keynes's psychological law does not apply at all to that part of national income that takes the form of undistributed corporate profits, for the propensity to consume out of income withheld by business firms is zero. In view of the growth during recent years in corporate profits, and in the proportion of profits withheld from distribution to stockholders, the psychological propensity to consume has a rather limited application in the economy as a whole. It remains relevant, however, to individual incomes. (These statements do not imply that Keynes neglected business savings in the *General Theory*.)

Expected Future Income. If an individual receives additional income, the proportion of this income that he will consume is determined in part by his expectations with respect to income in the future. If he expects subsequent additional increases in real income, he may feel safe in devoting a large part of any given increase to consumption. On the other hand, he may wish to accomplish his saving as quickly as possible, in which case he will postpone any expansion in his living standards until he actually receives the subsequent additions to income. Attitudes will obviously vary widely among different individuals according to their economic and personal circumstances, as well as to their individual attitudes toward saving. If a person regards the addition to income as only temporary, he may consciously avoid devoting any of it to consumption, on the ground that it is easier to save unexpected windfalls than to save out of currently budgeted income. On the other hand, many people regard temporary additional income as a consumption bonus, and consume the whole of it.

The Rate of Change of Income.   Generalization is impossible from specific cases. The rate at which income is changing exercises an important effect on the rapidity with which people will alter the proportion of income consumed. The reason is that they may lag in changing their living standards in response to changed income. The effect will differ not only according to differing attitudes among individuals, but also for the same individual, depending on how much time he has had to become wedded to a given way of life. Thus while Keynes's psychological law would say that if a man's income were to decrease he would lower his consumption, but not by as much as the decline in income, he might not in fact reduce his consumption immediately. Consequently, the rate at which income is changing is significant for the shape of the consumption function.

The Accumulation of Savings.   The size of a man's savings relative to income becomes important for his response to a change in income. If he has already saved enough to assure security, he may not decrease consumption when his income falls. If, on the other hand, his income rises, the possession of a large amount of assets may prompt him to spend the whole of the increase. But if the reason for his large savings was that his income was already so high as to enable him to save automatically, the whole of any increase may likewise be automatically saved.

The *liquidity* of savings also exercises an independent influence. Savings in the form of durable consumers' goods and fixed capital may not be regarded as sufficiently liquid to justify the spending of the whole of any increase in income. If savings are highly liquid, however, a person may feel safe in consuming a relatively large proportion of increased income. Since it is possible to borrow on the security of many types of illiquid savings, this point may not always be of great significance in practice.

Increases and Decreases in Income. The question must now be raised whether consumption responses to negative changes in income are in general parallel with those associated with positive changes. In view of the wide variety of the possible reactions to changes in income, there seems good reason to believe that the effects of increases and decreases in income on consumption are likely to be asymmetrical. For example, a public conditioned to the dangers of depression might be much more disposed to curtail consumption when income falls than to expand it when income rises. Conversely, after years of high-level income, the reverse might be true. Considerations of this kind have to be taken into account in any study of the practical value of analytical tools like the marginal propensity to consume and the multiplier. Unless there is an awareness of the possibility of asymmetries of this kind, the common mistake could be made of believing that estimates of the marginal propensity to consume arrived at on the basis of an examination of past experience could be automatically used for predictive purposes.

THE MULTIPLIER AND FISCAL POLICY

Because it is statistically difficult to ascertain the value of the multiplier, because the value of the consumption function (and therefore the multiplier) differs depending on whether we are concerned with short or with long periods of time, and because consumption is not a function of increases in income alone, one may have doubts as to the value of the concept as an analytical tool. It is true that the multiplier cannot be confidently used as a predictive device. Nevertheless, it is of great assistance to fiscal authorities in steering a course between inadequate or excessive use of public investment to bring about full employment. For the multiplier calls attention to the fact that the income effects of a net increase in investment or consumption spending do not immediately disappear. Therefore, an understanding of the role of the multiplier is a help to public morale during the depression, when there may be a tendency to overestimate the difficulties facing the government in raising the level of income; and knowledge of the existence and order of magnitude of multiplier effects reduces the temptation to continue the recipe of deficit spending too far into the upswing.

The marginal propensity to consume and the multiplier are also of help in the analysis of the effects of shifts in income from one income bracket to another, as well as between other group classifications in the national economy. To the extent that marginal propensities to consume differ as among different groups, net effects are produced on the level of consumption spending. By ascertaining these effects, we are in a position to take the next step, namely, to assess the effects on total spending (investment plus consumption spending) whenever a redistribution of income takes place.

► THE ACCELERATION PRINCIPLE

Attention has been called above to the fact that an increase in spending on consumption may engender an increase in the output of the plant and equipment required to produce them. This will occur, of course, only if there is no overcapacity in the capital goods industries. Again, an increase in output at a late stage of production may cause an increase in demand for the semifinished commodities produced at earlier stages. As we have seen, this is the principle of derived demand. Under certain circumstances an increase in the demand for a commodity involves a more than proportional, or accelerated, increase in the demand for the capital instruments that contribute to its manufacture. The existence of this phenomenon is borne out empirically by the observed fact that output in the producers' goods industries tends to fluctuate more violently over the cycle than does output in the consumers' goods industries. The case may be illustrated by the following *highly oversimplified* example.

EXAMPLE

Suppose that (1) there is neither excess capacity nor excess inventories, and (2) producers of capital equipment relate their output decisions strictly to the demand for goods in the industries using this equipment.[29] (These industries, incidentally, do not have to be consumers' goods industries. An increase in the demand for a certain type of machine tool, for example, affects the demand for the machine that makes this tool.) Suppose that 100 units of capital produce 1,000 units of a certain commodity per year, and that the plant wears out and is replaced at the rate of 10 per cent a year. Thus 10 units of capital have to be produced each year in order to maintain an output of consumers' goods of 1,000 per year. Now assume that there is an increase of 10 per cent in the demand for consumers' goods. This requires the production of new units of plant and equipment amounting to *10 per cent* of the original capacity, or 10 units. Thus the output of capital has *doubled,* from 10 to 20 units.

Obviously, the output of producers' goods, under these assumptions, fluctuates much more violently than does that of consumers' goods. It should be borne in mind that we have assumed that there is no idle plant. If, however, there is excess capacity, part or all of the additionally demanded consumers' goods can be produced out of equipment already in existence, and there may be little, if any, additional demand for capital goods. Moreover, for purposes of illustration we perhaps assumed a much greater increase in the demand for consumers' goods than is likely to be met with in practice unless demand has previously sunk to extremely low

---

[29] If these assumptions are not borne out, the derived demand (accelerator) principle will not operate in the manner described, and may not operate at all.

levels. The principle is the same, however, even if we assumed an increase in the demand for consumers' goods of 5 per cent rather than 10 per cent. Finally, producers of capital goods may respond sluggishly, if at all, to a rise in demand. They may regard the changed demand conditions as merely temporary.

We conclude that under our assumptions an increase in consumption spending can lead to a multiplied increase in investment, and therefore in income and employment, because of the more than proportional effect on the demand for producers' goods. But since the word "multiplier" has already been used to relate an increase in income to the increase in consumption or investment that caused it, a different term must be employed to describe this phenomenon. The term most commonly used is the "accelerator" or the "principle of acceleration."

The acceleration principle relates changes in consumption (or more generally, output) to changes in investment. We are concerned with the *induced* investment that results from fluctuations in the demand for commodities. A change in the level of induced investment can occur only when there is a change in output. At a stable level of output there is merely a steady demand for capital instruments as they wear out and are replaced at a constant rate.

Suppose, in the above example, that in the next year there is no further increase in the demand for consumers' goods. Demand therefore remains at 1,100 units of consumers' goods. Consequently there is a decline in the output of producers' goods from 20 to 10 units.[30] In practice the decline is not likely to be nearly so violent as this, for in the early stages of the upswing the existence of excess capacity would have probably made the actual increase in the output of capital in the previous year substantially less than that (from 10 to 20 units) in the example.

Table 15. Illustration of the Principle of Derived Demand

Period	Output of Finished Goods	Per Cent Increase	Capital Goods Required	Increase over Previous Period	Replacement Investment	Total Output of Capital Goods
1	1,000	—	100	—	10	10
2	1,100	10	110	10	10	20
3	1,155	5	115.5	5.5	10	15.5

The output of capital goods will likewise decline if the *rate of change* of output of finished goods, though still positive, declines. This is shown in Table 15, where in the third period a decline in the percentage increase in the output of finished goods from 10 per cent to 5 per cent produces

[30] Depreciation of capital is now at the rate of 11 units a year (10 per cent of 110). But none of the new capital will be replaced until ten years have elapsed.

an absolute decline in the output of capital goods from 20 units to 15.5 units.

Since a point may be expected in any upswing at which the rate of increase in output can no longer be maintained, it follows that the relation between the producers' goods industries and the consumers' goods industries is a source of economic instability.[31]

THE ACCELERATOR IN THE DOWNSWING

The accelerator may operate in the downswing in a manner that is not parallel to its behavior in response to increase output. Let us note two cases. The first illustrates a parallel situation. Suppose that instead of increasing, the output of consumers' goods declines by 10 per cent. Then in the example used above, only 90 units of capital are required to produce the lower output of consumers' goods of 900 units. Consequently, the machines that wear out in the current year are not replaced, and output in the capital goods industry has declined by 100 per cent, or by 10 units divided by 10. In this case the accelerator operates in the same way during a downswing as during the upswing.

Suppose, however, that demand for consumers' goods had declined by 20 per cent. It would then require only 80 units of capital to produce the 800 units of consumers' goods. But only 10 machines wear out during the year, so that the fall in capital goods output is the same as in the preceding case. In other words, gross output of capital goods cannot be less than zero. This type of limitation does not operate in the upswing, although other limits restrict the scope of the accelerator in that case. They are, however, less rigid. Labor and materials may not be easily available, but except at full employment the supply is not completely inelastic. Again, as we have seen, an important restriction on the investment reaction to increased demand for consumers' goods is the increasing difficulty of obtaining bank credit. Here again we are concerned not with a rigid ceiling, but with a type of limit that varies according to circumstances.

▶ INTERACTION BETWEEN THE ACCELERATOR AND THE MULTIPLIER

If there is a mutual interaction between consumption and investment, it is conceivable that a sufficient impetus to one or the other (or both) might set in motion a spiral that would lead out of depression to full employment, or, conversely, that would speed up a downswing. At the same time, if either of these spirals got out of control, there might be great difficulty in stopping at the full-employment level of national income,

---

[31] For similar tables illustrating the acceleration principle for consumers' durable goods and inventories, as well as durable capital goods, see Gordon, *op. cit.*, pp. 108–109.

or in preventing a recession from turning into a deep depression. There-fore, the possibility that a relatively small impetus might move a depressed economy toward full employment constitutes both a challenge and a threat to the use of fiscal policy as an instrument for doing away with mass unemployment.

What is the likelihood that the "leverage" effect of the interaction of these two principles may be adequate to relieve the government of the necessity of doing more than providing the initial toward impetus?[32] Is this effect likely to become more and more powerful as the upswing or downswing continues? Finally, is there reason to believe that this inter-action may itself produce a wave motion that is partly responsible for cyclical fluctuations in income and employment?

THE USE OF MODELS

Considerable work has been done by model-builders to show that different cyclical effects are produced under varying assumptions with respect to the values of the multiplier and the accelerator.[33] By making assumptions as to the response of the induced consumption expenditure of individuals to a net increase in deficit-financed government investment, and with respect to the amount of private investment in turn induced by the increase in consumption, we can calculate the total addition to national income caused by a given increase in public spending. Samuelson has pointed out that if the accelerator is zero, that is, if a rise in consumption causes no increase at all in the demand for plant and equipment, income rises by virtue of the action of the multiplier alone. Thus, if a given amount of new public investment is made *in each multiplier period,* the addition to national income approaches the product of the net increase in public investment and the multiplier.[34] With moderately high values of the accelerator, a constant level of government expenditures results in oscil-latory movements in national income, and with higher values of the accelerator and the multiplier the magnitude of the fluctuations in income increases. With very large values of the multiplier and the relation, national income rises continuously, even with a *single* act of net investment. This case corresponds with pump priming.[35]

---

[32] The combined multiplier-accelerator effect is sometimes referred to as the "super-multiplier." See Hansen, *Business Cycles and National Income,* p. 173. See also page 452, footnote 19, above.

[33] The first step was taken by Paul Samuelson, "Interactions between the Multi-plier Analysis and the Principle of Acceleration," *Review of Economic Statistics,* May, 1939, on a suggestion by Professor Hansen.

[34] It is important to bear in mind the assumption that the government is making the given amount of new investment in each multiplier period. If there has been only one impulse of net investment, income would have risen by the amount of the investment and then gradually fallen back to the original level.

[35] For a discussion of pump priming, see below. The term "relation" used above is synonymous with "accelerator."

EVALUATION OF THE MODELS

The mathematical treatment of the multiplier and the accelerator that lies behind this model-building requires the values of these terms to remain constant, or to change in a definite way, during the period under consideration. It is precisely here that the weakness of these concepts for purposes of prediction becomes apparent.[36] For just as we have seen in the case of the multiplier, the accelerator is certainly not constant, cannot be predicted, and may not even be known.

If these concepts are used for prediction it is like driving a locomotive with rubber connecting rods. They do not transmit power in a definite, predictable fashion. Thus, for example, if firms build ahead of demand in anticipation of the lower costs that will be possible when the market permits an expansion of output, they habitually maintain a certain amount of overcapacity. If demand for their product then increases they are not likely to feel it necessary to expand plant still further.[37] Again, expectations as to the likelihood of the continuance of increased demand must affect the output responses of producers of capital goods. Still another point is the fact that for technical reasons the reaction of producers of investment goods to an increase in demand varies enormously from industry to industry. The hesitancy of the steel producers to increase capacity at the outset of the Korean conflict is a case in point.[38]

Even if the multiplier and the accelerator operate differently in different circumstances, it may still be true that they reinforce one another, so that an initial injection of purchasing power by government or business into the income stream could put the economy on the road to full employment. Indeed, if the accelerator and the multiplier are defined considerably more broadly than is usually done, it is clear that the interaction between them is what in fact leads to full employment. This is no more than saying, of course, that it is the spread of economic changes from consumers' goods industries to producers' goods industries and back again that constitutes upswings and downswings. What we have to do is to inquire whether the values of the multiplier and the accelerator are likely to be great enough, at a time when a public works program for full employment is contemplated, so that after an initial injection of purchasing

---

[36] It should be carefully noted, however, that the use of models should not be judged on the basis of their capacity for prediction. They are analytical tools, and as such, are indispensable to clear thinking. The temptation to use them directly as a basis for policy recommendations has to be avoided until a great deal of empirical research on actual cases has been accomplished.

[37] H. B. Chenery, "Overcapacity and the Acceleration Principle," *Econometrica*, January, 1952.

[38] Many economists have warned against the assumption that the accelerator is "an immutable link between output and needed capital." See D. M. Robertson, "A Revolutionist's Handbook," *Quarterly Journal of Economics*, February, 1950, p. 12, and S. C. Tsiang, "The Accelerator, the Theory of the Firm, and the Business Cycle," *Quarterly Journal of Economics*, August, 1951, *passim*.

power the government can withdraw and leave the continuation of the recovery in private hands. In other words, can government spending "prime the pump"?[39]

▶ PRIMING THE PUMP

In the early days of the New Deal it was thought by some economists that increased deficit spending by the government might be able to engender a multiplied increase in consumption, and that this in turn would induce businessmen to increase their investment sufficiently so that an upward spiral of investment and consumption could be set in motion. It is often stated that pump priming failed during the thirties. The fact is that it was never really tried.[40] But would it have succeeded if the government had set out to achieve recovery by this route?

Since a characteristic of upswings and downswings is the mutual interaction of consumption and investment spending, an injection of purchasing power into the income stream by either government or business can be large enough to set in motion an upward spiral that is strong enough to carry the economy to full employment. If the public were convinced that deficit-financed government spending would be maintained at a sufficiently high level, business borrowing and investment might rise in anticipation of the assured demand. This rise might in turn make possible a subsequent decline in the government's contribution to spending. It is conceivable that full employment could be achieved by this route. There is nothing paradoxical in this effect of government spending, for it is exactly what happens when business itself becomes optimistic enough to start the economy on the road to recovery.

THE PROBLEM OF TIMING

There is, nevertheless, an important difference between a normal business recovery and pump priming. The pump-priming philosophy holds that an upswing can be inaugurated at will through a conscious policy adopted by a central planning board. This is a much more difficult matter, however, than simply waiting until the consensus of businessmen regards

---

[39] This expression owes its origin to the practice of using a small amount of water to make a seal when the column of water in a hand pump has drained away.

[40] Advocates of pump priming believed that by temporary deficit spending a sufficient increase in total spending could be brought about to cause private enterprise to borrow in order to expand investment. They hoped that the rise in income would automatically bring in to the Treasury sufficient tax revenues to retire the bonds sold to finance the deficit. Thus the pump primers believed that no fundamental defects of the economy caused depressions, but rather that all that was needed to return to full employment was to inject new money temporarily into the economy via government borrowing. The administration abandoned this policy early in the depression, when recovery was checked in late 1934. See A. E. Burns and D. S. Watson, *Government Spending and Economic Expansion* (Washington, D. C.: American Council on Public Affairs, 1940), Chap. IV.

the time as ripe for recovery. When business investment is the source of increased income, it is not anticipated that those firms which initiated the rise in investment will retire as soon as possible from the field in favor of others. Yet this is the expectation with respect to pump priming by the government. Therefore, possibly insoluble problems of timing exist that do not have to faced in a normal recovery.

On the one hand a decision has to be taken on the proper moment to inaugurate the plan, and on the magnitude of the government deficit. On the other hand, another conscious decision has to be made with respect to the correct moment for the government to withdraw. In neither case is there much reason to be optimistic that very accurate decisions can be made. The likelihood is great that the government will find itself either wasting its deficits in successive insufficient injections of purchasing power, or carrying the policy so far that a powerful tendency arises toward encroachment on the investment that the private sector would have been willing to make.

Timing of the inauguration of the program is made difficult by the fact that a feature of the early months of a depression is the existence of widespread excess capacity and idle stocks of goods. Hesitancy on the part of the government to unbalance its budget and inject new money into the system may permit the development of a deflationary spiral that is increasingly difficult to halt. Yet it is precisely at this phase of the recession that the accelerator is likely to have its weakest effects in stimulating a rise in incomes. Thus the government is in a quandary. If it does not act at once the depression may get out of hand. Even if the authorities do act immediately they are likely to find that a very large proportion of new purchasing power created by the deficit spending is quickly taken out of the income stream again at the points at which excess capacity and idle stocks exist.

A possible solution would be to aim government spending at those points in the economy at which little excess capacity or stocks exist. This is, however, precisely the direct intervention of the government into the day-to-day decisions of businessmen that it is the object of fiscal policy to avoid. Once the government starts to descend from the purely aggregative approach, bureaucratic officials necessarily commence to insist on a specific course of action from the firms that are receiving favorable treatment in the interest of public policy. In any event, most types of public works expenditures are almost inevitably directed toward a limited number of different projects. Thus it is difficult to take advantage of the existence of areas of limited excess capacity and low levels of inventories.

A FURTHER OBSTACLE

Another obstacle to successful pump priming is the doubt that exists in the minds of businessmen whether the government will continue the policy long enough to justify expansion of inventories, plant, and equipment. The same doubt exists, of course, in a normal business upswing with respect to private investment. But here again, whereas in a *business* recovery it is possible for a psychology to develop that is favorable to a continued rise in investment, an upswing that is initiated by government spending may never get over the "hump." Businessmen have to face the possibility that at any moment the government may change its policy and, as new elections approach, no one can be certain that the policy will be continued if there is a change of political parties. As in so many other instances of apparent similarity between the mechanics of action by the government and by free enterprise, the essential difference between the two may be important.

CONCLUSION

In conclusion it appears that not too much reliance ought to be placed on the possibility of inaugurating an upswing with government fiscal policy, while expecting to shift over to private investment as recovery progresses. It is not inconceivable that pump priming could work, but it is unlikely to do so except during a heavy rearmament program. Even in this case it is probable that increased private investment is the result of the expectation that the government will continue its high rate of spending, not curtail it.

The interaction of the multiplier and the accelerator can contribute substantially to a recovery only when the underlying conditions are favorable. These conditions may occur as the result of the wearing out of plant and equipment, the accumulation of inventions and innovations that await large-scale application, the gradual ironing out of cost-price dislocations, and the drawing down of consumer and business inventories. For the maintenance of a reasonable degree of control over income and employment, however, fiscal policy cannot be limited to pump priming.

► OTHER ALTERNATIVES

There are two other major possibilities for fiscal action. The federal government can establish a so-called compensatory spending policy. Fluctuations in private spending may be compensated for by fluctuations in the opposite direction of the net government contribution to the income stream. The objective of this device would be greatly to reduce, or even to eliminate, fluctuations in total spending. Alternatively, the government could spend such a large proportion of total national income that private spending would be a quantitatively small proportion of total spending. If the proportion of fixed government spending to total spending were large enough, variations in private spending would presumably have a relatively small effect on the level of income and employment.

Judging by the enormous increase in government spending during the last few decades it is not impossible that the second of these alternatives could actually come to pass. But the amount of government planning that it would imply is so great that not many supporters of the free-enterprise system would wish to adopt this route to economic stability. Compensatory spending, on the other hand, has considerable attraction for those who wish to minimize unemployment through fiscal means. Since it would have to be carried out within the framework of the federal budget, this device will be discussed in the following chapter, which relates the budget to economic stability. Another possibility that has to be considered is variable tax rates.

In the present chapter far more emphasis has been placed on the role of fiscal policy in stimulating recovery than on its effectiveness in preventing a boom and price inflation. This is not due to any belief that the depression case is necessarily the more important. Rather, the reason for the emphasis thus far is that the concepts that have been discussed were developed primarily in connection with the study of the role that fiscal policy might play in assuring high-level employment. In the following discussion of the function of the federal budget in economic stabilization, attention will be paid to the control of inflation through fiscal means.

► REFERENCES

BEVERIDGE, SIR WILLIAM H. *Full Employment in a Free Society.* New York: W. W. Norton & Company, 1945, Pt. IV, Sec. II, and the Appendix by N. Kaldor.

CLARK, J. M. *The Economics of Planning Public Works.* Washington, D. C.: U. S. Government Printing Office, 1935.

ESSAYS IN HONOR OF ALVIN HANSEN. *Income, Employment, and Public Policy.* New York: W. W. Norton & Company, 1948.

GORDON, R. A. *Business Fluctuations.* New York: Harper & Brothers, 1952, Chaps. IV and V (on the multiplier and accelerator).

HANSEN, A. H., and H. S. PERLOFF. *State and Local Finance in the National Economy.* New York: W. W. Norton & Company, 1944.

HARRIS, S. E., ed. *The New Economics.* New York: Alfred A. Knopf, Inc., 1947.

MACHLUP, F. "Period Analysis and Multiplier Theory," *Quarterly Journal of Economics,* November, 1939. Reprinted in American Economic Association, *Readings in Business Cycle Theory.* Philadelphia: The Blakiston Company, 1944, pp. 203–234.

SOMERS, H. *Public Finance and National Income.* Philadelphia: The Blakiston Company, 1949, Pt. VI, "Fiscal Policy and Economic Activity."

VILLARD, H. H. *Deficit Spending and the National Income.* New York: Rinehart & Company, Inc., 1941.

21 The Budget and Economic Control

► INTRODUCTION

In the three previous chapters a framework has been established for the discussion of the role of federal fiscal policy in the quest for economic stability. The conclusion has been reached that compensatory fiscal policy may offer the best route to this goal. This instrument requires, however, a large degree of freedom on the part of the budgetary authorities in manipulating public expenditure levels and rates of taxes.

Ideally, compensatory fiscal policy calls for the constant adjustment of public spending and taxing to variations in the rate of private spending above and below that level which corresponds to full employment. In practice it is doubtful if the operation can ever be quite this simple. Economic stability, important as it is, can only rarely be the sole criterion of budgetary policy. Congress and the President must at the same time give weight to the achievement of other control objectives as well. Therefore, different types of budgets are necessary which focus attention on one or another of these objectives.

► BUDGETARY CONCEPTS

The present chapter is concerned with the kind of information that is provided by the major alternative forms of the federal budget. In a sense they resolve themselves into different aspects of budgetary balance. Thus the budget may be balanced annually, biennially, or over a still longer period of years. Again, the budget may be balanced in a cash sense, which means that during the budgetary period the government is neither paying money into the income stream nor siphoning it out. On the other hand, the budget may be balanced in terms of taxing and spending commitments that extend beyond the current budgetary year. Balance may also be interpreted to take account of assets acquired by the government in the course of its financial operations. An increase in the national debt, for example, may be balanced by an equivalent increase in the value of its

471

holdings of installations, gold and exchange, public buildings, and the like. Finally, balance may be conceived of with respect to the economy as a whole, rather than from the point of view of the Treasury. In this case cash deficits and surpluses in the national budget are regarded as of no importance provided that aggregate public and private spending remains at the level which corresponds to full employment. This is the so-called economic budget.

In the crudest sense, budgetary balance would mean the equation of cash income and outgo over the budgetary planning period. The budget authority would simply be planning in such a way that total cash outgo was matched by total cash income. This concept of budgetary balance has little meaning. Short of a breakdown of the general functions of government, budgets are necessarily in balance in this sense. It is merely a technical problem to make certain that dollars flow to the Treasury at the same rate that the Treasury pays them out to the private sector. This is not to say that it is a simple matter, when public expenditures amount to a third of national income, to have the money on hand when it is needed.

▶ THE RATIONALE OF GOVERNMENT BORROWING

Until the depression of the thirties virtually all budgetary authorities had traditionally insisted on the analogy between the government and the private sector in their conception of what constitutes proper budgeting. Indeed, governments were likened to private individuals in that a large proportion of public borrowing was considered to be undertaken for financing consumption rather than investment. Unless all expenditures were financed by tax revenues, the public budget was regarded as out of balance. A budget was not balanced if any part of expenditures, even for purchases of capital assets that yield utilities over a period of years, was financed by borrowing.

This analogy with the private individual was in part justified. Whereas business borrows only for the purpose of facilitating production, governments and individuals borrow both to finance the acquisition of income yielding assets and to increase current consumption. The distinction between public consumption and public investment is hard to draw. In the past, conservative budgeting has avoided the necessity of making the distinction by regarding public investment as involving the acquisition of durable consumers' goods rather than durable producers' goods. The view that public borrowing is primarily consumption borrowing naturally strengthened the case for equating tax receipts and public expenditures on an annual basis. This does not mean, of course, that all government borrowing was proscribed.

Businessmen have always borrowed to purchase plant and inventories, and economic and accounting orthodoxy approved such borrowing because a flow of income in dollars was expected that would permit repayment of the debt. Even the consumer may safely borrow if he acquires a durable good (like a house or automobile) the market value of which equals or exceeds the size of the loan. The important question is whether his income is adequate to finance interest and amortization payments. Except for self-liquidating projects, the enterprises financed by government borrowing do not result in a flow of dollar income out of which the loan may be repaid. But the government has at its disposal the tax system, and so long as it is possible to levy taxes adequate to finance interest and amortization, the government has as much justification for borrowing as the firm.

THE FEAR OF INFLATION

The fear of inflation, sometimes irrational, has proved a powerful factor in the sentiment for balancing expenditures with tax revenues on an annual basis. During time of war the federal government has frequently been forced to borrow in order to meet the enormous rise in its current expenditures. At such times the level of business activity is likewise high as firms increase their bank borrowing in anticipation of war orders. Competition between private borrowers and the government for limited supplies of savings forces the latter to market a part of its securities with the reserve banks, and this results in a sharp increase in the money supply. At the same time marketable finished goods and factors of production become scarce as they are diverted to war uses. The consequence is a considerable degree of price inflation and the need for direct controls.

This had happened so often in the past that during the depression of the thirties many economists at first tended to fear the effects on the price level of a rise in the government debt associated with public works projects to stimulate recovery. As employment and incomes continued to fall despite rising federal deficits, however, it was gradually realized that a growing national debt does not necessarily result in a rising price level. Since the nation is not always in the midst of depression, the fear of inflation nevertheless remains one of the most potent factors influencing public opinion in favor of the annually balanced budget.

"SHIFTING THE DEBT BURDEN TO THE FUTURE"

Another argument for annual balance has been based on the contention that since the service and repayment of the debt may be spread over many years, the present generation of taxpayers is guilty of evading its financial responsibilities when the government borrows. The justice of taxing "generations yet unborn" to finance payments on a debt incurred before they could participate in the decision was held to be open to serious question. Of course, this consideration, even if valid, did not call for strict annual budgetary balance. It was relevant rather to a very large or continuous increase in the debt.

The existence of a national debt certainly means that higher tax *receipts* will be required in the future than would be needed in the absence of the debt. The same generation that pays a greater amount of taxes receives the equivalent, however, in interest payments on the debt, and as a whole bears no added burden. Whether or not higher tax *rates* are also required is quite a different question. Rises in tax rates may involve a special burden, for if rates of certain taxes become high enough, the disincentive effects on investment may stand in the way of material progress.

The service of a national debt may not, however, require a rise in rates. Those who stressed the inequity of "passing on the burden of the debt to future generations" ignored the possibility that the investment which gave rise to the debt might itself cause a rise in national income, and therefore obviate the necessity for higher tax rates. A good reason often existed, it must be confessed, for this pessimism. Most deficits incurred by national governments had been incurred in connection with financing wars, and no assets corresponding to the debt were created. Even in those cases where a successful war lead to the domination of areas rich in natural resources, the increase in real income in the conquering country was regarded as a sort of windfall. It was not associated with the debt created by war spending.

In conclusion, because government services are normally not sold, but are made available to the public outside the regular market for goods and services, people have in the past tended to think of the government more as an individual consumer than as a business. Therefore, annual balance in expenditures and tax revenues was regarded as the norm. Whatever one might think of the logic of this when applied without regard to the purpose of government spending, its effect in the United States throughout the greater part of the nineteenth century, at least, was to help retard the rate of growth of public expenditures.[1]

▶ THE FEASIBILITY OF ANNUAL BUDGETARY BALANCE

RECENT EXPERIENCE

The belief that the federal budget should be balanced annually still persists in many quarters despite the fact that circumstances exist in which this may prove to be impossible, and despite the many historical instances in which deficits have occurred during both war and peace. Experience from 1929 to 1933, for example, indicated that the rate of decline in business activity can be so great that no conceivable increases in tax rates

---

[1] For a further discussion of the economic implications of the public debt, see Chapter 25.

will balance the budget.[2] The higher rates of tax themselves may discourage private spending. If rising public spending for relief, for example, is matched by equally rising tax revenues, private spending may decline by more than public spending increases. Thus total spending and employment may fall. But the decline in total spending means a further decline in tax yields, which requires another round of tax rate increases. Thus the abortive attempt at balancing the budget is made at the cost of a larger volume of unemployment. The political reaction to this policy would naturally be negative, as Hoover and Roosevelt discovered in 1932 and in 1933.

Deficits are to be expected during time of war, since with the best of intentions finance ministers have found it politically impossible to pay for more than one third, or a little more, of war spending out of taxes. The public is "taxed" to the full amount, nevertheless, through the inequitable operation of price inflation. Of more serious concern, perhaps, are the deficits which are frequently incurred when a nation, though not at war, spends at a high rate during a period of prosperity. It may be inferred from a series of peacetime prosperity deficits that proposed increases in expenditures are not being tested against the pain of paying taxes. On the whole, however, public opinion is set against continuous deficits except during depressions and wars, and a refusal on the part of the public to be subject to higher taxes does not necessarily mean that expenditures, and therefore the national debt, will rise in any case. If the taxpayer shows himself to be completely amenable to increases in tax rates, a very necessary incentive to economy and efficiency on the part of government agencies, particularly the military, is removed.

ANNUAL BUDGETARY BALANCE TO CONTROL SPENDING

One way to discourage excessive increases in public expenditures, some have argued, is to forego the luxury of deficit spending. If the budget has to be balanced with taxes, the less urgent expenditures are more likely to be eliminated from the budget. Proposed expenditures will be judged in the light of the specific taxes that must be levied to finance them. Certainly much of the impetus to reduce Federal expenditures in 1953 arose out of the combined desire for lower taxes and a reduction in the size of the

---

[2] It must not be supposed that no one appreciated this fact at the time. As early as October, 1932, S. E. Leland of the University of Chicago was advocating that budgeting should take account of cyclical fluctuations in income, employment, and prices. (For a discussion of his proposal, see A. E. Buck, *The Budget in Governments of Today* [New York: Macmillan, 1934], pp. 118–119.) Leland advocated, in addition to the annual budget, a long-term budget which would merely seek to balance surpluses and deficits over a period of years. Cf. his paper "How Governments Can Best Meet the Financial Crisis," Convention of the International City Managers' Association, Cincinnati, October 24, 1932. He urged a similar course on President Roosevelt, who had taken office committed to the principle of annual budgetary balance.

deficit. The public simply made its view known that a portion of Federal spending could be advantageously released for disposition by the private sector. Implicitly it was expressing its alarm that while large deficits can continue for years without perceptibly undermining the economy, they at the same time can weaken our determination to assess carefully the alternative cost of government spending.

Unfortunately much of the agitation for an annually balanced budget is not based on an understanding of the economic and political realities described above. There is a disposition to confuse budgetary deficits with "national bankruptcy." This term has no clear-cut meaning. Governments may, of course, act in such a way as to bring about uncontrolled inflation. Again, they may repudiate their domestic or foreign debts. These events do not occur very often, however, except when a country is in the position of having to fight a war which is really beyond its economic powers or its financial acumen. In those circumstances the budget cannot be balanced in any event. There is no compelling reason to balance central government budgets annually. On the other hand, full responsibility must be undertaken by legislatures to justify the deficits.

▶ GOVERNMENT BORROWING FOR CAPITAL PROJECTS

In the United States it has been traditional to make a distinction between the circumstances that justify borrowing by the federal government and those that justify borrowing by the states and municipalities. The former borrows to finance wars and emergency relief expenditures during depression.[3] It may also borrow in order to bring total public plus private spending up to the level that corresponds to full employment.[4] But the federal government usually does not need to borrow in order to purchase capital assets that yield their income, in the form of either dollars or satisfactions, over a number of years.[5]

The reason for this is that the federal taxing power is adequate to

---

[3] Indirectly, however, the federal government may borrow for capital and other ordinary purposes. The Treasury holds securities issued by federal agencies and corporations. Such holdings totaled approximately $13 billion at the end of June, 1954, of which nearly one third consisted of securities issued by the Commodity Credit Corporation to finance the agricultural price-support program. Securities issued by the Rural Electrification Administration, and in connection with the housing programs, exceeded $4 billion. Cf. *Treasury Bulletins.*

[4] The latter instrument of policy has never actually been adopted in this country, although in the 1937–1938 downturn the President announced that he would give it a trial. It was not carried into effect, however, because of the rising employment connected with European rearmament.

[5] During 1955 the administration proposed a ten-year federal-state road program that would have cost $39.1 billion, of which $21 billion for an interstate system was to be financed by bonds not to be included in the national debt. Opposition to this proposal was largely based on this exclusion of a substantial amount of debt from the debt limit.

pay for government investment in land and buildings. The same reasoning applies, however, to any governmental unit large enough to undertake one or more items of new investment each year. If we assume a constant rate of new investment in building projects, the *annual* interest and amortization charges become in time as great as the investment cost of any one of them.

Thus a large city, starting a new school building every year or so, would finance the cost out of tax revenues rather than by borrowing. A smaller governmental unit, however, rightly borrows to build a new school every ten years. It needs the tax revenues of the intervening years to repay the debt. When the size of capital undertakings is large in relation to that of the governing unit, it is customary to finance them by borrowing. Since no capital project yet conceived, except war and unemployment relief, is large in relation to the taxing power of the federal government, it has ordinarily limited its net borrowing to years of war and depression.

▶ THE CAPITAL AND CURRENT BUDGETS

A business enterprise makes a distinction between capital and current accounts. In its statement of assets and liabilities it lists its debt obligations and the value of the assets that stand behind them. Naturally the meaningfulness of this statement depends on the accuracy of the valuation of the assets. But granting this, the distinction between capital and current accounts brings out the fact that capital expenditures do not have to be paid for out of current receipts so long as the business has the capacity to borrow in the market for savings. Why should not that part of government spending that results in the creation of capital instruments likewise be financed out of borrowing? If this were done, only the interest and depreciation related to purchases on capital account would be entered into the current budget, and thus financed out of tax revenues. In this way a distinction would be made between the capital budget and the current budget.

In recent years sentiment in some countries has arisen in favor of making this distinction.[6] Through the use of the capital budget it becomes obvious which expenditures should be financed out of current income, and which should be liquidated over the life of the capital instrument. This view of budgeting, however, requires an understanding of the difference between government investment spending and government consumption

---

[6] Cf. R. A. Musgrave, "The Nature of Budgetary Balance and the Case for the Capital Budget," *American Economic Review,* June, 1939, pp. 260–271; Alvin Hansen, *Fiscal Policy and Business Cycles* (New York: Norton, 1941), Chap. X.

For the origins of the practical application of the divided budget, and the important role played by the Scandinavian countries, see F. M. Marx, "The Divided Budget in Scandinavian Practice," *National Tax Journal,* June, 1955. See also Henry Laufenburger, "The Budget in the Frame of the National Economy: Evolution of Budgetary Structure and Technique in the Different Countries," *Proceedings* of the International Institute of Public Finance (Paris, 1950).

spending. It has been pointed out that much government spending is difficult to allocate as between consumption and investment, and the temptation is strong to assume that it consists mostly of consumption. There is, as we have seen, no sharp dividing line, for the bulk of government investment spending is not self-liquidating (i.e., does not yield income in terms of dollars, but rather in the form of a flow of utilities benefiting the public as a whole).

It is no coincidence that the concept of the capital budget originated, and has received its highest development, in those nations in which the self-liquidating state enterprise has achieved importance. The Scandinavian countries, particularly Sweden, have led the way. The latter was among the first to see the desirability of distinguishing between state investment and that portion of state spending that is essentially social consumption. Denmark also has taken the lead along these lines, with rather less emphasis on self-liquidating projects.

During the depression, the United States, Great Britain, and certain other countries also became interested in the dual capital-current budget. This interest, in the United States at any rate, did not originate primarily out of the increased importance of state enterprises. To be sure, the government corporation began to assume importance in those years. But the real reason in this country for growing interest in the capital budget seems to have been the desire to put as good a face as possible on the public investment that had to be undertaken during the depression in order to counteract the decline in employment in private enterprise. To the extent that such expenditures could be regarded as investment, which would yield income in the future, rather than as merely an instrument for the creation of current employment, the public would presumably be more favorably disposed to it.

DESCRIPTION

If a distinction is made between capital and current expenditures, two budgets are established. All current expenditures of the government, including interest on the debt, are entered in the current budget, and are financed out of tax revenues and earnings from government enterprises. Capital expenditures are reserved to the capital budget, and are paid for out of borrowing. Obviously, depreciation and obsolescence must be covered by current taxes or, if the project is self-liquidating, by the proceeds of the sales of the state-produced commodity (e.g., electricity). Just as in the case of private investment, the original capital sum financed by borrowing never has to be paid back so long as additional savings continue to seek investment outlets.

The characteristics of this arrangement are twofold: (1) Revenues related to capital purchases need only suffice to cover interest and depreciation charges. (2) Corresponding to increases in the debt are increases in government-owned plant and equipment. But the capital budget accomplishes no miracle. What it does is focus attention on the significant aspects of government investment spending and on the extent of the similarity between government and private investment. It thus supports the case for using methods of finance for government investment that are similar to those of private enterprise. In other words, the capital budget makes apparent the artificiality of the distinction between government and private financial practice when the circumstances happen to be the same. One of the recommendations of the Hoover Commission's report was the separation of current from capital outlays in the federal budget, and the Budget Bureau undertook to make this distinction in the 1951 budget (the "Character-Classification" budget).[7]

SELF-LIQUIDATING AND NON-SELF-LIQUIDATING INVESTMENT

As we have seen, the analogy between public and private investment is not complete. Thus a question arises whether the government should blindly adopt accounting practices developed for private enterprise. Since a very small proportion of government services is sold through the market, most public investment yields no dollar income to the government, but rather a combination of social consumption and cost reduction. There is no reason to think, or desire, that a given project will necessarily increase national income enough so that added tax revenues will automatically take care of interest and depreciation.

For example, it is true that better highways reduce transport costs and thus tend to increase profits and wages per unit of output in the industries using commodities and materials shipped by highway. If full employment is maintained, this cost reduction is equivalent to a rise in real income. The tax base may rise by more than enough to provide an automatic increase in revenues adequate to cover the cost of the public investment.[8] On the other hand, this may not occur. It depends on the nature of the investment. If only pleasure cars use the road, or if capital is substituted for labor, causing unemployment, and national income thus falls slightly, higher tax *rates* will be necessary to amortize the investment. Therefore, the government cannot be certain that a given investment can be financed entirely, or even in part, out of an automatic increase in tax yields from an increasing income base. This is not, of course, necessarily an argument against undertaking the investment.

---

[7] But a "character-classification" budget, which distinguishes items of capital expenditure within the budget, is not the same as a "capital-current" budget. The latter is a dual budget, whereas the former merely seeks to separate items of current spending from spending that produces assets. In his testimony before the subcommittee investigating monetary, credit, and fiscal policies in 1949, Budget Director Pace objected to the adoption of the capital budget. His reason was the difficulty of estimating depreciation for the complex operations of the federal government.

[8] Alternatively, a fall in production costs means that a given amount of revenues will command a greater volume of goods and services.

The *private* investor in plant and equipment does not count on the indirect effects of his investment on the level of national income for the income that will pay for depreciation and interest charges. He expects to attract a demand that is sufficient to cover all his costs. Should not the government, it might be asked, follow a similar policy and put into the capital budget only that portion of public investment that is self-liquidating, while paying currently out of taxes for that investment (e.g., parks, war plants) that can be amortized only out of tax receipts? The question resolves itself thus: Which should be the criterion for admitting a given item of public investment to the capital budget, durability or profitability?

Granted that the decision has been made to adopt the capital budget, the conclusion would seem to be justified that durability is the correct basis for distinguishing between current and capital expenditures. If the term "self-liquidating" were strictly interpreted, not many government capital projects would qualify for the capital budget. The proper criterion is evidently that the object of government expenditure should yield its satisfactions over a period of time greater than one year if it is to be included in the capital budget. Whether depreciation and interest charges are financed (1) solely out of the proceeds of sales, or (2) merely partly so, or (3) entirely out of general tax receipts, is irrelevant as a basis for granting or denying admission to the capital budget. The reason is that the purpose of the distinction between the capital and the current budget is merely to convey an understanding of the nature of the expenditure and the method of finance that is appropriate to it.

OBJECTIONS TO THE CAPITAL BUDGET

Objections have been raised to the use of the capital budget on several grounds. It is argued that whereas the performance budget rightly focuses attention on the functions to be performed, the capital budget diverts it from essentials. Since the federal government has ample borrowing capacity (from the reserve banks if need be), it is argued that there is no point in going through the motions of setting up depreciation and interest accounts for particular capital assets. Moreover, if a distinction is made between capital assets and current expenditures, when it is necessary to curtail expenditures the appropriations committees may reduce capital outlays without properly considering the relative utility of capital outlays to other types of departmental spending.[9] A doubtful inference might be that merely because certain expenditures resulted in the acquisition of capital assets, greater federal spending is necessarily to be condoned. Some writers have justified past increases in government spending on precisely these grounds, pointing to the gold in Fort Knox, for example, as evidence

---

[9] The problem is discussed by Jesse Burkhead, "The Outlook for Federal Budget-Making," *National Tax Journal*, December, 1949, pp. 295–296.

that the money was not wasted. If a capital-current budget classification is adopted, care must be taken to assure that it does not result in a less critical examination of proposed expenditures.

► THE EMERGENCY BUDGET

During the depression crisis of 1933, President Roosevelt introduced a new type of dual budget with his distinction between the ordinary and the extraordinary (or emergency) budgets. In the former were to be placed all the expenditures that would be made in the absence of depression. In the latter were included those expenditures that had to be undertaken, as a result of depression, for relief and for rehabilitation of the economy. By this distinction the President hoped to call attention to the (probably) temporary nature of such expenditures, and to convince the public that they should not be taken as indicating the adoption of a philosophy of deficit spending.

As compared with the adoption of a capital-current classification during depression, the use of the emergency budget has the advantage of honestly admitting more explicitly an inability to balance the budget. As we have seen, interest among American economists in the Danish and Swedish capital budgets was greatly stimulated as budgetary deficits mounted in the depression. It was suddenly discovered that much of federal spending gives rise to capital assets, and that since business borrows in order to produce capital assets, the government ought likewise to be permitted to do so. Although this may be perfectly true, the worst possible time to discover it, from the point of view of throwing light on budgetary practices, is precisely at the moment when public spending and debt are rising because of depression.

The emergency budget itself is not entirely free, of course, from the charge of weakening budgetary morality. Once this form of budget has been accepted, it becomes easy to throw into the extraordinary budget expenditures that may or may not be connected with the emergency. Alternatively, insistence on balance in the ordinary budget may mean that important ordinary functions are curtailed while less important extraordinary ones are expanded. Yet the emergency budget does provide a useful classification of the nature of expenditures.

The Roosevelt administration was accused of shifting certain ordinary expenditures to the emergency budget in 1933. Later on the procedure was reversed, when important relief programs (e.g., farm relief) were transferred to the ordinary budget. The emergency budget is apt to be used to enlist political support for an unbalanced budget, since the existence of a deficit can be played down by calling attention to the fact that the ordinary budget is in balance. This form of budget was abandoned by the Roosevelt administration as the depression lifted.

► CASH AND ACCRUAL ACCOUNTING

The accounts of the government may be kept on either a cash or a cash and accrual basis. The cash budget is merely a projection of cash receipts and expenditures. Accrual accounts, on the other hand, indicate not only cash receipts and disbursements, but also the "assets, liabilities, revenues, the extent to which the budget estimates of the revenues have been realized, appropriations, the rate at which the appropriations have been spent, the true available balance of each appropriation, and the accumulated costs of operation."[10]

In order to present a complete picture of planned spending and planned revenues, accrual accounting must set forth all commitments for spending, regardless of whether they call for any cash outgo during the current budgetary year; and it must indicate all sources of government income, likewise irrespective of when it accrues. For example, the European Recovery Program had involved a commitment of nearly $10 billion between 1948 and 1952.[11] Yet in the year in which the plan was inaugurated, only a fraction of the total ($1.4 billion) was actually spent. Clearly it is important to know what commitments the government has entered into for future years as well as for the current fiscal year.

Accrual accounting includes the cash budget. It must do so in order that the government may know what its cash commitments are, as well as the cash receipts on which it can count during the budgetary period. The cash budget, however, is important from another point of view. We are interested in the net contribution of government finance to the income stream, and therefore to the level of employment. Consequently, information is required on the expected magnitude of treasury disbursements and receipts in cash. If it is estimated that in a given year national spending (public plus private) must total a certain figure in order to assure full employment, the consolidated net cash budget is the relevant document. What we need to know is how much money the Treasury must pour into the income stream during the time period under consideration, in relation to the amount that will be withdrawn in the form of taxes, nontax revenues, and government borrowing.

► THE FULL-EMPLOYMENT BUDGET

John Maynard Keynes directed the attention of economists to the fact that mass unemployment is the consequence of the failure of total spending (that is, the sum of private consumption and investment spending, together

---

[10] Task Force, *Report on Fiscal, Budgeting, and Accounting Activities,* prepared for the Commission on Organization of the Executive Branch of the Government, January, 1949, App. F, p. 103.

[11] *Report* of the Secretary of the Treasury, 1952, p. 228.

with public spending) to remain at a level that corresponds to full employment. The *immediate* causes of a decline in private spending are twofold. On the one hand, the prospective return on investment in plant, equipment, and inventories may threaten to fall short of the cost of making such investment. On the other hand, either consumers may be receiving an inadequate share of national income, or they may be failing to spend a sufficient proportion of their income to take the current output of consumers' goods off the market.

In the first case employment falls in the investment goods industries, and in the second it declines in the consumers' goods industries. In either event unemployment may spread from one to the other, setting in motion a spiral of deflation. A possible remedy is for the central government to take steps to see that the gap is filled. This it may do either by enacting measures designed to increase the rate of private spending or by increasing its own net contribution to total spending. The former may be accomplished by fiscal or other legislation intended to raise the profitability of private investment, and thus to affect incentives. In the present section we shall be concerned with the government's own net contribution to income and employment.

The Keynesian analysis is also applicable to the situation in which total spending exceeds the flow of goods coming to market at the current price level. When this occurs prices are pushed up, and the smaller the response of the supply of goods to the excess of demand, the greater the rise in the price level. In this case the government can, if there is public support for the policy, restore equilibrium between the flow of purchasing power and the flow of goods and services by running a cash budgetary surplus and holding it idle.

If one accepts the approach outlined above as a politically acceptable attack on economic fluctuations, the first step is to break down total spending into its major elements. When this is done for a year already past it is possible to analyze the factors that actually determined the level of national income and the volume of employment in that year, including the contributions of public spending and taxation. If estimates of private spending plus ordinary government spending for a later year indicate that total spending will fall short of or exceed the full employment level of spending, the government may plan to make up the difference or reduce the excess by altering its own net contribution to total spending. Government spending, therefore, consists of two parts. First are ordinary government expenditures, determined independently of the objective of economic stabilization. Second are the expenditures undertaken as a balancing element in the economy.

THREE ALTERNATIVE ROUTES

Any deficiency in private spending (investment plus consumption spending) can be made up by three alternative routes: (1) by an increase in public spending, (2) by an increase in both spending and taxing, and (3) by the remission of taxes. An increase in public spending with no increase in tax receipts implies borrowing by the government, either from idle balances or from the banks. Thus income is increased either by the route of an increase in the quantity of money, or by an increase in velocity of circulation, or both. An increase in public spending accompanied by an equal increase in tax receipts is obviously a very difficult route to full employment, at least from a severe depression.

The third route, namely, the remission of taxes while holding government spending constant, in terms of purchasing-power flows is similar to the first. The increase in purchasing power results from a government deficit financed out of either an increased money supply or an increase in velocity of circulation of money. But the incentive aspects of tax remission are very different from those produced by increased government spending. They also differ according to the kind of tax that is remitted. Effects on investment spending will be of one sort, for example, if the tax reduction takes the form of lower taxes on corporate profits, another if the remitted taxes are sales taxes, and still another if income tax rates are reduced in particular income brackets. Yet in all these cases the net contribution of government to the income stream may be the same. The differences in their effects on private spending give a hint of the fact that the purchasing-power approach to stable employment is not adequate to solve all conceivable unemployment or overemployment problems.

If a given net contribution to the income stream by the government can have different effects on willingness to spend (and therefore on MV, the flow of purchasing power), depending on *how* the purchasing power is injected into or taken out of the income stream, then the maintenance of full employment may not be the simple matter of turning on and off the faucet marked "net government contribution to the level of income." Changes in the government's contribution may themselves cause changes in the rate of private spending. If this is so, then attempts by the government to regulate the level of national income either might be incompletely successful, or might bring about reactions in private spending that force the government to interfere still further with the private sector of the economy.

CONCLUSION

The full-employment budget, as we have seen above, makes it appear to be purely a matter of arithmetic as to how much the government must spend and tax in order to supplement or reduce private spending to achieve noninflationary full employment. But this makes the job to be done deceptively simple. The data are not readily ascertainable figures for spending of different kinds, but are estimates of probable future spending. Expected private spending is what a government bureau *thinks* private spending will be at a future date. Once this figure has been decided upon, though of course subject to change in the light of subsequent events, any gap is simply filled with government spending or tax remission.

As we have seen, however, government spending and taxing themselves affect private investment and consumption. Thus if, for example, an increase in government spending takes the form of investment in electrical capacity, private investment in this area may decline. If government consumption spending provides free consumers' goods (e.g., school lunches, subsidized housing, or free medical service), demand for these commodities from private producers may fall off. The concept of the full-employment budget is somewhat mechanical, and if applied without great discretion may lead to undesired results. For this reason the device has not as yet met with favor at the hands of politicians in the United States.[12] Instead, most practical proposals have consisted of watered-down versions. Budgetary management has usually been aimed at reducing the amplitude of cyclical swings in employment rather than completely eliminating them. This is known as cyclical budget management, which places reliance on a rough offsetting of deficits in depression years by surpluses in years of prosperity.

► THE CYCLICAL BUDGET

Toward the end of World War II Congress developed a lively interest in the possibility of evolving a permanent set of criteria for federal fiscal policy designed to bring an end to economic fluctuations. A bill (the Murray full-employment bill) aimed at establishing Congressional responsibility for full employment failed of passage, but the milder Employment Act of 1946 was finally approved. This provided for a semiannual report by the President to Congress on the economic state of the nation. The Council of Economic Advisers was established to help prepare this report, to sift the vast supply of statistics from all sources, and to make recommendations to the President with respect to economic policy.

One of the services of the CEA is to break down the figures for gross national product into various types of spending in order to show changes from year to year. The CEA does not, therefore, have responsibility for preparing a budget, but it is in a position to exert considerable influence on the economic policies advocated by the executive branch. Moreover, Congress stated in the Employment Act of 1946 that "it is the continuing policy and responsibility of the federal government to promote maximum

---

[12] For an evaluation of the attitude of the Eisenhower administration toward projections into the future of estimates for the levels of income, employment, and production that are an essential part of the "economic" budget, see P. J. Strayer, "Full Employment—1954 Model," *American Economic Review*, December, 1954, a review article of the *Economic Report* of the President and the Hearings and Report on the *Economic Report* (January–February, 1954), especially p. 885.

employment, production, and purchasing power." The manner in which it would do this was purposely left vague, and the word "maximum" was undefined; but the machinery that was set up invited debate over the extent to which federal fiscal policy should be used as an instrument of economic stabilization.

The Taft-Radcliffe amendment to the Murray full-employment bill would have provided that budgetary unbalance was not undesirable if in the interest of full employment. The bill did not pass, and in any event this was a very mild statement of purpose; but it did represent the existence in Congress of a strong feeling that the budget should not be balanced annually if depression made this difficult.

Despite the interest of Congress in cyclical fiscal policy (that is, the alternation of deficits and surpluses in order to offset at least partially cyclical swings in private spending), little real progress has been made in the direction of wholehearted adherence to this policy. A large gap exists between the acceptance of budgetary unbalance as an inevitable consequence of war and depression, and a planned budgetary unbalance intended to help stabilize employment and ward off inflation. The federal budget is unbalanced often enough, but little or no debt is repaid during periods of boom and inflation. Compensatory fiscal policy would require that this be done. This asymmetry between deficits and surpluses is the major objection to compensatory fiscal policy made by the Committee for Economic Development. They fear that acceptance of the policy would strengthen the present tendency for periods of rising public expenditures and debt to be succeeded by periods of prosperity unaccompanied by treasury surpluses and debt repayment.[13]

► THE STABILIZING BUDGET

The proposal made by the CED and others that the federal government pursue a limited, automatic, compensatory fiscal policy is based on the fact that both tax receipts and public spending respond to fluctuations in the level of national income. Suppose that the budget is balanced in a cash sense at a level of income which corresponds to full employment. Suppose further that all tax rates remain unchanged, and that government spending programs likewise are unaltered. If, then, for some reason the level of private spending rises, tax receipts will automatically increase. Income tax receipts will rise, and as spending increases, receipts from sales taxes and excises likewise rise. The response of different types of taxes will, of course, be varied. The greatest effects will be felt with respect to

---

[13] Committee for Economic Development, *The Stabilizing Budget Policy: What It Is and How It Works* (New York: The Committee, 1950). This committee is an organization of liberal businessmen who believe that the free-enterprise system must assist in finding a way to economic stability in the interest of its own survival.

the elastic taxes.[14] Of these, the corporate profits and personal income taxes will respond the most markedly. Corporate profits react strongly to changes in income, and the progressivity of rates under the personal income tax means that as personal incomes rise, many persons are thrown into higher bracket rates.

Changes in the level of national income would likewise affect the volume of public expenditures even if spending programs were held fixed over a period of time. As full employment is approached, unemployment benefits automatically decline. Once full employment is reached, these expenditures level off. However, in the later stages of an upswing the price level may begin to rise as successive bottlenecks are reached. This means an automatic increase in those public expenditures the magnitude of which is determined on the basis of programs rather than available funds. For example, if building costs rise during the course of construction of a school building, spending for this purpose will also rise. On the other hand, the response in many instances is likely to be delayed. Thus, when prices rise, legislative authorization is usually necessary before social security benefits can be increased. In the case of national social security programs this lag may be one of several years. It is because of this, incidentally, that the use of a price escalator has been advocated in some quarters in order to make social security benefits immediately responsive to cyclical changes in prices.

The net response of all types of public spending to changes in the levels of incomes, spending, and prices in the private sector is ambiguous. It depends on the relative magnitudes of the public spending programs which respond to a change in national income with a change in the same direction, and those which respond with a change in the opposite direction. Consequently, most of the stabilizing effect of automatic changes in fiscal magnitudes in response to fluctuations in the private sector may have to come about on the side of taxes.

Interest in the stabilizing budget became inevitable as a result of the decrease in personal income tax exemptions and the increase in rates and progression during World War II. Rising money income would be accompanied by a relatively large increase in tax receipts, and conversely with falling incomes. Current collection of income taxes also played its part by greatly accelerating the response of tax receipts to changes in the level of national income.

AUTOMATIC DEFICITS AND SURPLUSES

If the federal budget is balanced at or about full employment, divergences from full employment will automatically produce deficits and surpluses in the cash budget. Under certain circumstances these fluctuations

---

[14] Taxes whose yields fluctuate more than in proportion to changes in national income.

will tend to restore equilibrium. The deficits may be financed either through the creation of new money or by sales of government securities to savers. Unless private investment spending is discouraged, the effect is to cause a rise in total spending. This discouragement can be avoided by assuring an elastic money supply. Conversely, the proceeds of a cash surplus may either be held idle in the form of treasury cash or deposits with the federal reserve banks, or be used to repay treasury indebtedness. If treasury cash or deposits are increased, or if securities are brought back from federal reserve banks by the Treasury, the money supply is reduced as a result of the budgetary surplus, and the rise in national income and prices tends to be arrested. If, however, securities are bought back from commercial banks or savers, the effect is less clear-cut. It is unlikely that much or any of the proceeds of debt repayment to savers will be held idle during a period of high and rising national income. Again, commercial banks are likely to relend the proceeds to business firms. The most effective policy, therefore, would be to allow a rise in treasury cash or deposits, or to repurchase securities from the Federal Reserve System.

The proponents of the stabilizing budget plan recognize, of course, that fluctuations in income are required in order to give effect to the equilibrating forces. The surpluses and deficits are regarded as the balancing mechanism that will help to minimize, rather than eliminate, swings in business activity. Moreover, it is conceded that if the budget were balanced at a level of income corresponding to 100 per cent of full employment, the effect would probably be to encourage a creeping inflation. Consequently, the CED proposed that 96 per cent be taken as the norm.[15] It was hoped that this degree of flexibility would be effective in arresting the operation of the various price escalators, such as cost-of-living wage agreements.

EVALUATION

The stabilizing budget has one great advantage, offset by an equally significant disadvantage. The advantage is that "nothing is touched by human hands." No judgment is required to hold spending programs and tax rates stable. Therefore, this concept of budgeting appeals to those who wish to see the private-enterprise system preserved by minimizing the cyclical fluctuations that have caused impatience with it in the past. A limited advantage can be taken of the principle of compensatory fiscal policy without surrendering to an executive agency an amount of discretion

---

[15] In the interest of repayment of the federal debt the plan called for an estimated debt retirement of $3 billion annually at 96 per cent of full employment. The budget would be in balance at 93 per cent. The debt retirement aspect is not inherent in the principle of the stabilizing budget, but was introduced because of businessmen's fears with respect to the indefinite continuance of what they considered to be a huge national debt.

which it might be unable to exercise effectively. Moreover, the danger would be eliminated that more and more power might fall into the hands of such an agency.

The disadvantage is that there is no assurance, or even likelihood, that a given surplus or deficit will be adequate to bring the economy back into equilibrium. The implied analogy with a living room thermostat is not complete. A budgetary surplus, held idle, will be a brake on the continuance of an upswing. It will not necessarily reverse the movement, however, and it may not even slow it down noticeably. The same thing holds for the deficit produced by a downturn. Repayment of debt by business firms may well take place at a rate that is faster than the increase in government borrowing.

A technical difficulty with an automatic program of this sort is that factors unrelated to economic stability necessitate frequent changes in both spending programs and tax rates. The CED proposal recognizes this fact, and points out that the mechanism would have to be readjusted periodically. The question is, however, whether or not the tax system and spending programs could be let alone long enough for the mechanism to operate. Every session of Congress is occupied with the consideration of proposals to make substantial changes in spending programs. No mechanical device can limit the freedom of action of Congress to entertain proposals to change both spending programs and tax rates. The question boils down to whether economic stability is or is not the major criterion of policy. The fact is that the public does not regard it as such except during periods of obvious inflationary or deflationary tendencies. But an automatic device must operate continuously.

One advantage of the stabilizing budget as compared with a managed cyclical budget is that it removes the need to put reliance on treasury predictions with respect to tax yields. These are not easy to make accurately, since no method exists of predicting the future course of business activity, and therefore the tax base. It is true, on the other hand, that apart from this serious problem, the actual adoption of the cyclical budget would provide an impetus to the improvement of the technical competence of the treasury staff in forecasting revenue yields.

A number of weaknesses follow from the passiveness of the stabilizing budget as an instrument in the achievement of economic stability. It does not look beyond mere changes in purchasing-power flows as the cause of booms and depressions. Yet the business cycle is in part caused by psychological and other forces that may have an even greater effect on *future* purchasing-power flows than they do on the current levels of income and spending that determine the size of the deficit or surplus. Consequently, even on the unlikely assumption that the automatic deficits and surpluses would be quantitatively large enough to reverse an upward or downward movement in income, the stabilizing budget ignores the underlying dis-equilibrating forces that may be laying the basis for an even greater degree of instability of future income and employment.

This criticism, however, is equally applicable to managed compen-satory fiscal policy in the form of cyclical budgeting. The point is, however, that economic fluctuations arising out of price-cost and other dislocations can be neutralized if the government is able and willing to exploit com-pensatory fiscal policy to the fullest extent necessary. When deficits and surpluses are limited by the flexibility that happens to exist in the tax system and in public spending programs, they are not likely to be forceful enough to override the inflexibilities that may be responsible for dis-equilibrium.

A further defect of the stabilizing budget is that it assumes that under- and overemployment are cyclical in nature; in other words, that there is an equilibrium above and below which the level of income and employ-ment can oscillate. If those economists are correct who believe that under certain circumstances the economy may be subject to secular stagnation, an automatic deficit may be large without contributing anything substantial to the forces required to reverse the progress. Clearly, more positive policies would be required if the stagnationists are right.

A final difficulty may be considered. The stabilizing budget assumes that deflation and inflation are equal and parallel dangers in the minds of the public and of Congress. On the contrary, deflation and unemployment are much more feared than inflation. The consequence would be that whenever high income and rising prices produced a budgetary surplus, debate would inevitably arise over whether a policy of holding the surplus idle would not cause a downswing in business activity that could not easily be stemmed. The fact is that every boom and every depression must be subject to a separate analysis. Under these circumstances it is too much to expect that the government and the public will wish to stand idly by to wait for the automatic responses of the stabilizing budget.

► CONCLUSION

National budgets may be drawn up from a number of different points of view. One budgetary objective is the achievement of economic stability. Variations in taxes and public spending may be geared to the objective of offsetting fluctuations in private spending. Congress, however, has not been willing to accept the goal of full employment as the major objective of budgetary policy. Part of the reason for this hesitation has been a sus-picion that important Congressional powers might have to be transferred to executive agencies. Another objection is that in some circumstances criteria other than full employment may be important, and Congress has not wished to tie its hands in advance of unforeseeable situations.

On the basis of our experience with two recessions since the end of World War II (1948–1949 and 1953–1954), it can be inferred that the preponderance of Congressional sentiment favors the use of flexible policies for economic stabilization over the devices proposed by fiscal economists. Indeed, the executive branch has likewise indicated a preference for delaying the use of fiscal policy as long as possible. Two important practical considerations may detract from the social benefit derivable from rigid stabilization programs. In the first place, in our complex society they do not operate as neatly in practice as they do on paper. Therefore, a large measure of flexibility in their operation may be required in order to make them work at all. This makes fiscal policy for economic stability an art rather than a science. Second, the acceptance of a rigid program implies at least a temporary surrender of the power to guard against encroachment on the private sector. In the next chapter, then, emphasis will be laid on the practical and institutional problems that must be faced when using fiscal policy for economic stability.

► REFERENCES

BEVERIDGE, SIR WILLIAM H. *Full Employment in a Free Society*. New York: W. W. Norton & Company, 1945.

BISHOP, R. L. "Alternative Expansionist Fiscal Policies," in *Essays in Honor of Alvin Hansen*. New York: W. W. Norton & Company, 1948.

COMMITTEE FOR ECONOMIC DEVELOPMENT. *Taxes and the Budget*. New York: The Committee, 1947 (and its subsequent publications on the stabilizing budget).

Economic Reports of the President of the United States.

HANSEN, A. *Fiscal Policy and Business Cycles*. New York: W. W. Norton & Company, 1941, Chap. X, "Budgetary Theory and Practice."

MARX, F. M. "The Divided Budget in Scandinavian Practice," *National Tax Journal*, June, 1955.

SOMERS, H. *Public Finance and National Income*. Philadelphia: The Blakiston Company, 1949, Chap. XXIV, "Balanced and Unbalanced Budgets."

22 The Art of Fiscal Policy

In the preceding four chapters we have been concerned with establishing the conceptual basis for a fiscal policy aimed at economic stability. The approach, therefore, has been heavily weighted toward theory, with its consequent oversimplification of the problem of stabilization as it is met in practice. This emphasis on theory is indispensable, of course, as a prerequisite to the practice of fiscal policy. The executive agency charged with the task of managing a full-employment economy must be conversant with the potentialities of the instruments at its disposal. A by-product of the emphasis in these chapters on the aggregative approach, however, has been a heightened sense of its limitations.

► FISCAL POLICY AND FISCAL THEORY

The present chapter looks at fiscal policy for economic stability from the point of view of the practical problems that have to be solved when Congress and the President are faced with the prospect of actually using the fiscal instrument. No longer can the discussion run in terms of a theoretical treatment of the over-all effects of surpluses and deficits on private spending. Detailed analyses have to be made of the probable effects of alternative kinds of public spending and alternative taxes. The indirect as well as the direct effects have to be considered.

It is at this point, perhaps, that fiscal policy is discovered to be an art rather than a science. The empirical task of ascertaining all, or even a large part, of the information necessary for an effective stabilization policy is a very great one. We are concerned not with what ought to have been done in a past period to assure full employment, but with what must be done next month and next year. Therefore, fiscal theory gives us only limited help. Past experience is likely to be a treacherous guide to the future. Much use must be made of probabilities and even intelligent guesses. The preconditions for these judgments, however, are a firm grounding in fiscal theory and a wide knowledge of the practical effects of particular taxes and given forms of public spending.

The relation between fiscal theory and fiscal practice needs to be considered with respect to both taxes and public spending, and under conditions of both prosperity and depression. Empirical aspects of changes in the rates of the various taxes have been largely covered in the chapters on taxation. More needs to be said, however, of the cycle-sensitivity of particular taxes, of devices for increasing the response in the yields of various taxes to changes in income and spending, and of the feasibility of varying tax rates in the interest of economic stability. This will be done in the latter part of the chapter.

▶ PUBLIC SPENDING AND TAXATION

RELATIVE IMPORTANCE IN FISCAL POLICY

As of the present time the art of fiscal policy has become more highly developed with respect to public spending than to taxing. As an instrument of fiscal policy, public spending has, to be sure, yielded some ground in recent years to the device of variations in the rates and yields of taxes. During the thirties, advocates of fiscal policy for economic stabilization thought mainly in terms of public spending to restore prosperity. Consequently, a large literature grew up which put the emphasis on spending rather than on taxing. More recently, in part because the danger of inflation has succeeded unemployment as the chief enemy of stability, the economic role of taxes and the tax system has been more closely studied.

At the same time, however, there is some reason for believing that policy on public expenditures is likely to remain the major fiscal instrument for economic stabilization. One reason for this is that at the present stage of political thinking on government intervention to stabilize income and employment, the major decision at the federal level is how much to spend. If this is true, a discussion of the art of fiscal policy as it exists at the present time necessarily devotes most of the attention to the objective factors that determine the level and directions of public expenditures.

THE FLEXIBILITY OF PUBLIC SPENDING

To be effective in compensating for fluctuations in private spending, public spending itself must be capable of a wide degree of cyclical variation. Moreover, it must be possible to change the level of public spending very rapidly. Changes in the level of private investment may be sudden and substantial. Therefore, at least a part of public spending must be of the types that can be quickly altered. It is not necessary, of course, that the whole of it should be immediately flexible.

The factors which determine the flexibility of the many types of public spending are numerous and complex. Governments make expenditures in the form of the purchase of factors and commodities, and they make subsidies and transfer payments. The circumstances governing these two types of expenditure differ greatly in their adaptability to fiscal policy for economic stability. Certain types of transfer payment, e.g., interest on the debt, are subject to only slight variation. Others, such as subsidies to tightly organized pressure groups, can be curtailed only if sufficient political power can be mustered. Still others, benefiting less strongly knit groups, are more easily subject to reduction. Increases are always easier to negotiate; but if substantial increases were made in transfer payments to particular groups in order to stimulate spending, the demands of other groups to share in the "social dividend" might precipitate a political struggle that could reduce the effectiveness of public spending for economic stabilization.

Government expenditures for the purchase of factors (in other words, the expenses of running the government) can be varied within fairly broad limits. They are the subject of continuous legislative discussion. The great bulk of public spending, to be sure, is determined by a complex of (1) decisions made in the past, (2) considerations (like national defense) that have to be taken by the legislature as given, and (3) social and other programs on the need for which there is general agreement. Thus there is a large degree of inflexibility in public spending, at least in the downward direction.

More scope exists for increases in the size and number of public expenditure programs than for decreases. Therefore, compensatory public works programs are a better instrument for combating depressions than for arresting inflationary booms. A variety of new expenditure programs can be initiated to avert depression, but the political and practical obstacles to curtailing many types of spending programs may prove to be too great to permit the needed flexibility. At the present time hardly 10 per cent of the federal budget is subject to significant reduction. In other words, once obvious elements of waste and padding are eliminated, 90 per cent of federal spending cannot be dispensed with. The other 10 per cent consists of programs that might be substantially reduced, though obviously by no means eliminated.

State and local spending programs are perhaps more subject to trimming when the occasion is important enough. For example, during time of war, roads and buildings are simply allowed to deteriorate, and long-term programs intended to anticipate the rise in population are temporarily abandoned. This flexibility is not, however, of a nature that particularly lends itself to cyclical flexibility in public spending. The budgets of the states and municipalities are not coordinated under a central fiscal planning board. Consequently, reductions in their spending programs are hardly to be counted upon in a peacetime inflationary boom. Again, state and local spending is more apt to contract than to expand during depression. The concern of the lower governmental units to avoid bankruptcy works counter to a policy that advocates expanded public spending during a period of depression in the private sector.

▶ THE DETERMINANTS OF STATE AND LOCAL SPENDING

The bulk of public spending in recent years has been made by the federal government. Therefore, the fact that state and local expenditures are not easily amenable to a countercyclical public works policy is far less important than it was in the thirties. Nevertheless, state and local spending remains important in the area of fiscal control, for federal spending programs can be varied only within limits. Granted enough time, there is perhaps little obstacle to a substantial increase in public spending; but if a quick expansion in federal spending is required to avert a downswing, a contraction in state and local expenditures might have the effect of nullifying much of the increase. For this reason it is important to consider the factors that limit the variability of state and local spending.

In times of peace the states and localities do most of the ordinary public works spending. In the event of a depression, therefore, the possibility has to be reckoned with that only a fraction of total public works expenditures will have been centralized in the hands of the federal government. In past depressions it has been characteristic of state and local expenditure that fluctuations were the reverse of those required to help to offset a decline in private investment and consumption. On the basis of the knowledge gained in the depression of the thirties, however, it can be assumed that in the future the states and localities will be encouraged by the federal government to schedule their postponable expenditures in accordance with the requirements of economic stability. The limits on their power to cooperate in this, however, are set by their restricted financial resources. In terms of tax revenues alone, these limits are narrow. However, federal grants to the states, and state grants to the municipalities, provide a means of enlisting state and local cooperation in nation-wide public works programs.

SPENDING ON HIGHWAYS AND CONSTRUCTION

Most of the scope for cyclical variation in state and local public expenditures resides in spending on highways and investment in capital instruments. When these expenditures are broken down, it becomes apparent that substantial differences exist in the extent to which they are subject to compensatory variation. In an expanding economy it may be that the bulk of highway expenditures, for example, is for new construction. Once the basic network is built, on the other hand, most of the spending is for repair. How far should new construction and repair be determined by the objective of economic stability? It is precisely when private expenditures are high that more and better roads are needed. Much scope certainly exists for reducing expenditures on highways when private spending is high, and conversely when spending is low. But it is not unlimited. If a period of prosperity is prolonged, it is a poor allocation of resources if highways are allowed to run down.

Cyclical variation in state and local expenditures on construction other than highways is probably more defensible than fluctuations in spending on roads. The highway network is an indispensable precondition for commerce, and with the capture of much of the market of the railroads by trucks, its importance constantly rises. Expenditures on hospitals, penal institutions, and office buildings, on the other hand, are somewhat more adaptable to countercyclical variation. This is not true, however, of their upkeep. The greater the provision of state and local capital facilities, the greater the volume of expenditures which cannot easily be reduced when inflation threatens.

VARIATIONS IN CAPACITY FOR PUBLIC WORKS

The capacity of the various states and localities for public works varies greatly. A wide range of information is necessary in order to determine how far a particular governmental unit should go in either undertaking public works projects of its own or matching federal grants. On the one hand, complete data are necessary on financial condition; and on the other, information needs to be gathered on such matters as population trends and age distribution, on the possession of natural resources upon which future economic progress depends, and on the priorities to be attached to alternative programs of capital development. All these circumstances taken together determine the answer to the question whether or not an expansion of state or local public works in depression is advisable. In any event, the further question arises whether the program can be financed at the state or local level.

The sources of tax revenues for both the states and the municipalities are limited, particularly for the latter. Moreover, the market for state and local obligations is, of course, inferior to that for federal debt. It might also be pointed out that interest payments on state, and more particularly local, debt are likely to involve a drain of cash away to wealthy areas inhabited by the bondholders. This gives rise to a regional balance-of-payments problem. Although only the federal government enjoys an unlimited market for its obligations (through the creation of new reserve-bank and commercial-bank reserves), the states and localities may share in this market, for if the Treasury sells securities to the reserve banks during a depression, part of the newly created commercial-bank reserves may be devoted to the purchase of state and local securities. Since the states have sovereign powers they can borrow for public works. The localities, however, are not in the same position. Their borrowing powers are limited by the states, and at a given moment they are quite likely to have exhausted their legal borrowing powers. The possibility exists, however, of circumventing these limitations. One device which has been used is the revenue bond.

REVENUE BONDS

Increasingly the localities are financing public works through the sale of revenue bonds. These are securities issued against a self-liquidating public works project, like a toll road. They are outside the debt limitation. At the same time the interest on them is not taxable under the federal income tax. Consequently, they enjoy a market advantage over private issues. Since these securities are not backed by the general revenues, the rate of interest is somewhat higher than that on ordinary government bonds. On the other hand, the locality gains a measure of maneuverability in its ability to finance its capital projects.[1] The investor takes the risk that the project will remain self-liquidating.

A device that is being used to finance *non-revenue* producing projects (e.g., schools), without ascertaining the will of the voters on the debt limit, is the *lease-purchase agreement*. Here the locality asks for bids from private contractors. The successful bidder builds the facility, and then leases it to the locality for an annual charge that covers all expenses plus provision for gradual purchase.

The use of revenue bonds has expanded the capacity of the states and localities for public works expenditures. At the same time, this device has increased the interest of the lower levels of government in the maintenance of a high level of employment. Average income must remain high if toll roads, for example, are to be successfully financed. Revenue bonds do not appear, however, to offer much prospect of use for a compensatory public works plan during a depression. Their popularity with the investor presupposes the expectation of a high level of demand for the services being sold by the state or locality.

"PROSPERITY RESERVES"

An alternative to borrowing by the states and localities would be to use budgetary surpluses acquired during a period of prosperity to finance capital projects during depression. The proceeds of the surpluses would

---

[1] Nevertheless, some localities have included the general revenue backing in order to obtain the advantage of lower interest rates. Cf. The Tax Institute, *Tax Policy*, May–June, 1953. Revenue bond sales exceeded $1 billion in 1952, and comprised 18 per cent of state and local debt in that year. Revenue bonds are sometimes used for the construction of factories, which are then leased to private firms. This is a risky procedure, for the trend of business may be away from a particular region.

be invested in government securities until needed. Most states, however, do not permit their localities to make use of this device. A large "prosperity reserve" might tend to encourage the misuse of funds by local officials. Again, the existence of reserves encourages the demand for tax reduction. Therefore the reserves may have disappeared by the time they are needed. Prior to World War II only seven states permitted the localities to build up reserves for future projects. By the end of the war, however, nineteen states had granted the privilege.[2]

The idea of building up reserves during prosperity, out of which the states and municipalities could finance public works and relief payments during depression, is appealing. It looks like sound finance. Sweden, for example, provided for this form of financing during the depression. Some of the apparent advantages, however, are fictitious. The concept of the reserve implies that the business cycle is a regular oscillation around a full-employment level of income. If income rises above this level, the surplus is held idle. On the advent of depression these reserves are spent. If, however, depression years are predominant, the reserves become exhausted. Otherwise, they are greater than needed, and if held idle, they are deflationary. Even if the reserves are invested by the localities and states, it is conjectural whether on balance the accumulation of a prosperity reserve is economically advantageous. To the extent that the taxes rest on savings during a period of prosperity, the supply of savings to private enterprise is reduced and the cost of obtaining capital may be increased. To some extent, therefore, public investment is likely to be substituted for private investment. Unless the states and localities are associated with developmental enterprises designed to open up new areas of economic endeavor it is probable that the net effect of the reserve accumulation policy on national product is negative. While this is not a necessary consequence of the reserve program, it is one which has to be guarded against.

The question may also be raised whether anything is gained by building up reserves against depression during a period of prosperity. If we accept the view that during intervals of peace the economy faces alternate periods of prosperity and depression, it does not make much difference whether a government levies taxes during prosperity to repay debt incurred in a previous depression or to build up a reserve in anticipation of the next one. What is important is that prosperous times and high tax yields alternate with depression periods so that the increase in state and local debt can be kept within tolerable bounds. A steadily rising debt may ultimately become a serious matter, but a fluctuating debt is of little importance.

---

[2] The Tax Institute, *op. cit.* The impetus came, of course, from the inability of the lower governmental levels to maintain their normal capital expenditures during the restrictions of wartime. Most of the reserves thus accumulated were quickly dissipated after the war as labor and materials became available. Some of the surplus wartime revenues was devoted to debt retirement.

GRANTS-IN-AID

Neither taxation, borrowing, nor reserves accumulated in prosperity offer the states and localities the necessary financial means for varying their public works spending in accordance with the need for stabilizing total public and private spending over the years. The possibility exists, however, that the problem could be solved by federal grants-in-aid, timed to compensate for fluctuations in the level of private spending. An advantage of this device would be that the states and localities could proceed with confidence in the advance planning of those spending projects which they would reserve for periods of unemployment and idle capacity. Another advantage would be the reduced danger that a series of depressions over the years might result in undue centralization of power. For if the federal government were to retain the entire responsibility for depression public works, it might in time entirely absorb the function of civil public investment.

Up to the present time little thought has been given to gearing the level of federal grants to the maintenance of a full-employment level of spending. The origin and development of the grant-in-aid program has been independent of the goal of achieving economic equilibrium. Rather, the objective has been to assist the states and localities in providing the minimum standards of public service that Congress and the executive branch have come to regard as desirable.

Federal grants could, of course, be made to vary inversely to the cycle.[3] This might be accomplished either through conscious management or by gearing the grants to some index of income or employment. If this were done, however, federal agencies and others who are interested in particular subsidized programs could be counted upon to resist curtailment of funds during high-income periods. They naturally dislike to see their own programs curtailed merely because business and individual spending is rising. We would very likely have here another instance of the lack of parallelism in depression and boom policies that tends to nullify the effectiveness of fiscal policy as an instrument of economic control.

Grants-in-aid have had the effect of bringing about a gradual increase in the level of state and local public works expenditures. To the extent that this has occurred they have encouraged an increase in the ratio of public to total spending. The result has been to decrease somewhat the *need* for compensatory fiscal policy. The greater the ratio of permanent public spending to national income, the less is the scope for fluctuations in total expenditures. On the other hand, by the same token the area of choice open to the private consumer is reduced. Furthermore, an unplanned

---

[3] See the discussion of flexible grants-in-aid in James Maxwell, *Federal Grants and the Business Cycle* (New York: National Bureau of Economic Research, 1952), pp. 58, 67–71, 111.

expansion of federal grants results in an encroachment on the freedom of action of the states and localities. Only if the three levels of government get together under an integrated plan in which each has coordinate powers can the centralizing force of a grants program be avoided.

► THE FLEXIBILITY OF FEDERAL SPENDING

TIMING

The major conclusion of aggregative economics for public spending policy is that the government ought to compensate for fluctuations in private spending. Simple as this objective may appear when stated in terms of over-all purchasing-power flows, there are difficult problems in applying it in practice, and one of these problems is timing.

On a number of grounds the task of timing public investment projects to compensate for fluctuations in private spending is a difficult one. First, some government agency must be charged with the function of forecasting the level of national income and employment. Only if government money could be poured into the economy instantaneously, and at precisely the areas in which factors are unemployed, would it be possible to avoid the need for forecasting.

Second, the legislature has to authorize all expenditures; and the passage of appropriation bills takes time. It is true that in a major emergency the legislature is likely to look to the executive for leadership in combating depression. In these circumstances the required legislation can be quickly enacted. But in the event of a minor recession, before the sense of urgency has become general, legislatures are likely to be loath to surrender their right to debate. Yet compensatory spending operates most effectively when the decline in private spending is still small and tentative. Once the cumulative downswing sets in, it becomes very difficult to hit upon the correct volume of public spending to compensate for the increasing rate at which private spending is falling off.

When the necessary appropriations have been made, the task of spending falls to the executive branch. If spending is to be accomplished without delay, the machinery must have already been established. This machinery is complex, and not all of it can be set up without prior authorization by the legislature. For example, the expansion of public works expenditures requires the acquisition of sites. These cannot be required unless the legislature provides the funds in advance. Land must be condemned and purchased. To be sure, it ought not to be difficult to convince Congress of the necessity of accomplishing this step in advance of the crisis. There are, however, technical difficulties as well. Opposition to condemnation of land may make it politically preferable to resort to the much slower method of purchasing the land in the open market. The effect of this step, however, may be to encourage owners to demand excessive prices. Indeed, condemnation may also have this effect, for the public tends to sympathize with the owner.

The obstacles to the rapid acquisition of the necessary sites have led to the suggestion in some countries that all land be nationalized, or more modestly, that the development rights be nationalized. An alternative suggestion is that all land be owned by local authorities.[4] There is little sentiment for this step in the United States, though the situation is different in those countries that have been experimenting with nationalization.

A SHELF OF PUBLIC WORKS

A continuing task of the executive agency in charge of emergency public works would be the planning of projects by way of which newly created purchasing power could be injected into the income stream. Here the problem of timing merges with other criteria for the choice of public works projects. The public works authority must have at its disposal a variety of schemes on which money can be spent. Some of them may consist of longer-term plans—for example, irrigation projects—which will take a number of years to complete. If the program as a whole is to be flexible, however, other projects must be undertaken and completed rapidly. Much of its success will depend on the ease with which public expenditures can be tapered on and off as fluctuations in private spending may require.

The adoption of the principle that a reserve shelf of public works projects should be kept available at all times raises fundamental issues with respect to the optimum allocation of resources. It has often been argued by specialists in state and local spending that a tremendous deficiency exists in the provision of capital installation and equipment at these levels. It has been said that $100 billion or more could profitably be spent on bringing these up to the minimum desirable levels.[5]

This statement is somewhat akin to the contention frequently made in the depression that the demand for goods would be almost infinite if only the purchasing power could be got into the hands of those who desire, but cannot afford, to buy consumers' durable goods. The hitch was, of course, that their demand was not *effective,* and the problem was how to make it so without wrecking the system of price rationing which is the essence of the free-enterprise system.

Correspondingly, acceptance of the view that the backlog of capital needs of the states and localities ought to determine the direction of spending during a depression implies the obligation that all suggested pro-

---

[4] See the discussion in *Public Investment and Full Employment* (Montreal: International Labour Office, 1946), p. 297.

[5] See E. J. Howenstine, "An Inventory of Public Construction Needs," *American Economic Review,* June, 1948, p. 365. Howenstine estimated that at 1947 prices $120 billion was needed for construction in transport, education, rural electrification, housing, and public buildings.

grams should be carefully considered by the voters or their representatives. If the decisions are left to a public works committee—even a joint executive committee with representation at all three levels of government—no consideration is likely to be given to the possibility that the voter might have preferred that a part of depression spending take the form of consumer spending in the market for private goods. Obviously, opinions differ greatly on the need for civil public works. Advance planning for public works programs should be subject to legislative review, with adequate provision for hearing the views of those who do not have a vested interest in the long-term expansion of public works projects.

TECHNICAL ASPECTS OF TIMING[6]

The technical problem of contracting for, blueprinting, and getting projects under way offers a less serious obstacle to proper compensatory timing than do the considerations discussed above. The technical problem is not unimportant, however. Not only must decisions be made in advance on the projects to be undertaken, but detailed plans must be made. It might appear that all that is needed is to draw these plans up and pigeon-hole them for future reference. It is not quite this simple, however; with a growing population and rapid technological progress, plans made far in advance are likely to prove obsolete when the time comes to put them into effect. This means that the plans must be kept up to date. Therefore a trained staff must be constantly working on them, and this in turn requires that provision be made for attracting personnel. If several years pass without a depression the morale problem of the staff may become significant. Morale may be kept high, however, if the public works planning board is given responsibility for at least a proportion of the normal public works projects as well as that for emergency public works.

Another source of delay is the fact that the awarding of contracts takes time. If maximum participation by private firms is to be achieved, competitive bidding is necessary.[7] Advertisements have to be inserted more than once, and a waiting period is required before the contract is awarded. During the depression the delays were sometimes considerable, in some instances as long as two years. Much was learned, however, about the possibilities of reducing this lag. Moreover, the vast experience with the

---

[6] For a discussion of this problem with respect to federal experience in the depression, see National Resources Planning Board, *The Economic Effects of Federal Public Works Expenditures, 1933–1938,* November, 1940, Chap. VI, "Timing and Employment Flexibility of Public Works Construction."

[7] When the government's own labor force is used on a project, the time lags are much shorter. Obviously, the conflict between the principles of making maximum use of private firms and getting the expenditures made quickly when they are needed to put men to work can be resolved in favor of the former only if contracts are let in advance. But in a dynamic world the risk of price changes and supply problems makes this difficult.

letting of contracts in World War II has led to the elimination of much unnecessary legal and administrative red tape.

SECONDARY AND TERTIARY LAGS

A further source of time lags in achieving the full consequences of emergency public works spending arises out of the nature of the relation between the direct effects of the spending itself and the secondary and tertiary effects. The so-called process effects[8] on national income and employment are a composite of three types of influence. The primary effects consist of the "on-site" employment and income generated on the project itself and "off-site" employment and income created in connection with the supply of materials to the project. The secondary effects comprise the increase in the demand for consumers' goods by the workers on the project, together with the increased investment in investment goods industries in response to the demand for materials on the project. The tertiary effects consist of the investment that is induced by the secondary rise in private consumption and the consumption that is induced by the secondary rise in private investment.

Naturally, considerable reliance is placed on the multiplier and accelerator effects included in the secondary and tertiary effects of public spending. To the extent that they are not offset by multiplier and accelerator effects of opposite sign set in motion by increased taxes, there will be a magnified influence on income and employment. But the secondary and tertiary effects operate with varying lags. Some of the lags, to be sure, may be negative, since investment or consumption may be increased *in anticipation* of public works spending.

On balance, however, it may be supposed that time lags will be positive. Their magnitude will differ according to circumstances. For example, derived demand effects will be converted into accelerator effects only when inventories in the particular industries fall below the level that is regarded as the minimum under the prospective demand conditions. It is obvious that the lags at the tertiary stage are likely to be numerous and, in a severe depression, of considerable dimensions. They derive from the generalized excess capacity conditions that are met with relatively early in the course of depression. As the depression wears on, of course, this source of lag becomes less and less serious. In any event, there is not much that government can do about them, short of direct intervention in the private economy.

---

[8] As contrasted with the "product" effects in terms of the end product of the public investment itself. A useful glossary of the terms used in planning public works is given in International Labour Office, *op. cit.*, App. IV. See also Robert Dahl and Charles Lindblom, "Variation in Public Expenditure," in Max Millikan, ed., *Income Stabilization for a Developing Democracy* (New Haven, Conn.: Yale University Press, 1953).

One important source of lag at both the secondary and the tertiary stages, however, originates in the doubt in the minds of the spending and investing public about the intentions of the government in following through with its public works program. There is always the danger that a new administration and Congress might modify the program. Furthermore, in the event of economic recovery there is the possibility that projects already undertaken may be halted.

The danger that this may take place necessarily operates to dampen the enthusiasm of businessmen who might otherwise expand their inventories, plant, or equipment in anticipation of the direct and indirect spending effects of the project. During the depression it was frequently urged by public works advocates that even if projects are abandoned in the event that private spending subsequently rises, nothing is really lost. The social cost of unemployment, it was stated, exceeds that of abandoned public works projects. What was overlooked was the fact that there would not be much prospect of increased private investment if at any moment induced inventories and plant capacity might become superfluous.

A more sensible procedure would be to finish all projects that are physically undertaken, as well as those in anticipation of which private firms have expanded their inventories or equipment. The needed flexibility could be achieved by varying the rate at which new projects are undertaken. Naturally, it would be necessary to have in readiness projects of varying length, with an adequate number of short-term undertakings. In actual practice most of the flexibility is to be found in the kinds of projects undertaken by the municipalities. These ordinarily require less than a year to complete.

▶ PUBLIC RELIEF AND FLEXIBILITY

If it were deemed unimportant whether or not useful public works emerged from the spending program, the problem of the time lag would be of relatively small importance. A plan for relief payments could be legislated in advance, and Congress would make the necessary appropriations to take effect when the volume of employment fell below a certain level. No delay whatever would be necessary. As public works projects got under way, relief payments would automatically decline in response to the rise in employment.

IS PUBLIC RELIEF PREFERABLE TO PUBLIC WORKS?

Some economists would go farther than merely to advocate relief as a device for eliminating the time lags that are inevitable in a public works program. They argue that a basic cause of depression is the building up of greater investment capacity than is required in view of prospective levels of consumption. If this is so, a policy of full employment must rely to a large degree, or possibly even exclusively, on the underwriting of aggregate consumer expenditures.[9] A difficulty with public works spending is that certain narrow segments of the economy receive the initial impact of the additional demand. The construction industry obviously benefits immediately and predominantly from the very nature of public works expenditures. Yet costs and prices in this industry are likely to have been driven up greatly during the preceding boom. The consequence of directing public expenditure to construction may well be to prevent the decline in prices in this area that is a prerequisite to a well-balanced recovery. Therefore any rise in the incomes of the factors employed in this industry may be neutralized by the failure of prices to fall in the construction industry along with other prices.

Still other arguments have been advanced in favor of relief spending.[10] Consumption subsidies have the advantage over public works in that they leave in the hands of the individual the decision with respect to what to consume. If compensatory public works programs involved merely a rearrangement of public works over the cycle to compensate for variations in private spending, there would, of course, be no encroachment on private consumption decisions.

The argument for relief as against public works rests on the contention that the latter will actually replace some of the production for private markets that would otherwise have taken place. Since no one can know what the course of private investment would have been in the absence of public spending, this argument cannot be easily evaluated in a particular instance. The possibility of encroachment certainly exists, for as the government increases investment, it necessarily competes with private industry for those production factors that are limited in supply even during depression. Moreover, an increase in the supply of some types of publicly produced goods may reduce the demand for particular privately produced goods. For example, more parks may mean a smaller demand for entertainment.

PUBLIC WORKS, RELIEF, AND LEVERAGE EFFECTS

An important standard for comparing the efficacy of public works expenditures with relief is the relative leverage effects of each. It has been pointed out in Chapter 20 that the leverage effects of expanded private or

---

[9] See John H. G. Pierson, *Full Employment* (New Haven, Conn.: Yale University Press, 1941), p. 25, for the concept "national income insurance"; also, "The Underwriting of Aggregate Consumer Spending as a Pillar of Full Employment Policy," *American Economic Review*, March, 1944, pp. 21–55. The underconsumption interpretation of depression has, of course, a long history.

[10] Cf. Howard Ellis, "Economic Expansion through Competitive Markets," in *Financing American Prosperity* (New York: Twentieth Century Fund, 1945), pp. 133–136. Consult also P. A. Samuelson, "Fiscal Policy and Income Determination," *Quarterly Journal of Economics*, August, 1942, pp. 599 ff.

public investment are the aggregate multiplier and accelerator effects traceable to it. In other words, the leverage effects are the sum of the primary, secondary, and tertiary effects of additional private or public spending. A valid comparison of public works with relief spending on this count would have to evaluate certain kinds of indirect effects that are not easily identifiable. In part the problem is one of tracing indirect spending effects, but partly also it is one of paying attention to the differing psychological effects of the two methods on attitudes of both consumers and businessmen toward spending.

The immediate lifting effects of relief spending are probably greater than those of an equal amount devoted to public works. The marginal propensity to consume of relief recipients is unity, and the whole of the amount appropriated to relief comes into their hands. Under public works projects, on the other hand, part of the funds is devoted to the purchase of materials, and to the salaries of higher-paid experts (for example, architects and construction engineers), who merely shift from their previous jobs. The marginal propensity to consume of the businessmen and salaried workers who share in the benefits of a public works project is less than unity. However, this immediate advantage of relief over public works disappears after the first spending. Recipients of relief trade with the same merchants as do workers on public works projects. After the first spending, therefore, the possibility that the money will be held idle as merchants simply liquidate inventories is the same in the two cases.

It is not easy to make a clear-cut comparison between the lifting effects of relief and public works spending. On the one hand it can be argued that relief expenditures are devoted by the recipients to consumers' goods, and that they are thus spread very thinly over the economy. At the same time, public works expenditures are concentrated in the construction industry, and the likelihood is greater that new equipment will have to be purchased.

It may be questioned, however, whether it is worth while to try to exploit the strategic advantage of concentrating public expenditures on a limited number of projects. In recent years more and more support has been given to the view that the lower turning point of the cycle is reached when, throughout the economy, inventories have been drawn down, and plant and equipment have worn out, to the point at which replacement can no longer be deferred if firms are to be able to stay in business. If this is so, it may not make a great deal of difference at which points in the economy purchasing power is injected. The task during the depression may be, rather, to reduce capacity and inventories all along the line. One has the choice between striking a rough balance by raising the level of spending on the output of all industry, and concentrating expenditures in the construction industry. If there had been a great amount of private overbuilding in the preceding prosperity stage, the best chance for a balanced recovery might well be to avoid concentrating public spending at particular and obvious points in the economy.

The debate during and after the depression between the advocates of relief and those who supported public works perhaps gave a false impression that one method must be chosen to the exclusion of the other. The truth is, rather, that one or another form of public spending may be preferable at a particular moment, but that the over-all program may include both. Moreover, government subsidies to consumers during a depression may take a number of alternative forms. Consequently, it is necessary to consider their relative advantages and disadvantages from the point of view of economic stability.

► THE FORMS OF PUBLIC RELIEF

The two major forms of depression relief are home relief and unemployment compensation. Home relief, or the dole, suffers from the great disadvantage of giving the recipient a feeling of receiving charity, when as a matter of fact he is the victim of a failure on the part of the economic machine, for which he bears no responsibility. Furthermore, if a means test (proof of need of aid) is applied, the operation of the plan is likely to be unfair to those workers who are most deeply imbued with a sense of pride. By itself, moreover, the dole is unlikely to provide a very substantial boost to the demand for goods, and therefore to re-employment. Although it may be assumed that almost the whole of the relief payments will be passed on to storekeepers, the fact that only the unemployed are eligible means that benefits must be kept low. Furthermore, it may prove difficult to get workers off relief onto jobs again, for the dole is demoralizing.

UNEMPLOYMENT COMPENSATION

Unemployment compensation has much more to recommend it than does home relief. It is the duty of society to assure a man of steady work, and if this is impossible, to guarantee him a minimum annual income. The unemployment reserve fund is built up out of worker and employer contributions. No stigma attaches in the minds of the workers to the receipt of unemployment compensation. It is true, of course, that workers often welcome short periods of unemployment when they can count on receiving a weekly check. Employers, moreover, may take advantage of the unemployment compensation scheme to retain, at the expense of the reserve fund, a labor force that might otherwise drift to other industries. They do this by timing periods of unemployment so that each worker remains eligible for unemployment compensation payments. These are merely administrative problems, however, and are therefore not fundamental objections to the scheme.

UNEMPLOYMENT INSURANCE

Unemployment insurance offers the great advantage that the benefits vary inversely to, while payroll taxes rise and fall with, the level of employment. Thus unemployment insurance contributes to the built-in flexibility of the fiscal structure, and thus appeals to those who favor automatic over managed fiscal devices for economic stability. Unfortunately, since the states set standards with respect to both the size of payments and the length of time the worker may receive the payments, the effects vary greatly from state to state. On the other hand, the payments tend to be the most generous in the more highly industrialized states, in which unemployment may be greatest.

The essential difficulty with unemployment compensation schemes is that while they alleviate misery, they are not likely to be of sufficient quantitative importance to make a great contribution to halting the course of depression. For the most part agricultural workers are excluded. Moreover, payments per worker cannot be kept too high or he finds it better to be unemployed. Finally, if a depression is of long duration, more and more workers become ineligible for the benefits.

So long as unemployment compensation is viewed as unemployment *insurance,* the size of the reserve fund depends on the volume of payroll taxes collected from workers and employers during prosperous times. Since business cycles are not regular, it is impossible to set rates of contributions so that reserves are necessarily adequate to finance payments to all the unemployed during a depression. For this reason limits are set by the states on the period during which a worker may receive benefits after being laid off.

This difficulty could be avoided if the government were prepared to borrow freely from the banking system to finance any excess of benefits over the resources of the fund. For if this procedure were adopted, no time limit need be set to the receipt of benefits. Presumably the federal government would make grants-in-aid to the states for the specific purpose of replenishing the reserve fund. Since fluctuations in the size of these grants would be automatic, they would probably cause no alteration in the political power relations between the states and the federal government. The social justification for this procedure would be that not merely the employer and workers are responsible for periods of unemployment, but also society at large.

A "SOCIAL DIVIDEND"

Another means whereby purchasing power can be injected into the economy at those points at which the marginal propensity to consume is likely to be close to unity is the reduction of taxes on consumption. A difficulty with *general* tax reduction in achieving this goal is that taxes fall partly on savings, and during a depression the remitted savings are likely to be hoarded. The problem, then, is to discover those taxes the incidence of which is on individuals who would spend all, or nearly, all of the amounts remitted if the tax rates were reduced. Such taxes are, in general, the various sales and excise taxes on goods consumed by the mass of the public.

Tax remission, however, does not fall under the heading of public spending. If, on the other hand, tax rates are reduced to the point at which they become negative, a subsidy is involved that has similar economic effects to the dole. A scheme of this sort is too novel for practical consideration, but from time to time proposals have been made along these lines.[11]

The advantages urged for this sort of plan are these: (1) as much money as desired can be put into the hands of consumers merely by making the rates of tax sufficiently negative; (2) ease of administration—the income tax is already in operation; and (3) automaticity—the size of the benefits, once established, varies inversely with the level of income or employment. A disadvantage, however, would be the difficulty of taking account of variations in employment in different parts of the country. Whereas within limits public works projects can be directed toward areas in which unemployment is above average, "negative tax" subsidies would be determined by a general index of unemployment.[12]

OTHER FORMS OF CONSUMER SUBSIDIES

It has sometimes been urged that the government take the occasion of a depression to make increases in certain forms of transfer payments to consumer groups. The argument is that in the course of ordinary social progress these increases will come about in any event; therefore, they should be spaced in such a way that a maximum contribution is made to economic stability.

An example of this procedure would be the timing of increased social security coverage, or increases in the size of benefits, to coincide with periods of low income. To some extent this development tends to occur automatically. Thus the practice of replacing older with younger workers

---

[11] See, for example, Kenneth Boulding, *The Economics of Peace* (New York: Prentice-Hall, 1945), pp. 164 ff. His proposal is to allow variations in the income tax rate so as to make possible negative taxation, though he does not believe that deflation need be allowed to reach the point at which negative income tax rates would be necessary.

[12] Cf. Dahl and Lindblom, "Variation in Public Expenditures," *loc. cit.* However, with the development of more adequate indices of sectional prices, income, employment, and so on, there is no reason why allowance could not be made for regional differences in employment. One difficulty would be the discouragement placed on the exodus of factors from economically declining areas. It would be necessary to distinguish between general unemployment and unemployment ascribable to local conditions not associated with the general decline in national income. Even during periods of high unemployment this task is not easy.

during depression hastens retirement and increases old-age benefits. A similar effect is brought about if social security contributions (i.e., taxes) are reduced during a depression. This was provided, for example, in the British White Paper of May 26, 1944, which accepted in principle the policy of compensatory variations in social security premiums. Moreover, a given level of benefits in terms of dollars buys more goods when a depression is accompanied by a substantial price fall. Unless this increase in real income is offset by a fall in other types of income accruing to retired persons, the effect is to stimulate consumption by this group.

A policy of reserving increases in old-age security pensions, veterans' payments, and the like, for depression periods could hardly be successful. Political pressures operate whether or not the economy is depressed.[13] Indeed, the pressure for more generous subsidies is likely to be at its greatest during an inflationary period, when the real value of pensions and subsidies is declining. On the other hand, if the plan were rigidly adhered to, a long period of prosperity might unduly delay increases that ought to be made.

A TAX VARIANT ON THE CONSUMER SUBSIDY

A similar type of proposal would be to rely more heavily during depression on taxes that fall on saving. The argument runs that since it is then difficult to get businessmen to borrow savings, consumption should be encouraged at the expense of saving. The danger, however, is that the inducement to invest might be adversely affected by a policy so consciously directed at favoring the low-income consumer over the higher-income saver. No definite conclusions can be drawn as to the relative effects on investment resulting from (1) the accelerator effect of any increase in consumption, and (2) the discouraging effect of increases in the rates of the corporate and personal income taxes. In any case, it would be a very difficult thing to accomplish politically. A running battle is fought, throughout depression and prosperity, between the advocates of a federal sales tax and those who wish to exploit further the personal income tax on the middle and higher brackets. Finally, it would seem advisable to separate, so far as possible, policy with respect to the maintenance of full employment from measures designed to affect the distribution of income. Otherwise, unintended effects on the latter may be the result.[14]

If changes in taxes and the tax system are to be employed in the

---

[13] For example, during 1950–1952, receipts of the federal old-age insurance fund ran ahead of disbursements, and as a consequence benefits were raised by $5 a month. Cf. the discussion by J. R. Stark, "Equities in the Financing of Federal Old-Age and Survivors Insurance," *National Tax Journal*, September, 1953, pp. 287–288.

[14] In this connection it should be observed that public works exert an effect on the distribution of real income quite apart from the redistribution of dollar purchasing power. A low-cost housing program, for example, may permit low-income receivers to occupy better quarters at lower rents.

pursuit of economic stability, a more promising device is to vary the methods of financing the normal public works that are already being undertaken. A shift to deficit finance in depression and to tax-financed public works in prosperity would add to the built-in flexibility of the fiscal system. Since the bulk of civil public works during ordinary times is the responsibility of the states and localities, this scheme would necessitate an increase in federal grants-in-aid, financed out of sales of securities to the banking system. In addition, emergency public works spending would likewise be financed by inflationary borrowing. Here again a problem is to convince the businessman of the appropriateness of surrendering the objective of a balanced budget. It is important to remember that despite, or perhaps because of, the assurance of economists that the national debt is a minor matter in comparison with mass unemployment, the average citizen remains to this day convinced that a large debt threatens the national solvency.

► PUBLIC WORKS

Any future depression is likely to be combated with a combination of all the available fiscal and nonfiscal instruments. Therefore, so far as public spending is concerned, use will be made of both transfer payments, including various types of subsidies and payments to consumers, and government spending on public works projects. What ought to be the nature of such projects?

A BALANCED PUBLIC WORKS PROGRAM

Ideally, a public spending program should inject purchasing power into the income stream at precisely those points at which demand is deficient. The recognition of the need for a balanced public works program has resulted in a de-emphasis of the view, formerly widely held, that it does not make much difference where the new purchasing power enters the income stream. First, so far as possible, public works spending should be aimed at those spots where deficiencies in private and ordinary public spending occur. Second, emergency public works spending itself should not be allowed to cause very many instances of an excess of demand over supply of goods and production factors. Third, public works spending ought to offer as little rivalry as possible to competing types of private spending. Private investment is discouraged to the extent that the government produces goods and services that compete with, or may be substituted for, privately produced commodities.

AN INHERENT IMBALANCE

The major obstacles to the effective use of public works expenditures to eliminate unemployment and excess capacity are the ease with which public money can be spent for construction and the difficulties that face spending on nonconstruction industries. During a depression, excess capacity is a generalized phenomenon. The problem is to create a demand for unemployed factors, not merely to use a particular industry as a funnel through which to inject purchasing power into the income stream. If public works are restricted to the construction industry, the fact that cycles of activity occur in other industries as well is de-emphasized. Yet these industries may be as much the key to depression as is the construction industry.

Because of the operation of derived demand and the acceleration principle, the equipment industries, for example, are particularly hard hit by a recession. Indeed, they feel the effects of a decline in the *rate of increase* in aggregate income. Thus they may be the bellwether of an impending recession. Consequently, a balanced recovery program should take account of the relation of the construction cycle to that in the equipment industries. Indeed, since the cycle is not restricted to construction and investment goods production alone, but is a cycle in the production of durable goods production in general, it is this broader category of industries that has to be stabilized.[15]

The restriction of emergency depression spending largely to the construction industry "furnishes standing notice"[16] that the government will support demand and prices in an industry in which monopolized wages and prices are widespread. Knowledge that such support will be given whenever a recession develops obviously discourages the scaling down of the excessively high prices that may have been largely responsible for the downturn.

It is quite true that a depression in the residential construction industry is very likely to be due to overbuilding rather than primarily to high prices. If this is the case, however, public spending on housing is more likely to result in restoring that industry to a liquid position than it is to initiate a chain of new income payments that would spread from this industry to others. The effects will be more favorable, of course, if instead of devoting public money to housing projects, the government spends on roads and other nonresidential construction. In that event, resources tend to shift out of one segment of the construction industry into another. The accumulated surplus of housing accommodations is gradually liquidated as population rises and older houses are eliminated. Subsequently, then, the construction of residential housing can be resumed.

A BROADER CONCEPT OF BALANCE

The foregoing discussion assumes that the criterion of balance in a public works program is its capacity for re-employing resources without

---

[15] This point is made by John H. Williams, in his paper "Free Enterprise and Full Employment," in *Financing American Prosperity,* p. 361.

[16] The phrase belongs to J. M. Clark, *ibid.,* p. 106.

introducing new distortions that will ensure another depression. Still other considerations have to be taken into account, however, and a balance must be struck among conflicting objectives. The most urgent aim of a spending program is to get money into the hands of those who have been made destitute by the depression. Therefore, it may be necessary to sacrifice some portion of economic balance in favor of finding a solution to the immediate problem of relief.

Another criterion for emergency public works is their relative usefulness. It is not enough that income effects be maximized, or that all needy individuals be taken care of. In addition, the public must have confidence that the project is worth while. People will not remain content with make-work schemes, except for short periods during serious emergencies.

During the depression it was often argued that merely to dig postholes and fill them up again is justified if it gets money into circulation. In a limited sense this is true, but it ignores two circumstances. One is the many and obvious deficiencies in the supply of public facilities like hospitals, in the development of natural resources, and so on. The other is the highly adverse moral effect on the worker who is asked to devote his labor to a palpably useless undertaking. It is true, of course, that the definition of useful public works is very broad. In times past it has encompassed pyramids, the Acropolis, canal networks, and marble postoffices for small towns. It is quite reasonable that many projects pass the test during depression which would have to yield to higher priorities during a period of high-level employment.

► PUBLIC SPENDING AND INFLATION CONTROL

Suppose that private investment and consumption spending increase to the point at which full employment is approached. During the course of the upswing, emergency public works projects will have been tapered off. This is accomplished by reducing the rate of starts of new projects, rather than by leaving useful projects unfinished. A time may come, however, when inflation control requires that even normal or ordinary public works be curtailed. Otherwise, the principle of compensatory public spending is being observed in depression but not in prosperity.

Clearly, it may be difficult for the federal government to reduce its spending when private spending increases to the point of threatening inflation. It is easier to increase government spending in depression than it is to decrease it during a boom. While there is no obstacle to increasing public works spending except the physical problems involved in getting projects started, a reduction of public works during a boom might mean that the government would have to cut back its ordinary projects. Certain projects, it is true, can be deferred from prosperity to depression, but this device is limited in scope because cycles are unpredictable and irregular.

If a period of prosperity lasts long enough, it will be no longer politically possible to defer projects that are strongly desired by the public. Moreover, in the use of monetary policy the central-bank authorities have an instrument of control over private spending that is far more effective in restraining a boom than it is in encouraging private spending during a depression. Consequently, there may be a more pronounced tendency to try to restrain private spending through rediscount and open-market policy during a boom than to abridge public spending programs.

SHOULD PUBLIC SPENDING BE SUBORDINATED TO PRIVATE SPENDING?

The fact that the business cycle is not a regular oscillatory motion inevitably proves discouraging to a policy of so distributing public works spending over the cycle as to compensate for variations in private spending. If cycles were regular, the public's desire for government services could be satisfied by increasing government spending in depression and tapering it off in prosperity. Essentially, what compensatory spending policy calls for is a possible lengthy period of subordination of public expenditure to private investment and consumption spending. One should be clear on the implications of the policy for aggregate welfare. It means that the public works spending is the passive factor, that government spending decisions are determined in the light of what the private sector has decided to do. When consumers and businessmen collectively decide to make more intensive use of resources, the government is called upon to yield.

Public spending, however, cannot be regarded as simply a foil to private spending. The major reason is that under the legislative process in a democracy, decisions are constantly being made on the desired ratio of public to private spending. A compensatory public spending program might run counter to this principle. The fact is that except in the extreme circumstances of a very severe depression or a highly dangerous inflation, other considerations are likely to outweigh economic stability in the minds of legislators. This is consistent, moreover, with the principle of budgeting scarce national resources so as to maximize the aggregate welfare of society. It may be that from this point of view it would be preferable in a boom to force a reduction in *private* spending. Whether inflation is owing to an increase in private spending or in government expenditures, the decision with respect to which should be curtailed in the interest of economic stability has to be made on the basis of particular circumstances.

In addition to considerations of aggregate social welfare there are still other reasons why public spending may be difficult to curtail even in the face of inflation. These are summed up in the obvious fact that the precise considerations of marginal analysis are widely removed from the conditions of the real world. Both public and private expenditures are made largely without a close comparison of the relative advantages to be gained by society. Legislatures are rarely in a position to consider simultaneously the merits of alternative types of public spending, let alone those of the private spending that must be forgone to permit an increase in public spending. Again, their decisions are often forced by circumstances. Witness the fact that during a boom, when incomes and tax revenues are high, state and local governments find themselves in a position to undertake long-deferred projects.

We conclude that compensatory fiscal policy would have to consist of something more than compensatory government spending alone. Depending on circumstances, it may be preferable to rely on variations in tax rates or on a combination of both methods.

A DECREASE IN PUBLIC SPENDING VS. AN INCREASE IN TAXES

Under conditions of high-level employment a decrease in public spending is likely to have a greater disinflationary effect than an equal rise in tax receipts. Higher taxes, it is true, initially reduce disposable income. But this may not be the ultimate effect. An indirect effect of the tax increase may be to bring about an increase in incomes *before* taxes. Those who bear the burden of the increased taxes are likely in some degree to strive to maintain consumption by dipping into their savings accounts. The effect of this, under full-employment conditions, may be to reduce the availability of savings to businessmen and to consumers who purchase on installment credit. To the extent that these borrowers then turn to the commercial banks in order to maintain investment and consumption, the supply of money is increased. Thus prices may not have to fall back to their previous level.

AN EQUAL DECREASE IN SPENDING AND IN TAXES

Finally, we may consider the possible effects on the price level of an equal reduction of public spending and tax revenues. If in consequence of the tax reduction private spending were to increase by the same amount that public spending decreased, the immediate effect would be neither inflationary nor deflationary. There would be merely a transfer of purchasing power from the government to taxpayers. This conclusion assumes, however, that no effects are produced on the flow of salable goods to market. Actually, the substitution of private investment spending for government expenditures would be likely to increase the flow of goods relatively to spending. An expansion of productive capacity does not indeed result immediately in a rise in the goods flow, but once the new plant is built it does so. A comparable amount of government spending, even if it is clearly investment rather than consumption spending, is likely to consist at least in part of long-range development projects that require considerable time to bear fruit in the form of an increase in salable national product. Except for self-liquidating projects, they depend on their capacity for opening up new resources to exploitation by private firms. No additional goods flow to market until this exploitation is actually undertaken.

When taxes are reduced there is no assurance that the whole of the added purchasing power in the hands of taxpayers will be spent. Government spending declines by the full amount of the remitted taxes. Private *consumption* spending will rise by less than this amount, since a part of the taxes had fallen on savings rather than on consumption. That part of the remitted taxes which constitutes an addition to taxpayers' savings may or may not be spent on investment goods. To the extent that they are *not* invested, the net effect of the reduction in the size of the budget is deflationary. To the extent that they *are* invested, the purchasing-power effects are neutral, though, as stated above, there is likely to be an increase in the flow of goods to market as private investment is substituted for public investment.

A POSSIBLE ADVERSE EFFECT

The fact that not the whole of the remitted taxes may be returned to the income stream means that the government must exercise caution in reducing the size of the budget. Some disinflation is desired, but not too much. The problem is to give tax relief without at the same time lowering unduly the rate of total public plus private spending. So long as prospects for profits are bright, it is likely that the additional savings will be used to purchase investment goods. In this case, though private spending rises by as much as public spending falls, some disinflation should come about via increased productive capacity and output. Even during a period of inflation, however, it may be that underlying factors, not yet visible to the observer, are preparing the way for a downswing. If this downswing should happen to materialize during the months following the cut in the budget, the effect might be to encourage a deflationary spiral.

This is the enigma that faces the federal government during an inflationary period after years of budgetary increases. It is hard to reverse the process without initiating a depression. The difficulty with "disinflating" by means of a reduction in the budget is that no one knows exactly how far government spending was responsible for the maintenance of a full-employment level of income. Does the existing level of private investment depend in part on the knowledge that the government will continue to make itself responsible for a "core" of spending? If so, a reduction in the federal budget may result in a disinclination on the part of businessmen to invest the new savings now being made by those whose taxes have been reduced. This effect is not likely to be of great importance unless other deflationary forces are operating at the same time. But the possibility is always present.[17]

---

[17] This analysis should be compared with that in Chapter 20. There it was shown that an increase in the size of a balanced budget is *probably*, though not *inevitably*, inflationary. Here the converse is demonstrated, namely, that a decrease in the size of a balanced budget is probably deflationary.

► TAXATION AND ECONOMIC STABILITY

The contribution of taxation to economic stability depends on the extent to which the private sector relinquishes resources when tax receipts rise, and makes greater use of them when receipts fall. These reactions differ at different phases of the cycle, as well as in response to a variety of other influences. Consequently, the tax instrument, though useful for economic control, does not by any means operate in a precise fashion.

Taxes exert their effects in two ways. They affect disposable income, and thus the power to spend; and they modify incentives to earn income and to spend. Neither of these effects can always be closely controlled by the tax authorities. The purchasing-power effects must be estimated in advance, and therefore involve both economic forecasting and the estimation of lags in tax collections. The incentive effects may be ascertained after a fashion by an evaluation of reactions of taxpayers to similar fiscal changes in the past. But no two situations are ever exactly alike. Long experience is necessary for the successful practice of the art of tax policy for economic control.

Since the effect of taxes on the rate of use of resources by individuals and firms depends both on taxpayer reaction to the existence of the tax and on effects on disposable income, the impact of a tax on the level of national income is not measured solely by its power to produce revenues.[18] Tax receipts depend on both the tax rate and the base to which the rate is applied. In order to use tax policy for economic control, the tax authority must select taxes on the basis of their response to changes in the levels of income and spending; moreover, it must be politically feasible to manipulate tax rates and exemptions. This manipulation also includes the substitution of one tax for another, with no change in revenues, in order to take advantage of differing propensities to spend among taxpayers.

THE CYCLE-SENSITIVITY OF TAXES

Different tax structures differ in their reactions to changes in the levels of income and spending. As a first approximation it may be said that a progressive tax system will react more responsively to changes in income and spending than will a regressive tax system. A more careful statement, however, must take account of the fact that the distribution of income as well as the rate structure affects tax yields. Circumstances can be imagined in which a regressive tax system will respond more vigorously to changes in income than will a progressive tax system. This will be the situation if the rises in income are concentrated in the lower-income brackets, espe-

---

[18] As we saw in the case of the graduated spendings tax, the smaller the revenue yield, the greater may be the negative effect on individual spending. The incentive effects of such a tax override its purchasing-power effects.

cially if the wage rise is at the expense of profits and dividends to high-income receivers.[19]

Any pronounced rise in the level of income is not likely, however, to be restricted to the lower-income brackets. Indeed, inflation of incomes and prices ordinarily involves a lag of wages behind profits, despite efforts of unions to maintain or improve the relative position of the worker. Consequently, the more progressive rate structure may be expected to furnish the more elastic response, in terms of tax yields, to changes in income levels. Even taking account of the many regressive taxes at all levels of government in the United States, the great relative importance of the strongly progressive personal income tax makes the system as a whole at least somewhat progressive.

What scope exists for increasing the cycle-sensitivity of the American tax system? Are there tax devices at hand that are of sufficient quantitative importance so that changes in the levels of income and spending will cause a significant redistribution of resources between private and public sectors? The answer to this question depends on the extent to which the rates and base of each important tax are subject to manipulation. A further possibility is the timing of collection and refunds of taxes so that they reinforce rather than offset the sensitivity of the tax structure.

DEVICES FOR AFFECTING CYCLE-SENSITIVITY

One instrument for affecting the cycle-sensitivity of the tax system is the use of the schedular tax form under the personal income tax. In some countries different rates of tax are applied to different sources of income. For example, a higher rate may be applied to income received from interest and dividends. Profits fluctuate more violently than the level of income and employment; consequently, receipts from income taxes or corporate profits taxes likewise fluctuate more violently than the business cycle itself. If, in addition, higher rates are applied to dividends, the tax response to the business cycle is still further enhanced.[20] Even if the tax rates on investment income are no higher than those on ordinary income, an earned income credit of the type formerly in use under the federal income tax results in higher effective rates on dividend income.[21]

There is scope for making technical and administrative changes in certain taxes in order to increase or decrease their cycle-sensitivity.[22] If capital gains are subject to the income tax, an element is thereby included

[19] See the discussion by Carl Shoup in *Papers and Proceedings* of the American Economic Association, May, 1952, p. 161.

[20] This assumes that dividends and profits fluctuate together. To the extent, however, that corporations accumulate undistributed profits during periods of high corporate income and maintain dividends during depressions, higher tax rates on dividends would not contribute to the cycle-sensitivity of the tax system.

[21] Except, of course, to the extent that small amounts of interest and dividend income are regarded as earned income. This was the case under federal practice.

[22] The discussion here is based on Carl Shoup, "Taxation and Fiscal Policy," in Millikan, *op. cit.,* pp. 278 ff.

in the tax base that fluctuates more violently than wages and salaries. The inclusion of unrealized capital gains would still further increase the extent to which taxable income would rise during a business upswing. Again, if capital losses may be deducted from other income as well as from capital gains, the base of the income tax declines the more markedly in a downswing.

Carry-backs and carry-forwards of losses likewise redistribute the tax base over the cycle. Suppose that during a previous period of high income and employment firms have made high profits. If losses are subsequently incurred during a downswing, the privilege of carrying them back to earlier years means that tax refunds are forthcoming. Thus to the lower tax liability caused by declining profits is added the refund from taxes paid earlier. The net effect for some firms may be negative taxes during the downswing. A carry-forward, on the other hand, means that previous losses operate to reduce tax liability as profits rise, and thus reduce the cycle-sensitivity of the tax.

Ad valorem sales taxes are more sensitive to fluctuations in spending than are specific taxes. As prices change, tax liability changes as well. In a system that contains both per unit and ad valorem taxes, however, the effect is not as clear. Suppose that incomes and spending rise. Since the effective rates of ad valorem taxes will rise to a greater degree than will those of specific taxes, consumers are likely to shift their purchases at least to some extent away from commodities that are subject to the ad valorem tax. In other words, substitution effects have to be taken into account.

The property tax is a cyclically insensitive tax. Assessments lag both in the upswing and in the downswing. Increases and decreases in the rates of the tax are not rapid enough or great enough to make up for these lags. On the other hand, during a depression, much property may become delinquent. Although the tax liability remains, and indeed is for the most part ultimately satisfied, the revenues may for the time being fall off substantially. This effect is not likely to take place, however, unless the depression is severe. In any case, the property tax cannot be regarded as a cycle-sensitive device for automatic fiscal control.

Finally, it may be noted that the taxation of the passing of property at death provides little cycle-sensitivity. Fluctuations in prices and incomes do indeed affect substantially the size of taxable estates. Moreover, they greatly alter the real value of the exemption. Even so, the minute importance of death and gift taxation in the total tax structure virtually eliminates it as an instrument of economic control.

MANIPULATION OF THE TAX SYSTEM

Thus far we have concerned with the possibility of organizing the tax system so as to enhance the cycle-sensitivity of tax receipts. Once rates, base, and exemptions are set, they are let alone. The further possibility exists of making changes in various taxes during the course of fluctuations in order to minimize them. This procedure runs all the risks of management and of mistakes in forecasting. It is restricted, furthermore, by the limits on the scope for making frequent administrative and legal changes.

Examples of conscious management of the tax system follow.

1. A pay-as-you-go system might be introduced during an inflationary period to speed up tax payments, and abandoned during a severe depression in order to postpone tax liabilities. Obviously, such a procedure would be subject to the severe criticism of ignoring the major reason for pay-as-you-go, namely, keeping taxpayers current so that they do not dissipate funds to which the government rather than they themselves has title.

2. The rate at which certain taxes are due might be speeded up or retarded. In 1953, for example, this device was used with respect to the corporate income tax. A serious difficulty with this device is the fact that it adds still another risk to the hazards of doing business. Firms are faced with the prospect of having to meet unexpected tax liabilities. Possibly a more viable device would be to alter the rate at which tax refunds are made. To be sure, business faces the risk that refunds may be deferred, but in this case the carrot is used rather than the stick. Examples of tax refunds are those made after overpayment of the personal income tax, and the payments made to the taxpayer when losses are carried back to profits on which tax has been paid in an earlier year.

3. Rates and exemptions may be changed in response to changes in income levels. In theory there is wide scope for using this device to alter private business and consumption spending. In practice an obstacle is the reluctance of legislatures to turn this job over to executive agencies, which alone can act speedily enough to achieve the desired results. Even if this is done, however, there is the further difficulty that frequent changes in tax rates increase business risk and may therefore discourage investment. Moreover, in the case of commodity taxes, for example, unless the change in rates or exemptions is kept secret, much anticipatory buying may take place. The effect is, of course, to encourage the inflation that it is desired to mitigate. Secrecy is difficult under the American legislative system, although in Great Britain these secrets are kept until the budget is ready to be presented.

The changing of rates and exemptions always causes an inequity as between those who perforce incur tax liability during periods of high rates and low exemptions. The classic example of this injustice is the restriction of death taxes to time of war, but it is present whenever tax rates are temporarily increased. It has often been urged that payroll taxes under both the unemployment and the old-age security systems be reduced or eliminated during depression. Here again is a violation of equity, since not all workers are covered, and thus all do not benefit.

► CONCLUSION

The devices discussed above can serve to cause tax liability to vary in such a way as partially to offset the factors that make for economic instability. But because of administration and equity considerations, as well as because of their limited quantitative effects, it is questionable whether variations in tax rates and exemptions can contribute very much to stability. Moreover, built-in flexibility, while helpful, likewise makes only a limited contribution to stabilization.

It has been suggested by some that, if necessary, the whole tax system be suspended during a severe depression. This device is too novel to enlist much support. More than this, however, it is indiscriminate. To the extent that economic fluctuations are due to the presence of bottlenecks in the midst of unemployment, and to the resulting dislocations of cost-price relationships, a suspension of the tax system might well cause more harm than good. The effect might easily be a multiplication of rigidities and distortions. Reliance is solely on aggregative purchasing-power effects, and the possibility of specific maladjustments is ignored.

The appropriate relative roles of tax reduction and public works spending as instruments of economic control depend on the stage of the cycle, and on the relative importance of cyclical and secular factors in causing instability. One point should be emphasized. Tax reduction does not help very much, particularly if the economy is suffering from secular stagnation, unless the greater part of the remitted taxes had rested on consumption rather than on savings. If consumption is low, savings may be too high in relation to the demand for them. In these circumstances means have to be found either to raise the propensity to consume or to stimulate the rate at which new capital-using inventions are introduced; otherwise, the federal government must increase the level of its tax-financed public works spending.

► REFERENCES

CLARK, J. M. *Economics of Planning Public Works*. Washington, D. C.: U. S. Government Printing Office, 1935.

COLEAN, M. L., and R. NEWCOMBE. *Stabilizing Construction*. New York: McGraw-Hill Book Company, Inc., 1954.

HANSEN, A. *Fiscal Policy and Business Cycles*. New York: W. W. Norton & Company, 1941.

INTERNATIONAL LABOUR OFFICE. *Public Investment and Full Employment*. Montreal, 1946.

MAXWELL, J. *Federal Grants and the Business Cycle.* New York: National Bureau of Economic Research, 1952.

MILLIKAN, M., ed. *Income Stabilization for a Developing Democracy.* New Haven, Conn.: Yale University Press, 1953.

TWENTIETH CENTURY FUND. *Financing American Prosperity.* New York: The Fund, 1945.

23 Fiscal Policy and the Distribution of Income

► INTRODUCTION

Public spending, taxation, and debt management all affect the distribution of income. With the tremendous growth in recent years of the relative importance of public finance as compared with private finance, interest in the effects of the former on the distribution of income and wealth has risen substantially. At the same time a corollary of this interest has been an increasing concern with the role of the *private* sector of the economy in influencing the distribution of income.[1]

Important modifications are produced in the distribution of income by way of government control over monopoly and business practices. This method of achieving the desired income distribution has its limits, however. A whole battery of weapons is required, among which fiscal policy is of major importance. But fiscal policy, in turn, is hampered by the fact that some taxes tend to be made use of which produce undesired effects on income distribution. They are imposed because of their revenue-producing capacity, and all other considerations have been secondary. For the present time, at least, such taxes must be taken as given elements in fiscal systems. Therefore, the taxes that do lend themselves to manipulation in the interest of a conscious policy of income redistribution must perform a twofold function. In the first place they must counteract the undesired distribution effects produced within the fiscal system itself. Second, with their remaining power, they may be used to offset similar undesired effects in the private sector of the economy.

---

[1] It can be said that "almost every enterprise in our society is in part an arrangement to change the probability distribution of wealth." See Milton Friedman, "Choice, Chance and the Personal Distribution of Income," *Journal of Political Economy*, August, 1953, p. 281. While traditionally inequality in the distribution of income and wealth has been ascribed primarily to differences in ability and in inherited wealth, Friedman argues that there are grounds for believing that both private and public economic and social institutions can be regarded in part as "devices for achieving a distribution of wealth in conformity with the tastes and preferences of the members of society" (p. 290).

523

Much opposition has appeared in the past to the use of the fiscal system as a conscious instrument for controlling the distribution of income and wealth. In support of this point of view it must be admitted that such a use of the fiscal instrument undoubtedly intensifies the class struggle. An arena is provided in which conflicts arise that might not otherwise have come into existence. Against this view, however, it has to be pointed out that public finance affects the distribution of income, whether or not this is the intention. It can hardly be expected that those to whom a given tax or set of taxes is detrimental will indefinitely refrain from forcing the issue into the political arena.

More than this, tax systems have in the past favored savings at the expense of consumption. To this day many tax systems of the world rely almost exclusively on direct and indirect taxes on consumption. An increasing public knowledge of economics made it inevitable that this bias in favor of the income groups that are able to save would be gradually modified. There are simply more voters in the consuming than in the saving classes.

► THE MEANING OF OPTIMUM DISTRIBUTION

Once the public embarks on a policy of consciously modifying the distribution of income through fiscal and other governmental measures, an extremely thorny problem has to be solved. Agreement must be reached on what is optimum distribution of income. Individuals and groups view the economic system from their own positions in society. Unanimity of opinion is therefore impossible, and it is highly doubtful if an agreed concept of optimum distribution can be achieved. If such is the case, the actual effect of the fiscal system on the distribution of income will not be determined on the basis of a particular theory of optimum distribution, but rather as a result of the struggle between the dominant political forces at a particular moment of time. The result will be strongly modified, of course, by political decisions made in the past. This does not mean that theories will play no role whatever. Each group must have a rationalization of its position. And in the event that a particular group becomes politically dominant, the theory which it espouses may rise to the status of a dogma generally accepted by society.

If couched in sufficiently general terms, the concept of optimum income distribution can be accepted by everyone. It merely asserts that the distribution is best which maximizes aggregate economic welfare. To accept any other view would be to place individual interest over that of society as a whole. While individuals and pressure groups necessarily do place their own interests above those of society, they must take care to stress those aspects of their proposals which involve social advantage.

The possibility of legitimate differences of opinion over the welfare effects of government finance is enhanced by the fact that welfare is affected by both the level of aggregate real income and its distribution among the various income brackets. Welfare *may* be increased if output per capita rises.[2] Welfare may be increased also if a given output is redistributed from some income groups to others. In neither case do we know that welfare *will* be increased. The difficulty of measuring the effect on welfare of either an increase in output or a redistribution of a given volume of output means that arbitrary standards have to be applied. For example, it is usually simply assumed that increasing per capita output is socially desirable. Again, it may be assumed that a downward redistribution of income makes more people happy than unhappy. Neither assumption is necessarily true, but politicians may believe that these assumptions are more likely to appeal to the voter than are any alternative assumptions.

DIRECT AND INDIRECT WELFARE EFFECTS

The redistribution of income has both direct and indirect effects on the rate of flow of goods and services to each income group. The direct effect is the change in the share of each participating group in the national product as a result of the collection of taxes and government spending. The indirect effect results from the impact of this change on the proportion of national income saved and consumed. A change in the proportion of national income that is saved may affect real income *before* taxes and public spending.

Those who desire a redistribution of income on equity grounds, therefore, should concern themselves not only with the immediate effects on shares in income but also with the indirect effects on the size of income. They do not always take account of these income effects, however, for individuals do not measure their happiness solely in terms of their absolute standards of living. Most of us are also deeply concerned about the size of our incomes in comparison with the incomes of others. The growth in the power of the labor unions has encouraged the worker to think not merely of the level of his own income but also of his relative status in economic society. Consequently, the struggle for shares in national income may be carried on at the expense of the level of national income itself. The absolute real income of a particular group may fall while at the same time its relative share is rising. Yet the satisfaction accruing to this group may be greater than if the reverse were occurring.

CHANGES IN THE CONCEPT OF OPTIMUM DISTRIBUTION

The ambiguity of the concept of optimum distribution of income means that there is no abstract ideal to which an approach is to be made.

---

[2] It will not necessarily be increased, however, for an increase in output may hurt some people (e.g., the smoke nuisance of a new industrial plant) while it helps others. Since interpersonal comparisons of utility cannot be made, it is not always certain that the net effect on welfare is positive.

Our conception of the optimum distribution depends on circumstances obtaining at a given moment. For example, historically the nations of the world have for long periods of time stood in urgent need of rapid capital formation. This has been the situation during periods of war and military preparedness. It may also be the case for decades on end when a nation is attempting to convert from an agricultural to an industrial society. In these circumstances it is ordinarily conceded by all elements of the population that the proportion of national income saved should be maximized. This implies an unequal distribution of income, with a large proportion of total national income going to those whose incomes are high enough to permit saving.[3] On the other hand, once the urgency has passed, the situation changes. It may then be generally agreed that a rise in consumption is in order. Therefore, the distribution of income must be altered in the downward direction and quite another concept of the optimum distribution comes to be accepted.

ILLUSTRATIONS

The practical significance of changes in what constitutes an optimum income distribution may be illustrated by reference to recent experience in a few countries. In Great Britain, under the postwar Labour government, the desire for a more equal distribution of income led to the sponsorship of an economic legislative program that tended to encourage mass consumption at the expense of national savings. In Germany, on the other hand, the balance of political power kept in office a government which favored a rapid rate of saving in preference to a rise in consumption standards.[4] The same has been largely true in France and Italy, although the minority has been far more outspoken in those countries. For a time, until the eclipse of Malenkov, there appeared to be some disposition even in Russia to tip the scales slightly more in favor of consumption than had formerly been the case. However, the drive for investment and for de-emphasis of the production of consumers' goods has reasserted itself.

---

[3] It should be noted that it is not certain whether, or how far, a downward redistribution of income would result in a reduction in the proportion of national income that is saved. The *average* propensity to consume is, to be sure, higher for the lower-income receivers. A downward redistribution of income, however, is relevant to the *marginal* propensity to consume. It cannot be said in advance what proportion of additional income will be saved by the lower-income groups, nor do we know beforehand how the higher-income receivers will react to a reduction of income after taxes. See the article by H. Lubell, "Effects of Redistribution of Income on Consumers' Expenditures," *American Economic Review,* March, 1947; and Carl Shoup, "Taxation and Fiscal Policy" in Max Millikan, ed., *Income Stabilization for a Developing Democracy* (New Haven, Conn.: Yale University Press, 1953), pp. 269 ff.

[4] It is interesting to note that the German government in early 1954 recognized the desirability of a rise in consumption standards. At the same time, however, high-income receivers participated generously in the tax reduction of March, 1954. The government gave the appearance of being torn between two concepts of the optimum.

CONCLUSION

For practical purposes what society believes to be the optimum income distribution has to be inferred from the decisions taken by governments with respect to fiscal and other means of affecting distribution. This does not mean, however, that we have merely to stand by and watch events. Redistribution policies can be alternatively more or less intelligent. One of the ways to make them more so is to be certain that we have all possible knowledge of the true distribution of income prior to government fiscal interference. This is important both from the point of view of equity and from that of the maximization of national output.

Nothing can be known of the desirability, in terms of equity, of a proposed increase or decrease in public spending and taxing unless the public is in a position to have an opinion on the equity of the distribution of income *before* this step is taken. Again, unless we know the distribution of income that provides the most favorable basis for the maximization of real national income, any change in the level of public spending and taxing is as likely to discourage as to encourage production. For these reasons it is a mistake to argue in favor of either more or less equality of income distribution without first studying the distribution before the contemplated change.

► THE DEFINITION OF INCOME

Those who advocate a change in the distribution of income may be interested in either the equity aspects or the effects of such a change on the level of income and employment. In support of their proposals they necessarily make use of income distributions published by census takers or other investigators. Yet these distributions may be inaccurate, based on inadequate samples, and not inclusive of the entire income of the individual. It follows that a prerequisite to an intelligent fiscal policy for redistribution is a comprehension of what is involved in ascertaining the true distribution of income.

MONEY INCOME AND NONMONETARY INCOME

Comparisons of the distribution of income between two points of time, between two income groups, or between two geographical areas are ordinarily made in terms of money income. As a consequence, that portion of income which takes the form of directly consumable goods and services is excluded. This practice understates the economic well-being of those who receive a relatively large proportion of their incomes in nonmonetary form. Clearly nonmonetary income is as significant as income in the form of purchasing power when comparisons are to be made of equity between social groups.

It is less clear, however, that when we are concerned with the effect of the distribution of income on *economic stability* all nonmonetary forms of income ought to be taken into consideration. A change in aggregate money income can ordinarily be expected to cause an alteration in the volume of saving and investment. A change in nonmonetary income, however, in many instances exerts no direct effect on the rates of saving and investment, and therefore on the level of national income. For income in kind is often consumed directly.

When indirect effects are taken into account, on the other hand, it becomes apparent that no sharp line can be drawn between nonmonetary and monetary income from the point of view of effects on economic stability. The reason is that although some types of income in kind may have no effect on a man's propensity to consume, others may change the intensity of his desire for those goods and services which are obtainable only in exchange for dollars. Therefore, an effect is exerted on the proportion of his money income that he saves. For example, a housewife may increase her output of domestic services in the form of home beautification without causing a change in the level of spending of the household. On the other hand, an increase in the output of home-grown vegetables may (or may not) cause a reduction in the size of the family food budget. Although we are forced to the conclusion that nonmonetary income is not without an impact on personal spending, and therefore on the level of economic activity, the major significance of this form of income is to be found in its effect on the validity of comparisons of the distribution of income for purposes of comparing the relative welfare of two groups.

If a complete investigation is to be made of the relative welfare of two individuals, many types of income must be taken into account that may not be included in a census of income. Important examples are the services of housewives; work performed by the taxpayer himself, like painting the house; the imputed rent of an owned home; the flow of satisfactions deriving from the ownership of durable personal property; home-grown produce; leisure; and the psychological satisfaction accruing from pleasant working and living conditions. A very important item which is ignored in income estimates based on income tax returns is unrealized capital gains.

The fact that these types of income are not subject to the federal income tax makes it doubly important to take account of them. Comparisons made only in dollar terms fail to do this, and therefore must be interpreted with care. Errors due to failure to include all types of income appear throughout the entire income range. Exclusion of services performed by the consumer for himself (e.g., work done around the home) appears to be most important in the lower- and lower middle-income groups. Imputed income from the ownership of homes and durable consumers' goods increases with increasing income, though after a certain point probably at a decreasing rate. Unrealized capital gains accrue primarily to income receivers in the upper-middle and upper brackets.[5]

Perhaps one of the most significant gaps in any intertemporal comparison of income distribution by economic groups arises out of the fact that labor has taken, in the form of leisure, a large proportion of its share in the rising productivity of the economy during recent years. The average workweek outside agriculture declined from about fifty-five to forty-four hours in the thirty-year period ending in 1940. A comparison of labor income that was restricted to money income alone would overlook this highly important circumstance. The workweek of nonlabor groups has also declined, of course, but their hours were not as long.

The growth of leisure, it may be remarked in passing, provides an instance of the indirect effect on output of a shift in the distribution of income. The marked decline in the length of both the working day and the working week has provided the lower and lower-middle income groups with the leisure to consume goods other than necessities. In particular, many of the service industries owe much of their rapid development to the growing proportion of the worker's time that he is able to devote to leisure.

CONCLUSION

The above considerations lead us to conclude that (1) when we are considering the economic effects of a given distribution of income we are interested primarily in the distribution in terms of money, but (2) the fact that much income is not measurable in dollars makes it dangerous to draw very rigid conclusions from dollar comparisons of income distribution alone. Yet the impracticability of translating nondollar income into dollar income has forced investigators for the most part to make the easier but less meaningful comparison. This should be constantly borne in mind in the subsequent discussion of comparisons of distributions of income.

INCOME COMPARISONS IN TERMS OF DOLLARS

In addition to the fact that dollar comparisons of income distribution overlook a substantial part of real income, comparisons of distribution suffer from two further potential defects. The first is the difficulty of obtaining adequate data on the income, consumption, and saving of family units. The second is the problem of achieving an unambiguous measure of the concentration or inequality of income. Since there are a number of ways of measuring income inequality, each of which conveys a different impression, it is clear that serious obstacles may stand in the way of obtaining general agreement on the choice of a measure of the concentration of income.

---

[5] Moreover, it will be remembered that the higher-income groups, especially those who are in a position to take deductions for business expenses and to convert ordinary income into capital gains, enjoy the opportunity to minimize their money income for income tax purposes.

Everyone will wish to use the measure which gives the greatest support to his own view on the current distribution and the need for changing it.

Sources of Information.   Information on incomes in the United States comes from a number of different sources. One of these is *Statistics of Income,* published annually by the Treasury on the basis of income tax declarations. Another source is the decennial census, which depends for its accuracy on its completeness of coverage and on the faithfulness with which individuals report financial data to the census taker. Still another is the sampling study, carried out by experts in a limited number of localities, but with a much greater thoroughness and statistical sophistication than is possible in a general census of the entire population. Each method has advantages and weaknesses of its own. Consequently, interpretations differ, and the occasion arises for confusion. Moreover, if the results of a study are used by subsequent researchers for purposes that were not in the minds of those who made it, unwarranted inferences must be guarded against.

Major Difficulties.   Some of the major difficulties may be briefly mentioned.[6] The use of unduly small samples produces unreliable results; the incomes of individuals or families of a particular sample may differ greatly from those of the universe out of which the sample is selected. Again, a technical problem is involved in the choice of what constitutes a "family" for purposes of the sample. What should be the degree of relationship to justify the inclusion of an individual in a family? Should all related persons living in a single family dwelling be included? Or should family members who do not pool their income for major purposes of spending be regarded as separate individuals?

Still another difficulty is the fact that underreporting of income is far more likely than overreporting. Many persons fear that what they tell the census taker may become known to the Internal Revenue Service. Again, inferences with respect to the number of families falling within the lowest-income brackets convey a false impression if the fact is ignored that any particular family may be subject to a low income in a single year only. For example, it has been stated that "nearly 10 million of the families received total cash incomes of less than $2000 a year in 1948, or one-fourth the number of families."[7] Many families have low incomes only temporarily, owing to sickness or unemployment. Some individuals have low incomes because they are retired or are getting their education. Consequently, they should not be included in any income distribution that is used to demon-

---

[6] For a more complete discussion, see Selma Goldsmith, "Statistical Information on the Distribution of Income by Size in the United States," *Papers and Proceedings* of the American Economic Association, May, 1950.

[7] Statement made by the Staff of the Subcommittee on Low-Income Families of the Joint Committee on the Economic Report, *Low-Income Families and Economic Stability,* 81st Cong., 1st Sess., 1949, p. 2. This statement is often quoted without qualification, or any hint that *cash* income is often only a part of total family income.

strate that large numbers of people fall within income groups that are at or below subsistence.

THE DISTRIBUTION OF NONMONETARY INCOME

As we have seen, measures of the inequality of income necessarily concern themselves solely with income in terms of dollars. Therefore even if it were possible to evolve "the one best measure," it must be remembered that nonmonetary income would be excluded. Because of the importance of this difficulty it is desirable to consider the probable effect on the distribution of nonmonetary income of certain factors that have been operating in recent years.

Leisure. It has been remarked above that an important nonmonetary component of income that has rapidly grown in importance in recent decades is leisure. The shortening of the workweek has probably been somewhat to the advantage of the lower-income industrial worker, and therefore represents some downward redistribution of income.

The Distribution of Increments of Productivity. Another type of real income that is not reflected in dollar-income figures is the increase in the purchasing power of the dollar with respect to commodities that are sold at a lower price than before because of technological progress. Can it be said that any particular income groups have benefited more than others on this score? The evidence is not very clear, but certain types and qualities of goods are bought to a greater extent by some income groups than by others. Thus, mass production implies a mass market and a low price per unit. Moreover, the practice of charging high prices to cover the cost of developing a new product means that those who are subsequently enabled to buy a mass-produced commodity at a much lower price have been able to shift part of the development cost to the higher-income groups that are the first to buy the new product.

Neither of these cases, however, can be subjected to a quantitative analysis. With respect to the first, it would appear that it is not the *lowest*-income groups, but rather the lower middle-income groups, who are the ones that have benefited most from mass production. Workers who are not much above subsistence find themselves unable to buy mass-produced durable consumers' goods in appreciable amounts. The groups just above the lowest, however, are enabled to buy a variety of such goods that would have been otherwise unobtainable by them.

The upper-income groups would presumably benefit less from mass production, but there are two important qualifications to this statement. First, mass production is not necessarily synonymous with inferiority, and high-income receivers buy many mass-produced goods. Second, the cost of production of many commodities that are not mass-produced is lowered because of the mass production of parts and of the tools and machines used to produce them. One might be justified in concluding that on balance the lower middle- and middle-income groups have benefited most from mass production. However, one final and important qualification remains to be made. These groups account for the bulk of home ownership, and it is in home construction that the benefits of mass production and standardization have been felt the least.[8]

Price Discrimination.   Another way in which lower-income receivers have benefited, and which does not appear in statistics of income, is the practice of "price lining." A commodity, say automobile tires, comes in a number of grades differing in price. The difference in the value of two grades is not accurately reflected, however, by the difference in the price charged. A tire that costs twice as much as another of lower quality produced by the same firm is not likely to be twice as good. In other words, the practice of discriminating monopoly permits the lower-income consumer in this case to benefit at the expense of the higher-income receiver. Another widely used device occurs when a professional man or a hospital charges fees according to the income of the client or patient. This conscious but informal downward redistribution of income is not reflected in the statistics of income. It should be noted in passing that as the movement toward universal social security progresses, the scope and need for this type of downward redistribution decrease. Indeed, ambulance, X-ray, and other charges may actually be *raised* for low-income patients who are insured.

▶ A MEASURE OF INCOME INEQUALITY: THE LORENZ CURVE

A number of measures have been developed for exposing the inequality (or concentration) of income. Since the measure most frequently used in studies of the effects of taxation and public spending on the distribution of income is the Lorenz curve, discussion here will be limited to that measure.

For most purposes the arithmetic scale is preferable for showing income distribution. This is because equal weight is given to all levels of income. The Lorenz curve, which has had wide use as a device for the visual presentation of inequalities in the distribution of income, is drawn with cumulated percentages of total income plotted arithmetically against cumulated percentages of income receivers (or alternatively, consumer units).[9] It is apparent from Figure 17 that the line of complete equality

[8] Cf. M. L. Colean and R. Newcombe, *Stabilizing Construction: The Record and Potential* (New York: McGraw, 1952), pp. 60 ff.

[9] M. C. Lorenz, "Methods of Measuring the Concentration of Wealth," *Publications* of the Amercan Statistical Association, 1905, pp. 209–219. For recent work along these lines see R. Schutz, "On the Measurement of Income Inequality," *American Economic Review,* March, 1951, and G. Rosenbluth, "The Measure of Income Inequality," *American Economic Review,* December, 1951, and the literature there cited. See also G. L. Stigler, *The Theory of Price* (New York: Macmillan, 1952), Chap. XV, for a discussion of the relative advantages of different measures of concentration.

of income is *OAF*, since at any point on this line the cumulated percentage of income receivers is equal to the cumulated percentage of total income. For example, 10 per cent of the income receivers account for 10 per cent of total income, and 50 per cent receive 50 per cent of the total. Evidently, incomes are unequally distributed if the lower 50 per cent of income receivers receive less than 50 per cent of total income. This is illustrated by the lines *OBF, OCF, ODF,* and *OGF.* The more concave this line, the greater the concentration of income.

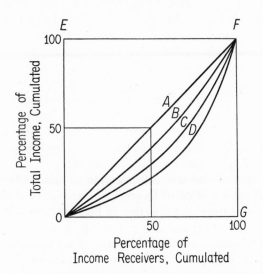

Fig. 17
THE LORENZ CURVE

The advantages of the Lorenz curve for some comparisons become disadvantages for others. No one measure is equally serviceable for all purposes. By making use of percentages the Lorenz curve conceals the number of income units in the different income brackets. Moreover, for some purposes a logarithmic scale has advantages over one that assigns equal importance to equal arithmetic differences in income. By reversing the scale, either upper- or lower-income brackets can be emphasized. One reason for the popularity of the Lorenz curve, as a device for measuring the effects of changes in the levels of taxing and government spending on the distribution of income, is that major changes in these levels require the passage of a comprehensive revenue or appropriations bill that is likely to affect all income groups. Consequently, a measure of inequality must be used that permits inferences with respect to all income brackets.

THE GINI MEASURE OF CONCAVITY

Through the use of a measure of concavity it is possible to avoid reliance solely on visual comparisons of Lorenz curves in order to draw inferences with respect to income distributions. Such a measure was devised by Gini. He divided the area *OBFA,* for example, by the maximum possible inequality *OGFA* (which means that the entire national income is received by one individual), to obtain a ratio that is greater the more concave the Lorenz curve. A measure of this kind is, however, an over-all average. It can therefore tell nothing about the extent to which inequality of distribution may be more marked in various segments of the income distribution.

For example, it may be that in some hypothetical country income is very equally distributed among the lower 90 per cent of income receivers, but that there are a few very high incomes. At the same time, assume that *all* incomes are well above subsistence. In this case the inequality might not give rise to any substantial pressure for redistribution of income. The fact that few persons are at or below subsistence might conceivably tend to weaken union aggressiveness, and it would probably make it difficult for a political party to make the distribution of income an issue. The situation might be rather different, however, if many individuals were receiving very low incomes and a sufficient number of upper middle-bracket individuals moved into the higher brackets so that the value of the Gini measure remained unchanged. The value of the measure would be concealing inequalities which society might not wish to permit.

Clearly, a measure is needed that will call attention to these various possible configurations in the distribution of income. The ambiguity of the Gini measure becomes apparent from an inspection of Figure 18, in which two very different income distributions are seen to yield the same measure of concentration. Curve *B* is more concave than curve *A* up to a point, and thereafter is less concave than curve *A*. Yet the Gini measure is the same in both cases. Evidently, for comparisons of income distributions that are to take account of differing relationships among the various income brackets, a table or a chart must be used.[10] No summary measure can take account of all changes in the data.

SUBJECTIVE ASPECTS

It will be noted that one cannot expect to tell by inspection of the curves just how unequal the distribution of income is. It is not possible to say whether a given concavity of the Lorenz curve implies greater or less equality in the distribution of income *than we are prepared to accept.* There is nothing to refer it to except the line of equality, *OAF,* the line of perfect inequality, *OGF,* or perhaps some other norm. In no country, however, is the distribution of income sufficiently close either to equality or to perfect inequality to make these standards of references appropriate. Subjective considerations are as likely to dominate in the interpretation of the Lorenz curve as they do in that of other measures of concentration. A given degree of concavity will appear to represent an intolerable inequality in the distribution of income to one observer and excessive equality to another.

---

[10] Cf. Rosenbluth, "The Measure of Income Inequality," *loc. cit.,* p. 935.

SUMMARY

We may summarize our conclusions thus far as follows. In order to justify government interference in the distribution of income it is desirable, even if not necessary, to know what the distribution of income is in the first place; and we must be able to measure the changes that are made in

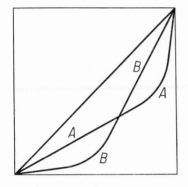

Fig. 18
AMBIGUITY OF THE GINI MEASURE

this distribution through fiscal policy or other devices at the disposal of the government. It is true that even if we cannot measure the distribution of income, general dissatisfaction with the existing degree of inequality or equality would justify attempts to change it. This dissatisfaction might be either greater or less if the concentration of income could be objectively measured. For example, on occasion zealous public agencies have tended to give the impression that larger numbers of workers receive incomes at or below subsistence than is the case. On the other hand, many people might feel a strong sense of irritation if they were aware of the extent to which upper-income groups receive incomes which (like unrealized capital gains and expense-account income) do not appear in the routine estimates of income distribution.

It must be confessed, however, that we probably would not reach a close agreement on income distribution policy even if we should succeed in establishing the true distribution of income. A change in the degree of inequality necessarily makes some people worse off and favors others. Consequently, there must always be two points of view with respect to whether a proposed change is too great or too little. Accuracy of measurement will not remove the conflict. In other words, no matter how precise the measure of income distribution might be, the ultimate comparison must be made on the basis of subjective considerations.

▶ FISCAL POLICY AND THE DISTRIBUTION OF INCOME

The fiscal system affects the distribution of income in two ways. First, taxes directly and indirectly reduce the disposable income of individuals. The direct effect is the reduction in the disposable income of the taxpayer, while indirect effects on the incomes of others are produced as a result of the reaction of the taxpayer to the tax. Second, government spending directly and indirectly affects the flow of benefits to individuals.

The problem is to evaluate these two types of effect. Obviously, this cannot be done for each individual. Rather, the effects must be ascertained for broad groups. For different purposes one or another basis of classification may be employed. The classical economists, for example, were interested in a classification according to land, labor, and capital. On the other hand, a particular state or other geographic region is interested in the interregional distribution of income. Again, the focus of interest may be on the effect of the fiscal system on the proportion of real income going to the individuals in the various income brackets. It may be felt that a gain in equity would result from a redistribution among the income brackets; or interest may stem from the conviction that a different distribution would bring about an improvement in the relation between aggregate consumption and aggregate saving and investment.

Government borrowing does not directly affect the distribution of income. Indirectly it may do so, however, by way of its relative effects on the level (and, therefore, the distribution) of national income, as well as by its effects on the distribution of income payments. The purchase of a government bond indeed represents a surrender of purchasing power by the individual. But since the bondholder now has a claim to repayment, he has merely changed the form in which he holds his savings. Similarly, at a later date when the security is redeemed, there is no effect on his income. As before, he is merely exchanging one asset for another.[11]

THE ALLOCATION OF TAX BURDENS

The allocation of tax burdens by income groups is, conceptually at least, a simple procedure. The first step is to obtain a distribution of income by income brackets. This is necessary in order that an effective tax rate can be calculated for each bracket. For example, suppose that in a given year 2 per cent of total income, or (say) $2 billion, was received by spending units (e.g., families) in the under-$1,000-a-year income bracket, and that they paid a total of $500 million in federal, state, and local taxes. Then the effective tax rate on this group would be 25 per cent. A similar effective rate would be calculated for each income bracket. It is clear that it is of great importance to make sure that the whole of the income accruing to spending units in each income bracket is actually imputed to it. The omission of income not received in the form of money, for example, would mean that the denominator of the above fraction would be relatively low when a large proportion of income is in a form other than money.

---

[11] The distribution effects of interest payments on the government debt are discussed below.

This in turn would make the ratio of taxes to income for that bracket appear too high.

The next step is to distribute the proceeds of all taxes, federal, state, and local, among the income brackets. This involves the making of assumptions on the incidence of each tax. In order to ascertain the effective rate the total taxes paid by those in each bracket are then divided by their total income received. In terms of effective rates, the tax system as a whole is progressive if this rate is higher for larger incomes, and regressive if it is lower. If data are available for a number of spending-unit income brackets, it is possible to show that the tax system may be regressive with respect to certain income ranges, and progressive and proportional in others.

For example, over a given range of income, progressive and regressive features of different taxes may roughly neutralize one another, so that the effective rate of tax would remain about the same for incomes between, say, $4,000 and $8,000. Thereafter the rate might be found to rise significantly. But any rise in the effective tax rate will be retarded (or even reversed) to the extent that higher individual incomes comprise a larger proportion of unrealized capital gains than do smaller incomes.

The method of allocating tax burdens by income brackets may be illustrated with reference to the tobacco tax. It is generally agreed that the bulk of this tax is paid by the consumer. If this view is accepted, the aggregate proceeds of federal, state, and local tobacco taxes are then distributed over the income brackets in accordance with tobacco consumption in each bracket. This operation depends on the existence of reliable statistical studies. Unfortunately, more dependable information is available on total spending than on spending for particular commodities. It may be assumed, however, that a continuing interest in this problem will ultimately result in the collection of data that are more nearly tailored to the purpose in hand.[12]

The problems involved in allocating tax payments by income brackets naturally differ for different types of tax. Differences of opinion on the procedure to follow, especially in the cases of the corporate income tax,

---

[12] On the basis of Bureau of Labor Statistics data, Musgrave allocated consumer expenditures on tobacco for 1948 as follows:

DISTRIBUTION FOR TAX ALLOCATION
(In percentages)

Spending-Unit Income Bracket
(In thousands of dollars)

	Under 1	1–2	2–3	3–4	4–5	5–7.5	7.5 and Over	Total
Consumer expenditures on tobacco:	3.9	11.4	21.1	22.9	14.3	14.1	12.2	100.0

R. A. Musgrave, et al., "Distribution of Tax Payments by Income Groups: A Case Study for 1948," National Tax Journal, March, 1951, p. 11.

property taxes, and social security payroll taxes, have led to controversy and subsequent compromise in the recent literature on this question. Changes in tax rates and in economic institutions and practices affect the reactions of taxpayers, and therefore the extent to which taxes are shifted. For this reason studies of the effects of taxes on the distribution of income must be made periodically. A brief indication of the nature of such studies will be given in a later section of this chapter.

THE ALLOCATION OF GOVERNMENT BENEFITS

The task of allocating government benefits by income brackets is a more difficult one. The government is in the business of providing benefits to the public as a whole. These benefits do not ordinarily accrue to particular individuals. A considerable proportion is not even allocable, except arbitrarily. The cost of military protection, for example, cannot be distributed over the income brackets on any logical basis. A number of alternative methods exist, each giving very different results, and each having an equal claim to recognition. Selection among them must be arbitrary. Should allocation be on a per capita basis, in which case each individual is regarded as receiving the same benefit as any other? Or should it be according to wealth, which would imply that the wealthy individual is receiving a greater benefit from protection than a poor man? Another possibility is to allocate certain types of benefits according to income. In this case a part of government spending would therefore be regarded as having no effect on the distribution of income. These alternatives will be considered further below.

It might seem that a way out of this difficulty would be to allocate the benefits provided by government on the basis of its money payments to the various income brackets. The aggregate of federal, state, and local spending is distributed in the form of payments to workers and contractors, subsidies, interest on the debt, and other transfers. There is no doubt who receives such payments. But this will not do. Government benefits do not consist of money payments of this kind, but rather of the services which the government makes available to its citizens. Moreover, the value of such services to the recipient may exceed their money cost. The following example will illustrate the distinction.

One form of government service is police protection. In large measure this protection accrues to property owners. To the extent that this is so, the benefit may be allocated among the income brackets according to their ownership of property. At the same time, however, money payments are made by the locality to policemen. To allocate the benefits according to money payments, then, would be to suppose that the benefits of police protection accrue solely to policemen. Consequently it is not the money-flow concept, but the benefit concept, which is relevant to the problem.

In certain instances, however, money payments by the government to individuals confer a benefit upon them which they would not otherwise receive. An example is relief payments to the unemployed. The money that is paid to them constitutes a net addition to their income, and thus such payments reduce the inequality of income. Here the money-flow and the benefit concepts can be used interchangeably.[13] The situation is different when the unemployed are put to work on public works projects. In this case there are two elements of income to allocate, namely, the wages paid to the previously unemployed, and the flow of benefits accruing to the public from the public works projects. The latter will be zero or negative only if government investment replaces private investment or if government investment actually encroaches on private enterprise.

INTEREST PAYMENTS ON GOVERNMENT DEBT

Interest payments on government securities are distributed in accordance with the holdings of the debt by income brackets. Therefore the distribution of a large federal debt has significant effects on the distribution of income. Formerly almost the whole of the debt was held by individuals in the above-$7,500 class. As a result of rising per capita real incomes, coupled with a scarcity of consumers' goods during the war, the debt is now rather more widely held.[14] It is often argued that the federal government should make every effort to lodge a considerable part of the debt with savers in the lower-income brackets. This would not result in a more equal distribution of interest payments, however, unless there were a net increase in savings by these groups. Such may be the case, of course, if the availability of a safe form of investment encourages them to decrease consumption.

A large part of the debt is held by institutional savers.[15] It is necessary, therefore, to undertake the task of imputing interest payments on this part of the debt to the individuals for whom the securities are held in trust. In the majority of instances this is not difficult. For example, interest paid on the bondholdings of insurance companies is allocable in accord-

---

[13] See John H. Adler, "The Fiscal System, the Distribution of Income, and Public Welfare," in K. E. Poole, ed., *Fiscal Policies and the American Economy* (New York: Prentice-Hall, 1951), pp. 360 ff.

[14] See Jacob Cohen, "Distributional Effects of the Federal Debt," *Journal of Finance,* September, 1951, pp. 267–275.

[15] Of total gross debt of $277 billion of federal securities outstanding at the end of April, 1955, the distribution was as follows:

U. S. government agencies	17.6%
Federal reserve banks	8.5
Commercial banks	23.8
Mutual savings banks	3.2
Insurance companies	5.5
Other corporations	7.4
State and local governments	5.7
Individuals	23.2
Miscellaneous	5.1

SOURCE: *Treasury Bulletins.*

ance with the total value of the policies held by the insured persons in each income bracket. Similarly, interest paid on securities issued to the Railroad Retirement Fund is attributable to the income brackets appropriate to retired railroad workers.

In some instances, however, there are conceptual difficulties. For example, the interest paid on federal securities owned by state and local governments is a form of revenue to the latter. How is it to be allocated to state and local taxpayers? Since it is not known which tax rates can be kept lower because of this income, it cannot be said which income groups benefit from the interest receipts. Similar difficulties face the allocation of interest paid to *corporate* holders of bonds. The stockholder effectively receives that portion of interest that is kept in the form of retained profits only if the price of his stock reflects the retention.

SURPLUSES AND DEFICITS

The *direct* impact of budgetary surpluses and deficits on the distribution of income is subsumable under the tax and spending effects. A deficit means that the public is receiving a volume of benefits from the government that exceeds the burdens it bears in the form of taxes. These benefits are distributed by income brackets. The total effects consist of the direct benefits together with indirect benefits accruing to individuals whose real incomes have increased as a result of the net cash contribution by the government to the income stream. It is important to note that at full employment these net effects depend on payments to factors by the government that differ from the payments that would have been made to them had purchasers of government securities lent to business firms instead of to the government. If the deficit is incurred under conditions of unemployment, on the other hand, payments are made to factors for the production of government services that would otherwise not have been produced. When national income rises because of a rise in employment, there is an increment of real income to be distributed according to income bracket. When *money* national income rises, the distribution of income by income bracket likewise changes. But in the latter case the effects are more difficult to trace, for we have to consider what the income of each factor would have been if employed in the private sector.

A budgetary surplus has effects that are opposite to those of a deficit. The burdens of taxes now exceed the benefits of public services. Moreover, if the effect of the surplus is to cause a fall in national income, a redistribution of income will occur in response to the development of unemployment of production factors. In order to take account of the effects on redistribution of a decline in national income, we must know the spots in the economy at which unemployment occurs, as well as the income brackets of the factors who become unemployed. Furthermore, there are indirect effects on the incomes of other factors as national income and spending fall.

► TAXATION AND THE DISTRIBUTION OF INCOME

If we are interested in the *total* effect of the fiscal system on the distribution of income, both taxing and spending effects must be considered. Under a balanced budget a change in either public spending or taxing must be accompanied by an equal change in the other. Deficits and surpluses are likely to be a relatively small proportion of total taxes or spending. Consequently, the greater part or the whole of the burden of taxes is offset by the benefits of public spending, and both must be considered if either is to be considered. On the other hand, interest may center in the *comparative* effects on the distribution of income of two or more different tax structures designed to yield the same revenue. In this case it is not necessary to distribute the *benefits* by income bracket.[16] The tax effects alone are important.

The first step in ascertaining the distribution of tax burdens by income group is to establish the incidence of each tax. The difficulties of doing this have been sufficiently emphasized in earlier chapters. Since it is impossible to follow through all the direct and indirect effects of taxation, the allocation "inevitably involves the use of grossly simplifying assumptions."[17] In some instances the allocation is fairly clear-cut, while in others room exists for considerable difference of opinion. Thus, most economists agree that the major part of sales and excise taxes is passed forward to the consumer. Therefore, it seems justified to allocate the proceeds of these taxes among the various income groups in accordance with their spending

---

[16] The two approaches are illustrated in the work of R. A. Musgrave and John Adler. Adler is interested in comparing the impact of the fiscal system on the distribution of income in two different years, 1938–1939 and 1946–1947.—Adler, "The Fiscal System . . . ," *loc. cit.* Musgrave, on the other hand, studies the *differential incidence* of the tax system for a particular year. Recognizing that "complete analysis of incidence must include both sides of the budget," he points out that we may be interested in the tax side alone. Taxes and expenditures are legislated in this country at different times and on the basis of different issues. The distributive effects of public spending are held to be secondary, while those of taxes are uppermost in the minds of tax legislators. Cf. Musgrave, "Distribution of Tax Payments . . . ," *loc. cit.,* pp. 7–8.

[17] Musgrave, *et al.,* "Distribution of Tax Payments . . . ," *loc. cit.,* pp. 2, 9, points (a)–(c). Musgrave takes account only of "items of loss associated directly with the sale (or purchase) of the taxed commodity or service." What this means in a particular instance is illustrated with the excise. Excise taxes are imputed to consumers according to consumption of commodities subject to the tax. But *income* effects are ignored. Thus, any effects on profits resulting from attempts to avoid the tax are excluded. If we are interested in the total effects on distribution of income this procedure is not legitimate. It is usual, however, to separate tax effects from the effects that are produced as the taxpayer adjusts to the imposition of the tax, and as those with whom he deals adjust to changes in his economic conduct, and so on.

on the articles subject to tax. On the other hand, the incidence of the corporate income tax is the subject of much disagreement. In his standard case, Musgrave allocated one third of this tax to consumers, one eighth to wage earners, and the remainder to profits. This allocation was arrived at on the basis of modifications in the "academic view" of the incidence of the corporate income tax, which is taken to be essentially correct.[18]

DIFFERENCES OF OPINION ON ALLOCATION

Obviously the assumptions that are chosen with respect to incidence will have a conclusive effect on the inferences ultimately drawn with respect to the impact of taxation on the distribution of income. On the one hand, the conclusion may be reached that the tax system is relatively progressive. This would weaken the case for the introduction of more progressive rates under the personal income tax and the estate and gift taxes. On the other hand, a conclusion that the tax system (federal, state, and local combined) bears heavily on the lower-income groups would make a strong case for the introduction of more progressive taxes. It is clear that the scientific investigator must bend over backward to avoid allowing his personal biases to intervene. The nature of the difficulty may be illustrated with respect to the corporate income tax, on which a particularly sharp difference of opinion exists.[19]

That part of the corporate income tax, if any, which is regarded as resting on the wage earner must be allocated among the income brackets in accordance with the share of total wage income received by wage earners in each income bracket. Since most wage earners are in the lower brackets, the greater the proportion of the tax that is regarded as shifted backward, the more regressive the tax will appear. Similarly, that part of the tax which is treated as shifted forward to the consumer is allocated to the various income brackets in accordance with their share of total spending

---

[18] *Ibid.*, pp. 15–16. The effects of substituting other shifting assumptions were tested. The assumptions were also made (1) that the entire tax is shifted forward to the consumer, and (2) that profits bear the whole burden of the tax. Complete backward shifting was considered too unlikely to merit consideration. By "academic view" Musgrave is referring to accepted incidence theory.

[19] The difficulties that face any attempt to reach definitive conclusions on the distribution of tax burdens have caused economists to restrict the area of their investigations to workable proportions. For example, in his study of the corporate income tax Richard Goode investigates the role of dividends in affecting the distribution of income and wealth. (See Richard Goode, *The Corporation Income Tax* [New York: Wiley, 1951], Chap. V, "The Corporation Income Tax and the Distribution of Income and Wealth.") In order to work from definite assumptions, he supposes that the tax rests solely on undistributed and distributed profits (p. 75). His justification for this procedure is the evidence previously adduced by him that in the short run this is actually the incidence of the corporate income tax. Quite apart, therefore, from considerations of long-run incidence, his approach throws light on the incidence of the tax immediately after a change in rates. This alone would be an important conclusion for tax policy, for a chain of economic effects is set in motion by virtue of the short-run incidence.

on consumers' goods. The greater the proportion of the tax that is believed to be shifted forward, the more regressive the tax appears to be, for consumers in general are likewise in the lower-income brackets. If none of the corporate income tax were shifted, however, the burden would rest on stockholders to the extent that dividends were smaller or that capital gains resulting from the retention of profits were smaller. Since stockholders are in higher-income brackets than are wage earners and consumers, the allocation of a relatively large proportion of the tax to stockholders would make the tax appear more progressive. Similar problems exist with respect to other taxes, but it is not necessary to discuss them all here.

ALLOCATION OF THE TOTAL TAX BURDEN

Although rather wide differences of opinion may exist among investigators on the distribution by income brackets of each separate tax, disagreement is substantially less when it comes to the tax system as a whole. The reason is, of course, that it will not be true that of two investigators, one will consistently ascribe the burden of each tax to a higher- (or lower-) income bracket than will the other. This is easily seen when note is taken of the number of federal, state, and local taxes to be allocated. The likelihood of at least a partial compensation of errors is graphically illustrated by the large number of separate allocations that have to be made under the property tax.[20] In Musgrave's study, fourteen separate types of property were considered, the proceeds of the property tax had to be broken down by type of property, and the yield from each type was allocated by income brackets on the basis of assumptions with respect to the incidence of each type.

Despite the fact that a considerable amount of neutralization occurs when the effects of all federal, state, and local taxes are aggregated, it remains true that different investigators are certain to arrive at different conclusions on the redistributive effect of the tax system. Because of the multiplicity of assumptions involved, space does not permit a detailed comparison here.[21] At any rate, it is generally agreed that a moderate progression in effective rates[22] occurs throughout the income brackets (for 1948) up to $7,500, and that thereafter progression becomes more rapid, even though unrealized capital gains are not taxed. This is on the assumption that a concept of income is adhered to which includes income in kind

---

[20] Cf. Musgrave, *et al.,* "The Distribution of Tax Payments . . . ," *loc. cit.,* Tables 5, 11, and 12.

[21] Musgrave's conclusions led to a controversy on methods of tax allocation. For a comparison of his views with those of Dr. Rufus Tucker see R. A. Musgrave, "Further Considerations of the Distribution of the Tax Burden: Rejoinder to Dr. Tucker," *National Tax Journal,* March, 1952, pp. 15–35.

[22] It will be remembered that the effective tax rate is the proportion of income taken in taxes.

as well as money income. If this is done, regression at the lower end of the income scale does not appear.

► GOVERNMENT BENEFITS AND THE DISTRIBUTION
OF INCOME

The problems faced in allocating government benefits by income bracket may be considered in the light of findings of the Adler study.[23] Government services are divided into three groups. The first includes benefits consisting mainly of monetary and nonmonetary payments to beneficiaries, including veterans' benefits, relief and general welfare, hospitals and health, social security, housing, benefits to agriculture, and interest payments on public debts. The procedure adopted here may be illustrated with respect to veterans' payments and services to agriculture in 1946–1947. It was assumed that veterans' payments were received equally by all consumer units with an income below $5,000 in that year. Thus $7.5 billion of veterans' payments was allocated in accordance with the number of consumer units in each income bracket up to $5,000 a year. Again, the benefits of services were assumed to be distributed according to the income distribution of farmers. These and similar assumptions are, of course, only attempts at approximating the true distribution. The investigator naturally decides upon the allocations that appear to him to be more nearly in accordance with the truth than any alternative allocations.

In the second group the author includes the public benefits which can be conceptually allocated on the benefit principle. For example, the cost of fire protection is allocated to the income groups in accordance with their real-property holdings. Educational expenditures are allocated on a per capita basis. The cost of road building is allocated to the various brackets according to the total income received by consumer units in each income bracket.

Finally, in the third group fall those indivisible government benefits which have to be allocated on some arbitrary basis. Examples are the general costs of government, national defense, the courts, and the like.[24] Three methods of allocation, each arbitrary, are (1) per capita, (2) proportionately to income or wealth, and (3) in accordance with the distribution of the total tax burden. The third alternative assumes that the benefit received by consumer units in each income bracket is measured by the taxes they pay. Therefore, for the "nonallocable" type of government

---

[23] Adler, "The Fiscal System . . .," *loc. cit.,* pp. 384 ff., and Appendix, Tables 44 and 45.

[24] As pointed out by U. K. Hicks, it may be less misleading to make no attempt to allocate indivisible public expenditures like the cost of maintaining an army or a system of courts. Cf. *Public Finance* (New York: Pitman, 1947), p. 297.

benefit, this third method of allocation would show no net downward redistribution of income as a result of fiscal operations.[25]

On the basis of the method described above it was found that in both 1938–1939 and 1946–1947 the distribution of benefits was markedly regressive.[26] Receipts of government services were a substantially larger proportion of lower than of higher incomes. Thus it is concluded that in each year both the tax system and the provision of public services contributed to reducing the inequality of income before taxes and spending. It is further pointed out that whereas legislators do keep the distribution of income more or less in mind in dealing with tax legislation, this is not so clearly the case with public spending. It is true that relief expenditures, public housing developments, and veterans' benefits are known to favor the lower-income brackets. Of these three types of spending, however, only the second can be regarded as a conscious downward redistribution. Most public spending is undertaken because it is felt that the private sector either will not provide the services in question or cannot do so as efficiently as the government can do it.

► CONCLUSION

There seems to be little doubt that the net effect of the allocable portion of public spending is to provide benefits which are a greater proportion of low than of high incomes. This is the result of a long-term development in the direction of increased governmental initiative in the provision of services which meet minimum acceptable social standards. Many services formerly purchasable only by the wealthy are now available entirely or partly free to all, or at least to the lowest-income groups. At the same time, not too much stress should be laid on moderate changes in the distribution of public benefits from one year to another. As with the allocation of tax burdens, many arbitrary decisions have to be made in the distribution of benefits by income groups. Changes in the relative importance of the *arbitrarily allocated portions* of benefits and taxes have the effect of changing the apparent distribution of income after taxes and public spending.

The effect of taxes, likewise, is to reduce moderately the inequality of income. Limited scope probably exists, however, for further use of progressive taxes. This means that further substantial extensions of govern-

---

[25] Adler allocates according to *income* in his standard case. Incidentally, as he points out, capital expenditures raise a problem for meaningful allocation. The benefits of a national highway, for example, are spread out over a number of years. This results in an overestimate in the year these expenditures are made, and an underestimate in later years, which is important if the rate of such expenditures is increasing rapidly. This will be the case in a growing economy.

[26] That is, *favored* the lower-income groups.—Adler, "The Fiscal System . . .," *loc. cit.*, pp. 390, 393.

ment benefits which accrue primarily to the lower-income groups may have to be financed largely by taxes borne by these same groups. The significance of this conclusion will be illustrated below, in the discussion of the economics of social security.

► REFERENCES

ADLER, J. H. "The Fiscal System, the Distribution of Income, and Public Welfare," in K. E. Poole, ed., *Fiscal Policies and the American Economy*. New York: Prentice-Hall, Inc., 1951.

AMERICAN ECONOMIC ASSOCIATION. "Capitalism and Equality of Income," *Papers and Proceedings,* May, 1950, pp. 321–370.

BOWMAN, M. J. "A Graphical Analysis of Personal Income Distribution in the United States," *American Economic Review,* September, 1945. Reprinted in American Economic Association, *Readings in the Theory of Income Distribution*. Philadelphia: The Blakiston Company, 1948.

COLM, G., and H. TARASOV. "Who Pays the Taxes?" TNEC *Monograph No. 3*. Washington, D. C.: U. S. Government Printing Office, 1941.

GOLDSMITH, S., *et al.* "Size Distribution of Income since the Mid-Thirties," *Review of Economics and Statistics,* February, 1954.

JOINT COMMITTEE ON THE ECONOMIC REPORT. *Selected Government Programs Which Aid the Unemployed and Low-Income Families*. Washington, D. C.: U. S. Government Printing Office, 1949.

"The Modern Income Tax," *Fortune* Magazine, December, 1948.

MUSGRAVE, R. A., *et al.* "Distribution of Tax Burdens by Income Groups," *National Tax Journal,* March, 1951, pp. 1–53. See also Reply by R. Tucker, *National Tax Journal,* September, 1951, and Rebuttal by R. A. Musgrave, *National Tax Journal,* March, 1952.

PEACOCK, A. T., ed. *Income Redistribution and Social Policy*. London: Jonathan Cape, Ltd., 1954.

TARASOV, H. "Who Does Pay the Taxes?" *Social Research,* Supplement IV, 1942.

WEAVER, F. "Taxation and Redistribution in the United Kingdom," *Review of Economics and Statistics,* August, 1950, pp. 201–213.

24 The Economics of Social Security

The security of its people is the primary objective of any government that recognizes the rights of man above those of the state itself. But concepts of security change with the times. Security may be limited to military and police protection. On the other hand, it may be extended to cover every conceivable risk faced by man. "Cradle-to-grave" security of the latter sort would obviously require a highly productive economy. Moreover, it presupposes that other, competing claims on annual national output do not too greatly reduce the residue of income available for social security. These competing claims have in the past been urgent, and they promise to be more so in the future. Preparation for military defense, demands for subsidies by powerful interests, and the competitive demands of capital and labor for shares in the annual increments to productivity, all conspire to make it difficult to foresee the extent of social security a generation or two hence.

There are three ways in which the needs of the individual for financial security throughout life can be met. These are private insurance, social insurance, and subsidies or public assistance. Private insurance is obviously available only to the extent that the individual is able to save, or to the extent that his employer is willing to do so for him. The failure of earlier European attempts to induce the worker to join private insurance schemes to provide for his social security was due to the lack of a sufficient margin of savings, though in part also to the time required to educate the public to accept the insurance concept. Consequently, if social security is to be available to all workers, the distribution of income must be fairly equal, or at any rate the average income receiver must have a real income substantially above the current definition of "subsistence."

Although the distribution of income after taxes and government spending is now far less unequal than formerly in this country, it is not so nearly equal that the average wage earner can hope to provide for any large proportion of his security needs through his own saving. Indeed, it is doubtful if complete equality of income in even a highly productive economy would provide an annual volume of personal savings adequate to finance all the desirable types of social security. The reason is that a rise in the disposable income of individuals provides an incentive, though possibly a delayed one, to raise consumption standards. As the public becomes accustomed to a higher level of consumption, a higher real income seems necessary to meet standards of "subsistence." The individual is usually willing to sacrifice a measure of security for a corresponding amount of current consumption. Clearly, therefore, no immediate prospect exists of financing the entire security needs of the individual out of his voluntary savings.

THE INSURANCE PRINCIPLE

Strictly speaking, social insurance financed by the insured persons implies a contributory system in which no subsidies are made out of general tax funds. Benefits depend on premiums paid in (the "benefit" principle). The role of the government is limited to (1) compelling the working individual to curtail consumption in order that he may receive an adequate income when he is for any reason incapacitated, and (2) providing the necessary administrative facilities.[1] Public assistance, on the other hand, is a direct subsidy to the needy from the public treasury. It differs from social insurance in that no pretense is made that funds need to be accumulated out of which benefits are to be paid. Since he has paid nothing, the individual has no inalienable right to public assistance. To be eligible he must pass a "need" test. The amount an individual receives depends on the funds voted by the legislature. Since the grants are usually inadequate, the view has become general that public assistance should only be invoked to fill the chinks in the social insurance system. Moreover, the amount a particular individual receives under public assistance is left to the discretion of officials, who are expected to apply a means test.

Social security systems usually start out with the insurance or "benefit" principle, but a tendency exists for them to develop into a mixture of compulsory self-insurance and subsidies out of the general tax funds.[2]

---

[1] In addition, contributions by *employers* are exacted if it is believed that on political or equitable grounds other elements in the economy should share in the cost of financing the social security of the worker.

[2] For a strong argument in favor of the benefit principle of financing social security, see W. Glenn Campbell, "The Economics of Social Security and the Theory of Government Finance," *National Tax Journal,* June, 1951, pp. 167–179.

In the United States the principle of government contributions was recognized in 1939, but it was repealed in the amendments of 1950. In the amendments of 1954, Congress retained the benefit principle in determining benefits and payroll tax rate schedules. (See W. J. Cohen, R. M. Ball and R. J. Myers, "The Social Security Amendments of 1954," *Social Security Bulletin,* September, 1954.) Whether or not an element of downward redistribution enters the old-age insurance scheme in future years will depend on the nature of the political balance in Congress, and on the scope for downward redistribution through taxes in the light of the ratio of total government spending to national income.

Although at first social security benefits may be regarded as merely supplementary to other savings of the individual, sentiment tends to develop for reducing the area of his responsibility. Moreover, conceptions of minimum standards of living tend to be revised upward. But the rise in benefits necessary to accomplish these objectives is greater than can be financed by contributions from the insured individual alone. This is so, at any rate, for present or foreseeable levels of real national product in any country, including the United States. Consequently, either redistribution of income downward through progressive taxes is necessary, or purchasing power must be transferred by way of taxes on consumers and active workers to those receiving social security benefits. Up to the present it is the latter that has been done in the United States, through a payroll tax levied on the employers and employees.[3]

SOCIAL SECURITY AND THE CONSUMER

It can be argued that the economic security of the worker throughout his entire life is a legitimate charge on those who consume his product. Rigidly interpreted, this would mean that the prices of all goods should be adjusted to reflect this added element of cost. If, then, the market for some articles declined or disappeared, this would only be consistent with a recognition of unwillingness on the part of the public to incur the full cost of these particular commodities. Factors of production would have to move out of these industries into those in which demand was sufficient to permit a price covering cost of production, including complete economic security for the worker.

In practice no attempt is made, of course, to make a precise charge for the cost of social security with respect to each commodity. An alternative procedure would be to levy sales taxes designed to transfer the required purchasing power from consumers at large to recipients of social security. In effect, consumers currently working and earning would have to restrict consumption in favor of the ill, the unemployed, and the retired. Still another alternative is to impose payroll taxes which are shifted to consumers, and thus are similar to sales taxes. It cannot be simply assumed, of course, that payroll taxes are shifted to consumers. To the extent that they are so shifted, consumers are contributing to the cost of social security in proportion to their purchases of the taxed commodities.

▶ THE INCIDENCE OF SOCIAL SECURITY TAXES

Old-age insurance in the United States is currently financed out of payroll taxes levied on both the employer and the employee, as well as on the self-employed. Unemployment insurance payroll taxes are now applied to the employer only (except in Alabama and New Jersey). The incidence

---

[3] The incidence of this tax is discussed below.

of these taxes is subject to the usual laws of shifting and incidence discussed in Chapter 7, but the special circumstances under which they are levied call for comment.

UNEMPLOYMENT INSURANCE

In the case of payroll taxes imposed on the employer under the unemployment insurance scheme, certain institutional factors play an important role in the determination of incidence. First is the circumstance that unless all employers come under the tax, those employers who are subject to it at full rates may be unable to shift it.[4] Thus the provision under the original act (designed to make for administrative simplicity) that excluded firms employing fewer than eight persons favored the very small firm. Again, when lower rates are granted in return for good employment records,[5] and when rates are lower in some states than in others, the limited application of the higher rates means that the benefiting firms can pass a relatively large amount of the tax forward to the consumers.

Similarly, firms subject to a higher payroll tax than their competitors are less able to pass the tax back to the employee. On the other hand, to the extent that unionization and a high level of national income permit labor to resist wage cuts, even the firms subject to the lower tax will find it difficult to pass the tax back to the worker. It is often pointed out that in an effort to reduce payrolls subject to tax, employers will use more machinery, and the lessened demand for labor will tend to facilitate backward shifting in the form of reduced wages. This assumes a degree of choice between hand and machine work, however, that may often exist to a greater extent in theory than in reality. Moreover, under conditions of high-level employment the dismissed labor will be quickly absorbed elsewhere, so that no pressure may be exerted on the remaining workers to accept lower wage rates.[6] Under the present state of knowledge with respect to the economic data involved, general statements cannot easily be made about the distribution of the incidence of unemployment insurance payroll taxes among the consumer, the employer, and the worker. The wide scope for variation in the institutional circumstances calls for a special study of each particular case.

OLD-AGE INSURANCE

Old-age insurance payroll taxes are uniform throughout the forty-eight states. Therefore, certain of the circumstances which obscure the incidence of unemployment insurance payroll taxes are not present. Old-age insurance legislation provides that payroll taxes be levied on both the

---

[4] However, if the price is set by the taxed firms, the effect would probably be a windfall to the firms not subject to the full payroll tax.

[5] "Experience rating" is discussed below.

[6] The substitution of capital for labor would involve an increase in employment in the capital goods industries.

employer and the employee, at equal rates, and on the self-employed at three fourths the combined employer-employee rate. The former pays a tax that is ultimately expected to rise to 4 per cent of his payroll, while an equal tax is deducted from the worker's pay envelope. The question arises whether the incidence of these legally distinct taxes actually differs.

The Employer's Payroll Tax. Under conditions of perfect competition the employer would not be able to bear any of the tax.[7] Average cost would rise above price, some firms would have to leave the industry, and the reduction in supply (leftward shift in the market supply curve) would result in a higher price of product. Similarly, demand for factors would fall, and unless their supply were completely elastic, some part of the tax would be shifted backward.[8]

In times of high-level total national spending, coupled with aggressive union bargaining, most or all of the tax will be shifted forward to the consumer. If demand conditions do not permit this, the firm will try to substitute capital for labor and improve efficiency in an effort to reduce cost. To the extent that workers simply move into industries producing equipment there is no net decline in the demand for labor. In this case a part of the tax can be covered through lower costs due to the use of more capital, and to the adoption of more efficient production processes.

Institutional considerations are of great importance in the determination of the incidence of the employer's payroll tax. In actual practice it does not appear likely that much of the tax will be shifted backward to labor. Trade unions will resist such a move on the part of the employers. Any direct attempt to bring this about will be met with the argument that the law provides that the employers pay that portion of the social security tax. It is true, however, that employers might struggle more strongly against wage rate rises because of the tax. A more likely result is a tacit agreement between employers and workers that the tax is a part of the cost of production, and thus should be borne by the consumer. Their intention is made effective through a reduction in supply. The incidence of the tax, therefore, is much like that of a system of excises.

The Employee's Payroll Tax. That part of old-age insurance payroll taxes that is levied on the employee looks very much like an income tax. The major difference is that personal exemptions and exemptions for dependents are lacking. In the United States, where most employed workers are significantly above the margin of income below which efficiency suffers, the lack of an exemption under the payroll tax does not result in a leftward

---

[7] We may neglect the effects of the spending of the proceeds of the tax if it is assumed that in the absence of payroll taxes the same revenues would be derived from some other source. If, however, we wish to know the absolute rather than the differential incidence, the effects on the firms' demand curves must be taken into account.

[8] For the response of firms subject to imperfectly competitive conditions to a rise in their cost curves, see Chapter 7.

shift of the supply curve. Thus, at first sight, price would not appear to rise, and the tax would not be shifted forward either to the employer or to the consumer. The effect is apparently that of an addition to withholding under the personal income tax.

Obviously there are limits, however, to the extent to which take-home pay can be reduced without producing a reaction on the part of labor. Purchasing power is being diverted from younger, able-bodied, and employed workers to the aged, the ill, and the unemployed. If the program is liberalized, resistance on the part of the employed worker seems certain. Under conditions of high-level demand, supported by private or public borrowing from the banks, labor would be in a position to try to force a rise in wage rates. The tax would then be pushed forward to the employer, who would try to shift as much as possible to the consumer. In other words, the elasticity of supply of labor is apt to rise to an extent depending on the level of employment, the level of income taxes already effective in the lower brackets, and the attitude of labor toward the desired rate of take-home pay. The latter, in turn, depends on the number and variety of deductions already being made from pay envelopes. Finally, as also in the case of the tax on employers, the tax is more likely to be shifted forward to the consumer if the proceeds are immediately put into the hands of the recipients of social security than if they are used to build up an idle cash-reserve fund.[9]

We conclude that the ultimate incidence of payroll taxes levied on the worker can only be allocated as among the consumer, the employer, and the worker (or other production factors) in the light of the particular circumstances existing at a particular time. Nevertheless, there seem to be grounds for believing that, assuming high-level employment and an elastic money supply, both forms of the payroll tax are likely to be borne largely by the consumer.

► SOCIAL SECURITY AND THE REDISTRIBUTION OF INCOME

Complete social security coverage includes old-age annuities, unemployment insurance, sickness and disability insurance, workman's compensation, and financial protection against those contingencies of life for which the average citizen finds it difficult to provide for adequately, for example, the special costs of birth, marriage, and death. It is possible to go still further and to include in social insurance the care of teeth, annual vacations, subsidy payments for children, and similar amenities.[10]

---

[9] It is not to be expected, of course, that a reserve fund would be held idle. Rather, it would be invested in government securities, and the proceeds paid into the income stream.

[10] Under the influence of the Beveridge plan, Britain's Labour government in 1946 provided for an extremely comprehensive conception of "minimum income," including even rights to false teeth, glasses, and wigs. Financial difficulties have

"Fringe" benefits of this nature tend to be in reality a means of downward redistribution of income and horizontal transfer payments rather than merely insurance. It is impossible at current levels of productivity, and with the present unequal distribution of income, for the individual dependent on wage income alone to insure himself adequately against every conceivable contingency. For example, prohibitive premiums would have to be paid to guarantee oneself a continuation of income in addition to medical and hospital expenses in the event of total disability.

In the United States social security has been expanded to take some account of the special circumstances of the aged and disabled dependents of deceased workers, orphans, and the blind. In view of the development of social security programs abroad, which serve as an example and an incentive, it seems reasonable to suppose that our own social security system will be gradually broadened to cover a greater number of personal contingencies. Therefore, so far as benefits are concerned, we may anticipate a further downward redistribution of income. On the other hand, the broader the coverage and scope of social security, the greater the proportion which must be paid by those who benefit. It seems probable that an expanded social security program will involve some redistribution downward from those in the lower middle-income brackets to the very low-income receivers. Relatively little opportunity exists for a further redistribution from the middle- and upper-income brackets.[11]

SOCIAL SECURITY BENEFITS AND THE INCOME TAX

The distribution effects of social security are complicated by the fact that if benefits are not subject to income tax they are worth more to a man with a high taxable income than they are to a poorer man. A dollar of old-age insurance benefit to a man with a large amount of interest and dividend income may be presumed to have a much lower marginal utility to him than a dollar to one who has no other income. Since the purpose of

---

enforced some retreat from the original program, but the Conservatives, in their campaign in the autumn of 1951, promised to retain the accepted philosophy of social security.

[11] The argument in the text states in effect that social security finance can make but little use of the ability-to-pay principle of taxation. On the other hand, in a wealthy economy real wages are high enough so that a considerable proportion of the cost of social security can be financed without a downward redistribution of income. It should be borne in mind that an important reason that the workers must pay for a large part of their social security benefits is the fact that tax rates are already extremely high in order to finance military expenditures. It is this fact which writers have in mind when they point out that even in Britain the beneficiaries of social security receive less in benefits than they pay in taxes. Cf. Findley Weaver, "Taxation and Redistribution in the United Kingdom," *Review of Economics and Statistics,* August, 1950, pp. 201–213, for the contention that a main feature of the development of redistributive programs after World War II in Britain has not been from higher- to lower-income groups. He finds, for example, that the increased cost of food subsidies, and health and education, has been covered by additional taxes on beer, tobacco, the purchase tax, and other indirect taxes.

social insurance is to provide against destitution as cheaply as possible, benefits should be subject to income tax. The granting of similar benefits to all, regardless of income, offers a device for avoiding a means test. By making the benefits taxable, however, account can be taken of the varying extent to which different individuals need such aid.

SOCIAL SECURITY AS A SHARE IN NATIONAL INCOME

Since the real income of the economy is not unlimited, the government must take account of the level and trend of national output in expanding the scope of its social security program. Per capita national product can be increased only gradually. The rate of technological advance is not subject to much change. Some scope does exist, it is true, for increases in productivity by way of greater personal efficiency. Social security itself contributes to the latter in a number of ways, but excessively generous social security benefits may have the opposite effect. Evidently considerable experience is necessary if an extensive social security system is to be conducted in a manner that will contribute to national efficiency rather than detract from it.

The future role of a social security system is strongly influenced by the extent to which competing claims to the national product are made effective. Social security benefits are only a single class among the numerous transfer payments included in governmental budgets. To the extent that they are financed out of taxes, they are an element in the complex of claims on the nation's taxable capacity. Therefore, beyond a certain point, the expansion of the coverage of social security would tend to meet with increasing pressure. Such pressure would not necessarily operate in a direct fashion, for public sentiment is likely to favor the policy of assuring a minimum living standard to all. It would take the form, rather, of price-level effects resulting from the attempt to allocate a greater real national income than is produced. In other words, if the competing claimants to the flow of real national output succeed in establishing a total of money claims that exceeds this flow at current prices, the latter must rise. A part of the apparent social security benefits therefore becomes fictitious, and a considerable lag is likely to intervene before Congress raises the benefits.

▶ DEVELOPMENT OF THE AMERICAN SOCIAL SECURITY SYSTEM

Comprehensive social security in the United States developed considerably later than it did in other advanced countries in the Western world.[12] On the other hand, once it was under way in the mid-thirties, its progress was rapid; moreover, owing to the high degree of productivity in

---

[12] In Europe, movements to abolish the profit system and to supplant the capitalist state with the socialist state hastened the adoption of social security measures designed to make the worker more contented with his lot. The failure of voluntary workers' insurance, even when assisted by high interest rates and subsidies, led to the

the American economy, it has the inherent capacity to develop further than in most other countries.

Important among the reasons for the relatively slow progress made in the United States toward social security before the great depression were the following factors.

1. Much of the energy of the economic liberals during the latter half of the nineteenth century was absorbed in the struggle for the progressive income tax, and for higher rates of pay, shorter hours, and better working conditions. The fear of socialism was particularly strong in this country, and until the decade of the nineteen thirties progress in relief to the worker was limited to the acceptance of the progressive income tax, shortening of the workweek, and higher wages. The improvement in working conditions was, indeed, primarily attributable to the high level of employment during World War I.

2. The American workingman shared with the businessman the belief that America was the land of equal opportunity for all, and that the best social security was the relative ease with which a man could rise from one income and social class to the next. There was a tendency to identify oneself with the successful Horatio Alger hero, and to overlook the fact that even where opportunities are great, the bulk of the workers must continue to perform low-paid types of work.

3. The popular distrust of government that kept Washington in the background of economic events during most of the nineteenth century extended to such proposals as government-sponsored social security. On the other hand, the combination of the rise of great fortunes and the abuses connected with monopoly, the unavoidable "dictatorship" of the federal government during World War I, and the failure of the private sector of the economy to assure continuance of the prosperity of the 1920's brought about a revolution in the attitude of the average citizen toward the economic role of the government.

4. The political representatives of the people hesitated to compromise the individuality of the American workman by placing him under the paternalistic influence of a federally administered social security system. One of the major reasons for the acceptance by Bismarck of the demands of German labor for old-age pensions was the fact that labor is bound to be more tractable if it has a pension to look forward to, and which it may lose unless it cooperates with the authorities.

---

idea of state compulsion. Germany, because of her rapid rate of industrialization, the absence of a laissez-faire philosophy, and the desire to cut the ground from the rapidly growing labor strength under the aegis of socialism, led the field in social insurance with the establishment of sickness and maternity insurance in 1883 and old-age and other benefits in 1889.

As a adjunct to veterans' aid, however, social security may be said to have originated very early in the United States. The budgetary surpluses that appeared after the War of 1812 gave impetus to generous treatment of Revolutionary War veterans, and pensions were granted on the basis of financial need as well as disablement.

The growth of the private pension system in the United States during the first thirty years of the present century did much to break down this opposition to publicly sponsored pension schemes; employers had been quick to appreciate that an employee who was qualified for pension rights that could not be transferred to another job was closely bound to the company. Presumably, it could have no more demoralizing effect on the independence of the worker if this system were replaced with a public insurance program in which the worker could carry his pension rights from one employer to another. It should be noted, incidentally, that Bismarck's confidence in the effects of social security on the independence of labor has not yet been borne out in this country.

CHANGING ATTITUDES

After the turn of the century, the rather indifferent attitude of the American public toward social security began to break down under the pressure of changing events. Until World War I immigration had kept the average age of the American worker comparatively low. The immigration laws reduced the flow to a trickle, however, and this development, combined with increasing life expectancy, made it apparent that in time the shift in the political balance of power would mean that something would have to be done for the security of the aged. An additional circumstance was the fact that decreased size of families, coupled with the increasing mobility of the worker, made it constantly more difficult for the aged to be cared for by their children. Finally, the factory system operated against the older worker. By the 1920's one began to hear that in many industries a worker was regarded as obsolescent at forty-five. Increasing worker interest in unemployment insurance was stimulated by the experience of England and other European countries. The depression brought into focus the need for assuring the continuance of a minimum income during hard times, and sentiment for unemployment insurance grew despite the example of the breakdown of the German system under the pressure of deep depression. The American public had gradually become convinced that we are all economically interdependent and that the only hope of economic security lies in social insurance.

SOCIAL SECURITY IN THE UNITED STATES[13]

Social security in the United States is characterized by great complexity. It is a mixture of private and public programs. Although the inadequacy of the private old-age and unemployment insurance (or employment guarantee) programs led to the inauguration of federal social

---

[13] For a more detailed treatment of the growth of social security in the United States, the following are a few of the titles which may be consulted: William Haber and Wilbur J. Cohen, *Readings in Social Security* (New York: Prentice-Hall, 1948); Earl E. Muntz, *Growth and Trends in Social Security* (New York: National Industrial Conference Board, 1949); S. E. Harris, *Economics of Social Security* (New

security, the limited coverage of the latter has permitted continued growth of industrially sponsored retirement schemes. The public social security programs are the joint responsibility of various levels of government. In carrying out their responsibilities the federal government and the states are partly independent of one another, but in part they cooperate in the same program. Legislation has been piecemeal, at times in response merely to political pressures for favors to particular groups like the veterans. Consequently, it is difficult to obtain a comprehensive idea of the system as a whole.

In addition to Old-Age and Survivors Insurance, social insurance comprises railroad retirement and unemployment insurance, workmen's compensation, state disability insurance, and state unemployment insurance. Moreover, the programs for veterans include pensions and other compensation, unemployment allowances, and self-employment allowances. Public assistance expenditure remains a very important element of the system, of which old-age assistance constitutes about two thirds. Inevitably, some groups are treated better than others in a system characterized by evolutionary growth, and the resulting vested interests and inertia make a thorough revision of the system difficult.[14] Yet it is of the highest importance ultimately to make such a revision so that the public can know exactly how much it is spending on social security and other subsidies. It is essential to effective budgeting that these important elements of federal receipts and expenditures be kept as simple and intelligible as possible.

THE FEDERAL PROGRAM

The federal social security program was set in motion in June, 1934, when President Roosevelt appointed a Committee on Economic Security to make recommendations for an act. The Social Security Act of 1935 established federally administered old-age insurance for those working in commerce and industry,[15] and empowered the states to enact unemployment insurance laws. It permitted federal grants to the states for old-age assistance, dependent children, and the blind, together with grants in support of state public health services, and maternal and child welfare programs. (Separate legislation had already provided for railroad retirement and unemployment, as well as veterans' security.) In 1939 survivors' benefits were added to the old-age insurance program, benefits were liber-

---

York: McGraw, 1941); and Eveline M. Burns, *The American Social Security System* (Boston: Houghton, 1949). For bibliography see Federal Security Agency, *Some Basic Readings in Social Security,* including the 1950 supplement.

[14] It is very important to note that many programs not nominally related to social security are nevertheless part of the collection of measures designed to guarantee to special groups minimum incomes during periods of adversity. Farm parity is a quantitatively important case in point.

[15] Thus many types of employment were excluded, for example, agricultural workers, domestic servants, and the self-employed.

alized, and coverage was extended in some directions though narrowed in others.

Between 1939 and 1950 no major changes were made in the act, but several provisions were enacted that had interesting economic and social implications. The persistent refusal of Congress to allow the contemplated rise in the payroll tax above the initial 1 per cent reduced the rate at which the old-age insurance reserve was built up, and increased the prospect of subsidies out of general tax funds. This prospect was made still more likely by the 1944 provision authorizing an appropriation whenever necessary out of general tax revenues to the reserve fund, but, as stated above, in 1950 Congress repealed the 1944 authorization for general revenues. In 1946 more liberalizations in the law were enacted, particularly to the benefit of veterans but also with respect to federal grants to the states for various types of assistance. The amendments to the act made in 1950 extended coverage under old-age insurance, and brought in an additional 10 million persons, including the self-employed, and most farm workers, employees of charitable organizations, and domestic servants. The 1954 amendments extended coverage to another 10 million persons, leaving as the major groups still not covered the following: doctors and dentists, members of the armed forces, the greater part of federal civilian employees, and policemen and firemen already covered by a government retirement system. In 1950, payroll taxes were applied to the first $3,600 of income instead of to the first $3,000 as previously, and the figure was raised to $4,200 in 1954.

PRICE DEFLATED BENEFITS: A PROPOSAL EVALUATED

In 1950 the maximum possible monthly benefit for the individual retired worker was raised to $80 (in 1952 to $85) and the maximum benefit including dependents, to $150 (in 1952 to $168.75). The previous maximums were $56 and $85, respectively. The amendments of 1954 further liberalized benefits. The minimum monthly payment for an individual was raised from $25 to $30. The maximum is now $108.50 for a retired worker, and $162.80 for a retired worker and eligible wife. Unfortunately, the doubling of the price level since 1939 has nearly eliminated the real value of the increase in dollar benefits, and has demonstrated the essential difficulty of attempting to assure recipients of social security payments a definite standard of living by defining monthly benefits in terms of dollars. For this reason sentiment is growing in some quarters for the use of a price index to stabilize ("price-deflate") the real value of social security payments over time.[16] However desirable this device may be from

---

[16] Such a proposal has been advanced in Sweden. Under this plan payments to retired persons would be geared to the price-deflated mean income of employed workers. See Alan Peacock, "Social Security and Inflation," *Review of Economic Studies,* No. 53, 1952–1953, pp. 169–173. It would be a separate task, of course, to *increase* the price-deflated social security benefit.

the point of view of social security recipients, one effect of its use would almost surely be an attempt to extend it to other types of income. It is already in use in escalator wage contracts and in farm parity payments.[17] The farther it is extended the greater the pressure that is put on other segments of the economy to demand a widening of its application.

This is not a conclusive argument against gearing social security payments to a price index. Obviously, some sort of inflation hedge is indispensable when prices continue to rise indefinitely. There are, however, great economic, political, and social dangers in the extension of purely automatic, rigid devices for guaranteeing any group a fixed real income. Guarantees couched in terms of real rather than money shares in national income tend to violate the principle that decisions with respect to the level and incidence of government spending and taxing must be subject to constant revision. Despite the claim on legislative time and energy, it might be preferable to use all changes in price indexes merely as signals requiring Congress to consider what changes should be legislated in subsidies and tax rates. There is no reason why absolute guarantees against change should be given in a world so dynamic that any completely rigid institutional setup is likely to produce undesirable economic and social effects.[18]

THE BRITISH AND AMERICAN SYSTEMS OF BENEFITS

In the American old-age insurance scheme benefits are related both to level of average earnings during the years of employment and to status with respect to dependents. Under the British system, on the other hand, workers in a given category make the same contributions and receive the same benefits (also geared to dependency) regardless of their earnings. The difference between the two is not as great as may at first appear, since the American system at present limits payroll taxes to the first $4200 of income, which is not much above the median. Moreover, under the benefit formula of the 1954 law, 55 per cent of the first $110 of monthly wage is included, but only 20 per cent of the next $240. This sharply reduces the effect of high average earnings in increasing a person's benefits.

At present, then, it may be inferred that both the British and the American systems accept the philosophy of a minimum benefit, which it is expected will be supplemented out of other savings by the insured individual. The minimum-benefit principle is acceptable only if those unable to accumulate adequate savings receive other assistance. In any case, in a

---

[17] Not to mention such devices as cost-plus contracts, percentage price markups, and price-escalated contracts.

[18] It should also be noted that if social security benefits were geared rigidly to cost of living, the beneficiaries would be denied their share in the productivity increments caused by technological progress. Another objection stems from the difficulty of obtaining a cost-of-living or consumers' price index that is regarded as adequate. Many problems face the use of an over-all index to measure changes in the cost of living.

country having large regional variations in income and price levels, and in customary standards of living, benefits should bear some relation to past earnings, and be geared to regional differences in price levels. Differences in living standards peculiar to different occupations can be maintained during retirement only if benefits are related to average earnings.

► THE FINANCING OF SOCIAL SECURITY

Social security legislation was based on the principle that unemployment and retirement benefits are insurance. Consequently, contributions were to be compulsory, in the form of a payroll tax, payable by both employers and employees in the case of old-age insurance, and by employers alone under unemployment insurance. The analogy with private insurance was carried still further in the provision for a reserve. An important part of the development of social security since its inception in 1935 has centered around the question of the extent to which the insurance principle should be maintained. Many of the risks faced by man are insurable. But the premiums are high where the risk is high, and the lower incomes do not permit substantial premium payments. Even in the middle-income groups there are many people who are "insurance-poor," i.e., they carry so many different kinds of insurance that their current living standard has become unduly low.

One great risk faced by the worker is not insurable, at least in the actuarial sense. This is unemployment. Since past experience of business fluctuations throws no light on their future course, no actuarial calculations can be made on the basis of which appropriate premiums can be established. That is, no matter how large a reserve might be built up out of employment taxes on the employer (or possibly also on the employee), a depression can be imagined which would be so deep and so prolonged that the reserve would be exhausted. However, the corollary of this fact is that in these circumstances the government should come to the relief of the unemployment reserve fund with subsidies out of general taxes, or, indeed, out of funds borrowed from the banking system.

A circumstance that undoubtedly influenced the Roosevelt administration in advocating the regressive payroll taxes, despite its interest in raising the standard of living of the low-paid worker, was the fact that coverage was very limited under the 1935 act. Thus those who benefited from insurance ought to finance it themselves. With large groups of workers excluded (for example, farmers, servants, the self-employed, many white-collar workers), the effect of financing old-age insurance out of general tax revenues would be the making of subsidies by some workers to others by way of the tax system. But with the great increase in coverage that has been effected in subsequent amendments, this argument in favor of payroll taxes has lost much of its force. Nevertheless, the tremendous growth in federal revenue needs since 1940 has emphasized the need for an essentially contributory social security system.

POLITICAL ATTITUDES TOWARD PAYROLL TAX INCREASES

On economic and other grounds there was some delay in acceptance of the principle of full employer and employee contributions to old-age insurance. The social security system was inaugurated during a period of much unemployment. An influential school of economists attributed to underconsumption much of the responsibility for the depression. Consequently to them the immediate adoption of payroll taxes (the incidence of which is largely on the consumer) adequate to finance a full-scale, old-age insurance plan was unacceptable. Congress was hesitant to permit the gradual rises in the rates of the payroll taxes provided for in the original legislation. Under the 1935 law the rate levied on both employer and employee was to be 1 per cent until 1939. Thereafter it was to rise by one-half per cent increases until it reached a maximum of 3 per cent of wages received after December 31, 1948. Successive revenue acts, however, postponed the additions to the 1 per cent rate through the year 1949. One of the milestones along the way was the afore-mentioned authorization by Congress in 1944 of appropriations from general tax funds to the social security accounts when benefits outran the resources of the fund. However, this was repealed in 1950 and a further step was taken toward self-sufficiency by amendments to the act which provided for a gradual increase in the rates from the 1½ per cent effective in 1950 and 1951 to a maximum of 3¼ per cent commencing in 1970. In January, 1954, the rate was allowed to rise to 2 per cent on the employer and the employee. The 1954 amendments provided for a rate of 2½ per cent from 1960 to 1964, 3 per cent from 1965 to 1969, 3½ per cent from 1970 to 1974, and 4 per cent thereafter. Thus it is contemplated that with expected benefit rates, and taking account of interest on the reserve, the old-age insurance system will be self-supporting.

Certain arguments in favor of employee contributions to old-age insurance have validity regardless of the extent of coverage of the population. If the worker who has the capacity to save has no personal concern with financing the costs of insuring himself against contingencies, many of which are eventually certain to occur, he inevitably sacrifices a measure of independence, for he is in the position of maintaining current consumption while leaving it to others to take care of his insurance. Therefore, it cannot be denied that certain portions of a man's current nonsubsistence consumption ought, on ethical grounds, to be forgone if his consumption at a later stage is to be maintained.

The problem, of course, is to determine what articles of consumption fall into this dispensable "luxury" category. The goods and services diverted to those receiving any of the various forms of insurance must be taken largely from those who are in the same income brackets. These are necessarily the mass of the workers, since the possibilities of downward redistribution of income are limited. Hence some proportion should clearly be financed by payroll taxes on the employee himself. Another consideration is that the interest of the citizen in good government is weakened when he has no responsibilities. If he feels that some of his own money is involved, he will use his vote more intelligently.[19]

THE RESERVE FUND AND THE EMPLOYEE'S PAYROLL TAX

The concept of the reserve likewise played an important part in the decision to finance old-age and unemployment insurance out of payroll taxes. Under private insurance schemes the need for a reserve is obvious. In the event that benefits temporarily rise to exceed premiums, a reserve is necessary to prevent bankruptcy of the fund. It was originally believed that an insurance plan operated by the federal government ought also to have a reserve, but it was finally realized that the possession of the power to tax (and to borrow, if necessary, during a depression) relieves the government of the necessity of maintaining a reserve fund.

There was, however, another argument in favor of such a fund. It was expected that by 1980, when the original old-age insurance system would reach maturity (i.e., when annual benefits would equal contributions), about 10 per cent of total annual payrolls would be required to finance benefits. Since under the plan maximum payroll taxes would be only 6 per cent, the differential would have to be made up out of interest payments on the accumulated reserve. The building up of this reserve, which by law had to be invested in government securities issued for the purpose, would require during the earlier years either an excess of payroll taxes over benefits or subsidies out of general tax funds.[20]

SHOULD THE WORKER CONTRIBUTE TO UNEMPLOYMENT INSURANCE?

Title IX of the Social Security Act made it possible for a state to levy payroll taxes for unemployment insurance without losing firms to states

---

[19] For justification of employee contributions, see *The Beveridge Report*, Cmd. 6404/42, ¶¶ 272–276. It should be noted that there is by no means general agreement that the insurance principle requires the use of payroll taxes. When taxes are already very high relative to national income, social security is financed mainly by the income groups which benefit from it. Consequently, the same individuals are forced to save for their old age under the one plan as under the other. Thus it is argued by Alan Peacock (*The Economics of National Insurance* [London: Hodge, 1952], pp. 99 ff.) that so long as most of the workers are contributing to the insurance program through general taxes, we have just as clearly a system of national social insurance as if contributions took the form of payroll taxes. The fact remains, however, that so long as there is reason to think that the incidence of the employee's payroll tax is actually upon the worker, there are important advantages from the point of view of morale and self-reliance in using this method of finance, though perhaps combined with subsidies out of the general revenues.

[20] An evaluation of this function of the reserve fund will be found on pages 571–573.

not having such plans. This was accomplished through the use of the federal credit, a device already familiar under the estate tax. All employers of eight workers or more,[21] in covered fields of employment, were required to pay a federal tax of 3 per cent on the first $3,000 of the wages of each worker. Employers could receive a credit against this tax of 90 per cent of payroll taxes paid under the state unemployment insurance law. The state could, if it liked, also impose a payroll tax on the employee, and for a time advantage was taken of this provision by as many as nine states. Both organized labor and the Social Security Board have opposed worker contributions under state unemployment insurance plans with experience rating, and the states levying worker payroll taxes have gradually given up the requirement. The trend away from worker contributions has been due partly to political pressure, and partly to the high level of employment in recent years, which has resulted in an accumulation of reserves, thus obviating the need for worker contributions.

One of the reasons for levying the tax on the employer alone is that it is his responsibility to provide steady employment to his employees. The tax would be an incentive to him to stabilize employment, since this would make for lower tax rates. Another point is that the cost of supporting the unemployed worker is part of the cost of production to be borne by the consumer. If the tax on the employer is passed forward, while that on the worker is borne by the latter, only the employer's tax should be used. If, on the other hand, both taxes are passed forward, it would not be important whether the tax were divided into two parts or imposed on the employer alone. Evidently, if there is doubt whether the worker's contribution can be shifted forward, the tax is properly placed on the employer alone. One point should be noted: even if the cost of unemployment is not regarded as a legitimate charge on the worker, he nevertheless bears his share in the form of the additional cost of consumers' goods owing to the forward shifting of the employer's payroll tax. The bulk of the cost of unemployment inevitably takes the form of lower real income to the worker.

EXPERIENCE RATING

The Social Security Act provided for a flat payroll tax to finance unemployment insurance. At the same time the law allowed the states freedom to lower the rate to firms having good employment records. A flat tax for all firms, applicable alike to industries with stable employment and

---

[21] The first significant change in coverage in nineteen years was made in 1954, when an amendment to the Federal Unemployment Tax Act extended coverage to about 3.7 million workers and 270,000 employers. Of this increase in coverage 1.4 million were brought in as a result of reducing the number of workers in the eligible firm from eight to four, and 2.5 million by including federal employees. More than 10 million workers were still excluded, comprising employees of firms employing less than four workers, agricultural and agricultural processing workers, domestic servants, employees of nonprofit organizations, and state and local government employees.——*Social Security Bulletin,* November, 1954.

those with fluctuating employment, would mean that the former were partially subsidizing the latter. Employment in much of industry necessarily fluctuates, and these fluctuations may be either cyclical or seasonal. Examples are the construction industry and agriculture. Naturally, firms in relatively stable industries dislike having their costs increased by a payroll tax to finance unemployment in other industries. Immediately after passage of the unemployment insurance program, pressure was exerted on state legislatures to take advantage of their right to lower tax rates in return for steady employment. This device, now in use in all states, is known as experience rating.

Effect on the Unemployment Reserve. Experience rating has greatly retarded the accumulation of an unemployment reserve. In 1940 the average rate of employer contributions for the four states operating under experience rating was 2.29 per cent. By 1947, with all the states using the device, the average rate had declined to 1.40 per cent. The estimated reduction in revenue from the use of experience rating was $1 billion in 1947.[22]

Unfavorable and Favorable Aspects. Experience rating has not remained as popular with some types of business as it was expected to be. The reason is that experience rating formulas fail to take adequate account of the reasons for unemployment in different industries. The objectives of experience rating are to encourage both seasonal and cyclical stability of employment, and to compel firms with relatively poor employment records to pay a more than proportionate share of the unemployment insurance bill. It may be no fault of the firm, however, that it is unable to stabilize employment. Moreover, a variety of formulas, of varying complexity, are in use in the several states. In some states a rate higher than 2.7 per cent is applied to firms with an unusually bad employment experience. It is difficult for the firm to perceive the connection between its employment experience and the rate of payroll tax to which it is subject.[23]

A further defect of experience rating, recently largely remedied, has been that new firms could not qualify for the lower rates. A clause in the federal law provided an employer to pay the taxes for three years before becoming eligible. As of January 1, 1955, however, this period was reduced to one year. It is the small new firm which, even in the absence of discrimination, finds it difficult to become established. The opposition stirred up by these considerations has led to a movement for the abandonment of

---

[22] Advisory Council on Social Security, _Unemployment Insurance_, A Report to the Senate Committee on Finance, 89th Cong., 2d Sess., Senate Document No. 206, 1948, p. 87.

[23] Among the complexities of experience rating formulas is the gearing of rates to the size of the states' unemployment reserve funds. Some states have suspended the reduced rates entirely for a period of time when the reserve balance has fallen below the minimum specified by their laws. For a detailed account of experience rating see Department of Labor, Bureau of Employment Security, _The Labor Market and Employment Security,_ July, 1952, and December, 1953.

the incentive aspects of unemployment insurance. Sentiment has been increasing for the determination of the payroll tax rate on the basis of the average record of all the firms in the industry rather than with respect to the individual firm.

The gearing of rates to the employment record might conceivably exert unwanted economic effects in the event of a depression. If rates were adjusted upward on the arrival of mass unemployment the effect would be to increase the burden of consumption taxation at the very moment when it should be reduced. This effect could be avoided, of course, by distinguishing between unemployment due to conditions within an industry and unemployment caused by a general failure of purchasing power. In practice this would not be easy, however. The many conceptual and administrative difficulties with experience rating have led some observers to urge its abandonment.

At the same time, many, if not most, of the criticisms of experience rating relate to practices which could be improved upon. The basic fact remains that awarding lower rates of tax for a good employment record stimulates employers to look about for ways to stabilize employment. Experience rating makes a contribution to the search for economic security inherent in labor's perennial demand for a guaranteed annual wage. A considerable part of past difficulties with experience rating emanates from the freedom with which the states have experimented with experience rating provisions. It may well be that the proper solution would be a concerted effort by the states to get together to write a "model law" rather than to accept the argument that the practice should be abandoned. At any rate, in a sustained period of high employment, sentiment for reduced rates for a good employment record tends to remain high.[24]

UNEMPLOYMENT INSURANCE BENEFITS

No standards of unemployment insurance benefits were provided for in the Social Security Act.[25] Consequently, a wide variety of formulas have been developed by the fifty-one states and territories. On the other hand, similarities as well as differences may be noted. Changes in benefit provisions are frequently enacted, usually in the direction of liberalization, and this constant flux tends to encourage uniformity in over-all philosophy if not with respect to details.

In recent years favorable employment experience has permitted the

---

[24] For arguments in favor of experience rating, see Elizabeth Brandeis, "The Role of Unemployment Compensation," *Social Service Review*, December, 1946, pp. 496–497.

[25] For a discussion of the details of benefit provisions of the states and territories see Department of Labor, Bureau of Employment Security, "Comparison of State Unemployment Insurance Laws as of August, 1954." See also, *The Labor Market and Employment Security*, November, 1953, pp. 20 ff., published by the same agency; and *Hearings* before the Committee on Ways and Means on Unemployment Insurance, April 14–15, 1953.

states to build up their reserve funds. However, a decline in the average employers' tax rate can exert a substantial effect on receipts. Thus, a decline from 1.3 per cent in the average rate paid by employers in 1953 to 1.2 per cent in 1954 was largely responsible for a decline in receipts from $1.3 billion to $1.1 billion. State reserve funds had reached $8.9 billion by the end of 1953, but because benefits exceeded tax receipts plus interest payments during 1954, the reserve had dropped slightly to $8.2 billion by the end of 1954.[26] The benefit picture, however, differs enormously from state to state. Sectional differences in employment records caused marked shifts in the distribution of both benefits and employment tax liabilities. Again, while the formulas for computing weekly benefits display a pronounced family resemblance, they vary greatly in details. Consequently, both total benefits and annual benefits per unemployed worker vary considerably.

In all states the amount payable for a week of total unemployment depends on the past wages of the worker, though it is limited by a minimum and a maximum. While most of the states base benefits on wages in that quarter year of the base period in which wages were highest, others make use of average weekly wages. Therefore, considerable variations exist in the maximum total benefits which may be received by an unemployed worker in a given year. Some states provide for dependents' allowances, and among these states the provisions differ substantially. Most of the states require a waiting period of one week before benefit payments are commenced.

► THE ECONOMICS OF THE RESERVE FUND

A private insurance company must build up a reserve out of premiums in order to be able to meet unforeseen contingencies. Actuaries can predict the incidence of death within narrow limits on the assumption that the future will behave in substantially the same way as the recent past. They cannot make any predictions about the effects of wars or plagues. No reserve fund can stand up against a major catastrophe. The protective function of the fund is to provide a cushion against likely contingencies, plus a reasonable factor of safety. So long as a disaster is localized, the company can protect itself and its policy holders by reinsuring with companies in other areas. A nation-wide or world-wide catastrophe means that only a percentage of benefits can be paid.

Obviously, the reason that a private insurance company has to accumulate a reserve fund is that no other source of income is available in a time of emergency. It is in this respect that national insurance schemes differ from those of private companies. Since the national government has

---

[26] Department of Labor, *The Labor Market and Employment Security*, February, 1955, p. 38.

sovereign tax powers, as well as the ability to borrow an unlimited amount of newly created money from the banking system, a national insurance agency needs no reserve beyond a relatively small one as a working balance, and for its psychological advantages in reassuring the public. A state insurance agency, on the other hand, stands in this respect somewhere between the national government and a private company. It does not have unlimited borrowing power, since it cannot make a market for its securities by drawing on the reserve-creating capacity of the Federal Reserve System. Moreover, although the state also has sovereign tax powers, it must compete for revenues with its own municipalities and the federal government. Therefore, a state insurance company, like a private insurance corporation, must build up a reserve.

▶ THE UNEMPLOYMENT INSURANCE RESERVE FUND

Unemployment insurance differs from retirement insurance in one important respect: whereas mortality rates are predictable, mass unemployment is not. Consequently, the states can never know when extraordinary sources of income will be necessary to keep the system solvent. A reserve can help them tide over minor recessions; but no matter how large the reserve, a depression can be imagined that is deep and prolonged enough to exhaust it. Even in times of high-level employment there are considerable differences from state to state in the size of the reserve funds and in unemployment.

In view of the limitations on state finance, the only extraordinary source of emergency payments to the reserve fund is a subsidy or a loan from the federal government. A federal loan for a period of, say, five years can provide a cushion against temporary unemployment, or unemployment peculiar to a particular area. When, during a depression, unemployment is country-wide, the unemployment relief problem is appropriately merged with the national recovery program.[27]

---

[27] See the Report to the Senate Committee on Finance from the Advisory Council on Social Security, *Unemployment Insurance,* 80th Cong., 2d Sess., Senate Document No. 206, 1948. Owing to the high employment rate in recent years, holdings of federal securities by the Unemployment Trust Fund rose from $3 billion in 1942 to over $8.5 billion ten years later.—*Annual Reports* of the Secretary of the Treasury.

An amendment to the Social Security Act in 1944 authorized Congressional appropriations to a fund from which states could borrow if their own funds became low. Under an amendment in 1954 the excess of collections from the federal unemployment tax over employment security administration expenses is to be devoted to the maintenance of a $200 million reserve in the federal unemployment account. This amount is to be available for non-interest-bearing loans to states having need of assistance. The amendment substitutes permanent for the earlier temporary financial assistance to the states. The loan is to be repaid either by a transfer from the state's trust fund account to the federal unemployment trust fund, or by a reduction in the allowable credit of 90 per cent against the 3 per cent federal tax.

In the past, instead of subsidizing the unemployment reserve fund, the federal government has made a "profit" from unemployment insurance payroll taxes. The law provides that 0.3 per cent of payrolls be segregated by the federal government as a basis for reimbursing the states for administrative expenses; yet these expenses have been much less than the proceeds of the tax. During the first ten years of operation an amount totaling $767 million was diverted to general treasury use by this device, which naturally caused considerable antagonism among the states.[28] A 1954 amendment forbids this practice.

► THE OLD-AGE AND SURVIVORS INSURANCE RESERVE FUND

Aside from a working reserve, no special fund is required under a federal old-age security program. Rates of contribution to the fund simply need to be adequate to finance current benefits. If benefits exceed contributions it is merely necessary to meet the deficiency out of general tax revenues. Rates can then be adjusted to provide for repayment, as well as for adequate contributions in the future. The dangers of insolvency that face private insurance companies, as well as those of subordinate governmental jurisdictions, are absent.

Although no reserve to maintain solvency is needed in a nationally administered program, a substantial reserve has nevertheless been accumulated. During the first five years after the passage of the Social Security Act, a lively debate went on over the validity of the reserve principle for federally administered old-age insurance. The act of 1935 provided for a schedule of payroll tax rates in relation to expected benefits that would have brought into being a reserve fund estimated at $47 billion by the time the fund reached maturity in 1980. Subsequent postponements in the dates on which increases in the tax rates were to take effect reduced the rate of increase in the size of the fund, which nevertheless by 1954 had passed $20 billion.

As a result of the debate over the reserve, the amendments to the act adopted in 1939 accepted the principle of a restricted reserve. A full reserve would be a fund large enough to cover all liabilities if the system were to be stopped at any time and no further contributions collected. A limited reserve is bound to be accumulated under a contributory system,

---

[28] Cf. the discussion by E. E. Muntz, *Growth and Trends in Social Security* (New York: National Industrial Conference Board, 1949), p. 24. It should be pointed out that although each state is treated separately with respect to its unemployment reserve fund, it was not thought wise to permit it to retain responsibility for administering the fund. Apart from the greater danger of inferior management when such funds are under the control of over fifty states and territories of vastly different size and resources, it was feared that in the event of a general depression all the states might simultaneously throw their assets on a weak market. This would at the same time demoralize the market for such assets and render the reserve funds largely fictitious.

however, because during the earlier years the volume of benefits is smaller than payroll tax collections. A reserve can be avoided only if the rate of contributions is constantly revised on the basis of the volume of benefits that are paid out in a particular year. If this is done, however, tax rates are so small in earlier years that the system is not contributory. If, instead of allowing payroll tax rates to rise each year as described above, a flat rate is enacted, a reserve fund is then automatically built up. The rate of increase of this fund can be held down by delaying the rise in social security tax rates and by paying liberal benefits in the earlier years. This device is not likely to appeal, however, to those who wish the system to be really contributory.

ARGUMENTS AGAINST A LARGE RESERVE[29]

Opponents of the large reserve had argued that (1) it would be a standing invitation to Congress to spend on objects unconnected with social security, and (2) if the reserve were held idle it would be deflationary. Each of these arguments needs to be examined.

In considering the first of these contentions it is necessary to distinguish between (1) a growing reserve and (2) a fixed reserve once the fund has reached maturity. Considering the latter case first, the only incentive to a higher level of Congressional appropriations would arise out of the knowledge that the workers had title, through the Trust Fund, to many billions of dollars of compulsory savings held for them by the government. The only difference between these and individual savings deposited in private savings institutions would be the fact that they were under the legislative control of Congress.

A Large Fixed Reserve.   Suppose that the reserve is invested entirely in federal securities. The securities could be converted into purchasing power in one of three ways. The Trust Fund could sell them to the Treasury, the latter financing the purchase out of increased general tax revenues. Obviously, this method would provide Congress with no incentive to increase public spending. Alternatively, the securities could be sold to private savers. All that has happened in this case is a transfer of government debt from one group of savers to another. No increase in the spending power of the government has occurred. Thirdly, part of the securities held by the Trust Fund might be sold via the Treasury to the banking system (assuming excess reserves). But, as before, this makes no new purchasing power available to the Treasury. In short, the only aspect of an old age or unemployment reserve fund which might encourage a higher level of federal spending would be the possibility of a misunderstanding by Congress of

---

[29] Under the 1939 amendments, the Board of Trustees of the Old-Age Fund was to report to Congress whenever the reserve looked as if it would exceed three times the highest expected annual outgo during a subsequent five-year period, as well as whenever the reserve appeared to be unduly small.

the financial significance of the fund. This is not likely to occur in view of our years of experience with social security finance.

A Growing Reserve. A growing reserve poses a different sort of problem. So long as the reserve is accumulating, payroll tax receipts exceed current benefits. In a sense this excess is a source of current receipts to the government. But it is a form of compulsory saving (probably in part replacing saving that would have been made even in the absence of the old-age insurance scheme) rather than tax revenue to the government. The conclusion does not follow, therefore, that the existence of this excess of compulsory contributions over benefits is likely to encourage a higher level of public spending. Compulsory saving does, however, absorb part of the taxpaying capacity of the groups which bear the burden of payroll taxes. Therefore, if tax rates are in general high, it may prove more difficult to raise income tax rates in the lower-income brackets, or to increase the scope of excise or sales taxation. Nevertheless, a contributory social security scheme can result in a higher level of current tax collections plus compulsory saving than would have obtained in its absence. If the total tax burden on the affected groups prior to the adoption of the program had been relatively low, the payroll taxes could constitute a net increase in the amount of purchasing power surrendered by individuals to the government. But it is the Trust Fund, not the Treasury, which has the function of disposing of this purchasing power.

A likely procedure is for the fund to buy government securities directly or indirectly from savers. The Treasury might make special issues to the fund, thus reducing its offers to other types of savers. In other words, since these tax receipts, or contributions, are the property of the fund, the government must borrow them if it wishes to make use of them. Federal spending might be larger than otherwise only if it were easier to borrow because of this device. Under particular circumstances this might indeed be the case, but the circumstances would be very exceptional.

In brief, the federal deficit is a residual item that is determined by the relation between tax receipts and expenditures. Congress decides on this relationship in the light of the political situation. If a deficit is accepted it is technically helpful that social security taxes exceed benefits; but it is not very important that they should do so, for the securities can always be temporarily sold to the federal reserve banks. The role of an annual surplus of receipts in the social security account is not that it permits the government to spend more, but that it may reduce the extent to which the Treasury has to rely on inflationary deficit finance.

IS THE RESERVE FUND DEFLATIONARY?

The foregoing discussion also throws light on the importance that should be attached to the second argument, namely, that a social security reserve might be deflationary. So long as the reserve is invested in government securities, the effect on the *volume* of money is nil. Purchasing power is surrendered to the fund by those who bear the incidence of the payroll taxes. A portion of the federal debt is shifted from the hands of private savers to those who save through the old-age insurance program. The only effect on *velocity* of money is to be found in the possible differences in rates of spending that result from a rise in the rate of (compulsory) saving on the part of payroll taxpayers. This effect is not likely to be significant.

If, on the other hand, the Treasury were forced to issue obligations merely to provide the reserve fund with a safe investment, the effect could be deflationary, but only if the Treasury were to delay in putting the money back into circulation. This result is unlikely, however. The normal procedure would be for the Treasury to reduce the offerings of government securities to other types of savers. As old issues matured they would be replaced, to the desired amount, by special nonnegotiable issues to the Old-Age Trust Fund. All that happens is that savings re-enter the income stream by a different route.

IS THE TRUST FUND A FICTION?

The argument has been made that the Old-Age Trust Fund does not really exist. Since the government spends the proceeds as they come in, it is contended, there is really no reserve at all. While private insurance reserves earn real interest income, old-age insurance and unemployment reserves are said to be merely a "record of future obligations" or "liabilities that do not represent assets."[30]

Under a contributory system the reserve possesses importance, quite irrespective of the form it takes, as a record of operations of the fund. On the other hand, it is unnecessary to go through the formality of establishing a fund merely in order to keep abreast of the equity of each insured person in the program. The real significance of the reserve fund is that compulsory savings, like all savings, are entitled to bear interest. An important source of income of private insurance companies is their receipts of interest. Insurance premiums are raised when interest rates decline. Does the interest income of a government trust fund have the same significance? The following points may be made.

1. The fact that the reserve is not kept in the form of cash is, of course, no basis for believing that the fund is fictitious. Private insurance funds are likewise invested in interest-earning assets. Institutional as well as private savers require the going rate of interest on their savings. Therefore, a government trust fund must be expected to take advantage of the same opportunity to earn interest.

2. The law requires that the reserves of government trust funds be

---

[30] See the discussion of this issue in L. Merriam and K. Schlotterbeck, *The Cost and Financing of Social Security* (Washington, D. C.: Brookings, 1950), p. 155.

invested in federal securities. This means that the interest payments are financed out of taxes. Is there anything in this circumstance that would justify the belief that the fund is fictitious? Certainly not, unless all reserve funds are to be so regarded if any of their assets take the form of government securities. Private insurance companies invest a large part of their reserves in government bonds.

3. The more extensive the scope of social security, the greater the proportion of the interest payments that is likely to have to be financed out of taxes on the insured persons themselves. These taxes consist of payroll and other taxes the incidence of which is on the insured individuals who, as a group, receive the interest payments. Under a full-coverage, high-benefit social security program, the taxable capacity of the middle and higher income groups may not be great enough to permit more than a limited proportion of the interest payments to be financed by taxing these groups. It might, therefore, be thought that the interest payments are in part a mere transfer of money from one pocket to another. The fact that the tax system as a whole may have to become more regressive under a large-scale social security program does not mean that the fund is fictitious, however, or, indeed, that the interest payments themselves are so. No one supposes that the interest payments to wealthy bondholders are illusory merely because they are financed in large part out of income taxes on the same groups. A person with a high income, and paying high income taxes, might not own any securities, and would be in a worse position than one who did.

THE ROLE OF INTEREST PAYMENTS

We conclude that the argument that the fund is fictitious is invalid. It remains to consider whether the interest payments on the reserve fund reduce the burden of old-age insurance by permitting lower payroll taxes.

An important argument advanced for the reserve at the time the Social Security Act was under discussion was that a large old-age insurance reserve would permit payroll taxes to be limited to a maximum of 3 per cent each on employer and employee. The rates of 8 per cent or more which would otherwise be necessary might, it was thought, prove to be intolerable.[31]

The entire cost of social security has to be borne out of taxes of one sort or another. It is conceivable, as stated above, that the whole tax burden might fall on the beneficiaries of social security. Assuming that the national

---

[31] That is, workers would have pressed for higher wages, and the program might thus prove to be inflationary. Alternatively, the contributory principle might be partially given up, possibly by lowering income tax exemptions or raising first bracket rates. This would be equivalent to extending the willingness of the insured persons to be taxed by dividing up their contributions into two or more types of tax. The scope for this is limited by the extent to which workers are concerned with their incomes after taxes rather than with payroll taxes alone.

debt is the same whether or not a reserve is built up, taxes required to service the debt are likewise the same in either case. The difference between the two is that under the reserve plan the taxes required for financing interest payments on the debt held in trust by the fund for the social security beneficiaries constitute a transfer to them, whereas under the no-reserve plan they flow to private savers outside the social security system. Thus interest payments on the reserve fund are a real source of financing social security benefits.

A GROWING RESERVE AND TAXABLE CAPACITY

Something should be said of the effects on taxable capacity that are produced by the act of building up a reserve of $25 to $50 billion. During the years when payroll taxes exceed benefits there are compulsory purchases, through the Trust Fund, of government obligations. These securities would otherwise be held by private savers outside the social security system. Does the accumulation of a security reserve imply a net increase in saving rather than merely a switch of the saving of payroll taxpayers from other repositories of savings into government securities?

The answer would appear to be in the affirmative. Payroll taxpayers would probably not have saved as much in the absence of the tax. Moreover, to the extent that taxes paid by the employer are passed forward to the consumer, some reduction in consumption may be expected. On the other hand, average family real income in the United States is high. This means that the average family has a margin available for saving, and this margin may be reduced by the reduction in take-home pay due to the payroll tax on employees, and by any rise in prices resulting from forward shifting of the payroll tax on the employer. It seems likely that some part, but not the whole, of the payroll taxes represent compulsory saving that is not offset by a decline in the voluntary saving of the community. The effects on economic growth, and therefore on long-run taxable capacity, are favorable if the total of government plus private investment in productive capacity is stimulated by the higher rate of saving. The opposite would be true during a period in which the economy was plagued by oversaving and underconsumption.

The conclusion seems justified that at the time an old-age insurance plan is set up, no one can say with assurance that the net economic effects of relatively high payroll taxes in the earlier years, and relatively low ones later, will be either beneficial or injurious to the economy. Since the welfare of the insured workers is bound up with that of the economy as a whole, it follows that the reserve may or may not on balance better their position. There remains, however, the question whether other considerations do not dictate the accumulation of a reserve. As a matter of fact, the special problems of the transition period, during which the fund is growing to maturity, do indicate the necessity for a reserve if the plan is to be contributory.

THE PROBLEMS OF THE TRANSITION PERIOD

As pointed out earlier, under the act establishing the system of old-age benefits it was provided that beginning in 1937 both employer and employee would pay a tax of 1 per cent on the employee's wages up to $3,000 a year. The rates were to be gradually increased to a maximum of 3 per cent each by 1949. Benefits were to become payable in 1942 to workers who were sixty-five or older. The benefit for a particular worker was to be calculated on the basis of his wages received in covered (i.e., insured) employment between 1936 and the year when the employee reached sixty-five years of age. Under this plan a reserve fund would commence accumulating in 1937. Since Congress would not start making annual appropriations to retired workers until 1942, and since few persons would be entitled to benefits in the earlier years, a large reserve fund would eventually be built up. Interest on this fund would preclude the danger that payroll taxes would have to be increased still higher, or that subsidies would have to be made to the fund. Nevertheless, it will be remembered that in 1944 Congress authorized such subsidies if and when necessary.[32]

The major problem of the transition period is to reconcile the interests of those who have entered the system late in their working life with those who spend a lifetime in covered employment. Indeed, no reconcilement is possible. If benefits are geared strictly to the total amount paid in to each worker's account, an old-age security system remains virtually worthless for many years to those reaching retirement. This situation would probably be politically impossible, since for a long time after the inception of the plan it would benefit little the very groups that have exerted the political pressure required to get the act on the books.[33]

On the other hand, the inequity to younger workers is obvious if a

---

[32] Estimates of the annual cost of the old-age insurance plan in a year of full operation vary widely depending on assumptions with respect to the number of people eligible and other factors. According to estimates submitted by the Senate Finance Committee (Report No. 1,669, to accompany H. R. 6,000, 81st Cong., 2d Sess., May 17, 1950, p. 39), under low-cost assumptions the level-premium cost would be about 4¾ per cent of payrolls, and under high-cost assumptions, 7¾ per cent. Low-cost and high-cost estimates in dollars were $8.5 and $13.3 billions, respectively (p. 41). Imperfectly predictable factors that will influence the results are immigration, the size of families, conditions of dependency, marriage rates, future payrolls, employment conditions, and the like.

It is important to remember that low-cost and high-cost calculations are intended as illustrations rather than as true estimates. This method gives a large range, and thus lessens the likelihood that actual cost will fall outside these limits. But the meaningfulness of the estimates is correspondingly reduced. For a discussion of the problems involved, see C. C. Killingsworth and G. Schroeder, "Long-Range Cost Estimates for Old-Age Insurance," *Quarterly Journal of Economics,* May, 1951, pp. 199–213.

[33] In this connection the strong political power of the Townsendites in the thirties may be mentioned. The aged were lobbying for their own benefit, not for that of the aged in future years.

man can become eligible to full benefits by paying social security taxes for only a year and a half before retirement. Yet it has been thought necessary to make this concession to the worker who is already advanced in years during the early years of the plan. A worker is regarded as fully insured if, under certain conditions, he has as few as six quarters of coverage; that is, if he has worked in covered employment for a year and a half. Another advantage to the older worker is that he does not become subject to the higher payroll tax rates contemplated as the system moves toward maturity. Thus until the system reaches maturity, younger workers (as well as employers and consumers) are subsidizing older ones.

The older worker suffers, however, from the fact that the principle of really adequate old-age insurance is being only gradually accepted in the United States. The original act, as well as its amendments up to the present time, assumed that old-age insurance benefits are merely a supplement to other income. The idea has been that in addition the worker will save out of his take-home pay. It seems almost certain that ultimately an adequate system of old-age insurance will be adopted in this country. If this proves to be the case, the advantage to workers who retire during the earlier years is reduced.

► SOCIAL SECURITY AND ECONOMIC STABILITY

The financing of old-age and unemployment insurance provides an opportunity for both automatic and managed economic stabilization. As the coverage of both forms of insurance becomes broader, and if taxes and benefits are significantly increased, the quantitative effects become large enough so that social security takes its place with other controls over the level of income and employment.

Social security finance contributes automatically to greater economic stability by virtue of the fact that when national income falls, social security tax receipts decline and benefits rise. On the one hand, a rise in unemployment reduces the tax base to which payroll taxes are applied; and on the other hand, more individuals become eligible for benefits. With respect to unemployment insurance it is clear that the magnitude of total benefits rises. It is not at first so clear, however, that old-age security benefits necessarily rise in a depression. Workers do not reach the age of retirement any more quickly. Nevertheless, individuals who might otherwise have remained in the labor force after retirement age undergo increasing pressure for their jobs from younger workers when unemployment rises. Therefore to some extent old-age benefits do respond to cyclical influences. Conversely, a condition of full or overfull employment implies a high level of payroll taxes and a decline in benefits.

The effect of the built-in flexibility of old-age and unemployment insurance is exercised through its impact on the income and spending streams. If benefits rise and payroll tax receipts fall during a *downswing*, either the excess of payroll taxes over benefits is reduced, or, after the reserve funds have reached maturity, the fund must sell government securities to finance net outpayments to insured individuals. In the former case, the two reserve funds must reduce their rate of purchase of government securities. Consequently, the reserve banks may be called upon to buy a larger proportion of federal debt in connection with a public works program. In the latter, the correct procedure is to make sales of securities to the Federal Reserve System. Although it is sometimes pointed out that this is indistinguishable from ordinary deficit finance, it should be remembered that in a depression it may be difficult to find appropriate places at which to inject new purchasing power. The existence of social security expands the possibilities. For example, it may be politically more difficult to achieve public acceptance of a given size of deficit created to finance public works alone than to finance a combination of public works, an increase in social security benefits or a decrease in tax receipts, relief subsidies, and so on. In short, the size of the deficit is not the only consideration: different types of public spending represent different degrees of encroachment on the private-enterprise system, and therefore different degrees of public acceptance of the program.

BENEFIT AND RATE VARIATIONS FOR ECONOMIC STABILITY

If *automatic* changes in payroll taxes and benefits in response to cyclical fluctuations in national income contribute to economic stabilization, *conscious* changes will make a still greater contribution to it. The difference between the two is similar to that between the stabilizing and the full-employment budgets, and the arguments pro and con are likewise similar. The principle of altering payroll tax rates in response to cyclical fluctuations was proposed in the British White Paper on Employment Policy in 1944,[34] and adopted *in principle* in the National Insurance Act of 1946, Sec. 3 (1). Some percentage of full employment (to be defined) would be taken as the norm, and payroll taxes on both employer and employee were to increase if employment rose above this level, and conversely if employment fell. Obviously, the effects would be to change (1) the disposable purchasing power of the worker, and (2) the level of costs to the employer.

The British plan described above is automatic, and its kinship is with the stabilizing budget proposal rather than with the full-employment budget. Discretion might be introduced, however, by giving an executive agency the power to vary rates of tax in accordance with its judgment on the probable seriousness of an upswing or a downswing in the level of private spending. On the credit side, this modification would improve the chances of really effective action by allowing, for example, a drastic reduction in

---

[34] Cmd. 6527.

payroll tax rates if it was believed that a serious downward spiral was in progress. On the debit side, however, is the fact that a great deal of power over the economy would be concentrated in the hands of a very few men.

As we have seen, under our philosophy of checks and balances, Congress would be slow to empower the Treasury or any other executive agency to alter tax rates in the interest of economic stabilization. The frequently cited power granted the executive to raise or lower the tariff rates (within limits) cannot be regarded as a precedent for the quantitatively far more important taxes involved in the financing of social security. It may be granted, however, that if a depression were severe enough, or if hyperinflation were to threaten the economic and political stability of the nation, Congress might well change its mind. But this implies merely an extraordinary rather than an ordinary use of the device.

VARIATIONS IN RATES OF BENEFITS

Little if any attention has been paid to the possibility of varying unemployment and old-age insurance *benefit* rates in response to changes in the level of income. The economic effects would be similar to those of the payroll tax on the worker. Old people and the unemployed would be provided with a larger number of dollars during depression, and conversely during a boom. Thus, provided the change in benefit rate were geared automatically to an index of unemployment, a further degree of built-in flexibility would be conferred on the fiscal system.

The reason for the lack of attention to this device is obvious. With respect to unemployment insurance, it would be a hardship on the unlucky unemployed or retired person during a period of relatively high employment to receive smaller dollar benefits merely because it is desired to arrest a boom. Obviously, it would be preferably to siphon off purchasing power by some other means. Conversely, there is no particular reason why insurance benefits to an unemployed person should be higher merely because many are unemployed.

Indeed, a better case can be made for pursuing a reverse policy. During a downswing the price level usually falls, and a given dollar of unemployment benefit will buy more commodities. There is no reason, as noted above, to permit an unemployed person to be better off because more workers are unemployed. Indeed, one of the phenomena of a downswing is the reduction in incomes of employed factors of production; and on grounds of equity the unemployed should be prevented from gaining relatively to the employed. Similar arguments apply in reverse to an upswing accompanied by a rise in prices.

► CONCLUSION

Discussions of old-age and unemployment insurance have been clouded by the introduction of what many would regard as a side issue, namely, its function in redistributing income. If the analogy of social insurance with private insurance is complete, the fact that social security taxes are paid primarily by the same groups that benefit is justifiable. Workers are simply saving for a rainy day; and to the extent that the taxes (or contributions) paid by themselves or by their employers are shifted to the consumer, essentially the same groups are still bearing the burden.

The conclusion is different, however, if it is demonstrable that the income of the average worker is insufficient for him to save for periods of unemployment and his old age. Since an enlightened society must certainly make sure that this job is done, a downward redistribution of income is inevitable, and those observers are correct who object if the entire cost of social insurance is financed through regressive taxes.

The truth must be somewhere between these two positions. Unemployment insurance is a matter that lies largely outside the purview of the individual worker. He cannot be held responsible for unemployment. Granted that he might be asked to contribute, along with the employer, to build up a fund to take care of brief periods of unemployment,[35] longer periods should be financed jointly by taxes according to ability to pay and by taxes ultimately borne by the consumer (who is, of course, largely synonymous with the worker). Unemployment is a charge on society, and the worker, as a part of society, bears his share of the cost.

Old-age insurance, on the other hand, must be regarded as largely, but certainly not entirely, the responsibility of the worker himself. He cannot be expected to do the whole job at current or prospective average real annual wages. On the other hand, it cannot be denied that the bulk of the workers in the United States are able to put by something for their retirement years. From the point of view of equity it makes little difference whether they do this through the employee's payroll tax, the tax on the employer, or sales taxes on articles widely consumed. It does make a difference, however, from the point of view of morale. The individual should be allowed the satisfaction of knowing that he is pulling his own weight. If he cares to think about it, he knows he is doing so, in part, if 3 or 4 per cent a year is deducted from his pay to finance benefits that cost upward of 10 per cent. If, however, his share takes the form of taxes that are shifted to him, he bears the burden without knowing it or getting the credit for it. This is the road to the paternalistic state.

► REFERENCES

BURNS, E. M. *The American Social Security System*. Boston: Houghton Mifflin Company, 1949.

FEDERAL SECURITY AGENCY. *Annual Reports*.

---

[35] The guaranteed annual wage can do part of the job, particularly with respect to seasonal unemployment.

HABER, W., and W. J. COHEN. *Readings in Social Security*. New York: Prentice-Hall, Inc., 1948.

HARRIS, S. E. *Economics of Social Security*. New York: McGraw-Hill Book Company, Inc., 1941.

MERRIAM, L., and K. SCHLOTTERBECK. *The Cost and Financing of Social Security*. Washington, D. C.: The Brookings Institution, 1950.

MUNTZ, E. E. *Growth and Trends in Social Security*. New York: National Industrial Conference Board, 1949.

PEACOCK, A. T. *The Economics of National Insurance*. London: William Hodge, Ltd., 1952.

————. "Social Security and Inflation," *Review of Economic Studies*, No. 53, 1952–1953, pp. 169–173.

25 The Economics of the Public Debt

► THE TREND OF THE FEDERAL DEBT

The federal debt had its origin in the indebtedness inherited by the new republic in 1789 from the Confederation. This debt, amounting to about $75 million, was held in part domestically and in part by foreigners, and included the obligations of the individual states. Hamilton insisted that the federal government should assume the state debts. They had been incurred in the interest of the nation as a whole, and the federal government ought to proceed at once to place its finances on a creditworthy basis.

Until recently the federal government has been able to repay large amounts, and at times virtually the whole, of its wartime debt. In this its experience has differed greatly from that of most countries. It will be recalled from Chapter 1 that up to the Civil War public opinion was strongly opposed to a high level of spending by the federal government. At the same time the country was relatively free from war for a period of about seventy-five years. The only important exception to this unbroken period of peace was the War of 1812, when the federal debt rather more than doubled, from $56 million in 1812, to $127 million in 1815.[1] A sizable portion was quickly repaid, however, and, except for one year, repayments were made steadily until the debt was virtually extinguished in 1834.

Although financial and economic crises contributed to a subsequent rise, in view of the rapid growth in population and national income, the interest-bearing federal debt remained insignificant until the Civil War. During that war it rose substantially (to $2.3 billion by 1866). Again, however, the debt was rapidly repaid as tax rates after the war remained for a time at high levels, and as a prolonged period of prosperity brought in revenues in excess of those needed by a government committed to a policy of relatively low expenditures.

---

[1] *Annual Reports* of the Secretary of the Treasury. The rise in the debt associated with the Mexican War, though greater in percentage terms, was smaller in terms of dollars, and much smaller in relation to national income.

The interest-bearing federal debt remained virtually constant at slightly under $1 billion from 1901 to 1916, and therefore became relatively less significant year by year. The great rise (to $25 billion) in World War I was again succeeded by a period of repayment in the twenties that had brought the interest-bearing debt down to $16.5 billion by 1931. Thereafter, the decline in revenues during the depression, coupled with various public works projects in the interest of relief and re-employment, again caused a sharp rise, this time to about $40 billion by 1939. Borrowing during World War II had lifted the debt to the enormous level of $268 billion by June, 1946, and although some of this debt could be repaid after the war (reducing the debt to $250 billion by June, 1948), events of the cold war and the war in Korea again reversed the trend.[2] As of May, 1955, interest-bearing debt of the federal government was $275 billion.

► BRITISH AND FRENCH EXPERIENCE

The contrast between American and European experience with debt repayment in the nineteenth and early twentieth centuries is striking. On grounds of political and military circumstances, as well as of attitudes toward a large national debt, the sense of urgency for debt repayment that characterized American thinking was absent in Europe.

For example, Britain's debt rose from around £15 million in 1700 to over £400 million in 1800. This rapid increase was continued throughout the Napoleonic Wars. Thereafter the debt leveled off at about £800 million, declining only slightly (except for a rise during the Boer War) to about £650 million by the eve of World War I.[3] During that war the debt rose precipitately to about £8 billion (by 1921). The trend of the debt in France throughout the nineteenth century was quite similar to that of Britain. In both countries the debt at the end of the nineteenth century stood far above its level in 1800. Although the rate of increase in the French debt was less during the years of increase, the long period of virtual stability in the British debt had no counterpart in the experience of

---

[2] In part this repayment of debt immediately after the war was fictitious. The debt had been inflated by the working balances carried by the Treasury in the commercial banks throughout the country, which at their peak in early 1945 reached $26 billion. Since they were no longer needed after the war they were quickly liquidated.

[3] Cf. A. H. Hansen, *Fiscal Policy and Business Cycles* (New York: Norton, 1941), pp. 136–137. It is interesting to note that whereas Napoleon financed a large share of the wars with England (1793 to 1815) by levies on occupied territory, England not only had to tax herself and borrow to support her armies, but also was forced to raise large sums to subsidize allies. The resemblance of her position to that of the United States since 1945 is obvious. Cf. E. J. Hamilton, "Origin and Growth of the National Debt in Western Europe," *Papers and Proceedings* of the American Economic Association, May, 1947, p. 128.

France. However, France's debt increased relatively more than did Britain's in World War I.

The major reason for the rise in the debts of the nations of Europe during these years was continual war and threat of war. An additional reason was the growth of the idea that it is a proper function of government to furnish a wide variety of services to the public. These services, though made necessary by the progress of industrialism, could not be provided by the private sector. Again, the rise of the public school occurred largely in the nineteenth century; a minimum education was needed to make possible an effective industrial working force. Moreover, governments increasingly borrowed for the purpose of making capital improvements, for example, railways. At the same time, advantage was not taken of periods of high income to reduce debt levels.

▶ THE NATIONAL DEBT AND GROSS NATIONAL PRODUCT

It is, of course, misleading to trace the trend of the national debt solely in terms of dollars. A different impression is derived by relating the debt to gross national product, and still another if interest payments on the debt are compared with GNP. A secular rise in GNP reduces the relative importance of each dollar of debt. Moreover, if debt is not repaid, taxes have to be found only for the interest payments. If interest rates are gradually falling, the tax burden falls correspondingly, and conversely if interest rates are rising.

On both the above counts, the real burden of each dollar of federal debt has been declining in recent years. Consequently, there has been *some* degree of rise in the debt that could be financed without any increase in tax burdens. Recognizing that over-all ratios conceal many things, we may nevertheless glance at the relevant statistics.

National debt was a slightly smaller percentage of GNP at the end of World War I than at the end of the Civil War (35 and 40 per cent, respectively).[4] After a sharp drop during the prosperous twenties, the ratio rose to 45 per cent in 1939. The financial methods used in World War II pushed the ratio up to a peak of 127 per cent in 1946. The postwar price and income inflation, however, contributed to a rise in GNP that had reduced the ratio to 91 per cent by 1950, and to 76 per cent by 1954.[5] In the absence of further substantial increases in the debt, the ratio would gradually decline.

The downward trend in the average rate of interest payable on the interest-bearing debt has helped to hold down the interest burden of the

---

[4] Cf. Henry Murphy, in K. E. Poole, ed., *Fiscal Policies and the American Economy* (New York: Prentice-Hall, 1951), p. 163.

[5] *Economic Reports* of the President; *Annual Reports* of the Secretary of the Treasury.

federal debt. In 1920 the annual interest charge amounted to 4.2 per cent of the interest-bearing debt, whereas the percentage had declined to slightly less than 2.0 by 1943. The decline in interest rates was due to a complex of factors, including changes in savings and demand for investment funds during these years, and in the thirties also to the pressure on rates exerted by the huge increase in excess commercial-bank reserves, caused jointly by the gold inflow from Europe and by federal reserve policies. It was also attributable, after 1939, to a change in the composition of the debt in favor of securities bearing a lower rate of interest.

The true rate of interest on government debt has declined even further than the nominal rates, because no part of the interest on the federal debt now being issued is exempt from the federal income tax. Finally, however, it should be noted that as a result of federal reserve pressure for higher interest rates, there was some tightening after 1950. In any case, little if any scope exists for further relief through declining rates.

▶ STATE AND LOCAL DEBT

HISTORICAL

State and local borrowing has taken a markedly different course from that which characterizes federal borrowing. The dislike of public spending that prevented a substantial increase in federal debt during the first half of the nineteenth century did not extend to state and local finance. The states played a dominant role in the vast capital investment required to finance the transportation facilities that made possible westward expansion in the second quarter of the century. Per capita state debt increased from $2 in 1829 to over $10 in 1839.[6]

Unfortunately, the states counted on financing their borrowing through the income from their railroads, roads, and canals,[7] but the financial panic of 1837 forced the abandonment of many of these enterprises. Defaults followed, which in the case of foreign bondholders gave rise to bitter feelings against some of the American states. This experience did not prevent a subsequent recurrence of heavy state borrowing, and the constitutions of a number of the states were revised to prohibit a repetition of past excesses.

The localities, too, were under much pressure to expand their expenditures, and, therefore, in view of their limited capacity to tax, their borrowing. In addition to borrowing for local construction, they made subsidies to railroads and even engaged in experiments in municipal ownership of public utilities. The fact that the municipalities require the per-

---

[6] P. Studenski and H. Krooss, *Financial History of the United States* (New York: McGraw, 1952), pp. 7, 129.

[7] The popularity of state investment in internal improvements was due partly to the great success of the Erie Canal, which had paid for itself within ten years of its completion in 1825.—*Ibid.*, p. 129.

mission of the states in order to increase the statutory level of their borrowing was no serious obstacle, for this permission was usually obtainable during the era of great expansion.

Another period of heavy state and local borrowing occurred during the years 1900 to 1930. In the twenties, for example, the decline in federal debt was offset by increased state and local borrowing. This time the reason was the rapid expansion in the services required in connection with the growth of automotive transportation and rapid urbanization. A road network had to be built, and increasing population density and the changing conceptions of the services required to maintain the population in health and security forced a rise in expenditures which could not be financed out of current taxes. Per capita state debt rose from $3.56 in 1913 to $18.91 in 1932.[8] The relative rise in per capita local debt between 1913 and 1932 was not as great (from $35.75 to $121.88).

As the depression came to an end the finances of both the states and the localities gradually improved. Per capita state debt (as of 1942) had risen only slightly above that of 1932 (to $20.42), while per capita local debt had dropped substantially to $109.16. Because of the extremely low level of national income in 1932, the ratio of state and local debt to income rose sharply, but rising income as the depression lifted brought about a reversal of the movement. Taking state and local debt together, the decline in this ratio between 1932 and 1942 was from 37.1 per cent to 14.9 per cent.

The finances of the states and the municipalities were further strengthened during World War II. On the one hand, tax yields were stimulated by income and price inflation. On the other, expenditures were necessarily curtailed because of the unavailability of resources for construction. Much debt was retired during the war, and surpluses were built up that permitted a delay in the rise of property and other state and local tax rates after 1945.

Since the war, however, the trend of debt has been sharply upward. So far as state debt is concerned, cash bonuses to veterans have been largely responsible for this movement. Much of the postwar construction of highways, hospitals, schools, and the like, by states and municipalities has been financed out of surpluses built up during the war, but the prospect is for increased borrowing for these purposes in the future. Indeed, it can be argued that total welfare would be increased if state and local borrowing for construction purposes were to be increased even at the expense of a measure of business borrowing for expansion of plant.

NONGUARANTEED DEBT

Not the whole of state and local debt is backed by the "full faith and credit" of the borrowing government. As of June, 1952, for example, about

---

[8] Bureau of the Census, *Historical Review of State and Local Government Finances*, June, 1948, p. 33.

$5 billion was nonguaranteed, of which cities owed about 50 per cent. The remainder had been issued by special districts and state institutions and agencies.[9] Since 1937 the popularity of this type of debt has been increasing. By the end of 1952, out of total state debt of $6.6 billion, 26 per cent was nonguaranteed debt.[10] This was a rise of nearly half a billion dollars over the previous year. Much of this nonguaranteed debt represents borrowing for self-liquidating enterprises; but for the states, for example, nearly half of it has arisen in connection with the ordinary activities of government.[11]

The issuance of nonguaranteed debt permits evasion of a constitutional prohibition or limitation on borrowing. The debt is serviced out of the proceeds of an earmarked tax.[12] For example, nonguaranteed state debt for highway construction may be serviced out of gasoline tax receipts. The use of these revenue bonds has the further advantages that capital projects can be undertaken without recourse to the electorate and that nonguaranteed debt does not affect the creditworthiness of the state's ordinary debt issues. The latter advantage would disappear, however, if a nonguaranteed issue actually came to be in jeopardy. In order to maintain its general credit standing, the state would have to support the issue. Other disadvantages are the danger that the device might be abused, and that the earmarking of taxes for special purposes disintegrates the budget, thus impairing budgetary control.

► PRINCIPLES OF DEBT REPAYMENT

Central governments not only possess the power to tax, but they also have the exclusive right to create money. Consequently, they are not always under the pressure to repay debt that operates to induce business firms and individuals to minimize indebtedness. As we have seen, a given level of public debt represents a decreasing burden, in terms of taxes for debt service, as population and national income grow. Nevertheless, it is a fact that a rise in the debt ordinarily means a higher volume of interest payments and, for a time at least, the need for higher tax rates. Moreover, the feeling is strong that governments ought to adopt the same sense of responsibility toward their debts that is expected of private borrowers. The consequence is that Congress and Presidents have habitually remained alert to opportunities to repay debt.

---

[9] Bureau of the Census, *Government Debt in 1952,* p. 2; and the same agency's *Debt of Governments, 1953.*

[10] Bureau of the Census, *Summary of State Government Finances in 1952,* p. 16.

[11] Cf. G. P. Smith, "Who Owes State Debt?" *Tax Review,* August, 1950.

[12] The device has also been used at the federal level. An example is Commodity Credit Corporation borrowing at commercial banks in 1953 and 1954, which was done in order to avoid exceeding the federal debt limit. Another is the indirectly guaranteed financing of public housing.

The decision with respect to debt repayment rests, of course, with the ultimate budgetary authority. In this country that authority is in the hands of Congress. Borrowing and debt repayment are the resultant of prior decisions to spend and to tax. Technical devices designed to facilitate the repayment of debt can operate successfully only if there is a budgetary surplus.

Suppose, for example, that bonds are issued to be redeemed serially in subsequent years. Clearly, unless there is a budgetary surplus, new bonds must be issued to replace those which are maturing, and on balance nothing is accomplished. A similar device is the statutory sinking fund, which provides that a certain amount of taxes be allocated each year to the redemption of the outstanding debt. Because of the popularity of this device in the past (it has not been used for twenty years at the federal level, but is extensively employed in state and local government finance), it deserves a brief mention.

The most obvious criticism of a statutory sinking fund is that unless revenues exceed spending it is meaningless.[13] One security is issued to redeem another. But a sinking fund requirement may be worse than meaningless. It may raise the interest cost to the government. This will be the case if interest rates rise, and the government is forced to retire lower-interest-bearing debt with funds realized through the issue of new debt at a higher rate of interest.[14]

REFUNDING AND CONVERSION

Any reissuance of debt is known as refunding. Refunding is met with most commonly when an excessive amount of short-term securities matures in a given budgetary period. In these circumstances, the debt must either be repaid, be replaced with new short-term issues, or be replaced with long-term issues. From the point of view of the Treasury, this is a

---

[13] Probably the most famous sinking fund was that of Prime Minister Pitt, who in 1786 allowed himself to be argued by the persuasive Dr. Price into reestablishing Walpole's sinking fund. The financial strain of the Napoleonic Wars required new borrowing far in excess of the annual statutory debt retirement. Despite the transparency of the fiction, Pitt's sinking fund was continued until 1830. See A. W. Acworth, *Financial Reconstruction in England, 1815–1822* (London: King, 1925), Chap. IV.

[14] The federal government took the sinking fund seriously from the days of the Funding Act of 1790 until the passage of the National Industrial Recovery Act in 1933. Hamilton regarded the sinking fund as an instrument of fiscal policy. If the fund borrowed from the banks, treasury cash would be built up, and credit would be contracted. Conversely, the fund could purchase government securities, and thus pour hitherto idle cash into the economy. Cf. Studenski and Krooss, *op. cit.*, p. 53. Much more recently, the National Industrial Recovery Act provided that an amount equal to 2½ per cent of public works expenditures be appropriated each year to a sinking fund. Since a large deficit was being incurred each year, this provision meant that the debt was simply being partially refunded. The practice was halted in 1937, the Treasury commencing to exercise discretion on the amount of debt retired each year under the sinking fund provisions.—*Ibid.*, p. 427.

delicate operation. When long-term securities are issued to replace maturing short-terms, the price at which the new securities are issued, and therefore their interest rate, is at the mercy of the market. Since the purpose of refunding in this case is to obtain permanent lodgment of the debt in the hands of savers, federal reserve support purchases can be relied on only temporarily as a means of assuring orderly marketing.

The pattern of interest rates may be such that an interest saving will be made if long-term, higher-interest debt is replaced with notes and certificates bearing a lower rate of interest. This course was adopted, for example, in 1949, with a resulting saving in interest charges. An adverse effect, however, is the greater vulnerability of the Treasury to changes in interest rates. Because of the increased frequency of maturities it is forced to keep close contact with the money market, and may therefore be induced to attempt to maintain control over interest rates. Efforts in these circumstances to support the price of government bonds may result in excessive money market liquidity and a tendency to inflation.[15]

TRADITIONAL ATTITUDES TOWARD NATIONAL DEBTS

1. "The Debt as a Mortgage on the Future."   Events in recent years have brought about a marked change in the public attitude toward government debt. Traditionally debt has been regarded as a burden, and as a "mortgage on the future." Interest has to be paid on the debt, and taxes must therefore be levied on individuals who may not have been born when the decision to borrow was taken. The burden is still greater if debt is repaid. Thus, it was thought, not only is debt burdensome, but a particular generation may be the more willing to incur debt if people are secure in the knowledge that repayment must be made by those who come later. It was not appreciated that when debt is repaid, bondholders in a given generation receive purchasing power that has been taken from taxpayers *in the same generation.* In the period when the government borrows, savers surrender purchasing power to the government, and thus spare the taxpayer from having to do so. The reverse occurs when the debt is serviced or repaid.

In one sense, however, the burden of a debt may be shifted from one generation to another. The taxes necessary to amortize the debt may have to be superimposed on other taxes that are already weakening incentives to produce. It is clear that, if this is so, *other things being equal,* the later generation would have been better off if the earlier one had refrained from incurring as great a debt. But the phrase "other things being equal" is the key to the whole problem. Other things cannot be equal, since government spending of the proceeds of the borrowing must inevitably have affected the military and economic potential of the borrowing nation. Later generations might be still worse off if the country had lost a war; or, for that

---

[15] The bond-price-support program is discussed in a later section of the chapter.

matter they might be economically better off. Again, the proceeds of the borrowing in earlier years might, or might not, have been spent in such a way as to cause a more rapid increase in productivity than would have occurred had the savings been lent to private borrowers.

2. *"Government as Analogous with a Business Firm."* The traditional attitude toward debt, which even at the present time is shared by a large proportion of the general public and businessmen, was that the government is similar to a private business and ought to finance its operations on the same principles.[16] Indeed, it was thought that the government should be even more cautious in its borrowing policies than private enterprise. The application of more rigid standards of orthodoxy to government finance is easy to understand in the light of the history of public expenditures and public borrowing. Much public borrowing is "unproductive" in the narrow sense in which it is used by businessmen. It does not result in the creation of capital equipment that can be amortized out of the sales of the end product. For many years the businessman's view had the authority of men like Adam Smith, who cast their eyes over the palpably unproductive expenditures of the sovereigns of Europe throughout the great age of wars and royal self-indulgence from the early part of the sixteenth century onward. It was concluded that any increase in public debt necessitates a corresponding decrease in the availability of capital for productive uses by private enterprise.[17]

3. *"Priority in Borrowing Resides with Business."* One further point should be made in connection with the traditional view of businessmen and bankers that government borrowing ought to be kept at a minimum. Implicit in the classical position was a feeling that business should have a priority in the market for loans. Thus John Stuart Mill called attention to the frictional losses that occur when capital is transferred from the private market to the government.

Under certain circumstances it is true that an increase in government borrowing can drive up the rate of interest. This will occur if the Treasury ignores the existence of a lively business demand for savings. Thus savers

---

[16] It may be noted in passing that the tendency in recent years for corporations to finance their capital needs from internal funds (undistributed profits and depreciation reserves) has arisen out of their *ability* to do so rather than because of any fixed conviction that it is inherently inadvisable to borrow.

[17] Much interesting material on the growth and role of public debt can be found in A. H. Hansen, *Fiscal Policy and Business Cycles* (New York: Norton, 1941), Chap. IX; P. Studenski and H. Krooss, *Financial History of the United States* (New York: McGraw, 1952); S. E. Harris, *National Debt and the New Economics* (New York: McGraw, 1947), Chap. IV; W. F. Stettner, "Sir James Steuart on the Public Debt," *Quarterly Journal of Economics,* May, 1945; *Papers and Proceedings* of the American Economic Association, May, 1947, Papers on public debt; H. Fisk, "History of the National Debt Prior to the World War [I]," in M. C. Mills and G. W. Starr, *Readings in Public Finance and Taxation* (New York: Macmillan, 1932); and C. J. Bullock, *Selected Readings in Public Finance* (Boston: Ginn, 1924), Chap. XXIII (on early views on the public debt).

would gain through higher yields on private and public issues at the expense of the businessman and the taxpayer. Yet exactly the same thing happens when one firm competes with another for loans. If the supply of loanable funds is fixed, any increase in demand drives up rates.

Evidently the real point being made is not that government borrowing drives up interest rates. Rather, it is being contended that government borrowing is inferior from the welfare standpoint to private borrowing. Furthermore, if the argument is made without respect to the prevailing level of business activity, there is an implied assumption that the supply of savings is fixed.

As recently as 1931–1932, it was argued that any substantial increase in government borrowing to finance public works expenditures would necessarily tighten interest rates, and thus prolong the depression. The assumption was, apparently, that the phenomenon of oversaving cannot exist or, alternatively, that the supply of loanable funds is fixed. The argument ignores the fact that the government can borrow newly created purchasing power so that the increase in the demand for loanable funds can be matched with an increase in supply, with zero or even negative effects on the interest rate. Again, if hoarded savings are activated, the added demand impinges on an elastic supply with no effect on interest rates.

4. "The Debt Promotes Inequality of Wealth." It was thought by some that a large government debt, by providing high-income savers with a safe form of investment, would contribute to the rise of an idle rentier or coupon-clipping class. However, the growth of the idea that all able-bodied citizens ought to have a gainful occupation has diminished the importance of this contention. Nevertheless, the argument might still be made that interest payments on the debt would encourage greater inequality of wealth.

The validity of the latter argument depends on the acceptance of the view that the higher-income groups would not be able to save at all if they were denied the opportunity to save in this particular form. They can, of course, put their savings into direct investment, real estate, stocks, and bonds. If their losses would have been greater under the latter alternatives than if they had invested in government securities, it follows that the existence of a government debt favors the saving classes. We do not have adequate information to say with confidence whether in the last one hundred years, for example, the yield net of risk on government securities was higher or lower than that on the various forms of private investment.

5. "A Rising Debt Encourages Spending." It is argued that once the principle of a rising public debt is accepted, an important weapon has been placed in the hands of those who advocate increased public spending. The constitutional prohibition on borrowing in effect in some states was introduced partly to discourage excessive spending. Certainly, the knowledge that expenditures can be financed by borrowing must on occasion encourage some degree of laxness in expenditure control. It should be noted, however, that at the federal level, at any rate, the major increases in public spending and the debt have occurred as a result of circumstances not subject to financial control, namely, wars and depressions. Moreover, until World War II, periods of war and rising public debt have been followed by periods of reduced spending and debt repayment.

6. *"A Large Public Debt May Necessitate a Capital Levy."*   A capital levy is a (usually) nonrecurrent tax on the various forms of wealth, ordinarily imposed after a war in an effort to reduce the burden of the debt. Naturally, it is an unpopular tax. In recent times capital levies have also served the purpose of helping to equalize the financial burdens of war by recapturing a portion of the wealth accumulated by those who have made high profits. Again, the capital levy is a means of equalizing the burden between those who have suffered war damage and those who have been fortunate enough to escape it.

Ordinarily a country which has accumulated a very large debt during time of war has also sold much of it to the banking system, or has issued a large volume of non-interest-bearing debt in the form of fiat currency. If this is so the real burden of the debt is reduced in proportion to the rise in the price level resulting from overissue. A capital levy is therefore unnecessary as a means of reducing the burden of the debt. A true capital levy is not restricted to the debt, but includes in its base all forms of property. The proceeds of the levy can be devoted, of course, to the reduction of the debt. But other taxes, for example the personal income tax, are better suited to the constant flow of revenues to the Treasury over the years that is required to reduce significantly a large war debt.

7. *"A Large National Debt Is Inflationary."*   A large debt may encourage the government to replace debt maturing in the hands of savers with new issues to the banking system. If new purchasing power is thus created during a period of high employment, the resulting price rise will amount to a haphazard form of taxation that is more inequitable than those taxes would have been that were consciously levied in the first place. An important reason for the unpopularity in some European countries of bond issues having a definite maturity is the fear that a large amount of debt might come due for redemption at a time that is fiscally inexpedient, thus forcing the debt into the banking system for monetization. The advantage to a government of a debt that does not mature on a given date is that the holder can liquidate it only at its market value. The holder, therefore, not the issuer, takes the risk of price fluctuations, although market price does affect the terms of *new* issues.[18] If maturing debt must be redeemed

---

[18] The British debt has in part consisted of "consols" (consolidated annuities), first used in 1751. They were issued without a fixed maturity date, to bear given rates of interest, and their market price has fluctuated in accordance with the supply and demand of loanable funds. In September, 1797, for example, the price quoted for consols was 47⅜, while in 1896 it rose to 114. Much of the former British penchant for sinking funds is attributable to the fact that part of the national debt

on a fixed date, a temptation necessarily exists for the government to look with favor on a rising price level, since this reduces the burden of the debt.

In a democracy a cold-blooded attempt to inflate in order to relieve the Treasury is not likely to be met with except in extremely abnormal circumstances, for it would have to run a gantlet of public opinion in which creditors as well as debtors would be represented. Yet it is true that public authorities cannot be unaware of the fact that an inflation engendered for quite other reasons facilitates the problem of debt management. Therefore, resistance to inflationary financial policies may well be lowered when the debt is extremely large.[19] Moreover, one must not underestimate the appeal of the argument that prices should be allowed to rise at least slightly during periods of rising public debt in order to favor the groups that are actively producing.[20]

▶ SELF-LIQUIDATING AND NON-SELF-LIQUIDATING DEBT

Debt may be classified according to whether it is self-liquidating or non-self-liquidating. The distinction relates to the sources out of which interest payments are financed and the principal amortized.

Self-liquidating debt is incurred in connection with those types of public investment which yield a return in dollars. The services sold by a publicly owned hydroelectric installation, for example, may be priced

---

had no maturity date, a circumstance which stimulates the search for automatic repayment devices. The reason for the high price of consols in 1896, for example, was automatic operation of the sinking fund, together with a high rate of saving and substantial debt repayment. Cf. the article "National Debt," *Encyclopaedia Britannica* (11th ed.; Chicago: Encyclopaedia Britannica, 1910), especially pp. 268–270.

[19] S. E. Harris points out that about three quarters of the Civil War debt was repaid at prices averaging one third lower than those which obtained when the debt was contracted, and that the average price level during the nineteen twenties was 21 per cent below that of 1918–19.—Harris, *op. cit.,* pp. 130–131. The experience after World War II has been the reverse, but there is no evidence that a desire to minimize the burden of the debt has ever played a significant role. It should be borne in mind that the burden of debt is not to be reckoned solely in terms of relative price levels during periods of borrowing and repayment. Account must also be taken of movements in productivity, population, and real national income. The incentive to inflate in order to reduce the burden of the debt would be greatest during a period of declining population and falling per capita real national income.

[20] This is the argument of Harris, *op. cit.,* p. 134: "The gains of progress should not go to those who receive interest on the basis of past commitments. . . . Rather the gains should go to the workers, the managers and the investors—to those, in short, who determine current output, not past output." This view involves a curious division of a man's life into its productive and nonproductive periods, which would appear to be hard to justify during an age of rapid technological progress and lengthening life span. A man might live through fifteen or twenty years of retirement, watching the annual increments to productivity going to younger managers and workers, who were making no greater contribution to progress than he had done, but were merely fortunate enough to be born later. On the other hand, it has to be admitted that medical progress may so lengthen the period of a man's inactive life that without a secular rise in prices an unduly large proportion of real national income each year will be paid to those who have retired. This problem is of importance in connection with the financing of social security.

high enough to yield the going rate of return for this kind of project after all costs have been covered. In this case, with the undertaking free of public subsidy, there is no economic difference between the government debt created to finance an expansion of plant and equipment and private debt incurred for the same purpose.

Non-self-liquidating debt arises out of government investment which yields no direct return in dollars but lowers costs and increases the productivity of the private sector of the economy. Examples are reforestation, the building of roads, airports, and communications facilities, and the exploitation of natural resources. Less obvious but equally valid examples are investment in secondary school education, aid to universities, and public health programs. Spending of this sort is a necessary condition for a high level of real income in a modern industrial state. Therefore, public debt incurred in order to make the private sector of the economy more efficient may contribute to a higher level of tax revenues out of which the debt can be amortized. If the effect is to increase money income and spending, tax receipts rise automatically. Alternatively, if the effect is to lower cost of production, the Treasury's dollar will buy more.

It has to be noted, however, that although developmental public investment is a necessary condition for a high level of income, it is not a sufficient condition. For example, an increase in the efficiency of labor due to higher educational and health standards cannot result in a higher level of income unless labor is kept fully employed. Again, there is no definite connection between (1) the cost of government borrowing in order to improve the physical and institutional framework within which the private-enterprise system operates and (2) the automatic rise in public revenues which accompanies any resulting increase in the level of income. All we can say is that a part of the annual increment to productivity is ascribable to government spending, and that this may justify borrowing for projects that are not necessarily self-liquidating.

Non-self-liquidating debt includes what used to be commonly known as dead-weight debt. This is debt incurred to finance public investment which results in neither additional tax receipts nor decreased costs to the government. Examples are borrowing to build a dam that is subsequently washed away, and debt incurred for relief payments, the prosecution of war, and the like.

HOW USEFUL IS THE CONCEPT "DEAD-WEIGHT DEBT"?

The distinction between self-liquidating and non-self-liquidating debt clarifies thinking on the welfare considerations involved in borrowing for public projects. The usefulness of the concept of dead-weight debt as synonymous with "paying for a dead horse," particularly when related to government debt but not to private debt, is open to question. It is easier to recognize apparently dead-weight public debt than it is to know when private borrowing has resulted in abortive investment. Anyone can see, for example, that military equipment must either be destroyed or become obsolete. But private investment likewise may be misdirected, and thus wasted. In the case of the latter, however, it may take an expert to perform the task of evaluating the profit prospects of the firm before we can know whether its investment policies have been successful or not.

The correct evaluation of the economic cost of borrowing requires a clear knowledge of how far apparently dead-weight public debt actually represents an investment that makes no contribution to national efficiency. For example, debt originating out of the payment of relief to the unemployed may not be associated with an absolute rise in income. On the other hand, as a result of the relief payments the level of real income may not have fallen as much as would have been the case if the consuming power of the unemployed had not been sustained. Therefore, tax yields may be higher than they would have been in the absence of the relief payments. Moreover, there might conceivably have been a further loss of real national income as a result of political tension if the government had done nothing for the unemployed.

War debt, likewise, is similar in some ways to private debt. Although the physical commodities produced for war purposes may have been destroyed,[21] the cost of the war can be regarded as a charge on the economy similar to certain of the costs included in the prices paid for privately produced goods. There is no great distinction between private investment to protect business property against fire and theft, and government investment in protection against attack from abroad.

Still another point may be made. Much war spending is devoted to the development of new products and techniques that are later converted to peacetime use. Although no attention whatever is paid to the relation between the cost of such investment and the direct and indirect dollar return that it may later yield, it is not entirely different from risky private investment. When forward-looking investment is made by private enterprise no market yet exists. It must be created. The close calculations of marginal analysis may therefore be nearly as inappropriate as in the case of government investment in military equipment and in production techniques that are in part later adapted to private use.

THE SIGNIFICANCE OF ASSETS BEHIND THE DEBT

The attempt to justify a large government indebtedness has sometimes led to a listing of the assets behind the debt. The idea is that to the extent that such assets exist, the public debt is put on a par with that of private industry. Certainly if a case can be made for business firms to

---

[21] Government war spending may cause a rise in *real* income. This occurred in the United States during the first two years of World War II. Thus not all of war debt can be regarded as "dead weight."

carry the asset backing of their debt on their books at *cost of acquisition,* the practice would hold equally well for the government. In neither case is the practice justified, however. For a business firm the ability to service debt depends on the earning capacity of the enterprise. The value of the assets is derived by the capitalization of earnings. For the government, except for truly self-liquidating debt (which, because of political pressures for subsidies is rarely found at the national level), there is little relationship between a given amount of the debt and the value of its asset backing.

Behind the depression debt there were, of course, a number of assets, of a very miscellaneous nature, some of which might conceivably be liquidated.[22] By 1937 government corporations and credit agencies had accumulated assets of nearly $4 billion. A "profit" of $2 billion, resulting from the devaluation of the dollar, was held in the exchange stabilization fund. Moreover, some of the public works projects were self-liquidating, and many more resulted in the creation of assets. Although the cost of these assets was known, their value was ambiguous. The social advantage might be small or great, but this consideration has no significance for debt backing.

CONCLUSION

We conclude that except for self-liquidating debt different standards have to be employed in judging the desirability of undertaking different items of debt-financed government and private investment. Whatever the ultimate success of private investment, decisions to invest and incur debt are based on calculations of discounted cost and total returns over the life of the investment. Public investment and borrowing, on the other hand, have to be undertaken in the light of the valuation put upon the benefits and costs by the public as interpreted by the budget-making authorities. Although economic considerations play an important part, the matter may become primarily political.

► A DEBT HELD BY FOREIGNERS

THE MECHANISM OF REPAYMENT

In assessing the economic effects of public borrowing for investment purposes, a sharp distinction must be made between public debt held domestically and that which is held by foreigners.[23] As we have seen, one of the arguments commonly made by those who minimize the seriousness of a large domestically held public debt is that "we owe it to ourselves."

---

[22] Cf. W. Withers, *The Public Debt* (New York: John Day, 1945), p. 53.

[23] Since the governmental debt of the United States is held domestically, this problem is not of direct interest to us. Our concern stems from the fact that we have made loans to foreign countries in connection with postwar reconstruction. The question is whether there are special obstacles to the repayment by foreign countries of their foreign-held debt.

Although this view oversimplifies the problem,[24] it is nevertheless true that when a debt is held outside the borrowing country, the debt service problem is more serious.

When debt is held by foreigners, interest payments and debt repayment can be effected only if supplies of exchange (i.e., the national currency) of the creditor country are available to those individuals in the borrowing country who must make the payments. Here difficulties arise which do not appear in connection with the service of domestically held debt. Foreign currencies must be purchased in the foreign exchange market, and the many influences that affect the international value of a nation's currency in the absence of a gold standard add greatly to the debtor's risk. Moreover, the act of debt service itself involves the purchase of the currency of the creditor country, and is therefore a factor tending to depress the value of the currency of the debtor nation.

If there were no obstacles to trade and to the movement of long- and short-term capital across national boundaries, this pressure would be eliminated. Decline in the relative value of the currency of the debtor country would make it a cheaper country to buy in, and foreign demand for its currency would rise. The currency of one nation, however, does not circulate within another, and there are international barriers to the free movement of commodities and capital. Consequently, a "transfer" problem arises that is much more serious than the similar problem that must be faced when a loan is repaid by individuals in one section of a country to creditors living in another part of the same country.

THE TRANSFER PROBLEM

If a relatively undeveloped country, for example, borrows from savers or from the treasury of a more industrialized nation, the debt can be serviced only if the lending country, either directly or through third countries, makes it possible for the borrower to obtain supplies of its currency. This it can do in a variety of ways, for example, through new loans, tourist travel, and immigrant remittances; and by purchasing more goods from the borrowing country than it exports to it. Ultimately, of course, it is expected that the loan will result in lower cost of production in the borrowing country, so that the debt can be serviced through the payments in foreign currency which it receives for its additional exports. This cannot occur, however, unless the lending country is willing to admit imported goods in competition with the output of domestic producers.[25]

---

[24] It neglects the frictional and disincentive effects involved in taxing to service the debt. See the review by J. E. Meade (*Economic Journal*, April, 1945, pp. 47–69) of Abba Lerner's *Economics of Control* (New York: Macmillan, 1944).

[25] The total credits and debits of any country or region are necessarily always in balance. This is inherent in the notion of a balance of payments. If, for example, a country has an excess of imports over exports which is not offset by an excess of demand for its currency arising out of such items as emigrants' remittances, expendi-

Moreover, when loans are granted for the reconstruction of war-devastated industries, costs do not necessarily fall enough to assure that the borrowing country will have an export surplus to the lending country. In this case special measures may have to be taken to assist the borrowing country to service its debt.

There is, of course, a transfer problem within a country as well as between two countries. If businessmen in Region A borrow from bankers in Region B, reserves flow from banks in the latter to those in the former. Later, when the loan is repaid, the flow is in the other direction. If Region A has an adverse balance of trade with Region B it experiences a loss of reserves. In this case, one or more items in the interregional balance of payments must be found to bear the burden of the adjustment. If the debtor region cannot attract those types of industries whose product is demanded outside its boundaries, then money income must fall until a balance has been restored. This is likely to entail a long period of painful readjustment, and perhaps a loss of population. The point is, however, that the adjustment can be made in the interregional case. As between nations, however, adjustment may be impossible. International barriers to the movement of commodities, capital, and population may prevent it. It is largely for this reason that delays and defaults so frequently occur in the repayment of international loans. If the loans have been formalized into long-term obligations, these defaults react adversely on a nation's credit standing. Consequently, it has become popular in recent years for borrowing countries to try to minimize this danger by persuading the lending country to accept payment in commodities, or in the borrower's currency, rather than insisting on repayment in its own.

▶ ADVANTAGES OF A PUBLIC DEBT

Although prior to the thirties the weight of opinion in the United States had traditionally held that a public debt is a disadvantage, many economists pointed out that both public and private debt have certain advantages as well.[26] The fact was not overlooked that the rise of European

---

tures of foreign tourists, formal loans, and the like, it must be that other countries are holding supplies of its currency that it has used to pay for the excess of imports. But when one country holds supplies of another country's currency it is lending on short term for an indefinite period. This is the balancing item, a residual item whose magnitude is necessarily equal, and opposite in sign, to the net imbalance in all the other items in the balance of payments.

Even though total payments must always be in balance, this does not preclude the fact that a currency may be under selling pressure that tends to push down its value in terms of other currencies. This can be illustrated as follows. If we imagine a market for perishable goods (fruit), under competitive conditions the market must be cleared at the end of the day. Yet the price of fruit will rise or fall depending on the relative eagerness of sellers and buyers.

[26] See the collection of views on the public debt in Harold Groves, *Viewpoints on Public Finance* (New York: Holt, 1948), Chap. XI.

public debts in the eighteenth and nineteenth centuries was accompanied by an unprecedented accumulation of capital. Unfortunately, the frequent occurrence of wars, and the inability of governments to maintain the service of their debts, gave public borrowing a bad name that should have been reserved for the refusal of national populations to permit themselves to be taxed adequately during emergencies. The question remains to be answered whether the rise in public debts actually facilitated the rise in real income.

A SAFE INVESTMENT

One of the advantages claimed for a large public debt is the opportunity it provides for savers to be assured of the safety and liquidity of their assets. The argument runs that if wealthy savers can protect part of their savings, they are more likely to be willing to venture the remainder in risky enterprises. This advantage is enhanced to the extent that the Treasury appeals to different types of savers by issuing a wide range of securities, of varying maturities and terms of redemption, and carrying different rates of interest.

Against this argument it can be contended that if savers are protected from loss of savings in terms of dollars, they may prefer to play safe and withdraw entirely from the risky types of ventures which promise the most in the way of technological advance. Any clear-cut decision between these two points of view is complicated by the tremendous rise in *both* private investment and holdings of government securities in recent years. In any case, many business firms find it possible to finance investment outlays out of undistributed profits, without the necessity of recourse to the stock market or other sources of personal savings.

THE DEBT AND THE MONEY SUPPLY

The major advantage of the debt is the role it plays in permitting an increase in the money supply. Unless the quantity of money increases at a rate that is appropriate to the secular rise in the volume of transactions, a deflationary effect is exerted on the price level.[27] This in turn tends to cause windfall losses and thus discourages investment. Since population may be expected to continue to rise in the foreseeable future, and because a continued secular growth in transactions for money is to be anticipated, a corresponding secular growth in the money supply is necessary.

Modern monetary systems are based on debt. Both private and public debt may be monetized by being sold to the commercial banks. The banking system purchases the debt obligations with excess reserves, thereby creating new money. An elastic money supply is possible if private firms increase secularly the amount of their borrowing from the banks. Otherwise

---

[27] Assuming a constant velocity of circulation and no economies in the *use* of money.

government borrowing must step in to fill the gap. In any event, the proportion of total business borrowing which is represented by borrowing from commercial banks is not determined solely in the light of the monetary needs of the economy as a whole. Loans to business firms are made on the basis of thousands of separate business and banking decisions. These decisions are in no way concerned with the over-all adequacy of the money supply. Consequently, there is no reason to suppose that their aggregate effect on the volume of demand deposits will be such as to provide the economy with the appropriate amount of money at a given level of prices.

Table 16. Estimated Ownership of the Federal Debt, 1939, 1946, and 1955
(In billions of dollars)

Type of Holder	December 31, 1939	February 28,[a] 1946	April 30, 1955
Banking system			
Commercial banks	15.9	93.8	65.7
Federal reserve banks	2.5	22.9	23.6
Total	18.4	116.7	89.3
Other than banks			
Individuals	10.1	63.9	64.1
Insurance companies	6.3	24.4	15.0
Mutual savings banks	3.1	11.1	8.8
Corporations	2.2	19.9	20.6
State and local governments	0.4	6.7	15.7
U. S. government agencies and trust funds	6.5	28.0	48.9
Miscellaneous[b]	0.7	9.1	14.2
Total	29.3	163.1	187.3
All holders	47.7	279.8	276.7

[a] The date of the wartime peak.

[b] The item "Miscellaneous" includes such institutional investors as savings and loan associations, nonprofit institutions, corporate pension trust funds and brokers, and investments of foreign balances and international accounts in this country. The marked rise is explained by the rise in dollar national income, together with the liking of savings institutions for U. S. government obligations.

SOURCE: U. S. *Treasury Bulletin.*

The relation between bank loans to business and the money supply may be illustrated with reference to the two cases of war and depression. Between 1941 and 1945 a tremendous increase in the money supply was required in order to finance the expansion of output in connection with the war. Demand deposits adjusted for all insured commercial banks rose from

$38 billion at the end of 1941 to $75 billion at the end of 1945. Their total loans increased only from $21 billion to $26 billion in the same interval, while total investments in United States government obligations rose from $21 billion to $89 billion.[28] It can, of course, be argued that under the circumstances of war, firms were not permitted to expand borrowing; and that if they had been, bank loans to business would have risen sufficiently to provide all the additional money that was needed. Indeed, in the absence of adequate credit controls a demand inflation would have arisen in the private sector of the economy. To get a more complete picture, therefore, it is necessary to take a look at the role played by the banks with respect to the money supply during the depression.

Total loans of all commercial banks declined from $35.7 billion in June, 1929, to $15.7 billion in June, 1934. At the same time, commercial-bank holdings of United States government obligations rose from $4.9 billion to $10.3 billion.[29] By 1939 loans had increased by only $1.5 billion, while holdings of federal debt had risen by a further $6 billion. Yet from 1934 to 1939 gross national product rose from $64.9 billion to $91.3 billion. The role of the federal debt in permitting the increase in the money supply required to finance rising transactions during the recovery years is clear. The money supply was becoming increasingly based on public debt. The assertion that economic growth requires a rise in the volume of monetized debt is subject, however, to an important qualification. Changes in banking practice and in the nature of financial assets permit economies in the use of money. Therefore, while it is true that the existence of monetizable public debt is an important source of elasticity in the money supply, it would not be correct to say that long term growth in the transactions demand for money can be satisfied only by debt monetization.

▶ STRUCTURE OF THE FEDERAL DEBT

Debt management is concerned with the conditions of issue and redemption of public securities. Because of the large number of federal financial programs, the national debt is very complex. Moreover, it is not a simple matter to ascertain the total direct and contingent liabilities of the national government. The debt consists of both interest-bearing and non-interest-bearing securities. Of the interest-bearing debt, a part consists of marketable and nonmarketable issues, while the rest comprises a wide variety of special securities issued under many different government programs.

In addition to its direct debt the national government is responsible

---

[28] *Federal Reserve Bulletin.*
[29] *Midyear Economic Report* of the President, July, 1952, Table B–26.

on a contingent basis for a substantial number of programs sponsored by it. The quantitatively important contingent liabilities are unpaid obligations against appropriations; federal reserve notes; life, crop, and deposit insurance; and various type of loan guarantees.[30] A contingent liability does not have the same significance, of course, as the direct debt. Thus, although unpaid obligations against appropriations are in fact a part of the debt at a given moment, the expectation is that they will be liquidated in due course. Again, a contingent liability is a guarantee that the debt will be paid; it is not a debt in itself. The real significance of the contingent debt is that, with the growth of federal agencies, much of the borrowing that is done by them would otherwise have been undertaken by the government itself. Consequently, it is difficult to make a proper assessment of the importance of changes in the size of the direct federal debt.

When an increase occurs in the federal debt, a variety of judgments have to be made with respect to the form in which new debt is to be issued. Decisions must be reached on interest rates, maturities, negotiability, and terms of redemption. It has to be decided how far special appeals are to be made to various types of investors, and whether a particular issue may be held by commercial banks. Conversely, as debt matures, further decisions have to be made on the terms of reissue and, if the debt is being reduced, which issues are to be retired.[31]

OBJECTIVES OF DEBT MANAGEMENT

In the broad sense there is no disagreement over the proper objective of debt management. It is generally accepted that the national debt ought to be managed so as to make a maximum contribution to public welfare. Here the agreement ends, however, for a sharp cleavage of opinion exists on what constitutes public welfare, and on what role the debt plays in welfare economics.

One group of economists has argued that welfare is maximized if the debt is so managed that it exerts the minimum possible effects, either intended or unintended, on the economy.[32] They do not exclude the use of debt management to contribute to price stability; but aside from this limited objective they adhere to the view that a positive program of debt management designed to do more than this is likely to affect welfare negatively. Underlying this position, of course, is the conviction that the government

---

[30] See the discussion in C. C. Abbott, *The Federal Debt: Structure and Impact* (New York: Twentieth Century Fund, 1953), pp. 197 ff.

[31] Cf. Henry C. Murphy, *The National Debt in War and Transition* (New York: McGraw, 1950), for a discussion of the problems of debt management.

[32] Leading representatives of this view are Henry Simons, "On Debt Policy," *Journal of Political Economy,* December, 1944, pp. 356–361 (reprinted in *Economic Policy for a Free Society* [Chicago: University of Chicago Press, 1948]), and C. C. Abbott, *Management of the Federal Debt* (New York: McGraw, 1946). See also H. C. Wallich, "Debt Management as an Instrument of Economic Policy," *American Economic Review,* June, 1946, pp. 292–310, who regards debt management as more adapted to long-run techniques than to the mitigation of cyclical fluctuations.

should do no more than provide the basis for economic stability. If it goes farther than this, it may encroach on the private sector.

A contrary position is taken by those who believe that full employment cannot be assured merely by eliminating the rigidities and other

Table 17. The Federal Debt, 1946 and 1955
(In billions of dollars)

	February, 1946[a]	May, 1955
TOTAL FEDERAL DEBT	279.8	277.5
INTEREST-BEARING PUBLIC DEBT	277.9	274.8
Public marketable issues	199.8	158.4
Bills	17.0	19.5
Certificates	41.4	17.0
Notes	19.6	40.7
Bank eligible treasury bonds	68.2	81.1
Bank restricted treasury bonds	53.4	—
Public non-marketable issues	57.2	74.2
U. S. savings bonds	48.7	58.3
Treasury savings notes	8.0	2.8
Treasury bonds, investment series	—	12.6
Special issues	22.3[b]	42.2
Federal Deposit Insurance Corporation	0.1	0.8
Federal Home Loan Banks	—	0.2
Federal Old-Age and Survivors Insurance Trust Fund	5.9	17.7
Federal Savings and Loan Insurance Corporation	0.05	0.1
Government Employees' Retirement Fund	2.2	5.9
Government Life Insurance Fund	0.7	1.2
National Service Life Insurance Fund	5.2	5.2
Postal Savings System	0.8	0.1
Railroad Retirement Account	0.7	3.4
Unemployment Trust Fund	6.7	7.5

a Wartime peak.   b June, 1946.
SOURCE: *Treasury Bulletin*, July, 1955.

factors that limit the free play of market prices. They advocate a positive policy designed to make all possible use of the potentialities of debt management as one of the instruments of control,[33] and are not opposed to a major role for government in the determination of the level of national income.

Evidently, agreement would be much easier to obtain during a period when the debt is a relatively small proportion of national income. The

[33] For example, Harris, *op. cit.*, Chap. XXIV.

effects of debt management on the level and distribution of income would then be small, and its objectives would be mainly technical. They would be limited to (1) maintaining a relatively low interest rate in order to hold down the tax burden and to avoid any suspicion of a subsidy to bond-holders, who as a class need it least; (2) maintaining the debt at par value in order to facilitate flotation of new issues; (3) spacing maturities so as to assist in stabilizing the market; and (4) tailoring the types and maturities of the government obligations to the requirements of the various classes of savers who prefer to invest in government debt. In brief, when the debt is small, principles of debt management are not unlike those which govern the private borrower.

DEBT MANAGEMENT AND TREASURY CONVENIENCE

Many economists have argued that treasury convenience ought to rank low in the criteria for debt management. It is merely a technical matter to arrange maturities, interest rates, terms of convertibility, and so on, in such a way that the Treasury avoids the embarrassment of finding the market unprepared to take up its issues. Therefore, the federal government should take a broader view. Thus, it is contended that fitting the security to the investor is a more important objective than treasury convenience. The government is said to assume a sort of moral obligation to provide a satisfactory array of securities to the various types of savers, for it diverts a large proportion of total savings out of the private sector during depression and war years when the debt is rapidly increasing. The Treasury has indeed borne the needs of savers in mind in determining the terms of its securities issues. But convenience to savers is actually simply an aspect of marketing. It contributes to the assurance of a firm market for government obligations, and thus minimizes the need to rely on federal reserve purchases. Any borrower on the open market behaves in the same manner. The Treasury considers the needs of various types of savers in much the same way that an investment banker does so.

MINIMIZATION OF INTEREST PAYMENTS

Once the Treasury has adopted the practice of issuing a wide variety of securities, the volume of interest payments can be minimized by carefully exploiting the differences in the elasticities of demand for different types of public debt. In other words, the Treasury finds itself somewhat in the position of a discriminating monopolist. The existence of a wide variety of government securities permits the Treasury to take advantage of the compartmentalization of the market for loanable funds.

The extent to which the government should indulge in this practice depends on the relative consideration to be given to the interests of the types of savers who purchase government obligations and to those of the taxpayer. In view of the wide range of types of purchasers of government obligations, and of the even wider range of taxpayers, no strong case seems to exist for favoring savers, and the conclusion seems reasonable that the Treasury is justified in minimizing interest payments on the debt by means of discrimination on the basis of elasticity of demand.

► DEBT MANAGEMENT AND ECONOMIC STABILITY

Debt management has been defined above as the establishment of the conditions of issue and redemption of public securities. Government obligations may be held by savers, the commercial banks, and the reserve banks. Outstanding debt will be held by these three types of purchasers in a proportion that varies depending on a complex of economic considerations. Treasury debt management policy is an important element in these considerations, for the terms of issue will influence individual and business savers, as well as the commercial banks, in their decisions to hold or sell government securities. Thus debt management policy controls the degree of monetization of the debt, and therefore exerts a potential effect on the interest rate and the level of private spending. For when outstanding debt is sold to the commercial banks, excess reserves are absorbed; and when it is sold to the federal reserve banks, reserves are made available to the commercial banks.

In a technical sense the effects of debt management ought to be distinguished from the effects of budgetary cash deficits and surpluses when we are considering effects on the level of national spending.[34] If a deficit is incurred, two things happen. The Treasury pays out into circulation more money than it receives in taxes; and a joint decision is made with the market for savings with respect to the ownership of the newly incurred debt. In practice, debt management effects and fiscal effects are apt to be associated. Thus, if there is a budgetary surplus, the Treasury could devote the proceeds either to the retirement of debt held by savers, to the purchase of securities from the commercial banks, or to purchases from the reserve banks. Conversely, a deficit can be financed by sales of securities to savers, to commercial banks, or to the reserve banks.

When securities are sold to savers, purchasing power which, assuming a high level of employment, would have been made available to purchasers of inventories and equipment is diverted to the Treasury. The Treasury keeps a balance at the reserve banks that is sufficient for only a few days' expenditures, and draws all its checks on these accounts. Therefore, although the proceeds of the sales of securities to savers are deposited at the reserve banks, they are shortly checked out again. This is important because a rise in treasury deposits at the reserve banks decreases member-

---

[34] This point has been discussed from time to time in the literature on debt management in recent years. A recent reference is the review by Earl R. Rolph of C. C. Abbott's *The Federal Debt* (New York: Twentieth Century Fund, 1953), in *American Economic Review,* December, 1953, pp. 962–964.

bank reserves. But this decrease is only temporary, since the deposits are soon withdrawn. In any event, at the present time it is the policy of the Federal Reserve System to neutralize the effects of treasury financing on member-bank reserves. In brief, federal reserve policy is to prevent sales of treasury securities to savers from substantially affecting member-bank excess reserves.

Sales of securities to commercial banks absorb member-bank reserves. Provided the banks do not allow a corresponding amount of loans to private enterprise to run off, there has been a net monetization of debt. Here again the deposit of the proceeds of the sales of securities at the reserve banks would, in the absence of corrective action by the latter, draw down member-bank reserves. If the commercial banks did not have excess reserves they would be forced to demonetize private debt. In practice, however, the reserve authorities counteract this temporary pressure on bank reserves. Sales of securities to the banks are inflationary when the existence of excess reserves permits them to hold the new government debt in addition to the public and private debt already in their possession. In other words, bank-financed deficits are inflationary because new money is injected into the flow of purchasing power.

Finally, it may be that both savers and the commercial banks are simultaneously decreasing their debt holdings. In this case it is necessary that the reserve banks add to their portfolios unless the Treasury is willing to allow interest rates to rise sufficiently to permit the new debt to be marketed. Alternatively, it may be desired that the reserve banks purchase the debt in order to make new resources available to the member banks. Since 1951 the reserve authorities have not purchased all amounts of federal securities offered to them at set prices. In other words, the Federal Reserve System reclaimed its control over bank reserves. It would appear, however, that the system has not been insensitive to the financing needs of the Treasury. The correct policy during a depression, of course, would be to sell securities to the reserve banks. This would result in a rise in member-bank excess reserves, and thus would make certain that Treasury deficit finance did not drive up the interest rate to private borrowers.

EFFECTS OF TREASURY REPURCHASE

The financing of a budgetary surplus can likewise be accomplished in three ways. If securities are bought back from savers with the proceeds of tax receipts, savers' demand deposits rise and taxpayers' deposits decline. There is no effect on member-bank reserves because the increase in treasury deposits at the reserve banks due to the excess of tax receipts over budgetary expenditures is canceled by the decline when the Treasury repurchases securities from the savers. Any temporary effects on bank excess reserves are avoided by federal reserve open-market operations.

Repurchases of securities from commercial banks provide the latter with reserves which they are now free to relend. If the banks have not been loaned up, the result may simply be a rise in idle reserves. Thus a certain amount of debt has been demonetized. Alternatively, the banks may have been loaned up, in which case the proceeds of the redeemed debt may be relent to business borrowers, and no decrease occurs in the money supply. In this case, the deflationary effects anticipated from the budgetary surplus are prevented by debt management policy.

Lastly, the budgetary surplus may be devoted to repurchase of securities held by the reserve banks. In effect, deposits of taxpayers are drawn down at commercial banks, and reserves of the latter are reduced by a corresponding amount. If the banks are loaned up, and required reserves are, say, 20 per cent of demand deposits, a multiple contraction of loans and deposits in the banking system results. If, however, it is feared that a reduction in bank reserves may precipitate a recession, the reserve authorities can counteract the decline in reserves through open-market purchases. The latter alternative represents a combination of three separate policies: fiscal policy (the budgetary surplus), debt management (repurchases of securities from the reserve banks), and monetary policy (counteraction of the decline in bank reserves by open-market purchase of securities).

DEBT MANAGEMENT IN DEPRESSION AND BOOM

Debt management is a relatively minor instrument of control during a depression. It is largely restricted to creating a favorable monetary situation on which an expansion of investment and income can be based. Treasury sales of securities to the reserve banks increase the deposits and reserves of the commercial banks, and with a fractional reserve requirement the latter are thus in a position to add to their own portfolios. New money is created, but the effects of this operation on the willingness of investors and consumers to spend are very tenuous.

Money plays a more important role during prosperity than it does during depression. The task of debt management is then a more difficult one, but at the same time, it is likely to be more effective in stimulating or retarding spending. In combating inflation the problem is one of maximizing the proportion of the federal debt that is lodged in the hands of savers. This program has to be carried on in the light of competing private demands for funds. A debt management crisis is likely to appear during a period of prosperity occurring immediately after a major war.[35] Appeals to patriotism begin to lose some of their effect, and new issues of the Treasury are likely to meet increasing resistance from the market. Indeed, as corporate bondholders feel the need for cash to facilitate reconversion

---

[35] Thus the Treasury raised the rate for its new issue in April, 1953, to 3¼ per cent. The intention was to arrest the forces of inflation and "to channel new savings into government." The issue was opposed by those who foresaw, as a result, the tightening of interest rates to business borrowers.

to civilian production, government securities are disposed of in a market which may be already saturated.

It is at this point that a series of annual budgetary surpluses proves particularly helpful. During the five-year period ending June 30, 1951, for example, the Treasury retired about $27 billion of securities held by the commercial and federal reserve banks. It did this partly out of budgetary surpluses ($8 billion), to a large extent out of increased holdings of debt by savers, ($12 billion), and in part by a reduction of its own cash balance ($7 billion).[36] This reduction was roughly equal to the increase in commercial-bank holdings of private debt, and thus operated to offset the inflationary effects of the latter.

Repurchase of government securities from the commercial banks, however, leaves them in the position to relend the proceeds to business. The effect may therefore not prove on balance deflationary. Repurchase from the reserve banks, on the other hand, brings about a reduction in member-bank reserves and, if the banks are loaned up, forces them to curtail loans. Reserve-bank holdings of securities fell from $23.8 billion in June, 1946, to $18.3 billion in June, 1950. In the next year, however, they rose to $23 billion, while holdings of commercial banks continued to fall. Federal reserve cooperation with the Treasury in maintaining the price of government securities forced the acceptance of a passive open-market policy during this period.

LODGING DEBT WITH SAVERS

The large increases in government debt which occur during wartime can be kept out of the banks and placed in the hands of savers in two ways. Savers can be forced to invest part of their savings in government debt, or they can be encouraged to do so by making government debt an attractive form of investment as compared with the available alternatives.

One way of discouraging the holding by banks of government issues is to sell nonnegotiable, nonredeemable securities to savers and savings institutions. If government securities are nonnegotiable, they cannot be sold directly or indirectly to either the commercial banks or the federal reserve banks. If they are not redeemable, the saver cannot force the Treasury to reissue them to the banks. Once bought, they take the form of compulsory investment.

Obviously, this device cannot be used in a free market. Savers would hardly buy new issues if their old holdings were frozen. It is a device, however, that can be used in a free-enterprise economy during time of war. In such circumstances, motives of patriotism, coupled with the unavailability of both consumers' goods and productive resources, provide an

---

[36] Joint Committee on the Economic Report, *Monetary Policy and the Management of the Public Debt*, 82d Cong., 2d Sess., February, 1952, Statement by Secretary Snyder, Pt. I, pp. 11–12.

incentive to savers to retain their government securities. A diluted version of compulsory investment in government securities used in the war was the payroll deduction plan, which contained elements of coercion. A much stronger device is to require individuals to invest in government securities a portion of the savings which they involuntarily make during a period of consumer-goods rationing. During World War II Germany utilized this method of "freezing" the savings of individuals.

If no use is to be made of compulsory investment in government securities, the alternative is to work out a means of assuring that Treasury emissions are not only taken up by savers but are held until such time as budgetary surpluses permit redemption. This may be difficult to accomplish. The terms of issue of government debt during World War II complicated in two ways the postwar task of keeping the debt lodged in the hands of savers. First, a large proportion of the debt took the form of short-term issues, thus advancing the date when the Treasury would have to meet the test of the market. Second, a considerable number of bonds were issued with a maturity of ten years. This assured the bunching of maturities in the first half of the decade of the fifties. Both these circumstances kept the Treasury constantly involved in the problem of marketing its debt. The nature of the problem can be best appreciated if we take a brief glance at the debt situation in the years immediately preceding and during the war.

► DEBT AND THE DEPRESSION OF THE THIRTIES

The events of the thirties conspired to bring about an unusual pattern[37] of interest rates. During that decade a large increase in commercial-bank reserves, coupled with a low depression level of business demand for investable funds, resulted in declining interest rates. At the same time the desire for liquidity by investors and the commercial banks resulted in a far greater percentage decline in short-term than in long-term interest rates. This is shown in Table 18. We entered the war, therefore, with a highly unusual pattern of interest rates that had been established as a result of an extraordinary set of circumstances in the thirties.

Commercial-bank reserves grew steadily from 1934 onward. Large amounts of gold flowed into the country, primarily because of the flight of capital from Europe that accompanied the growth of power of the Nazis. The Federal Reserve System naturally became fearful of the ultimate inflationary potential of the growth in commercial-bank reserves. Notwithstanding a doubling of reserve requirements by 1937, excess reserves grew until they had reached $7 billion in 1940. As a result, despite the rapid

---

[37] Note the definition of the pattern of rates given by Murphy: "The 'pattern of rates' on United States securities consists of the market yields obtainable *on the same date* [his italics] on securities of different maturity."—Poole. *op. cit.*, p. 186.

growth in the federal debt caused by depression deficits, both long- and short-term rates trended downward.

Federal financial methods during the thirties played a role in preserving the low rate which had become established on short-term securities

Table 18. Bond Yields and Interest Rates, 1931 and 1940[a]
(Per cent per annum)

Type of Security	1931	1940	Percentage Decline
Long-term			
Corporate AAA bonds (Moody)	4.58	2.84	38
Long-term treasury bonds (partially tax exempt)	3.34	2.26	32
Short-term			
Treasury bills	1.40	0.014	99
Commercial paper (4–6 months)	2.64	0.56	79

[a] The federal reserve rediscount rate was 2.11 per cent in 1931 and 1.00 per cent in 1940.

SOURCES: Midyear *Economic Report* of the President, July, 1952, Table B–30; *Annual Report* of the Secretary of the Treasury, 1951, p. 818.

at the beginning of the decade. During the earlier part of the period, to be sure, most of the increase in the federal debt took the form of short-term securities, a development which worked in the direction of strengthening the short-term rate.[38] Thereafter, however, the bulk of the increase was in the form of (marketable) bonds. The result was twofold. The supply of short-term securities came to be deficient relative to the demand. Their prices therefore rose sharply, the effective interest rate at times going below zero.[39] At the same time the commercial banks' portfolios were so loaded with long-term federal obligations that the banks became more and more sensitive to the long-term rate of interest, and it was necessary for the Federal Reserve System to make certain that the long-term securities market remained stable, or "orderly."

The greater fluctuations that can occur in the prices of long-term

---

[38] The supply of short-terms tended to be in excess of the demand, thus driving down their market price and raising the effective interest rate.

[39] The reason that the interest rate on a security can go below zero is that the purchaser may have to redeem at par a security which he bought in the market at a price above par. If the interest which he collects during the period that he holds the security is less than the capital loss, his effective interest rate is negative. It will be recalled that if charges on checking accounts exceed the actual cost to the bank of maintaining the account, the interest rate payable on demand deposits is likewise negative.

securities, coupled with their strategic position in the portfolios of the banks, increased the importance of the function of the reserve banks in stabilizing the prices of government securities.[40] In brief, the country entered the war with short-term interest rates abnormally low, and faced a situation in which it seemed necessary to preserve this relationship in the interest of the holders of the outstanding debt, in particular the banks. It was feared that to allow a change in the pattern of short- and long-term rates might create uncertainty in the minds of investors, and thus delay the rate at which subscriptions were made to new loans.

▶ WORLD WAR II

It is not surprising that the Treasury did nothing prior to 1940 to encourage a rise in interest rates. The low rate held down interest charges on the debt. At the same time it was an advantage to keep interest rates low during a period of reluctant recovery from depression. Prior to Pearl Harbor the interest rate policy of the Treasury was passive. Thereafter, however, an active program was adopted to preserve the pattern of interest rates which existed on the eve of the war.[41]

It was agreed by the Treasury and the reserve authorities that interest rates should not be allowed to rise. Higher interest rates would increase bank profits at the expense of the Treasury. More important than this, however, would be the discouraging effect on war bond sales to savers if any hint were given that long-term interest rates would subsequently be permitted to rise.[42] The effects on public morale of the failure of a war bond issue might be serious. Stabilization of the pattern of rates removed this possibility, and among the steady purchasers of treasury bonds were the commercial banks themselves, which naturally preferred the higher interest-bearing issues to bills and certificates. The consequence was that the reserve banks tended to load their portfolios with the latter, at the same

---

[40] This discussion is based on *Annual Reports* of the Board of Governors of the Federal Reserve System, and Exhibit E, "Relation of Federal Reserve Policies to Fiscal Policies and Debt Management, 1946—October 1949," in Joint Committee on the Economic Report, *Monetary Policy and the Management of the Public Debt*, 82d Cong., 2d Sess., Document No. 123, 1952, Pt. I, pp. 351 ff. (reply to the Patman questionnaire by Chairman McCabe).

[41] In the fall of 1942 the Treasury indicated its intention to stabilize the rate pattern as follows:

90-day bills	⅜ per cent
1-year certificates	⅞
4–4½ year notes	1½
8–10 year bonds	2
Long-term bonds	2½

See P. A. Samuelson, "The Turn of the Screw," *American Economic Review*, September, 1945, p. 674.

[42] That is, those who bought at the higher price (lower interest rate) would experience a capital loss.

time providing new reserves to the commercial banks for a shift to longer-term issues.

As the war progressed, the abnormal prewar volume of excess bank reserves began to diminish, and the Treasury became concerned to make certain that the banks continued able and willing to purchase government securities. By the end of 1941, excess reserves of member banks had dropped to $3 billion, and they fell by another $1 billion in 1942. This meant that an increasing number of banks had little or no excess reserves. If they were to subscribe to war bond issues they would either have to curtail their higher interest-bearing loans to business or become indebted to their regional reserve bank. Since neither of these courses was attractive to the banks, other means had to be devised.

This was done as follows. On the one hand, reserves were made available to the banks through reserve purchases of government securities. On the other, federal deposits and short-term securities were subjected to more favorable terms than those accorded to private persons. For example, the reserve requirement against government demand deposits with member banks was removed. Consequently, if a bank shifted from private to public obligations, reserves would be released for further purchases of government securities. Thus additional earnings were provided which would offset the loss from the sacrifice of higher-interest-bearing private loans. Again, legislation in 1942 permitted the Board of Governors to change the reserve requirements of central reserve-city banks independently of those of reserve-city and country banks. By lowering the reserve requirements of central reserve-city banks, the board would be in a position to release reserves in the New York and Chicago districts, where particularly large sales of government securities were being made. Another expedient was the introduction of a preferential discount rate on fifteen-day advances by the reserve banks, secured by short-term government securities.[43]

THE FIXED PATTERN OF RATES AND THE MONEY SUPPLY

These various methods of favoring bank purchases of government securities were aimed at stimulating the market for short-term governments, and thus minimizing purchases by the Federal Reserve System. The maintenance of a wide spread between long- and short-term rates, however, meant that the banks would prefer the long-term, higher-rate issues. Thus the short-terms gravitated to the reserve banks. The repurchase option offered by the Federal Reserve System on the three-eighths per cent treasury bills made these securities the equivalent of cash, since the banks

---

[43] Devices were also used to restrict the granting of bank credit for nonessential purposes, and therefore to release reserves for the purchase of government securities. The major step in this direction taken in 1942 was Regulation W, which served to increase restrictions on consumer credit.

could sell them at any time to the reserve banks at par. Therefore the system lost control over the money supply.

Despite measures taken to prevent securities originally sold to savers from ending up in the commercial banks, reserve-bank purchases of the short-term securities had the effect of pegging their rates. Increased bank purchases of long-term securities drove down the long-term rate of interest. In other words, if long- and short-term securities are virtually interchangeable in bank portfolios, so that one is as liquid as the other, investors will prefer the security that bears the higher rate of interest. Therefore, the pattern cannot be preserved unless the Treasury sells long-term debt at a rate fast enough to prevent a decline in the long-term interest rate.[44]

THE DEBT, THE TREASURY, AND THE FEDERAL RESERVE SYSTEM

During World War II the point of view of the Treasury quite naturally carried greater weight than did that of the monetary control authorities. The main business was to win the war. Inflation control therefore necessarily played a secondary role. Given the size of the war effort, and the volume of tax revenues and borrowing from savers, the federal government must gain command over any deficiency of purchasing power regardless of the inflationary effects of its spending.

The requirement that the reserve banks support the prices of treasury obligations made a large part of the vastly increased debt virtually the equivalent of money. On the other hand, the methods of borrowing used in World War II were superior to a full-blown system of direct central-bank loans to the Treasury, for the views of the reserve authorities were interposed into the chain of events which brought about an increase in the money supply. Although the monetary authorities could not prevent an increase, they could publicize it, and, by striving for compromise, even slow it down. Moreover, direct controls over prices and production obviated the danger of an inflationary spiral during the war.

The question remaining unsolved, however, was the nature and extent of monetary control after the cessation of hostilities. Direct controls ought to be abandoned as soon as possible in order to permit a return to a normal peacetime free-enterprise system. Not only this, but if all price and other controls were abolished, how could one justify the continuance of a policy of keeping interest rates lower than they would have been if market forces were allowed to come into play? Again, would there be reason to think that the pattern of interest rates established prior to the

---

[44] As Murphy says: "When the market acquires absolute confidence in a given pattern of rates, it can no longer be maintained."—Poole, op. cit., p. 192. Chairman McCabe decided that the idea of stabilizing the level of rates during the war was a good one, but that it was not necessarily advisable to stabilize the abnormal structure of rates that existed at the end of 1941.—Joint Committee on the Economic Report, op. cit., p. 357.

war, and retained throughout the period of hostilities, would be appropriate during the subsequent period of peace?

THE ROLE OF THE FEDERAL RESERVE SYSTEM

One of the conditions of a free-enterprise economy is central-bank control over the money supply. Without that control, fluctuations in income and employment may be so great as to stimulate sentiment for direct controls over prices and output. The retention of the Treasury's power to require federal reserve support of the government securities market would postpone the time when the Federal Reserve System could effectively control the monetization of the debt. As matters stood in 1945, an un-anticipated combination of events might result in a sudden monetization of large amounts of securities. At the very moment when corporations and other businesses were selling government securities in order to finance plant expansion and renovation, millions of small savers might decide to purchase hitherto unavailable homes and durable consumers' goods.

THE ROLE OF THE TREASURY

Obviously both the Treasury and the Federal Reserve System must share responsibility for controlling the quantity of money. The Treasury possesses a number of powers which inevitably affect the volume of bank reserves and deposits. Since the days of Alexander Hamilton, Secretaries of the Treasury have been conscious of these powers, and on a number of occasions have used them to increase or decrease the money supply. Although at times protests have been raised against the exercise of mon-etary powers by the Treasury, it appears likely that its role will not diminish significantly.[45] Indeed, in some of the "welfare" states the central bank has been placed under the control of the Ministry of Finance. In the American type of mixed economy, however, the reserve authorities must have an important say in matters of monetary control. Only the Federal Reserve System is solely occupied with the control of the interest rate and the quantity of money in order to preserve economic stability.

▶ THE TREASURY–FEDERAL RESERVE CONTROVERSY

After the close of World War II a cleavage of opinion arose between those who thought the wartime pattern and level of interest rates was artificial and should be modified, and those who objected to any change in

---

[45] For example, protests against the right of the Treasury to switch deposits between the commercial banks and the reserve banks. An increase in treasury deposits at the latter causes a decrease in member-bank reserves. This result may be contrary to the desires of the reserve authorities. A fully coordinated Reserve-Treasury policy would, of course, remove the difficulty. Moreover, there is no objection to the use of the device to minimize the impact of tax collections and debt operations on the money market.

policy. The Treasury subscribed to the latter view, and the federal reserve authorities to the former. Both were able to find economists to support their positions.[46] A sharp rise in interest rates would involve bondholders in losses, and it was argued that this not only might threaten the solvency of the banks but also could greatly complicate the problem of debt management. The market should be kept "orderly." But did an orderly market mean rigid supports under government security prices? If so the Federal Reserve System could not regain control over the money supply. Federal reserve purchases to support the prices of government securities, and thus to prevent the interest rate from rising, would continue to make the debt freely convertible into money.

The point was often made by treasury spokesmen that if the rise in the interest rate (fall in the prices of treasury issues) were to be more than very minor, it might reflect on the credit of the federal government. If, on the other hand, the rise were small, it would do little good in arresting an inflation. It was also pointed out that a rise in the interest rate would increase the cost of servicing the debt. If Congress refused to vote additional taxes, therefore, the Treasury might be forced into further borrowing. This would offset, or more than offset, the anti-inflationary effects of the removal of supports from government securities prices.

Opponents of the treasury view argued that the important thing was not interest rate as *cost*; no one supposed that a moderate increase in the interest rate would result in a halt in the rise in investment during a generally inflationary period. The significance of the rise in the interest rate rested, on the contrary, on the fact that holders of government securities could no longer depend on the reserve banks to buy them at par. In other words, they would no longer be equivalent to money.

The area of disagreement between the Treasury and the federal reserve authorities was not as great as one would have supposed from reading contemporary newspaper reports of statements by representatives of the opposing camps. Both favored a monetary policy aimed at economic stability, and both realized that the stability of federal security prices could not be left to the whim of the investor. Much of the warmness which sometimes characterized the public statements issued by spokesmen for each agency is attributable to the growing pains that inevitably accompanied the tremendous rise in the debt during a period of war, superimposed on several years of deficit finance during depression. The dispute was

---

[46] See the discussion in C. C. Abbott, *The Federal Debt: Structure and Impact,* Twentieth Century Fund, 1953, pp. 27 ff., as well as the references to L. H. Seltzer, "Is a Rise in Interest Rates Desirable?" *American Economic Review,* December, 1945, pp. 831–850, and L. V. Chandler, "Federal Reserve Policy and the Federal Debt," *American Economic Review,* March, 1949, pp. 405–429. The controversy aroused such interest that a thorough airing of the problem was provided for the use of the Joint Committee on the Economic Report. See *Monetary Policy and the Management of the Public Debt,* Hearings before the Subcommittee on General Credit Control and Debt Management, and the Replies to the questionnaire, Pts. I and II.

finally settled in favor of the reserve authorities in the so-called Accord of March 4, 1951, and the debt was unpegged, though orderly market conditions were to be maintained in a less rigid sense than that of the Treasury. Since that time the Federal Reserve System has been in a position to pursue an active policy with respect to monetary control. Its role reverted to its prewar status. It must be borne in mind that the reserve authorities had traditionally taken into account the need for a dependable market for government debt.

► A PROPOSAL FOR AVOIDING DEBT MONETIZATION

The difficulty of keeping the government debt in the hands of savers when strong competition for savings is offered by the private sector has led some economists to search for a more dependable device than the interest rate.[47] One proposed solution would be for the Treasury to issue only two types of securities instead of the complex structure of "tailored" debt that has grown up in recent years. An earnest advocate of this approach was Henry Simons, who urged that federal securities should consist of only two types, currency and consols.[48] Currency is defined as the non-interest-bearing certificates of indebtedness (greenbacks) of the federal government, and would be the only type of debt, either public or private, that could be monetized.[49] The amount of debt thus monetized would be determined by the monetary needs of the economy at that level of national income which corresponds to full employment. Consols are interest-bearing government debt issued to savers without a definite maturity, whose price is allowed to fluctuate freely in the market for savings.

By issuing consols the Treasury would, like other borrowers, accept the rate of interest that is established in the market for loanable funds. Among the forces which would depress the price of consols, and thus raise the cost of government borrowing, would be an attempt to borrow more savings than are flowing to market. Thus the Treasury would be recognizing that the interest rate has the function of rationing a limited annual increment of savings. By allowing the interest rate to fluctuate freely, it would cease the practice of subsidizing the taxpayer at the expense

---

[47] Not all economists would agree that a proposal as novel as the one discussed in this section is worthy of consideration. Nevertheless, it serves as a useful benchmark for a discussion of Treasury–Federal Reserve relationships.

[48] Cf. his article "On Debt Policy," *Journal of Political Economy*, December, 1944, reprinted in the collection of his essays entitled *Economic Policy for a Free Society* (Chicago: University of Chicago Press, 1948).

[49] Simons urged that reserve requirements against demand deposits be raised to 100 per cent. This would prevent the new currency issued to the banks from increasing bank reserves. With 100 per cent reserve requirements the quantity of money would increase by the exact amount of the treasury currency issued to the banks. Control would then be complete, and the entire attention of the monetary authority could be concentrated on providing the "correct" money supply.

of the saver. In thus refraining from laying claim to savings that do not exist, the Treasury's debt management policy would cease to be inflationary.

In evaluating the Simons proposal it may be pointed out that, apart from administrative difficulties, an obstacle to the acceptance of simple and logical devices is that they often avoid meeting political issues which cannot be pushed aside. The point at issue is not merely to find a means of exempting the Federal Reserve System from supporting the market for government securities. Rather, it is whether or not the public approves of a federal tax-spending policy which on occasion requires government securities to be bought with bank-created new money. If so, it is idle to hope that the only reason for monetizing debt will be the monetary needs of the economy. Granted an adequate tax policy, and a recognition by the government that the annual increment to savings is limited, and must be shared with the private sector, the need for the Simons device would be much less.[50]

▶ MONETARY POLICY AND DEBT MANAGEMENT
EXPERIENCE SINCE THE "ACCORD"

The new federal reserve policy inaugurated as a result of the Treasury–Federal Reserve "Accord" of March, 1951, has now been tested under conditions of wartime boom, peacetime full employment, and recession. The stated objective of the Federal Reserve Board during this period has been to promote "a reasonable degree of stability and growth in the economy."[51] To this end open-market operations have been directed toward influencing member-bank reserves in accordance with the objective of stable economic growth. The support of government securities has no longer been the objective of open-market policy. On the other hand, purchases of short-term government obligations have been made in order to steady the market. After the middle of 1951 very few long-term government bonds were purchased. Consequently, the Treasury was "on its own" in competing in the market for long-term investable funds. From the point of view of the problem of federal debt management, a major test of the new policy came on the occasion of the treasury issue of $1 billion of thirty-year, 3¼ per cent bonds in the spring of 1953. These securities were issued at a time when competing demands of state, local, and private borrowers were large; their new issues exceeded $7 billion in the first half

---

[50] It should also be observed that measures to stabilize the money supply are not intended to eliminate *all* the causes of fluctuations in spending. The latter are a function of the whole of the assets of individuals and firms, not merely of those assets which are to be regarded as money or near money.

[51] For a review of federal reserve policy through the end of 1954, see the answers of Board Chairman Martin to the questions posed by the Subcommittee on Economic Stabilization of the Joint Committee on the Economic Report, *Hearings,* entitled *United States Monetary Policy: Recent Thinking and Experience,* 83d Cong., 2d Sess., December 6 and 7, 1954, pp. 218 ff.

of the year. Under the new policy the Treasury was not given a guarantee that the new issue would succeed; rather it was expected to arrange its terms so that it could compete successfully for the available supply of savings. This offering went to a discount before the date of issue.

The action of the Federal Reserve Board in reducing its commitments to the success of treasury finance has been the subject of a good deal of discussion. In order to emphasize its abandonment of the support policy in operation during World War II and until the spring of 1951, the board changed its interpretation of the objective of maintaining "orderly conditions in the government securities market." Instead of committing itself to "maintaining orderly conditions," it adopted the milder policy of "correcting a disorderly situation." At the same time, the board directed the Open Market Committee to confine its operations to the short end of the market. Thus no direct support would be given to new treasury issues or to the refinancing of old issues. The new policy has been criticized on the ground that the board is refraining from using all its powers, and that greater control over the range of interest rates, and therefore over the economy, is desirable in the interest of economic stability.[52]

The board has argued that orderly conditions in the government bond market would be more easily obtainable if the Open Market Committee limited its operations to the market for short-terms. The reason given is that stability in the bond market requires that private bond dealers be prepared to make a market for bonds (i.e., buy and sell out of their own resources), and to undertake arbitrage operations. But if the Federal Reserve System were to intervene in the bond market, it is argued, this would increase uncertainty, limit the activities of private bond dealers, and, by producing a thin market in government bonds, increase the amplitude of fluctuations in their prices. The New York Federal Reserve Bank disagreed with this position, and Hansen[53] regards the argument that open-market operations increase the uncertainties facing bond dealers as a "curious" one. It would be difficult to evaluate the board's argument by simply observing the fluctuations in security prices, for other considerations besides open-market operations help determine the "depth, breadth, and resiliency" of the market (to use the phrase favored by the board). But it is difficult to see why federal reserve operations in government bonds could not be handled in such a way as to contribute to, rather than detract from, the willingness of bond dealers to buy and sell bonds on their own account, and thus help to stabilize the market. Whether one agrees with

---

[52] Cf. Alvin Hansen, "Monetary Policy," *Review of Economics and Statistics,* May, 1955, pp. 110–119, and "Comment" by Sidney Weintraub, *Review of Economics and Statistics,* August, 1955, pp. 292–296; Elmer Wood, "Recent Monetary Policies," *Journal of Finance,* September, 1955, pp. 315–325; and the testimony of Allan Sproul, President of the Federal Reserve Bank of New York, Subcommittee on Economic Stabilization, *op. cit.,* pp. 223–225.

[53] Hansen, *op. cit.*

the board or with its critics, the lively interest displayed in monetary policy in recent years has been a natural result of the substitution of inflation control for the war against depression as the focus of attention for the economic control authorities. Monetary policy has taken its position beside fiscal policy as one of the instruments of indirect economic control. We have not yet, however, had a full test of the efficacy of monetary policy in the presence of a $275 billion federal debt.

▶ REFERENCES

ABBOTT, C. C. *The Federal Debt.* New York: The Twentieth Century Fund, 1953.

AMERICAN ECONOMIC ASSOCIATION. *Papers and Proceedings,* May, 1947, Papers on the Economics of the Public Debt, pp. 118–276.

———. *Readings in Fiscal Policy.* Homewood, Ill.: Richard D. Irwin, Inc., 1954, Pt. IV.

BULLOCK, C. J. *Selected Readings in Public Finance.* Boston: Ginn and Company, 1924, Chap. XIII (for early views on the public debt).

FFORDE, J. S. *The Federal Reserve System, 1945–1949.* New York: Oxford University Press, 1954.

GROVES, H. *Viewpoints on Public Finance.* New York: Henry Holt and Company, 1948, Chap. VI (views on public debt).

HANSEN, A. H. *Fiscal Policy and Business Cycles.* New York: W. W. Norton & Company, 1941, Chap. IX, "The Growth and Role of the Public Debt."

HARRIS, S. E. *National Debt and the New Economics.* New York: McGraw-Hill Book Company, Inc., 1947.

JOINT COMMITTEE ON THE ECONOMIC REPORT. *Monetary Policy and the Management of the Public Debt,* 82d Cong., 2d Sess., Document No. 123, 1952.

MURPHY, H. C. *The National Debt in War and Transition.* New York: McGraw-Hill Book Company, Inc., 1950.

26 Public Finance and Economic Growth

▶ THE NATURE OF THE INTERACTION BETWEEN
PUBLIC FINANCE AND GROWTH

Since the end of World War II economists have been extremely interested in the phenomenon of economic growth. The fever pitch which this
interest has reached is explainable in part by the enormous stimulus to
investment and growth provided by World War II. Two wars within a
generation greatly accelerated scientific and material progress, giving us the
external economies of simultaneous and rapid development on a wide front.
Accelerated growth is also explainable in part by the revolution in the
position of the underdeveloped countries throughout the world, which has
vastly lifted the horizon of material progress within these economies, and
thus also that of the advanced industrial countries which depend on them
for raw materials and markets for their products. Changing colonial policies,
medical progress, higher standards of living, technological advances, higher
educational standards, emulation of more advanced countries—all these
and a host of associated phenomena have conjoined to hasten the rate of
exploitation and development of hitherto backward areas.

Growth is most rapid when resources are utilized in an optimum
fashion, and we can therefore specify the conditions under which the rate
of material progress is maximized. Employment must remain constantly at
a high level. The relation between consumption and saving must be such
as to maintain full employment and at the same time permit a smooth flow
of savings into those forms of investment which maximize the rate of
economic progress. On a wider stage, the public must be kept satisfied that
adequate attention is being paid to the living standards of the present
generation, and that the desired rate of growth is consistent with the long-
term interests of the people living within the nation as well as with those
of the nation as a political entity.

The fiscal system, by affecting the allocation of resources and eco-

618

nomic incentives, plays an important part in the determination of the rate of economic growth. Taxes, public spending, and debt management exert a combination of favorable and unfavorable effects on the allocation of resources and on the level of economic activity. The ascertaining and the evaluating of these effects are, of course, the object of the study of public finance. Basically, the financial role of government in the economy is to bring about an optimum distribution of resources between public and private sectors, as well as to make a selection among different objects of public expenditure and among the various taxes chosen to make this expenditure possible.

At every stage of our discussion we have been either explicitly or implicitly concerned with the problem of the impact of public finance on output efficiency, the optimum relationship between consumption, saving, and investment, the level and stability of income and employment, and the rate of economic growth. Moreover, particularly in the historical parts, it has become apparent that economic growth, in turn, exerts important effects on the development of the fiscal systems of the federal, state, and local governments. This concluding chapter will summarize briefly the major considerations that relate to the reciprocal impact of the finance of government and fiscal policy, on the one hand, with economic growth, on the other. We may first indicate the effect of growth on the nature of the fiscal system.

► THE IMPACT OF ECONOMIC GROWTH ON THE
FISCAL SYSTEM

In part the rise in public spending and tax receipts brought about by economic growth is automatic. Large economic units require large amounts of all types of goods and services, including those provided by governments. Again, on the revenue side, a high level of national income, spending, and property values means a high yield of tax receipts at given tax rates; and new types of taxes become available as a maturing economy adds more and more economic activities. But economic growth is also likely to be responsible for a more than proportional rise in government spending and tax receipts. This is the sort of thing that Adolph Wagner had in mind in his contention that there is a "law" of increasing public expenditures. The question is, of course, whether or not such a law has empirical validity.

Historical evidence indicates that in some form such a law may hold, at least during certain periods of time. To the extent that growth is associated with a rapid rate of technological development, with increasing complexity of political, social, and economic relationships, and with rising economic pressures on resources and increasing political pressure on neighboring populations, there is a strong possibility that there will be periods when the functions of government will multiply at an even greater rate than the activities of the private sector of the economy. So long as underlying forces are working to bring this about, opposing philosophies of public spending are not likely to have a substantial effect in modifying the increase in the proportion of national product devoted to public use. We have seen this to be the case, for example, in connection with Republican attempts to decrease the importance of the federal government in the economy during the decade of the twenties. Moreover, attitudes toward public spending may change radically over time in response to changes in the underlying economic and political data. The views of the conservative of the nineteen fifties toward the economic role of government are very different from those of the conservative of the eighteen eighties, or even of the nineteen twenties.

ECONOMIC GROWTH AND PUBLIC DEBT

One aspect of the impact of economic growth on public finance which has received much more recognition since the great depression than had been formerly accorded to it is the significance of a growing economy for the burden of the debt. Although there is no particular reason why economic growth should necessarily be associated with a rise in governmental debt, the burden of a debt of given magnitude is likely to be reduced in correspondence with a secular rise in per capita national product. We have seen that there have frequently been periods (for example, the episode of Britain at the end of the Napoleonic Wars) when the national debt appeared to be too large to bear. But these worries gradually disappeared as the century wore on. With the passage of time, provided no further substantial increase in the debt or in the rate of interest payable on the debt occurs, interest payments become a smaller and smaller proportion of national income. Thus growth comes to the rescue and deflates the dire prophecies of those who fear the consequences of a "legacy of debt to future generations." More importantly, a secular rise in the bases of the various taxes in response to economic growth is an automatic mechanism which reduces the real burden of a given level of interest payments. The layman has difficulty to this day in comprehending this fact, for the analogy of the government with the individual or the firm as a debtor is too tempting for the superficial observer to resist. Since World War II, however, the phenomenal growth in all those aspects of the economy which reduce the real burden of a national debt has gone far to convince even the public and the conservative press that debt burden is a relative matter.

THE OPTIMUM RESPONSE OF PUBLIC FINANCE TO GROWTH

A good deal of thought has been given by political scientists and economists to the questions involved in ascertaining the optimum relationship between economic growth and the level and direction of public spending. As we saw in Chapter 3, it is much easier to state the problem in general terms than it is to give practical answers. The level and directions of public spending should be such as to equalize the marginal social benefit of the last dollar of each type of spending in the public and private sectors of the economy. But the task of legislative bodies and executive budgetary authorities in putting this precept into practice is an immense one. The job is consciously undertaken, as it must be; but budgetary policy is necessarily a complex of long- and short-term decisions, characterized by much reconsideration and day-to-day makeshift expedients that are often arrived at on the basis of highly imperfect knowledge.

On the tax side it is perhaps somewhat simpler to devise a fiscal system which adapts itself fairly closely to the economic changes associated with long-term growth. The reason is that tax decisions are to a considerable extent a *result* of these economic changes. Economic growth has a logic of its own when related to tax systems. It is the constant aim of the tax authority to examine the tax revenue potentialities of all newly appearing tax objects as they are born into the economic system. Whenever a potential new tax base appears, consideration is given to taxing it. Political pressures are quickly established that force an adaptation of the tax system to the development of the economy.

For example, the growth of the corporate form of enterprise has taken place along with the increasing use of the corporate income tax, until this source of revenue has become one of the two or three major federal taxes. Again, the phenomenon of mass consumption of durable goods has provided all levels of government with a made-to-order source of tax revenues, and the development of the limited-access highway has encouraged the use of the toll. And so on. Although it is true that every extension of a tax, or introduction of a new tax, inaugurates a vigorous debate over the merits of alternative tax policy, the generally accepted practice of taxing wherever there is a base to tax operates to gear the development of the tax system quite closely to the expansion of economic activity that characterizes growth. The possibilities of variation in the response of taxes and tax rates to economic progress should not, of course, be underestimated. Wide diversity of opinion exists over the manner in which the tax system *ought* to respond, and the selection of one tax instead of another will exert real or fancied effects on the subsequent course of economic growth.[1]

▶ THE IMPACT OF PUBLIC FINANCE ON ECONOMIC GROWTH

The effect of the fiscal system on growth has to be considered in two distinct aspects. In the first place, a given constellation of taxes, public

---

[1] An example of a strong expression of opinion on the relation of the tax system to economic growth is the publication of the National Association of Manufacturers, entitled "A Tax Program for Economic Growth" (New York: The Association, January, 1955).

expenditures, and debt management practices will produce its own set of effects on the significant economic variables that relate to growth. In the second place, fundamental political decisions taken at a crucial stage in the economic and political development of a nation will determine the future role of government in the exploitation of resources and in the development of national economic potentialities. The tax system may to a large extent simply grow with, and adapt itself to, the growing economic organism. On the spending side, however, it is frequently impossible to avoid making a very basic decision on the extent to which the government will henceforth participate in the aggregate investment and consumption spending of the economy. Once the decision is made, a chain of events may be set in motion that is not reversible. The underlying principle in the determination of the level and direction of public expenditures remains, of course, the maximization of social benefit and the minimization of social cost. The comparisons at the margin, however, must henceforth be made in the light of a prior decision on the kind of political and economic system that is desired.

In many underdeveloped countries the fundamental decisions on the role of government in determining the use made of resources in the interest of healthy and balanced economic growth are now being taken. Frequently, these decisions are being made rather hurriedly, as a corollary of strenuous efforts to escape the former subservient position occupied by these nations with respect to the more developed economies. The consequence has been a tendency on the part of many governments to play the role of protector to the economy. Savings may be collected by state financial institutions and allocated among competing private and public investment projects, import-export policies may be state-controlled, factor shares in the national product may be modified by government action. These functions of government must be financed, and the joint effect of spending, taxing, and debt management may be to alter significantly the directions of subsequent growth as compared with the probable developments had the government's role been substantially less important. The situation is quite different in a highly industrialized, free-enterprise economy, where the complex of political pressures determines the economic role of government on a fairly continuous basis (unless one party succeeds in staying in office for decades, or there is a political landslide). In mature economies one might speak of an adaptation of taxes and expenditures to the underlying political and social predilections of the public as expressed in their countless manifestations. The vigor with which bickering goes on between individuals and groups over tax and expenditure legislation can be taken as evidence of a continuous attempt to make this "fit" as complete as possible.

FISCAL POLICY FOR FULL EMPLOYMENT

The use of fiscal policy for full employment clearly has significance for the rate of growth. For, if needed and successful, a tax-expenditure policy geared to the criterion of full employment eliminates the loss of momentum associated with economic stagnation. The question that has to be decided, however, is just what sort of fiscal policy for full employment is best calculated to encourage a maximum rate of balanced growth. The short-period objective of such a fiscal policy is to take men off the rolls of the unemployed. The long-period aim is something more. It becomes important to utilize full-employment fiscal measures in such a way that the best possible use is made of our economic resources. We have seen that full employment can be achieved, theoretically at least, by both the deficit finance and the balanced budget routes. Deficits can be created either by holding spending programs fixed and reducing tax rates or by holding tax rates fixed and enlarging spending programs (or by a combination of both). The level of employment can also be affected by an increase or a decrease in the level of government spending balanced by an equal change in the magnitude of tax receipts.

The choice among these four fiscal policies obviously depends on our assessment of the underlying economic situation that has led to the appearance of unemployment. And this is the point at which differences of opinion become inevitable. For example, on the basis of the balanced-budget theorem it can be argued that in certain circumstances a rise in government spending, financed by an equal rise in tax receipts, will result in a rise in national income and employment. On the other hand, it can be shown that in other circumstances a *fall* in spending and tax receipts will have an employment-creating effect. In the first case reliance is placed on the inflationary effects of a refusal of the taxpayer to reduce consumption by an amount as great as the tax. In the second case it is being argued that the reason for a deficiency in aggregate spending is an unduly high tax-rate structure, which impairs investment incentives. Thus a reduction in the rates of these taxes, even when accompanied by a corresponding decline in government spending, is believed to have net beneficial effects on private spending incentives.

It is clear that the choice that is made among these policies is crucial to the success of a fiscal plan for full employment. But it is also true that even if full employment can be reached by more than one of these routes, the probable effects on long-term growth may dictate the selection of one method rather than another. If, for example, a rise in public spending can take the form of the kind of public works that will provide external economies to the private sector (power, transport, and communications installations, for example), the effects on growth will be superior to those achieved if the public works must take the form of sumptuous public buildings, post offices, parks, and elaborate Sunday-driver highways. Again, if it can be successfully argued that the reason for a recession is a repressive tax system, a choice is called for between a reduced *balanced* budget and a reduction in tax receipts *not balanced* by a corresponding reduction in government spending. The effect of the choice made between these two alternatives will be determined by the effect on economic growth of the public expenditures that are forgone if it is elected to reduce not merely tax rates but also public spending. Only through consideration of particular instances can we say how far the reduction in public expenditures is likely to imply a use of economic resources that would contribute more to growth than would the same amount of spending left in the hands of the government.

ORDINARY PUBLIC EXPENDITURES

The events of the past fifteen years have made it clear that it is by no means always necessary to worry much about the development of serious unemployment. When the prospect is for continuing full employment, debate over the impact of public finance on growth assumes an aspect which differs from that which characterizes it in a depression. When the alternative to increased public expenditures is a lower level of private spending, the alternative cost of public expenditures becomes a matter of great importance. Not all public or private spending conduces to growth. Many examples can be cited with respect to both types that must be classed as not contributing to the economic potential of the nation. Moreover, of those public and private expenditures which do make a contribution, some make more of a contribution than others.

The acceleration of the rate of growth in recent years has itself operated to raise the importance of certain types of public spending relative to private spending in stimulating growth. Many costly and risky projects can be undertaken only by the state, or under its sponsorship. Examples are atomic energy installations, port authorities, interstate or international schemes like the St. Lawrence Seaway and vast irrigation projects, and plans for the accelerated industrialization of underdeveloped economies. One should not, however, too easily assume that all large projects are necessarily the province of national or state governments. Those who stand strongly for private enterprise would say that the burden of proof lies with the government when it expands the range of its economic activities. A case in point is the bitter debate that went on throughout 1954 and 1955 over the Dixon-Yates contract, which gave a private firm a franchise to supply electrical energy in the Tennessee Valley area. The depth of the cleavage of opinion on the role of government in economic growth was sharply illustrated in this episode, which was only one of a long line of similar occurrences extending back to the founding of the Republic. It will be remembered that Alexander Hamilton believed that economic growth could best be fostered by giving the national government a prominent role in the economic life of the nation. His opponents, equally interested in growth, preferred to see it fostered in the private sector, while a third view (associated with the name of Jackson) favored public works, but at the hands of the states.

Before leaving the role played by ordinary public expenditures in economic growth, a word should be said of the question of balance within the sphere of public spending. An expansion of federal government spending cannot be analyzed in aggregative terms only. Questions of the maintenance of regional economic balance arise. Moreover, the indirect effects may interact with other variables to such an extent that their quantitative importance greatly transcends that of the original impetus. As an example may be cited the complex of federal measures that were enacted increasingly after the War of 1812, and which worked to the advantage of the industrial North. One of the important factors leading to the Civil War was the disproportion thus fostered between the economic strength of North and South. A consequence was a growing regional cleavage of interest that was ultimately settled on the battlefield. It would be fruitless to attempt to evaluate an episode of this sort in terms of its impact on growth. On the one hand, the losses incident to the war itself were enormous. On the other, the Civil War was a vast laboratory for the testing of all sorts of military and other techniques which contributed immeasurably to the emergence of the United States as a great power. This example is cited only in order to call attention to the elusive character of the indirect effects of economic measures on growth. Those who enter wholeheartedly into the pursuit of growth as the major objective of economic systems often ignore many of the side effects which may, at a future time, have more importance for aggregate satisfaction than growth itself.

TAXES FOR REVENUE

The fundamental purpose of taxes for revenue is to divert real resources from the taxpayer to the government. In a world of scarcities the government cannot increase its command over resources without a corresponding decrease in the power of private individuals and firms to command resources. In the present section the assumption of scarce resources will be adhered to, and it will be therefore assumed that there is no problem in maintaining full employment. Under given assumptions with respect to the desirable level of public expenditures a corresponding quantity of resources must be diverted from private use. The impact of taxation for revenue on the rate of growth of the economy is therefore determined by the contribution that the taxpayer would have made to economic growth had he remained in possession of his tax money, as compared with the contribution that would have been made by the payer of alternative forms of tax. It is this question that is constantly being debated by those who are concerned with the purchasing-power effects and incentive effects of any particular federal-state-local tax structure.

An influential segment of business opinion has long taken the position that the tax system, particularly the federal tax system, operates to take an unduly large part of its revenue from the middle-income and wealthy groups. It is in the middle brackets, of course, that is to be found the bulk of the taxpaying capacity, as well as the bulk of the saving that is required to finance public and private investment enterprises. For example, the National Association of Manufacturers, in the pamphlet cited above, argues that the top rate under the corporate income tax should not exceed 35 per cent; that the personal income tax likewise should be gradually reduced until the top bracket rate is 35 per cent, the whole of this reduction coming about in the progressive element of each rate bracket; that the taxation of capital gains should be eliminated; that the federal estate and gift taxes should be repealed; and that the selective excise system should be replaced by a uniform rate system, with the uniform excises serving to remove any temptation to make "income tax rates even more severe" than they are at present.

Implicit in this program is the belief that economic progress depends on a high rate of saving, and that the tax burden should therefore be shifted more largely to the consumer. Likewise implicit in the argument is the view that consumers (i.e., the lower-income groups) would not be adversely affected in an *absolute* sense by the enactment of the recommended changes in the federal tax law, because taxable national income and spending would be higher than it would be under the present rate structure.

It would be difficult to deny that so long as full employment is virtually guaranteed in a period of cold war or even a period (like the present) dominated by an arms race, economic growth is maximized when the proportion of national income that is saved is maximized. Testimony to this point of view is amply provided in the West German experience since the currency reform of 1948. In that country consumer purchasing power has been kept down by a combination of low wage rates and high consumer taxes. The consequence has been that Germany presents the spectacle of having one of the highest rates of capital formation in the world, and her rate of growth in the past seven years has been phenomenal. The trade unions have been restive under this iron economic regime, but it seems safe to assume that wage rates will not be raised to such an extent that any marked reduction in the rate of saving and investment will occur. But the fact that a substantial part of Germany's brilliant recovery from the prostration of 1945–1948 has been made at the expense of the worker and to the advantage of the producer is obvious to any observer. In every country the differential impact of the tax system on the several income brackets will be determined by the resultant of the views of the various interest groups as reflected in the decisions of cabinets and legislatures. If maximization of the rate of growth is the sole objective in the choice of taxes, then so long as full employment can be assumed the tax system should aim at maximizing the rate of saving. It is the essence of tax maneuvering, however, that, taking account of all points of view, maximization of the rate of growth is not the sole objective of legislatures in making decisions with respect to the structure of the tax system. Current living standards need also to be taken into account.

When full employment is not guaranteed (for example, by virtue of unstable international political relations), the view can no longer be accepted that maximization of the rate of saving assures a high rate of growth. On the contrary, a balance between consumption and saving is then a prerequisite to the continuous investment of savings, and after a lengthy period of rapid investment in plant and equipment it may be indispensable to encourage a high level of consumption by all possible means, including a shift toward greater taxation of savings relative to consumption.

THE PUBLIC DEBT AND GROWTH

Public debt can influence the rate of economic growth in a number of different ways. Long-term securities provide the saver with an alternative to private debt and stock purchases. In certain circumstances the availability of this alternative may prove discouraging to those forms of private investment that compete closely with government debt for the available savings. The result will be to retard economic growth, provided that private investment would have contributed more than public investment to national economic potential. But since this is not necessarily the case, we cannot say that even if government borrowing encroaches on private borrowing the effect is to retard growth. Moreover, government debt does not compete closely with the more risky types of private investment, and it is these which make a particularly large contribution to growth. Therefore, a rapidly growing public debt may not be incompatible with considerable investment in forward-looking private undertakings. Again, the availability of a safe form of debt obligation may induce the more wealthy savers to devote part of their savings to a more risky type of investment.

The availability of a large amount of liquid assets can affect the community's propensity to consume, and therefore the rate of saving. The willingness of individuals to spend on consumption is dependent, among other things, on the extent to which they believe their liquid assets to be adequate to meet all likely contingencies. During a major war millions of persons experience a rise in their holdings of highly liquid government securities, and thus may be much more disposed to spend for consumption than would have been the case had a greater proportion of the cost of the war been financed out of taxes. In a long war a policy of compulsory purchases of government securities, coupled perhaps with provisions for the postwar return of a proportion of taxes (for example, excess-profits and income tax rebates), will set the stage for a relatively high postwar level of aggregate consumption. On the other hand, a rush to convert these liquid assets into money will be price-inflationary, and a given amount of spending will not result in as high a level of real consumption in the postwar period as the security holders had anticipated. However, the public has actually shown itself to be loath to sacrifice part of its savings in this way.

Finally, the public debt plays an important part in the determination of the rate of output, and therefore indirectly in the rate of economic growth, through its contribution to economic stability and to a smooth growth in the volume of money. Greater or smaller amounts of public debt will be monetized, depending on the decisions that are made as to the proportion of the debt that is to be held by the banking system. The debt can be managed in such a way that interest rates are either tightened or forced down. The optimum contribution to economic growth is made when the amount of public debt that is monetized, combined with private debt monetization, is such that the means of payment corresponds to the volume of business that is being contracted at the current price level. That is, the money supply should be flexible, but it should not abet inflation. This statement is subject to one qualification. It may be that a small degree of continuous inflation will slightly increase the proportion of national income that is saved. If this is true, at full employment investment and the rate of growth are therefore encouraged.[2]

► CONCLUSION

By virtue of its function in the allocation of resources the fiscal system plays a basic role in the determination of the rate of economic growth. Taxes and public spending at all levels of government operate directly, along with private investment and consumption spending, to distribute factors of production among manifold alternative uses. Public borrowing substitutes government decisions for those of businessmen in the allocation of that part of national product that is not consumed. Again, public spending, taxes, and debt management all exert effects on economic incentives, and thus also affect the rate of growth by modifying the nature of decisions in the private sector of the economy. Finally, public finance may operate to intensify or diminish fluctuations in business activity, and thus influence the rate of capital formation and growth.

► REFERENCES

HANSEN, A. *Fiscal Policy and Business Cycles.* New York: W. W. Norton & Company, 1941, pp. 38–46 (on the stagnation thesis).

---

[2] Obviously we would not anticipate a favorable effect on economic growth through gradual price inflation unless anticipations with respect to a continued price rise did not lead to a flight from the dollar into goods. For the conditions under which a continuous and gradual price rise is consistent with stability and sustained economic growth, see William Vickrey, "Stability through Inflation," in K. K. Kurihara, ed., *Post-Keynesian Economics* (New Brunswick, N. J.: Rutgers University Press, 1954).

JOINT COMMITTEE ON THE ECONOMIC REPORT. *Federal Tax Policy for Economic Growth and Stability.* (Papers submitted by panelists appearing before the Subcommittee on Tax Policy.) 84th Cong., 1st Sess., November 9, 1955.

MILLIKAN, M., ed. *Income Stabilization for a Developing Democracy.* New Haven, Conn.: Yale University Press, 1953.

SPENGLER, J. "Prospective Population and Income Growth and Fiscal Policy," *National Tax Journal,* March, 1950, pp. 36–63.

WALLICH, H. C., and J. H. ADLER. *Public Finance in a Developing Country: El Salvador—A Case Study.* Cambridge, Mass.: Harvard University Press, 1951.

Index

Index